ALLOCATING INTERNATIONAL RESPONSIBILITY BETWEEN MEMBER STATES AND INTERNATIONAL ORGANISATIONS

The ever-growing interaction between member States and international organisations results, all too often, in situations of non-conformity with international law (eg peacekeeping operations, international economic adjustment programmes, counter-terrorism sanctions). Seven years after the finalisation of the International Law Commission's Articles on the Responsibility of International Organisations (ARIO), international law on the allocation of international responsibility between these actors still remains unsettled. The confusion around the nature and normative calibre of the relevant rules, the paucity of relevant international practice supporting them and the lack of a clear and principled framework for their elaboration impairs their application and restricts their ability to act as effective regulatory formulas.

This study aims to offer doctrinal clarity in this area of law and purports to serve as a point of reference for all those with a vested interest in the topic. For the first time since the publication of the ARIO, all international responsibility issues dealing with interactions between member States and international organisations are put together in one book under a common approach. Structured around a systematisation of the interactions between these actors, the study provides an analytical framework for the regulation of indirect responsibility scenarios. Based on the ideas of the intellectual fathers of international law, such as Scelle's 'dédoublement fonctionnel' theory and Ago's 'derivative responsibility' model, the book employs old ideas to add original argumentation to a topic that has been dealt with extensively by recent commentators.

Volume 70 in the series Studies in International Law

Studies in International Law

Recent titles in this series

International Law and Child Soldiers
Gus Waschefort

The Contractual Nature of the Optional Clause
Gunnar Törber

Non-State Actors in International Law
Edited by Math Noortmann, August Reinisch and Cedric Ryngaert

The Rule of Law at the National and International Levels: Contestations and Deference
Edited by Machiko Kanetake and André Nollkaemper

Human Rights Obligations of Non-State Armed Groups
Daragh Murray

Security and International Law
Edited by Mary E Footer, Julia Schmidt and Nigel D White

Complicity and its Limits in the Law of International Responsibility
Vladyslav Lanovoy

Complicity in International Criminal Law
Marina Aksenova

Arctic Law and Governance: The Role of China and Finland
Edited by Timo Koivurova, Qin Tianbao, Tapio Nykänen and Sébastien Duyck

States, the Law and Access to Refugee Protection: Fortresses and Fairness
Edited by Maria O'Sullivan and Dallal Stevens

Revisiting the Concept of Defence in the Jus ad Bellum: The Dual Face of Defence
Johanna Friman

The International Legal Protection of Persons in Humanitarian Crises
Dug Cubie

The International Committee of the Red Cross and its Mandate to Protect and Assist: Law and Practice
Christy Shucksmith

The Impact of Investment Treaty Law on Host States: Enabling Good Governance
Mavluda Sattorova

For a complete list of titles in this series, see www.bloomsburyprofessional.com/uk/series/studies-in-international-law

Allocating International Responsibility Between Member States and International Organisations

Nikolaos Voulgaris

•HART•
OXFORD • LONDON • NEW YORK • NEW DELHI • SYDNEY

HART PUBLISHING

Bloomsbury Publishing Plc

Kemp House, Chawley Park, Cumnor Hill, Oxford, OX2 9PH, UK

HART PUBLISHING, the Hart/Stag logo, BLOOMSBURY and the Diana logo are trademarks of Bloomsbury Publishing Plc

First published in Great Britain 2019

A catalogue record for this book is available from the British Library.

Library of Congress Cataloging-in-Publication data

Names: Voulgaris, Nikolaos, author.

Title: Allocating international responsibility between member states and international organisations / Nikolaos Voulgaris.

Description: Oxford, UK ; Chicago, Illinois : Hart Publishing, 2019. | Series: Studies in international law ; volume 70 | Includes bibliographical references and index.

Identifiers: LCCN 2018059642 (print) | LCCN 2018060032 (ebook) | ISBN 9781509925735 (EPub) | ISBN 9781509925728 (hardback)

Subjects: LCSH: Tort liability of international agencies. | Government liability (International law) | United Nations. International Law Commission. Draft Articles on the Responsibility of International Organisations. | BISAC: LAW / International.

Classification: LCC KZ4850.3 (ebook) | LCC KZ4850.3 .V68 2019 (print) | DDC 341.2—dc23

LC record available at https://lccn.loc.gov/2018059642

ISBN: HB: 978-1-50992-572-8
ePDF: 978-1-50992-574-2
ePub: 978-1-50992-573-5

Typeset by Compuscript Ltd, Shannon

A Salomon saith: there is no new thing upon earth. So that as Plato had an imagination, that all knowledge was but remembrance; so Salomon giveth his sentence, that all novelty is but oblivion.

Foreword

THIS BOOK DEALS with one of the most important topics in the law of international organisations. It is no exaggeration to say that the nature of international organisations depends to a very large extent on the juridical relationship between organisations and member states, and that central to this relationship are questions about the allocation of responsibility between them. These have always been issues of great theoretical complexity. They involve both conceptual challenges and thorny arguments about the foundations of international law.

With the expansion in the functions and importance of international organisations, a justified sense of urgency about questions of allocation of responsibility has emerged: from peacekeeping missions to multilateral relief operations, the potential for wrongful acts has become more apparent – and so has the need to understand who, between the organisation and its members, is responsible for wrongful acts in what circumstances and to what degree.

Dr Voulgaris approaches these issues in a thoroughly analytical, thoughtful and engaged manner. He begins by considering some of the underlying theoretical and conceptual issues in the first two chapters; but the heart of the book is doctrinal with much attention devoted, as it needs to be, to the work of the International Law Commission on the Responsibility of International Organisations. As the Commission itself found, this is a difficult field to systematise doctrinally, characterised by international institutional and state practice that is negligible in places and idiosyncratic in others.

Dr Voulgaris's ordering idea is to look at the nature of the underlying interactions between the organisation and the member states. It is no easy feat. Interactions between international organisations and their members are a matter of both law and fact, with the latter known to prevaricate over the former. These situations – e.g. where states manage to direct the conduct of an organisation outside and sometimes in breach of the institutional rules – are problematic at every stage in the process of responsibility, from attribution to causation (and implementation too, although implementation falls outside the scope of this book). Some of the examples discussed by Dr Voulgaris, for example in the final chapter, bring these difficulties into sharp relief.

Dr Voulgaris is critical of the work of the International Law Commission, but accepts that there would be little point in trying to reinvent the wheel, and argues that his concerns, important though they are, can be addressed interpretatively. As with the Articles on State Responsibility, we have a framework of rules – some leaving more questions unresolved than others, some benefitting from more practice and guidance than others – that can now grow, organically as is often said, through interpretation and application. Of course, a lot can happen (and sometimes not happen) during what passes for organic growth. The experience with the Articles on State Responsibility shows the importance of the first generation of post-Articles scholarship in contributing to those developments. On the defining and critically important question of the allocation of responsibility between international organisations and their members, I have no doubt that Dr Voulgaris's book deserves to be one of those shaping future developments.

Professor Guglielmo Verdirame QC
King's College London
20 Essex Street Chambers

Acknowledgements

THIS STUDY IS an edited version of the doctoral thesis I defended at King's College London in December 2015. Thankfully, both the PhD and the final manuscript were not written in clinical isolation and numerous people supported me throughout.

Professor Guglielmo Verdirame has not been a supervisor but a mentor in the true sense of the word. I am indebted for our conversations irrespective of their subject and I am looking forward to more in the future. His support and encouragement is something I will not be able to repay. His future students are lucky to have him. Dr Philippa Webb has always been there for me whenever I sought her advice or help, not only with her immense support, she is an exemplary colleague, the best one can ask for.

The King's PhD family has given me great courage with their support and good company. Among them, Adrienne Yong and Ermioni Xanthopoulou deserve a special reference. Special thanks also go to Anastasios Gourgourinis, Panos Merkouris, Akis Papastavridis, Orfeas Hassapis-Tassinis and Sotiris Lekkas for the endless conversations. I hope they will never end.

My family's love and encouragement cannot be returned. This thesis is dedicated to Dimitra, Aristidis, Areti and Thodoris.

A special mention is due to the late Professor Stavros Tsakyrakis. He taught me how to think, how and when (not) to speak and how to write. He was like a father to me and this book is also devoted to his loving memory.

Contents

List of Abbreviations

AJIL	American Journal of International Law
ARIO	Articles on the Responsibility of International Organizations
ARIO Comment	ARIO with Commentaries
ASR	Articles on State Responsibility
ASR Comment	ASR with Commentaries
BYBIL	*British Yearbook of International Law*
CIA	Central Intelligence Agency (US)
CJEU	Court of Justice of the European Union
CUP	Cambridge University Press
ECHR	European Court of Human Rights
ECJ	European Court of Justice
ECtHR	European Court of Human Rights
EHRR	European Human Rights Reports
EJIL	*European Journal of International Law*
ESA	European Space Agency
EU	European Union
FYROM	Former Yugoslavian Republic of Macedonia
GATT	General Agreement on Tariffs and Trade
HVD	High Value Detainee
IACmHR	Inter-American Commission on Human Rights
IACtHR	Inter-American Court of Human Rights
ICESCR	International Covenant on Economic, Social and Cultural Rights
ICJ	International Court of Justice
ICLQ	*International and Comparative Law Quarterly*

ICTY	International Criminal Tribunal for the Former Yugoslavia
IDI	Institute of International Law (Institut de Droit International)
ILC	International Law Commission
ILM	International Legal Materials
ILO	International Labour Organization
ILOAT	Administrative Tribunal of the International Labour Organization
IMF	International Monetary Fund
IOLR	*International Organizations Law Review*
ITC	International Tin Council
ITLOS	International Tribunal for the Law of the Sea
ITU	International Telecommunication Union
LOSC	Law of the Sea Convention
NATO	North Atlantic Treaty Organization
OPCW	Organization for the Prohibition of Chemical Weapons
OUP	Oxford University Press
PCIJ	Permanent Court of International Justice
RCADI	Recueil des Cours de l'Academie de Droit International
RFMO	Regional Fisheries Management Organisation
SRFC	Sub-Regional Fisheries Commission (West Africa)
UN	United Nations
UNGA	United Nations General Assembly
UNMIK	UN Mission in Kosovo
UNSC	United Nations Security Council
WHO	World Health Organisation
YBILC	*Yearbook of the International Law Commission*

Table of Cases

ICJ and PCIJ

European Court and European Commission of Human Rights

CJEU

Other

Table of Treaties and Unilateral Acts

UN Resolutions

1

Introduction

I. INTRODUCTION

INTERNATIONAL ORGANISATIONS HAVE emerged in the United Nations era as prominent actors in the international arena. Within a very limited time-span, they have grown considerably in number but also in size and scope. But as their competences augment, so do their obligations. The transformation of International Organisations is so evident that the remark of the United Nations International Law Commission (ILC) that 'it must not be forgotten that, by their very nature, international organizations normally behave in such a manner as not to commit internationally wrongful acts' hardly reflects the present state of affairs.[1] Nevertheless, International Organisations coexist and interact with other subjects of international law and mainly with States who are (to a great extent) their members.

International Organisations are all the more frequently accused of behaving in a manner inconsistent with their international obligations and such behaviour more often than not impacts their member States. Recent international practice abounds with relevant examples. UN Nepalese peacekeepers admittedly were the source of a cholera outbreak in Haiti in 2010 that afflicted nearly a tenth of the country's population and may have caused over 9,000 deaths.[2] The International Monetary Fund (IMF)'s engagement with the euro area, focusing on its surveillance and crisis management in Greece, Ireland and Portugal, had a major impact on human rights standards in those States. The list grows to cover illegal conduct during military operations where NATO participates, and recommendations by the World Health Organization (WHO) proven to be harmful and without significant clinical effect that are followed by its member States. Given the gravity of such situations, it is only pertinent to ask whether international law possesses the necessary normative toolkit to address such scenarios.

To pose in other words the research question I will endeavour to answer in this book: how does international law regulate (if at all) the international

[1] ILC, *Report of the International Law Commission on the Work of Its 27th Session (5 May–25 July 1975)*, UN doc A/10010/Rev.l (1975), reproduced in (1975) 2(1) *YBILC* 47, 87, [3].

[2] Secretary-General, *A New Approach to Cholera in Haiti*, UN doc A/71/620 (25 November 2016).

responsibility of both the members States and the International Organisation of which they are members when these two subjects interact? And in case international law leaves the matter unsettled or unregulated, how is this potential gap in international law to be filled? So, this book is essentially a law-identification exercise. Overall, I do not aim just to identify international law, but also to suggest, where the law is not yet formed, how it should be developed, how its content should be determined.

The ILC purported to answer these questions in its Articles on the Responsibility of International Organisations (ARIO).[3] Within its mandate to codify and progressively develop international law,[4] the Commission produced this set of Articles that contains two Chapters directly relevant for present purposes: namely, Chapter IV of Part Two entitled 'Responsibility of an international organization in connection with the act of a State or another international organization' and Part Five entitled 'Responsibility of a State in connection with the conduct of an international organization'. Since the ARIO constitute the most authoritative text to date on the matter but also lay the essential background for integrated answers, it is only pertinent to ask how the ILC should have drafted the provisions that regulate the international responsibility of both the member States and the International Organisation of which they are members in scenarios when these two subjects interact.

When drafting the ARIO, the ILC faced a considerable challenge: the paucity of relevant international practice, be it judicial or institutional.[5] The precedents are rare and poorly documented (eg unreported institutional documentation or unpublished case law) and this was underlined by the ILC itself,[6] the Special Rapporteur[7] and several International Organisations which commented during the drafting process.[8] Consequently, the Commission concluded that

[3] See ILC's ARIO in ILC, *Report of the International Law Commission in the Work of Its 63rd session (26 April–3 June and 4 July-12 August 2011)*, UN doc A/66/10 52 (2011). See commentaries to the ARIO in ibid 67.

[4] UN Charter, Art 13(a) Charter of the United Nations (adopted 26 June 1945; entered into force 24 October 1945) 1 UNTS XVI; Statute of the International Law Commission, Art 1(1), UNGA, Resolution 174(II) (21 November 1947), UN doc A/RES/174(II).

[5] See eg G Hafner, 'Is the Topic of Responsibility of International Organizations Ripe for Codification? Some Critical Remarks' in U Fastenrath, R Geiger, DE Khan, A Paulus, S von Schorlemer and C Vedder (eds), *From Bilateralism to Community Interest, Essays in Honour of Judge Bruno Simma* (OUP, 2011) 695, 700–4; VJ Proulx, 'An Uneasy Transition? Linkages Between the Law of State Responsibility and the Law Governing the Responsibility of International Organizations' in M Ragazzi (ed), *Responsibility of International Organizations, Essays in Memory of Sir Ian Brownlie* (Martinus Nijhoff, 2013) 109, 114.

[6] ARIO Comment, 67–68, [5]: 'relevant practice resulting from exchanges of correspondence may not be always easy to locate, nor are international organizations or States often willing to disclose it'. For examples of unpublished case law, see ibid notes 109, 143, 146 and 189.

[7] G Gaja, *Third Report on Responsibility of International Organizations*, UN doc A/CN.4/553 (2005), reproduced in (2005) 2(1) *YBILC* 7, 9, [3] ('Gaja Third Report'); G Gaja, *Eighth Report on Responsibility of International Organizations*, UN doc A/CN.4/640 (2011) 5–6, [6] ('Gaja Eighth Report'): 'only a few instances of unpublished practice have been contributed by States and international organizations in order to facilitate the Commission's study'.

[8] ILC, *Responsibility of International Organizations: Comments and Observations Received from International Organisations*, UN doc A/CN.4/568 (2006) and Add 1 reproduced in (2006)

most provisions incorporated in the ARIO constitute progressive development of the law, rather than its codification.[9] This lack of relevant State and International Organisation practice is a prominent feature of all provisions that will be examined throughout this book, and address the issue of interaction between member States and International Organisations.[10] I hold the view that the provisions under examination do not form part of customary international law and the intention of the Commission when drafting them was to reflect the progressive development of the law. Having proven this, I intend to assess whether the relevant ARIO provisions, in the way they are drafted, indeed provide for the progressive development of the law. If this is not the case, I will examine how the law has developed and therefore to what extent the provisions deviate from the development of the law.

As a caveat, I should stress that I intend to confine my study to the level of establishment of international responsibility, irrespective of its implementation, since this is what the ILC had in mind when drafting the relevant ARIO provisions. And by implementation it is not necessarily meant enforcement through the courts or through the settlement of claims (while this will most often be the case), but any type of enforcement of international responsibility against the responsibility bearer.[11] While the two have been mixed up by some theorists,[12] the former is completely independent of the latter. This is so, because these two aspects of international responsibility operate at different levels.[13]

2(1) *YBILC* 125, 128 (WHO); ILC, *Responsibility of International Organizations: Comments and Observations Received from International Organisations* UN doc A/CN.4/609 (2009), reproduced in (2009) 2(1) *YBILC* 97, 98 (WHO); ILC, *Responsibility of International Organizations: Comments and Observations Received from International Organizations*, UN doc A/CN.4/637 (2011) 10–11 (Joint submission) and 14 (World Bank); ILC, *Responsibility of International Organizations: Comments and Observations Received from International Organizations*, UN doc A/CN.4/637/Add 1 (2011) 4–5 (United Nations).

[9] ARIO Comment, 68, [5]. According to Wood this assertion by the ILC is 'the most important point made in the general commentary' of the ARIO, as it seeks to explain the legal status of the Arts, M Wood, '"Weighing" the Articles on Responsibility of International Organizations' in M Ragazzi (ed), *Responsibility of International Organizations, Essays in Memory of Sir Ian Brownlie* (Martinus Nijhoff, 2013) 55, 60.

[10] On the significance of International Organisations' practice with respect to the identification of international customary law, see M Wood, *Second Report on the Identification of Customary International Law*, UN doc A/CN.4/672 (2014) [43]–[44]; M Wood, *Third Report on the Identification of Customary International Law*, UN doc A/CN.4/682 (2015) [68]–[79]; M Wood, 'International Organizations and Customary International Law' (2015) 48 *Vanderbilt Journal of Transnational Law* 609.

[11] A Tzanakopoulos, *Disobeying the Security Council: Countermeasures Against Wrongful Sanctions* (OUP, 2011) 6.

[12] S Chesterman, *Who Needs Rules? The Prospects of a Rules-Based International System* (2005), available at www.iilj.org/research/documents/panel_2_report.pdf 7; TM Franck, 'The United Nations as Guarantor of International Peace and Security' in C Tomuschat (ed), *The United Nations at Age Fifty: A Legal Perspective* (Kluwer, 1995) 25, 37.

[13] ILC, 'Draft Articles on the Responsibility of States for Internationally Wrongful Acts with Commentaries' (2001) 2(2) *YBILC* 31, 67, [11]: 'Article 16 does not address the question of the admissibility of judicial proceedings to establish the responsibility …'.

For many decades, for example, no means were put in place to enforce within the international legal system a violation of the prohibition of genocide. This does not *ipso facto* mean that international responsibility for such violations was not established before a competent tribunal could render a relevant finding.[14] While they remain distinct, the two aspects are undoubtedly related, for a robust implementation of international responsibility can only depend upon clear and coherent rules regulating its establishment. The lack of enforcement through the courts is, it has been suggested, the main obstacle preventing accountability of International Organisations in general.[15] I agree that this is a problem that merits deep reflection, but it exceeds the remit of the present study.

II. INTERACTION BETWEEN INTERNATIONAL ORGANISATION AND MEMBER STATES

Interaction between member States and the International Organisation of which they are members is addressed by Chapter IV of Part Two and Part Five of the ARIO. For present purposes, interaction involves the establishment of international responsibility by virtue of a particular relationship between two subjects of international law. Given that the victim is by definition not involved in the establishment of international responsibility, interaction in these provisions is reflected in the relationship between the perpetrator of wrongful conduct and the responsibility bearer. This is evident from the titles of both ARIO Chapters; Chapter IV regulates the responsibility of an International Organisation 'in connection with the act of a State or another international organisation', while Part V the corresponding responsibility of a State 'in connection with the conduct of an international organization'.

Throughout the book, I distinguish between two types of such interaction. The criterion that separates one from the other is the basis on which this interaction occurs. In the first type, interaction occurs on the basis of the particular member State-International Organisation relationship (or on the basis of membership), while in the second it occurs outside this relationship. In the latter case, the two subjects interact as independent subjects of international law.

[14] R McCorquodale, 'International Organizations and International Human Rights Law: One Giant Leap for Humankind' in KH Kaikobad and M Bohlander (eds), *International Law and Power: Perspectives on Legal Order and Justice, Essays in Honour of Colin Warbrick* (Nijhoff, 2009) 141, 151; D van Zyl Smit, 'Punishment and Human Rights in International Criminal Law' (2002) 2 *Human Rights Law Review* 1. See also S Talmon, 'A Plurality of Responsible Actors: International Responsibility for Acts of the Coalition Provisional Authority in Iraq' in P Shiner and A Williams (eds), *The Iraq War and International Law* (Hart, 2008) 185, 219: 'The fact that no judicial machinery exists to hold the United Nations responsible should not be allowed to obscure the fact that the United Nations remains responsible for its internationally wrongful acts'.

[15] J Wouters, E Brems, S Smis and P Schmitt, 'Introductory Remarks' in J Wouters, E Brems, S Smis and P Schmitt (eds), *Accountability for Human Rights Violations by International Organisations* (Intersentia, 2010) 1, 11.

First, member States interact with International Organisations on the basis of membership. This mode of interaction is in place when two conditions are present: first, member States exercise competence that lies with the International Organisation; and second, member States do so in accordance with the rules of the International Organisation. This is the case, for example, when a State exercises its right to vote within decision-making procedures of an International Organisation. ARIO, Articles 58(2), 59(2) and 62 capture this type of interaction. Unsurprisingly, they have no corresponding provision within the United Nations' Articles on State Responsibility (ASR).[16] Only when both these conditions are present, member States will *act as members* of the International Organisation. The main feature of this mode of interaction is that member States disappear behind the international personality of the International Organisation – or 'under the organisational veil' – and, as a result, do not bear international responsibility for internationally wrongful acts even when they contributed to their causation.

On the other hand, member States interact with the International Organisation of which they are members as independent subjects of international law in every case that does not fulfil both the aforementioned conditions. Throughout this book, I examine instances where one of the two conditions is present, ie when member States exercise competences that originate from the International Organisation but lie with member States in a particular instance (eg the request by a domestic court to the Court of Justice of the European Union for a preliminary ruling), and instances where member States operate within procedures of the International Organisation but not in accordance with its rules (eg exercise of political influence over decision-making procedures). In none of these scenarios do member States and International Organisations interact on the basis of their particular relationship.

On these occasions, *member States act as States*, do not disappear 'under the organisational veil' and thus their international responsibility can be established. The three provisions on 'aid or assistance', 'direction and control' and 'coercion' incorporated in ARIO, Articles 14, 15, 16, 58(1), 59(1) and 60, address this type of interaction. These provisions were transposed into the ARIO 'lock, stock and barrel' from the corresponding Chapter IV of the ASR and they capture all the possible ways in which two independent subjects may interact. Further, an analysis of the scope of application of ARIO, Articles 17 and 61 that have no corresponding ASR provision clearly demonstrates that they fall under the second type of interaction too.

It is the use of competence on a particular instance that points to the type of interaction in play, and the criterion that separates one from the other is

[16] UNGA, Resolution 56/83 (12 December 2001) 'Articles on the Responsibility of States for their Internationally Wrongful Acts', UN doc A/RES/56/83, Annex, and corrected by UNGA, Resolutions and decisions adopted by the General Assembly during its fifty-sixth session, UN doc A/56/49(Vol.I)/Corr.4.

purely functional. In this sense, the two bases of interaction are mutually exclusive. At the same time, the second type is broad enough to encompass all instances of interaction that do not fall under the first type and hence these two cover all possible interaction scenarios.

III. A DESCRIPTION OF THE PROBLEM

The provisions of ARIO, Chapter IV and Part Five, and the ASR, Chapter IV provisions which they replicate, possess certain characteristics that set them apart from other ILC provisions dealing with international responsibility (in both the ASR and the ARIO). They differ in their scope of application but also in the way international responsibility is established in these cases.

First, they are applicable to scenarios involving three legal actors. Generally, responsibility concerns only the relationship between a wrongdoer and a victim.[17] Such cases will be referred to as involving 'direct responsibility'. ARIO, Chapter IV and Part Five provisions, however, deal with situations in which, between the wrongdoer and the victim, a third intermediate legal subject is placed who is in some way linked to the wrongdoer.[18] While the ILC refers to such triangular relationships as involving 'derived responsibility',[19] I will use the term 'indirect responsibility' instead, not only because of the presence of the intermediate subject, but also as an antithesis to the situation of 'direct responsibility'.[20]

Second, the establishment of international responsibility in cases covered by indirect responsibility is considered to arise in an exceptional way. The establishment of international responsibility in direct responsibility is dependent upon the objectively determined conditions of breach and attribution.[21] Under ARIO, Chapter IV and Part Five, the establishment of responsibility depends on the presence of subjective requirements such as knowledge or intent.[22]

[17] ASR, Art 2 and ARIO, Art 4.

[18] J Fry, 'Coercion, Causation and the Fictional Elements of Indirect State Responsibility' (2007) 40 *Vanderbilt Journal of Transnational Law* 611, 615.

[19] ASR Comment, 65, [8].

[20] Inconsistent terminology is a source of confusion surrounding indirect responsibility norms and clarification of the terminology is undoubtedly a necessary prerequisite of a robust analysis. The ILC refers to indirect responsibility rules as 'derived responsibility' provisions (ASR Comment, 65) while Tzanakopoulos refers to them as 'derivative responsibility' rules (Tzanakopoulos, *Disobeying the Security Council* (n 11) 47). The term 'indirect responsibility' which I use throughout the book has been used in contrast with direct responsibility since C de Visscher, *La Responsabilité des Etats, Bibliotheca Visseriana Dissertationum Ius Internationale Illustrantium* (Brill, Lugduni Batavorum, 1924) vol 2, 91. For a thorough examination of the terms 'direct' and 'indirect' responsibility in international law, see H Fox, 'The International Court of Justice's Treatment of Acts of the State and in Particular the Attribution of Acts of Individuals to the State' in N Ando, E McWhinney and R Wolfrum (eds), *Liber Amicorum Judge Shigeru Oda* (Kluwer Law International, 2002) 147ff.

[21] ASR, Art 2 and ARIO, Art 4, with commentaries.

[22] eg ASR, Art 16(a).

The introduction of such notions is prima facie in contrast with the ILC's two projects, which intend to confine the establishment of international responsibility to objectively determined prerequisites.[23] What is more, there is general consensus that indirect responsibility norms, in contrast to the rest of the international responsibility provisions, provide directly for the attribution of responsibility[24] without the prior attribution of conduct.

Due to the aforementioned features, indirect responsibility provisions have been perceived to be 'anomalies' or exceptions within the law of international responsibility.[25] The absence of a solid doctrinal background in the ASR for those provisions has been perpetuated in the ARIO, with Special Rapporteur Gaja opting to follow the indirect responsibility approach of the ASR and thus failing to bridge this doctrinal gap.[26] Since the problematic features of the indirect responsibility provisions have not been adequately explained, they appear to cause incoherence within the law of international responsibility. It has been argued that this incoherence, in turn, is detrimental to the validity and prestige of the international responsibility edifice as a whole.[27] Thus, it is questioned whether international responsibility as an accountability mechanism possesses the necessary doctrinal rigour to address complex scenarios such as those resulting from the interaction between member States and International Organisations.

Further, the confusion around the nature of the indirect responsibility provisions has practical ramifications. It impairs their application, and impedes their effective functioning as regulatory formulas for triangular scenarios. For example, it remains unclear whether the provisions provide for shared, joint, joint and several, or parallel responsibilities for the legal subjects involved in such triangular situations.[28] Thus, international courts and tribunals experience a certain unease when applying such provisions and need more guidance as to their proper interpretation and application.

[23] On the ramifications of the adoption of such an objective model of international responsibility, see J Crawford and S Olleson, 'The Nature and Forms of International Responsibility' in M Evans (ed), *International Law* (OUP, 2003) 443, 451.

[24] ASR Comment, 64, [5]; R Ago, *Eighth Report on State Responsibility* UN doc A/CN.4/318 (1979) and Add 1 to 4 reproduced in (1979) 2(1) *YBILC* 4, 22–24, [38]–[42] '(Ago Eighth Report'); Fry, 'Coercion, Causation and the Fictional Elements' (n 18) 631; Tzanakopoulos, *Disobeying the Security Council* (n 11) 45–46. Referring to these norms, the ILC suggested that 'responsibility of an international organization may in certain cases arise also when conduct is not attributable to that international organization', ARIO Comment, 83, [2].

[25] Ago Eighth Report (n 24) 5–6, [4]: 'the abnormal phenomenon of indirect responsibility'; ASR Comment, 64, [5]: 'Chapter IV of Part One defines these exceptional cases where …'.

[26] Gaja Third Report (n 7) 11.

[27] J d'Aspremont, 'The Articles on the Responsibility of International Organisations: Magnifying the Fissures in the Law of International Responsibility' (2012) 9 *IOLR* 15, 17, 24–25: 'the concept of responsibility falls short of capturing complex situations of non-conformity'; N Nedeski and A Nollkaemper, 'Responsibility of International Organisations in Connection with Acts of States' (2012) 9 *IOLR* 33, 43–48.

[28] See the commentaries to the provision on direction and control, ASR Comment, 69.

Because understanding indirect responsibility provisions as *sui generis* norms has always been the 'orthodoxy' among international lawyers and the ILC,[29] so far no commentator has managed to adopt a holistic perspective on indirect responsibility. On the contrary, the ILC has relied heavily on the exceptional character of these norms in order to avoid offering a normative explanation of the way they operate;[30] and in so doing, it has precluded the systematic incorporation of those norms into the law of international responsibility. In fact, the ILC has relied upon considerations external to the law on international responsibility, such as policy arguments, or arguments that pertain to liability, in order to justify these provisions.

Overall, the ILC lacks a principled argumentative basis for the elaboration of such rules. This is why it was uneasy about drafting provisions that were not backed by the adequate *opinio juris* and State or institutional practice. Likewise, the literature has evoked divergent grounds to assess whether the Commission has effectively delivered its function and drafted provisions that indeed reflect the progressive development of the law. For example, commentators have suggested that the ILC should have elaborated these norms on the basis of their accordance with (admittedly scarce) State, institutional and judicial practice, by way of analogy with the concomitant provisions on the ASR, or on the basis of other pragmatic or policy considerations such as usability.[31] This lack of a guiding drafting framework, along with the heterogeneity of the provisions under examination, have confused both the ILC and the academic discussion that sparked after the provisions were finalised in 2011; the provisions were drafted by the ILC on an unprincipled and ad hoc basis and commentators have failed to articulate a comprehensive criticism since they lack the necessary framework to do so. As otherwise put by Rao, a member of the Commission:

> Recalling the opinion of Oliver Wendell Holmes, Jr., that the life of the law was not logic but experience, [Mr Rao] personally believed that, in the absence of practice, logic could help to move the debate forward and might even lead to the creation of practice. Yet while much of the Commission's work in the area of the responsibility of international organizations was premised on logic, many of the real problems did not fit neatly into a logical framework.[32] (footnote omitted)

[29] Both bibliography and ILC documentation consider indirect responsibility norms as exceptional and incoherent with the overall responsibility framework, see n 25 above. Commentators who have dealt with the issue of EU international responsibility also share this view, eg E Paasivirta and PJ Kuijper, 'Does One Size Fit All? The European Community and the Responsibility of International Organisations' (2005) 36 *Netherlands Yearbook of International Law* 169, 214ff. I am not aware of any commentator that does not share this view.

[30] An explanation of normativity as used throughout this book is provided in Chapter 2, n 8ff and accompanying text.

[31] For a discussion of the analogy argument, see FL Bordin, *The Analogy Between States and International Organizations* (CUP, 2018).

[32] ILC, *Provisional Summary Record of the 2891st Meeting*, UN doc A/CN.4/SR.2891 (2006) reproduced in (2006) 1 *YBILC* 145, 153–54, [59] (Rao).

IV. ADDRESSING THE PROBLEM

A. Aim of the Book

My aim is to assess whether international responsibility is an accountability mechanism that can effectively address scenarios of interaction between member States and International Organisations. In order to do so, I first offer a principled and logical framework upon which practice can be based, and subsequently I assess whether the indirect responsibility provisions under scrutiny are aligned with it. I reject the *sui generis* approach described above, and I endeavour to offer an integrated analysis of all ARIO, Chapter IV and Part Five provisions by putting forward a new understanding of the ILC international responsibility edifice. The principled analysis I attempt throughout the book is, I believe, the key to understanding the operation of indirect responsibility provisions and hence to legally addressing concomitant judicial or extra-judicial cases.

My main argument is that international responsibility is the expression of certain basic legal rules. And I characterise as 'legal' those rules that possess binding force according to the sources of international law.[33] In the second chapter, I define the particular features of those rules that constitute the foundations of international responsibility. These rules take the form of normative principles: what the Permanent Court of International Justice (PCIJ) has termed 'principles of international law' in the *Lotus* case,[34] or what the Study Group of the ILC and the International Court of Justice (ICJ) have named 'general international law'.[35] These terms capture both the 'general principles of law' according to ICJ Statute, Article 38(1)(c) and the 'principles of international law' that have the status of customary international law according to ICJ Statute, Article 38(1)(b). The ICJ evokes a common method of identification for both categories and that is why for practical reasons it is pertinent to group them in one. My aim is not

[33] On the relationship between normativity and the legal character of a rule, see Chapter 2 nn 12–16 and accompanying text.

[34] *Case of the SS Lotus* (*France v Turkey*) [1927] PCIJ Ser A, no 10, 3, 16: 'Now the Court considers that the words "principles of international law", as ordinarily used, can only mean international law as it is applied between all nations belonging to the community of States'. For an analysis of the reference to legal principles in the PCIJ and the ICJ case law, see G Gaja, 'General Principles of Law' in *Max Planck Encyclopedia of Public International Law* (OUP online ed, 2013) [20] and G Schwarzenberger, 'The Fundamental Principles of International Law' (1955) 92 *RCADI* 195, 204.

[35] ILC, *Fragmentation of International Law: Difficulties Arising from the Diversification and Expansion of International Law [Report of the Study Group]*, UN doc A/CN.4/L.682 (13 April 2006) 254. This term has been used by the ICJ, eg *Legal Consequences of the Construction of a Wall in the Occupied Palestinian Territory* (Advisory Opinion) [2004] ICJ Rep 136, 197, [150]. Gourgourinis, who conducted a survey in the use of the term in international practice, concludes that 'general international law' refers to norms which are 'binding on and, in principle, applicable to all the subjects of the international legal system', A Gourgourinis, 'General/Particular International Law and Primary/Secondary Rules: Unitary Terminology of a Fragmented System' (2011) 22 *EJIL* 993, 1011.

to ground the law of international responsibility *in toto* upon 'general principles of law' as B Cheng tried to do.[36] It is far more modest than that.

I argue that those 'principles of international law'/'general international law' determine the nature of international responsibility, the basic premise of the whole ILC international responsibility edifice. Since these legal principles underlie the law of international responsibility as a whole, the latter cannot progressively develop against these binding rules. And arguably all ARIO provisions, due to lack of relevant practice, have been drafted as reflections of the progressive development of the law and not of existing law. Therefore, my analysis rests upon those 'principles of international law' I identify in Chapter 2 as the legal basis of international responsibility. The elaboration of any provision that regulates international responsibility can only be based on, and respect, these rules. By contrast, a provision that runs counter to them does not reflect the progressive development of the law. Overall then, I aim to justify the development of the law on the basis of its accordance with its normative premises.

Theorising indirect responsibility provisions as exceptions to such principles affects the normative status of such provisions. This is so, because they are conceptualised as running counter to the essential legal basis upon which the whole international responsibility edifice is constructed. And unless they are proven to exist as *lex lata*, exceptions to existing law cannot constitute the progressive development of the law, all the more when, as is the case with the ARIO, no relevant practice exists.

It is not only the content of the provision drafted but also the argumentative basis upon which the ILC infers the 'progressive development' that should be congruent with the legal premises of international responsibility. And in the case of both the ASR and the ARIO, this argumentative basis is provided mainly by the commentaries and by the drafting history of the respective provisions. Thus, the book argues for a rethinking of indirect responsibility provisions on the basis of the legal rules underpinning every provision that deals with international responsibility so that the latter forms a coherent and principled whole.

I believe that if the ILC had elaborated the indirect responsibility provisions on such normative grounds it would have achieved a double goal. Most importantly, it would have got the law's development right and consequently it would have forestalled the breadth of criticism and the ensuing distrust that targeted these provisions after the final reading of the ARIO. The novel understanding of international responsibility on the basis of legal principles put forward here explains the operation of these provisions and clarifies their relationship with other responsibility provisions. The analysis demonstrates that scenarios

[36] B Cheng, *General Principles of Law as Applied by International Courts and Tribunals* (CUP, 2006) 163–256.

of interaction between member States and International Organisations are not necessarily regulated by exceptional or anomalous responsibility provisions, but rather by norms consistent with the whole responsibility framework.

Finally, the raison d'être of these provisions is their use by interested actors, be they courts and tribunals in relevant cases, or International Organisations and member States when justifying their conduct and addressing reparation claims. But as formulated at present, some of these provisions do not represent the progressive development of the law and are thus of limited practical usefulness for those actors. So, by proposing new interpretations of existing rules or alternative formulations of them, I intend to offer rules that can help courts, International Organisations or States address cases of indirect responsibility. I do not propose that the ILC reconsiders the wording of the ARIO, because the latter are now finalised and in the hands of the General Assembly. Hence, the rules I propose throughout the book as reflections of the progressive development of the law are intended to function primarily as interpretative guidelines of the existing ARIO provisions. Only to the extent that harmonisation through interpretation is impossible, the rules proposed here will serve as substitutes of the ARIO provisions. Instead of putting forward an overhaul of the whole system of responsibility, I examine what can be done within the corners of the existing legal framework.

While most of the discussion in the book revolves around the ARIO, it is not exclusively confined to the analysis of the provisions drafted by the ILC. The book aims to answer any legal question pertinent to the allocation of responsibility between International Organisations and member States. The issues that arise by virtue of the research question are guiding the analysis and not the ILC's treatment of the matter. The Commission has not tackled every issue (eg no member responsibility rule)[37] or has got the law wrong with respect to others (eg Article 61).[38] Thus, in dealing with scenarios where the ILC's approach has proven defective, the analysis will move beyond the ARIO.

B. Progressive Development of International Law in the ARIO

The ILC in its Statute is mandated not only to identify or codify existing law (*lex lata*), but also to record international law's progressive development (*lex ferenda*) in matters when no identifiable legal rules exist. Article 15 of the ILC Statute defines 'progressive development' as 'the preparation of draft conventions on subjects which have not yet been regulated by international law or in regard to which the law has not yet been sufficiently developed in the practice of States', while 'codification' entails 'the more precise formulation and

[37] See Chapter 3.
[38] See Chapter 6.

systematisation of rules of international law in fields where there already has been extensive State practice, precedent and doctrine'.[39] The separation between the two exercises, reflected in Chapter II of the Commission's Statute 'has proved impractical'[40] or 'unworkable'[41] and the Commission's modern practice has de facto pushed the distinction to one side.[42] With this in mind, the ILC reluctantly shied away from expressing an overall opinion on the legal status of every ARIO provision. On the other hand, it was satisfied with a generic statement that 'the provisions of the present draft articles do not necessarily yet have the same authority as the corresponding provisions on State responsibility'.[43] This oracular statement suggests that, absent any characterisation from the ILC or collectively from States, the normative standing of the Articles remains uncertain, just like Schrodinger's cat.[44] So, it falls upon the consumers of the ILC's work to determine their legal validity.

Despite the aforementioned statement, not every single provision in the ARIO exists, in the absence of an observer, in a state of 'quantum superposition'. As will be explained in the next chapter, the ILC has implicitly, albeit clearly, suggested that ARIO, Articles 3 to 5 constitute rules of general applicability that exist as *lex lata*. And my argument is that these rules, in turn, affect the normative status of the remaining ARIO provisions that have been drafted as reflections of international law's progressive development.

The elaboration of the progressive development of international law has not been extensively analysed by legal scholarship. And this may be so because it is believed to be a political and not a legal exercise since it 'involves controversial policy choices'.[45] However, this *ipso facto* does not mean that existing law has no say in it. To the extent that progressive development of the law constitutes *lex ferenda*, a separation between *lex lata* and *lex ferenda* is in order. As Thirlway explains, the establishment of *lex lata* is dependent upon objective determination, while *lex ferenda* is a subjective assertion that some rule should

[39] ILC Statute, Art 15.

[40] H Lauterpacht, 'Codification and Development of International Law' (1955) 49 *AJIL* 16, 30.

[41] A Watts, 'Codification and Progressive Development of International Law' in R Wolfrum (ed), *Max Planck Encyclopedia of Public International Law* (OUP, 2007) [20].

[42] Crawford characterised the modern approach as 'a functional hybrid between codification and progressive development', J Crawford, 'The Progressive Development of International Law: History, Theory and Practice' in D Alland, V Chetail, O de Frouville and JE Vinuales (eds), *Unity and Diversity of International Law, Essays in Honour of Professor Pierre-Marie Dupuy* (Martinus Nijhoff, 2014) 1, 19.

[43] ARIO Comment, 67–68, [5].

[44] By presenting a cat that may be simultaneously both alive and dead, Schrodinger intended to explain a state known as 'quantum superposition'. According to the latter, a quantum system can exist as a combination of multiple states corresponding to different possible outcomes until it interacts with, or is observed by, the external world, E Schrodinger, 'Die gegenwartige Situation in der Quantenmechanik' (1935) 23 *Naturwissenschaften* 807.

[45] K Daugirdas, 'The International Law Commission Reinvents Itself?' (2014) 108 *AJIL Unbound* 79, 80.

be part of positive law.[46] So, the ILC in the ARIO records the rules on responsibility of International Organisations *which the ILC thinks* ought to be law.

The question that arises is whether the ILC remains completely unrestrained to propose any provision it sees fit as the progressive development of the law, or whether this is qualified in some way. To put this differently, can the content of a proposed rule affect its standing as progressive development of the law? When discussing *lex ferenda* in general, Thirlway suggests that there are 'numerous possible ideas and rules' that do not qualify for *lex ferenda* 'inasmuch as they would not be desirable as law'.[47] Targeting solely the ILC, Pellet has argued that the Commission's 'duty is to try to understand the logic of existing rules and to develop them in the framework of this logic, not to change the underlying logic'.[48] If existing law forms part of the framework (or the underlying logic) for developing rules, then it is conceivable that it imposes restraints on law's progressive development.

With respect to the indirect responsibility ARIO provisions examined in this book, the Commission has no relevant practice it can 'build on' but it rather has to construe provisions seemingly *ex nihilo*. As stated above, Article 15 of the ILC Statute suggests that progressive development can occur in two instances: with respect to 'subjects which have not yet been regulated by international law or in regard to which the law has not yet been sufficiently developed in the practice of States'.[49] ARIO, Chapter IV and Part V provisions clearly fall under the first category. Since no indications of practice direct the future development of the law, the Commission has to start *almost* from a 'blank sheet'. Nevertheless, the sheet is not entirely blank, for certain fundamental legal rules of general applicability impose some limitations to the ILC's work.[50]

The thrust of my argument is that with respect to the law on international responsibility, the ILC is not unrestricted when delivering its function of progressive development. The ILC cannot use its mandate of progressive development to draft *lex ferenda* provisions that run counter to foundational legal rules underpinning the ILC's project as a whole.[51] By setting the legal foundations

[46] H Thirlway, 'Reflections on Lex Ferenda' (2001) 32 *Netherlands Yearbook of International Law* 3, 4.

[47] ibid.

[48] A Pellet, 'Between Codification and Progressive Development of the Law: Some Reflections from the ILC' (2004) 6 *International Law FORUM du Droit International* 15, 16–17.

[49] ILC Statute, Art 15.

[50] Similar proposition from Boyle and Chinkin: 'even in those topics where the element of progressive development of new law is necessarily larger … there are usually some indications of state practice and general principles, however fragmentary, on which to build … Rarely, if ever, is the Commission starting from a blank sheet', A Boyle and C Chinkin, *The Making of International Law* (OUP, 2007) 174–75.

[51] See the similar argument by Ahlborn, who suggests that: 'analogies have … a limiting effect on progressive development if they are incoherent with established principles or underlying reasons accepted in a given legal order', C Ahlborn, 'The Use of Analogies in Drafting the Articles on the Responsibility of International Organizations: An Appraisal of the "Copy-Paste Approach"' (2012) 9 *IOLR* 53, 65.

for the ARIO edifice, in the form of *lex lata* Articles 3 to 5, the Commission has self-imposed certain limitations on what it can identify as *lex ferenda* in the rest of the ARIO. It should respect those legal rules applicable to the law of international responsibility in its entirety. If it does not, it does not record the progressive development of the law, for *lex ferenda* does not gradually develop in defiance of *lex lata*.

In a similar vein, Guideline 9(2) of the recent ILC Guidelines on the Protection of the Atmosphere reads:

> States should, to the extent possible, when developing new rules of international law relating to the protection of the atmosphere and other relevant rules of international law, endeavour to do so in a harmonious manner.

While this provision is addressed to States in their capacity as international legislators and not to the ILC, and pertains to the relationships between rules emanating from different legislative texts, it confirms the applicability of the principle of systemic integration when progressively developing the law.[52] According to this principle, legal reasoning 'builds systemic relationships between rules and principles by envisaging them as parts of some human effort or purpose'.[53] The so-called presumption against normative conflict that emanates from this principle dictates that rules do not conflict and 'when creating new obligations, States are assumed not to derogate from their obligations'.[54] Since no single legislative will can be discerned in international law, this principle promotes harmonisation, coherence and uniformity in the application, interpretation and development of international law.

As a matter of logic, this principle applies more forcefully in the case of ARIO provisions. If relationships are built between two or more rules that emanate from different texts, shouldn't this be the case between rules that emanate from the same text? The Commission clearly intends to draft rules that form a coherent whole and can coexist harmoniously. Also, if rules with the same normative value are presumably in accordance with each other, shouldn't a developing *lex ferenda* rule presumably accord with a *lex lata* rule? Especially when this *lex ferenda* rule comes as an assertion based on extra-legal considerations and not as the reflection of a developing practice or a concomitant *opinio juris*. This means that in the absence of a legal indication to this direction, the ILC cannot infer that exceptions to existing law constitute the law's progressive development. It would be self-contradictory and against any systemic conceptualisation of the law, if the latter were to undermine itself in such a way. So, the presumption against conflict applies not only to a *lex lata–lex lata* conflict but also to a *lex ferenda–lex lata* conflict, when the former constitutes

[52] ILC, *Report of the International Law Commission on the Work of Its 69th Session* (1 May–2 June and 3 July–4 August 2017), UN doc A/72/10 (2017) ch VI, 147, 161, [14].

[53] ILC, *Fragmentation of International Law* (n 35) 24–26, [35]–[38].

[54] ibid [38].

the progressive development of the latter and no *legal* indication (ie existing practice or *opinio juris*) points to the opposite direction.

If the qualification to the progressive development of ARIO rules stands, then the ILC is not entitled to ignore ARIO, Articles 3 to 5 when recording international law's progressive development in the field of responsibility of International Organisations. If it does, the Commission is stepping beyond its mandate, is recording provisions that do not reflect the development of international law, and abuses the confidence placed in it by the General Assembly.[55] However, it must be reminded that the Commission is not a law-maker but rather a law-identifier.[56] The hardening of *lex ferenda* into *lex lata* falls upon the legislators of the international legal order, be they States or International Organisations.[57] So, what are the consequences that follow from a determination that certain ILC provisions do not reflect the progressive development of international law and hence the Commission is acting *hors mandat*?

Arguably, the normative status of such provisions is affected. They constitute legislative proposals but with no claim to normativity. They no longer ought to transform into existing law and in this sense they are dispossessed of their 'deontic' characteristic.[58] This change of status may be utterly insignificant should law-makers decide to act upon those rules and transform them into customary *lex lata*. Nevertheless, it is of the outmost significance when such rules are to be applied from international courts and tribunals. And the ARIO, for lack of a more authoritative alternative, already play an important role in judicial practice (ie the *Nuhanovic* judgments before Dutch courts and the European Court of Human Rights (ECtHR) *Behrami* decision).[59] It is essential, then, for courts to have a guiding light in cases where the law is in a state of formation, and arguably the ILC Articles fulfil this role.[60] Judicial bodies should not resort to provisions that cannot constitute the progressive development of the law in order to fill gaps in existing law.

Being a law-identification exercise, this book purports to serve as a point of reference for courts and tribunals that must determine legal issues related

[55] UN Charter, Art 13(1)(a).

[56] Pellet, 'Between Codification and Progressive Development' (n 48) 16.

[57] On the role of International Organisations in international law-making, see N Voulgaris, 'International Organizations as Autonomous Actors in the Formation of Customary International Law' in S Droubi and J d'Aspremont (eds), *Perspectives on International Organisations and Formation of Customary International Law* (Manchester University Press, forthcoming).

[58] 'Deontic' originates from the ancient Greek word 'δέον', present participle of the verb 'δεῖ', which means 'being necessary to', HG Liddell and R Scott, *An Intermediate Greek-English Lexicon* (Clarendon Press, 1889).

[59] For an analysis of those cases, see Chapters 4 and 6, respectively.

[60] The tendency of international courts to uncritically rely on the ILC's work has been argued by Boyle and Chinkin: 'This has also enabled the ICJ and other tribunals to rely on ILC conventions without overtly enquiring whether particular articles represent existing law, revision of existing law or a new development of the law', *The Making of International Law* (n 50) 200. For an analysis of the use of ILC Articles by international courts and chiefly the ICJ, see G Gaja, 'Interpreting Articles Adopted by the International Law Commission' (2015) 85 *BYBIL* 10.

to the allocation of international responsibility between International Organisations and member States. From a practical perspective, this constitutes this book's contribution. The ILC rules that presumably constitute the progressive development of the law in such cases will be used as a starting point of the analysis. In order to test whether they indeed reflect *lex ferenda*, the book will analyse whether they can be interpreted to align with *lex lata*. If harmonisation through interpretation is impossible,[61] alternative formulations that accord with existing law will be proposed as accurate reflections of international law's progressive development.

C. Structure of the Argument

This book is divided into six substantive chapters and my argument is structured around the afore-mentioned types of interaction.

In Chapter 2, I set the scene for the analysis that follows. Since indirect responsibility provisions will be scrutinised against the basic premises of the law of international responsibility, my objective is to identify these premises. In this way, I aim to fill a doctrinal gap that has been haunting the ILC's work since it embarked upon its 50-year quest to draft the ASR.[62] The Commission has done very little to set out the common foundations of its two projects. Had it pondered over them, the ILC would have formulated a legal accountability mechanism with unitary nature in both the ASR and ARIO. In this way, the Commission would have provided solid foundations to its international responsibility edifice.

It is of fundamental importance to determine why these common foundations should exist in the first place. The function of international responsibility provides guidance in this respect. According to the ILC, international responsibility for internationally wrongful acts is the legal accountability mechanism of the international legal order with respect to States and International Organisations. This will be the case, however, if this mechanism can be attached to both subjects of international law. Respectively, international responsibility's nature, comprised of its content and its applicability *ratione personae* and *ratione materiae*, should possess a unitary character in order to be compatible with this function. Since it is the content of international responsibility that determines its applicability, I test whether the former possesses such conceptual unity in both the ASR and ARIO.

[61] '[I]t is a rule of interpretation that a text emanating from a Government must, in principle, be interpreted as producing and intended to produce effects in accordance with existing law and not in violation of it', *Case concerning Right of Passage over Indian Territory* (*Portugal v India*) (Preliminary Objections) [1957] ICJ Rep 125, 142.

[62] The Commission began the study of State responsibility at its seventh session in 1955 and concluded it in 2001, ILC, 'Analytical Guide to the Work of the International Law Commission' available at legal.un.org/ilc/guide/9_6.shtml.

This will be the case only if this content is constructed upon rules that are sufficiently generic to attach to both entities. As constructed by the ILC, the content of international responsibility is indeed based on such rules. According to the Commission, the content of responsibility is inherently linked with the notion of an internationally wrongful act. I argue that the latter is the expression of generally applicable legal principles that admit of no exceptions. It follows that international responsibility possesses the necessary conceptual unity to attach to both States and International Organisations and fulfil its function. This understanding of international responsibility's nature I put forward, determined by legal principles and applicable to both subjects of international law, constitutes the foundation of the ILC's responsibility edifice.

Part 1 of the book, comprised of Chapter 3, focuses on member State-International Organisation interaction on the basis of their particular relationship. For every relationship, I will examine it from each side, discussing both the position of the member States and that of the International Organisation. Interaction occurs on this basis when member States exercise competence that lies with the International Organisation in accordance with the latter's rules. This type of State conduct puts the organisational veil in operation and shields member States under it by virtue of a personality merging.

The starting point for the analysis of this subject-matter is Article 62, although the ILC's ARIO Articles deal with it after the other provisions which are examined in this book. In this sense, the analysis begins from the end. The provision incorporates the rule that member States do not bear international responsibility for internationally wrongful acts of the International Organisation. I suggest that the ILC should have clearly premised the drafting of both limbs of Article 62 (ie Article 62(1)(a) and (1)(b)) and the commentaries to it on the understanding of the member State-International Organisation relationship outlined above. The ARIO, however, fail to articulate an elaborate analysis of the member State-International Organisation relationship and that is why the loosely justified 'exclusive International Organisation responsibility' rule (in the commentaries) and its exceptions (Article 62(1)(a) and (1)(b)) must be understood under this prism. What is more, Article 62 in the way advocated in the ARIO, further entangles international responsibility with the relative notion of liability and perpetuates the confusion surrounding their establishment and function. On the normative basis provided by the member State-International Organisation relationship and the foundational principles of international responsibility, I suggest how the provision and the commentaries should have been drafted, so that both the 'exclusive International Organisation responsibility' rule and the one valid exception to this rule are justified.

The second Part is centred around the other type of interaction: that between member States and the International Organisation as independent subjects of international law. The first chapter in this Part (Chapter 4) turns the focus on these ARIO provisions regulating such interaction, which were drafted according to the respective ASR template. In the way advocated by the ILC and analysed by commentators, these provisions exist in a problematic relationship with the premises of international responsibility. The provision on 'aid or assistance' has seemingly eradicated the prerequisite of breach for the establishment of an internationally wrongful act and thus of international responsibility, while both 'direction and control' and 'coercion' provisions seemingly suggest that an internationally wrongful act can arise without attribution of conduct. I reinterpret the provisions through the prism of the general principles I identified in Chapter 2 and thus realign them with the nature of international responsibility.

The main argument running throughout the chapter suggests that indirect responsibility provisions operate according to specific responsibility models. Apart from the 'independent responsibility' model, which is attached to direct responsibility, it is submitted that two more normative schemes, attached to indirect responsibility, can be identified: derivative responsibility and complicity. The complicity model addresses scenarios in which an actor participates in the internationally wrongful act of another and the derivative responsibility model regulates the responsibility of an actor for the conduct of another. The normative elements found in both 'direction and control' and 'coercion' place these provisions under the derivative responsibility model, while the complicity model is attached to 'aid or assistance'. Arguably, the two must be distinguished and kept apart, as they each affect differently the responsibility of the relevant subjects. On the basis of these models, I propose new interpretations of the provisions reflective of the progressive development of the law.

The next two chapters deal in turn with two mirroring situations. Articles 17 and 61 were adopted following several reformulations of their wording and heated debates during their drafting. They revolve around the notion of circumvention and give expression to the basic principle that one cannot do through another what one cannot do oneself. While they do not find a parallel in inter-State relations, they regulate interaction between member States and the International Organisation of which they are members as independent subjects of international law. This is why they operate according to the responsibility models I identify in Chapter 4.

Article 17 pertains to circumvention of obligations binding an International Organisation through decisions and authorisations issued by the International Organisation that are addressed towards its member States. The second chapter in Part II (Chapter 5) explains how the provision under scrutiny fits within the responsibility models attached to indirect responsibility, and how its wording is to be realigned with the foundations of international responsibility. Arguably, there is a strong case to draw parallels between Article 17 and the two indirect responsibility models identified in the previous chapter. Paragraph 1 of Article 17, referring to binding decisions, makes sense when seen under the lens of derivative responsibility, while paragraph 2 clearly references complicity. Such analogies, it is contended, provide adequate answers to underlying questions of shared, joint or parallel responsibility which were too complicated for the ILC to directly address. Since analysis of the provision as a whole would result in deeper confusion, the disentanglement put forward here is a prerequisite for a normative explanation of Article 17. Through this prism, the provision finds a perfect fit within the law of international responsibility; it reflects the progressive development of the law and is of use for international courts and tribunals.

The new understanding of Article 17 proposed here provides an efficient approach to the regulation of recurring scenarios. The application of the provision in UN targeted sanctions cases suggests that Article 17 provides a just and effective regulatory basis for the resolution of conflicts of obligations that have been (to date) too complex for courts to handle. Even if it is not yet *lex lata*, it is submitted here that a consistent application of the provision by interested actors (States, International Organisations and courts) can have an effect on its normative status and transform it into a customary rule. Beyond the normative analysis, I argue that due to the broad range of cases it covers and the practical ramifications that come with its application, Article 17 should be seen as an opportunity to initiate a change in the way International Organisations operate in the international arena.

Article 61, on the contrary, is a strange combination of the indirect responsibility models analysed in Chapter 4. In Chapter 6, I argue that, as it stands at present, Article 61 does not reflect the progressive development of the law. The lack of normative analysis behind the drafting of the provision, is evinced by two factors. First, the Commission sought to accommodate a wide array of scenarios by drafting a 'package-deal' provision and Article 61 incorporates both indirect responsibility models in one single provision. This is why I argue that, like its counterpart (ie Article 17), Article 61 should have been split into two paragraphs, each one addressing a different model. Second, the ILC should have avoided any reference in the commentaries to ECtHR case law. The latter pertains to direct responsibility and therefore does not incorporate valid authoritative statements in support of Article 61. This relationship between Article 61 and existing case law, the ILC has established, is the main reason that provoked some misplaced criticism and a inaccurate understanding of the provision. Instead, a rule on circumvention of State obligations through member State conduct on the basis of the present analysis would have constituted the progressive development of the law and could potentially transform into a customary rule of international law.

In the last Part, comprised of Chapter 7, I test how my theoretical framework applies in practice. With this in mind, I use decision-making procedures within International Organisations as a case-study. The scenarios analysed do not cover only member States' votes but any type of influence a State can exert during these procedures. A thorough understanding of the establishment of international responsibility in the context of decision-making procedures of International Organisations is premised on a *tour d'horizon* of most issues discussed throughout the book. And I think it is only pertinent to conclude the argument through an applied synthesis of all intermediate findings.

The starting and end-point of the analysis will be the regulation of the matter within ARIO, Articles 58, 59 and 61, but also within existing case law. It is fitting to do so with respect to decision-making, for three main reasons: first, it is timely to bring Articles 58(2) and 59(2) into the analysis, as such procedures were the main reason why these provisions were inserted in the ARIO. The criterion of accordance of State conduct with the rules of the International Organisation they incorporate echoes the threshold I advocated in Chapter 3 for the occurrence of interaction on the basis of membership. Second, State conduct during decision-making procedures could occur both inside and outside the particular member State-International Organisation relationship. The type of interaction then shifts in these procedures, and that is why they provide a good illustration of both types of interaction and a figurative way to keep the cleavage as clear as possible. Third, while international responsibility can be established on certain occasions, it will seldom substantiate as jurisdictional bars will inhibit its fruition before a court. Decision-making procedures, then, are pertinent to keep clear another distinction – that between establishment and implementation of international responsibility.

2

The Function and Nature of International Responsibility

I. INTRODUCTION

THE RESEARCH QUESTION I aim to answer in this book pertains to the international responsibility rules regulating interaction between States and International Organisations. In order to provide a doctrinally sound answer to the research question, two issues must be clarified from the outset: whether international responsibility can attach to both entities and how the rules that regulate the establishment of international responsibility should be drafted. Given the International Law Commission (ILC)'s attempt to elaborate such rules, it is assessed here whether the Commission has laid the essential groundwork for a joint examination of responsibility issues. The Commission has done very little to clarify the nature of international responsibility, and voices from within the Commission and commentators have suggested, for example, that States and International Organisations cannot be subject to common responsibility rules.[1] What is more, the arguments employed by the ILC in the elaboration of these rules do not have a common thread and it seems as if the Commission is lacking a principled argumentative basis.

A reflection upon the function and nature of international responsibility as an accountability mechanism provides the necessary background to address such issues. Being the only legal accountability mechanism attached to States and International Organisations, I argue that international responsibility is a necessary element of the international legal order, as it substantiates the 'normative characteristic' of international legal rules. Respectively, international responsibility's nature, comprised of its content and its applicability *ratione personae* and *ratione materiae,* should be compatible with this function.

[1] See ILC, *Provisional Summary of the 3081st Meeting*, UN doc A/CN.4/SR.3081 (2011) 6 (McRae); R McCorquodale, 'International Organizations and International Human Rights Law: One Giant Leap for Humankind' in KH Kaikobad and M Bohlander (eds), *International Law and Power: Perspectives on Legal Order and Justice, Essays in Honour of Colin Warbrick* (Nijhoff, 2009) 141, 148.

II. FUNCTION OF INTERNATIONAL RESPONSIBILITY: 'NO RESPONSIBILITY, NO LAW'

Legal theorists have long debated whether the international order presents a legal quality and any attempt to provide an answer in a few lines is deemed to fail.[2] It is pertinent only to remark that a commonplace criticism against the legal quality of international law revolves around the lack of enforceability of its legal rules.[3] Nevertheless, it exceeds the scope of the argument presented here to explain whether international law constitutes a legal system (or a legal order, the two terms will be used interchangeably) in the first place, and thus whether the above mentioned criticism has merit.[4]

But arguably, the legal quality of a system of rules can be inferred when the violation of the rules it prescribes results in foreseeable legal consequences.[5] The Permanent Court of International Justice (PCIJ) has famously traced the generation of such legal consequences to a legal 'principle of international law'.[6] So long as there exists a system that lays down in rules the rights and obligations of the subjects it regulates,[7] this system will be of a legal nature if it prescribes legal consequences for those subjects – independently of their will – when they commit conduct that runs counter to such rules. Therefore, the fact that the violation of international legal rules results in consequences is a characteristic that derives from the legal character of the international order.

The latter must not be confused with the legal character of the rules of this order. And by legal character of rules, I understand their feature to provide binding commands to their addressees. This is what I shall call the 'normative characteristic' of international legal rules.[8] It is the sources of the international

[2] Kelsen strongly affirms that international law is 'a juridical order', H Kelsen, *The Legal Process and International Order* (New Commonwealth Institute Monograph Series, 1935) 11. Hart, on the other hand, argues that an ultimate rule of recognition lies on the basis of any legal order, and such a rule is absent with respect to international law, HLA Hart, *The Concept of Law* (Clarendon Press, 1961) ch X.

[3] I accept the positivist assumption that a legal system is comprised of legally valid rules, J Beckett, 'Countering Uncertainty and Ending Up/Down Arguments: Prolegomena to a Response to NAIL' (2005) 16 *EJIL* 213, 218.

[4] Dominicé concludes that international law exists as a legal system on the basis of a 'mere observation of reality' and the maxim *ubi societas ibi jus*. His assertion 'is buttressed by the finding that there is a sort of collective opinio juris, a conviction that international law exists and that States could not do without it', C Dominicé, 'Methodology of International Law' in R Bernhardt (ed), *Encyclopedia of Public International Law* (OUP, 1997) 354, 355.

[5] Pellet suggests that responsibility is 'the best proof' of international law's existence, A Pellet, 'The Definition of Responsibility in International Law' in J Crawford, A Pellet and S Olleson (eds), *The Law of International Responsibility* (OUP, 2010) 3, 3–4.

[6] *Factory at Chorzów (Germany v Poland)* (Jurisdiction), PCIJ, 26 July 1927, Ser. A (No 9) 21.

[7] H Thirlway, 'The Sources of International Law' in M. Evans (ed), *International Law* (OUP, 2014) 91.

[8] I understand normativity to go hand in hand with bindingness, J Raz, *The Authority of Law, Essays on Morality and Law* (Clarendon Press, 1979) 149: 'The best route to the understanding of "legally valid" is by attending to the fact that it is used interchangeably with "legally binding". A valid rule is one which has normative effects, that is legal effects'. Similar definition by

legal order that provide to legal rules their normative characteristic and determine the validity of a rule in the first place.[9] Their function, then, is to determine whether a rule, as posited, qualifies as an international legal rule.

The International Law Commission of the United Nations, which has the mandate for both the codification and the progressive development of international legal rules, axiomatically assumes that the international order possesses a legal quality in order to proceed with its task.[10] In the two sets of Articles it has produced, the Commission concluded that the mechanism that provides for the legal consequences from the violation of international legal rules incumbent upon States and International Organisations is termed 'international responsibility', and the illegal conduct that triggers this mechanism 'internationally wrongful act'.[11]

International responsibility rules, then, perform a different function within the international legal system; they substantiate the normative characteristic of international legal rules. Since international responsibility is the legal accountability mechanism in international law insofar as States and International Organisations are concerned, it puts into effect the normative characteristic of international legal rules incumbent upon those subjects: it enforces the legal obligation to be followed.[12] The same function is performed by individual criminal responsibility insofar as individuals are the addressees of international legal norms.[13] By prohibiting conduct through the mechanism of international responsibility and individual criminal responsibility, the international legal system provides a legal reason against performing it that would otherwise be absent.[14] In this sense, the preservation of the normative characteristic of international legal rules effectuated by the mechanisms of responsibility helps bolster the authority, legitimacy and efficacy of international law.

Overall, a rule is posited as law because the sources dictate so, but the breach of the rule results in legal consequences because this rule functions in the context of a legal order. This is why, if one denies the idea of legal responsibility in international law, one necessarily is forced to deny the existence of an

J d'Aspremont, *Formalism and the Sources of International Law: A Theory of the Ascertainment of Legal Rules* (OUP, 2011) 29.

[9] Thirlway, 'The Sources of International Law' (n 7) 93.

[10] 'In sources discourse … the legal order is always already presumed', D Kennedy, 'The Sources of International Law' (1987) 2 *American University Journal of International Law and Policy* 1, 95.

[11] ASR, Art 1 and ARIO, Art 3.

[12] Nollkaemper suggests similarly that 'responsibility is inherent to the notion of obligation', A Nollkaemper, *Responsibility*, Amsterdam Center for International Law Research Paper 2017-03 (2017), available at papers.ssrn.com/sol3/papers.cfm?abstract_id=2914250 6.

[13] J Crawford and J Watkins 'International Responsibility' in S Besson and J Tasioulas (eds), *The Philosophy of International Law* (OUP, 2010) 283, 284. The assumption in this statement is that individual criminal responsibility is the only form of legal accountability attached to individuals as subjects of international law.

[14] ibid 286; J d'Aspremont, 'The Idea of "Rules" in the Sources of International Law' (2014) 84 *BYBIL* 103, 109.

international legal order.[15] Pellet has summarised this in the maxim 'No responsibility, no (international) law'.[16] So, while it is not easy to make an assessment on whether international law constitutes a legal order in the first place, it is clear that international responsibility operates in the context of such an established order. Thus, my argument traces the existence of international responsibility in the presumed existence of the international legal order/system.

The above explains why the ILC selected State responsibility as one of the topics for codification at its inaugural session in 1949. The ILC was anxious to ensure the bindingness of international law, to provide for the enforcement of international obligations without an international policing force, and thus the restoration of international legality.[17]

The Commission tried to separate the rules on international responsibility from other international legal rules on the basis of their function. This was effectuated by Roberto Ago in 1970. He mentioned that '[i]t is one thing to define a rule and the content of the obligation it imposes and another to determine whether that obligation has been violated and what should be the consequences of the violation'.[18] So, he made the following distinction:

> the rules of international law which … impose particular obligations on States … may, in a certain sense, be termed 'primary', as opposed to the other rules – precisely those covering the field of responsibility – which may be termed 'secondary', inasmuch as they are concerned with determining the consequences of failure to fulfil obligations established by the primary rules.[19]

This separation between the two categories has been adopted and employed by the ILC in both the Articles on State Responsibility (ASR)[20] and the Articles on the Responsibility of International Organizations (ARIO).[21]

I believe that keeping in mind this distinction is crucial in order to clarify the function of international responsibility rules. This categorisation need not necessarily align with the archetype Hartian view on the matter.[22] But, it spells out the role of international responsibility rules in the international legal order

[15] R Ago, *Third Report on State Responsibility* UN doc A/8010/Rev.l (1971) and Add 1 to 3 reproduced in (1971) 2(1) *YBILC* 199 ('Ago Third Report') 205.

[16] Pellet, 'The Definition of Responsibility in International Law' (n 5) 4. See Verdross in a similar vein: 'A denial of this principle would destroy international law, since the negation of responsibility for a wrongful act would also do away with the duty of States to behave in accordance with international law', A Verdross, *Volkerrecht* (Springer, 1964) 373 (translation by the United Nations Secretariat). In the words of Brownlie, international responsibility 'put[s] a harder edge on legal rights and duties' and thus constitutes the heart and lungs of international law, I Brownlie, *System of the Law of Nations: State Responsibility, Part I* (Clarendon Press, 1983) 87.

[17] Pellet, 'The Definition of Responsibility in International Law' (n 5) 15.

[18] Ago Third Report (n 15) 200.

[19] R Ago, *Second Report on State Responsibility*, UN doc A/CN.4/233 (1970), reproduced in (1970) 2(1) *YBILC* 177, 179, [11] ('Ago Second Report').

[20] ASR Comment, 31, [1].

[21] ARIO Comment, 67, [3].

[22] Hart, *The Concept of Law* (n 2) 92.

and it is sufficiently clear in that the two categories are mutually exclusive, they cannot coexist in one rule. Notwithstanding the analysis in Chapter 4,[23] and because I do not intend to engage in a philosophical analysis about the primary/secondary norms distinction in international law, I will employ throughout the book the ILC's view on the matter. Therefore, this distinction Ago put forward between primary norms (the obligations themselves) and secondary norms (consequences of breaching any such primary obligation), emphasises that 'the secondary rules of State responsibility were the international equivalent of domestic sanctions'.[24]

III. INTERNATIONAL RESPONSIBILITY AND THE SUBJECTS OF INTERNATIONAL LAW

According to the ILC, 'international responsibility' pertains to the legal relations which arise under international law by reason of an internationally wrongful act.[25] The Commission held that a mechanism of such nature delivers the above-mentioned function and substantiates the normative characteristic of international legal rules. And this is the case according to the ILC with respect to both States and International Organisations, as entities endowed with international legal personality. I do not argue that the ascription of the ability to incur or to invoke international responsibility is constitutive of subjecthood in international law.[26] For the purposes of this book, it suffices to note that the ILC has attached this accountability mechanism to two distinct categories of international legal subjects.

Perforce then, conceptual unity should be a feature of the notion of responsibility in international law insofar as it pertains to States and International Organisations. If this is proven, it finds a two-level expression: first, the notion of international responsibility should be the mechanism that provides legal consequences for violations of primary obligations incumbent upon States and International Organisations (applicability *ratione materiae*); and second, its content should not be tailored to addressing the position of States but it rather should apply to International Organisations as subjects of international law also (applicability *ratione personae*). It is pertinent to assess, then, whether the ILC, with the drafting of the ASR and the ARIO, has codified such a mechanism. The analysis thus turns to revealing the nature of international responsibility.

[23] See Chapter 4 at III A ii.

[24] A Nissell, 'The ILC Articles on State Responsibility: Between Self-Help and Solidarity' (2006) 38 *International Law and Politics* 355, 356; M Koskenniemi, 'Solidarity Measures: State Responsibility as a New International Order?' (2002) 72 *BYBIL* 337, 339.

[25] ASR Comment, 32, [1].

[26] Nollkaemper, *Responsibility* (n 12) 10.

IV. NATURE OF INTERNATIONAL RESPONSIBILITY

A. International Responsibility as the Expression of Legal Principles Without Exceptions

It should be noted as a caveat that apart from the fundamental principle that international responsibility (as a mechanism that attaches to legal rules their normative characteristic) exists in international law, all other principles that determine international responsibility's nature need some justification that they belong to the *corpus* of rules of international law. The only accepted pedigree test for the determination of the normative force of rules in international law is incorporated in Article 38(1) of the Statute of the International Court of Justice (ICJ).[27] Any other test would lack the shared acceptance of international lawyers and its applicability would be questioned. Arguably, then, the ILC's approach in the ASR and the ARIO to assess the normative force of the rules of international responsibility according to the sources of international law is justified. This consideration nevertheless determines the argumentative method to be employed. Since the sources identify the law based on issues susceptible of objective determination, when arguing for the normative force of the rules of international responsibility, the ILC should put aside moral and policy argumentation.[28] It is solely normative argumentation that identifies the legal quality of rules.

The rules that determine the nature of international responsibility possess two key characteristics that render them foundational legal rules underpinning both the ILC's ASR and ARIO: general applicability and normative force of law. Chapter 1 of Part One of the ASR and Chapter I of Part Two of the ARIO which address this issue, are comprised of three mirroring provisions and are both entitled 'General Principles'. ASR, Article 1 and ARIO, Article 3 provide that a State's or an International Organisation's international responsibility is established when this subject commits an internationally wrongful act. ASR, Article 2 and ARIO, Article 4 specify breach and attribution as the constituent elements of such an act of either a State or an International Organisation. Finally, according to ASR, Article 3 and ARIO, Article 5, the characterisation of a given act as internationally wrongful is governed by international law.

[27] It is commonly accepted that this provision incorporates the sources of international law, see generally Thirlway, 'The Sources of International Law' (n 7) 93. The ICJ has called the rules incorporated in ICJ Statute, Art 38(1) 'positive law tests', *North Sea Continental Shelf* (*Germany v Denmark and the Netherlands*) [1969] ICJ Reports 3, 29, [38]. Article 38(1) reads: 'The Court, whose function is to decide in accordance with international law such disputes as are submitted to it, shall apply: (a) international conventions, whether general or particular, establishing rules expressly recognized by the contesting states; (b) international custom, as evidence of a general practice accepted as law; (c) the general principles of law recognized by civilized nations; (d) subject to the provisions of Article 59, judicial decisions and the teachings of the most highly qualified publicists of the various nations, as subsidiary means for the determination of rules of law'.

[28] Raz, *The Authority of Law* (n 8) 152.

Seen together, these three provisions determine the nature of international responsibility as it applies to both States and International Organisations.

The commentaries to ASR, Articles 1 to 3 and ARIO, Articles 3 to 5, clarify two things with respect to these provisions. First, they are principles generally applicable to the law of international responsibility and admit of no exceptions. The Commission holds that the first two constitute 'basic principle[s] underlying the articles as a whole'.[29] The same inference is drawn with respect to the third one, since this provision 'makes explicit a principle already implicit in' the second provision.[30]

As a clear-cut distinction between principles and rules has not yet been elaborated in international doctrine or case law, the use of the term 'principles' denotes the general nature of the norm in question.[31] Principles express 'general truths'[32] or maxims of the law.[33] In this way, the ILC implicitly suggests that these provisions are abstractions or generalisations from all legal rules that pertain to the establishment of international responsibility.[34] Or, they remain 'in the background', controlling the way more specific rules are being interpreted and applied.[35] What is more, when the more specific rules do not possess a clear normative status (as is the case with the rest of the ARIO), the general principles control not only directly the content of the specific rules, through interpretation and application, but also indirectly, as explained in the previous chapter, their normative status.[36] There is no specific test in international law that determines the establishment of a generally applicable principle without exceptions and that is why the ILC made these assertions without justifying them in any way.

[29] ASR Comment, 32, [1], 34, [1] and 36, [9]; ARIO Comment, 78, [1] and 79, [1].

[30] ASR Comment, 36, [1]; ARIO Comment, 80, [1].

[31] G Gaja, 'General Principles of Law' in *Max Planck Encyclopedia of Public International Law* (OUP online ed, 2013) [31]; ILC, *Fragmentation of International Law: Difficulties Arising from the Diversification and Expansion of International Law [Report of the Study Group]*, UN doc A/CN.4/L.682 (13 April 2006) [28]; R Wolfrum, 'General International Law (Principles, Rules, and Standards)' in *Max Planck Encyclopedia of Public International Law* (OUP online ed, 2010) [6]; R Kolb, 'General Principles of Procedural Law' in A Zimmermann, K Oellers-Frahm, C Tomuschat and C Tams (eds), *The Statute of the International Court of Justice: A Commentary* (OUP, 2012) 871, 872–73.

[32] *Gentini (of a General Nature)*, Italy-Venezuela Mixed Claims Commission, Decision of 29 August 1903 (1960) 10 *Reports of International Arbitral Awards* 551, 725.

[33] During the drafting process of Art 38(3) of the PCIJ Statute, the precursor of Art 38(1)(c) of the ICJ Statute, which refers to general principles of law, Philimore, who proposed the formula, explained that by general principles of law he meant 'maxims of law', PCIJ Advisory Committee of Jurists, *Procès-verbaux of the Proceedings of the Committee, June 16–July 24th 1920 with Annexes* (Van Langenhuysen, 1920) 335.

[34] G Schwarzenberger, 'The Fundamental Principles of International Law' (1955) 92 *RCADI* 195, 201. Crawford suggests that they are of an axiomatic nature, J Crawford, 'State Responsibility' in *Max Planck Encyclopedia of Public International Law* (OUP online ed, 2013) [17].

[35] ILC, *Fragmentation of International Law* (n 31) [31].

[36] See Chapter 1 at IV B.

Nevertheless, it is logic first of all that justifies the unexceptional character of these provisions. A rule that determines the nature of international responsibility perforce will underpin all rules that deal with the establishment of this accountability mechanism and in this sense the provisions under scrutiny are principles of general application.[37] Further, an examination of these provisions in turn demonstrates that no exceptions can be read into them. ASR, Article 1 and ARIO, Article 3 are clear in that international responsibility arises exclusively by virtue of an internationally wrongful act. It may be that the ILC wanted to limit the scope of application of both the ASR and ARIO to international responsibility that arises by virtue of an internationally wrongful act. Nevertheless, if the Commission held that there exists a different set of circumstances that triggers international responsibility, it should have clearly stated it and exclude these scenarios from the scope of the ASR and ARIO. To the contrary, the Commission suggested that with respect to conduct that does not fulfil the criteria to be characterised as internationally wrongful, different accountability mechanisms apply.[38] This limitation necessarily implies that under no other circumstances will international responsibility come into play. The same goes with respect to the other two principles. The violation of any primary rule always 'raises the two basic questions identified in' ASR, Article 2 and ARIO, Article 4,[39] and the term 'internationally wrongful act' constitutes a *terminus technicus* in international law so only the latter can define its content as per ASR, Article 3 and ARIO, Article 5. It follows from the above that the ILC intended to draft two sets of Articles with internal coherence since each one of them is based on principles that admit of no exceptions.

The second feature of these rules pertains to their legal status. The ILC cites extensive State practice in the commentaries to ASR, Articles 1 to 3 in order to justify these rules. Given the extent of State practice evoked by the ILC, it is safe to assume that they have attained customary law status according to Article 38(1)(b) of the ICJ Statute. Further, the ICJ recently confirmed that ASR, Article 3, whereby 'the characterization of an act of a State as internationally wrongful is governed by international law' is a rule of customary law.[40] Since they combine the two aforementioned characteristics, ASR, Articles 1 to 3 are generally applicable and are binding principles of customary law.

And while these provisions are normatively justified with respect to the ASR, the problematic aspect with the ILC's ARIO project is that it does not clearly explain nor justify the legal status of the provisions regulating the nature of international responsibility of International Organisations. This is why several members of the ILC called for such a clarification in the general commentary on

[37] FA Mann, 'Reflections on a Commercial Law of Nations' (1957) 33 *BYBIL* 20, 36.

[38] ASR Comment, 31, [4] lit c; ARIO Comment, 70, [5].

[39] ASR Comment, 35, [8] and 36, [9].

[40] *Case concerning the Application of the Convention on the Prevention and Punishment of the Crime of Genocide* (*Croatia v Serbia*) (Merits) [2015] ICJ Reports 3, 55 [128].

the ARIO.[41] The Commission cannot argue that these principles, which admit of no exceptions, form part of customary international law since the necessary international practice for such an assertion is lacking.[42]

The ILC holds in the commentaries that the principles incorporated in ARIO, Articles 3 to 5 constitute specific manifestations of other more general principles and from the latter they derive their existence and normative justification.[43] The Commission assumes that such general principles exist as a matter of logic and does not argue for them in normative terms. As said before, however, every rule needs some justification that it belongs to the *corpus* of rules of international law and thus the legal status of these general principles cannot be presumed. The ILC, then, should have provided a more cogent explanation as to why the principles incorporated in ARIO, Articles 3 to 5 possess normative value.

Most likely, the Commission implies that the general principles upon which ARIO, Articles 3 to 5 rest constitute 'general principles of law as recognised by the civilised nations' according to Article 38(1)(c) of the ICJ Statute. It is commonly agreed by commentators that principles, irrespective of their origin in national law, international legal relations or legal logic, can constitute binding rules of international law by virtue of Article 38(1)(c).[44] In this sense, the reference to recognition by 'civilised nations' as the sole origin of such principles has nowadays lost its significance and must be considered obsolete. Nevertheless, as reflections of the conscience of the international community,[45] some form of recognition by the latter is necessary for their transformation into international legal rules. This is so, because consent is considered the 'wellspring of all international legal obligations', but for the (still unsettled) exception of *jus cogens* norms.[46] Thus, recognition by the international community is the element that provides 'general principles of law' with their consensual or voluntary character,[47] and the ILC had to provide evidence of such recognition in the commentaries to ARIO, Articles 3 to 5.

[41] See the suggestions by McRae, Nolte and Wood in *Summary of 3081st Meeting* (n 1).

[42] Nollkaemper, *Responsibility* (n 12) 9.

[43] ARIO Comment, 78, [1] and 79, [1].

[44] C Rousseau, *Principes généraux du droit international public*, vol I, *Sources* (Pedone, 1944) 891; Gaja, 'General Principles of Law' (n 31) [32]; Wolfrum, 'General International Law' (n 31) [28]; H Mosler 'General Principles of Law' in R Bernhardt (ed), *Encyclopedia of Public International Law* (North Holland, 1984) vol 7, 90; *Pulp Mills on the River Uruguay (Argentina v Uruguay)*, Separate Opinion of Judge Cançado Trindade [2010] ICJ Reports 135, 143–45, [20]–[25]; M Nolan and F Gilles Sourgens, 'Issues of Proof of General Principles of Law in International Arbitration' (2009) 3 *World Arbitration and Mediation Review* 505, 508; O Schachter, *International Law in Theory and Practice* (Martinus Nijhoff, 1991) 51.

[45] GM Danilenko, *Law-Making in the International Community* (Martinus Nijhoff, 1993) 7, 17, 175 and 186–87; Mosler, 'General Principles of Law' (n 44) 90–92 and 95.

[46] E Criddle and E Fox-Decent, 'A Fiduciary Theory of Jus Cogens' (2009) 34 *Yale Journal of International Law* 331, 332.

[47] Wolfrum, 'General International Law' (n 31) [54].

The form of this recognition may vary. It is more commonly demonstrated through acceptance in the jurisprudence of international courts or tribunals. In this way, a principle transforms to a legal principle with normative value in international law whenever international jurisprudence – and chiefly the ICJ – decides that this is the case.[48] Such principles of international law may also be recognised by resolutions of International Organisations or policy statements of international conferences, such as world summits.[49] An example in this respect is the general principle of prevention in the context of international environmental law that was recognised by the UN Conferences of Stockholm (1972) and Rio de Janeiro (1992).[50]

Arguably, the principles determining the nature of international responsibility of International Organisations are recognised by the international community as principles with normative value per ICJ Statute, Article 38(1)(c). They may not appear in judgments of international tribunals or in statements of international conferences, but States, International Organisations and commentators unequivocally accept them as valid statements of existing law. This is why a member of the Commission, when commenting on ARIO, Articles 3 to 5, considered it unnecessary for the ILC to give numerous examples of practice in order to justify those 'norms that he considered as being close to general principles of international law'.[51] As will be demonstrated below, this is the case with all three relevant provisions. Like their ASR counterparts, they combine the two aforementioned characteristics: they constitute legally binding principles that are generally applicable.

The establishment of their characteristics is of cardinal importance, for these foundational principles guide the elaboration of all ARIO provisions. Due to their general applicability, principles serve as mechanisms that unify different legal provisions.[52] And this overarching character is strengthened further when they possess normative value and are established as binding commands. Thus, given their binding and unexceptional nature, no ARIO provision can

[48] The ICJ makes recourse to general principles of law without elaborating further on such principles and how they emanate. Fitzmaurice criticised this unfettered discretion of the ICJ to invoke general principles: 'the concept of the general principles is so fluid that a quasi-legislative element would often be introduced into the Court's decisions by any "bold" application of them, and … considerable harm might be done to the desideratum of increased resort to the Court unless a reasonable predictability as the basis of its decisions can be maintained', G Fitzmaurice, 'The Future of Public International Law and of the International Legal System in the Circumstances of Today' in Institute of International Law, *Livre du centenaire 1873–1973: Evolution et perspectives du droit international* (Karger Bâle, 1973) 196, 325. Cançado Trindade laments in his separate opinion the reluctance on behalf of the Court to further elaborate on these principles, Cançado Trindade, Separate Opinion (n 44) [49].

[49] Wolfrum, 'General International Law' (n 31) [55].

[50] N de Sadeleer, 'The Principles of Prevention and Precaution in International Law: Two Heads of the Same Coin?' in M Fitzmaurice, D Ong and P Merkouris (eds), *Research Handbook on International Environmental Law* (Edgar Elgar, 2010) 182.

[51] *Summary of 3081st Meeting* (n 1) 9–10 (Nolte).

[52] Wolfrum, General International Law' (n 31) [63].

run counter to ARIO, Articles 3 to 5. Especially, those provisions that constitute progressive development of the law and do not as yet possess the status of a legally valid rule can transform into existing law only if they do not contradict these fundamental principles. If these principles are respected, then perforce all international responsibility provisions will form a system of rules with a coherent content, as the law does not progressively develop against its own premises.[53] A rule cannot acquire a *lex ferenda* normative value if it runs counter to generally applicable binding rules that form its basis.

In the sections that follow, I will analyse how these principles, and particularly those incorporated in ARIO, Articles 3 and 4, give form to the nature of international responsibility of International Organisations. Article 5 prohibits a *renvoi* to national law for the determination of an internationally wrongful act and and it only negatively affects the content of the term. Because this principle can be inferred from ARIO, Article 4 as the ILC suggests,[54] it should be considered a specific elaboration of the principle incorporated in this provision. Without devaluating the normative value of ARIO, Article 5 or its character as a general principle that admits of no exception since it determines the nature of international responsibility of International Organisations, I hold the view that the ILC should have incorporated its wording within ARIO, Article 4.

B. Content of International Responsibility

According to the ILC, international responsibility 'covers the new legal relations which arise under international law by reason of an internationally wrongful act'.[55] According to this definition, it is exclusively an internationally wrongful act that will give rise to international responsibility.[56] The legal ramification from the establishment of an internationally wrongful act is the automatic attribution of new obligations to the responsible subject.[57] Thus, the legal obligations incumbent upon the responsible subject arise under international law independently of their invocation by another subject of international law.[58] If there exists at least one subject entitled to invoke the performance of these obligations,[59] then automatically a new legal relation is formed. For the sake of

[53] See Chapter 1 at IV B.

[54] ARIO Comment, 80, [1].

[55] ASR Comment, 32, [1]; Pellet, 'The Definition of Responsibility in International Law' (n 5) 8.

[56] ASR Comment, 32, [4] lit c; ARIO Comment, 69, [4]; ILC, *Report of the International Law Commission on the Work of Its 25th Session (7 May–13 July 1973)*, UN doc A/9010/Rev 1 (1973), reproduced in (1973) 2 *YBILC* 161, 175, [10].

[57] These are, according to the ASR, the continued duty of compliance (Art 29), the cessation of the wrongful conduct and the offer of assurances and guarantees of non-repetition by the responsible State (Art 30), and the obligation to provide reparation (Art 31), ASR Comment, 87, [2].

[58] ASR Comment, 116.

[59] Sometimes not only one but multiple States are entitled to invoke international responsibility, see ASR, Art 46 and ARIO, Art 49.

the argument and without engaging in a philosophical conversation whether an obligation is correlative with a right in international law, I will assume that this condition is always present and an internationally wrongful act triggers a new legal relationship.

The content of international responsibility as described above has been established as a legal rule of international law by the case law of international courts and tribunals;[60] it is endorsed unanimously by commentators and features in the title of the ILC's ASR.[61] For example, in the *Phosphates in Morocco* case, the PCIJ had to declare whether a decision of the Moroccan Department of Mines not to recognise the rights of an Italian citizen to prospect for and to work phosphates was issued in violation of France's international obligations (Morocco was a French protectorate at the time). The Court held that:

> it is in this decision that we should look for the violation of international law a definitive act which would, by itself, directly involve international responsibility. This act being attributable to the State and described as contrary to the treaty right of another State, international responsibility would be established immediately as between the two States.[62]

Because of its general acceptance by the international community, its status as a general principle of law as per Article 38(1)(c) has been accepted for a long time.[63] By virtue of its binding force, the content of international responsibility has normative value.

The definition of international responsibility is clear in that the presence of an internationally wrongful act is indispensable for the triggering of international responsibility, but it does not clarify the exact connection between the subject that bears international responsibility and the subject that commits an internationally wrongful act. First, ASR, Article 1 and ARIO, Article 3 suggest that there exists a close connection between international responsibility and internationally wrongful act; every subject's internationally wrongful act triggers this subject's international responsibility (international responsibility for own internationally wrongful act).[64] An important feature of a subject's international responsibility for its own internationally wrongful act is that the new obligations incumbent upon the responsible entity arise automatically and do not depend on the responsible subject's consent or will to be bound by them. The presence of a circumstance precluding wrongfulness (ASR, Articles 20–25

[60] ASR Comment, 32–33, [2]; *Factory at Chorzów* (n 6) 29.

[61] The exact title of the Articles is 'Responsibility of States for Internationally Wrongful Acts'.

[62] *Phosphates in Morocco* (*Italy v France*) (Preliminary Objections), PCIJ, 14 June 1938, Series A/B, no 74 10, 28.

[63] B Cheng, *General Principles of Law as Applied by International Courts and Tribunals* (CUP, 2006) 163–80; *Avena and Other Mexican Nationals* (*Mexico v United Slates of America*) (Jurisdiction and Admissibility) [2004] ICJ Reports 12, 59, [119].

[64] This is according to the ILC a 'basic principle' of the law of international responsibility, ASR Comment, 32, [1]; ARIO Comment, 78, [1].

and ARIO, Articles 20–25) does not constitute an exception to this principle, since no internationally wrongful act is formed in these scenarios.[65]

Apart from this straightforward scenario, nevertheless, the ILC in the ARIO has endorsed a more lax connection between international responsibility and internationally wrongful act as sufficient for the triggering of international responsibility. ASR, Article 1 states that every internationally wrongful act 'of a State entails the international responsibility of *that* State', thus confining international responsibility to international responsibility for own internationally wrongful act (emphasis added). Article 1 ARIO expands this principle in both paragraphs 1 and 2. Article 1(1) ARIO for example stipulates that the articles 'apply to the international responsibility of an international organization for *an* internationally wrongful act' (emphasis added). The ARIO thus leave enough room to include scenarios when international responsibility arises for *another subject's* internationally wrongful act.

And this is so because the legal relations covered by international responsibility can be formed in a different manner: consensually. It is a general principle of international law that all legal 'rights or obligations are within the dispensation of States' when they consent to them.[66] Nothing can prevent a subject of international law from voluntarily assuming the obligations that arise by virtue of an internationally wrongful act, and the ILC has recognised this possibility in ARIO, Article 62(1)(a).[67] An example of this rather unlikely scenario is provided by recent practice. Assuming that the 1999 bombing of the Chinese embassy in Belgrade during NATO's military involvement in the Yugoslav crisis was an internationally wrongful act of that International Organisation, and not an internationally wrongful act of the United States, then the compensation awarded to China from the United States was an instance of acceptance of international responsibility. This incident does not prove that NATO is incapable of committing an internationally wrongful act, but rather that States are capable of voluntarily assuming international responsibility for another subject's internationally wrongful act.[68] The only necessary prerequisite for the engagement of international responsibility in this scenario is that the responsible entity is capable of assuming international obligations, thus that it possesses international legal personality.

[65] These circumstances provide 'a shield against an otherwise well-founded claim for the breach of an international obligation', ASR Comment, 71. Since no breach is present, no internationally wrongful act is established. For the necessary prerequisites for the establishment of an internationally wrongful act, see below.

[66] ASR Comment, 122, [2].

[67] ARIO, Art 62(1)(a) provides: 'A State member of an international organization is responsible for an internationally wrongful act of that organization if: it has accepted responsibility for that act towards the injured party'. For more on this, see Chapter 3.

[68] Against T Gazzini, 'NATO Coercive Military Activities in the Yugoslav Crisis (1992–1999)' (2001) 12 *EJIL* 369, 424–25, who questions NATO's international legal personality and consequently argues that each NATO member State bears international responsibility 'for the acts committed by its forces engaged in NATO operations'.

Therefore, apart from the exceptional scenario envisaged in ARIO, Article 62(1)(a), the rest of the provisions in the ASR and ARIO should provide for international responsibility for own internationally wrongful act. If this is not the case and international responsibility is deemed to arise for another subject's internationally wrongful act with respect to other scenarios, then the triggering of international responsibility can only be explained by reference to exceptional circumstances.

Resort to such arguments, however, denotes that the ILC's project lacks coherence. If the establishment of international responsibility arises by virtue of exceptional circumstances, it cannot be explained by reference to legal principles. This suggests that international responsibility degenerates to a mechanism without a principled basis. Such unprincipled theorising is not germane to notions that possess a unitary and coherent content. Since international responsibility is such a key feature of the international legal order, it is of cardinal importance to assess whether the framework provided by the ILC rests on a principled and coherent basis. Because if international responsibility as presently constructed does not possess this characteristic, it is ill-adapted to address certain scenarios with doctrinal rigour. Then, maybe there is a case for a rethinking of international responsibility or its re-construction on new principles.[69]

It has been made clear that the establishment of international responsibility is always dependent upon the existence of an internationally wrongful act. An assessment of international responsibility's nature then inevitably requires an examination of the respective nature of an internationally wrongful act.

The content of an internationally wrongful act is necessarily comprised of two elements according to the ILC.[70] First, conduct must be attributable to a subject of international law (attribution element).[71] This conduct can consist of both actions or omissions.[72] But, a legal person,whether this is a State or an International Organisation, is an abstract entity that acts through human beings. It should be assessed, then, by virtue of a normative operation,[73] by which persons should be considered (for legal purposes) to act on behalf of this legal subject. After this operation, one is able to identify whether an 'act of an international legal person' has occurred. Second, this attributed conduct should constitute a

[69] Upon this premise rests the SHARES project, see D Jacobs and A Nollkaemper, 'Shared Responsibility in International Law: A Conceptual Framework' (2013) 34 *Michigan Journal of International Law* 359.

[70] ASR, Art 2 and ARIO, Art 4.

[71] The principle that attribution is the link between conduct and a legal subject is endorsed in ASR Comment, 35, [6]: 'In speaking of attribution to the State what is meant is the State as a subject of international law'.

[72] ASR Comment, 35, [4], where the ILC cites the *Corfu Channel* case (*United Kingdom v Albania*) (Merits) [1949] ICJ Reports 4) as an example of attribution of an omission; ARIO Comment, 79, [1].

[73] D Anzilotti, *Corso di diritto internazionale* (CEDAM, 1955) vol I, 222, as cited in F Messineo, 'Attribution of Conduct' in A Nollkaemper and I Plakokefalos (eds), *Principles of Shared Responsibility in International Law: An Appraisal of the State of the Art* (CUP, 2014) 60, 70.

breach of an international obligation incumbent upon this legal subject (breach element). The character or provenance of the international obligation is indifferent for the purpose of establishment of an internationally wrongful act and thus conduct contrary to any international obligation is considered 'wrongful'. Combined together, these elements form an 'internationally wrongful act'.

The next question is whether these elements are also sufficient for the establishment of an internationally wrongful act. As a result of the so-called 'Ago revolution',[74] injury (ie material or moral damage) was dropped as a condition generating an internationally wrongful act.[75] It may be that injury will always be inherent within the breach element of an internationally wrongful act and in this way it is implicitly incorporated within an internationally wrongful act.[76] The inclusion of injury within the concept of an internationally wrongful act was advocated by certain writers based mainly on cases of State responsibility for injuries to aliens.[77] The ILC held that even in such cases, injury is indispensable because it is dictated by the primary obligation violated and not because it forms part of the content of an internationally wrongful act.[78]

In this sense, it is dependent upon the content of the primary obligation whether injury will be required or not in a particular case and not upon the secondary norm that determines the content of an internationally wrongful act.[79] For example:

> the obligation under a treaty to enact a uniform law is breached by the failure to enact the law, and it is not necessary for another ... party to point to any specific damage it has suffered by reason of that failure.[80]

On the other hand, the obligation incumbent upon States not to commit genocide requires the infliction of injury. Therefore, no infliction of injury in this case suggests that no violation of the particular obligation has taken place and thus the breach element has not been fulfilled. This concept of an internationally wrongful act limited to breach and attribution has been endorsed by the ILC in both the ASR and the ARIO.[81]

[74] A Pellet, 'The ILC's Articles on State Responsibility for Internationally Wrongful Acts and Related Texts' in in J Crawford, A Pellet and S Olleson (eds), *The Law of International Responsibility* (OUP, 2010) 75, 76.

[75] On the development of the concept of international responsibility in international law, see G Nolte, 'From Dionisio Anzilotti to Roberto Ago: The Classical International Law of State Responsibility and the Traditional Primacy of a Bilateral Conception of Inter-state Relations' (2002) 13 *EJIL* 1083; ASR Comment, 36, [9].

[76] Pellet, 'The ILC's Articles on State Responsibility' (n 74) 74.

[77] See AV Freeman, *The International Responsibility of States for Denial of Justice* (Longmans, 1938) 22; E Jimenez de Arechaga, *International Responsibility: Manual of Public International Law* (Sorensen, 1968) 534.

[78] Ago Third Report (n 15 above) 223, [73].

[79] ARIO Comment, 78–79, [3].

[80] ASR Comment, 36, [9].

[81] ibid; ARIO Comment, 80, [3].

The excision of injury from the concept of an internationally wrongful act suggests that the latter's content is conducive to a purely objective determination. Arguably, it would have been practically impossible for the ILC to formulate exhaustive criteria for the existence of material or moral damage, for their elaboration rests necessarily upon a subjective assessment. Contrariwise, the establishment of both attribution and breach rests on the observation of facts conducive to objective determination.[82] While attribution is sometimes referred to as the 'subjective' element of international responsibility, the establishment of both conditions depends solely on events occurring in the world that do not admit of a subjective, moral or psychological assessment.[83] And the ILC has tried to exhaustively formulate the criteria for the occurrence of both of them.

According to the ILC, a binding legal rule provides for the afore-mentioned content of an internationally wrongful act in international law. The commentaries to ARIO, Article 4 affirm without further elaboration that there exists a general principle to this effect.[84] With the exception of some French writers,[85] this view is shared almost unanimously by commentators,[86] and by States.[87] What is more, International Organisations, when commenting on the drafting of the ARIO, did not question the applicability of this general principle.[88] Given the general acceptance and thus recognition that the rule enjoys in the international community, it is safe to assume that it has attained the status of a general principle of international law, and therefore the content of an internationally wrongful act has legal value.

To sum up, the content of the term 'internationally wrongful act' has two hallmarks that must be kept separate; it is both objectively determined and possesses normative force. It is objectively determined since the presence of its constituents can be assessed through an examination of social facts; and it has normative value to the extent that a binding rule provides that this is the content

[82] ASR Comment, 34, [3].

[83] For more on what constitutes a fact and how it is distinguishable from morality, see J Hund, 'Are Social Facts Real?' (1982) 33 *British Journal of Sociology* 270ff.

[84] ARIO Comment, 79, [1].

[85] J Combacau and S Sur, *Droit international public* (Monrchrestien, 2004) 519; G Cottereau, 'Systèmes juridiques et notion de responsabilité' in Colloque du Mans, *La responsabilité dans le système international* (Pedone, 1991) 21; E Decaux, 'Responsabilité et réparation' in ibid 147. They all suggest that injury should have been incorporated in the definition of an internationally wrongful act.

[86] Ago Third Report (n 15) 215, [53]; Pellet, 'The ILC's Articles on State Responsibility' (n 74) 77.

[87] ILC, *State Responsibility: Comments and Observations Received from Governments*, UN doc A/CN.4/488 (1998), Add 1 to 3, reproduced in (1998) 2(1) *YBILC* 81; ILC, *State Responsibility: Comments and Observations Received from Governments*, UN doc A/CN.4/492 (1999), reproduced in (1999) 2(1) *YBILC* 101. Exceptions to this are Argentina and France, see ibid 1998 *Comments and Observations*.

[88] The IMF has explicitly endorsed this principle, ILC, *Responsibility of International Organizations: Comments and Observations Received from Governments and International Organizations* UN doc A/CN/4.556 (2005), reproduced in (2005) 2(1) *YBILC* 27, 35–36.

of an internationally wrongful act. The objective determination of the content of an internationally wrongful act should not be confused with the objective determination of its normative character as a rule of international law. The former pertains to whether an internationally wrongful act has been established and the latter to whether this particular way of establishing an internationally wrongful act exists as a legal rule. This conclusion implies that international responsibility's normative content is also susceptible to objective determination.[89] In the case of international responsibility for own internationally wrongful act, this is self-evident. But also when international responsibility for another subject's internationally wrongful act is in play, the condition of consensual assumption of obligations is objectively determined by observable facts.

Having concluded a *tour d'horizon* of the inherent characteristics of international responsibility's content, it is pertinent to assess how this affects international responsibility's applicability *ratione personae* and *ratione materiae*.

C. Applicability of International Responsibility

Since the content of international responsibility is clearly defined, it is pertinent to assess whether this content can provide international legal rules incumbent upon States and International Organisations with their normative characteristic. This is dependent, as stated earlier, upon the applicability *ratione personae* and *ratione materiae* of international responsibility.

(i) Applicability Ratione Materiae

According to its content, international responsibility is in some way based on an internationally wrongful act. The general commentary to both the ASR and ARIO limits their scope to this accountability mechanism that arises by virtue of an internationally wrongful act.[90] As explained, the latter is established following the violation of a primary rule of international law. The ASR and ARIO thus provide the framework for determining the consequences of a failure to fulfil obligations established by primary rules.[91] Until a primary international obligation has been violated, the secondary international responsibility rules are not engaged. As a consequence of this distinction, the 'secondary' rules are posited in neutral terms, ie without regard to the nature and content of the

[89] The ILC thus attempted to maximise uniformity in the determination of responsibility. Ago clearly states: 'The principle to be established from the outset is the unitary principle of responsibility, which it should be possible to invoke in every case', Ago Second Report (n 19) 185.

[90] ibid; ARIO Comment, 70, [5], 'the present Articles do not address the question of liability for injurious consequences arising out of acts not prohibited by international law'.

[91] ASR Comment, 31, [4].

primary rules. The Articles are indifferent to primary norms, and apply generally to the entire *corpus* of international obligations assumed by States and International Organisations.[92] This occurs by operation of the law, ie the very fact of the breach of an international obligation renders the secondary rules on responsibility applicable.

What is more, international responsibility is *the* legal accountability mechanism in international law as far as States and International Organisations are concerned. First, it has a legal character since it is a control mechanism attached to legal rules.[93] As noted by the International Court of Justice (ICJ): 'it is a principle of international law, and even a general conception of law, that any breach of an engagement (nb a primary norm) involves an obligation to make reparation'.[94] Also, it is the only accountability mechanism of legal character attached to these subjects of international law. The ILC clarified that conduct that does not qualify as internationally wrongful triggers different accountability mechanisms such as liability. International law, then, does not attach further legal consequences to a violation of its legal rules by States and International Organisations apart from those envisaged by the establishment of international responsibility.

(ii) Applicability Ratione Personae

The starting point of the analysis is again the concomitant features of an internationally wrongful act. The fact that an internationally wrongful act is a term with a unified and specific content does not *ipso facto* mean that it applies with respect to both States and International Organisations. It has been argued that with the excision of damage the ILC has left behind a purely State-centric view of an internationally wrongful act, and with this content, an internationally wrongful act can become attached to different subjects of international law.[95] The applicability *ratione personae* of an internationally wrongful act will depend on the respective applicability of its constituent parts. First, the definition of attribution as a nexus between conduct and a subject of international law, suggests that its sole prerequisite is that the subject under examination possesses international legal personality.[96] Second, a breach of international obligations can only occur by a subject capable of bearing such obligations, that is, a subject with international legal personality. So both conditions of an internationally

[92] ibid 31, [1].

[93] A Tzanakopoulos, *Disobeying the Security Council: Countermeasures Against Wrongful Sanctions* (OUP, 2011) 6.

[94] *Factory at Chorzów* (n 6) 4, [21].

[95] Pellet, 'The Definition of Responsibility in International Law' (n 5) 15.

[96] For example, if the World Bank's Partnership Programmes lacks international legal personality, decisions of their governing bodies will not be attributable to any subject, A Angelini, 'A Trouble Shared is a Trouble Halved: How the Structure of Cooperation Matters for the Engagement of Responsibility in the World Bank Partnership Programmes' (2016) 13 *IOLR* 171, 190.

wrongful act have only one and the same prerequisite, and hence an internationally wrongful act can be attached to every subject of international law.

Since it has already been established that according to a general principle of law, an internationally wrongful act gives rise to legal obligations, it logically follows that an internationally wrongful act generates such obligations for every subject of international law who commits it and leads to the establishment of international responsibility. Rightfully then, the ILC delimits the ARIO's scope of application only to International Organisations that possess international legal personality and are subjects of international law.[97]

Some argue that this applicability of an internationally wrongful act reflects a general principle of international law,[98] and others that it is a rule of international customary law.[99] The ILC, which has researched the matter since Ago formulated the content of an internationally wrongful act, concluded in the ASR that only insofar as States are concerned, a principle of customary law exists in international law to this respect. The Commission arrived at this conclusion by citing both case law of the ICJ and its precursor, the Permanent Court of International Justice,[100] but also writings of scholars from Anzilotti to Brownlie and Dupuy.[101] In the ARIO, however, the Commission had very limited practice at its disposal to justify a rule of customary law with respect to International Organisations. So, in the commentary to Article 3, the ILC resorted to a general principle applicable to all subjects of international law, on which to base its inference that international responsibility for internationally wrongful acts is also applicable with respect to International Organisations.[102] Without any elaboration, the Commission assumes that such a general principle exists as a matter of logic and does not feel compelled to justify it in legal terms.[103] As stated earlier, due to its unanimous acceptance by the international community, the status of this foundational rule as a general principle of law as per ICJ Statute, Article 38(1)(c) has been accepted for a long time.

The applicability *ratione personae* to all subjects of international law is an attribute of international responsibility also. Given the strong connection between international responsibility and internationally wrongful act, this

[97] ARIO, Art 2(a).

[98] MH Arsanjani, 'Claims Against International Organizations' (1981) 7 *Yale Journal of World Public Order* 131ff.

[99] M Hirsch, *The Responsibility of International Organizations Toward Third Parties: Some Basic Principles* (Martinus Nijhoff, 1995) 8; ILA, *Accountability of International Organizations: Final Report, Berlin Conference 2004*, 26, available at www.ila-hq.org/en/committees/index.cfm/cid/9.

[100] ASR Comment, 32–33, [2].

[101] ibid 33, [3].

[102] The ILC also referred to authorities that support a relevant customary norm tailored to International Organisations. In particular, the ILC cited a peacekeeping report of the United Nations Secretary-General and a *dictum* from the ICJ's Advisory Opinion on *Difference Relating to Immunity from Legal Process of a Special Rapporteur of the Commission on Human Rights*, Advisory Opinion [1992] ICJ Reports 62; ARIO Comment, 78–79, [2]–[3].

[103] ARIO Comment, 78, [1].

is evident with respect to international responsibility for *own* internationally wrongful acts. Accordingly, the ILC assumes that a general principle exists in international law according to which the subjects of international law bear international responsibility.[104] With respect to its previous work on the Articles on State Responsibility, Special Rapporteur Ago found that such a concomitant principle existed but it was confined to the international responsibility of States:

> there is no need to justify or establish this fundamental principle by deducing it from other principles. Despite certain variations in its formulation, it is expressly recognised, or at least clearly assumed by doctrine and practice unanimously.[105]

Ago insightfully inferred that the existence of international responsibility for States as a legal accountability mechanism in international law does not need a justification by reference to some other principle or to the sources of international legal rules, since it is inferred directly from the original presumption that international law possesses a legal quality. Similarly, Schwarzenberger held that international responsibility was one of the five fundamental principles of international law that formed the international public order.[106] Since the justification for the existence of the principle lies in the legal quality of the international order as a whole, international responsibility should attach to all entities that fall under international law's authority.

But international responsibility can also arise for another subject's internationally wrongful act and, as stated earlier, the only prerequisite for the establishment of international responsibility in these cases is the capacity to assume international obligations. This explains why the ILC concludes that '[i]t may be that the notion of responsibility for wrongful conduct is a basic element in the possession of international legal personality'.[107]

The ARIO endorse the general *ratione personae* applicability of international responsibility and set up the general framework of rules on international responsibility of International Organisations, based on the concomitant State responsibility provisions. It follows that ARIO, Articles 3 and 4, as specific formulations of legal principles, are themselves binding rules of international law. The ILC, then, was not progressively developing international law, but rather codifying existing law when drafting these provisions.

[104] By the term 'subject of international law', I mean every entity that possesses international legal personality and thus is a bearer of rights and obligations enforceable at law. See also M Shaw, *International Law* (CUP, 2008) 195ff; A Cassese, *International Law* (OUP, 2005) Pt II.

[105] Ago Third Report (n 15) 206. As stated by the Italy-United States Conciliation Commission, no State may 'escape the responsibility arising out of the exercise of an illicit action from the viewpoint of the general principles of international law', *Armstrong Cork Company*, Italian-United States Conciliation Commission, Decision of 22 October 1953 (1965) 14 *Reports of International Arbitral Awards* 159, 163.

[106] The other ones being the principle of consent, good faith, self-defence and the freedom of the seas, G Schwarzenberger, 'The Fundamental Principles of International Law' (1955) 92 *RCADI* 195, 376.

[107] ASR Comment, 34.

Some very strong policy arguments have been evoked in order to justify the applicability of the State responsibility principles to International Organisations. Most common among them is that coherence between the two sets of international responsibility Articles is necessary to evade a risk of fragmentation in this field of international law.[108] Pellet suggests that it would be 'unreasonable for the Commission to take a different approach',[109] and the ILC itself suggests that '[t]here seems to be little reason for formulating these principles in another manner'.[110] And these can be very persuasive arguments, but they identify the law based on subjective extra-legal considerations (need for coherence, reasonableness) and thus their strength is relative.[111] But normativity does not lie in the eye of the beholder. Normative arguments are absolute in the sense that they identify the law through objective pedigree tests elaborated by the legal system.[112] Thus, policy arguments are unnecessary when the law is determined by normative arguments. Consequently, these principles are not binding because they have been drafted *mutatis mutandis* with the concomitant ASR provisions, but because they rest upon binding general principles of international law. Insofar as the ARIO reflect the nature of international responsibility and of an internationally wrongful act, the drafting of their provisions by analogy is not a 'fitting choice' because of its advantages (eg it promotes coherence), it is rather dictated by legal reasons.

The argumentation provided by the ILC to justify why it drafted ARIO, Articles 3 and 4 in a similar way to the concomitant ASR provisions was not convincing, though, and it sparked strong academic criticism.[113] Moreover, the

[108] M Möldner, 'Responsibility of International Organizations, Introducing the ARIO' (2012) 16 *Max Planck Yearbook of United Nations Law* 281, 323. Endorsed by the Commission, ILC, *Report of the International Law Commission on the Work of Its 54th Session (29 April–7 June and 22 July–16 August 2002)*, UN doc A/57/10 (2002) 232, [475].

[109] A Pellet, 'International Organizations are Definitely Not States: Cursory Remarks on the ILC Articles on the Responsibility of International Organizations' in M Ragazzi (ed), *Responsibility of International Organizations, Essays in Memory of Sir Ian Brownlie* (Martinus Nijhoff, 2013) 41, 43.

[110] ARIO Comment, 78, [1].

[111] For a member of the ILC, for example, '[c]oherence among the instruments prepared by the Commission was not a very compelling reason for adopting a particular formulation', *Summary of 3081st Meeting* (n 1) 7 (McRae).

[112] I accept the 'social thesis' of positivism that regards law-ascertainment rules as social facts, Raz, *The Authority of Law* (n 8) 37. This thesis is, I believe, implicitly or explicitly endorsed by most international law commentators making normative arguments, since the foundations of this legal order are essentially positivist and this theory dominates international legal argumentation about the validity of norms, G Gaja, 'Positivism and Dualism in Dionisio Anzilotti' (1992) 3 *EJIL* 123.

[113] Alvarez is the most fervent critic of the ARIO, see J Alvarez, 'Revisiting the ILC's Draft Rules on International Organization Responsibility' (2011) 105 *American Society of International Law Proceedings* 344; J Alvarez, 'Misadventures in Subjecthood', *Ejil:Talk!*, 29 September 2010; J Alvarez, 'International Organizations: Accountability or Responsibility?', address at the Canadian Council of International Law, 27 October 2006, available at www.asil.org/aboutasil/documents/CCILspeech061102.pdf. See other criticisms by G Hafner, 'Is the Topic of Responsibility of International Organizations Ripe for Codification? Some Critical Remarks' in U Fastenrath, R Geiger, DE Khan, A Paulus, S von Schorlemer and C Vedder (eds), *From Bilateralism to Community Interest, Essays in Honour of Judge Bruno Simma* (Oxford, 2011) 695; J Wouters and J Odermatt, 'Are All

ARIO 'represent an autonomous text' and any provisions drafted similarly to the ASR should be justified 'on appropriate reasons and not on a general presumption that the same principles apply'.[114] The ILC correctly pointed out that ARIO, Articles 3 and 4, rest upon general principles of international law, but provided no authorities whatsoever to support these principles. It rather axiomatically inferred their existence.[115] This argument was essentially correct, but very weak as to its elaboration. What is more, academics supported the ILC's approach on an axiomatic basis and not on the basis of normative argumentation.[116]

Arguably, such reasoning possesses limited argumentative value and has inevitably given rise to criticism. McCorquodale, for example, suggests that insufficient evidence supports the view that State responsibility principles can be elevated to general international responsibility principles, thus questioning whether the ASR establish the basic framework of international responsibility for internationally wrongful acts.[117] He then argues that the ASR incorporate such a State-centric view of international responsibility to conclude 'that all or parts of the law of State responsibility cannot apply – or apply with considerable differences – to international organisations'.[118] It should be noted that McCorquodale and all other commentators who share his opinion do not specify exactly which parts of the ASR are inapplicable to International Organisations. I believe that the ILC would have addressed this criticism, if it had supported these provisions with the normative argumentation cited above.

The same goes for another line of criticism, particularly popular among those unsympathetic to the ILC's *mutatis mutandis* approach. The argument points to the difference in nature between States and International Organisations to suggest that the ARIO do not recognise sufficiently the different attributes of

International Organizations Created Equal? Reflections on the ILC's Draft Articles of Responsibility of International Organizations' (2012) 9 *IOLR* 7; VJ Proulx, 'An Uneasy Transition? Linkages between the Law of State Responsibility and the Law Governing the Responsibility of International Organizations' in M Ragazzi (ed), *Responsibility of International Organizations, Essays in Memory of Sir Ian Brownlie* (Martinus Nijhoff, 2013) 109.

[114] ARIO Comment, 69, [4]. It is commonplace for the Commission to indicate that the word 'international organization' has been substituted for 'State', point to some analogies based on the ASR, refer to the commentaries to those Articles, or underscore that a specific provision in the project on the responsibility of International Organisations has drawn heavily on the ASR.

[115] A Pronto, 'An Introduction to the Articles on the Responsibility of International Organisations' (2011) 36 *South African Yearbook of International Law* 94.

[116] C Yamada, 'Viability of the ILC's Articles Formulated on the Basis of the Articles on State Responsibility' in M Ragazzi (ed), *Responsibility of International Organizations, Essays in Memory of Sir Ian Brownlie* (Martinus Nijhoff, 2013) 89, 92; CF Amerasinghe 'An Assessment of the ILC's Articles on the Responsibility of International Organizations' in ibid 71, 76; CF Amerasinghe, 'Comments on the ILC's Draft Articles on the Responsibility of International Organizations' (2012) 9 *IOLR* 29.

[117] McCorquodale, 'International Organizations and International Human Rights Law' (n 1) 141, 148.

[118] ibid 149.

these two subjects of international law.[119] The criticism levelled seemingly has merit because it rests on a solid basis, the ICJ's *Reparation for Injuries* Advisory Opinion, where the Court stated that:

> [w]hereas a State possesses the totality of international rights and duties recognised by international law, the rights and duties of an entity such as the Organization must depend upon its purposes and functions as specified or implied in its constituent documents and developed in practice.[120]

The so-called 'principle of speciality' suggests that International Organisations possess international legal personality but their rights and obligations are limited when compared to those of States. As was the case with the previous criticism, advocates of this argument fail to substantiate it and to offer concrete examples where specific characteristics of International Organisations dictate a different approach from the one taken by the ILC.[121] Nor have they suggested how this discrepancy of attributes should have been dealt with.[122] There appears to be an assumption that any difference, regardless of its nature should lead to different outcomes. As I elaborated, however, international legal personality, that is, the capacity to bear rights and obligations, is the only and necessary condition for the establishment of international responsibility for internationally

[119] This was suggested by all commentators cited in n 113 above but also by ILC members during the drafting process, ILC, *Summary Record of the 2800th Meeting*, UN doc A/CN.4/SR.2800 (18 May 2004), reproduced in (2004) 1 *YBILC* 65, 69, [17] (Matheson); ILC, *Summary Record of the 2801th Meeting*, UN doc A/CN.4/SR.2801 (19 May 2004), reproduced in (2004) 1 *YBILC* 73, 75, [20]–[22] (Pambou-Tchivounda) and 80, [64] (Escarameia); by members of the Sixth Committee, ILC, *Report of the International Law Commission on the Work of its 55th Session (2003): Topical Summary of the Discussion Held in the Sixth Committee of the General Assembly during its 58th Session, prepared by the Secretariat*, UN doc A/CN.4/537 (2004) 6–8, [7] and [10]–[12]; ILC, *Report of the International Law Commission on the Work of its 57th Session (2005): Topical Summary of the Discussion Held in the Sixth Committee of the General Assembly during its 60th Session, prepared by the Secretariat*, UN doc A/CN.4/560 (2006) 18, [76]; and by International Organisations commenting on the ARIO, ILC, *Responsibility of International Organizations: Comments and Observations Received from International Organizations*, UN doc A/CN.4/637 (2011) 8, [1] (International Labour Organization) and 10–11, [2] (Joint Submission by 14 International Organisations). For an account cautioning against 'blindly copying rules on responsibility that may work for other actors properly but not for' International Organisations, see N Carrillo, 'The Links Between the Responsibility of International Organizations and the Quest Towards a More Reasonable and Humane International Legal System' (2010) 7 *IOLR* 441, 443.

[120] *Reparation for Injuries Suffered in the Service of the United Nations*, Advisory Opinion [1949] ICJ Reports 69.

[121] Pellet, 'International Organizations are Definitely Not States' (n 109) 48. It should be noted that some commentators (undoubtedly a minority) have acknowledged that the principle of speciality is pertinent mainly with respect to the applicable primary obligations than to the secondary rules on international responsibility. See M Wood, '"Weighing" the Articles on Responsibility of International Organizations' in M Ragazzi (ed), *Responsibility of International Organizations, Essays in Memory of Sir Ian Brownlie* (Martinus Nijhoff, 2013) 55, 62; Pronto, 'An Introduction to the Articles' (n 115) 113–16.

[122] Pellet regretted having criticised the ARIO on this general basis, 'International Organizations are Definitely Not States' (n 109) 49, note 35.

wrongful acts. For the purposes of ARIO, Articles 3 and 4, then, the principle of speciality, which refers to the extent of rights and obligations that a subject of international law may bear, is irrelevant and any criticism that rests upon it cannot be given merit.

In order to obviate these concerns, the ILC should have engaged in some preventive action. Specifically, the Commission never clarified in the ARIO how International Organisations compare to States in matters of international responsibility, or how the ARIO relate to the ASR more generally, and this reluctance on behalf of the ILC is disappointing.[123] It conveys the impression that 'the Commission uncritically elected the [ASR] as a starting point',[124] and that principles germane to the international responsibility of States were transposed 'lock, stock and barrel' into the ARIO.[125] This is why it has been suggested, and I certainly agree, that the Commission should have conducted an in-depth study around the nature of international responsibility of International Organisations, before contemplating the prospect of codification.[126]

Unsubstantiated and of an equally general nature is a third interrelated criticism based on the heterogeneity of International Organisations. The idea of diversity between International Organisations has been a recurrent theme in academic writings,[127] but mainly in the comments of International Organisations to the ARIO.[128] According to both, the ARIO cannot accommodate all types of International Organisations and hence they should have differentiated between them. Again, the argument is an easy one to make since it is premised on a truism. Nevertheless, the only concrete elaboration of this argument was offered by the European Union (EU), who advocated for special attribution rules in Regional Economic Integration Organisations such as itself.[129] Even if this consideration is given merit, though, it does not affect the basic premise of the law on international responsibility, namely, that the possession of international

[123] C Ahlborn, 'The Use of Analogies in Drafting the Articles on the Responsibility of International Organizations: An Appraisal of the "Copy-Paste Approach"' (2012) 9 *IOLR* 53, 62.

[124] Proulx, 'An Uneasy Transition?' (n 113) 120.

[125] Pellet, 'International Organizations are Definitely Not States' (n 109) 43.

[126] Hafner, 'Is the Topic of Responsibility of International Organizations Ripe for Codification?' (n 113) 717; Wouters and Odermatt, 'Are All International Organizations Created Equal?' (n 113) 14.

[127] See E Paasivirta and PJ Kuijper, 'Does one Size Fit All? The European Community and the Responsibility of International Organisations' (2005) 36 *Netherlands Yearbook of International Law* 169, 169–226; N Blokker, 'Preparing Articles on Responsibility of International Organizations: Does the International Law Commission Take International Organizations Seriously? A Mid-Term Review' in J Klabbers and A Wallendahl (eds), *Research Handbook on the Law of International Organizations* (Edward Elgar, 2011) 313, 335.

[128] UNGA 58th Session, Sixth Committee, *Summary Record of the 14th Meeting*, UN doc A/C.6/58/SR.14 (2003) 4, [13] (EU); 2005 *Comments and Observations* (n 88) 26 (International Criminal Police Organization); 2011 *Comments and Observations* (n 119) 10, [3] (IMF) and 11, [1] (NATO).

[129] ILC, *Responsibility of International Organizations: Comments and Observations Received from International Organizations*, UN doc A/CN.4/545 (2004), reproduced in (2004) 2(1) *YBILC* 19; UNGA 66th Session, Sixth Committee, *Summary Record of the 18th Meeting*, UN doc A/C.6/66/SR.18 (2011) 4, [18].

legal personality is the only prerequisite for the establishment of a subject's international responsibility. As otherwise put by a member of the ILC:

> [t]he question of diversity was an interesting philosophical topic, but it was of no relevance to the codification of the responsibility of international organizations. Once an international organization had legal personality it had to be responsible for its acts.[130]

V. CONCLUSION

The ILC's reluctance to ponder over the foundations of its ARIO project is regrettable. I believe that the Commission would have benefited in a twofold way if it had reflected on the legal basis of international responsibility's nature. First, for inward-looking reasons: it would have clarified the keystones of its project and thus the drafting of international responsibility rules, based on solid foundations, would have been clearer and more effective. The ILC would have in this way prevented criticisms, such as that of Jacobs and Nollkaemper, who caution with respect to indirect responsibility rules: 'The foundations of this construction of responsibility are undertheorized, and their relationship with the normal conditions of wrongfulness not at all well articulated'.[131] Second, for reasons of projecting its work to the international community: to these actors who have an impact in the rule-making process at the international level, be they States and International Organisations that commented during the drafting process, or academics who through their writings lamented the drafting of international responsibility rules, especially with respect to the ARIO. The ILC would have forestalled a wide array of criticism which had the effect of debasing the authority of its work.

To address the two issues outlined in the Introduction above: (a) international responsibility for internationally wrongful acts is, according to the ILC, the legal accountability mechanism of the international order that attaches to both States and International Organisations; and (b) when drafting the rules that regulate the establishment of international responsibility of these subjects, the ILC cannot contradict the generally applicable legal principles that determine the nature of the concept.

As opposed to many domestic legal systems, international law draws no distinction between responsibility *ex delictu* and *ex contractu*.[132] Further, internationally responsibility is neither civil, nor criminal but *sui generis*.[133] It has a

[130] *Summary of 3081st Meeting* (n 1) 14 (Melescanu).

[131] Jacobs and Nollkaemper, 'Shared Responsibility in International Law' (n 69) 390–91.

[132] Crawford, 'State Responsibility' (n 34) [12].

[133] *Case concerning the Difference between New Zealand and France concerning the Interpretation or Application of Two Agreements Concluded on 9 July 1986 between the Two States and which related to the Problems arising from the Rainbow Warrior Affair* (*New Zealand v France*), Ruling of 6 July 1986, (1990) 20 *Reports of International Arbitral Awards* 215, 251, [75]; Pellet, 'The Definition of Responsibility in International Law' (n 5) 12–15.

normative content in international law sufficiently general and coherent to function as the sole legal accountability mechanism of this legal order for States and International Organisations. Being a notion with normative content, international responsibility's establishment can only be determined through respective argumentation. This content of international responsibility, which rests upon legal principles of international law, is something that the ILC could not have altered with respect to its ARIO project.

Part I

Member State-International Organisation Interaction on the Basis of the Particular Member State-International Organisation Relationship

3

Reassessing the Particular Member State-International Organisation Relationship

I. INTRODUCTION

THIS FIRST PART of the book focuses on those Articles on the Responsibility of International Organizations (ARIO) provisions which regulate interactions between member States and International Organisations arising from membership. These interactions can be examined from two different perspectives, that of the member State and that of the International Organisation. Commentators, nevertheless, have for the most part focused on the responsibility of the member State and only incidentally on the responsibility of the International Organisation.[1] They focus on member States and examine scenarios whereby their international responsibility arises either for acts of the International Organisation or for own acts. I contend here that it is equally important to look at the other side and assess the international responsibility of International Organisations in such instances. It is often forgotten that the so-called 'institutional (or organisational) veil'[2] that defines the member State-International Organisation relationship has important ramifications for the international responsibility of the latter subject too.

The starting point for the analysis of this subject-matter is Article 62. The provision forms part of ARIO, Part V (Articles 58–63), a set of provisions inserted in the ARIO in order to fill in a gap that was intentionally left unregulated by the Articles on State Responsibility (ASR).[3] Article 62 deals with

[1] C Ryngaert and H Buchanan, 'Member State Responsibility for the Acts of International Organizations' (2011) 7 *Utrecht Law Review* 131, 139–45; A Stumer, 'Liability of Member States for Acts of International Organizations: Reconsidering the Policy Objections' (2007) 48 *Harvard International Law Journal* 553, 556; J d'Aspremont, 'Abuse of the Legal Personality of International Organizations and the Responsibility of Member States' (2007) 4 *IOLR* 91, 94–101; O Murray, 'Piercing the Institutional Veil: The Responsibility of Member States of an International Organization' (2011) 8 *IOLR* 291, 291–347.

[2] C Brölmann, *The Institutional Veil in Public International Law: International Organisations and the Law of Treaties* (Hart Publishing, 2007).

[3] ASR, Art 57 states: 'These articles are without prejudice to any question of the responsibility under international law of an international organization, or of any State for the conduct of an international organization'.

the 'responsibility of a State member of an international organization for an internationally wrongful act of that organization'.

At the heart of the provision lies the relationship between the International Organisation and its member States. Hence the basic proposition in Article 62, formulated in the commentaries. can be seen from two mirroring angles: the rule that member States do not bear international responsibility for the acts of the International Organisation is either a 'no member State responsibility' or an 'exclusive International Organisation responsibility' rule. No matter which perspective one adopts, the examination of the provision requires first and foremost a clarification of the nature of the relationship between member States and the International Organisation of which they are members. As suggested by Klabbers, the assignment of international responsibility:

> presupposes that it is clear that those agents actually had something to do with the matter … and that it is reasonably clear what part of the action was theirs. This now is problematic with international organizations, precisely because it is not always clear where the organization begins and its member states end.[4]

Article 62 then, is a convenient starting point for the clarification of the member State-International Organisation relationship and the consequent assignment of international responsibility.

The chapter is divided into three sections. The first section examines the position of member States within the idiosyncratic member State-International Organisation relationship. The next adopts the opposite perspective and focuses on the ramifications for the International Organisation of taking part in this relationship. Having set the framework for analysis, I then address the justification and normative status of both the general rule of international responsibility latent in Article 62, and the exceptions thereto (which are found in Article 62(1)(a) and (1)(b)). The principal objective of this chapter is to develop a legal framework for the analysis of Article 62 and clarify its legal status; as drafted, does it represent existing international law or its progressive development? And if it does not, how should it have been drafted in order to reflect the progressive development of the law?

II. RELATIONSHIP FROM AN INSIDE-OUT PERSPECTIVE: STATES IN AN ORGANISATIONAL SETTING

The common feature of the scenarios examined in this section is their occurrence within the idiosyncratic relationship between member States and International Organisations. As pointed out by Judge Lachs in the ICJ case *Interpretation of the Agreement of 25 March 1951 between the WHO and Egypt*, an International Organisation 'acquires a special status' vis-à-vis its member States

[4] J Klabbers, *An Introduction to International Organizations Law* (CUP, 2015) 310.

and the same goes for member States vis-à-vis the International Organisation.[5] Several commentators found in the words of Victor Frankenstein 'You are my creator, but I am your master; obey!' a fitting metaphor that describes the member State-International Organisation relationship.[6] In order to proceed with the examination of the scenarios in play under the law of international responsibility, it appears timely to assess – in less dramatic terms, however – the special features of such relationship.

As suggested quite paradoxically a long time ago, '[i]nternational organizations belong to all members, and to none'.[7] States are the masters of International Organisations, for they decide whether or not to establish an International Organisation in the first place and they also determine to a large extent the fate of their creation. If States prefer not to cooperate with respect to certain State functions, or if they prefer to cooperate by concluding a treaty without giving birth to a new legal entity, no International Organisation is created. If they establish an International Organisation but no longer consider it useful, States can dissolve the International Organisation or render it inactive. In this sense, International Organisations belong to their members.[8]

At the same time, every International Organisation constitutes a legal order of its own, so State conduct should occur within the confines of this order. In 1982, for example, a significant number of member States of the International Telecommunication Union (ITU) proposed the suspension of Israel's membership rights and privileges, despite the absence of such a clause in the ITU's constituent instrument.[9] Such assumed freedom was rejected by the International Court of Justice (ICJ) in its Advisory Opinion on *Conditions of Admission of a State to Membership in the United Nations*, where the Court held:

> The political character of an organ cannot release it from the observance of the treaty provisions established by the Charter when they constitute limitations on its powers or criteria for its judgment. To ascertain whether an organ has freedom of choice for its decisions, reference must be made to the terms of its constitution.[10]

[5] *Interpretation of the Agreement of 25 March 1951 between the WHO and Egypt*, Advisory Opinion, Separate Opinion of Judge Lachs [1980] ICJ Reports 108, 110.

[6] Klabbers, *An Introduction to International Organizations Law* (n 4) v; J Alvarez, 'International Organizations: Accountability or Responsibility?', address at the Canadian Council of International Law, 27 October 2006, available at www.asil.org/aboutasil/documents/CCILspeech061102.pdf 6; S Yee, 'The Responsibility of States Members of an International Organization for its Conduct as a Result of Membership or Their Normal Conduct Associated with Membership' in M Ragazzi (ed), *International Responsibility Today, Essays in Memory of Oscar Schachter* (Brill, 2005) 435, 451; Murray, 'Piercing the Institutional Veil' (n 1) 345.

[7] J Lorimer, 'Le Problème final du Droit International' (1877) ix *Revue de Droit International et de Législation Comparée* 161.

[8] N Blokker, 'International Organizations and Their Members: "International Organizations Belong to All their Members and None", Variations on a Theme' (2004) 1 *IOLR* 139, 139–61.

[9] H Schermers and N Blokker, *International Institutional Law: Unity Within Diversity* (Martinus Nijhoff Publishers, 2011) 1210.

[10] *Conditions of Admission of a State to Membership in the United Nations*, Advisory Opinion [1948] ICJ Reports 57, 64.

The constitutional confines of an International Organisation, as demarcated by its constituent instrument, determine the actions of its organs.

It only stands to reason that the same restriction should apply to the conduct of member States vis-à-vis the International Organisation. States operate within the constitutional confines of an International Organisation when they exercise competence that lies with the organs of the International Organisation by virtue of the rules of the International Organisation. It is argued here that such action, that lies within the confines of the constituent instrument of the International Organisation, is what defines membership as a legal status for States. In this sense, States act as members of an International Organisation. For example, when the Permanent Representative of a State at the General Assembly of the United Nations is voting for the adoption of a Resolution, this State organ is exercising UN competence in accordance with the UN Charter. Thus, the State the organ represents is acting as a member of the UN. In such cases, member State and International Organisation interact in the context of the idiosyncratic member State-International Organisation relationship.

On the other hand, members act as States if their conduct, while based in International Organisation rules, pertains to competence that does not lie with the organs of the International Organisation, or where this conduct, while within the procedures of the International Organisation, is not based on the rules of the latter. In these cases, International Organisations and States interact as independent subjects of international law.[11] Instances of such interaction when members act as States are provided, for example, by ARIO, Articles 17 and 61. This is the case in the ITU example cited above, or in the case of State political influence over International Organisation decisions that exceed the rules of the International Organisation, which will be discussed in Chapter 7.[12] This, however, does not mean that member States and the International Organisation cannot interact as independent subjects outside the context of the International Organisation and this possibility is envisaged in ARIO, Articles 14–16, 58(1), 59(1) and 60.

The ramifications of this distinction on the establishment of international responsibility will be examined throughout the next chapters with respect to different scenarios. For present purposes, it is important to note two things. First, not all State conduct that occurs within the procedures of the International Organisation is necessarily member State conduct and thus conduct that

[11] As noted by the International Labour Organization: 'a member State may interact with an international organization beyond the scope of its constitutional obligations as a member of the organization; in such cases, the State and the organization relate to each other as two independent subjects of international law', ILC, *Responsibility of International Organizations: Comments and Observations Received from International Organisations*, UN doc A/CN.4/568 (2006) and Add 1, reproduced in (2006) 2(1) *YBILC* 125, 142; in the same vein, see the observations of UNESCO, ibid 144–45.

[12] See Chapter 7 at II B.

must be examined by reference to the constituent instrument of the organisation. Second, a functional dualism underpins State operation within the procedures of the International Organisation. When States act as members, these subjects interact in the context of the specific member State-International Organisation relationship, and when members act as States they interact as independent subjects of international law as if the interaction was occurring outside the constitutional context of the International Organisation.[13]

These two roles performed by States bring to mind Scelle's *dédoublement fonctionnel* theory.[14] In his attempt to explain the particular way in which the international community is organised, Scelle vests national members of the executive, as well as State officials, with a 'dual' function: they act *qua* State organs whenever they operate within the national legal system; they act *qua* international agents when they operate within the international legal system. In this way, State organs transform into legislative, judicial and enforcement organs of the international community. Similarly, according to my argument, States can wear two different hats when joining an International Organisation as each one pertains to the exercise of a different competence/function.[15]

Nevertheless, the position of member States as advocated here goes beyond the purview of Scelle's conceptual straitjacket. In Scelle's view, the law of *dédoublement fonctionnel* applies solely to a typical 'interstate society' which lacks international collective organs or institutions capable of either passing binding legal standards or of enforcing them (what he calls 'abovestate society').[16] Scelle clearly did not have in mind an explanation of the functioning of States within International Organisations such as the European Union (EU), the UN or the International Criminal Court (ICC). Therefore, the functional dualism that explains State operation within procedures of the International Organisation, as analysed above, can be regarded as an adaptation of Scelle's theory to the present stage of development of the international community.

[13] Distinction put forward by Rao, ILC, *Provisional Summary Record of the 2891st Meeting*, UN doc A/CN.4/SR.2891 (2006), reproduced in (2006) 1 *YBILC* 145, 153, [58].

[14] G Scelle, 'Le phénomène juridique du dédoublement fonctionnel' in W Schätzel and JJ Schlochauer (eds), *Rechtsfragen der Internationalen Organisationen* (Festschrift Hans Wehberg, 1956) 324, 324–42.

[15] The Janus-faced interests of representatives of member States when voting in decision-making procedures of an International Organisation is aptly demonstrated in a 2008 report prepared by the Independent Evaluation Office of the IMF. The self-perception of Board members was described as follows: 'More than half of Board members reported that they occasionally face a conflict between their role as representatives of their authorities and their role in upholding the Fund's institutional interests … while in practice all Directors clearly understand their representational role, their *status* as officers of the Fund is less clear', IMF, Independent Evaluation Office, *Governance of the IMF: An Evaluation* (2008) 16, available at www.ieo-imf.org/ieo/pages/CompletedEvaluation110.aspx.

[16] G Scelle, 'Quelques réflexions sur l'abolition de la competence de guerre' (1954) *Revue générale de droit international public* 5, 9.

III. RELATIONSHIP FROM AN OUTSIDE-IN PERSPECTIVE: RAMIFICATIONS OF THE INTERNATIONAL ORGANISATION'S LEGAL PERSONALITY

A. Organisational Veil

The main reason why the particular member State-International Organisation relationship merits special treatment is the independent legal personality of the International Organisation. This legal fiction seems to function as a veil, directing any ensuing international responsibility towards the International Organisation, and prima facie barring any international responsibility claim against member States for conduct performed in the context of procedures of the International Organisation. A set of questions automatically arises: under which conditions can the behaviour of States within the processes of an International Organisation, as such, be considered relevant for international responsibility purposes? Could such behaviour possibly lead to conduct being attributed to the member States rather than to the International Organisation? What exactly are the criteria to determine that States actually acted in the framework of the International Organisation's operations? I will immediately turn the analysis towards this direction.

As said before, the main reason why it is fitting to examine the provisions in a reverse order is because Article 62 incorporates (albeit implicitly) the general starting point for an inquiry on the relationship between the international responsibility of an International Organisation and that of its member States. The provision reads as follows:

> Responsibility of a State member of an international organization for an internationally wrongful act of that organization
>
> 1. A State member of an international organization is responsible for an internationally wrongful act of that organization if: (a) it has accepted responsibility for that act towards the injured party; or (b) it has led the injured party to rely on its responsibility.
> 2. Any international responsibility of a State under paragraph 1 is presumed to be subsidiary.

The rule latent in the wording of the Article is clearly spelled out in the commentaries. The latter provides that 'membership does not as such entail for member States international responsibility when the organization commits an internationally wrongful act'.[17] The Commission thus made it clear that the separate international legal personality of the International Organisation affects the international responsibility of member States so long as International Organisations

[17] The reason why the rule does not appear in the text of a provision is because the ARIO (and the ASR for that matter) do not identify scenarios 'when responsibility is not deemed to arise', ARIO Comment, 162, [2].

are 'in principle the *only* subjects that bear international responsibility for their international wrongful acts'[18] (emphasis added).

The aforementioned general rule of 'exclusive International Organisation responsibility'/'no member responsibility' presupposes that there exists a strong connection between the International Organisation's separate legal personality and its separate international responsibility. Legal personality is in general a cloth, a legal fiction that enables subjects to bear rights and duties in a legal system.[19] At the international level, International Organisations are capable of acquiring such personality and thus of having a separate existence from their member States.[20] This principle was recognised by the ICJ in the 1949 *Reparation for Injuries* case[21] and reiterated by the same court in 1980[22] and 1999.[23] Attribution of international personality to a legal subject signifies not only that the latter can be bound by international obligations but also that its acts are directly attributable to that subject. It logically follows that when an International Organisation commits an internationally wrongful act, its international responsibility will be triggered.[24] This is why for the ARIO, international personality is a defining feature of an International Organisation.[25] The question that arises is whether the International Organisation's personality creates a veil that shields member States and justifies the International Law Commission (ILC) general rule on 'no member responsibility'. In simpler terms: is the separate international responsibility of the International Organisation for own internationally wrongful acts necessarily exclusive?

As simple and logical as the link between the personality veil and international responsibility may seem, the rule of exclusive international responsibility

[18] ARIO Comment, 130, [1]. This principle will be referred to in this book as the 'exclusive International Organisation responsibility' or the 'no member responsibility' rule, as opposed to the 'member responsibility' rule according to which member States are responsible for acts of the International Organisation by virtue of membership alone. For the use of these terms, see Yee, 'The Responsibility of States Members' (n 6) 329.

[19] M Shaw, *International Law* (CUP, 2008) 195.

[20] ARIO Comment, 74, [10]. Wilde rightly observes that 'legally, they [ie International Organisations with legal personality] are more than the sum of their (State) parts', R Wilde, 'Enhancing Accountability at the International Level: The Tension Between International Organization and Member State Responsibility and the Underlying Issues at Stake' (2006) 12 *ILSA Journal of International and Comparative Law* 395, 401.

[21] 'It must be acknowledged that its Members, by entrusting certain functions to it, with the attendant duties and responsibilities, have clothed it with the competence required to enable those functions to be effectively discharged … Accordingly, the Court has come to the conclusion that the Organization is an international person', *Reparation for Injuries Suffered in the Service of the United Nations*, Advisory Opinion [1949] ICJ Reports 49, 178–79.

[22] *Interpretation of the Agreement of 25 March 1951* (n 5) 89–90.

[23] *Difference relating to Immunity from Legal Process of a Special Rapporteur of the Commission on Human Rights*, Advisory Opinion [1999] ICJ Reports 62, 89.

[24] ARIO, Arts 3 and 4. *A contrario* the ICJ in the *Certain Phosphate Lands in Nauru* case held that the Administering Authority of Nauru possessed no such personality and hence every State involved in it could be sued individually before the Court, *Certain Phosphate Lands in Nauru (Nauru v Australia)* (Preliminary Objections) [1992] ICJ Reports 240, 258–59.

[25] ARIO, Art 2(a) defines an International Organisation as: 'an organization established by a treaty or other instrument governed by international law and possessing its own legal personality'.

of International Organisations only gradually developed in the course of the twentieth century. In contradiction with the perception that dominated legal scholarship in the pre-UN era, International Organisations are considered nowadays 'non-transparent'.[26] Back in 1928, Eagleton presumed that member States will be responsible for acts of International Organisations, as the separate international personality of International Organisations had not crystallised at the time.[27] The *dictum* of the ICJ in the *Reparation for Injuries* case was therefore a watershed. With the personality of International Organisations taken for granted, legal scholarship in the UN era addresses the issue by drawing parallels between International Organisations and corporations possessing personality under national laws.[28]

A necessary inference drawn from this analogy is that the responsibility of an International Organisation for its own wrongful acts must be exclusive. This is only logical, otherwise the separate legal personality of the International Organisation, distinct from its member States, would be little more than a fiction.[29] Since no authoritative legal statement has resolved the issue, commentators have invoked such policy considerations in order to back up the 'no member responsibility' rule. In the same vein, it has also been suggested that a 'member responsibility' rule would jeopardise the efficient and independent functioning of International Organisations and would unduly expose third parties to loss and damage.[30] Based on these arguments, the Institute of International

[26] Brölmann remarks that the once 'transparent image of organisations ... now is squarely at odds with the organisations' separate legal identity', Brölmann, *The Institutional Veil in Public International Law* (n 2) 68.

[27] C Eagleton, *The Responsibility of States in International Law* (New York University Press, 1928) 220–29.

[28] According to this analogy, States are equated with shareholders of a body corporate, CF Amerasinghe, 'Liability to Third Parties of Member States of International Organizations: Practice, Principle and Juridical Precedent' (1991) 40 *ICLQ* 259, 274–75; HT Adam, *Les organismes internationaux spécialisés, contribution à la théorie générale des Etablissements publics internationaux* (Librairie Générale de Droit et de Jurisprudence, 1965) 130; I Seidl-Hohenveldern, *Corporations In and Under International Law* (CUP, 1987) 120–21.

[29] Lauterpacht notes: 'But if, in such cases, provision is made for direct recourse against Members, it should be recognized that this will involve in some marked degree a departure from the notion of an integrated and effective personality in international law', E Lauterpacht, 'The Development of the Law of International Organizations by the Decisions of International Tribunals' (1976) 152 *RCADI* 381, 412–13. In a similar vein, Higgins as the Special Rapporteur of the Institute of International Law notes: 'If members were liable for the defaults of the organization, its independent personality would be likely to become increasingly a sham', R Higgins, Special Rapporteur, 'Report on the Legal Consequences for Member States of the Non-fulfilment by International Organizations of Their Obligations toward Third Parties' (1995) 66 *Yearbook of the Institute of International Law* 419; N Blokker, 'Member State Responsibility for Wrongdoings of International Organizations: Beacon of Hope or Delusion?' (2015) 12 *IOLR* 319, 321–29.

[30] See Stumer, 'Liability of Member States for Acts of International Organizations' (n 1) 564–69; Ryngaert and Buchanan, 'Member State Responsibility' (n 1) 136–38; Higgins, 'Report on the Legal Consequences for Member States' (n 29) 419; Klabbers, *An Introduction to International Organizations Law* (n 4) 288–89. Amerasinghe argues that international responsibility of member States has significant repercussions in international cooperation through International Organisations, CF Amerasinghe, *Principles of the Institutional Law of International Organizations* (CUP, 2005) 443.

Law (IDI) concluded that a rule on 'no member liability' exists in international law.[31] The work of the Institute on the *Legal Consequences for Member States of the Non-fulfilment by International Organizations of Their Obligations toward Third Parties* proved to be very influential for the ILC's work. Special Rapporteur Gaja endorsed the Institute's policy concerns[32] and the ILC relied on the IDI's conclusion to justify the 'no member responsibility' rule.[33]

Others, without invoking normative arguments, have advocated for the exact opposite principle. Narula, for example, argues for the establishment of the international responsibility of member States in the case of international financial institutions violating rights contained in the International Covenant for Economic Social and Cultural Rights (ICESCR).[34] She suggests that member States can be held responsible for the institutions' failure to the extent that they are bound by such obligations.[35] However, she fails to explain on what basis member States are responsible or to provide any authorities that would support such a solution to what she considers to be a 'yet unsettled question'.

The ILC relied on two more sources in order to provide authority for the exclusive responsibility rule. First, this rule was 'defended by several States in contentious cases'.[36] This may be true, but no international court has so far endorsed this argument and thus it is 'too slender a reed' to provide authoritative support for the rule.[37] Secondly, according to the ILC, this view was taken incidentally by British courts in the litigation that followed the collapse of the International Tin Council (ITC). As I will explain in detail below, the view taken by the British courts and the IDI are valid authorities for a 'no member liability' but not for a 'no member responsibility' rule.[38]

I argue here that the rule latent in Article 62 derives from legal argumentation and not from the policy concerns described above. First of all, if the international responsibility of member States is established by virtue of an internationally wrongful act of an International Organisation, then it cannot be inferred that member States, merely because they are members of the International Organisation, consent to be bound by the obligations that arise by virtue of that internationally wrongful act. If that was the case, ARIO, Article 62(1)(a) and (1)(b), which regulate such consensual assumption of obligations, would not be considered as exceptional scenarios. Second, the international responsibility

[31] See Art 6(a) of the IDI's 1995 Resolution, included in Higgins, 'Report on the Legal Consequences for Member States' (n 29) 445.

[32] G Gaja, *Fourth Report on Responsibility of International Organizations*, UN doc A/CN.4/564/(2006) and Add 1 and 2, reproduced in (2006) 2(1) *YBILC* 103, 124, [94] ('Gaja Fourth Report').

[33] ARIO Comment, 163, [5].

[34] S Narula, 'The Right to Food: Holding Global Actors Accountable under International Law' (2006) 44 *Columbia Journal of Transnational Law* 691.

[35] ibid 744.

[36] ARIO Comment, 162, [3].

[37] Yee, 'The Responsibility of States Members' (n 6) 333.

[38] See III B below.

of member States does not arise for own internationally wrongful act either. To put it in terms of the law of international responsibility, an application of the attribution rules contained in ASR, Chapter II suggests that there is no reason why conduct of an International Organisation should be attributable to a member State by virtue of its membership only.[39] Attribution of conduct, as a normative operation, ensues from some sort of control or organic link established between a subject and certain conduct.[40] And in the present scenario of mere membership, neither of the two is in play.

While the above are legal arguments that justify the shielding of member States, I believe that an integrated understanding of the institutional veil's functioning reveals the true justification for the provision. The rationale behind the shielding of member States was given by the Special Rapporteur in his Fourth Report and pertains to the protection of the International Organisation's independent legal personality. In this report, the Special Rapporteur referred to the special member State-International Organisation relationship and explained that: '[t]he influence … has to be used by the State as a legal entity that is separate from the organization [in order to trigger the member State's international responsibility]'.[41]

Within this *dictum* lies the legal explanation of the protective function of the institutional veil. According to the Special Rapporteur, member States are in fact legally inseparable from the International Organisation when they influence the latter in accordance with its rules, that is, when they act as members. In fact, they merge with the international legal personality of the International Organisation on these occasions and this is why they do not bear responsibility for the influence exercised. *Mutatis mutandis*, when the International Organisation sets up an entity in accordance with its rules and endows it to carry out certain functions of that organisation, 'there is little doubt that this entity can be qualified as an organ or agent of the organization'.[42] Thus, the lack of a distinct legal personality is the reason for no distinct member State responsibility. The question that automatically comes to mind then is: why does this merging occur?

[39] See Higgins, 'Report on the Legal Consequences for Member States' (n 29) 283. Same assertion by Advocate General Darmon in a limb of the ITC litigation, before the ECJ. Darmon argued that 'the mere fact of the Community's being a member of the ITC does not, in view of the ITC's separate personality, enable the wrongful acts and omissions of the ITC to be imputed to the Community', C-241/87 *Maclaine Watson & Co Ltd v Council and Commission of the European Communities* (1990) 96 International Law Reports 226.

[40] ASR Comment, 47, [3], [4]; ARIO Comment, 86–87, [5], [7].

[41] Gaja Fourth Report (n 32) [62]. Same principle in ibid [67]: 'The role that a member State may have within the organs of an international organization would not justify attribution of responsibility to the State for the conduct of the organization: this would be tantamount to denying the separate legal personality of the organization'.

[42] P Palchetti, 'Applying the Rules of Attribution in Complex Scenarios: The Case of Partnerships among International Organizations' (2016) 13 *IOLR* 37, 42. See also G Gaja, *Eighth Report on Responsibility of International Organizations*, UN doc A/CN.4/640 (2011) [29].

It is considerations of autonomy that dictate the answer to this question. Autonomy, as the expression of separate juridical will,[43] exists in a dialectic relationship with separate legal personality; without autonomy, legal personality is not conceivable and vice versa.[44] In the *Phosphate Lands in Nauru* case, the ICJ denied to attribute international legal personality to the tripartite Administering Authority for Nauru on the justification that the Administrator 'was at all times appointed by the Australian Government and was accordingly under the instructions of that Government' and that his acts 'were subject to confirmation or rejection by the Governor-General of Australia'.[45] The Court concluded that the Administering Authority did not possess a distinct will and therefore an international legal personality distinct from those of the States that comprised it.[46] It is thus the expression of a separate will with respect to certain competence, and not the conferral of competence as such, that bestows legal personality upon the International Organisation.[47] The General Agreement on Tariffs and Trade (GATT), for example, in its early stages was refused International Organisation status because it did not possess such *volonté distincte*.[48] Two different types of autonomy are germane to the present context: the autonomy International Organisations enjoy from member States and conversely the autonomy member States enjoy from the International Organisation.

As far as the first is concerned, autonomy of an International Organisation is defined by the constituent instrument of the International Organisation, and hence the rules of the International Organisation which are enacted in accordance with this instrument. When drafting the constituent instrument of the International Organisation, members intend to bestow legal personality upon

[43] P Reuter, *Institutions internationales* (Paris Presses Universitaires, 1955) 195: 'En tant qu'organisation il ne peut que s'agir d'un groupe susceptible de manifester d'une manière permanente une *volonté juridiquement distincte* de celle de ces membres' [Only a group capable of manifesting in a permanent way a *will that is legally distinct* from that of its members can be considered an organisation] (author's translation) (emphasis added).

[44] Schermers and Blokker, *International Institutional Law* (n 9) 34–35; P Sands and P Klein, *Bowett's Law of International Institutions* (Sweet and Maxwell, 2001) 16; G Verdirame, *The UN and Human Rights: Who Guards the Guardians?* (CUP, 2011) 59–60. Autonomy derives from the Greek word αυτονομία that literally means the 'freedom to use one's own laws', HG Liddell and R Scott, *An Intermediate Greek-English Lexicon* (Clarendon Press, 1889).

[45] *Phosphate Lands in Nauru* (n 24) 257.

[46] ibid 258.

[47] The International Court of Justice referred to International Organisations as 'subjects of law endowed with a certain autonomy', *Legality of the Use by a State of Nuclear Weapons in Armed Conflict*, Advisory Opinion [1996] ICJ Reports 66, 75, [19]; C Ahlborn, 'The Rules of International Organizations and the Law of International Responsibility' (2011) 8 *IOLR* 397, 416; K Schmalenbach, 'International Organizations or Institutions, General Aspects' in *Max Planck Encyclopedia of Public International Law* (OUP online ed, 2014) [7]: 'international organizations have at least one organ with the capacity to generate a will attributable to the organization alone'; R Wessel and I Dekker, 'Identities of States in International Organizations' (2015) 12 *IOLR* 293, 306.

[48] Schermers and Blokker, *International Institutional Law* (n 9) 35. White suggests that the G7 is denied legal personality because of the lack of a separate will, N White, *The Law of International Organizations* (Manchester University Press, 2005) 31.

the International Organisation, and consequently every decision of the International Organisation adopted in accordance with the rules of the International Organisation is necessarily an expression of the separate juridical will of the International Organisation.[49] To uphold the opposite would be tantamount to suggesting that International Organisations can have legal personality without possessing autonomy at the same time.

This is why it cannot be upheld that International Organisations lose their autonomy when member States operate in accordance with the rules of the International Organisation.[50] For example, in the 2011 ICJ *Interim Accord* case,[51] NATO's decision not to invite the Former Yugoslav Republic of Macedonia to join the International Organisation, was rendered autonomously by the International Organisation, albeit Greece's de facto veto was the catalyst to the International Organisation's stance. Accordingly, the fishing quotas set by the plenaries of regional fisheries management organisations (RFMOs) are undeniably decisions of the latter International Organisation attributable only to it even if they are in fact the aggregated decisions of member States.[52] Therefore, the formation of the separate will of the International Organisation, through the processes envisioned in its rules, cannot undermine the autonomy of the International Organisation.

Being so closely tied to the formation of a separate juridical will through specific processes which are different in every International Organisation, autonomy, when attached to International Organisations, is a relative concept without a fixed meaning. This is why it is an elusive trait to establish and, in general, writers have not elaborated on how it should be identified.[53] However, the fact that an International Organisation will enjoy autonomy from members with respect to the processes covered by its rules does not render autonomy a quantitative value.[54] No such thing as 'a large measure' of autonomy is conceivable when

[49] Ahlborn, 'The Rules of International Organizations' (n 47) 403, 415.

[50] D'Aspremont argues in a similar vein that no abuse of the International Organisation's legal personality occurs in such instances, d'Aspremont, 'Abuse of the Legal Personality of International Organizations' (n 1) 110. Sarooshi suggests that International Organisations cannot be considered as agents of member States when the latter exercise control within the confines of the decision-making processes of the International Organisation, D Sarooshi, *International Organizations and Their Exercise of Sovereign Powers* (Oxford University Press, 2007) 45. Neither of them, however, explains in normative terms why this is so. See also T Gazzini, 'The Relationship Between International Legal Personality and Autonomy' in ND White and R Collins (eds), *International Organisations and the Idea of Autonomy* (Cavendish-Routledge, 2010) 199ff.

[51] *Application of the Interim Accord of 13 September 1995 (Former Yugoslav Republic of Macedonia v Greece)* (Merits) [2011] ICJ Reports 644.

[52] S Guggisberg, *The Use of CITES for Commercially-exploited Fish Species: A Solution to Overexploitation and Illegal, Unreported and Unregulated Fishing?* (Springer, 2016) 165.

[53] White has offered some indicia of existence of a separate will, N White, 'Discerning Separate Will' in W Heere (ed), *From Government to Governance: The Growing Impact of Non-State Actors on the International and European Legal System*, Proceedings of the 2004 Hague Joint ASIL/NVIR Conference (2004) 31, 31–38.

[54] Against Gazzini, 'The Relationship Between International Legal Personality and Autonomy' (n 50) 200.

it comes to conferring competence to an International Organisation.[55] Because, as said earlier, such a proposition suggests that no personality is conferred to the International Organisation with respect to specific competence, which is clearly not the intention of the members.

When it comes to the autonomy of member States from the International Organisation, if the outcome of a process is an expression of the International Organisation's autonomous will, the same outcome (for example, a decision by the Organisation's plenary organ) cannot be the expression of the separate juridical will of member States at the same time. Since a process pertains to the exercise of certain competence, when the International Organisation exercises autonomously this competence, member States necessarily lose their autonomy with respect to the said competence and hence the separateness of their legal personality.[56] States are inseparable from the International Organisation in such instances. This, however, does not mean that States lose their legal personality altogether; this will be the case only to the extent that their conduct is not an autonomous exercise of certain competence.

A recent example that brings to the fore the operation of the organisational veil is the 2015 Advisory Opinion of the International Tribunal for the Law of the Sea (ITLOS) in a request submitted by the Sub-Regional Fisheries Commission (SRFC).[57] The SRFC, an International Organisation that reinforces cooperation between its West-African member States and coordinates their fisheries policies, submitted, inter alia, the following question to the Tribunal:

> Where a fishing license is issued to a vessel within the framework of an international agreement with the flag State or with an international agency, shall the State or the international agency be held liable for the violation of the fisheries legislation of the coastal State by the vessel in question?

In order to rephrase the question in the terminology used throughout this book, the Tribunal clarified that in the context of the particular question 'liability' signifies international responsibility[58] and 'international agency' is coterminous with International Organisation.[59] As far as International Organisations are concerned, the question was exclusively addressed to the EU, as it is the only organisation of such nature that concludes international fisheries agreements

[55] J Alvarez, *International Organizations as Law-Makers* (OUP, 2005) 129; A Cassese, *International Law* (OUP, 2005) 137.

[56] Geslin suggests that it is the International Organisation that loses its autonomy when member States control its actions, A Geslin, 'Réflexions sur la répartition de la responsabilité entre l'organisation internationale et ses Etats membres' (2005) 109 *Revue Générale de Droit International Public* 539, 564.

[57] *Request for an Advisory Opinion Submitted by the Sub-Regional Fisheries Commission*, Advisory Opinion, ITLOS Case no 21, 2 April 2015, available at www.itlos.org/en/cases/list-of-cases/case-no-21.

[58] ibid [145].

[59] ibid [152].

with third States on behalf of its member States.[60] The latter have transferred their competence with regard to the conservation and management of sea fishing resources and hence the capacity to enter into external undertakings with third States exclusively to the EU.[61] In fact, the members States of the SRFC have entered into such bilateral agreements with the EU, whereby it is stated that all relevant activities shall conform to the fisheries laws and regulations of the coastal State.[62] Thus, the Tribunal had to determine whether it is the EU or its member(s) that will be held internationally responsible for violations of those agreements committed by vessels that fly the flag of the member(s).

Without referring to autonomy *eo nomine*, the ITLOS concluded that the EU will be exclusively responsible for such internationally wrongful acts committed by vessels flying the flag of an EU member State. The starting point of the Tribunal's analysis was the notion of competence and its close connection to international responsibility.[63] Specifically, the Tribunal held that:

> in cases where an international organization, in the exercise of its exclusive competence in fisheries matters, concludes a fisheries access agreement … the obligations of the flag State become the obligations of the international organization.[64]

Member States then, are not capable of assuming international obligations when an entity whose conduct is attributable to that State (in this case a vessel flying its flag) is exercising competence that has been transferred exclusively to an International Organisation. It is competence that dictates where autonomy will lie and hence when the organisational veil will effectively come into play.

The understanding of autonomy is only functional and thus legal subjects can at the same time be autonomous with respect to certain competence but not with respect to others. The existence of different types of autonomy (territorial, cultural, etc) corroborates this functional understanding of the notion.[65] During the *interbellum*, for example, Estonia implemented the Cultural Autonomy Law which vested certain ethnic groups with autonomy only in the field of education, culture, sports and youth affairs.[66] Since autonomy is attached to legal

[60] United Nations Convention on the Law of the Sea, Art 305[1(f)], Art 306 Agreement relating to the Implementation of Part XI of the United Nations Convention on the Law of the Sea (adopted 28 July 1994; entered into force 16 November 1994) 1836 UNTS 3 and Annex IX, 10 December 1982, 1833 UNTS 397.

[61] *Request for an Advisory Opinion* (n 57) [164]; Consolidated Version of the Treaty on the Functioning of the European Union, Art 3(1)(d) [2012] OJ C326/47; Declaration made pursuant to Art 5(1) of Annex IX to the Convention and to Art 4(4) of the Agreement, 1998 UNTS 227–35.

[62] See the bilateral agreement between the EU and Mauritania, Protocol setting out the fishing opportunities and financial contribution provided for in the Fisheries Partnership Agreement between the European Community and the Islamic Republic of Mauritania for a period of four years, Art 1(3) [2015] OJ L315.

[63] *Request for an Advisory Opinion* (n 57) [168]. See analysis by E Paasivirta, 'The Responsibility of Member States of International Organizations? A Special Case for the European Union' (2015) 12 *IOLR* 448, 457–59.

[64] *Request for an Advisory Opinion* (n 57) [172].

[65] HZ Heintze, 'On the Legal Understanding of Autonomy' in M Suksi (ed), *Autonomy: Applications and Implications* (Kluwer Law International, 1998) 7, 17–24.

[66] ibid 21.

personality, when States limit their autonomy by merging with the International Organisation, this impacts their capacity to bear separate international personality and hence responsibility.

As has been argued with respect to International Organisations: 'Without *volonté distincte* international organizations cannot incur *responsabilité distincte*'.[67] It is suggested here that this proposition can be reversed and apply to States also. When conferring competence to an International Organisation, States vouchsafe their autonomy with respect to the exercise of specific competence in the benefit of the International Organisation. This is why no internationally wrongful act of member States is established and thus their international responsibility is not triggered. And since State autonomy vanishes when they behave as members within the context of an International Organisation, it is only logical that the same occurs when they do not perform any act. A 'no member responsibility' rule, then, does exist in international law, however its justification does not lie in the sources cited in the ILC's commentaries.

In a different line of argument, Brölmann suggests that the 'institutional veil' can be used as a descriptive tool.[68] She identifies four possible responsibility contexts where the veil applies, with different legal ramifications for member States.[69] In this sense, the 'institutional veil' is not the reason for the occurrence of such ramifications, but rather the veil's shape adapts to the prevailing trend as to the allocation of responsibility in each scenario. For example, if the ILC reverses the rule latent in ARIO, Article 62, the veil's protective scope automatically changes. In an unsettled legal issue, nevertheless, where the legal trend alters, this notion is subject to continuous development and it is only a fitting metaphor with explicative but without any normative value per se.

Such unprincipled theorising only perplexes further the issue and does not offer insights into the understanding of the legal relationship between member States and the International Organisation. I believe that a change of perspective is necessary. The focus of the legal discussion should turn to the reason why the veil exists and thus to clarifying the connection between the International Organisation's legal personality and the establishment of the 'institutional veil'. The explanation of the functioning of the 'institutional veil' proposed here rests on a legal basis. I contend that it protects member States whenever their conduct is not an autonomous exercise of certain competence, because on such occasions member States do not possess international legal personality distinct from that of the International Organisation. There exists a clear legal reason – the lack of a separate international legal personality – why the veil exists and member States disappear under it.

[67] Ahlborn, 'The Rules of International Organizations' (n 47) 479.

[68] C Brölmann, 'Member States and International Legal Responsibility: Developments of the Institutional Veil' (2015) 12 *IOLR* 358, 360ff.

[69] ibid.

B. On Liability and Responsibility: 'Exclusive International Organisation Responsibility' Rule

The most problematic aspect of the provision is that it conflates the notion of international responsibility with that of liability and to this extent Article 62 is based on a false premise. And while this confusion may result in the correct outcome when it comes to drafting the general underlying rule, the same does not necessarily hold true when it comes to drafting the exceptions to this rule.

Undoubtedly, the discussion about the issue at hand has been marred by the mingling between liability and international responsibility. This section will demonstrate that the issues of member State liability and that of member State international responsibility for an internationally wrongful act of an International Organisation are conceptually different and should be kept apart.[70] It is considerations of liability, at best 'tangential' to the law of international responsibility,[71] that have unnecessarily perplexed a basic international responsibility question. The ILC in the ARIO has implicitly endorsed this intersection of the two accountability mechanisms and instead of looking for answers in some basic premises of the law of international responsibility, has transposed the debate on member State liability to the international responsibility framework.

This confusion was fostered during the academic and judicial debate that followed the collapse of the ITC in the mid-1980s.[72] On 24 October 1985, the ITC, an International Organisation and the operative arm of the Sixth International Tin Agreement, announced that it was unable to repay its debts or to fulfil its contractual obligations to purchase tin. When the International Organisation's creditors turned to the member States for payment, the latter refused to pay any of the ITC's debts, which were estimated at £900,000,000.[73]

[70] I am not aware of any commentator who attempts to separate the two forms of accountability in the present debate.

[71] Bronwlie has insightfully noted that the Articles of the IDI on member State liability have 'a curiously tangential character' when it comes to regulating the matter of member State responsibility, I Brownlie, 'The Responsibility of States for the Acts of International Organizations' in M Ragazzi (ed), *International Responsibility Today, Essays in Memory of Oscar Schachter* (Brill, 2005) 355, 356.

[72] For academic commentary on the collapse of the ITC, see R Sadurska and C Chinkin, 'The Collapse of the International Tin Council: A Case of State Responsibility?' (1989–1990) 30 *Virginia Journal of International Law* 845; I Mallory, 'Conduct Unbecoming: The Collapse of the International Tin Agreement' (1990) 5 *American University Journal of International Law and Policy* 835; E McFadden, 'The Collapse of Tin: Restructuring a Failed Commodity Agreement' (1986) 80 *AJIL* 811, 815–21; P Sands, 'The Tin Council Litigation in the English Courts' (1987) 34 *Netherlands International Law Review* 367; I Seidl-Hohenveldern, 'Piercing the Corporate Veil of International Organizations: The International Tin Council Case in the English Court of Appeals' (1989) 32 *German Yearbook of International Law* 43.

[73] For a detailed analysis of the facts see S Chandrasekhar, 'Cartel in a Can: The Financial Collapse of the International Tin Council' (1989) 10 *Northwestern Journal of International Law and Business* 309.

Thus, the creditors sued the International Organisation in order to reclaim their money and the tin crisis was transferred before domestic UK[74] and US courts[75] but also before the European Court of Justice (ECJ).[76] This litigation process revealed the problems facing third party creditors dealing with International Organisations when the latter are unable to meet their obligations.

The most extensive and informed debate, pertinent for present purposes, took place before the UK courts. The House of Lords finally upheld the ITC's immunity and ruled that such matters were not justiciable before UK tribunals. Setting aside questions of jurisdictional immunity of International Organisations, a lively debate revolved around the question of member State liability for acts of International Organisations. Academics commented extensively on the findings of the UK courts and the pertinent questions taken up by courts and commentators were aptly summarized by Schermers and Blokker:

> First, in situations in which an international organization is liable, are the member states simultaneously liable? ... Secondly, if the organization is liable, can it recover the costs from the member states? ... Thirdly, if the creditors are unable to recover their money from the organization ... should they be entitled to file a claim with the member states?[77]

English courts suggested that member State liability, if it existed, was established in international law.[78] Thus, when English courts ruled on member State liability for acts of the ITC they had in mind the international liability of States as an accountability mechanism. At that time, however, international liability had not crystallised as a term of art. The ILC had only clarified that State liability, in contradistinction to State international responsibility, was deemed to arise out of certain acts not prohibited by international law.[79] Since no further

[74] *Arab Banking Corp v International Tin Council*, UK High Court, Queen's Bench Division, Judgment of 15 January 1986; *In Re International Tin Council*, UK High Court, Chancery Division, Judgment of 22 January 1987; *JH Rayner Ltd v Department of Trade and Industry and Others*, UK High Court, Queen's Bench Division (Commercial Court), Judgment of 24 June 1987; *JH Rayner Ltd v Department of Trade and Industry and others and Related Appeals*, UK Court of Appeal, Judgment of 27 April 1988; *JH Rayner v Department of Trade and Industry and others and Related Appeals*, UK House of Lords, Judgment on Appeal of 26 October 1989; *Maclaine Watson & Co v Department of Trade and Industry*, UK House of Lords, Judgment of 2 January 1989. The litigation process before UK courts will be referred to here as the *Tin Council* case.

[75] *International Tin Council v Amalgamet Inc*, US Supreme Court, New York County, Judgment of 25 January 1988.

[76] See n 39 above.

[77] Schermers and Blokker, *International Institutional Law* (n 9) 1010.

[78] Lord Griffiths, House of Lords, Judgment on Appeal of 26 October 1989, transcript, 10.

[79] ILC, *Report of the International Law Commission on the Work of Its 25th Session, 7 May–13 July 1973*, UN Doc A/9010/Rev.1 (1973), reproduced in (1973) 2(1) *YBILC* 161, 169, [39]. According to Boyle: 'What distinguishes international liability from other forms of responsibility is that it does not presuppose wrongful conduct or breach of any obligation', A Boyle, 'State Responsibility and International Liability for Injurious Consequences of Acts not Prohibited by International Law: A Necessary Distinction?' (1990) 39 *ICLQ* 1, 3. In a similar vein, Barboza refers to the terms as *ex delicto* responsibility and *sine delicto* liability, implying that liability is not premised upon

clarifications were made as to the nature of this mechanism, it is safe to assume that the starting point for English courts was the correlative domestic concept of liability for the adjudication of the matter at hand.

More importantly, English courts did not reflect upon the distinction between international responsibility and liability in an international context.[80] Given the difference in nature between these accountability mechanisms, it should not be lightly presumed that any finding pertaining to member State liability for acts of International Organisations can be transposed *mutatis mutandis* to international responsibility of member States for internationally wrongful acts of International Organisations. Nevertheless, the ILC and commentators have used the *Tin Council* case in order to draw inferences with regard to the matter of international responsibility of member States for the internationally wrongful acts of International Organisations.[81]

The statement underlying this terminological leap from liability to international responsibility is that the establishment of the two mechanisms arises by virtue of the same argumentation. Therefore, before turning to the substance of the arguments put forward in order to answer the questions in play, the relationship between liability and international responsibility must be addressed. Because if the underpinnings of international responsibility are totally unrelated to those of liability, then it may be that the findings of the courts in this debate are not germane to the present issue.

The two mechanisms must be kept separate for two reasons. First, the rules governing each scheme are so different by nature, that 'a joint examination of the two subjects could only make both of them more difficult to grasp'.[82] Both the ASR and the ARIO supposedly deal solely with secondary rules.[83] This means that they provide the framework for determining the consequences of a failure to fulfil obligations established by primary rules.[84] In the same vein, the commentaries to the ARIO expressly state that:

> [t]he reference in paragraph 1 [of ARIO, Article 1] to acts that are wrongful under international law implies that the present draft articles do not address the question of liability for injurious consequences arising out of acts not prohibited by international law.[85]

wrongful conduct, J Barboza *The Environment, Risk and Liability in International Law* (Brill, 2011) 3; same line of argumentation adopted by S Sucharitkul, 'State Responsibility and International Liability under International Law' (1996) 18 *Loyola of Los Angeles International and Comparative Law Review* 821, 821–22.

[80] Sadurska and Chinkin imply that the terms can be used interchangeably and thus English courts had international responsibility rather than liability in mind when dealing with the *Tin Council* case, 'The Collapse of the International Tin Council' (n 72) 857.

[81] ARIO Comment, 162–63, [4]; Stumer, 'Liability of Member States for Acts of International Organizations' (n 1) 553.

[82] ILC, *Report of the International Law Commission on the Work of Its 30th Session, 8 May–28 July 1978*, UN doc A/33/10 (1978), reproduced in (1978) 2(2) *YBILC* 74, 75–75, [79].

[83] For a critique of this perception see III A ii below.

[84] ASR Comment, 31, [4].

[85] ARIO Comment, 70, [5].

Thus, the Articles are indifferent to primary norms, the breach of which gives rise to responsibility.[86]

In comparison with the above, liability rules themselves constitute primary norms of international law.[87] As the purpose of the rules on international liability is to assert obligations without a prior finding of wrongfulness,[88] the concept of international liability consists of a 'compound "primary" obligation'; the four duties to be found within the concept are according to the ILC the duty to prevent, to inform, to negotiate and the duty to repair.[89] Under international law then, liability and international responsibility operate at distinct levels and that is why they have not been treated under a common legal framework.

Second, the establishment of the two schemes comes about via different routes. The basis for the establishment of international liability is that a state is liable for the harmful effects of activities under its control or within its jurisdiction. According to the ILC, liability in an international law context revolves around the concept of damage, while international responsibility revolves around that of an internationally wrongful act.[90] The Commission also stressed that both liability regimes it drafted on prevention of harm for transboundary hazardous activities and on transboundary environmental harm 'should be without prejudice to the relevant rules of international responsibility of States adopted by the Commission in 2001'.[91] It is clear, then, that while international responsibility and liability can coexist, the establishment of the two is dependent upon different conditions. Since the rules on international responsibility examined here are clearly detached from the concept of liability, would it be safe to bring into the international responsibility debate inferences from the previous debate on liability?

Despite the effort of the ILC to keep the cleavage as clear as possible, the confusion between the two notions is apparent in the text of treaties as well as the work of many commentators, especially of those that have dealt with the matter at hand.[92] A strong separation between them appears in the IDI's

[86] ibid 76, [3]. This distinction was put forward by the ITLOS in *Request for an Advisory Opinion* (n 57) [145].

[87] ILC, *Draft Principles on the Allocation of Loss in the Case of Transboundary Harm Arising Out of Hazardous Activities, with Commentaries*, UN Doc A/61/10 (2006), reproduced in (2006) 2(2) *YBILC* 59, 62, [6] ('ILC, Harm Principles').

[88] R Quentin Baxter, *Fourth Report on International Liability for Injurious Consequences Arising Out of Acts Not Prohibited by International Law*, UN doc A/CN.4/373(1983), reproduced in (1983) 2(1) *YBILC* 201, 201–2, [1]–[2].

[89] ibid 220, [65].

[90] In its liability Principles regarding transboundary harm, the Commission stated that: 'for the purpose of the principles, the focus is on the consequences of the activity and not on the lawfulness of the activity itself', ILC Harm Principles (n 87) 62, [5]; ILC, *Draft Articles on Prevention of Transboundary Harm from Hazardous Activities, with Commentaries*, UN Doc A/56/10 (2001), reproduced in (2001) 2(2) *YBILC* 144, 150.

[91] ILC Harm Principles (n 87) 60, [7].

[92] NLJT Horbach, 'The Confusion About State Responsibility and International Liability' (1991) 4 *Leiden Journal of International Law* 47ff.

1995 report,[93] nevertheless critics have used these notions interchangeably.[94] For example, Stumer suggests that: '[t]he terms secondary liability and concurrent liability are used … to refer to the attribution of responsibility of a State merely by virtue of its membership in an international organization'.[95] Boyle has criticised the ILC for unnecessarily perplexing the regulation of 'accountability mechanisms' through the inclusion in its work of the term liability.[96] A paradigmatic example of a synonym use of these notions can be found in Article 263(2) and (3), and Article 235(1) of the 1982 Law of the Sea Convention.[97] The fact that the provision does not place any emphasis on the distinction between the two schemes is evident from its title: while entitled 'Responsibility and Liability' in English, the respective French and Spanish titles are 'Responsabilité' and 'Responsabilidad'. It may be that these languages do not have an equivalent term for liability,[98] but they would have invented one if the two terms had a different connotation within the text of the provision.

From a different perspective, Goldie equated liability not with international responsibility but rather with legal redress once responsibility and injury arising from a failure to fulfil that legal responsibility have been established.[99] This same approach was seemingly adopted by Article 139(2) of the 1982 Law of the Sea Convention which reads:

> Without prejudice to the rules of international law and Annex III, Article 22, damage caused by the failure of a State Party or International Organisation to carry out its responsibilities under this part shall entail liability.[100]

[93] In her report on behalf of the IDI, Special Rapporteur Higgins wondered whether 'the general principles of state responsibility [are] illuminating in regard to the problem before us', implying in that way that the Institute was in fact addressing the problem of liability, 'Report on the Legal Consequences for Member States' (n 29) 254.

[94] Ryngaert and Buchanan, 'Member State Responsibility for the Acts of International Organizations' (n 1) 133. Crawford also uses the terms interchangeably, J Crawford, *State Responsibility: The General Part* (CUP, 2013) 395ff.

[95] Stumer, 'Liability of Member States for Acts of International Organizations' (n 1) 553.

[96] Boyle, 'State Responsibility and International Liability' (n 79) 21–24.

[97] Law of the Sea Convention (LOSC), Art 263: '2. States and competent international organizations shall be responsible and liable for the measures they take in contravention of this Convention … 3. States and competent international organizations shall be responsible and liable pursuant to article 235 for damage'; Art 235: '1. States are responsible for the fulfilment of their international obligations concerning the protection and preservation of the marine environment. They shall be liable in accordance with international law'.

[98] Crawford and Watkins observe that the same holds true for the other three official UN languages, J Crawford and J Watkins, 'International Responsibility' in S Besson and J Tasioulas (eds), *The Philosophy of International Law* (OUP, 2010) 283, 284 note 3.

[99] L Goldie, 'Concepts of Strict and Absolute Liability and the Ranking of Liability in Terms of Relative Exposure to Risk' (1985) 16 *Netherlands Yearbook of International Law* 175, 175–76.

[100] See also the comments by the UN Secretariat to the ILC Codification Division of 3 February 2004, which state: 'an act of a UN peacekeeping force … if committed in violation of an international obligation entails the international *responsibility* of the Organization and its *liability in compensation*', ILC, *Responsibility of International Organizations: Comments and Observations Received from International Organizations*, UN doc A/CN.4/545 (2004), reproduced in (2004) 2(1) *YBILC* 19, 28, [3] (emphasis added).

This latter view has not been endorsed by the ILC,[101] but it is instructive as it brings to the forefront the main point of convergence between the two concepts.

This is, namely, the duty of reparation owed to the victim. Undoubtedly, the rationale behind both schemes is that the victim must be redressed and without such a legal duty, the establishment of international responsibility or liability would fall down to an academic exercise. However, this duty of reparation must be regarded as a secondary obligation in the context of international responsibility of States and as a primary one in the context of State liability. As the ILC very clearly explains:

> it is one thing to define a rule and the obligation it imposes, and another to determine whether there has been a breach of that obligation and what should be the consequences of the breach. Only the second aspect comes within the sphere of responsibility proper; to encourage any confusion on this point would be to raise an obstacle which might once again frustrate any hope of successful codification.[102]

This means that reparation results from the rules established by the ILC when international responsibility is in play and from arbitrary considerations of causation when liability is triggered. The level of causation required is determined ad hoc in every case by the relevant primary norm. For instance, in the *Tin Council* case, English courts asserted that membership of an International Organisation is not a sufficient causal link in order to hold member States liable for damage suffered from acts of the International Organisation. In a different vein, in the case of damage caused by space objects, a sufficient causal link is presumed to exist between the state that has launched the object and the damage occurred.[103] Thus, the threshold for the establishment of liability varies. It is based upon an ad hoc causative assessment of the relationship between the wrongdoer and the harmful consequences. Nevertheless, this causation element, that justifies the imposition of a duty to repair, will be different according to the context. Contrariwise, international responsibility is not dependent upon the context and is triggered upon the existence of an internationally wrongful act. And the determination of such an internationally wrongful act rests upon the prerequisites of attribution and breach that, according to the ILC, are objectively determined.[104]

[101] '[Liability] is not used to mean only the consequences of an obligation, but rather to mean the obligation itself, which – like "responsibility" – includes its consequences', R Quentin-Baxter, *Preliminary Report on International Liability for Injurious Consequences Arising Out of Acts Not Prohibited by International Law*, UN doc A/CN.4/334 (1980) and Add 1 and 2, reproduced in 2(1) *YBILC* 247, 250, [12].

[102] 1973 Report of the ILC (n 79) 170, [41].

[103] Convention on the International Liability for Damage Caused by Space Objects, Art II, 961 UNTS 187. Because of the absence of a causal link, it has been suggested that the provision establishes a principle of absolute liability, see V Kayser, *Launching Space Objects: Issues of Liability and Future Prospects* (Kluwer Academic, 2001) 50.

[104] The establishment of both attribution and breach is objective since it is based on observable facts, see Chapter 2 nn 82–89 and accompanying text. Further, the rules whereby these requirements

This distinction *ipso facto* means that the establishment of these mechanisms is susceptible to different argumentation, otherwise the separation between the two in international law is devoid of any meaning. Liability is based upon a subjective assessment of the relationship between the wrongdoer and the damage done to the victim. International responsibility revolves around the existence of an internationally wrongful act, which is comprised of two clearly identifiable elements. The latter are exhaustively analysed in the rules established by the ILC and do not rest upon a subjective assessment of causation. The ILC in its ASR, for example, held that Article IV(1) of the Convention on International Liability for Damage Caused by Space Objects does not provide a valid authority for ASR, Article 47 as 'it concerns liability for lawful conduct rather than international responsibility in the sense of the present articles'.[105] From a theoretical and a judicial point of view, then, the establishment of one scheme or the other rests upon a substantially different inquiry. Under this prism, no clear points of convergence between the two mechanisms can be traced, on the contrary there are good grounds to keep them separate. The necessary implication of this disentanglement is that a finding on international responsibility of member States cannot prejudice any finding on member State liability.

To return to the previous discussion, the inclusion in the ARIO of the 'no member responsibility' rule based on authorities that are germane to a rule on liability is problematic in a twofold way. First, it transposes the tangled debate on member State liability to the international responsibility framework and in this way the ILC unnecessarily perplexes a matter that it should have addressed by reference to basic international responsibility rules. More importantly, though, the Commission perpetuates the confusion that it has so strongly condemned. Secondly, from a legal standpoint, the exclusive responsibility rule rests in ARIO not only on a false but also on a weak basis which renders the rule amenable to criticism.[106] Arguably, the matter of member State liability for acts of an International Organisation is still unsettled and any pronouncement on the matter is at best a progressive development of the law. For these reasons, the ARIO would have been better without the 'no member responsibility' rule in the way it was spelled out in the commentaries to Article 62.

Overall, it is fitting to quote Amerasinghe's observations on the distinction between liability and international responsibility:

> What is important in any context is that it be made clear in what sense terms are being used. Uniformity is not an end in itself but consistency is a virtue that cannot be overemphasized and, if possible, avoidance of variance in the same context is desirable in order that clarity may be achieved.[107]

are met are exhaustively listed in the ASR (Part One Chapters II and III) and the ARIO (Part Two Chapters II and III).

[105] ASR Comment, 125, [5].

[106] Yee, for example, suggests that the authorities cited by the ILC are not sufficient to definitely conclude that a 'no member responsibility' rule exists, 'The Responsibility of States Members' (n 6) 332–35.

[107] Amerasinghe, *Principles of the Institutional Law* (n 30) 386 note 5.

The ILC's approach is, in the way described above, inconsistent and the ensuing lack of clarity affects not only the underlying rules but also the rules incorporated in Article 62, as will be analysed in the following section.

IV. EXCEPTIONS TO THE 'EXCLUSIVE INTERNATIONAL ORGANISATION RESPONSIBILITY' RULE

A. Acceptance of Responsibility

The first exception provided in Article 62(1)(a) provides that a member State will be responsible for an internationally wrongful act of an International Organisation, if it 'has accepted international responsibility for that act'. The exception suggests that member States when drafting the International Organisation's constituent instrument or the International Organisation itself at a later stage, can dictate where international responsibility for a given conduct will lie, thus bypassing all ASR and ARIO norms on attribution and breach. It is generally argued that the Article 62(1)(a) exception requires certain member State conduct for the triggering of international responsibility and the latter does not result from mere International Organisation membership.[108] As will be demonstrated in the next section, however, in exceptional circumstances of implied acceptance, mere membership can be a sufficient condition for the triggering of international responsibility.[109]

This first exception incorporated in Article 62 was deemed to be 'the least controversial' during the debates in the ILC.[110] The main reason why the exception was regarded as self-evident is its contiguity with the ASR, Article 11 attribution rule. According to this provision, which has acquired customary law status,[111] certain conduct will be attributable to a State when the latter 'acknowledges and adopts the conduct in question as its own'.[112] The example *par excellence* of acknowledgment and adoption is the *Tehran Hostages* case before the ICJ.[113] In that case, the armed attack on the US Embassy by private militants, the ensuing seizure of its premises and inmates as hostages were considered acts of the State of Iran since they were approved and endorsed on multiple occasions by organs of the Khomeini regime.[114] The question that

[108] Stumer, 'Liability of Member States for Acts of International Organizations' (n 1) 562; Ryngaert and Buchanan, 'Member State Responsibility' (n 1) 141.

[109] See IV B below.

[110] ARIO Comment, 163, [6]; Gaja Fourth Report (n 32) 103, 123, [91]; d'Aspremont, 'Abuse of the Legal Personality of International Organizations' (n 1) 98.

[111] Stumer, 'Liability of Member States for Acts of International Organizations' (n 1) 561; Ryngaert and Buchanan, 'Member State Responsibility' (n 1) 141.

[112] ASR, Art 11 provides as follows: 'Conduct which is not attributable to a State under the preceding articles shall nevertheless be considered an act of that State under international law if and to the extent that the State acknowledges and adopts the conduct in question as its own'.

[113] *United States Diplomatic and Consular Staff in Tehran* (*United States of America v Iran*) (Jurisdiction and/or Admissibility) [1980] ICJ Reports 3.

[114] ibid 35, [74].

automatically comes to mind is, in what sense is the Article 62(1)(a) exception different from the rule incorporated in ASR, Article 11 that justifies its inclusion as a separate rule within ARIO?

The obvious difference that derives from the text of the provisions is that Article 11 refers to acknowledgement and adoption of conduct while Article 62 to acceptance of international responsibility. Even if acceptance is considered a specific instance of acknowledgment and adoption, the objective of the two rules is different.[115] The former refers to attribution of conduct while the latter to attribution of international responsibility. This could be a very refined distinction to make, as such scenarios of attribution of conduct through acknowledgment and adoption will on most occasions lead to the establishment of responsibility. However, equalising the one with the other would be tantamount to cancelling the distinction between them. As the ICJ held in the *Tehran Hostages* case, adoption, and hence attribution, of conduct does not automatically lead to international responsibility; the establishment of international responsibility will also depend on the compatibility of the conduct in question with the international obligations of the subject to be held responsible.[116] Seen under this prism, Article 62 is indeed different from Article 11 and its inclusion in the ARIO is justified.

There are nevertheless good grounds to assume that Article 62(1)(a), as supported in the ARIO, is completely external to the law of international international responsibility, as it is essentially reminiscent of the perplexing member State liability debate referred above. The only authority invoked by the ILC to support this exception is Lord Gibson's opinion before the Court of Appeal during the *Tin Council* litigation.[117] As noted in the previous section however, the judicial debate in this case revolved around the matter of member State liability and Lord Gibson referred to 'direct secondary liability … [that] might be found in the terms, express or implied, of the constituent document of the organisation'.[118] What is more, the ILC did not provide any example from institutional practice that could support such an exception. A rule that could be

[115] Both Stumer, 'Liability of Member States for Acts of International Organizations' (n 1) 561 and Ryngaert and Buchanan, 'Member State Responsibility' (n 1) 141 consider Art 62(1)(a) a specific instance of the Art 11 rule. While Crawford does not take the argument that far, he notes that the two rules 'would appear similar in character', Crawford, *State Responsibility* (n 94) 428.

[116] Specifically, the court held that: 'First, it must determine how far, legally, the acts in question may be regarded as imputable to the Iranian State. Secondly, it must consider their compatibility or incompatibility with the obligations of Iran under treaties in force or under any other rules of international law that may be applicable', *Tehran Hostages* (n 113) 29, [56]. See also ASR Comment, 53, [7].

[117] ARIO Comment, 163, [7].

[118] *JH Rayner (Mincing Lane) Ltd v Department of Trade and Industry and others and Related Appeals* [1989] Ch 72, 242–43. The ILC clarified that acceptance may not only result from the constituent instrument but also from other rules of the International Organisation, ARIO Comment, 163, [7].

of relevance is Article 6(2) of Annex IX to the UN Law of the Sea Convention which provides thus:

> Any State Party may request an international organization or its member States which are States Parties for information as to who has responsibility in respect of any specific matter. The organization and the member States concerned shall provide this information. Failure to provide this information within a reasonable time or the provision of contradictory information shall result in joint and several liability.

While the provision suggests that it falls upon the International Organisation and the member States to decide who will be responsible with respect to a certain violation of the Convention, it merges international responsibility with liability, thus rendering it unreliable for a pronouncement on a rule on either liability or international responsibility.[119] Therefore, it must be assumed that the rule incorporated in Article 62(1)(a) is a *mutatis mutandis* inference transposed into the ARIO from a different context, to cover a rather unlikely scenario.

And while such an approach to international responsibility is not valid in the ARIO given the difference in nature between liability and international responsibility, it is submitted here that acceptance of international responsibility is indeed a valid exception to the rule of exclusive International Organisation responsibility, but on a different basis altogether. This is so, because acceptance is an expression of some form of consent on behalf of the interested party.[120] Consent has been seen as the primary source of obligations in international law since Vattel.[121] The general principle of law that all legal 'rights or obligations are within the dispensation of States' when they consent to them was recognised by the ILC.[122] The central role of consent in the determination of legal obligations in the international sphere was also affirmed by the PCIJ in the *Lotus* case.[123] Notwithstanding modern criticism of the reliance of the international system on consent,[124] the principle that consent generates legal obligations is regarded as a fundamental principle of international law.[125] And since the legal

[119] The same holds true for both Arts 235 and 263 of the LOSC. Jacobs and Nollkaemper suggest that Art 6 of Annex IX refers to international responsibility in the way evoked by the ILC, D Jacobs and A Nollkaemper, 'Shared Responsibility in International Law: A Conceptual Framework' (2013) 34 *Michigan Journal of International Law* 359, 412. Even if this were the case, given the terminological inconsistency in its wording, the provision is an authority with limited usefulness.

[120] The ICJ uses this language in its Nicaragua judgment: 'in international law there are no rules, other than such rules as may be accepted by the states concerned, by treaty or otherwise', *Military and Paramilitary Activities In and Against Nicaragua* (*Nicaragua v United States of America*) (Merits) [1986] ICJ Reports 14, 135, [269].

[121] E de Vattel, *The Law of Nations* (Liberty Fund, 2008 [1797]) 17: 'There is another kind of law of nations [in addition to the law of nature], which authors call *arbitrary*, because it proceeds from the will or consent of nations'. On the importance of consent for modern international law, see L Henkin, 'International Law: Politics, Values, and Functions' (1989) 216 *RCADI* 9, 27 and 46.

[122] ASR Comment, 122, [2].

[123] *The Case of the S.S. Lotus* (*France v Turkey*) (1927) PCIJ, Ser A, No 10, 3, 18.

[124] A Guzman, 'Against Consent' (2012) 52 *Virginia Journal of International Law* 747.

[125] J Crawford, *The Creation of States in International Law* (Clarendon Press, 1979) 32.

consequences deriving from the establishment of international responsibility are the attribution of new obligations to the responsible State,[126] it would run counter to this basic principle to deny these obligations to the legal subject that has expressed its will to be bound by them. The international responsibility of a member State which has accepted international responsibility with respect to the conduct of an International Organisation is therefore established, due to the voluntary character of the assumption of obligations.

The primacy given in Article 62(1)(a) to the consent of the parties when allocating international responsibility is not a novel concept in international law. The ILC has already recognised such a principle in the ASR when it noted that: '[t]he principle of independent responsibility reflects the position under general international law, in the absence of agreement to the contrary between the States concerned'.[127] If agreement is the expression of mutual consent, then this element is the primary factor to be taken into account when allocating responsibility. Acceptance is unqualified but in most occasions it will stem expressly and *a priori* from the International Organisation's constituent instrument.[128] This, however, does not preclude implied acceptance, acceptance *a posteriori* or acceptance through other rules as the source of member State responsibility.[129]

Arguably, consent provides the only reason why the ILC had to expand the scope of ASR, Article 1 in the concomitant first Article of the ARIO. ASR, Article 1 holds that every internationally wrongful act 'of a State entails the international responsibility of *that* State'[130] (emphasis added). ARIO, Article 1(2) expanded this principle and stipulated that the Articles 'apply to the international responsibility of a State for *an* internationally wrongful act in connection with the conduct of an international organization'[131] (emphasis added). The ARIO thus leave enough room to include scenarios where

[126] See Chapter 2 n 55.

[127] ASR Comment, 124, [3].

[128] ARIO Comment, 163, [7]; d'Aspremont, 'Abuse of the Legal Personality of International Organizations' (n 1) 98. Several examples on acceptance of member State liability can be found at M Hartwig, 'International Organizations or Institutions, Responsibility and Liability' in *Max Planck Encyclopedia of Public International Law* (OUP online ed, 2011) [26].

[129] No acceptance of responsibility rules exists in multilateral treaties. There do exist, however, certain relevant rules on liability. Several examples appear in in Hartwig, ibid [27], ie Art XXII(3) of the Convention on International Liability for Damage Caused by Space Objects (n 103) that provides for joint and several liability of member States and International Organisation for damage caused by the International Organisation. The provision provides: 'If an international intergovernmental organization is liable for damage by virtue of the provisions of this Convention, that organization and those of its members which are States Parties to this Convention shall be jointly and severally liable; provided, however, that: (a) any claim for compensation in respect of such damage shall be first presented to the organization; (b) only where the organization has not paid, within a period of six months, any sum agreed or determined to be due as compensation for such damage, may the claimant State invoke the liability of the members which are States Parties to this Convention for the payment of that sum'.

[130] This is what I termed 'international responsibility for own internationally wrongful act' in Chapter 2 n 64 and accompanying text.

[131] For the expansion effectuated by Art 1(1), see Chapter 2 at IV B.

international responsibility of a State does not arise for this State's internationally wrongful act (and thus incorporate international responsibility for another subject's internationally wrongful act). To the extent that Article 62(1)(a) does not premise the establishment of a member State's international responsibility upon the existence of this State's internationally wrongful act, it justifies the expansion effectuated by ARIO, Article 1(2). It constitutes the *exemplaire* of international responsibility for another subject's internationally wrongful act. This should have been acknowledged by the ILC in the commentaries to both ARIO, Articles 1 and 62.

The problem that arises is how the acceptance of international responsibility by member States will affect the international responsibility of the International Organisation. First, acceptance should not have the effect of writing off legal obligations by excluding or limiting international responsibility. This is so because such limiting of international responsibility will not be opposable towards injured third parties without their consent.[132] Brownlie argues that such limitation of international responsibility by delegation is unacceptable and 'stems directly from the normal concepts of accountability and effectiveness'.[133] For one reason or the other, the international responsibility of the International Organisation should remain intact. For example, a provision on the constituting instrument of an International Organisation whereby acceptance of international responsibility by member States for internationally wrongful acts of an International Organisation will automatically lead to exclusive member State responsibility, will only produce effect with the consent of the injured third state.

The judgment of the Dutch Court of First Instance in the Srebrenica massacre case dealt in passing with an issue that falls under the ambit of this exception.[134] The question put to the court was whether a troop-contributing UN member State can be held internationally responsible by virtue of an agreement that apportions international responsibility to the member State in case of gross negligence by members of the deployed troops. The national court suggested that the agreement through which a State accepts international responsibility for any harmful outcome resulting from the gross negligence of its contributing troops does not affect the secondary rules on attribution and is a purely contractual arrangement.[135] This arrangement then does not deprive from nor does it create rights for third parties, notably the victims of such gross negligence, under

[132] Vienna Convention on the Law of Treaties, Art 35, 23 May 1969, 1155 UNTS 341; See also Ahlborn, 'The Rules of International Organizations' (n 47).

[133] I Brownlie, 'State Responsibility: The Problem of Delegation' in K Ginther, G Hafner, W Lang, H Neuhold and L Sucharipa-Behrmann (eds), *Völkerrecht zwischen normativem Anspruch und politischer Realität* (Duncker and Humblot, 1994) 299, 300–1.

[134] *Hasan Nuhanovic and others v Netherlands (Ministry of Defence and Ministry of Foreign Affairs)*, First Instance Judgment, Decision no LJN: BF0181, Case no 265615 International Law in Domestic Courts 1092 (NL 2008), 10 September 2008, District Court, [4.13].

[135] P d'Argent, 'State Organs Placed at the Disposal of the UN, Effective Control, Wrongful Abstention and Dual Attribution of Conduct' (2014) 1 *Questions of International Law* 17, 19.

the law of international responsibility.[136] Thus, the Netherlands are responsible by virtue of this agreement, but this *ipso facto* does not exclude the triggering of the UN's international responsibility in this instance.

This is why the ILC suggested that acceptance can only entail 'subsidiary' or 'joint and several' responsibility and not the exclusive responsibility of any subject involved.[137] The second paragraph of Article 62 adopted the former solution and created a presumption in favour of subsidiary responsibility in such scenarios of acceptance of responsibility.[138] The ILC, apparently in an exercise of its function of progressive development, indeed attempted through the inclusion of the notion of subsidiary responsibility to tackle the problem of the International Organisation shielding its member States.[139]

The characterisation of such international responsibility as subsidiary has led Klabbers to argue that the (secondarily responsible) member States on such occasions 'may be responsible *if* the organization itself is unwilling or unable to bear responsibility'[140] (emphasis added). Yet, such a view is problematic for two reasons. First, it asserts that the international responsibility of an international subject is dependent upon the triggering of the international responsibility of another subject. Such an argument however was, implicitly but no less unequivocally, rejected by the ICJ in the *Corfu Channel* case.[141] According to the Court, Albania's international responsibility for failure to warn passing British warships of the presence of mines in its territorial waters was not reduced or precluded by reason of the concurrent responsibility of Yugoslavia.[142]

Second, it suggests that in subsidiary responsibility scenarios, the establishment as such of the international responsibility of member States is conditional, while the ILC has stated that only the invocation of international responsibility is conditional. This latter point has been made clear in ARIO, Article 48(2), which defines subsidiary responsibility as follows: 'Subsidiary responsibility may be invoked insofar as the invocation of the primary responsibility has not led to reparation'. Therefore, the incurrence of subsidiary responsibility essentially means two things: first, that primary responsibility, ie that of the International

[136] As pointed out in ARIO Comment, 85, [3]: 'The agreement appears to deal only with distribution of international responsibility and not with attribution of conduct. At any event, this type of agreement is not conclusive because it governs only the relations between the contributing State or organization and the receiving organization and could thus not have the effect of depriving a third party of any right that that party may have towards the State or organization which is responsible under the general rules'.

[137] ARIO Comment, 164–65, [13]. Both 'subsidiary' and 'joint and several' responsibility are not problematic in this respect, as they only broaden the scope of possible responsible entities.

[138] Art 62(2) states: 'Any international responsibility of a State under paragraph 1 is presumed to be subsidiary'.

[139] T Grant, 'International Responsibility and the Admission of States to the United Nations' (2009) 30 *Michigan Journal of International Law* 1095, 1142.

[140] Klabbers, *An Introduction to International Organizations Law* (n 4) 302.

[141] *Corfu Channel Case* (*United Kingdom v Albania*) (Merits) [1949] ICJ Reports 4.

[142] ibid 22–23. See also ASR Comment, 124, [1] and 125, [8].

Organisation for its internationally wrongful act, remains unaffected.[143] Second, that while its invocation is conditional, subsidiary responsibility of member States for internationally wrongful acts of International Organisations has arisen since 'State responsibility arises under international law independently of its invocation by another State'.[144] In a different vein, Martin does not distinguish between invocation and establishment of international responsibility and thus he is forced to argue that subsidiary responsibility is incompatible with the principle of independent responsibility in ASR, Article 47.[145] Acceptance of responsibility in the way analysed above is a scenario whereby multiple subjects are concurrently responsible, as both the member States and the International Organisation are responsible for the same internationally wrongful act. Therefore, it should be stressed that the term 'subsidiary' does not characterise international responsibility in a qualitative sense, nor does it alter its nature.[146] It rather sets a temporal priority as to the vindication of the claims connected with the invocation of international responsibility.

Finally, acceptance of international responsibility will produce legal effects if it is made 'towards the injured party'. Since acceptance automatically leads to the establishment of responsibility, as argued earlier, what does this qualification add to the provision? To assess whether this requirement is justified, one must first examine the legal relationship established between the injured party and the responsible member State in this scenario.[147]

The distinction between establishment and invocation of international responsibility is again of cardinal importance. The previous analysis demonstrated that the international responsibility of a member State accepting international responsibility for the internationally wrongful act of an International Organisation has indeed been established, but this does not *ipso facto* necessarily create a legal relationship between the injured State and the member State. The establishment as such of the international responsibility of a member State only attributes obligations to the responsible member State (ie obligations of cessation and non-repetition), it does not identify the subject that will be able to vindicate these obligations.[148] In order to form a legal relationship, the injured party must be identified as the subject 'towards which the responsible State's obligations … exist'.[149] Only then will a relationship come into being and the injured party will be able to invoke the international responsibility of the member State.

[143] ARIO Comment, 164–65, [13].
[144] ASR Comment, 116, Chapeau of Part Three.
[145] JMC Martin 'The Responsibility of Members Due to Wrongful Acts of International Organizations' (2013) 12 *Chinese Journal of International Law* 679, 715, [65].
[146] The ILC suggests that 'Paragraph 2 addresses the nature of the responsibility', ARIO Comment, 164–65, [13]. Such a dictum though is incompatible with the analysis of 'subsidiary responsibility' as presented in ARIO, Art 48(2).
[147] ARIO Comment, 163, [7].
[148] ibid 142, [2].
[149] ASR Comment, 94, [1].

According to ASR, Article 33, obligations will be owed to the injured party 'depending in particular on the character and content of the international obligation and on the circumstances of the breach'.[150] To the extent that obligations are correlative with rights,[151] the provision echoes Article 36 of the Vienna Convention on the Law of Treaties, according to which implied or express acceptance by the third party is needed for the conferral of rights to the latter.[152] This explains why Article 62(1)(a) requires that acceptance of international responsibility be made 'towards the injured party'; because otherwise, this party will not be able to invoke the (otherwise established) international responsibility of the member State and vindicate the fulfilment of the relevant obligations.

B. Third Party Reliance

The second exception to the exclusive International Organisation responsibility rule is found in Article 62(1)(b). According to this provision, a member State is responsible for an internationally wrongful act committed by an International Organisation if 'it has led the injured party to rely on its responsibility'. As in the previous scenario of acceptance of responsibility, the consent of the parties remains the basis of the present enquiry. Thus, a provision in the International Organisation's constituting instrument stating that member States are not responsible for the internationally wrongful acts of the International Organisation would be effective in defeating an allegation of international responsibility founded on Article 62(1)(b). Further, the lack of relevant institutional practice shows that the occurrence of a scenario on third party reliance is equally unlikely as the previous one on acceptance.

According to the Commission, the impression of reliance necessarily rests upon prior member State conduct.[153] However, it is open to interpretation what this conduct consists of, as the ILC has not done much to clarify this notion. Contrary to the exception of acceptance that refers specifically to a consensual assumption of obligations, third party reliance can be triggered by different types of member State conduct. On a general note, the ILC suggested that

[150] ASR, Art 33 provides thus: 'The obligations of the responsible State set out in this Part may be owed to another State, to several States, or to the international community as a whole, depending in particular on the character and content of the international obligation and on the circumstances of the breach'.

[151] WN Hohfeld 'Some Fundamental Legal Conceptions as Applied in Judicial Reasoning' (1913) 23 *Yale Law Journal* 16, 30. Hohfeld uses the term 'duty' instead of 'obligation', but he accepts them as interchangeable, ibid 53.

[152] Vienna Convention on the Law of Treaties, 23 May 1969, 1155 UNTS 341. See also *North Sea Continental Shelf* (*Germany v The Netherlands and Denmark*) (Merits) [1969] ICJ Reports 3, 25–26, [28].

[153] ARIO Comment, 164, [8].

such reliance is to be inferred either from an implied acceptance of obligations on behalf of member States or, without acceptance of obligations, from an ad hoc general assessment of relevant factors.[154] The first set of scenarios is arguably covered by Article 62(1)(a), for this provision does not distinguish between express and tacit acceptance, as noted above.[155] Thus, to the extent that third party reliance refers to tacit acceptance, its inclusion within the ARIO is redundant.

It is worth examining, though, whether the other scenarios addressed by the provision provide for a valid exception to the exclusive responsibility rule. In order to make such an assessment, it is important to examine whether a reason exists (from a legal point of view) why member States should be held responsible for the internationally wrongful acts of the International Organisation without their consent.

The ILC has not invoked many authorities in the commentaries in order to support the drafting of the Article 62(1)(b) exception and all of them are pertinent to the member State liability debate. Third party reliance was advocated by Amerasinghe and Klein,[156] and endorsed by the second arbitral award in the dispute concerning *Westland Helicopters*.[157] Like the *Tin Council* litigation, *Westland Helicopters* was decided on the basis of liability and the case need not be analysed further, as its findings are not pertinent to the present debate, for the same reason why the *Tin Council* case's findings are not pertinent. According to these sources, third party reliance liability rests upon policy arguments, and more specifically on the basis that member States had become guarantors of the obligations incumbent upon the International Organisation. This approach, however plausible from a liability perspective, does not explain the establishment of the international responsibility of member States for acts of the International Organisation without acceptance of the ensuing obligations.

Commentators have argued that the provision rests upon the general principle of estoppel or *venire contra factum proprium* and thus can be explained as the establishment of the international responsibility of member States in scenarios of third party reliance.[158] The essential aim of this principle 'is to preclude a party from benefiting by his own inconsistency to the detriment of another party who has in good faith relied upon a representation of fact made

[154] The only relevant factor cited by the ILC is the small size of membership, ibid 164, [10].

[155] See n 129 and accompanying text.

[156] See authorities cited at ARIO Comment, 164, note 357.

[157] *Westland Helicopters Ltd v Arab Organization for Industrialization and others*, Arbitral Award of 21 July 1991, [56], quoted by Higgins, 'Report on the Legal Consequences for Member States' (n 29) 393. *Westland Helicopters*, like *Tin Council*, was adjudicated before several jurisdictions. Characteristic of that case is that on first instance, the arbitral tribunal upheld a presumption of member State liability for acts of the International Organisation, which was, however, overturned on appeal.

[158] Stumer, 'Liability of Member States for Acts of International Organizations' (n 1) 563; Ryngaert and Buchanan, 'Member State Responsibility' (n 1) 145; Crawford, *State Responsibility* (n 94) 419.

by the former party'.[159] The ICJ dealt extensively with this principle for the first time in the *Preah Vihear* case and Percy Spender defined estoppel as follows:

> [T]he principle operates to prevent a State contesting before the Court a situation contrary to a clear and unequivocal representation previously made by it to another State, either expressly or impliedly, on which representation the other State was, in the circumstances, entitled to rely and in fact did rely, and as a result that other State has been prejudiced or the State making it has secured some benefit or advantage for itself.[160]

In an international responsibility context, estoppel does not function as a procedural bar for the vindication of a claim before a tribunal, but rather as a source of a subject's international responsibility.

Since the *Preah Vihear* case, the content of the principle has crystallised in public international law through the case law of the ICJ which has adopted a restrictive notion of estoppel.[161] According to this view, the establishment of estoppel is premised upon two conditions: (a) very definite and unequivocal representation of a state of fact; and (b) detriment for the party relying on the representations or benefit for the party making the representation. Crawford notes that the condition of detriment has been dropped in Article 62(1)(b);[162] a justified moderation since the establishment of international responsibility is not conditioned upon the prerequisite of damage or injury.[163] Further, the ILC has suggested that the impression of reliance in the ARIO necessarily rests upon prior member State conduct,[164] and in this sense the exception comes very close to what Bowett has identified as 'estoppel by conduct'.[165] A combination of all the above provides the form of estoppel incorporated within Article 62(1)(b) that suffices to bind member States and establish international responsibility; a very definite and unequivocal representation of a state of fact established through member State conduct.

With this definition of estoppel in mind, the assessment of reliance that rests on general factors, as the commentaries suggest, is problematic on a twofold

[159] DW Bowett, 'Estoppel Before International Tribunals and its Relation to Acquiescence' (1957) 33 *BYBIL* 176, 177.

[160] *Case concerning the Temple of Preah Vihear* (*Cambodia v Thailand*) (Merits), Dissenting Opinion of Judge P Spender [1962] ICJ Reports 101, 143–44.

[161] Restrictive estoppel requires a very definite, very consistent course of conduct in order to produce binding effects upon third parties, *North Sea Continental Shelf* (n 152) 25–26, [28]–[30]; *Case concerning Delimitation of the Maritime Boundary in the Gulf of Maine Area* (*Canada v United States of America*) (Merits) [1984] ICJ Reports 246, 303–12, [126]–[154]; *Case concerning the Land and Maritime Boundary Between Cameroon and Nigeria* (*Cameroon v Nigeria*) (Preliminary Objections) [1998] ICJ Reports 275, 303–4 [57]; T Cottier and JP Müller, 'Estoppel' in *Max Planck Encyclopedia of Public International Law* (OUP online ed, 2007) [6].

[162] Crawford, *State Responsibility* (n 94) 429.

[163] ASR Comment, 36, [9].

[164] ARIO Comment, 164, [8].

[165] Bowett defines 'estoppel by conduct' as: '[r]epresentations of a state of fact … made expressly or impliedly where, upon a reasonable construction of a party's conduct, the conduct presupposes a certain state of fact to exist', Bowett, 'Estoppel Before International Tribunals' (n 159) 183.

basis. First, it seemingly fails to surpass the threshold of restrictive estoppel since it is questionable whether the assessment proposed in the commentaries amounts to a clear and unequivocal representation. Even if that were the case, the Commission pointed towards the oral comments made by Belarus during the drafting procedure in order to establish the factors to be assessed.[166] The representative of that State suggested small membership and/or limited resources as factors indicating 'a high level of [member State] control over the organization's activities'.[167] Then it was not on considerations of estoppel, but rather on the basis of the control exercised over the activities of the International Organisation (as per ARIO, Article 59(1)) that Belarus proposed the establishment of international responsibility of member States in International Organisations with limited resources and/or small membership.

Second, the establishment of international responsibility on such occasions is not necessarily premised on member State conduct and the ILC indirectly brings back mere membership as a sufficient condition for the triggering of responsibility.[168] This is clearly implied from the *Westland Helicopters* quote cited by the ILC in the commentaries to support the exception:

> The panel found that the special circumstances of the case invited: 'the trust of third parties contracting with the organizations as to its ability to cope with its commitments because of the constant support of the member States'.[169]

The 'special circumstances' of the case were the limited resources of the International Organisation and its small membership (four member States). 'Constant support' was inferred from member State conduct in the exercise of competences of the International Organisation and under the limitation of its rules (conduct of States as members). As *Westland Helicopters* was decided in all fora through the prism of liability, the weight given to this case aptly demonstrates how influential the debate on liability has been for the drafting of the ARIO.

Arguably then, the ARIO would have been better without the Article 62(1)(b) exception, for this provision does not adequately address the two scenarios it intends to regulate. Implied acceptance of international responsibility is covered by Article 62(1)(a) and the establishment of international responsibility based on a general assessment of relevant factors brings to the forefront issues of international responsibility for 'direction and control' and international responsibility for mere membership that have been dealt with respectively in ARIO, Article 59 and the commentaries to ARIO, Article 62.

[166] UNGA, 60th Session, Sixth Committee, *Summary Record of the 12th Meeting*, UN doc A/C.6/60/SR.12 (2005) 9, [52] (Belarus).

[167] ibid.

[168] As noted in the previous section, such a proposition has been clearly rejected in the commentaries to Art 62, ARIO Comment, 162, [2].

[169] ARIO Comment, 164, [9].

On the basis of the analysis attempted in this chapter, the following rule reflects the progressive development of the law in the matter at hand:

> Responsibility of a State member of an International Organisation for the Organisation's internationally wrongful acts
>
> A State member of an International Organisation will be responsible for the internationally wrongful act of this Organisation when it consents to be bound by the legal obligations that arise by virtue of this act.

I believe that Article 62(1)(a) can be interpreted so as to accord with this rule, while Article 62(1)(b) adds nothing to the present discussion, it only perplexes the matter unnecessarily.

V. CONCLUSION

This chapter attempted to examine the particular member State-International Organisation relationship and infer its ramifications with respect to the establishment of international responsibility of both subjects involved in it. Arguably, such a relationship is formed when member States exercise competence that lies with the International Organisation in accordance with the latter's rules. This type of State conduct puts the organisational veil in operation and shields member States under it by virtue of a responsibility merging. I suggest that the ILC should have clearly premised the drafting of both paragraphs and the commentaries to Article 62 with these considerations. The ARIO, however, fail to articulate an elaborate analysis of the member State-International Organisation relationship and that is why the 'exclusive International Organisation responsibility' rule (in the commentaries) and the exceptions to it (Article 62(1)(a) and (1)(b)) are loosely justified.

What is more, Article 62, in the way advocated in the ARIO, further entangles international responsibility with the notion of liability and perpetuates the confusion surrounding the establishment and function of both notions. A sound regulation of the scenarios scrutinised here from an international responsibility perspective, is, I believe, clearly premised upon legal – and not policy – arguments. The disentanglement of the ideas of international responsibility and liability, attempted in this chapter, exposes the policy arguments evoked to address the issue at hand and at the same time it turns the focus on legal argumentation. Consequently, the approach adopted here serves a dual goal; it furthers conceptual clarity, on the one hand, and on the other, it promotes coherence in the law of international responsibility.

On the legal basis provided by the member State-International Organisation relationship and the basic principles of international responsibility, I suggested how the provision should read in order to reflect the progressive development of the law and be of potential use for international courts. Since the redrafting of Article 62 is no longer possible, Article 62(1)(a) should be interpreted in accordance with this rule. On the other hand, Article 62(1)(b), to the extent that it pertains to responsibility for mere membership and responsibility for 'direction and control', cannot be interpreted accordingly and does not capture the progressive development of the law. I attempted to offer a normative justification for the 'exclusive International Organisation responsibility' rule and to demonstrate that there in fact exists only one valid exception to this rule.

Part II

Member State-International Organisation Interaction as Independent Subjects of International Law

4

The Applicable Responsibility Models

I. INTRODUCTION

THIS CHAPTER WILL focus on these Articles on the Responsibility of International Organizations (ARIO) provisions that regulate interaction between member States and the International Organisation of which they are members as independent subjects of international law, that were drafted according to the respective Articles on State Responsibility (ASR) template. It is pertinent to assess whether ARIO, Articles 14, 15, 16, 58(1), 59(1) and 60 reflect the progressive development of the law. The scope of application of these provisions under the ASR was rather limited, in that such scenarios were not particularly common in inter-State relations. The same is true with respect to the ARIO and this has been duly recognised by the International Law Commission (ILC).[1]

It is important to assess whether the wording of the relevant provisions reflects a doctrinally consistent formulation. After all, if the wording has been chosen with a purely practical view to regulate real-life scenarios, thereby putting aside doctrine, there is no point in looking for coherence in chaos. I argue that the provisions, as instances of the progressive development of the law, should respect the fundamental principles of international responsibility I have identified in Chapter 1. Thus, a legal analysis to this effect is in order.

Contrary to what the ILC has maintained,[2] incorporation of the provisions in play within the international responsibility edifice rests upon the premise that they provide for international responsibility for own internationally wrongful acts. As explained in the previous chapter, any provision that does not establish international responsibility through the consent of the responsible entity (responsibility for another subject's internationally wrongful act), should be explained on the basis of responsibility for own internationally wrongful act. If that is not the case, then international responsibility lacks a principled basis.

Arguably, there are different responsibility models that provide for responsibility for own internationally wrongful act and they will be analysed throughout this chapter. Apart from the 'independent responsibility' model,

[1] ARIO Comment, 100, [1].

[2] Both the ARIO and the ASR suggest that indirect responsibility arises for another subject's internationally wrongful act, ARIO Comment, 69–70, [4]; ASR Comment, 64, [5].

which is attached to direct responsibility,[3] it is submitted that two more schemes, attached to indirect responsibility, can be identified: the complicity[4] and the derivative responsibility models. These two models are applicable to different triangular relationships that the direct responsibility model cannot capture. The complicity model addresses scenarios in which an actor participates in the internationally wrongful act of another, and the derivative responsibility model regulates the responsibility of an actor for the conduct of another. While in both models international responsibility arises in connection with the conduct of another, the two situations should be kept distinct. It is argued here that the lack of legal analysis of indirect responsibility has triggered the misunderstandings surrounding the regulation of scenarios falling within the scope of these two models.

I will put into perspective these two models that apply in the context of indirect responsibility, by juxtaposing them with the independent responsibility model that operates in the context of direct responsibility. Because both the ASR and ARIO provisions use identical wording, the following analysis is based on the archetypical ASR, Chapter IV Articles.[5] Nevertheless, whenever necessary, a special reference will be made to the replica set of rules.

This chapter will be divided into two sections, and will present the argument along the following lines. After a rudimentary exposition of the direct responsibility model, the two indirect responsibility models will be analysed in turn in the order they appear in the ASR and ARIO. The normative elements found in both 'direction and control' and 'coercion' place these provisions under the derivative responsibility model, while the complicity model is attached to 'aid or assistance'. For the sake of brevity, I will use the acronyms P (perpetrator of wrongful conduct), R (responsibility bearer) and V (victim) throughout the chapter, but at the same time I will enrich my analysis with concrete examples from international practice.

It has to be clarified from the outset that the provisions examined here regulate interaction between independent subjects of international law. This is evident since they were copied and pasted from the ASR, and in inter-State relations only such type of interaction is in play. No personality merging occurs then, and all actors involved retain their legal personality during their interaction and thus their international responsibility can be established.

[3] Referred to as 'independent responsibility' by the Commission in ASR Comment, 64, [1].

[4] The term 'complicity' is generally avoided in the context of international responsibility since it is not a term of art in international law and is primarily associated with international criminal law. Lanovoy explains that Special Rapporteur Ago used the term 'complicity' but dropped it after criticisms from States and some ILC members, V Lanovoy, *Complicity in an Internationally Wrongful Act*, SHARES Research Paper No 38 (2014) 4. I use it here just for labelling, with no normative connotation.

[5] cp ASR, Arts 16–18, with ARIO, Arts 14–16 and 58(1), 59(1) and 60.

II. DIRECT RESPONSIBILITY: RESPONSIBILITY IN CONNECTION WITH OWN CONDUCT

As explained in the previous chapter, the two bases of international responsibility are: responsibility for own internationally wrongful act and responsibility for the internationally wrongful act of another.[6] An internationally wrongful act in turn is dependent upon the cumulative presence of two conditions: first, that certain conduct of a subject of international law, whether an act or an omission, must be in breach of this subject's international obligations; and second, that this conduct must be attributable to that same subject. This principle has been recognised by all subjects of international law, it has been applied in a uniform manner from international tribunals and no exception to it has yet been established in international law.[7] Thus, the term 'internationally wrongful act' has acquired a specific binary normative content in the law of international responsibility.[8] Both the elements of breach and attribution are indispensable for the establishment of an internationally wrongful act of any subject of international law, and they form the double basis of an internationally wrongful act. Since this is a general principle of international law, it forms part of the foundation of the whole international responsibility edifice. Because it is a rule of general application with normative value, the interpretation of all other international responsibility rules should respect this fundamental principle.

Direct and indirect responsibility differ as to the establishment of this double basis of an internationally wrongful act; that is, the particular rules according to which this basis is established. Their difference lies in the connection required between the actor who performs the wrongful conduct (P) and the responsibility bearer (R). The distinctive feature of direct responsibility is the very close connection between the two. If one were to break down the constituent elements of this model, direct responsibility would be found in accordance with the following pattern: an international obligation must be incumbent upon a subject of international law, and this international actor must thereafter violate the international obligation through own conduct.[9] The connection required is so tight that the model falls short of addressing scenarios in which P and R do not correspond.[10]

[6] For more on these terms, see Chapter 2.

[7] ASR Comment, 34, [2] and 36, [9].

[8] For an analysis of the nature and content of the term 'internationally wrongful act', see Chapter 2.

[9] See ASR, Chapter II of Part 1 (Arts 4–11) and the corresponding ARIO, Chapter II of Part 2 (Arts 6–9).

[10] As d'Aspremont argues, 'the concept of responsibility falls short of capturing complex situations of non-conformity', J d'Aspremont, 'The Articles on the Responsibility of International Organisations: Magnifying the Fissures in the Law of International Responsibility' (2012) 9 *IOLR* 15, 24.

III. INDIRECT RESPONSIBILITY: RESPONSIBILITY IN CONNECTION WITH THE CONDUCT OF ANOTHER

The ILC intended to fill the gap left by the direct responsibility model, and to address any scenarios that could not fit within the direct responsibility bilateral paradigm. The principal justification for incorporating such provisions in the ASR and ARIO is to 'ascribe responsibility for conduct which would not otherwise trigger responsibility'.[11] While this is clear enough, the ILC went on to perplex the matter by confusing the concepts of 'internationally wrongful act' and 'conduct' in its commentary.

According to the Commission, Chapter IV of the ASR lists the situations in which State responsibility arises from the implication of an actor in the internationally wrongful act of another.[12] Chapter IV provisions then constitute a fragment in the principle embodied in Article 1 of the ASR, which provides that every internationally wrongful act of a State entails the international responsibility of that State.[13] Having this in mind, the ILC broadened the formulation of the ARIO principle that corresponds to ASR, Article 1. ARIO, Article 1(1) provides that the international responsibility of an International Organisation can be triggered for an internationally wrongful act. Thus, the provision leaves enough room to incorporate those ARIO provisions that provide for responsibility 'in connection with' the internationally wrongful act of another, within the general framework of these rules. In this way, the ARIO open up the bases upon which international responsibility can be established; an own internationally wrongful act or the internationally wrongful act of another.[14]

I argue that the broadening effectuated by ARIO, Article 1(1) is not linked with indirect responsibility provisions since ARIO, Chapter IV and Part Five provide for responsibility in connection with the *conduct* of another and not in connection with the *internationally wrongful act* of another.[15] Like the other international responsibility provisions, indirect responsibility rules retain the strong linkage between the responsibility bearer and the subject who commits an internationally wrongful act and thus establish an own internationally wrongful act as the basis of international responsibility. The Commission then did not make clear the cleavage between the double basis of an internationally wrongful act and the basis of international responsibility, and this mingling has deepened the confusion surrounding these provisions.

The ILC drafted three provisions to regulate different triangular situations that address the aforementioned relationship. The first addresses cases of 'aid

[11] HA Aust, *Complicity and the Law of State Responsibility* (CUP, 2011) 239.

[12] ASR Comment, 64, [5].

[13] ARIO Comment, 69, [4].

[14] N Nedeski and A Nollkaemper, 'Responsibility of International Organisations in Connection with Acts of States' (2012) 9 *IOLR* 33, 41–43.

[15] Against: Nedeski and Nollkeamper, who suggest that the broadening in ARIO, Art 1 was necessary to encompass Chapter IV provisions, ibid 42–43.

or assistance', in which the responsibility bearer is responsible for its participation in the perpetrator's internationally wrongful act (ASR, Article 16). The remaining two refer to situations of either 'coercion' or 'direction and control', whereby the responsibility bearer is responsible for the perpetrator's wrongful conduct (ASR, Articles 17 and 18). Note that in the latter scenarios, unlike that of 'aid or assistance', an internationally wrongful act on the perpetrator's behalf is not a prerequisite for the triggering of the responsibility bearer's international responsibility. While the provisions have been drafted to address the responsibility bearer's responsibility, they also present legal implications for the perpetrator of wrongful conduct.

As noted above, the main perception with respect to indirect responsibility norms is that they are exceptional and, like all exceptions, they should not be abused: resort to them should remain limited.[16] This exceptional nature has confused commentators, who tend to group together all forms of indirect responsibility under the umbrella of the same responsibility model and they also use inconsistent terminology when doing so. It is maintained in this chapter that there is good reason to distinguish between two models of indirect responsibility, in large part due to the different real-life situations triggering each one.

The key to understanding indirect responsibility provisions is to understand that they perform a double function. Compared to the other responsibility provisions, they are applicable only in particular – triangular – scenarios. Thus, the first task for those provisions is to define the scenarios in which their application is triggered. The two functions that must be kept separate are the delimitation of their scope of application, and the determination of the legal consequences arising from their application. While incurring international responsibility under these provisions is a two-stage process, only the second function corresponds to what has been defined in Chapter 2 as the establishment of international responsibility. However, the two functions described above are entangled within the wording of the provisions, so it is critical to disentangle them in order to understand their operation.

It must be clarified from the outset that international responsibility in indirect responsibility provisions does not rest upon subjective elements, and thus does not cause doctrinal incoherence within the overall framework of international responsibility.[17] This needs to be clarified, because these elements form part of the scope of application of the provisions and, as stated above, the

[16] D'Aspremont, 'The Articles on the Responsibility of International Organisations' (n 10) 25; N Blokker, 'Abuse of the Members: Questions Concerning Draft Article 16 of the Draft Articles on Responsibility of International Organisations' (2010) 7 *IOLR* 35, 42–48; Nedeski and Nollkaemper, 'Responsibility of International Organisations' (n 14) 43–48.

[17] The discarding of subjective elements for an effective operation of international responsibility was suggested a long time ago by Anzilotti: PM Dupuy, 'Dioniso Anzilotti and the Law of Responsibility of States' (1992) 3 *EJIL* 139. On the objective nature of international responsibility, see Chapter 2.

distinct concepts of scope of application and basis of responsibility are entangled within the wording of these Articles. Thus, the use of subjective notions in order to explain a real-life situation that triggers the application of a specific provision does not cause doctrinal incoherence, so long as the double basis of the internationally wrongful act is upheld. The analysis that follows demonstrates that the internationally wrongful act in the case of ARIO, Chapter IV and Part Five provisions can be explained on the basis of the traditional conditions of breach and attribution.

A. Complicity Model

(i) Scope of Application

(a) Knowing Intention to Facilitate

The first model regulates international responsibility for participation in the internationally wrongful act of another. According to the ILC, the terminology 'aid or assistance' covers those instances of international responsibility in which help or support is given in the commission of an internationally wrongful act. It is the interrelationship between the aid provided and the internationally wrongful act committed that puts the complicity model in operation. The underlying assumption of the provision is that R (the aiding subject) is autonomously responsible for its own act of aiding or assisting, and not for P's (the aided subject's) act.[18] The peculiarity of the present model is that R's behaviour is per se lawful and only acquires its wrongful character when undertaken in connection with P's internationally wrongful act.

In order to understand the scenarios falling under the 'aid or assistance' provision's ambit, it is necessary to delimit the scope of 'aid or assistance': that is, the scope of the provision's application. There is general agreement that the aid provided must be material and not psychological, since incitement of any kind is a lawful influence in international law.[19] The ILC has not done much to clarify this notion in the commentaries by stipulating that 'the aid or assistance must be given with a view to facilitating the commission of the wrongful act, and must actually do so'.[20] This statement lends to the apparent conclusion that aid or assistance is tantamount to facilitation. However, it raises two issues in its description of the 'facilitation' required for the provision to be triggered.

[18] The wording of ASR, Art 16 is unequivocal in that R is responsible 'for doing so'; see also B Graefrath, 'Complicity in the Law of International Responsibility' (1996) 29 *Revue Belge de Droit International* 371, 374–75.

[19] ASR Comment, 65, [9]; R Ago, *Seventh Report on State Responsibility*, UN doc A/CN.4/307 (1978) and Add 1-2 and Corr 1-2, reproduced in (1978) 2(1) *YBILC* 31, 55.

[20] ASR Comment, 66, [3].

First, an element of causality has to be fulfilled, meaning that R's conduct must have actually caused P's internationally wrongful act. The ILC has formulated the criterion of 'significant contribution' but not too much should be read into this, as considerations of causality are case-specific and the formulation of exhaustive normative criteria are practically impossible.[21] Nevertheless, a caveat applies: if this element is exceeded, the threshold of 'contribution' may be inappropriate and the actor may instead find itself within the boundaries of co-authorship. This occurs when both R and P are independently responsible for the commission of the main conduct.[22] By contrast, in a situation involving only the provision of aid or assistance, R's conduct, seen independently from P's internationally wrongful act, is not sufficient to hold R responsible for the main conduct. Thus, the demarcation of what constitutes the provision of aid or assistance through the application of objective standards has provided only a maximum threshold ('co-authorship'), as a result of which the ILC has needed to have recourse to a second, alternative criterion in order to clearly delineate the *contours* of this notion.

Secondly, the ILC has limited the scope of the provision's application by introducing a subjective requirement that informs the relationship between R and P's internationally wrongful act. According to the ILC commentaries, to fall within the provision, R must provide its assistance 'with knowledge of the circumstances of the internationally wrongful act'[23] and 'with a view to facilitating [P's] internationally wrongful act'.[24] These statements have led most commentators to suggest that both an element of knowledge (be it actual, constructive or that of 'wilful blindness') and one of intent (while not present in the wording of the provision) is necessary for the incurring of R's responsibility.[25] It is crucial, then, that R not only was aware of what P was about to commit, but also that additionally it wanted to facilitate the resulting act. Thus, the subjective element required to trigger the application of the complicity model could be summarised as 'knowing intention'.

The presence of both these components of knowledge and intention is indispensable for the operation of an 'aid or assistance' provision. First, if R was unaware of the circumstances surrounding P's internationally wrongful act, it would be illogical and unjust to charge R for complicity in an act the commission

[21] Aust, *Complicity* (n 11) 210–19.
[22] ASR, Art 47 and ARIO, Art 48.
[23] ASR, Art 16(a).
[24] ASR Comment, 64, [4] and 66, [1], [3]. See also J Quigley, 'Complicity in International Law: A New Direction in the Law of State Responsibility' (1986) 57 *BYBIL* 77, 109ff.
[25] For an analysis of the subjective element in Art 16 and a summary of the relevant literature, see H Moynihan, 'Aiding and Assisting: the Mental Element Under Article 16 of the International Law Commission's Articles on State Responsibility' (2018) 67 *ICLQ* 455, 455–71. The ICJ, when considering the provision on complicity in the Genocide Convention by analogy with ASR, Art 16, stated that complicity requires 'at least' knowledge, *Case concerning the Application of the Convention on the Prevention and Punishment of the Crime of Genocide* (*Bosnia and Herzegovina v Serbia and Montenegro*) (Merits) [2007] ICJ Reports 43, 218, [421] ('*Genocide Case*').

of which he was not aware. In the same vein, in its 2007 *Genocide* case, the International Court of Justice (ICJ) held that Serbia was not fully aware of the circumstances of the Srebrenica massacre, and – to that extent – it could not be held responsible as an accomplice to genocide.[26] Second, the provision on 'aid or assistance' cannot be functional without an intent requirement, as it would otherwise be difficult to see how one could distinguish between ordinary forms of cooperation and aid or assistance in the commission of a wrongful act.[27] The element of knowing intention provides the minimum threshold for complicity in a subjective form. The formulation of a material one is practically impossible due to the case-specific way in which the provision is applied.[28] Reinisch suggests that the subjective element is of such importance in this responsibility model that causation requirements should be dropped as a result of their indeterminacy.[29] In contrast with situations involving derivative responsibility, in which the presence of the subjective element is presumed,[30] situations of complicity require the establishment of the element of intent.[31]

Therefore, complicity is triggered by the real-life situation that lies in the space between co-authorship and unintentional participation in another subject's internationally wrongful act. For present purposes, it is important to keep in mind that once a nexus of knowing intention to facilitate P's internationally wrongful act has been established, the essential groundwork is laid for triggering responsibility for complicity.

(b) Opposability Requirement

The delimitation of the provision's scope of application, however, did not stop there. Subparagraph (b) limits the scope of application to situations where both

[26] A broad discussion about the *mens rea* in complicity was initiated by the *Genocide Case* (n 25). It suffices here to say that the Court's doctrinal analysis of the provision's scope of application is consistent with the present analysis. For further discussion of this issue, see M Milanovic, 'State Responsibility for Genocide: A Follow-Up' (2007) 18 *EJIL* 669, 680–84; A Gattini, 'Breach of the Obligation to Prevent and Reparation Thereof in the ICJ's Genocide Judgment' (2007) 18 *EJIL* 695, 702–5.

[27] Aust and Nolte argue for such an interpretation of Art 16, G Nolte and H Aust, 'Equivocal Helpers-Complicit States, Mixed Messages and International Law' (2009) 58 *ICLQ* 1, 14–15. *Contra* M Jackson, *Complicity in International Law* (OUP, 2015) 160–62.

[28] Lowe argues for the necessity of such a minimum threshold but does not develop the argument further, AV Lowe, 'Responsibility for the Conduct of Other States' (2002) 101 *Japanese Journal of International Law and Diplomacy* 1, 5.

[29] Au Reinisch, 'Aid or Assistance and Direction and Control Between States and International Organisations in the Commission of Internationally Wrongful Acts' (2010) 7 *IOLR* 63, 71. In favour of substituting any material requirement with the criterion of participatory intentions, see C Kutz, 'Responsibility' in J Coleman and S Shapiro (eds), *The Oxford Handbook of Jurisprudence and Philosophy of Law* (OUP, 2002) 458, 463.

[30] See [14]–[18] of the commentaries to the former Draft Art 27, ILC, *Report of the International Law Commission on the Work of Its 30th Session, 8 May–28 July 1978*, UN doc A/33/10 (1978), reproduced in (1978) 2(2) *YBILC* 74, 101–5.

[31] ibid; Lowe, 'Responsibility for the Conduct of Other States' (n 28) 7.

the aiding and assisting entity and the aided and assisted entity, are bound by the same international obligation.[32] In other words, the ILC suggests that there is nothing wrong with aiding or assisting a breach of an international obligation by which one is not bound. Since the wrongfulness of R's conduct is attached to the wrongful character of P's act, one wonders why the ILC has inserted this opposability requirement. From the discussions that led to the adoption of this requirement in the ASR, it is evident that States were not favourable to its inclusion[33] and it was the Special Rapporteur that convinced the Commission to incorporate such a requirement.[34] Analogous was the situation in the discussion that preceded the drafting of the ARIO,[35] however, it was a policy choice on behalf of the ILC not to deviate from the ASR for reasons of consistency.

Special Rapporteur Crawford convinced the ILC that the rule on responsibility for aid or assistance could not 'be applied to bilateral obligations in an unqualified form'.[36] The justification for the insertion of the requirement was weak in normative terms. Despite the lack of relevant international practice, the Special Rapporteur gave particular weight to the *pacta tertiis* rule of Article 34 of the Vienna Convention on the Law of Treaties (VCLT).[37] Under this provision, a bilateral obligation does not create any duties for third states and that is why R is free to act for itself in a way which is inconsistent with the obligations of P vis-à-vis the victim, V.[38] What is more, the Special Rapporteur appealed to the principle whereby '[a] State cannot do by another what it cannot do by itself'.[39] While this principle is legally valid, it pertains to circumvention scenarios that are not regulated by ASR, Article 16.[40] To further support his thesis, the Special Rapporteur cautioned that '[w]ithout the inclusion of paragraph (b), Article 16

[32] Crawford clarifies that in fact what is required by Art 16(b) is not the identity of norms or sources of the obligation but rather the wrongfulness of the conduct, J Crawford, *State Responsibility: The General Part* (CUP, 2013) 410.

[33] Sweden being the only exception, ILC, *State Responsibility: Comments of Governments on Part 1 on the Draft Articles on State Responsibility for Internationally Wrongful Acts*, UN doc A/CN.4/342 (1981) and Add 1 to 4, reproduced in (1981) 2(1) *YBILC* 71, 77.

[34] V Lanovoy, 'Complicity in an Internationally Wrongful Act' in A Nollkaemper and I Plakokefalos (eds), *Principles of Shared Responsibility in International Law: An Appraisal of the State of the Art* (CUP, 2014) 134, 157.

[35] ILC, *Responsibility of International Organizations: Comments and Observations Received from Governments*, UN doc A/CN.4/636 16 (2011) (Cuba); UNGA 60th Session, Sixth Committee, *Summary Record of the 12th Meeting*, UN doc A/C.6/60/SR.12 (2005) 11, [67]–[69] (Russian Federation).

[36] J Crawford, *Second Report on State Responsibility*, UN doc A/CN.4/498 (1999) and Add 1 to 4, reproduced in (1999) 2(1) *YBILC* 3 ('Crawford Second Report'), 51, [186].

[37] Vienna Convention on the Law of Treaties, 23 May 1969, 1155 UNTS 331 (VCLT), Art 34. See also DJ Bederman, 'Third Party Rights and Obligations in Treaties' in DB Hollis (ed), *The Oxford Guide to Treaties* (OUP, 2012) 328.

[38] Lauterpacht held otherwise in 1936, but we have to recognise that his arguments were tailored to the circumstances of his era and are potentially not applicable today, H Lauterpacht, 'Contracts to Break a Contract' (1936) 52 *Law Quarterly Review* 494.

[39] Crawford Second Report (n 36) 51, [188].

[40] For more on the regulation of circumvention scenarios, see Chapters 5 and 6.

could become a vehicle by which the effects of well-publicized bilateral obligations are given universal extension'.[41]

The last policy argument was strongly objected to by ILC members and commentators on multiple bases. It has been suggested that this 'bilateralisation' of complicity, reproduces a monolithic view of reciprocal normativity in international law.[42] Aust argued that the ILC favoured the complicit State's interests over the interests of the injured State[43] and Lanovoy that it failed to capture the social need of the international system as a whole.[44] Lowe, finally laments the overly cautious approach taken by the ILC that has unnecessarily restricted via the inclusion of the opposability requirement an already limited scope of application.[45] This last point is of particular significance with respect to ARIO, Articles 14 and 58(1), as very seldom an International Organisation will be bound by the same obligation as its member States, thus rendering the incurrence of complicity a rather remote possibility.[46]

Even if one disagrees with these policy objections, it is argued here that the inclusion of the opposability requirement makes no sense from a legal point of view. First, the justification for its inclusion is based on a private-law approach to international responsibility,[47] while the latter is neither civil, nor criminal but *sui generis*.[48] When the obligation breached by the main act is of a public or criminal character, the unjust results of the opposability requirement are readily apparent. Lowe has invoked an example in this respect; R (a persistent objector to claims to extended security zones at sea) assists P (which has acquiesced in such claims) to engage in unlawful military activities within the security zone of V.[49] The exculpation of R per ASR, Article 16 in this set of

[41] Crawford, *State Responsibility* (n 32) 410.

[42] Some members of the ILC were indeed deeply opposed to the inclusion of such requirement, eg ILC, *Summary Record of the 2577th Meeting* (25 May 1999), reproduced in (1999) 1 *YBILC* 67, 68, [5] (Economides); Aust, *Complicity* (n 11) 254; Lanovoy, 'Complicity in an Internationally Wrongful Act' (n 34) 157–60.

[43] Aust, *Complicity* (n 11) 254.

[44] Lanovoy, 'Complicity in an Internationally Wrongful Act' (n 34) 159.

[45] Lowe, 'Responsibility for the Conduct of Other States' (n 28) 7.

[46] Alvarez uses this argument in order to suggest that the ARIO in general 'might not produce the results that proponents of accountability want', J Alvarez, 'Revisiting the ILC's Draft Rules on International Organization Responsibility' (2011) 105 *American Society of International Law Proceedings* 344, 347–48.

[47] ILC, *Summary Record of the 2672nd Meeting* (3 May 2001), reproduced in (2001) 1 *YBILC* 34, 42, [52] (Lukashuk).

[48] *Case concerning the Difference Between New Zealand and France concerning the Interpretation or Application of Two Agreements Concluded on 9 July 1986 Between the Two States and which related to the Problems arising from the Rainbow Warrior Affair (New Zealand v France)*, Ruling of 6 July 1986, (1990) 20 Reports of International Arbitral Awards 215, 251, [75] ('in international law there is no distinction between contractual and tortious responsibility'); A Pellet, 'The Definition of Responsibility in International Law' in J Crawford, A Pellet and S Olleson (eds), *The Law of International Responsibility* (OUP, 2010) 3, 12–15.

[49] Lowe, 'Responsibility for the Conduct of Other States' (n 28) 7–8.

facts seems indeed unacceptable. A solution would be to restore the distinction between *traités-lois* and *traités-contrats* and attach different legal consequences to the violation of each of them.[50] This dichotomy, however, is no longer applicable, and according to the modern construction of international responsibility the establishment of the latter is indifferent to the nature of the obligation violated.

Since international responsibility is of a *sui generis* nature, only an assessment of the opposability requirement on the basis of general principles of law is pertinent for a safe judgement. VCLT, Article 34 provides that a treaty is not binding on third States, and thus a third State enjoys discretion on how it will behave towards the parties to the treaty. Nevertheless, this discretion is not unqualified. The arbitrary and unreasonable exercise of this discretion amounts to an abuse of rights when the rights of a third State are encroached on in bad faith.[51] The duty to act in a way that does not cause deliberate damage to another is an aspect of good faith and considered a general principle of international law.[52] To the extent that the opposability requirement legalises aid or assistance provided with the intention of infringing international law, it runs counter to this general principle and hence it cannot be justified from a legal perspective.[53]

I argue that the opposability requirement does not form part of the customary rule because it runs counter to a general principle of international law. To admit the contrary would be tantamount to arguing that there can be exceptions to the general principle of good faith. ASR, Article 16 then provides an example where the law has been recognised to exist against its premises, since the ICJ in its 2007 *Genocide* case held that this provision *in toto* forms part of customary law.[54] I believe that the only reason why the ICJ has not disentangled this requirement from the rest of the provision is because it has not yet faced such a set of facts. Subparagraph (b), then, should not have formed part of the archetype of Article 16, or of ARIO, Articles 14 and 58(1) which followed its wording.

[50] H Triepel, *Völkerrecht und Landesrecht* (Scientia Antiquariat, 1958) 65.

[51] T Hassan, 'Good Faith in Treaty Formation' (1980) 21 *Vanderbilt Journal of International Law* 443, 448; G Fitzmaurice, 'The Law and Procedure of the International Court of Justice' (1953) 30 *BYBIL* 1, 53; M Byers, 'Abuse of Rights: An Old Principle, a New Age' (2002) 47 *McGill Law Journal* 389, 423; GDS Taylor, 'Content and Rule Against Abuse of Rights in International Law' (1972) 46 *BYBIL* 324ff.

[52] B Cheng, *General Principles of Law as Applied by International Courts and Tribunals* (CUP, 2006) 130; S Reinhold, *Good Faith in International Law*, Bonn Research Chapters on Public International Law, Ch No 2/2013, 8–12. International case law supports this conclusion, see eg *Trail Smelter Arbitration* (*United States of America v Canada*), Awards of 16 April 1938 and 11 March 1941 (1949) 3 Reports of International Arbitral Awards 1965.

[53] See similar arguments by Lanovoy, 'Complicity in an Internationally Wrongful Act' (n 34) 160.

[54] *Genocide Case* (n 25) 217, [420].

(ii) Establishment of Responsibility

Before analysing the basis of R's internationally wrongful act in scenarios of complicity, it is important to assess whether the provision on 'aid or assistance' imposes a particular obligation on R, and if it thereby constitutes a primary norm. I do not wish to burden the theoretical debate on international responsibility with the primary/secondary rules dichotomy, but I rather wish to explain the operation of the normative elements found within the text of the 'aid or assistance' provision. If R's internationally wrongful act arises for own conduct as per the direct responsibility model, it is crucial to determine whether the conduct is unlawful because it is in breach of R's international obligations or it becomes unlawful through its connection with P's internationally wrongful act.

A point of criticism in relation to the drafting of all three provisions on indirect responsibility is that they blur the distinction between primary and secondary norms that has long been established in relation to international responsibility; primary norms lay down obligations and secondary norms provide for the consequences of the breach of primary obligations.[55] And since the ILC codified solely secondary rules in the ASR and ARIO, the Commission recognised the confusion surrounding the nature of Chapter IV provisions by stating in the commentaries that '[a] feature of this Chapter is that it specifies certain conduct as internationally wrongful'.[56] The inclusion of such provisions is then hastily justified by reference to their exceptional character.

The provision blurs the boundaries between primary and secondary norms and does not seem to fit adequately within one of the two categories, at least if one adopts a Hartian understanding of the distinction.[57] Primary norms in international law are those 'customary or treaty rules laying down substantive obligations for States [or International Organisations]'.[58] Some commentators have thus argued that Article 16 of the ASR sets out a primary norm as it 'is clearly conceived as giving rise to a distinct obligation'.[59] However, the ILC has not hesitated to leap the barrier of the distinction between primary

[55] R Ago, *Second Report on State Responsibility*, UN doc A/CN.4/233 (1970), reproduced in (1970) 2 *YBILC* 177 ('Ago Second Report'), 306.

[56] ASR Comment, 65, [7].

[57] HLA Hart, *The Concept of Law* (Clarendon Press, 1961) 79–99. On the classification of primary/secondary norms in international law, see also N Bobbio, 'Nouvelles réflexions sur les normes primaires et secondaires' in N Bobbio (ed), *Études de théorie du droit* (LGDJ, 1988) 198; J Combacau and D Alland, 'Primary and Secondary Rules in the Law of State Responsibility: Categorizing International Obligations' (1985) 16 *Netherlands Yearbook of International Law* 81; E David, 'Primary and Secondary Rules' in J Crawford, A Pellet and S Olleson (eds), *The Law of International Responsibility* (OUP, 2010) 27; A Marschik, 'Too Much Order? The Impact of Special Secondary Norms on the Unity and Efficacy of the International Legal System' (1998) 9 *EJIL* 212.

[58] A Cassese, *International Law* (OUP, 2005) 244.

[59] D Jacobs and A Nollkaemper, 'Shared Responsibility in International Law: A Conceptual Framework' (2013) 34 *Michigan Journal of International Law* 359, 409.

and secondary norms:[60] in this respect, Special Rapporteur Crawford adopted a purely functional understanding of the relationship between primary and secondary norms, whereby the latter acquire their character as a result of their generality.[61] Taking the argument further, Linderfalk suggests that such distinctions are merely an anachronism, because rules falling under both categories become all the more interdependent in modern international law.[62] Perhaps then, the use of the primary/secondary distinction in the international responsibility framework does not reflect a purely Hartian analysis, and was 'designed solely as a methodological vehicle'.[63]

Be that as it may, I hold the view that the provision is of a mixed nature, but that disentanglement of the two sub-norms latent within the wording of the rule is possible. Based on the way in which the provision has been analysed here, the primary sub-norm is relevant to the provision's scope of application and the secondary is relevant to the establishment of the double basis of internationally wrongful act. Thus, the obligation incumbent upon R in the inter-State construction of ASR, Article 16 would be 'to not facilitate with knowing intention the commission of an internationally wrongful act of another State when the same act would have been in breach of your international obligations if committed by you'. In this sense, the presence of the subjective element of knowing intention is justified, as it forms part of a primary rule of conduct. The secondary sub-norm in its turn pertains to the consequences flowing from the breach of the aforementioned norm: that is, the establishment of an internationally wrongful act and the incurring of international responsibility.

This separation of the two rules encrypted within the text of the provision clarifies the basis of R's internationally wrongful act in cases that fall under the complicity model. The norm breached is the prohibition on knowing and intentional facilitation without the opposability requirement: 'to not facilitate with knowing intention the commission of an internationally wrongful act of another subject of international law'. Furthermore, R's conduct, through which the breach has materialised, is attributable to itself, since R is the actual author. In this way, the two conditions of breach and attribution are met and R's internationally wrongful act is clearly established through the application of

[60] ILC, *Summary Record of the 1519th Meeting* (18 July 1978), reproduced in (1978) 1 *YBILC* 237, 240 (Ago).

[61] J Crawford, 'The ILC's Articles on Responsibility of States for Internationally Wrongful Acts: A Retrospect' (2002) 96 *AJIL* 874, 879.

[62] U Linderfalk, 'State Responsibility and the Primary-Secondary Rules Terminology: The Role of Language for an Understanding of the International Legal System' (2009) 78 *Nordic Journal of International Law* 53, 72.

[63] A Gourgourinis, 'General/Particular International Law and Primary/Secondary Rules: Unitary Terminology of a Fragmented System' (2011) 22 *EJIL* 993, 1018. Boyle reiterates this approach: 'The designation of obligations as either primary or secondary is not itself important, for it is merely a helpful way of expressing a distinction between the content of rules of law and the results of their breach', A Boyle, 'State Responsibility and International Liability for Injurious Consequences of Acts Not Prohibited by International Law: A Necessary Distinction?' (1990) 39 *ICLQ* 1, 10–11.

the two-part test for direct responsibility. The defining feature of the complicity model is the operation of the facilitation primary norm it incorporates and not the content itself of the primary norm.

The final point requiring clarification is how the nexus of the 'knowing intention to facilitate' affects P's international responsibility. I hold the view that there is no reason to preclude P's international responsibility for the commission of its internationally wrongful act. Provisions on joint responsibility require the incurring of responsibility 'for the same wrongful act', which is not the same requirement as that for 'aid or assistance'.[64] Since P's international responsibility arises with respect to an internationally wrongful act which is different from R's, complicity is a straightforward case of independent international responsibilities running in parallel.

The rule based on the complicity model that reflects international law (or its progressive development in the case of International Organisations) could take the following form:

> 'Aid or Assistance': A State or an International Organisation which facilitates with knowing intention the internationally wrongful act of another State or another International Organisation, is responsible for doing so.

(iii) Responsibilities Running in Parallel: Rendition Operations Before the ECtHR

The judicial application of ASR, Article 16 has proven problematic, especially in a strain of cases regarding rendition operations before the European Court of Human Rights (ECtHR). The relevant case law of the Strasbourg Court is not that extensive (six cases arising from three sets of facts), but it highlights in an exemplary way the misconceptions surrounding application of the complicity model by international judicial bodies.

El-Masri

The earliest relevant judicial example in this respect is the *El-Masri* case.[65] According to the Court, the applicant was subjected to a secret rendition operation, in which agents of the Former Yugoslavian Republic of Macedonia (FYROM) had arrested him and handed him over to CIA agents at Skopje Airport. From there, he was transferred to a CIA-run secret detention facility in Kabul, where he had been ill-treated for over four months. The Court, in holding that FYROM was internationally responsible under the European

[64] The ILC statement that 'joint responsibility … is envisaged in [ARIO] Articles 14 to 18' is inappropriate not only in reference to 'derivative responsibility' scenarios, but also in relation to complicity scenarios, ARIO Comment, 142, [1].

[65] *El-Masri v Former Yugoslav Republic of Macedonia*, Application no 39630/09, ECtHR Grand Chamber, Judgment of 13 December 2012.

Convention on Human Rights (ECHR) for a violation of, inter alia, Articles 3 and 5, utilised particularly obfuscatory reasoning that rendered the judgment somewhat problematic.[66]

The judgment holds FYROM responsible for the applicant's ill-treatment and detention by US agents in both a territorial and an extra-territorial context. Had the Court instead opted to attribute to the respondent State its own agents' inactivity and failure to act, and thus find a violation of an obligation to prevent the occurrence of the harm, the Court's reasoning would have made perfect sense: FYROM would have been directly and independently responsible under Articles 3 and 5 of the ECHR for the violation of a primary norm incumbent upon its own organs, and for the conduct of its own organs.[67] That, however, is not what the Court had in mind.

The reasoning of the Court suggests that it understood the scenario as one of indirect responsibility. First, within FYROM's jurisdiction, the ECtHR explained that the respondent State is responsible under the ECHR for acts of torture performed by foreign officials on its territory with the acquiescence or connivance of its authorities since its agents actively facilitated the applicant's treatment.[68] The ECtHR clearly held in para 206 of the judgment that 'the treatment suffered by the applicant at Skopje Airport at the hands of the special CIA rendition team is imputable to the respondent State'. When adjudicating upon a similar set of facts, the Human Rights Committee adopted the same approach in the *Alzery* case.[69]

Extra-territorially, the ECtHR distinguished between the violation of ECHR, Articles 3 and 5. A similar approach was taken by the Court with respect to the applicant's subsequent detention (ECHR, Article 5) in Kabul. The ECtHR asked 'whether the applicant's subsequent detention in Kabul is imputable to the respondent State'.[70] On the basis that '[t]he FYROM authorities … actively

[66] Main point of criticism in A Nollkaemper, 'The ECtHR Finds FYROM Responsible in Connection with Torture by the CIA, but on What Basis?' *Ejil:Talk!*, 24 December 2012.

[67] This is also Jackson's suggestion: 'A better solution would be to interpret the rights guaranteed by human rights instruments as imposing a correlative duty of non-participation in violations of human rights carried out by other actors. In this way, states would be held responsible for their own contribution to wrongdoing', Jackson, *Complicity in International Law* (n 27) 200.

[68] *El-Masri* (n 65) [211].

[69] *Alzery v Sweden*, United Nations Human Rights Committee, Decision of 10 November 2006, UN doc CCPR/C/88/D/1416/2005. The applicant was ill-treated by Egyptian agents at Bromma airport. Paragraph [11.6] holds: 'On the issue of the treatment by the author at Bromma airport, the Committee must first assess whether the treatment suffered by the author at the hands of foreign agents is properly imputable to the State party under the terms of the Covenant and under applicable rules of State responsibility. The Committee notes that, at a minimum, a State party is responsible for acts of foreign officials exercising acts of sovereign authority on its territory, if such acts are performed with the consent or acquiescence of the State party (see also Article 1 of the Convention against Torture). It follows that the acts complained of, which occurred in the course of performance of official functions in the presence of the State party's officials and within the State party's jurisdiction, are properly imputable to the State party itself, in addition to the State on whose behalf the officials were engaged'.

[70] *El-Masri* (n 65) [235].

facilitated his subsequent detention in Afghanistan', the ECtHR attributed US conduct in Kabul to FYROM.[71] In this way, the Court inevitably concluded that FYROM was to be held responsible for violating the applicant's rights under Article 5 during the entire period of his captivity.

What the Court did then is to conflate the complicity model with the derivative responsibility model. On the one hand, it clearly articulates intentional facilitation as the element that triggers FYROM's international responsibility (complicity model), but it suggests that FYROM is legally responsible for the physical conduct performed by US agents. In other words, facilitation is conceptualised by the Court as a criterion of attribution of State conduct.[72] And while such an argument can be made with respect to private conduct,[73] it is *contra legem* when it comes to inter-State cooperation. And this does not strike as absurd to the extent that US conduct is committed within FYROM's jurisdiction, but it is far-fetched with respect to extra-territorial acts that lie beyond the jurisdictional reach of the respondent State.

It is submitted that the complicity model was applicable, given the circumstances of the case and FYROM's responsibility should have been understood to arise for participation in the internationally wrongful acts of the United States, not for the US agents' physical acts. An analysis of ASR, Article 16 should result in the Council of Europe member State being held responsible for the facilitation itself. This then results in the main internationally wrongful acts (the ill-treatment for the purposes of Article 3, or the detention for Article 5) being attributable to the United States. In this way, two separate independent responsibilities with respect to two distinct acts can arise.

Nevertheless, the Court's approach excludes this interpretation, and it would be interesting to see how the Court might tackle a future case in which the State, whose breach of the Convention has been facilitated by a second State, is itself bound by the ECHR. If the Court were to follow the *El-Masri* precedent, then it is bound to attribute the main wrongful conduct (the ill-treatment/ detention itself in *El-Masri*) to both States: to the State in the position of FYROM due to its facilitation, and to the State in the position of the United States because it (or its organ) is the author of the acts. This outcome of joint attribution, and hence joint responsibility, in complicity cases for the commission of the main wrongful act[74] does not find support among commentators,[75] and is in stark contrast to the wording of ASR, Article 16.

[71] ibid [239].

[72] Jackson, *Complicity in International Law* (n 27) 194.

[73] D Amoroso, 'Moving Towards Complicity as a Criterion of Attribution of Private Conducts: Imputation to States of Corporate Abuses in the US Case Law' (2011) 24 *Leiden Journal of International Law* 989.

[74] ASR, Art 47.

[75] Aust, *Complicity* (n 11) 280–81 and the authorities cited therein.

Finally, it is submitted that there is another practical reason why the ECtHR should have engaged in an analysis of the responsibility model it applied. Despite its complexities, the Court in the *El-Masri* case was significantly helped to its conclusion due to the United States' status as a non-State party to the ECHR. Since joint responsibility was not at play, there was no issue as towhether FYROM would be responsible for the internationally wrongful acts of the United States or for participation in the acts of the US agents. In either case, the outcome would have been the same: FYROM's responsibility under Articles 3 and 5 would have been triggered.

What the Court did then was not only to conflate, but also to equate, both responsibility models. It is of little importance whether this was the result of an oversight or an overly refined distinction the Court did not need to make. Rather, the true importance of the case lies in the statement underlying this equation of responsibility models. This conflation of complicity and derivative responsibility suggests that, with a view to reparations, it does not make a difference which model is triggered. Effectively, the Court implies that a violation of two different primary rules incorporated within the same provision – in the case of responsibility for, and for participation in, the act of another – has identical legal consequences.[76] Compensation for damage, however, is awarded on an equitable basis.[77] After all, it is one thing to violate the prohibition against torture, and quite another to violate the prohibition against the facilitation of torture.[78] Therefore, because the adoption of one responsibility model or another has practical repercussions for the measure of compensation potentially available to a victim, this in and of itself is a good enough reason for clearly distinguishing between the two responsibility models.

Despite the fact that the complicity model was the applicable responsibility model in this case from a doctrinal point of view, the ECtHR could not have affirmed FYROM's responsibility on that basis due to jurisdictional limitations. The nature of the Court's jurisdiction prevents applications when the principal issue requires a determination of the legal position of a State that is not a party to the proceedings.[79] The so-called *Monetary Gold* (or indispensable third parties) principle reflects the well-established principle that a Court

[76] Article 3 is a typical example of a provision that incorporates different primary norms, for it is vertically divided into three component parts according to the severity of the suffering: 'torture', 'inhuman treatment' and 'degrading treatment', see M Evans, 'Getting to Grips with Torture' (2002) 51 *ICLQ* 365, 370.

[77] *Tsirlis and Kouloumpas v Greece*, Application nos 19233/91 and 19234/91, ECtHR, Judgment of 29 May 1997, [80].

[78] As the violation of torture or inhuman treatment may affect the amount of compensation awarded under ECHR, Art 41, it is argued here that the violation of torture or complicity to torture should entail in principle different legal consequences, see M Addo and N Grief, 'Does Article 3 of the European Convention on Human Rights Enshrine Absolute Rights?' (1998) 9 *EJIL* 510, 511–12.

[79] *Monetary Gold Removed from Rome in 1943 (Italy v France, UK and USA)* (Preliminary Question) [1954] ICJ Reports 19, 32; NS Klein, 'Multilateral Disputes and the Doctrine of Necessary Parties in the East Timor Case' (1996) 21 *Yale Journal of International Law* 305, 315–16.

cannot exercise jurisdiction over a State without its consent.[80] It may be that the ECtHR has applied the indispensable parties rule rather pragmatically,[81] nevertheless it has endorsed this principle in all but name.[82] In *El-Masri*, the lawfulness of FYROM's complicit conduct rests upon the determination of the legal position of the United States. This does not mean that FYROM's responsibility for this conduct does not arise, it only means that FYROM's responsibility for this conduct cannot be implemented before this particular Court.[83] This is a practical reason why the Court should have dealt with the matter in the context of direct responsibility by focusing on primary norms.

Abu Zubaydah and Al-Nashiri (Stage One)

The judicial adventure of Mr Zayn Al-Abidin Muhammad Husayn (also known as Abu Zubaydah) and Mr Abd Al Rahim Husseyn Muhammad Al Nashiri unfolded in two stages. The applicants were the subjects of two separate rendition operations as both were classified by the CIA as 'High Value Detainee' (HVD).[84] They were captured in Asia and before ending up in Guantanamo they were held exclusively by CIA agents in different secret detention centres around the globe, one of them being Stare Kiejkuty in Poland. Other intermediate stops within Council of Europe territory were Lithuania for Mr Abu Zubaydah and Romania for Mr Al Nashiri. The ensuing cases, two against Poland decided on 24 July 2014[85] (Stage One) and two more against Romania and Lithuania decided on 31 May 2018[86] (Stage Two) were based on identical claims and reasoning.

[80] ICJ Statute, Art 36.

[81] M den Heijer, 'Procedural Aspects of Shared Responsibility in the European Court of Human Rights' (2013) 4 *Journal of International Dispute Settlement* 361, 373–78.

[82] *Soering v United Kingdom*, Application no 14038/88, ECtHR Grand Chamber, Judgment of 7 July 1989 (1989) 11 EHRR 439, [86]; *Cruz Varas and others v Sweden*, Application no 15576/89, ECtHR Grand Chamber, Judgment of 20 March 1991, (1992) 14 EHRR 1, [60]; *MSS v Belgium and Greece*, Application no 30696/09, ECtHR Grand Chamber, Judgment of 21 January 2011, [67]; *Saadi v Italy*, Application no 37201/06, ECtHR Grand Chamber, Judgment of 28 February 2008, (2009) 49 EHRR 30, [126]. Standard phrasing in these cases: 'the Convention does not govern the actions of States not Parties to it, nor does it purport to be a means of requiring the Contracting States to impose Convention standards on other States'.

[83] On the relationship between the *Monetary Gold* principle and ASR, Art 16, see ASR Comment, 67, [11].

[84] For more on the CIA's 'High Value Detainees Program', see CIA, Office of the Director of National Intelligence, *Summary of the High Value Detainees Program*, available at www.defense.gov/pdf/thehighvaluedetaineeprogram2.pdf, and the relevant report of the Human Rights Council, *Joint Study on Global Practices in Relation to Secret Detention in the Context of Countering Terrorism*, UN doc A/HRC/13/42 (19 February 2010) 45–59.

[85] *Al-Nashiri v Poland*, Application no 28761/11, ECtHR, Judgment of 24 July 2014, (2015) 60 EHRR 16; *Husayn (Abu Zubaydah) v Poland* Application no 7511/13, ECtHR, Judgment of 24 July 2014, (2015) 60 EHRR 16.

[86] *Al Nashiri v Romania*, Application no 33234/12, ECtHR, Judgment of 31 May 2018 (*Al-Nashiri* (Stage Two)) and *Abu Zubaydah v Lithuania*, Application no 46454/11, ECtHR, Judgment of 31 May 2018 (*Abu Zubaydah* (Stage Two)).

This is why they are considered twin cases and when analysing them I will refer only to *Al-Nashiri*.

In the first set of cases against Poland, the ECtHR fine-tuned the understanding of 'aid or assistance' in an extra-territorial context as put forward in *El-Masri*. The aspect that differentiates these cases from *El-Masri* is that Poland did not actively facilitate the treatment of the applicants but kept a passive attitude by allowing US organs to operate within its jurisdiction.

Resting on the *El-Masri* precedent, the applicants asked the Court to declare that:

> [s]ince Poland had actively facilitated the applicant[s] detention and transfer, it was also responsible for [their] ill-treatment and unlawful, secret detention for the period following [their] transfer from Poland.[87]

The Court omitted any reference to facilitation as a ground for attribution and reiterated its dictum from the *Soering* case; namely, that a State will be responsible for own conduct to the extent that it exposed the applicant to a serious risk of further ill-treatment and conditions of detention.[88] On this basis, the Court carefully concluded that Poland was responsible 'in respect of both [the applicants'] detention on its territory and [their] transfer from Poland'.[89] It may have been that Poland's stance did not surpass the *El-Masri* 'active facilitation' threshold and this is why it was not responsible for the applicants' extra territorial treatment. As the distinction between active and passive facilitation is irrelevant as to the establishment of international responsibility, it would have been helpful for the ECtHR to clarify whether it has abandoned the criterion of 'active facilitation' altogether.

Nasr and Ghali

In *Nasr and Ghali v Italy*, the same court had to rule on the extraordinary rendition of Egyptian national Osama Mustafa Hassan Nasr (also known as Abu Omar).[90] The ECtHR was presented with a set of facts that undoubtedly qualified as 'active facilitation', nevertheless the ECtHR shied away from the *El-Masri* precedent. The events of the case concerned the abduction and the subsequent detention of Abu Omar, once more in the context of the CIA 'High Value Detainees' program.[91] Mr Nasr is an Egyptian national, imam and member of an Islamist group who was residing in Italy with his wife Ms Ghali since he was granted political asylum status in that State. After his abduction in Milan in 2003, he was flown from the Aviano US base through Germany to

[87] *Al-Nashiri* (n 85) [445].
[88] ibid [531]; *Soering* (n 82) [90], [91], [113].
[89] *Al-Nashiri* (n 85) [531].
[90] *Nasr and Ghali v Italy*, Application no 44883/09, ECtHR, Judgment of 23 February 2016.
[91] For a detailed account of the events, see ibid [6]–[151].

Cairo. There he was ill-treated and detained without charge for approximately four years in unhygienic conditions. The Milan public prosecutor's office, after the abduction, immediately initiated a judicial investigation. The information obtained both in the investigation and during the ensuing judicial procedure before Italian courts confirmed, first, that 26 US citizens (CIA members and diplomats) and one Italian policeman had been involved in the operation, and second, that six senior officials of the Italian military intelligence agency had been aware of the CIA's plan to abduct Mr Nasr.

The Court found Italy responsible for the violation of Articles 3 and 5 of the ECHR by fine-tuning the approach to responsibility adopted in *El-Masri*. The defendant alleged that the facts of the case, irrespective of whether they happened intra- or extra-territorially, were not attributable to it since the entire operation was planned, organised and executed by the US government through its agents and the Italian policeman involved in the abduction was acting in his personal capacity.[92] The reasoning of the judgment does not engage with attribution but rather attaches importance to Italy's knowledge or intentional participation in the events. Being aware of the operation necessarily means that Italian authorities knew the potential dangers posed to the applicant by virtue of it. Since the Italian courts had affirmed that the defendant had full knowledge of the operation and its nature, the Court shared their findings. Regarding the events that occurred in Milan, then, the subjective element was not used by the Court to infer Italy's responsibility for the treatment the applicant suffered in the hands of CIA agents, but for its failure to prevent it from happening and thus exposing the applicant to a real risk of suffering treatment contrary to Article 3 of the Convention.[93] In this way, no indirect responsibility model was implicated and Italy was held directly responsible for its own wrongdoing.[94]

The Court tried to adopt an analogous approach with respect to the applicant's extra-territorial detention in Egypt. Paragraph 302 of the Court's judgment provides the reasoning and it is worth quoting it in full here:

> Dans le cadre de l'examen du grief du requérant sous l'aspect matériel de l'article 3, la Cour a déjà jugé que l'Italie savait que le requérant avait été transféré hors de son territoire dans le cadre d'une 'remise extraordinaire' et que les autorités italiennes, en permettant à la CIA d'enlever le requérant sur le territoire italien, l'ont sciemment exposé à un risque réel de traitements contraires à l'article 3 (paragraphe 290 ci-dessus). Elle estime que ces con- clusions sont également valables dans le contexte du grief tiré par le requérant de l'article 5 de la Convention et que la responsabilité de l'Italie est engagée eu égard tant à son en- lèvement qu'à l'ensemble de la détention consécutive à sa remise aux autorités américaines. (El-Masri, précité, § 239 and

[92] ibid [229].

[93] ibid [289]. Note the reference to *El-Masri* (n 65) [211] as a supporting authority for this statement, where the Court used 'acquiescence or connivance' by the territorial State as an attribution criterion. The Court is struggling to demonstrate consistency in its case law where there is none.

[94] See nn 67 and 88 and accompanying text.

> Al Nashiri, précité, § 531). [When examining the applicant's complaint under the material aspect of Article 3, the Court has already held that Italy knew that the applicant had already been transferred as part of an 'extraordinary rendition' [operation] out of its territory and that the Italian authorities by allowing the CIA to abduct the applicant in Italian territory, have knowingly exposed him to a real risk of treatment contrary to Article 3 (paragraph 290 above). The Court holds that these conclusions are equally valid in the context of the applicant's complaint under Article 5 of the Convention and that Italy's responsibility is triggered with respect to his abduction and the entirety of his detention following his rendition to the American authorities (El-Masri, above § 239 and Al Nashiri, above § 531).] (author's translation)

It is not clear which primary norm Italy had violated in the context of ECHR, Article 5 and whether indirect responsibility was in play according to this reasoning. I believe that since the Court drew parallels between the violation of Article 3 and the applicant's extra-territorial detention, it had in mind the violation of a concomitant 'due diligence' obligation. Apparently, the Court did not intend to attribute the detention in Cairo to Italy and render the latter responsible for the detention itself, as it did in *El-Masri*. Nevertheless, the open-ended last sentence of paragraph 302 and the reference to paragraph 239 in *El-Masri* could support the opposite interpretation. In any case, a more elaborate analysis that would not leave us to speculate would certainly be welcome.

Abu Zubaydah and Al-Nashiri (Stage Two)

The same blurred justification appears also in the latest set of rendition cases decided by the ECtHR. In the second part of the *Abu Zubaydah/Al-Nashiri* saga, the Court's reasoning lacks the clarity and meticulousness of a well-constructed judgment. The attempt to present all previous case law on the issue as a coherent strain of cases is testament to that.[95] A close examination of the ECtHR's chain of thoughts demonstrates the entanglement of direct and indirect responsibility which permeates both judgments. For example, the Court announced, on at least two occasions (three in *Abu-Zubaydah* (Stage Two)),[96] that it would deal with the issue of attribution of the acts complained of, but it never delivered on its promise. Since the Court did not clarify whether Romania was responsible for its participation in the HVD programme running in its territory, or because it failed to exercise 'due diligence', it is inevitable that it cannot provide an attribution analysis but rather a mesh of thoughts.

Paragraph 677 of the *Al-Nashiri* (Stage Two) judgment which summarises the basis of Romania's responsibility with respect to ECHR, Article 3 is

[95] *Al Nashiri* (Stage Two) (n 86) [594] and [689]. In the latter paragraph, the Court held: 'In the previous cases concerning similar allegations of a breach of Art 5 arising from secret detention under the CIA HVD Programme in other European countries, the Court found that the respondent States' responsibility was engaged and that they were in violation of that provision on account of their *complicity* in that programme and cooperation with the CIA' (emphasis added).

[96] *Al Nashiri* (Stage Two) (n 86) [602] and [669]; *Abu Zubaydah* (Stage Two) (n 86) [411], [587] and [633].

characteristic. The ECtHR emphasises that, while the CIA was in charge of the operation of the HVD programme in Romanian territory, Romania knew about the programme, facilitated its operation, and thus it was responsible 'on account of its "acquiescence and connivance"'.[97] The Court did not make any further inferences from this and assumed that acquiescence and connivance provided sufficient justification for the establishment of Romania's responsibility. At the same time, though, the primary obligation incumbent upon Romania was 'to take measures designed to ensure that individuals within its jurisdiction were not subjected to torture or inhuman or degrading treatment or punishment'. The above have led journalists to report that both Romania and Lithuania have been held responsible as accomplices to the CIA's secret rendition programme.[98] In legal terms, however, responsibility for complicity is most probably not what the Court had in mind.

The Court wished to kill two birds with one stone. One the one hand, it was anxious to demonstrate consistency with its previous case law; hence, the *El Masri* 'acquiescence and connivance' reference which was presented as a basis for the direct responsibility model. On the other, the Court wanted to structure its reasoning in terms of breach of primary obligations and attribution of conduct in accordance with the ILC responsibility framework. Alas, to have both is impossible.

If the Court wishes to abandon the 'active facilitation' criterion altogether and establish responsibility for own conduct in both a territorial and an extraterritorial context, it should explicitly say so. This will hopefully be clarified by future case law, however, the latest approach of the ECtHR, despite its blurred reasoning, must be welcomed for it demonstrates a clear tendency to align with the ILC's international responsibility framework.

B. Derivative Responsibility Model

(i) Scope of Application

(a) Knowledgeable Restriction of Freedom of Action

The other scheme that can be extracted from this Chapter of ILC provisions is the responsibility of an actor for the conduct of another. Both provisions on

[97] *Al Nashiri* (Stage Two) (n 86) [677]. The same paragraph makes explicit reference to complicity: 'on the basis of their own knowledge of the CIA activities deriving from Romanian's complicity in the HVD Programme'.

[98] A Cowell and C Savage, 'Lithuania and Romania Complicit in C.I.A. Prisons, European Court Says', *New York Times*, 31 May 2018, available at www.nytimes.com/2018/05/31/world/europe/lithuania-romania-cia-torture.html; Amnesty International, *Landmark Rulings Expose Romanian and Lithuanian Complicity in CIA Secret Detention Programme* (31 May 2018), available at www.amnesty.org/en/latest/news/2018/05/landmark-rulings-expose-romanian-and-lithuanian-complicity-in-cia-secret-detention-programme.

'direction and control' as well as 'coercion' operate according to this model. In such situations, the establishment of an internationally wrongful act is dependent upon the restriction of freedom imposed upon international actors when they exercise their rights and duties.[99] As advocated by Ago, the effect the relationship between responsibility bearer and perpetrator of wrongful conduct has on the freedom of the latter is the decisive element for the establishment of international responsibility in such scenarios.[100] The present analysis echoes Ago's view and suggests that the legal classification of an indirect responsibility scenario as one of either derivative responsibility or complicity rests on P's freedom to perform the wrongful conduct or the restriction thereof. Arguably, the notion of freedom provides a fitting threshold for present purposes, as it is an absolute notion; the idea of partial freedom or semi-freedom is, as I perceive it, a *contradictio in terminis*. Freedom, then, functions as an on-off switch that points in triangular scenarios either in the direction of complicity if it exists, or to that of derivative responsibility if it does not.

An impairment of freedom results from some sort of control that R exercises over P, the degree of which need not necessarily exceed a minimum threshold for present purposes. It is a well-established maxim in international law that responsibility derives from control in one way or another.[101] In both the *Nicaragua* and *Tadic* cases, the ICJ and the International Criminal Tribunal for the Former Yugoslavia (ICTY), respectively, in fact recognised this customary rule, although they interpreted it in a different manner and that is why they ended up with different control tests.[102] The controlling link established, however, must exceed the level of mere incitement, as such an influence is hardly a form of restriction of an actor's freedom and is not so reprehensible as to trigger the responsibility of the inciting state.[103]

In the *Nicaragua* case, for example, it was proven before the International Court of Justice that the CIA had produced a manual on 'Psychological Operations', which was used to train Nicaraguan guerrilla fighters for some six months from December 1983 to May 1984.[104] The manual contained specific advice

[99] 'A State may be held responsible, as a subject of international law, only to the extent that it has rights and duties which it is free to exercise', C Eagleton, *The Responsibility of States in International Law* (New York University Press, 1928) 43.

[100] R Ago, *La responsabilita indiretta nel diritto internazionale* (CEDAM, 1934) 59. To this end Ago had proposed one single provision to encompass both direction and control and coercion, see R Ago, *Eighth Report on State Responsibility*, UN doc A/CN.4/318 (1979) and Add 1 to 4, reproduced in (1979) 2(1) *YBILC* 4 ('Ago Eighth Report') 25–26, [45].

[101] C Eagleton, 'International Organization and the Law of Responsibility' (1950) 76 *RCADI* 319, 385.

[102] P Merkouris, *Article 31(3)(c) of the VCLT and the Principle of Systemic Integration: Normative Shadows in Plato's Cave* (Brill Nijhoff, 2015) 176–83. He explains that the discrepancy between the ICJ's 'effective control' and the ICTY's 'overall control' attribution standards, results from diverging interpretations of the same customary norm.

[103] ASR Comment, 65, [9].

[104] *Military and Paramilitary Activities In and Against Nicaragua (Nicaragua v United States of America)* (Merits) [1986] ICJ Reports 14, 67, [119].

on how to neutralise certain carefully-selected and planned targets, including judges, police officers, State Security officials, and so on. The ICJ held that such encouragement, even though prohibited per se by the rules of international humanitarian law, was not sufficient to hold the United States responsible for the relevant guerrilla atrocities.[105]

The key question is whether a restriction of freedom should take a particular form. This is a delicate matter, as a restriction may result either from a legal relationship or from a factual relationship. For present purposes, however, restriction of freedom is relevant only as an objective outcome, and therefore it is logical to assume that it should make no difference whether the nature of the control is legal or factual.[106] It is also of no legal significance whether the control exercised will necessitate P's action through forcing his will or by eliminating his capacity to act in a certain way.[107]

In the ASR, the ILC opted for a narrow construction of both derivative responsibility provisions it contains, and excluded legal relationships from their ambit. Specifically, it held that only factual relationships may trigger application of the derivative responsibility provisions: the concepts of 'direction and control' and 'coercion' lead to this conclusion;[108] and is also evidenced in the relevant ILC commentaries.[109] However, the specific examples provided by the ILC in the ASR that pertain to factual control, such as dependency relationships, should today be considered obsolete.[110]

In the ARIO, the ILC position has changed. According to the Commission, de jure control will be equated with de facto control when the binding decisions adopted are coupled with an adequate enforcement mechanism 'so that normative control would correspond in substance to factual control'.[111] The restriction of P's freedom of decision in and of itself then seems irrelevant for the purposes of derivative responsibility. It becomes relevant only to the extent

[105] The ICJ held *obiter* that: 'The question here does not of course relate to the definition of the circumstances in which one State may be regarded as responsible for acts carried out by another State, which probably do not include the possibility of incitement', ibid 119, [255].

[106] Ago Eighth Report (n 100) 26; A Orakhelashvili, 'Division of Reparation Between Responsible Entities' in J Crawford, A Pellet and S Olleson (eds), *The Law of International Responsibility* (OUP, 2010) 647, 651.

[107] cp the concepts of 'direction and control' (Art 17 is limited to cases where a dominant State actually directs and controls conduct, ASR Comment, 68, [2]) with that of 'coercion' ('[n]othing less than conduct which forces the will of the coerced State will suffice, giving it no effective choice but to comply with the wishes of the coercing State', ASR Comment, 69, [2]) in the ASR.

[108] Blokker, 'Abuse of the Members' (n 16) 39; Nedeski and Nollkaemper, 'Responsibility of International Organisations' (n 14) 40.

[109] ASR Comment, 68, [6]: 'Article 17 is limited to cases where a dominant State actually directs and controls conduct'. And with respect to coercion: 'Nothing less than conduct which forces the will of the coerced State will suffice, giving it no effective choice but to comply with the wishes of the coercing State', ibid 69, [2].

[110] ibid 68–69, [2]–[3], [5]–[6].

[111] G Gaja, *Third Report on Responsibility of International Organizations*, UN doc A/CN.4/553 (2005), reproduced in (2005) 2(1) *YBILC* 7, 16.

that it effectively leads to a conditioning of P's act: that is, when it results in the restriction of P's freedom of action. In essence, if R decides that P must act in a certain manner, R may only be held derivatively responsible for P's conduct if R's decision effectively resulted in a restriction of P's freedom of action.

This broadening of the notion of control to encompass legal relationships has radically expanded the scope of application of the derivative responsibility provisions under the ARIO. This is because the ILC has opened the door for legally binding decisions of International Organisations to be viewed as constituting 'direction and control' or – very rarely – 'coercion' when such decisions do not permit any discretion in their implementation.[112] Given that most International Organisations adopt binding decisions because they lack operational capacity, this scenario could be considered to arise particularly frequently in modern practice.[113]

Moreover, apart from the link between responsibility and freedom, which is clearly present in the ILC Articles concerning both 'direction and control' and also 'coercion', a determination of responsibility also turns upon the presence of a subjective element. R is exculpated when it is unaware of the circumstances surrounding the commission of the act. The presence of such requirement is valid and justified, as R should be afforded a defence when it bears responsibility for conduct that is not its own. In practice, however, R's knowledge will generally be presumed in such circumstances, due to the high degree to which P's freedom is restricted.[114] Importantly, the introduction of a knowledge requirement in a framework of norms that has attempted to eradicate subjectivity is logical and justified, as it forms part of its scope of application and does not cause doctrinal confusion.

In combining the two aforementioned findings, it is evident that the ILC utilises one party's knowledgeable restriction of another's freedom of action in order to delimit the scope of application of derivative responsibility.

The scenarios examined in this section bring to mind 'agency relationships'. This concept, of private law origin, describes the relationship established 'between two persons, one of whom ["principal"] expressly or impliedly consents that the other ["agent"] should act on his behalf so as to affect his relations with third parties, and the other of whom similarly consents so to act or so acts'.[115] The concept was long time since transposed in international law to describe inter-State relationships,[116] and more recently interactions between

[112] ARIO Comment, 103–4, [4]–[5] and 105, [4]–[5].

[113] See next chapter for the regulation of such scenarios.

[114] Dominicé argues for a presumption of knowledge in such cases, but from a different point of view, C Dominicé, 'Attribution of Conduct to Multiple States and the Implication of a State in the Act of Another' in J Crawford, A Pellet and S Olleson (eds), *The Law of International Responsibility* (OUP, 2010) 281, 288.

[115] FMB Reynolds, *Bowstead & Reynolds on Agency* (Sweet & Maxwell, 2006) 1.

[116] AP Sereni, 'Agency in International Law' (1940) 34 *AJIL* 638.

States and International Organisations.[117] The most typical example of such an agency relationship between an International Organisation and a State or States which has been extensively covered by commentators is that of peacekeeping operations.[118]

The agency relationship rests upon the premise of a consensual establishment in the form of an implicit or explicit agreement of the relevant parties.[119] To the extent that the agent in an agency relationship acts upon the instructions or the orders of the principal, thus restricting its freedom, the ensuing conduct will be covered by derivative responsibility. In such cases, restriction of freedom has been agreed to *a priori*. If, on the other hand, the principal's involvement with the agent's conduct does not surpass this threshold, derivative responsibility does not ensue but complicity could come into play. Agency relationships, then, do not provide any assistance with respect to the normative analysis conducted in this book since the interaction between agent and principal could fall under the scope of both the responsibility models outlined above.

(b) Opposability Requirement

The ILC has adopted a controversial stance on this matter in ASR, Articles 17 and 18. The two provisions point in different directions, thus generating a discrepancy as to the spectrum of scenarios covered by each one.[120] The 'direction and control' provision follows the logic of ASR, Article 16 and 'for ease of application' holds that R's responsibility will arise only if it is bound by the obligation that prohibits the main act,[121] while Article 18 provides that R's responsibility is established irrespective of such a prerequisite. In this way, the 'direction and control' provision excludes from its ambit scenarios where the directing and controlling subject dominates an act that does not run counter to its own obligations.

An example will clearly highlight this discrepancy. During the First World War, certain oil storage and other facilities owned by a US company in Roma-

[117] D Sarooshi, 'Conferrals by States of Powers on International Organizations: The Case of Agency' (2003) 74 *BYBIL* 308; I Couzigou, 'International Organisations and States Within an Agency Relationship: The Distribution of Responsibility' (2014) 61 *Netherlands International Law Review* 335.

[118] See M Moelle, *The International Responsibility of International Organisations: Cooperation in Peacekeeping Operations* (CUP, 2017).

[119] T Gazzini, 'Personality of International Organizations' in J Klabbers and A Wallendahl (eds), *Research Handbook on the Law of International Organizations* (Edward Elgar, 2011) 33.

[120] This largely escaped the attention of academics and of States commenting on the ASR, the only exception being Argentina in ILC, *State Responsibility: Comments and Observations Received from Governments*, UN doc A/CN.4/515 (2001) and Add 1 to 3, reproduced in (2001) 2(1) *YBILC* 33, 53, [2]–[5].

[121] Crawford Second Report (n 36) 54, [202].

nia were destroyed on the orders of the Government of Romania.[122] The claim of the United States was originally addressed to the British Government. The United States claimed that the Romanian authorities had been compelled by Great Britain to take the measures in question and the latter has to assume international responsibility for the destruction of the facilities. Let us assume *arguendo* that the destruction led to the violation of a bilateral obligation between Romania and the United States for the provision of oil to the latter State. If the British influence amounted to coercion then its responsibility for the latter violation would have been established. On the contrary, if Great Britain had exercised direction and control over the conduct it would have escaped responsibility for this particular violation.

The opposability requirement is problematic in Article 17 for the same reason as the complicity scenario. It implies that conduct that deliberately forces another subject of international law to violate its obligations can sometimes be tolerated by the international legal order. As said earlier, such conduct runs counter to the general principle of good faith, irrespective of whether R is bound by the obligation that prohibits the main act or not.[123] To the extent that the opposability requirement legalises direction and control rendered with the intention of infringing international law, it cannot be justified from a legal perspective. The direction and control provision, then, should have followed Article 18 and 'not allow for an exemption from responsibility ... in circumstances where the coercing [or directing and controlling] State is not itself bound by the obligation in question'.[124]

Therefore, derivative responsibility covers scenarios that involve knowledgeable restriction of P's freedom of action, irrespective of whether the ensuing act runs counter to R's international obligations.

(ii) Establishment of Responsibility

What remains unclear from the wording of both provisions is whether R satisfies the attribution and breach requirements necessary for the establishment of the double basis of an internationally wrongful act. The caveat is that the elements of breach and attribution are entangled in the derivative responsibility model, and separation thereof proves to be a challenge. At this point, it must be stressed that R is not responsible for the direction and control or coercion itself but rather for the conduct committed under the circumstances of restricted freedom.

[122] *Romano-Americana Company Case (United States v Romania and Great Britain)* (1943) 5 G *Hackworth, Digest of International Law* 840.

[123] See III A ii b above.

[124] ASR Comment, 70, [6].

(a) Attribution

In this situation, a peculiarity arises in that if one were to follow the standard rules on attribution, P's conduct would not be attributable to R.[125] After all, since derivative responsibility arises when one party is held responsible for the conduct of another, it would seem that the wrongful conduct is, and should be, prima facie attributable to P, which has committed the relevant act or omission. Thus, it seems as if international responsibility is invoked in this scenario without the requisite and prior attribution of P's actions to R.

However, when commenting on its rules on attribution of conduct, the ILC reiterates time and again that attribution depends on control of some sort.[126] The ILC has clarified that it does not specifically provide for negative attribution criteria,[127] however, it has implicitly recognised that the lack of control over specific conduct functions as a negative attribution criterion.[128] This element functions as a trump card in ARIO, Article 7, which reads:

> The conduct of an organ of a State or an organ or agent of an international organization that is placed at the disposal of another international organization shall be considered under international law an act of the latter organization if the organization exercises effective control over that conduct.

According to the commentaries, in such cases the factual control exercised 'channels' attribution to the controlling entity and severs any attribution link the organ may have with the relevant contributing State or International Organisation.[129] It has been argued that such severance does not ensue since both entities may simultaneously exercise effective control over the same conduct.[130] I believe that the latter 'bifocal' interpretation, unjustifiably broadens the notion of 'effective control' for it is difficult to see how effective is a control that is not exclusive.

The textbook example of such a situation is that of State military organs placed at the United Nations' disposal for peacekeeping operations. In July 1995, the unit of the United Nations Protection Force stationed at the 'safe area' of Srebrenica was comprised of Dutch contingents, who later abandoned their post and failed to protect Bosnian Muslims when attacked by Serbian

[125] The only pertinent rule is ASR, Art 6, but the narrow wording of the provision reserves its operation only for cases of 'dual allegiance' in the sense that P as an organ is attached at the same time to both R and P, see A Tzanakopoulos, *Disobeying the Security Council: Countermeasures Against Wrongful Sanctions* (OUP, 2011) 38. This is clearly not the case here.

[126] ASR Comment, 47, [3]–[4]; ARIO Comment, 86–87, [5], [7].

[127] ARIO Comment, 81, [5].

[128] In this case the organ's conduct would clearly be attributable only to the receiving organisation, ibid 85, [3].

[129] ibid 86, [5]. The opposite interpretation has been proposed, whereby dual attribution is possible in effective control scenarios. For an analysis of the relevant debate, see T Dannenbaum, 'Dual Attribution in the Context of Military Operations' (2015) 12 *IOLR* 401, 405–6.

[130] T Dannenbaum, 'Public Power and Preventive Responsibility: Attributing the Wrongs of International Joint Ventures' in A Nollkaemper and D Jacobs (eds), *Distribution of Responsibilities in International Law* (CUP, 2015) 192, 200, 207.

forces, resulting in the massacre of approximately 8,000 Bosnians.[131] For the purposes of attribution, the failure to prevent the massacre is not attributable to the Netherlands, despite the fact that those military contingents are clearly a State organ. When faced with a petition by relatives of some of the victims, the Hague District Court explained, 'these acts and omissions should be attributed strictly, as a matter of principle, to the UN', since the Netherlands had placed its forces under UN command and the UN had exercised 'operational command and control' over the contingents.[132] It is debatable whether this standard is tantamount to effective factual control as per ARIO, Article 7.[133] What is important for present purposes is that the Court perceived that this was the case and thus concluded that '[a]ttribution of acts and omissions by Dutchbat to the United Nations therefore *excludes attribution* of the same conduct to the State'[134] (emphasis added). This ruling was reversed by the Court of Appeal, and verified by the Supreme Court, who held that: 'the possibility that more than one party has "effective" control is generally accepted'.[135] As d' Argent notes, this *dictum* contrasts the ARIO, Article 7 'effective control' criterion as a factual element 'shifting' attribution from the lending State to the International Organisation.[136] Thus, the control exercised may serve to sever any organic ties, and channel attribution accordingly.

Since attribution in the law of international responsibility pertains to a relationship between certain conduct and a subject of international law, when this relationship is governed by conditions of impairment/restriction of freedom, no link is established between the two. It would be safe to assume, then, that the application of all the provisions on attribution of conduct rests on the prerequisite that the subject under examination adopts a certain course of action under conditions of freedom.[137] If this is not the case, the normative operation of attribution is affected.

In principle, the same channelling occurs in situations involving derivative responsibility. The restriction of freedom of action functions as a carrier that transfers the conduct of one actor to another, thus attributing P's conduct to R.[138] As P's freedom of action has been impaired, no act can be attributable to

[131] For more on the facts of the case, see *Genocide Case* (n 25) 43.

[132] *Hasan Nuhanovic v Netherlands (Ministry of Defence and Ministry of Foreign Affairs)*, First Instance Judgment, Decision No LJN: BF0181, Case No 265615, International Law in Domestic Courts 1092 (NL 2008), 10 September 2008, District Court, [4.8].

[133] Dannenbaum, 'Public Power and Preventive Responsibility' (n 129) 411–12.

[134] *Nuhanovic* (n 132) [4.13].

[135] *Hasan Nuhanovic v Netherlands,* Appeal Judgment, LJN:BR5388 International Law in Domestic Courts 1742 (NL 2011), 5 July 2011, Court of Appeal, [5.9].

[136] P d' Argent, 'State Organs Placed at the Disposal of the UN, Effective Control, Wrongful Abstention and Dual Attribution of Conduct' (2014) 1 *Questions of International Law* 30.

[137] Eagleton has expressed the similar view that responsibility, and hence attribution, is based on freedom, 'International Organization and the Law of Responsibility' (n 101) 385.

[138] An argument that these norms provide for attribution of conduct is put forward by Reinisch, 'Aid or Assistance and Direction and Control' (n 29) 76. Lowe seems to suggest the same but with rather obscure language, 'Responsibility for the Conduct of Other States' (n 28) 4.

it. This derivative attribution rule is the reason why P does not commit an internationally wrongful act in coercion scenarios. The ILC has equated coercion with *force majeure*, a circumstance precluding wrongfulness, and thus held that lack of wrongfulness and not of attributability explains P's exculpation.[139] I suggest to the contrary that it is the condition of attribution and not that of a breach of a primary obligation that is not satisfied in such instances.[140] Therefore, a latent rule in relation to the derivative attribution of conduct operates within this model, a characteristic that defines this particular responsibility model.

The restriction of P's freedom generates a *sui generis* situation that is hard to conceptualise, because certain conduct is not attributable to the legal subject who physically commits it, but rather to the subject that restricts the first subject's freedom. The author of an act committed in the real world is thus incongruent with the author of the act for legal purposes. From a doctrinal point of view, this attribution rule is justified because attribution 'is a pure result of the law; a will or an act are attributable to a given subject only because a legal provision says so'.[141] Accordingly, the identities of the physical actor and the legal actor need not necessarily align. For this reason, I take issue with the ILC's position in the ARIO with regard to indirect responsibility: that is, that in cases of indirect responsibility, R is held responsible 'not for having actually committed the wrongful act but for its causal contribution to the commission of the act'.[142] While this *dictum* may be true for situations involving complicity, in the situations under examination R is responsible as the actor(although in a legal, and not a physical, sense) and is responsible for his own internationally wrongful act.

The most recent example of derivative responsibility provided by the ILC is the belligerent occupation of Italy by Germany during the Second World War. During the occupation, Italian police in Rome operated under the control of the occupying Power. Thus, the forcible entry by police forces into the territory of the Holy See in February 1944 cannot be attributed to Italy. According to the previous analysis, the act is derivatively attributed to Germany by virtue of a latent rule on attribution, and the control exercised severs any attribution link that may otherwise exist between Italy and the police forces.

Most commentators explain the operation of the derivative responsibility provisions in a different way. They begin from the premise that ARIO, Chapter IV provides for international responsibility for another subject's internationally

[139] ASR Comment, 65 note 267.

[140] A detailed examination of the circumstances precluding wrongfulness exceeds the scope of the research question. But, to the extent that *force majeure* pertains to conduct 'which is beyond the control of the State concerned' I argue that it excludes attribution of conduct to the entity that is unable to control its conduct. Thus, it is not a circumstance precluding wrongfulness, but rather a circumstance precluding attribution or a negative attribution criterion, ASR Comment, 76, [2].

[141] D Anzilotti, *Corso di diritto internazionale* (CEDAM, 1955) vol I, 5.

[142] ARIO Comment, 101, [2].

wrongful act. Thus, it is commonly argued that these provisions provide for the attribution of international responsibility rather than conduct, and it is international responsibility that is channelled from P to R.[143] The approach rests on the premise that P's international responsibility has actually arisen with respect to its own conduct (P has committed an internationally wrongful act), and that this international responsibility is then subsequently redirected to and imposed on R. Under this prism one can explain the ILC's proposition in its commentaries to the ARIO that in indirect responsibility, R's international responsibility can arise without prior attribution of conduct to R.[144] The way this is stated, however, is misleading and has led the International Monetary Fund (IMF) to believe that the ILC has eradicated attribution as a prerequisite for the establishment of an internationally wrongful act.[145] The attribution of international responsibility explanation is simpler than the one provided in this chapter, results in the same outcome (the establishment of R's international responsibility) and would seem to suggest that the construction of a latent attribution rule is an unnecessary legalistic trick.

Nevertheless, this dominant approach is not favoured in this book for three reasons. First, the premise upon which it rests cannot be accepted. As explained earlier, Chapter IV provisions stipulate for international responsibility for own internationally wrongful act. But even if one accepts that the provisions at hand provide for international responsibility for P's internationally wrongful act, the 'attribution of responsibility' argument is problematic with respect to each of the two derivative responsibility provisions. On the one hand, the 'coercion' provision stipulates that P's conduct is not wrongful and thus no internationally wrongful act is established that could give rise to P's international responsibility. On the other, the requirement in the 'direction and control' provision that the relevant act must be wrongful for R in order to trigger R's responsibility becomes automatically superfluous. Why should the conduct be required to be contrary to R's obligations (the breach element) to trigger its responsibility, if it is international responsibility (attribution and breach) that is allocated to it through the operation of the provision?

[143] J Fry 'Coercion, Causation and the Fictional Elements of Indirect State Responsibility' (2007) 40 *Vanderbilt Journal of Transnational Law* 611, 631; Tzanakopoulos, *Disobeying the Security Council* (n 125) 45–46; PJ Kuijper, 'Introduction to the Symposium on Responsibility of International Organisations and of (Member) States: Attributed or Direct Responsibility or Both?' (2010) 7 *IOLR* 9, 30.

[144] ARIO Comment, 100–1, [2].

[145] ILC, *Comments and Observations Received from Governments and International Organizations*, UN doc A/CN/4.556 (2005), reproduced in (2005) 2(1) *YBILC* 27, 35–36: 'It is therefore surprising that the commentary should now assert that "responsibility of an international organization may in certain cases arise also when conduct is not attributable to that international organization". IMF does not recognize the validity of such a proposition and sees no legal basis on which to accept this statement as codifying either a general principle of international law or as representing a proposal for its progressive development' (footnote omitted).

Lastly, the 'attribution of responsibility' argument does not explain in legal terms why P's international responsibility is directed to R. As explained in the previous chapter, a principled exegesis is needed when international responsibility is established for the internationally wrongful act of another. The legal ramification from the establishment of international responsibility is the attribution of new obligations to the responsible subject. Let us assume *arguendo* that P has committed an internationally wrongful act and its international responsibility has in fact been established. If R has not expressed its consent to be bound by P's obligations, then how will R be bound by them? The 'attribution of responsibility' argument then makes sense only in the exceptional circumstances of a voluntary assumption of obligations.[146] This is why 'attribution of responsibility' is a term with very limited value within the law of international responsibility, and its thoughtless invocation merely causes doctrinal confusion.[147]

(b) Breach

Prima facie, it should be indifferent whether the ensuing conduct runs contrary to P's obligations in derivative responsibility scenarios. The accordance of the conduct with P's international obligations cannot affect the establishment either of P's nor of R's international responsibility. P's international responsibility cannot be established in the first place as no conduct can be attributed to it under conditions of restriction of freedom, as explained above. Further, each subject's internationally wrongful act is established individually, by reference to its own international obligations.[148] If R then is the legal author of the conduct in question, the wrongfulness of such conduct is judged solely against the background of R's, and not P's, international obligations.

Nevertheless, both provisions depend the establishment of R's responsibility upon the wrongfulness of the ensuing conduct for P. The ILC held that in both Articles, R's responsibility is established for P's internationally wrongful act and that is why they are aligned in this respect.[149] According to the provision on 'direction and control', the ensuing conduct must be contrary to the obligations of both R and P. ASR, Article 18(a) also provides: 'the act would, but for the coercion, be an internationally wrongful act of the coerced State'.[150]

[146] See the analysis of ARIO, Art 62(1)(a) in Chapter 2.

[147] Chen characterises attribution of responsibility as 'a general social institution of rectificatory justice', Y Chen, 'Attribution, Causation and Responsibility of International Organizations' in D Sarooshi (ed), *Remedies and Responsibility for the Actions of International Organizations* (Brill, Nijhoff, 2014) 33, 37.

[148] ASR Comment, 125, [8].

[149] ASR Comment, 68, [1] and 69, [1].

[150] In this case coercion is equated with *force majeure*, ASR Comment, 65 note 267.

The ILC, however, offers no justification as to why R is responsible for P's internationally wrongful act. It fails to explain how R assumes the international obligations that automatically arise by virtue of the internationally wrongful act of another. Since R has not expressed its consent to do so, derivative responsibility scenarios provide for responsibility for own internationally wrongful act. It follows that P's conduct does not have to be internationally wrongful for R's responsibility to arise. R's responsibility will be established if and only if R violates an international obligation incumbent upon it. Such scenarios, then, should be analysed under this prism.

Most restriction of freedom scenarios will present no problem as to the occurrence of the breach prerequisite for R. In the *Romano-Americana* case, for example, the destruction of the oil facilities is illegal for R (Great Britain) also and hence the latter's internationally wrongful act is automatically established. The situation gets more complicated, however, when the ensuing act is not illegal for R. From the preceding analysis, a paradoxical situation arises in such instances. On the one hand, they fall under the scope of derivative responsibility, ie the bilateral obligation hypothesis in the *Romano-Americana* case cited above. On the other hand, in such scenarios R should not bear international responsibility as it seemingly does not violate its international obligations.[151] So the question arises: how is the condition of breach established on such occasions?

I believe that the solution to this question comes from the realm of primary norms. The British Government which forces Romania to breach its obligation to export oil to the United States breaches its obligation not to procure a breach of Romania's international obligation towards the United States by restricting this subject's freedom of action. Great Britain, in this example, cannot be held responsible for the breach of an obligation it never assumed (ie to export oil to the United States). Great Britain is responsible for causing the breach of Romania's bilateral obligation. As per complicity, the ILC should have incorporated in the ASR and ARIO a primary rule that prohibits restriction of freedom per se in cases where the ensuing conduct is not wrongful for R.[152] The primary rule that R violates then could be: 'not to knowingly restrict the freedom of action of another subject in order to cause the violation of the latter subject's obligations'. So, the wrongfulness of the ensuing conduct for P becomes relevant for the establishment of R's responsibility in this scenario, although not

[151] See Argentina's comment to the same effect, ILC, *State Responsibility: Comments and Observations Received from Governments*, UN doc A/CN.4/515 (2001) 53, [3].

[152] The ILC had suggested prohibiting direction and control per se in an earlier draft, Crawford Second Report (n 36) 56: 'Article 27. Assistance or direction to another State to commit an internationally wrongful act. A State which aids or assists, or directs and controls, another State in the commission of an internationally wrongful act is internationally responsible for doing so if: (a) That State does so with knowledge of the circumstances of the internationally wrongful act; and (b) The act would be internationally wrongful if committed by that State'.

because R is responsible for P's internationally wrongful act, as the ILC suggests, but because it forms part of the primary rule incumbent upon R.

As explained with respect to complicity scenarios, the inclusion of a primary norm in the ASR does not cause doctrinal confusion within the law of international responsibility. This is so because it pertains to the delimitation of the provision's scope of application and not to the establishment of responsibility per se. The fact that R is bound by a primary obligation that can be found within the ASR or the ARIO does not mean that its responsibility arises by virtue of exceptional rules.

Therefore, the ILC should have distinguished between two derivative responsibility scenarios. Not on the basis of the intensity of the restriction of freedom exercised, as it finally did, as both direction and control and coercion lead to the derivative attribution of the ensuing conduct; rather, on whether R is bound by the obligation that prohibits P's conduct or not, as in each case the breach element is established differently and with respect to a different act. According to the analysis above, with respect to derivative responsibility scenarios, the progressive development of the law is reflected in the rule that follows:

Derivative Responsibility

1. A State or an International Organisation which restricts the freedom of action of another State or another International Organisation, is responsible for the conduct committed under conditions of restriction of freedom if:
   (a) it had knowledge of these conditions; and
   (b) the ensuing act would have been wrongful if committed by the former subject.
2. A State or an International Organisation which restricts the freedom of action of another State or another International Organisation, is responsible for doing so, if:
   (a) it had knowledge that the ensuing act would violate the latter subject's international obligations; and
   (b) the ensuing act would not have been wrongful if committed by the former subject.

(iii) An Instance of Joint Responsibility?

The last point that calls for clarification is the establishment of P's international responsibility. This problem has troubled academics for two main reasons: the wording of the provisions is silent on the matter;[153] and the ILC has adopted contradictory positions in this respect. The commentaries to Article 47 of the ASR suggest that, of all the Chapter IV provisions, joint and several responsibility

[153] ARIO, Art 19, which stipulates that '[t]his Chapter is without prejudice to the international responsibility of the State or international organization which commits the act in question', does not provide much guidance.

arises only in situations involving direction and control.[154] The ARIO, on the other hand, take this one step further, and in the Article 48 commentaries, the ILC accepts that all provisions on indirect responsibility are instances of joint responsibility.[155] Commentators have also adopted conflicting views on the issue.[156] This confusion is generated mainly due to the lack of a uniform and integrated explanation of how these provisions operate.

The wording of the two derivative responsibility provisions suggests that they should be dealt with separately. Coercion is equated with *force majeure*, by which P's act does not give rise to its responsibility because it is not wrongful. Having this in mind, the ASR commentaries seem to arrive at the correct outcome but with the wrong justification. The ARIO, on the other hand, do not sufficiently explain how P will be responsible without having committed some wrongful conduct. On the contrary, in relation to their respective 'direction and control' provisions, both commentaries suggest that joint responsibility is possible as, in such situations, restriction of freedom is not equated with a circumstance precluding wrongfulness.

However, the preceding analysis suggests that P will not be responsible under the derivative responsibility model as its conduct fails to meet the attribution test. It is maintained that establishing restriction of freedom has legal ramifications for both actors: not only does it trigger R's responsibility, but it also exculpates P. In accordance with the above, Ago notes that the outcome of exclusive, and not joint or parallel, responsibility is dictated by the nature of derivative responsibility and State practice.[157] In this sense, the ILC's view that 'the pertinent provisions ... do not affect attribution of conduct to the [S]tate which is ... under the direction or control, or under coercion' is, I believe, inaccurate.[158] In all likelihood, the ILC probably wanted to emphasise the 'without prejudice' clause of Article 19 of the ARIO, insofar as P's international responsibility is concerned.[159] According to this provision, P's international responsibility may be triggered by virtue of the remaining responsibility provisions. However, as noted earlier, restriction of freedom functions as a trump card that severs any attribution link. Hence, P's conduct cannot be attributable

[154] ASR Comment, 69, [9] and 124, [2]. It should be noted that according to the ILC, joint responsibility will arise when two or more subjects are responsible for the same act, ASR, Art 47 and ARIO, Art 48.

[155] ARIO Comment, 142, [1].

[156] Dominicé, for example, argues – and I agree – that in situations of direction and control, P should be exculpated, Dominicé, 'Attribution of Conduct to Multiple States' (n 114) 284–88. Fry, on the other hand, suggests that even in scenarios of coercion P maintains a certain degree of freedom that could trigger its responsibility, 'Coercion, Causation and the Fictional Elements' (n 143) 639.

[157] Ago Eighth Report (n 100) 26. Dominicé argues that lack of freedom is incompatible with responsibility, 'Attribution of Conduct to Multiple States' (n 114) 288.

[158] ARIO Comment, 100–1, [2].

[159] According to this provision, P's responsibility will arise according to the other responsibility provisions, ibid 109, commentary to Art 19.

to it by virtue of the attribution provisions in Chapter II of either the ASR or the ARIO.

This section on derivative responsibility has aimed to outline a doctrinal approach that is applicable in circumstances involving both coercion and direction and control. The interpretation of both provisions demonstrated that the basis of responsibility and the consequences flowing from the engagement of responsibility are identical. Despite the difference in their scopes of application, it is submitted that this difference does not justify separate provisions.[160] The restriction of P's freedom of action, when done with the knowledge of the circumstances and irrespective of the form it takes (whether de jure/de facto, or of high or low levels of intensity), suffices to trigger the application of the derivative attribution rule. It is the breach element that is established via different routes depending on whether R is bound by the obligation that prohibits the ensuing conduct or not. Based on this distinction, the formulation of ARIO, Articles 15, 16, 59(1) and 60 contradicts the principles of international responsibility identified in Chapter 2 and does not reflect the progressive development of the law.

IV. CONCLUSION

This chapter has focused on some of the ARIO provisions that regulate interaction between member States and the International Organisation of which they are members as independent subjects of international law, most particularly on those provisions that have been slavishly copied from the ASR and form part of ARIO, Chapter IV and Part Five. Their main feature is that they are applicable to scenarios involving three legal actors covering the field of indirect responsibility.

This aspect of the law of international responsibility has troubled both academics and the ILC, as the relevant Articles in the ASR and the ARIO have been characterised as exceptional and abnormal, and have been severely criticised for causing doctrinal inconsistency within the international responsibility framework. More specifically, the ILC held in both the ASR and the ARIO that Chapter IV provisions constitute a fragment in ASR, Article 1 that stipulates international responsibility for own internationally wrongful act as the only basis of international responsibility. This chapter takes issue with the Commission's position that international responsibility in ARIO, Chapter IV arises for another subject's internationally wrongful act and suggests that international responsibility in the provisions at hand arises for own internationally wrongful act. By providing a systemisation of all models that can be found within international responsibility's legal framework, this chapter has suggested that the

[160] Ago had suggested one provision that would capture both scenarios, see the former ASR, Art 28 discussed in Ago Eighth Report (n 100) 26.

provisions exist in a problematic relationship with the premises of the international responsibility edifice.

On the basis of this edifice, I have identified the general principles incorporated in ASR, Articles 1 and 2 and ARIO, Articles 3 and 4. According to these principles, responsibility is triggered upon the presence of an internationally wrongful act, which in its turn is established only when its two constituents are present. An analysis that deviates from these principles is unacceptable, for it violates international legal rules that admit of no exceptions. The main argument running throughout the chapter suggests the separation between the responsibility models found within indirect responsibility, while upholding these fundamental general principles. Arguably, the derivative responsibility and the complicity models, according to which indirect responsibility operates, must be distinguished and kept apart, as they each affect differently the responsibility of the relevant subjects. An explanation of the way in which these models operate has also demonstrated that the real-life scenarios triggering each one are visibly different and clearly identifiable. On the basis of these models, I suggested how the ILC should have formulated the relevant ARIO provisions in order to reflect the development of the law. As is the case with Article 62, redrafting of the ARIO provisions is no longer an option, hence these alternative formulations aim to function as interpretative guidelines for the existing ARIO provisions.

5

Circumvention of Obligations through Member States

I. INTRODUCTION

WHILE MOST INTERNATIONAL Organisations do no more than influence their members' conduct through non-binding acts, some have the power to take decisions that are binding upon them. With increased interaction between various legal subjects in the international arena nowadays, situations of non-conformity are becoming all the more frequent. The (in) famous *Behrami and Saramati* cases,[1] the *Kadi I* and *Kadi II* cases[2] and the *Nada* case[3] are just a few pertinent examples of cases in which the relationship between a State and an International Organisation has been contested and examined.

Until now, international and domestic courts have struggled to develop a consistent approach to deal with such situations, but to no avail. It is symptomatic that in both the *Nada* and *Kadi* cases, the relevant tribunals followed divergent paths with respect to questions of international responsibility. For example, while in its judgment of 14 November 2007, the Swiss Federal Court absolved Switzerland of committing a wrongful act in relation to the implementation of the UN-endorsed targeted sanctions against Mr Nada,[4] the European Court of Human Rights (ECtHR) subsequently held otherwise. What is more, these scenarios have often given rise to problematic situations involving the conflict of obligations, which can arise when an International Organisation

[1] *Behrami and Behrami v France/Saramati v France, Germany and Norway*, Application nos 71412/01 and 78166/01, ECtHR Grand Chamber, Decision of 2 May 2007,(2007) 45 EHRR SE10.

[2] Joined Cases C-402/05P and C-415/05P *Yassin Abdullah Kadi, Al Barakaat International Foundation v Council of the European Union, Commission of the European Communities, United Kingdom of Great Britain and Northern Ireland* (Judgment), European Court of Justice (GC) [2008] ECR I-6351 ('*Kadi I*'); Joined Cases C-584/10P, C-593/10P and C-595/10P *European Commission and United Kingdom of Great Britain and Northern Ireland v Yassin Abdullah Kadi* (Judgment), Court of Justice of the European Union (GC) [2014] All ER (EC) 123 ('*Kadi II*').

[3] *Nada v Switzerland*, Application no 10593/08, ECtHR Grand Chamber, Judgment of 12 September 2012,(2013) 56 EHRR 18.

[4] *Youssef Nada v State Secretariat for Economic Affairs and Federal Department of Economic Affairs*, Case no 1A 45/2007, Swiss Federal Court, 14 November 2007, International Law in Domestic Courts 461 (CH 2007).

adopts a decision that binds its members to undertake actions prohibited by some other international norm. This chapter therefore seeks to identify an approach in such scenarios that could effectively accommodate even extreme situations involving the conflict of obligations.

This chapter will examine how the law of international responsibility regulates this particular type of interaction, which does not have a parallel in inter-State relations. Both binding and non-binding decisions of International Organisations can only be addressed towards their members (be they States or International Organisations).[5] Nevertheless, this does not *ipso facto* suggest that member States and the International Organisation of whom they are members operate in the context of the particular member State-International Organisation relationship in these instances. I will argue to the contrary that member States and International Organisation interact as independent subjects of international law in these cases and thus the responsibility models analysed with respect to indirect responsibility are pertinent to the present analysis.

The International Law Commission (ILC) took these problematic scenarios into account when drafting the Articles on the Responsibility of International Organizations (ARIO), and developed a provision that could function as an effective regulatory formula in such situations. Article 17 of the ARIO reads as follows:

> Circumvention of an international obligation through decisions and authorizations addressed to members
>
> 1. An international organization incurs international responsibility if it circumvents one of its international obligations by adopting a decision binding member States or international organizations to commit an act that would be internationally wrongful if committed by the former organization.
> 2. An international organization incurs international responsibility if it circumvents one of its international obligations by authorizing member States or international organizations to commit an act that would be internationally wrongful if committed by the former organization and the act in question is committed because of that authorization.
> 3. Paragraphs 1 and 2 apply whether or not the act in question is internationally wrongful for the member States or international organizations to which the decision or authorization is addressed.

While commentators uniformly agree that the ILC had to deal with scenarios of binding decisions and authorisations issued from International Organisations

[5] *Legal Consequences for States of the Continued Presence of South Africa in Namibia (South West Africa) Notwithstanding Security Council Resolution 276* (Advisory Opinion) [1971] ICJ Reports 16, 56, [126]. See the interpretation by K Widdows, 'Security Council Resolutions and Non-Members of the United Nations' (1978) 27 *ICLQ* 459, 461–62; P Cahier, 'La Charte des Nations Unies et les Etats tiers' in A Cassese (ed), *Current Problems of International Law* (1975) 81, 99–100.

in the ARIO, the way in which the ILC in fact addressed the matter was not welcomed.[6]

Article 17 was included in the ARIO in order to deal with the problematic situation in which decisions and authorisations of an International Organisation are addressed to its member States (or member International Organisations). It should be noted that it is uncertain whether this provision reflects customary law or whether it was drafted as a progressive development of the law.[7] I agree with Nedeski and Nollkaemper that Article 17 'seems therefore more a proposed ("progressive") development ... than a codification of customary law', mainly due to the scant practice supporting the drafting of this provision.[8] Even if it is not yet *lex lata*, it is submitted here that the provision is of use for international courts and tribunals since it accurately reflects international law's progressive development and through uniform practice can potentially transform to a customary rule.

This chapter explains how the provision under scrutiny fits within the responsibility models analysed in the previous chapter, and how its wording is to be realigned with the context in which it operates. It will be argued that Article 17 operates according to these responsibility models, and hence the following analysis is permeated by a distinction. The first two paragraphs of Article 17 will be dealt with separately, in the two main sections. The third paragraph informs the scope of application of both of the previous paragraphs and will therefore be inherent in the analysis of both sections.

Arguably, there is a strong case to draw parallels between Article 17 and the two indirect responsibility models, derivative responsibility and complicity. With this in mind, the provision will be cut in half: the first part of the provision will be analysed under the rubric of the derivative responsibility model, while the second under that of complicity. Such analogies, it is contended, provide adequate answers to underlying questions of shared, joint or parallel responsibility that were too complicated for the ILC to directly address. Since analysis of the provision as a whole would result in deeper confusion, the disentanglement put forward here is a prerequisite for a legal explanation of Article 17.

[6] See the various criticisms by N Blokker, 'Abuse of the Members: Questions Concerning Draft Article 16 of the Draft Articles on Responsibility of International Organisations' (2010) 7 *IOLR* 35; J d'Aspremont, 'The Articles on the Responsibility of International Organisations: Magnifying the Fissures in the Law of International Responsibility' (2012) 9 *IOLR* 15; N Nedeski and A Nollkaemper, 'Responsibility of International Organisations in Connection with Acts of States' (2012) 9 *IOLR* 33; PJ Kuijper, 'Introduction to the Symposium on Responsibility of International Organisations and of (Member) States: Attributed or Direct Responsibility or Both?' (2010) 7 *IOLR* 9; A Tzanakopoulos, *Disobeying the Security Council: Countermeasures Against Wrongful Sanctions* (OUP, 2011) 45–54.

[7] The Commission did not provide any guidance in this respect. It must be recalled that the ILC proceeds 'on the basis of a composite idea of "codification and progressive development"', and thus it very seldom explains whether a particular provision falls under the rubric of 'codification of existing law' or that of the 'progressive development of the law', ILC, 'Other Decisions and Conclusions of the Commission' (1996) 2(2) *YBILC* 84, 86, [156]–[157].

[8] Nedeski and Nollkaemper, 'Responsibility of International Organisations' (n 6) 41.

Under this prism, the provision fits within the law of international responsibility, accurately depicts the progressive development of the law, and can be useful for international courts. The new understanding of Article 17 proposed here provides an effective approach to the regulation of the perplexing scenarios highlighted above. The application of the provision in UN targeted sanctions cases suggests that Article 17 provides a just and effective regulatory basis for the resolution of conflicts of obligations that have been (to date) too complex for courts to handle. Beyond the legal analysis, I argue that due to the broad range of cases it covers and the practical ramifications that come with its application, Article 17 should be seen as an opportunity to initiate a change in the way International Organisations operate in the international arena.

Therefore, this chapter adopts a contextual approach to analysing Article 17 and emphasises two main points. First, the coherence of the system of rules constructed by the ILC is not compromised through the inclusion of provisions that prima facie appear to fit only awkwardly within the law of international responsibility. Second, the understanding of Article 17 advocated offers a twofold opportunity that courts may grasp: first, an opportunity to effectively tackle cases that have until today troubled them; and second, an opportunity to change the way States and International Organisations interact in the international arena.

In order to proceed with the examination of the provision, it has to be clarified from the outset what is the basis of the member State-International Organisation interaction in Article 17. This provision does not have a precedent in the Articles on State Responsibility (ASR) and one would expect that it pertains to interaction that occurs on the basis of the particular member State-International Organisation relationship. It is true that both decisions and authorisations issued by an International Organisation can only be addressed to their members, and in this sense only a State that has joined the International Organisation can be involved in such a scenario. As the effect of the particular relationship is the shielding of member States by virtue of the personality merging, it should be assessed whether member States act as members when acting upon the normative acts of the International Organisation, that is when the International Organisation circumvents its obligations.

This will be the case only when member States exercise competence that lies with organs of the International Organisation according to the rules of the latter.[9] By the time that the International Organisation either decides that a member State shall perform certain conduct or authorises a member State to perform such conduct, the competence for the performance of this conduct lies with the member State. The latter does not act instead of an organ of the International Organisation in these cases but rather performs the conduct it was

[9] For an analysis of the particular International Organisation-member State relationship, see Chapter 3.

instructed or authorised to commit. For example, Security Council Resolution 1244 authorised UN member States and relevant International Organisations 'to establish the international security presence in Kosovo'.[10] It may be that the United Nations is the International Organisation charged with the preservation of international peace and security and thus it was the sole subject in the international legal order competent to give this authorisation. However, member State conduct taken by virtue of this authorisation is the exercise of competence that lies with the member State, and the same goes with binding decisions. Therefore, the institutional veil does not cover member States in either case; member States and International Organisations do not interact on the basis of the particular member State-International Organisation relationship and the responsibility models identified with respect to indirect responsibility are potentially applicable.

II. ARIO, ARTICLE 17(1) AND THE DERIVATIVE RESPONSIBILITY MODEL

A. Intentional de Jure Restriction of Freedom of Action

This first section here will focus on Article 17 paragraph 1 and the next on paragraph 2 since the two operate on the basis of different responsibility models. If it is accepted that there exists a need to address the possible international responsibility of an International Organisation for conduct of a member State (or a member International Organisation) resulting from the International Organisation's normative acts, the second question that arises is whether the three ARIO provisions copied from the ASR adequately cover the relevant potential scenarios that might arise. Since Article 17 does not have a corresponding ASR provision, it seems that the ILC did not consider that the situation of circumvention was covered by the rest of the ARIO's indirect responsibility provisions. The delimitation of the provision's scope of application is pertinent, in order to address both these issues in turn.

First, it should be assessed whether the scope of application of paragraph 1 of Article 17 totally overlaps with that of other responsibility provisions (a partial overlap would not render it superfluous).[11] The scope of application of paragraph 1 is comprised of two elements: the subjective element of circumvention, and the compliance by the member States with, or the adoption or implementation by the member States of, a binding decision issued by the International Organisation. If these elements adequately place paragraph 1 under the derivative responsibility umbrella of 'knowing restriction of freedom of

[10] UNSC Resolution 1244, UN doc S/RES/1244 (10 June 1999) [7].
[11] ARIO Comment, 106–7, [5]–[7].

action', it needs to be examined whether the provision on 'direction and control' already covers such scenarios, thereby rendering paragraph 1 unnecessary. Coercion as an extreme form of control is unlikely to arise in this context: while the ILC does not exclude this possibility, neither does it offer an example of such a situation.[12]

A binding decision of an International Organisation will only effectively restrict a member State's freedom of action, and hence lead to a situation of control that is relevant for the establishment of derivative responsibility, when it predetermines an exact course of action to be taken by the member State. The decision must leave no choice to a member State but to adopt the relevant specific act through which the violation of the obligation occurs. Of particular importance then is the notion of discretion, because it defines the normative control exercised: the perpetrator of wrongful conduct has no room to manoeuvre at the stage of implementing the normative act, and the decision effectively results in a restriction on the member State's freedom of action.[13] The phrase 'decision binding' under paragraph 1 does not refer to the imposition of a general or abstract obligation, but rather to the imposition of a targeted one.

It is therefore submitted that a normative act defined as a binding decision under the rules of the International Organisation, might not fall within paragraph 1 when it imposes obligations upon member States that do not predetermine an exact course of action. For example, an EU Directive stipulating that member States shall kill all communists within their jurisdictions would not fall under the ambit of paragraph 1, even though it is a binding decision under the rules of the International Organisation. This is so because the Directive does not specify by name the persons to be executed; instead, it falls upon member States to do so. If Greece decides on its own initiative that a certain Mr Stalinides is a communist and therefore must be executed, it cannot be sustained that the European Union has normatively controlled Stalinides' death. Arguably, such scenarios are better accommodated through the prism of paragraph 2, as the degree of discretion afforded to member States brings such scenarios closer to the category of authorisations.[14] It suffices to note at present that not all decisions that create obligations will automatically lead to the application of paragraph 1.

The control link that resurfaces here is not factual or operational; rather, it is of a legal nature.[15] Nevertheless, as stressed earlier, the restriction of the

[12] ibid 106–7, commentary to Art 16.

[13] ibid 107, [7]; M Hirsch, *The Responsibility of International Organizations Toward Third Parties: Some Basic Principles* (Martinus Nijhoff, 1995) 87. Blokker argues that the title of the provision is misleading to the extent that it does not define the decisions under [1] as binding, See Blokker, 'Abuse of the Members' (n 6) 42.

[14] This will become clearer in the discussion of the *Nada* and *OMPI* cases in II B i and III B below, respectively.

[15] Otherwise called 'normative control', Tzanakopoulos, *Disobeying the Security Council* (n 6) 40. Hoffmeister argues, in a different vein, that an International Organisation will exercise normative

member State's freedom of action per se is of interest. This is why the decision must be acted upon. When this ensues, de jure control is equated with de facto control and gives rise to derivative responsibility.

The ILC, however, took the argument one step further, holding that international responsibility will arise for the International Organisation even if a member State does not commit any act. This has troubled both commentators[16] as well as International Organisations who have commented on former drafts of the provision,[17] as it suggests that an International Organisation can bear responsibility for an act that has not yet taken place. The ILC commentaries indicate the justification for this provision is that paragraph 1 will operate as a deterrent for the said International Organisation, because the latter 'would have to refrain from placing its members in the uncomfortable position of either infringing their obligations under the decision or causing the international responsibility of' an International Organisation.[18] While understandable from a practical angle, this justification does not explain from a theoretical point of view how an International Organisation will be responsible for the member State's conduct in the event that such conduct never occurs.

Given that ARIO, Chapter IV provides for international responsibility in connection with the conduct of another, it is hard to conceptualise this bizarre construction. After all, this set of norms presupposes that some conduct actually takes place. The ILC has effectively created a presumption in which the member State's implementing conduct is deemed to have been committed by the time the International Organisation's decision became binding for the member State. In this way, the ILC seemingly equates responsibility arising from the legislation of an obligation, that is, the adoption of a binding decision, with the responsibility arising from the compliance with or implementation of such obligation.

The question to be asked at this point is whether the presumption created by the ILC is sustainable from a theoretical perspective. In more concrete terms: are there good grounds to presume that a member State has acted upon the International Organisation's binding decision, from the time the latter has been

control when it 'governs both the substantive legality of and the available remedies for a measure', F Hoffmeister 'Litigating Against the European Union and its Member States: Who Responds under the ILC's Draft Articles on International Responsibility of International Organisations?' (2010) 21 *EJIL* 723, 742. Hoffmeister adapts in a normative context the interpretation of effective control put forward by Dannenbaum, in T Dannenbaum, 'Translating the Standard of Effective Control into a System of Effective Accountability: How Liability Should be Apportioned for Violations of Human Rights by Member State Troop Contingents Serving as United Nations Peacekeepers' (2010) 51 *Harvard International Law Journal* 113. Dannenbaum suggests that 'effective control … is held by the entity that is best positioned to act effectively and within the law to prevent the abuse in question', ibid 157.

[16] Tzanakopoulos describes this aspect as 'baffling', *Disobeying the Security Council* (n 6) 50.

[17] ILC, *Comments and Observations Received from International Organisations*, UN doc A/CN.4/568 (2006) and Add 1, reproduced in (2006) 2(1) *YBILC* 125, 139–45.

[18] ARIO Comment, 106, [5].

adopted? According to the ILC, the presumption is upheld because the member State is expected to comply with the decision.[19] The ILC's answer is germane to the nature of binding decisions, by which an obligation is created because the enforcer wants it to produce real effects. The obligation demands certain conduct and this restriction of freedom in the implementation of the act is an element that defines the derivative responsibility model. From a legal standpoint, a member State cannot disobey the International Organisation's decision as it is bound to follow certain conduct. Otherwise, the decision will not produce any effects and will be de facto stripped of its binding character. Hence, the presumption is upheld because of the decision's nature. Be that as it may, the triggering of responsibility before actual implementation will in practice seldom take place.[20]

The material standard is thus fulfilled, as is the subjective element. Circumvention is, according to the Commission, an 'intention … to avoid compliance with an international obligation'.[21] At first, this requirement appears to be different from that of 'knowledge' required in situations of derivative responsibility. Indeed, it sets a higher threshold for the application of the provision. However, it should be stressed that knowledge is the minimum subjective requirement for triggering derivative responsibility. As intent presupposes knowledge, an *a minore ad maius* argument has to be accepted whereby the strict formulation (ie intent) is contained within the general rule (ie knowledge).

From a practical perspective, the ILC admitted that circumvention is presumed upon adoption of a binding decision.[22] This presumption renders the inclusion of the subjective element almost superfluous, and it has been pointed out that the requirement of circumvention adds nothing to the provision.[23] Be that as it may, for present purposes the scope of application of paragraph 1 brings the provision within the ambit of derivative responsibility.

However, an interpretation that views paragraph 1 as a provision that deals with derivative responsibility does not automatically render paragraph 1 a provision dealing with direction and control. To this end, the ILC has explicitly distinguished between the two.[24] By virtue of the opposability requirement it incorporates, Article 15 of the ARIO does not cover situations involving the circumvention of obligations in which a member State is not bound by the norm its conduct violates.[25] Paragraph 3 of Article 17 of the ARIO effectively

[19] ibid.

[20] 'If the normative act has not yet been implemented … there is little chance of any real life impact of the act in the "real" world, and responsibility for it, while engaged, may remain theoretical', A Tzanakopoulos, 'Sharing Responsibility for UN Targeted Sanctions', *Ejil:Talk!*, 14 February 2013.

[21] ARIO Comment, 106, [4].

[22] ibid 107, [7]: 'Paragraph 1 assumes that compliance with the binding decision of the international organization necessarily entails circumvention of one of its international obligations'.

[23] Blokker, 'Abuse of the Members' (n 6) 42–43.

[24] ARIO Comment, 103–4, [4]–[5].

[25] ibid.

fills this gap.[26] As noted earlier, this will most likely be the case in circumvention scenarios, in which the International Organisation, in wanting to outsource its obligations to its member States, would rather the member States not be bound thereby. Hence, the overlap between paragraph 1 and the provision on direction and control is only partial. The adoption of binding decisions will amount to direction and control only if the member State is simultaneously bound by the obligation prohibiting the conduct mandated in the aforementioned binding decision.

Article 17's raison d'être within the ARIO makes it desirable to place this analysis into perspective, and to examine the ways in which the interpretation of Article 17 put forward by this chapter would regulate real-life scenarios.

B. Article 17(1) as an Opportunity to Change the Operation of International Organisations

(i) United Nations 1267 Sanctions Regime in the Nada *Case: A Derivative Responsibility Paradigm*

Since the provision operates according to the derivative responsibility model, the International Organisation will be responsible for breaching the norm that prohibits the member State's conduct and the latter will be exculpated. The example utilised here to demonstrate how such a model works in practice is the UN 1267 targeted sanctions regime, under which member States are obligated to sanction individuals and legal entities associated with terrorist activities. This regime, imposed by UN Security Council Resolutions, has recently attracted a lot of attention, especially since it has given rise to situations that have proved difficult for courts to address. Indeed, the obligations imposed by the Security Council are so strictly conditioned that member States are afforded no discretion with respect to their implementation, which effectively restricts the States' freedom of action. These obligations are particularly problematic when they place member States in situations that give rise to conflicting obligations. The latter occur when the course of action mandated by the Security Council Resolution is prohibited by some other pre-existing international obligation incumbent upon the member States. The relevant case law is far from consistent, and courts have adopted contradictory decisions, often with overly-obfuscatory reasoning.

In *Nada,* the applicant who resided in the Italian enclave of Campione in Switzerland was added, along with a number of organisations with which he was associated, to the list maintained by the UN 1267 Sanctions Committee. Pursuant to Security Council Resolution 1390, individuals on the list were subject

[26] Ibid, 108, [14].

to an entry and transit ban.[27] This Security Council Resolution was implemented at the national level through an Ordinance issued by the Swiss Federal Council, effectively confining the applicant to the Campione region. The applicant, in taking the case to the ECtHR, alleged that the travel ban was contrary to his rights under Articles 5 and 8 of the European Convention on Human Rights (ECHR). Although the Court ultimately held Switzerland to be internationally responsible under the ECHR, it struggled to reach this conclusion.

The facts of the case clearly place it within the scope of application of paragraph 1. The normative decision adopted creates legal obligations for Switzerland. Indeed, the language of both Security Council Resolutions 1267 and 1390 is uncontroversial in this respect.[28] The obligation imposed is so tight that Switzerland effectively had no margin of discretion in its implementation.[29] Effectively, the Security Council de jure clearly and intentionally restricted Switzerland's freedom of action. This lack of latitude and discretion as to the sanctions' implementation was noted by judges Malinverni, Bratza, Nicolaou and Yudkivska in their concurring opinions,[30] but the majority of the Court held otherwise.

The ECtHR's entire argument was based on the proposition that, in implementing the Security Council Resolution, the respondent State 'enjoyed some latitude, which was admittedly limited but nevertheless real'.[31] Consequently, the Court considered that Switzerland was free to choose the means for transposing the Resolution into its domestic legal order.[32] In this way, the Court '*pretend[ed]* that the state implementing conduct was *not* conditioned by the UN act', and thereby attempted to disentangle the domestic measure from the international resolution.[33] It is clear that the Court struggled to arrive at this conclusion, leading one to conclude that the ECtHR was intentionally finding a way to review Switzerland's conduct.

While correctly holding that the latitude left to Switzerland was an important feature of the particular case, the judgment's analysis is flawed for two main

[27] UNSC Resolution 1390, UN doc S/RES/1390 (16 January 2002) [2].

[28] UNSC Resolution 1267, UN doc S/RES/1267 (15 October 1999) [4]: '[The SC] [d]ecides further that, in order to enforce paragraph 2 above, all States shall: (a) Deny permission'. And in UNSC Resolution 1390, [2]: '[The SC] [d]ecides that all States shall take the following measures'. In the *Nada* case, the UK Government for example, held in its written submissions to the Court that the Security Council had used 'clear and explicit language' to impose specific measures on States, see *Nada* (n 3) [111].

[29] Tzanakopoulos, 'Sharing Responsibility for UN Targeted Sanctions' (n 20).

[30] *Nada* (n 3) Joint Concurring Opinion of Judges Bratza, Nicolaou and Yudkivska, [5], [7] and [8]. Judge Malinverni in his concurring opinion concludes that 'it is difficult, in my opinion, to sustain the argument that Switzerland had any room for manoeuvre in the present case. The situation here was undeniably one of *mandatory* power and not one of *discretionary* power', *Nada* (n 3) Concurring Opinion of Judge Malinverni, [10].

[31] *Nada* (n 3) [180].

[32] ibid.

[33] Tzanakopoulos, 'Sharing Responsibility for UN Targeted Sanctions' (n 20).

reasons. On the one hand, it attached legal consequences to the wrong type of latitude. There are two different types of latitude evidenced in this example. The first is the latitude granted to Switzerland to choose the means through which the obligation will produce an effect in its national order; and the second is the latitude granted to Switzerland to determine the content of the obligation, and hence define its course of action. As reiterated above, what is of interest in circumstances of legal control is the restriction of action as an outcome, and not the means through which the restriction is imposed. Thus, Switzerland would have determined its own action only if it had the discretion to alter the substance of the UN-imposed obligation. It is only in such a limited circumstance that the national measure can be disentangled from the international one.

In *Nada*, the lack of such discretion was evident. The UN-imposed obligation is one of result: Switzerland must impose a travel ban on Mr Nada. Failure to give effect to this specific outcome inevitably violates the obligation. It is irrelevant, then, as to how Switzerland effectuates the sanction (decree, ordinance or law) since the latitude as to the means of implementation does not in any way affect or negate the obligation to impose the sanctions. Nevertheless, the Court held that the existence of the latitude as to the means of implementation was sufficient to conclude that the national measure was not conditioned by the international one, and to keep them separate.

Secondly, the Court never distinguished between establishment of its jurisdiction and attribution of the said conduct to Switzerland. According to the judgment, the disentanglement between the national and the international measure was a condition for reviewing Switzerland's conduct, because it gave the Court the green light to proceed with the examination of the applicant's claim on the merits.[34] On this basis, the Court correctly asserted that the applicant had rights vis-à-vis Switzerland and hence it could exercise its jurisdiction according to ECHR, Article 1. This, however, is a wholly different matter of whether the measures taken are attributable to Switzerland.[35] And in this lies the second flaw of the judgment.

The Court conflated the two issues of attribution and jurisdiction in its analysis. In examining the jurisdiction *ratione personae* question, it also asserted laconically that the '[t]he alleged violations of the Convention are thus *attributable* to Switzerland'[36] (emphasis added). It is for this reason that the judgment failed to identify the separation between the two measures and, hence, the latitude relevant for attribution purposes. The analysis of derivative responsibility in Chapter 3 suggests that a restriction on the freedom of action of a State, such

[34] *Nada* (n 3) [122].

[35] On the distinction between jurisdiction and attribution see Chapter 6 at III A, and M Milanovic, *Extraterritorial Application of Human Rights Treaties: Law Principles and Policy* (OUP, 2011) 41–53.

[36] *Nada* (n 3) [121]–[122].

as the restriction imposed on Switzerland in this case, is the main reason why Switzerland's conduct is not attributable to that State. Instead, the conduct in question should be attributed to the controlling subject, being in this case the United Nations. The Court and commentators however, found it unthinkable to preclude the attribution of the implementing measures to the physical author, Switzerland.[37]

In the *Al-Dulimi* Chamber judgment before the ECtHR, Judge Sajó expressed a view that vividly demonstrates the confusion surrounding the establishment of jurisdiction and admissibility.[38] In a comparable set of facts, he asserted in his partly dissenting opinion that the application regarding Switzerland's implementing acts of Security Council sanctions should have been declared inadmissible *ratione personae*.[39] He did not advance his syllogism further, but his proposal was perceived by commentators as an argument on attribution: meaning that the acts reviewed by the Court are not attributable to Switzerland, not that the applicant had no rights vis-à-vis Switzerland.[40] The same point of view was advanced by the defendant State and the intervening States before the Court's Grand Chamber in the context of the same proceedings.[41] The Court, in both a Chamber and a Grand Chamber formation, rejected this convoluted argument with a convoluted approach similar to the one it adopted in *Nada*.[42] I believe that this uneasiness results from the absence of a clear formula to be followed in such cases, which in turn encourages judges to rule intuitively.

This main flaw is shared by all judgments dealing with UN targeted sanctions. In the *M & Co* case before the (now defunct) European Commission of Human Rights,[43] in the *Ahmed* case before the UK Supreme Court,[44] and in the *Abdelrazik* case before the Canadian Federal Court,[45] the relevant tribunals hastened to attribute the implementing conduct to the member State as to do otherwise would mean that State responsibility could not be engaged and

[37] ibid [121]; M Milanovic, 'European Court Decides *Nada* v *Switzerland*', *Ejil:Talk!*, 14 September 2012, arguing that the sanctions 'were undoubtedly attributable to Switzerland'.

[38] *Al-Dulimi and Montana Management Inc v Switzerland*, Application no 5809/08, ECtHR, Judgment of 26 November 2013, Partly Dissenting Opinion of Judge Sajó.

[39] ibid.

[40] A Peters, 'Targeted Sanctions after *Affaire Al Dulimi et Montana Management Inc c Suisse*: Is There a Way Out of the Catch-22 for UN Members', *Ejil: Talk!*, 4 December 2013; L Gasbarri, 'Al-Dulimi and the Competing Concepts of International Organizations' (2016) 1 *European Papers* 1119.

[41] *Al-Dulimi and Montana Management Inc v Switzerland*, Application no 5809/08, ECtHR Grand Chamber, Judgment of 21 June 2016, (2016) 55 ILM 1023, [85], [86], [89], [90]. In particular, [86]: 'Switzerland had acted in this matter as a sort of agent of the United Nations … had no control over the addition or deletion of names to or from the sanctions list'.

[42] ibid [93]–[96].

[43] *M and Co v Federal Republic of Germany*, Application no 13258/87, European Commission of Human Rights, Decision of 9 February 1990, 64 Decisions and Reports 138.

[44] *HM Treasury v Ahmed and others*, UK Supreme Court, Judgment of 27 January 2010, 2.

[45] *Abousfian Abdelrazik v Minister of Foreign Affairs and the Attorney General of Canada*, no. T-727-08, Federal Court of Canada, Judgment of 4 June 2009.

the injustice towards the applicant would not be remedied.[46] Thus, judgments rendered in such cases often sacrifice the doctrine in order to deliver justice.

The same slip is discernible in the reasoning of the Court of Justice of the European Union (CJEU) and its precursor (the European Court of Justice (ECJ)) in both *Kadi* judgments.[47] The applicant's saga before EU judicial institutions was triggered by EU acts implementing Security Council sanctions against him by virtue of the 1267 regime.[48] The reasoning of *Kadi I*, reaffirmed in *Kadi II*, held that the UN-imposed obligation 'leaves the Members of the United Nations *a free choice among the various possible models for transposition of those resolutions into their domestic legal order*'[49] (emphasis added). As in *Nada*, discretion was invented by the Court,[50] but minor importance was attached to this consideration.

The disassociation between the two measures was essentially rooted in the disassociation between the EU and international legal orders. So long as the primacy of a Security Council Resolution is not called into question at the international level, EU institutions are required to review the lawfulness of any EU measures implementing such Security Council acts irrespective of their nature.[51]

[46] The argument that 'each jurisdiction decides questions on responsibility very much against the procedural background of available respondents' is articulated in Hoffmeister, 'Litigating Against the European Union' (n 15) 738.

[47] See n 2 above. Each judgment by the higher EU court was preceded by a judgment from the lower General Court of the EU (previously named Court of First Instance). However, as these rulings were overruled by the subsequent CJEU judgments and so as not to complicate the matter further, they will not be examined here.

[48] The EU measures challenged by the applicant before the ECJ and the CJEU were the Council Common Position 2001/931/CFSP (27 December 2001) on the application of specific measures to combat terrorism [2001] OJ L344/93; and Council Regulation (EC) 2580/2001 (27 December 2001) on specific restrictive measures directed against certain persons and entities with a view to combating terrorism [2001] OJ L344/70 and corrigendum, [2010] OJ L52/58. For a complete review of the complex history of the case and further discussion see PJ Cardell, D French and N White, 'Kadi v Council of the European Union' (2009) 58 *ICLQ* 229; A Johnston, 'Frozen in Time? The ECJ Finally Rules on the Kadi Appeal' (2009) 68 *Cambridge Law Journal* 1; L Palombella, 'The Rule of Law Beyond the State: Failures, Promises and Theory' (2009) 7 *International Journal of Constitutional Law* 442; P de Sena and Ch Vitucci, 'The European Courts and the Security Council: Between Dédoublement Fonctionnel and Balancing of Values' (2009) 20 *EJIL* 193; G de Burca, A Nollkaemper and I Canor, 'The European Courts and the Security Council: Between Dédoublement Fonctionnel and Balancing of Values: Three Replies to Pasquale De Sena and Maria Chiara Vitucci' (2009) 20 *EJIL* 853; P de Sena and C Vitucci, 'The European Courts and the Security Council: Between Dédoublement Fonctionnel and Balancing of Values: A Rejoinder to Gráinne de Burca, André Nollkaemper and Iris Canor' (2009) 20 *EJIL* 889; A Reinisch, 'Should Judges Second-Guess the UN Security Council' (2009) 35 *IOLR* 257; A Tzanakopoulos, '*Kadi* Showdown: Substantive Review of (UN) Sanctions by the ECJ', *Ejil:Talk!*, 19 July 2013.

[49] *Kadi I* (n 2) [298].

[50] It has been suggested that the ECtHR and CJEU are influencing one another and their interaction, under the looming accession of the EU to the ECHR, has been instrumental to ensure the effectiveness of the protection of due process standards in the European multilevel human rights architecture, V Sanxhaktari, 'The Implications of the Accession Agreement of the EU to the ECHR' (2014) 5 *Mediterranean Journal of Social Sciences* 135, 135–36.

[51] *Kadi II* (n 2) [67]. On this basis the ECJ was criticised as introvert and overly narrowly dualist, see P Šturma and V Bílková, 'Targeted Anti-Terrorist Sanctions and Their Implications for

The overall relationship between two legal orders, the one imposing the obligation and the other executing it, is of no relevance for attribution purposes. What is important, though, is the relationship between the act reviewed by the court and the subject that commits this conduct in the real world. If this relationship is governed by conditions of impairment of freedom, then the conduct is not attributable to the subject at hand.[52] In the *Kadi* case, the EU had no discretion when implementing the UN acts that imposed the listing of Mr Kadi in the relevant list of the Sanctions Committee. Hence, the EU's international responsibility does not arise in this instance, as no act can be attributed to this International Organisation.

It should be noted that the analysis here does not preempt the question of the standard of review applicable by EU courts in reviewing UN-imposed sanctions. This was the main issue discussed by the CJEU in both *Kadi* judgments.[53] This standard has to do with the different question of whether the EU normative acts were in breach of the EU's international obligations and thus it pertains to the breach element. I argue here that the CJEU should not have examined this question in the first place, for reasons germane to the attribution element. The Court should have pointed the finger at the United Nations by declaring the measures reviewed by the Court attributable to the world organisation.

The approach advanced in this chapter saves the doctrine by upholding an applicable formula consistent with the overall framework of international responsibility, which simultaneously resolves the impossible norm conflict situation faced by member States in such circumstances. In the present case, for instance, Switzerland's implementation of the UN sanctions would violate its concomitant obligations under the ECHR. On the other hand, failure to implement the travel ban runs counter to the obligation imposed by the UN. According to the present understanding of Article 17(1), a member State will be exculpated when implementing an obligation imposed on it by another subject. Thus, from a responsibility perspective, member States clearly have the option of adopting the course of action that incurs no legal consequences. Further, from the perspective of an International Organisation, the latter will think twice when imposing upon member States obligations that will give rise to its international responsibility.

In this way, the present approach effectively tackles complex situations of non-conformity as presented in *Kadi* or *Bosphorus*,[54] which have long troubled courts and commentators. In these cases, the implementation of targeted

International Law Normative and Institutional Coherency' in A Constantinides and N Zaikos (eds), *The Diversity of International Law, Essays in Honour of Professor Kalliopi K. Koufa* (MNP, 2009) 217ff.

[52] See the analysis of the derivative responsibility model in Chapter 4.

[53] Tzanakopoulos, '*Kadi* Showdown' (n 48).

[54] *Bosphorus Hava Yollari Turizm v Ireland*, Application no 45036/98, ECtHR Grand Chamber, Judgment of 30 June 2005, (2006) 42 EHRR 1.

sanctions passed through the intermediate EU level, and the obligations on UN member States already had direct effect in the relevant EU national legal orders by the time the EU issued a regulation in this respect. Effectively, what happened in these instances was the disassociation of the obligation from its source, not at the national level, as was the case in *Nada*, but at the regional level. This does not, however, alter the basic outcome, in that the imposition of a UN obligation is, in one way or another, still binding upon member States. The fact that the imposition of the sanction finally became binding in the national order through one or countless levels of ordinances, or none at all, makes no difference insofar as the source of the obligation is identifiable. Indeed, the UN normatively controls both the EU and its member States when it imposes sanctions upon the latter, sufficing to trigger the UN's international responsibility.

At this point, a practical caveat must be considered: the engagement of UN responsibility (as with that of other International Organisations) remains, to a large extent, theoretical, as there exists to date no tribunal competent to rule upon it. The adoption of the approach put forward here, then, becomes counter-intuitive for domestic and regional tribunals that want to reverse any injustice arising in respect of an applicant. Since such courts cannot rule on UN actions, it inevitably falls upon member States to compensate the victim of a targeted sanction.

It has been argued that a way to overcome this lack of adjudicatory mechanism and implement International Organisations' responsibility is through decentralised pressure.[55] The *Kadi* case provides a pertinent example in this respect. After the ECJ's judgment indicated that the UN was responsible for the implementation of 1267 sanctions, the Security Council introduced the independent and impartial 'Office of the Ombudsperson'. Under this system, the UN was forced to introduce a delisting procedure, through which individuals who have been listed and who are therefore subject to 1267 sanctions can seek recourse.[56]

The premise of this argument lies in the fact that International Organisations value their international image and reputation, which is certainly true. An International Organisation with a tarnished public image will lack legitimacy in the eyes of its member States, for whom it will undoubtedly be easier to disobey the diminished decisions of the International Organisation.[57] It is thus in the best interests of International Organisations to take into account the reactions of all international players, including international and domestic courts,[58] and change potentially problematic conduct.

[55] Tzanakopoulos, 'Sharing Responsibility for UN Targeted Sanctions' (n 20).

[56] ibid.

[57] K Daugirdas, 'Reputation and the Responsibility of International Organizations' (2014) 25 *EJIL* 991.

[58] Arguing that domestic courts are in fact players in the international arena, see A Tzanakopoulos, 'Domestic Courts in International Law: The International Judicial Function of National Courts' (2011) 34 *Loyola of Los Angeles International and Comparative Law Review* 133.

An opportunity for change in the operation of International Organisations is provided by the application of Article 17 in situations involving conflicts of obligations. If courts were to adopt the course of action proposed in this chapter, they would find the Security Council responsible for injustices done to victims of the sanction. As the UN would increasingly be found to be responsible, it is safer to assume that a change may take place. However, change will not come without the concomitant sacrifice. A concession must be made: until forced to change, the Security Council would operate as an emperor *legibus solutus* and justice will most probably be sacrificed to save doctrine. Nevertheless, previous experience has demonstrated that political communities do not often tolerate unrestrained power for long, and there is no reason this should differ for the international community.

As indicated above, targeted sanctions often confront UN member States with a 'lose or lose' situation, in which it seems impossible to uphold both doctrine and justice at the same time in the present international legal order. While doctrine can be described as a consistent legal pattern or approach that promotes legal certainty, justice is the alleviation of injustices towards victims. Finally, it should be noted that the relationship between these two elements is causal: justice can never be served through inconsistent and obfuscatory reasoning. Thus, the proposal of a legal approach that would fill this gap certainly indicates that steps are being taken in the right direction. Once adopted by courts, the proposed approach would lay the basis for exerting pressure on International Organisations, and de facto implement their responsibility by forcing them to change.

(ii) A Special Provision for the European Union?

Like Security Council-generated law, EU-imposed legislation is implemented almost exclusively through EU Member States.[59] Thus, international lawyers dealing with the particular circumstances presented by the EU have suggested that the EU is an International Organisation of a *sui generis* nature which deserves special treatment in relation to situations involving legal control.[60] It has been argued that the EU constitutes 'a legal order of its own, with comprehensive legislative and treaty-making powers, deriving from transfers of competences from the member States to the Community level'.[61] According to the European

[59] Declaration (No 19) on the Implementation of Community Law, Annexed to the Final Act of the Treaty on European Union (TEU) done at Maastricht on 7 February 1992 [1992] OJ C191/1 95. TEU, Art 4(3) provides: 'The Member States shall take any appropriate measure, general or particular, to ensure fulfilment of the obligations arising out of the Treaties or resulting from the acts of the institutions of the Union'.

[60] This was pointed out for the first time as early as 2003, UNGA 58th Session, *Sixth Committee, Summary Record of the 14th Meeting*, UN doc A/C.6/58/SR.14 (2003) [13].

[61] A Sari and RA Wessel, 'International Responsibility for EU Military Operations: Finding the EU's Place in the Global Accountability Regime' in B Van Vooren, S Blockmans and J Wouters (eds), *The Legal Dimension of Global Governance: What Role for the EU?* (OUP, 2013) 126, 130.

Commission, such transfers of competence 'ha[ve] implications for the freedom of European Union member States to act in the international sphere'.[62]

This is why both the EU, in its comments on the drafting of the ARIO,[63] as well as commentators[64] have argued that Member State measures adopted pursuant to the implementation of exclusive EU competences should be attributed solely to the International Organisation and engage the latter's international responsibility. From a policy standpoint, the EU wishes to assume responsibility for breaches arising from actions taken pursuant to EU law in judicial proceedings (World Trade Organization (WTO), ECtHR, International Tribunal for the Law of the Sea (ITLOS)) in order to encourage respect for the supremacy of EU law by Member States even where compliance results in breaches of other legal regimes.[65] The European Commission suggested that the ILC should either incorporate in the ARIO special attribution rules, or a special exception or saving clause in order to address the distinct features of the EU and similar International Organisations.[66] In the same vein, commentators have also suggested the inclusion in the ARIO of a special attribution provision linked to the operation of a regional economic integration organisation, such as the EU.[67]

The ILC, however, has not taken a clear-cut stance on this matter. Even though it has not decided to propose a special rule for the attribution of Member States' conduct to the EU in scenarios of normative control, it did somewhat open a

[62] ILC, *Responsibility of International Organisations, Comments and Observations Received from International Organisations*, UN doc A/CN.4/637 (14 February 2011) 37.

[63] ibid.

[64] Hoffmeister, 'Litigating Against the European Union' (n 15) 746; S Talmon, 'Responsibility of International Organisations: Does the European Community Require Special Treatment?' in M Ragazzi (ed), *International Responsibility Today, Essays in Memory of Oscar Schachter* (Brill, 2005) 405; P Eeckhout, 'The EU and its Member States in the WTO: Issues of Responsibility' in L Bartels and F Ortino (eds), *Regional Trade Agreements and the WTO Legal System* (OUP, 2006) 453–55; E Paasivirta and PJ Kuijper, 'Does One Size Fit All? The European Community and the Responsibility of International Organisations' (2005) 36 *Netherlands Yearbook of International Law* 169.

[65] A Sarvarian, 'The EU Accession to the ECHR and the Law of International Responsibility' in V Kosta, N Skoutaris and V Tzevelekos (eds), *The EU Accession to the ECHR* (Hart, 2014) 91. For an analysis of the latest practice concerning the EU's international responsibility, see C Contartese, 'Competence-Based Approach, Normative Control and the International Responsibility of the EU and Its Member States: What Does Recent Practice Add to the Debate? (2018) 15 *IOLR* (forthcoming).

[66] The EU falls within the category of 'regional economic integration organisations'. An International Organisation will belong to this category if it 'is composed of several sovereign states, and to which its Member States have transferred competence over a range of matters, including the authority to make decisions binding on its Member States in respect of those matters', Talmon, 'Responsibility of International Organisations' (n 64) note 58.

[67] Hoffmeister, for example, proposes the following rule: 'The conduct of a State that executes the law or acts under the normative control of a regional economic integration organization may be considered an act of that organization under international law, taking account of the nature of the organization's external competence and its international obligations in the field where the conduct occurred', Hoffmeister, 'Litigating Against the European Union' (n 15) 746.

back-door for such an exception by accepting such a rule as a *lex specialis* under ARIO, Article 64. The commentaries to this provision do not clearly stipulate whether such a rule has arisen specifically with respect to the EU; rather, they simply cite the relevant case law, which is indeterminate, do not take the argument further, and thus leave the matter in limbo.

A relevant discussion has ensued from the attempted accession of the EU to the European Convention on Human Rights. Negotiations about the modalities of the accession started in July 2010 and ended in April 2013 with the presentation of a draft agreement that was subsequently endorsed by the Council of Europe's Steering Committee on Human Rights ('Accession Agreement').[68] The Accession Agreement sets up a complex co-respondent mechanism in Article 3. According to this mechanism, both the EU and its Member State(s) can potentially be parties in ECtHR cases where it may not be clear whether it is the EU which is responsible for the alleged human rights violation, or a particular Member State which is implementing EU law or taking a decision connected to EU law.

The Accession Agreement also provides for particular responsibility rules that will regulate the establishment of international responsibility in such cases. Notably, Article 1(4), inserted under EU initiative,[69] dictates that conduct by an EU Member State in implementation of EU law will be attributable to this particular State. This new approach taken by the EU constitutes a major departure from the EU stance in the ARIO and it is difficult to see what triggered this change of heart.[70] Further, Article 3(7) stipulates a default rule on joint responsibility (unless the Court decides otherwise) in cases where the co-respondent mechanism is in effect. The Accession Agreement never came into force, however, as the CJEU in its 2/13 Opinion found it incompatible with EU law and thus stalled the process.[71] Since the rules incorporated therein are not themselves

[68] The draft Agreement and its Explanatory Report can be found in Council of Europe, *Fifth Negotiation Meeting Between the CDDH Ad Hoc Negotiation Group and the European Commission on the Accession of the Europena Union to the European Convention on Human Rights. Final Report to the CDDH*, Council of Europe doc 47+1 (2013)008rev2 (10 June 2013) Appendix I and Appendix 5. For a detailed account of most international law issues arising from the accession, see Kosta et al, *The EU Accession to the ECHR* (n 65).

[69] Council of Europe, *Third Negotiation Meeting Between the CDDH Ad Hoc Negotiation Group and the European Commission on the Accession of the European Union to the European Convention on Human Rights: Meeting Report*, Council of Europe doc 47+1(2012)R02 (9 November 2012) 2, [4].

[70] G Gaja, 'The "Co-respondent Mechanisms" According to the Draft Agreement for the Accession of the EU to the ECHR' in V Kosta, N Skoutaris and V Tzevelekos (eds), *The EU Accession to the ECHR* (Hart, 2014) 341, 343.

[71] Opinion 2/13, Accession of the European Union to the European Convention for the Protection of Human Rights and Fundamental Freedoms, ECJ (18 December 2014) ECLI:EU:C:2014:2454. For a thoughtful criticism of the opinion, see P Eeckhout, 'Opinion 2/13 on EU Accession to the ECHR and Judicial Dialogue: Autonomy or Autarky' (2015) 38 *Fordham International Law Journal* 955.

binding, it is only pertinent to ask whether they reflect the emerging special responsibility rules regarding the EU as per ARIO, Article 64.

The explanatory report to the Accession Agreement sheds light on the reasoning behind the drafting of the relevant provisions. Article 1[4] was drafted as such 'for the sake of consistency' with EU law that allegedly provides for default attribution to Member States when they implement EU law.[72] Nevertheless, rules of an International Organisation pertaining to its relation with its member States are of an internal nature and cannot affect the functioning of the general regime on responsibility.[73] Respectively, Article 3[7] was perceived as a 'normal' consequence deriving from the special features of the EU legal system.[74] Thus, both responsibility rules were drafted on the basis of internal rules and practices of the EU and not on account of sources pertaining to the establishment of international responsibility of the EU and/or its Member States. It is safe to assume, then, that they provide limited guidance as to any emerging *lex specialis* rules under ARIO, Article 64.

The interpretation of derivative responsibility provisions that has been advanced in the previous chapter however, suggests that the present formulation of the ARIO sufficiently addresses the issue of EU legal control over its Member States. The latent rule on derivative attribution, put into operation in situations involving legal control, suggests that the special provision advocated by the EU and relevant commentators is already implicit within the ARIO. In other words, the special provision sought by the EU under Article 64 is not 'special' but rather already implicit within ARIO, Articles 15 and 17(1).

This militates against the inclusion of a special provision for regional economic integration organisations in the Articles. The approach taken here is based on the ensuing restriction on freedom of action. The fact that EU Member States have *a priori* abolished their competences in favour of the EU does not render the latter a *sui generis* International Organisation, at least with respect to the application of the ARIO. Nor does it justify special treatment, for the outcome of decisions taken at the EU level is similar to that of obligations imposed by the Security Council, resulting in the restriction of Member States' freedom of action.

[72] Explanatory Report (n 68) [23]. It is debatable whether EU law indeed provides for such attribution rules, J d' Aspremont, 'A European Law of International Responsibility? The Articles on the Responsibility of International Organizations and the European Union' in V Kosta, N Skoutaris and V Tzevelekos (eds), *The EU Accession to the ECHR* (Hart, 2014) 75, 80.

[73] ILC, *Report of the International Law Commission on the Work of Its 23rd Session, 26 April–30 July 1971*, UN doc A/8410/REV.1 (1971), reproduced in (1971) 2(1) *YBILC* 275, 287–88; d' Aspremont, 'A European Law of International Responsibility?' (n 72) 80–81; C Ahlborn, 'The Rules of International Organizations and the Law of International Responsibility' (2011) 8 *IOLR* 397, 428.

[74] Explanatory Report (n 68) [62].

III. ARIO, ARTICLE 17(2) AND THE COMPLICITY MODEL

A. Authorisation as Facilitation

The second paragraph of Article 17 deals with the responsibility of an International Organisation for 'authorizing member States or international organizations to commit an act that would be internationally wrongful if committed by the former organization'. Two elements define this second paragraph: the authorisation addressed to a member State (or a member International Organisation), and the subjective element of circumvention found also in paragraph 1. Unlike binding decisions, authorisations leave the member States a margin of discretion in the implementation of the normative act, in that the member States' conduct is not predetermined and conditioned by the authorisation. The ILC considered that this was reason enough to keep the two paragraphs of Article 17 separate.[75] It is the link between the authorisation and the ensuing internationally wrongful act that triggers responsibility in Article 17(2), hence it is safe to assume that it has been perceived as a scenario of responsibility for participation in the internationally wrongful act of another.

The original drafting of paragraph 2 also comprised responsibility for recommendations; however, this was excluded from the final draft. Strictly speaking, recommendations lack any normative weight, as they only exert influence on members and hardly meet the 'significant contribution' criterion set by the ILC for cases of aid or assistance.[76] It would be safe to assume, then, that recommendations are similar to incitement, a lawful influence in international law, especially as they do not restrict the freedom of the addressee in the sense of creating binding obligations. All International Organisations stressed in their written observations to the Commission that this overly broad feature of paragraph 2 would lead to unjust outcomes for the recommending International Organisation.[77] The Special Rapporteur himself recognised that no clear examples exist in practice to lend support to such a provision.[78] Thus, the part of the provision concerning international responsibility for recommendations was shelved, in light of its lack of tenability from both a theoretical and practical perspective.

[75] ARIO Comment, 107, [7].

[76] ILC, *Report of the International Law Commission on the Work of its 61st Session (4 May–5 June and 6 July–7 August 2009)*, UN doc A/64/10 (2009), reproduced in (2009) 2(2) *YBILC* 1, 44 [8]–[9].

[77] See the observations of the IMF in ILC, *Responsibility of International Organizations: Comments and Observations Received from International Organizations*, UN doc A/CN.4/582 (2007), reproduced in (2007) 2(1) *YBILC* 17, 24–25; and of Interpol in ILC, *Responsibility of International Organizations: Comments and Observations Received from International Organizations*, UN doc A/CN.4/568 (2006) and Add 1, reproduced in (2006) 2(1) *YBILC* 125, 139–42.

[78] G Gaja, *Third Report on Responsibility Of International Organizations*, UN doc A/CN.4/553 (2005) ('Gaja Third Report'), reproduced in (2005) 2(1) *YBILC* 7, 13–14, [27]–[28].

While authorisations do not create legal obligations, they were also distinguished from recommendations in that their normative calibre is fundamentally different. According to the ILC, authorisations delegate, confer or otherwise provide 'certain functions to the member or members concerned so that they would exercise these functions instead of the organization'.[79] In essence, the member State is vested with functions and competences it did not previously hold. However, the crucial aspect of an authorisation is that it affects the legal status of its addressee.

If the functions conferred on a member State are consistent with its other international obligations, authorisations affect the member State's legal status from a perspective that is the opposite of binding decisions, namely, they take away the wrongfulness of certain conduct.[80] A clear-cut example is that of Security Council authorisations concerning the use of force. The UN organ decides that the obligation deriving from UN Charter, Article 2(4) will not apply in a particular instance. Since no other international norm prohibits member State conduct in this instance, certain conduct that would prima facie be unlawful becomes lawful for member States pursuant to that authorisation. Such preclusion of wrongfulness is most common when an authorisation is provided, and it is evident that in such cases the authorisation will have legal consequences for the members of an International Organisation.

Things get more complicated when the functions delegated to or conferred on a member State do not have the effect of rendering the member State's conduct lawful. This will be the case if the functions conferred by the authorisation cannot 'put aside' the application of all norms that prohibit the conduct at hand. In the imaginary scenario in which the use of force would be prohibited by another international norm (that is, apart from Article 2(4)) outside the UN context, a relevant Security Council authorisation would not *ipso facto* render State conduct lawful. In this case, too, the legal position of a member State would be essentially different as a result of the authorisation: only one international norm, not two, would prevent them from using force after the authorisation has become effective. While this scenario will be further scrutinised below, it suffices to note here that in both scenarios there are good grounds for distinguishing authorisations from recommendations, as the former effectively alters the legal position of their addressee by writing off legal obligations.

As noted, the fulfilment of the material standard of aid or assistance will always be case-specific. However, the conferral of a certain competence to perform a particular act is presumed to be a form of facilitation in every case: it is certainly easier to perform an act for which a green light has been given, even if it does not necessarily render the conduct lawful. However, this is insufficient to place paragraph 2 under the umbrella of the complicity model highlighted above. To this end, it will be examined if the established nexus between member States

[79] ARIO Comment, 107, [8].
[80] Blokker, 'Abuse of the Members' (n 6) 45.

and International Organisation in cases of authorisations under paragraph 2 fulfils the elements of causation and intent analysed in Chapter 4.

The International Organisation's authorisation will facilitate member State conduct when it causally contributes to its commission. The wording of the provision clearly stipulates the presence of such a direct, causal relationship when it states that a member State's act must be committed 'because of that authorization'. According to the commentaries, the authorisation should play a role in determining member State conduct.[81] This connection does not render the International Organisation either co-author in the commission of the act or the manipulator of member State conduct. Therefore, the causality established falls below the maximum threshold of co-authorship in the complicity model and outside the derivative responsibility model as no targeted legal obligation is created through authorisations. Hence, there is no ensuing restriction on a member State's freedom of action.

The connection between member State and International Organisation will satisfy the 'knowingly intend to facilitate' element if it surpasses the minimum threshold of knowing intention. It is here that the element of circumvention, which implies an intention to avoid compliance, becomes relevant. The subjective element in para 2 operates differently from para 1 because its presence is not presumed; rather, it must be proven in every case as 'discretion … does not imply circumvention'.[82] This may incommode the provision's use before a court, as a victim may face potentially insurmountable difficulties in proving the subjective element.[83] Nevertheless, the subjective requirement remains indispensable for the operation of the complicity model, as was explained in the previous chapter.

If paragraph 2 falls within the scope of application of the complicity model, it has to be assessed whether it overlaps with Article 14 of the ARIO on 'aid or assistance'. As mentioned, an authorisation will on some occasions eradicate the wrongful nature of the member State's act: that is, when the conduct authorised is not prohibited by another norm of international law. This is explicitly stipulated in paragraph 3 of Article 17. This feature, however, is in stark contrast to an essential prerequisite for the application of ARIO, Article 14, namely, the wrongfulness of the main act. Paragraph 2 captures situations involving the participation in a lawful act, whereas the provision on 'aid or assistance' applies only in situations involving participation in an internationally wrongful act. Therefore, the overlap between the two provisions is only partial and the inclusion of paragraph 2 is clearly justified.

While the eradication of wrongfulness is a hard pill to swallow, this aspect of paragraph 2 makes perfect sense if one bears in mind the operation of authorisations. In such situations, the International Organisation has aided or assisted

[81] ARIO Comment, 107, [11].
[82] ibid 107, [7].
[83] Nedeski and Nollkaemper, 'Responsibility of International Organisations' (n 6) 48.

the commission of an act by altering the nature of the act itself: the authorisation in this case *is* the facilitation. The conduct is prima facie wrongful, but its nature has been altered due to the facilitation. Thus, assisting the commission of lawful conduct is not permitted when the assistance rendered consists solely in depriving the conduct of its wrongful character.

The scenario envisioned by paragraph 2 is peculiar to the functioning of International Organisations, and this norm arguably has a raison d'être within the ARIO. In the framework of State responsibility, such a scenario did not present itself, because no State has the relevant competence to alter the legal position of another State. From all of the foregoing, it is evident that the inclusion of this paragraph in the ARIO fills an existing gap, as it does not overlap totally with Article 14 and it regulates a situation that is particularly common in the modern operation of International Organisations.

B. Article 17(2) Applied in the UN 1373 Sanctions Regime

Paragraph 2 of Article 17 operates according to the complicity model, under which an International Organisation will be independently responsible for the authorisation, and the member State's direct responsibility for the main act will arise only if the authorisation does not alter the wrongful nature of the member State's conduct. On the contrary, if the authorisation is the element that renders the main act lawful, a member State cannot be responsible for the commission of lawful conduct.

Considering a real-life application of the provision is useful. As such, this section of the chapter will focus on the UN targeted sanctions 1373 regime as implemented in the *OMPI* case, in order to put paragraph 2 to the test.[84] Like the 1267 sanctions regime, the 1373 sanctions regime has been considered by regional and domestic courts alike.[85] Further, the applicable UN Resolution does not have the effect of rendering member State conduct lawful. Thus, member State responsibility is still in play, making the circumstances being scrutinised more interesting and complex. Finally, it is appropriate to formulate a clear methodology for the resolution of these situations, given that existing case law on the matter has not yet formulated one.

The facts of the present case resemble those of *Nada*, discussed above. Paragraph 1 lit (c) of Security Council Resolution 1373 provides that all States must freeze without delay funds, assets or economic resources of persons and

[84] Case T-228/02 *Organisation des Modjahedines du Peuple d'Iran v Council of the European Union*, Court of First Instance, Judgment of 12 December 2006, [2006] ECR II-4665 ('*OMPI*').

[85] See eg *A, K, M, Q and G v HM Treasury*, Case No PTA 13, 14, 15, 17, 19/2007, High Court of Justice, Queen's Bench Division, Administrative Court, Judgment of 24 April 2008, [2008] EWHC 869 (Admin).

entities associated with terrorist activities.[86] The Resolution does not specify by name the persons, groups and entities subject to these measures, leaving it incumbent on member States to fill this gap. The Resolution was implemented at the European Community (now EU) level through a Common Position and a Regulation that was directly applicable in all member States. These normative acts established a list of persons and entities associated with terrorism, which was regularly updated by European Council decisions.

The applicant's name was added to the list on 2 May 2002 and its assets were frozen. Subsequently, OMPI brought an action before the Court of First Instance (CFI) seeking annulment of those normative acts, arguing that its right to a fair trial had been violated in that it had had no opportunity to effectively question the asset freeze or to defend its rights before a court. The CFI indeed found a violation of the right to a fair hearing and quashed the sanction.

The obligation imposed on member States under the present regime does not amount to the restriction of their freedom of action and can clearly be distinguished from the obligation imposed under the 1267 regime. The critical aspect of the case, as the CFI noted,[87] was that UN members are free to direct the implementation of the sanction at will. In this case, the Security Council did not compel the EU to freeze OMPI's assets in particular: it was the regional organisation itself which, on its own initiative, decided to sanction that specific entity. It is one thing to oblige members to 'implement a sanction towards OMPI or Mr Nada' and quite another to compel them to freeze the assets of whomsoever they deem necessary in the context of combating terrorism. In the first case, the obligation imposed clearly and unequivocally predetermines the wrongful act, while in the second it does not.[88] This latter type of obligation does not effectively condition the implementing conduct, as members have real latitude in defining the outcome of their conduct. Thus, the Court correctly disentangled the international from the EU implementing measure and went on to review the latter on its merits.[89]

In such instances, the Security Council is in fact assisting members to target those entities they wish to target. This more closely resembles an authorisation than a Security Council-imposed obligation necessitating certain conduct.[90]

[86] UNSC Resolution 1373, UN doc S/RES/1373 (28 September 2001) [1]: '[The Security Council] Acting under Chapter VII of the Charter of the United Nations ... Decides that all States shall: ... (c) Freeze without delay funds and other financial assets or economic resources of persons who commit, or attempt to commit, terrorist acts or participate in or facilitate the commission of terrorist acts; of entities owned or controlled directly or indirectly by such persons'.

[87] *OMPI* (n 84) [101]–[102].

[88] The two regimes correspond to the distinction put forward by Special Rapporteur Crawford in an earlier draft of the ASR, which was dropped at the final reading of the Articles, see J Crawford, *Second Report on State Responsibility*, UN doc A/CN.4/498 (1999) and Add 1–4, reproduced in (1999) 2(1) *YBILC* 3, 20–27.

[89] *OMPI* (n 84) [107].

[90] As clarified by the ILC, '[t]he principle expressed in paragraph 2 also applies to acts of an international organization which may be defined by different terms but present a similar character to an authorization as described above', ARIO Comment, 107, [9].

The EU and its Member States are obliged to investigate the association of individuals or entities with terrorism, and only upon positive identification of such associations are they bound to implement the sanctions envisioned in paragraph 1 lit (c). Thus, the EU and Member States would have complied with their 1373 obligations even where they had undertaken a fruitless investigation that did not result in the implementation of any sanctions. This example demonstrates that, in essence, the role of the UN under the 1373 regime is to give members the green light to impose sanctions by vesting in them the relevant competence. From this perspective, the facts of the present case and of all sanctions implemented under the 1373 regime are such that they can be placed within the scope of application of paragraph 2.

The complicity model provides a clear approach to be followed, which promotes legal certainty. The United Nations will be responsible for assisting the freezing of OMPI's assets, while the EU assumes responsibility for its own act. The troubling aspect of this scenario is that EU conduct remains wrongful despite the lawful transfer of functions. The conduct of the two responsibilities runs in parallel, and not jointly, seeing as they arise with respect to different acts. Consequently, this analysis demonstrates that the CFI's approach, though correct, is of limited utility. It would be a welcome change if courts, in analogous cases, were to apply the complicity model in the manner laid out above.

IV. CONCLUSION

Based on legal analysis, the operation of Article 17 of the ARIO within the context of indirect responsibility has become clearer. Paragraph 1 of Article 17, referring to binding decisions, makes sense when seen under the lens of derivative responsibility, while paragraph 2 clearly references complicity. Drawing parallels of this kind promotes a triple goal: it sustains coherence in the law of international responsibility; it provides courts with a clear legal approach that effectively regulates complex scenarios of non-conformity; and it offers a valuable opportunity to initiate change in the way in which International Organisations currently operate and interact with their member States. I believe that the understanding of Article 17 in the way proposed here provides for the progressive development of the law on this issue. Even if the provision has not yet attained the status of customary law, it is the key to solving complex legal puzzles and advancing legal certainty in a strain of cases that has, to date, been rather too problematic for courts to handle.

6

Circumvention of Obligations through the International Organisation

I. INTRODUCTION

ARTICLE 61 HAS been one of the most controversial, and certainly one of the most amended, provisions of the Articles on the Responsibility of International Organizations (ARIO). The provision reads:

> Circumvention of international obligations of a State member of an international organization
>
> 1. A State member of an international organization incurs international responsibility if, by taking advantage of the fact that the organization has competence in relation to the subject-matter of one of the State's international obligations, it circumvents that obligation by causing the organization to commit an act that, if committed by the State, would have constituted a breach of the obligation.
>
> 2. Paragraph 1 applies whether or not the act in question is internationally wrongful for the international organization.

The commentaries to this provision stipulate that the inclusion of the provision mainly addresses scenarios of transfer of powers/competences from member States to the International Organisation.[1] This view is corroborated by the drafting history of the provision and shared by most commentators.[2] In the final chapter, I will argue for a potential usage of Article 61 in political influence scenarios over decision-making procedures. In the present chapter, I will examine instances of provision of competences where Article 61 is potentially applicable.

Nevertheless, the analysis here is not driven by the need to examine the adaptation of Article 61 to the particular scenarios, but rather from the necessity to examine whether the terms of the provision are justified from a legal standpoint and consequently whether it adequately reflects the progressive development of

[1] ARIO Comment, 161, [6].
[2] ibid 159–60, [3]–[4] and authorities cited therein.

the law. To this end, by examining the relationship between Article 61 and existing case law, I will put it to the test and assess whether it can effectively regulate the circumvention scenarios in play. Responsibility at the level of the provision of competence through the prism of Article 61 will be used, then, as a case-study that will drive the legal analysis conducted here.

The argument will run in two parts. In the light of the commentaries and the analysis of the mirroring Article 17, I will delimit the provision's scope of application and examine how responsibility is established according to the general principles of international responsibility. Then, I will juxtapose Article 61 with relevant European Court of Human Rights (ECtHR) case law in order to evaluate how the discrepancy between the two affects the normative status of the provision. As noted earlier, it is the aim of this chapter to test whether the provision reflects, in the way it is formulated, the progressive development of the law.

II. A LEGAL ANALYSIS OF ARIO, ARTICLE 61

The legal analysis of the provision will follow that of previous ARIO Articles. To make sense of it, it is crucial to disentangle the scope of application from the terms that pertain to the establishment of international responsibility.[3] This distinction is fundamental in order to explain from a legal standpoint the operation of the elements present in the provision. The ones attached to the scope of application form part of a primary norm and do not cause doctrinal incoherence within the law of international responsibility. Under this prism, the analysis attempted here will follow the methodology invoked with respect to Article 17 above.

And while it may seem a replica provision of Article 17, the International Law Commission (ILC) constantly changed its wording and commentators have struggled to put it into context.[4] This is probably the case, because it combines a weird mixture of elements: a scenario in which it is not clear neither whether member States participate as members or as States nor whether the incurring responsibility is direct or indirect. Having this in mind, in this first section, I will try to clarify the operation of Article 61 and answer the following questions: on what basis do member States and International Organisations interact in

[3] The ILC failed to do so in the commentaries where it lists three conditions necessary for the incurrence of responsibility, thereby entangling elements that pertain to the conditions of breach and attribution with those germane to the provision's scope of application, ARIO Comment, 70, [6] – [7]. An understanding of the methodology used here is provided in Chapter 2.

[4] O Murray, 'Piercing the Institutional Veil: The Responsibility of Member States of an International Organization' (2011) 8 *IOLR* 291; C Ryngaert and H Buchanan, 'Member State Responsibility for the Acts of International Organizations' (2011) 7 *Utrecht Law Review* 131; J d' Aspremont, 'Abuse of the Legal Personality of International Organizations and the Responsibility of Member States' (2007) 4 *IOLR* 91.

the cases identified in this provision? Is the provision superfluous in the sense that both its scope of application and its secondary norms are covered *in toto* by other ARIO provisions? Because it is not clear which scenarios fall under the ambit of the Article 61, the first question can only be answered after the provision's scope of application has been determined.

In order to make sense of the practical instances covered, I will use as a recurrent theme the example given by the Special Rapporteur in his Fourth Report,[5] namely, that of a State that is a party to a treaty which forbids the development of certain weapons and that indirectly acquires control of those weapons by making use of an International Organisation which is not bound by the treaty.

A. First Attempt to Delimit the Provision's Scope of Application

The wording of Article 61 is similar to its mirroring Article 17, for they intend to cover reverse situations.[6] It was suggested in the Sixth Committee that 'States should not be able to hide behind the conduct of the international organization' in the same way as International Organisations should not be allowed to avail themselves of the personality of their member States.[7] To this effect, Special Rapporteur Gaja proposed the inclusion in the ARIO of a provision titled: 'Use by a State that is a member of an international organization of the separate personality of that organization'.[8] The abuse of the International Organisation's separate personality and the ensuing 'piercing' of its veil still remains at the thrust of the provision even if not expressly spelled out under the present formulation. In both provisions, the abuse is masked under the notion of 'circumvention of obligations' which expresses an intention to take advantage of the separate legal personality of the International Organisation in order to avoid compliance.[9] The underlying *ratio*, then, is identical and one would expect that the two provisions would respectively have mirroring scopes of application.

[5] G Gaja, *Fourth Report on Responsibility of International Organizations*, UN doc A/CN.4/564 (2006) and Add 1 to 2, reproduced in (2006) 2(2) *YBILC* 103 ('Gaja Fourth Report') [66]–[67].

[6] ARIO, Art 17 reads: 'Circumvention of international obligations through decisions and authorizations addressed to members 1. An international organization incurs international responsibility if it circumvents one of its international obligations by adopting a decision binding member States or international organizations to commit an act that would be internationally wrongful if committed by the former organization. 2. An international organization incurs international responsibility if it circumvents one of its international obligations by authorizing member States or international organizations to commit an act that would be internationally wrongful if committed by the former organization and the act in question is committed because of that authorization. 3. Paragraphs 1 and 2 apply whether or not the act in question is internationally wrongful for the member States or international organizations to which the decision or authorization is addressed.'

[7] UNGA 60th Session, Sixth Committee, *Summary Record of the 13th Meeting*, UN doc A/C.6/60/SR.13 (2005) [45].

[8] Gaja Fourth Report (n 5) [65] and [74].

[9] ARIO Comment, 106, [4] and 159, [2].

While the thrust of the provision was clear from the beginning, the ILC has oscillated before delimiting the provision's scope of application. First, it was agreed that the International Organisation should have competence in relation to the subject-matter of the circumvented obligation. As International Organisations do not possess, in contrast with States, a general presumption of competence, they can only perform acts covered by such competences. This was not an issue with respect to Article 17, because States possess the presumption of competence and International Organisations can circumvent their obligations by causing States to perform any act.

What is of importance here, is that the circumvented obligation covers the area in which the International Organisation is provided with competence, while it is irrelevant how the International Organisation acquired such competence. Thus, provision of competence may not be the only way of State-initiated circumvention and the ILC decided not to qualify it in any way.[10] As it will be explained in the next chapter and as has been suggested by theorists, circumvention at the decision-making level is also covered by Article 61.[11] What is more, commentators suggested that provision of competences limits the operation of Article 61 to the level of the creation of an International Organisation.[12] While this will certainly be the case on most occasions, it cannot be excluded that States can transfer competences to International Organisations at a subsequent stage. In our example, the International Organisation should possess the competence to acquire weapons, while it is indifferent if such competence was provided for in its constituent instrument, it was conferred by an institutional act or a re-interpretation/re-definition of the constituent instrument.[13] Seen from this perspective, this generic terminology in Article 61[14] leaves open the range of possible scenarios covered by the provision and excludes from its ambit only those fields that go beyond the competences of the International Organisation.

The question that troubled the ILC the most when drafting Article 61 was what level of member State involvement would trigger its responsibility in

[10] ARIO Comment, 161, [6]. It should be noted that earlier formulations of the provision made explicit reference to the provision of competence to the International Organisation, thus excluding other scenarios from their ambit, See ILC, *Provisional Summary Record of the 3015th Meeting*, UN doc A/CN.4/SR.3015 (15 July 2009), reproduced in (2009) 1 *YBILC* 109, 117–18, [59].

[11] See next chapter and d'Aspremont, 'Abuse of the Legal Personality of International Organizations' (n 4) 100.

[12] Murray, 'Piercing the Institutional Veil' (n 4); d'Aspremont, 'Abuse of the Legal Personality of International Organizations' (n 4); E Paasivirta, 'Reponsibility of a Member State of an International Organization: Where Will It End? Comments on Article 60 of the ILC Draft on the Responsibility of International Organizations' (2010) 7 *IOLR* 49.

[13] A great example in this respect is NATO's extension of constitutional mandate. NATO radically expanded its competences through the adoption of 'Strategic Concepts' (most prominent among them, those of 1991 and 1999) and thus altered its purpose and nature. For an analysis, see B Simma, 'NATO, the UN and the Use of Force: Legal Aspects' (1999) 10 *EJIL* 1.

[14] The provision is applicable when the International Organisation 'has competence in relation to the subject-matter of one of the State's international obligations'.

circumvention scenarios. To return to our example, what type of conduct is sufficient in order to link the member State with the acquisition of weapons from the International Organisation? The different functioning between States and International Organisations suggests that these international subjects would employ different means in order to achieve circumvention. Instead of addressing normative acts to International Organisations (as per Article 17), member States will most likely cause International Organisations to act upon competences where they (the member States) have undertaken international obligations. The Commission struggled to provide an answer to this question because it hadn't clarified whether member State responsibility is direct or indirect in these instances. In other words, how are the conditions of breach and attribution met in these scenarios? I will now turn the analysis in this direction.

B. Responsibility Models in Article 61

The main argument advanced here is that member States incur indirect responsibility in circumvention scenarios. For this to be proven, however, it should be assessed first whether member States and the International Organisation of which they are members interact as independent subjects of international law or on the basis of the particular member State-International Organisation relationship in the context of Article 61. Because if the latter is in play, member States are hidden behind the institutional veil, their legal personality vanishes and they cannot bear international responsibility in the first place.

As noted previously, when joining an International Organisation, States act as members (and thus interact in the context of the particular member State-International Organisation relationship) when they exercise competence that lies with the organs of the International Organisation by virtue of the rules of that International Organisation. On the other hand, members act as States and hence interact with the International Organisation as independent subjects of international law, in any other case. In the way formulated, Article 61 limits State-initiated circumvention to member States, and only to a subject-matter that lies in the remit of the competences of the International Organisation. However, this does not *ipso facto* mean that when initiating circumvention member States are acting as members of the International Organisation. As was the case with Article 17, the member State conduct that initiates circumvention is not an exercise of competence that lies with the International Organisation but solely with the acting State.[15] Also, if the opposite was accepted, and member State-International Organisation interaction in Article 61 is based on the particular member State-International Organisation relationship, it will be

[15] For an example, see the *Kokkelvisserij* case (n 63) and accompanying text.

impossible for member States to bear international responsibility since their personality will have merged with the International Organisation's.[16] The ILC then limited circumvention scenarios to instances where members operate as States and they interact with the International Organisation outside the particular member State-International Organisation relationship.

I believe that Article 61 operates according to both indirect responsibility models: member State responsibility for conduct of the International Organisation (derivative responsibility) and for participation in the internationally wrongful act of the International Organisation (complicity). Depending on the level of causation involved in every particular case, the application of each model will be pertinent. Article 61 accommodates both models of indirect responsibility, as if paragraphs 1 and 2 of ARIO, Article 17 were joined together. This is why the provision should be analysed through the prism of both indirect responsibility models. It is the ECtHR case law on the matter which has perplexed this issue and has sidetracked the attention of the ILC and commentators.

A careful reading of Article 61 shows that certain member State conduct is required for the triggering of member State responsibility. The provision stipulates that the member State must cause the act of the International Organisation that would have constituted a breach of that State's international obligations. An objective link – causation – between the conduct of the circumventing member State and the ensuing act of the International Organisation is necessary. In the absence of a member State act or omission, contributive to the commission of the ensuing act of the International Organisation, member State responsibility would arise without any member State conduct. This would have been problematic from a normative perspective, as it runs counter to Article 2 of the Articles on State Responsibility (ASR) which requires State conduct for the incurrence of State responsibility for own internationally wrongful act. Therefore, a member State which transfers to the International Organisation in bad faith the competence to acquire weapons, but then does nothing to promote this cause within the International Organisation, will not be responsible for the acquisition of weapons that may occur in the future. Irrespective of the exact level of causation required, the link required demonstrates beyond dispute that member State responsibility arises for conduct attributable to the member State.

There are two inferences to be drawn from this. First, member State responsibility does not arise for an act attributable to the International Organisation, and second, it is indirect. It was heavily debated in the ILC whether some form of causation is necessary in the provision. In 2006, the Commission clearly stated that there is no requirement that the State caused the International Organisation to commit the act in question.[17] No reference to causation was deemed

[16] On the issues of personality merging of member States, see Chapter 3.

[17] ILC, *Report of the International Law Commission on the Work of Its 58th Session, 1 May–9 June and 3 July–11 August 2006*, UN doc A/61/10 (2006), reproduced in (2006) 2(2) *YBILC* 1, 129, [6].

necessary at the time because attention was centred around the ensuing act of the International Organisation. After the discussions at the Drafting Committee the position has altered, a reference on causation was inserted, but it is not clear what prompted this change of heart.[18]

No explanation was given for this, however, the ILC's perseverance to retain causation in respect of the conduct of the International Organisation as a prerequisite for the establishment of responsibility is telling.[19] Had the Commission perceived Article 61 as a direct responsibility scenario, this prerequisite would have been absent from its wording. It would have been indifferent if the International Organisation has in fact committed the act or not since direct responsibility scenarios are not triangular; the incurrence of responsibility is not dependent on the relationship with the conduct of a third subject.[20] A NATO member State, bound by the Treaty on the Non-Proliferation of Nuclear Weapons not to contribute to the acquisition of such weapons,[21] which introduces a resolution to this respect at the NATO Council would be responsible for a violation of the treaty even if the resolution fails. If the requirement of the link with the International Organisation act was dropped, Article 61 would have been a mere statement that member States bear direct responsibility for own acts when they operate within the context of an International Organisation.[22]

I have established that Article 61 addresses indirect responsibility scenarios and hence an analysis akin to indirect responsibility must be followed. The perception that the provision establishes a primary norm and thus finds an awkward fit within a set of secondary norms is dominant among commentators. Paasivirta holds that Article 61 introduces 'a new primary rule',[23] while Murray states that it replicates the general principle of good faith.[24] I reject this approach, by arguing here that the provision is of a mixed nature, -like the complicity provisions in ASR and ARIO, and not a primary norm extraneous to the international responsibility framework. Within the provision, there operate both a latent secondary norm on derivative attribution (as per the derivative responsibility model) alongside a latent primary rule (as per the complicity model). Article 61 then has a scope of application broad enough to cover both. Before proceeding with the exact delimitation of this scope, it is crucial to keep in mind that member State responsibility arises indirectly for conduct adopted by *members as States*.

[18] ILC, *Summary Record of the 3015th Meeting* (n 10) 24.

[19] ARIO Comment, 161, [8].

[20] In fact, it was proposed that a State should be held responsible 'if it had sought to gain an illicit advantage by using the organization's competence, whether or not the organization had committed the act in question', but the proposal was rejected as overly relying on intent, ILC, *Summary Record of the 3015th Meeting* (n 10) 24.

[21] Treaty on the Non-proliferation of Nuclear Weapons (adopted 1 July 1968; entered into force 5 March 1970) 729 UNTS 161.

[22] This was already suggested in the commentaries to Arts 58 and 59, ARIO Comment, 157, [5].

[23] Paasivirta, 'Reponsibility of a Member State of an International Organization' (n 12) 61.

[24] Murray, 'Piercing the Institutional Veil' (n 4) 320.

C. Second Attempt to Delimit the Provision's Scope of Application

In these scenarios, two factors have to be balanced on a razor's edge: the objective link between the conduct of the circumventing member State and the ensuing conduct of the International Organisation (causation) and the subjective element of member State intention to avoid compliance with its obligations. It is a fine balance indeed, because both elements are indispensable for the operation of the provision and at the same time neither of them can be overstressed.

First, the elimination of either of them from the wording of Article 61 would lead to unacceptable results.[25] As explained above, the establishment of member State responsibility for own internationally wrongful acts without member State conduct is incongruent with the double basis of the internationally wrongful act. The eradication of the subjective element, on the other hand, would result in the triggering of member State responsibility when the ensuing act is regarded as the unintended result of member State conduct.[26] The Special Rapporteur, in his Seventh Report, explained that the provision of competences to an International Organisation per se does not necessarily imply an intention to avoid compliance. The transfer, he explains, could well have occurred in good faith, while the opportunity for circumventing an international obligation may have appeared only at a later stage.[27] Member State intentions will on most occasions be clear and easy to infer from the circumstances, ie when the State votes or otherwise participates in organs of the International Organisation. It is difficult to think of an example where a member State unintentionally causes an act of the International Organisation, no matter how low one sets the causation threshold. However, it would be just to protect a member State in the extreme scenario that it proved its good faith and had no intention to cause the act of the International Organisation.

Seemingly, the focus is on the double subjective standard; intention is inherent in both 'circumvention' and 'taking advantage'. It was long debated in the ILC how much emphasis, if at all, should be given to the subjective element. During the drafting process, several States had pushed for the introduction of a 'bad faith', 'deliberate intent' or 'misuse' element.[28] Others favoured a turn towards objectivity,[29] while the Special Rapporteur himself seemed reluctant to

[25] Murray correctly suggested that prior formulations of the provision that have discarded both elements lead to the imposition of 'strict liability' upon member States ibid (n 4) 314.

[26] ARIO Comment, 159, [2].

[27] G Gaja, *Seventh Report on Responsibility of International Organizations*, UN doc A/CN.4/610 (2009), reproduced in (2009) 2(1) *YBILC* 73 ('Gaja Seventh Report'), 88–89, [81]–[82].

[28] See UNGA, 61st Session, Sixth Committee, *Summary Record of the 13th Meeting*, UN doc A/C.6/60/SR.13 (2006) [45], [46] (Ireland); UNGA, 61st Session, Sixth Committee, *Summary Record of the 14th Meeting*, UN doc A/C.6/61/SR.14 (2006) [50] (Spain); ibid [3] (Germany); UNGA, 61st Session, Sixth Committee, *Summary Record of the 15th Meeting*, UN doc A/C.6/61/SR.15 (2006) [30] (United Kingdom).

[29] UNGA, *Summary Record of the 15th Meeting* (n 28) [3] (Switzerland).

introduce a high subjective standard in the provision.[30] For reasons of consistency, circumvention incorporates in this context the same subjective standard as in Article 17, but the Commission finally held that an intention to take advantage of the International Organisation's competence, absent from the wording of Article 17, should also be present. A close examination of the two aforementioned elements demonstrates that they are in fact tautological. It is the International Organisation's competences that the State will use in any case in order to achieve the intended result. At the macro-scale, this is described as availing of the International Organisation's separate personality. The member State takes advantage of the fact that the International Organisation has competence in relation to the acquisition of weapons and intentionally causes the acquisition. Had the Commission overstressed the subjective element, the provision would have been inoperable in most probability. Therefore, the level of subjective member State involvement is similar to the one required in both paragraphs of ARIO, Article 17.

The problematic standard to clearly define is not the subjective but rather the objective one. This is so, because the ILC has done very little to clarify it. In the commentaries, the Commission suggests that: 'Should the act of the international organization be wrongful and the act be caused by the member State, there could be an overlap between the cases covered in draft article 61 and those considered in articles 58, 59 and 60'.[31] This demonstrates that the wording on causation selected in Article 61 was intended to be as generic and all-encompassing as possible in order to cover the whole spectrum from coercion (extreme form of control) to complicity (facilitation). Since incitement is not unlawful, every type of member State influence over an act of an International Organisation that surpasses the latter threshold falls under the objective standard of the provision. Even if the member State's act is not the catalyst in the adoption of the act of the International Organisation (eg by exercising a veto vote), any act in this direction that can be characterised as an essential contribution to the internationally wrongful act of the International Organisation would suffice. A member State pleading at the International Organisation's council in favour of the adoption of an decision of the International Organisation to acquire certain weapons is not essentially contributing to the adoption of a wrongful decision of the International Organisation and hence the member State will not be responsible for its stance.

The level of causation, nevertheless, will indicate the responsibility model applicable in every situation. When a member State, through conduct it adopts as a State, restricts the freedom of the International Organisation's action, it bears responsibility by virtue of the derivative responsibility model. The ensuing conduct of the International Organisation is then attributable to the

[30] Gaja Seventh Report (n 27) 27.
[31] ARIO Comment, 161, [10].

member State by virtue of the derivative attribution rule and that is why the said act should run counter to the obligations of member States. This would also have triggered member State responsibility under ARIO, Article 59(1). But as explained above, the inclusion of Article 61(2) covers scenarios where the conduct in question is not internationally wrongful for the International Organisation, a situation not covered by Article 59(1). The ILC did not provide an example in this respect and it is difficult to think of one apart from the abuse of legal personality through political influence described in the next chapter. The relationship between the two provisions would have been a great deal clearer if the Commission had provided instances of some relevant institutional practice. What is more, for reasons of legal consistency, the ILC should have distinguished between derivative responsibility and complicity within Article 61.

On the other hand, the member State act may only facilitate the ensuing conduct of the International Organisation, in which case the complicity model is put in operation. Perhaps without realising it, Murray adheres to this approach when she states with respect to Article 61: 'the Special Rapporteur proposed a new rule on state *complicity*, based on the notion of "circumvention"'[32] (emphasis added). The primary rule violated by the member State in this situation, as in Article 17(2), derives from the synthesis of the elements that pertain to the provision's scope of application: 'to not cause, with an intention to avoid compliance, an act of an International Organisation which would have run counter to your international obligations if committed by you'. It must be noted that the primary norm incorporated in Article 61 differs from the one latent in the provisions examined in the previous chapter as it prohibits under certain circumstances also facilitation of lawful conduct.[33] To the extent that this lies in the realm of primary obligations, it is not incompatible with the complicity model since, as stated earlier, it is not the content of the primary norm that defines this model but rather the operation of this norm within the provision.

Again, the complete lack of institutional practice renders difficult the complete apprehension of the provision but also its relationship with ARIO, Article 58(1). An example of such facilitation is arguably provided by the ECtHR *Kokkelvisserij* case, which will be analysed in the following section. It is also maintained here that the primary rule in Article 61 is different from the one in Article 58(1) as it prohibits the facilitation not only of unlawful but also of a lawful conduct as suggested by Article 61(2).[34] Thus, when acting as a State, a member State which facilitates certain conduct of an International Organisation is violating the latent primary rule within Article 61, and the 'piercing' of the institutional veil that occurs is explained from a legal point of view.

[32] Murray, 'Piercing the Institutional Veil' (n 4) 313.

[33] ARIO, Art 61(2).

[34] Note the different focus of the analysis that pertains to the complicity model between Arts 17(2) and 61. In Art 17(2) it is hard to understand that authorisation amounts to facilitation in order to place the provision under the complicity model, see Chapter 5. Here, it is not evident that the latent primary rule is different from the respective rule within Art 58(1).

It is pertinent, now, to put the preceding analysis into perspective and juxtapose it with the case law of the European Court of Human Rights. The latter has been used by the ILC as an essential basis for the drafting of Article 61. What is more, States and International Organisations heavily relied upon it during the drafting process, and, finally, commentators have used it as a point of reference for any criticism they have addressed towards the drafting of the provision.

III. ECtHR CASE LAW AND ARTICLE 61: A RELATIONSHIP LOST IN CAUSATION

The perplexed wording of Article 61 was further obfuscated in the commentaries where the ILC cited ECtHR case law as supportive to the rule it wanted to formulate. It is not entirely clear what inferences the ILC has drawn from this case law and how it has affected the drafting of Article 61. It is suggested here that these particular cases do not provide adequate guidance for the provision, as they purport to address scenarios different from those regulated by the provision. Apart from being unhelpful, the citing of this case law has resulted in further confusion; it has brought about some academic criticism which in its turn has only perplexed a matter that is rather simple.[35] The purpose of this section is to make sense of the responsibility models applied by the Strasbourg Court in order to see how they fit with Article 61. To this end, I will attempt a return to the basics and disentangle ECtHR case law from Article 61, by exposing their points of divergence.

A. An Outline of ECtHR Case Law

The ECtHR can only affirm the international responsibility of member States of the Council of Europe and not that of International Organisations.[36] The Strasbourg Court has extensively dealt with the issue of member State

[35] C Ryngaert, 'Oscillating Between Embracing and Avoiding *Bosphorus*: The European Court of Human Rights on Member State Responsibility for Acts of International Organisations and the Case of the EU' (2014) 39 *European Law Review* 176; G Pinzauti, 'It Takes Two to Tango: States' Conferral of Powers on International Organizations and Its Implications for the Responsibility of the Organization and Its Members' in D Sarooshi (ed), *Remedies and Responsibility for the Actions of International Organizations* (Brill, Nijhoff, 2014) 113; JA Uriarte, 'The Responsibility of International Organizations and International and European Courts and Tribunals: Judicial Review of Security Council Resolutions' in ibid 321; C Ryngaert, 'The European Court of Human Rights' Approach to the Responsibility of Member States in Connection with Acts of International Organisations, (2011) 60 *ICLQ* 997; G Verdirame, 'Breaches of the European Convention on Human Rights Resulting from the Conduct of International Organisations' (2008) 2 *European Human Rights Law Review* 209; Murray, 'Piercing the Institutional Veil' (n 4); Paasivirta, 'Reponsibility of a Member State of an International Organization' (n 12).

[36] The EU is the only International Organisation that will potentially accede to the ECHR, however the latest draft accession agreement was found incompatible with EU law by the CJEU.

responsibility in a field where they have attributed competence(s) to an International Organisation. Nevertheless, the ECtHR fails to address certain doctrinal issues with the necessary rigour, thus rendering it hard to draw systematic inferences from this strain of relevant cases.[37] In particular, the Court's approach in these cases is flawed in a twofold way: there is no principled distinction between attribution and State jurisdiction throughout the Court's case law, and further the attribution rules applied by the Court are not clearly discernible. For these reasons, one struggles to clarify how international responsibility arises in every case.

A basic point of convergence between Article 61 and Strasbourg case law that renders their juxtaposition possible, is that they both provide for a common basis of international responsibility. All relevant case law examined in this chapter pertains to international responsibility for own internationally wrongful act, as does Article 61. Thus, attribution of conduct to a Council of Europe member State is a *conditio sine qua non* for the arising of this member State's responsibility. In other words, the ECtHR only reviews conduct attributable to a Council of Europe member State.

Before proceeding with the analysis of the case law, the notions of attribution and State jurisdiction should be kept separate from the outset. Different tests apply with respect to each of them as they focus around different relationships: State jurisdiction revolves around State control over the victims of human rights violations, while attribution around the State's control over the perpetrators of such violations.[38] This means that, for present purposes, in the examined case law these two concepts pertain to different conduct.[39] Jurisdiction answers the question whether the applicant has rights vis-à-vis the respondent State(s).[40] If this is not the case, the obligations arising from the European Convention on Human Rights (ECHR) are not applicable and

See Opinion 2/13, Accession of the European Union to the European Convention for the Protection of Human Rights and Fundamental Freedoms, ECJ (18 December 2014) ECLI:EU:C:2014:2454 and the analysis in Chapter 5 at II B ii.

[37] Commonplace criticism in all the authorities cited in n 35 above; T Lock, 'Beyond Bosphorus: The European Court of Human Rights' Case Law on the Responsibility of Member States of International Organisations under the European Convention on Human Rights' (2010) 10 *Human Rights Law Review* 529; G Verdirame, *The UN and Human Rights: Who Guards the Guardians?* (CUP, 2011) 108–22 and 359–72; G Verdirame, 'A Normative Theory of Sovereignty Transfers' (2013) 49 *Stanford Journal of International Law* 371.

[38] M Milanovic, *Extraterritorial Application of Human Rights Treaties: Law Principles and Policy* (OUP, 2011) 51; A Sari, 'Untangling Extra-Territorial Jurisdiction from International Responsibility in Jaloud v Netherlands: Old Problem, New Solutions?' (2014) 53 *Military Law and the Law of War Review* 287.

[39] To the extent that the tests relate to different acts, I disagree with Milanovic that attribution can be a prerequisite for State jurisdiction, ibid.

[40] *R (on the application of Al-Skeini and others) v Secretary of State for Defence*, Judgment of 13 June 2007, [2007] UKHL 26, [2008] AC 153, [64] (per Lord Rodger): 'It is important therefore to recognise that, when considering the question of jurisdiction under the Convention, the focus has shifted to the victim or, more precisely, to the link between the victim and the contracting state'.

the ECtHR cannot judge a case. State jurisdiction is a preliminary issue and its establishment depends upon the link between the conduct allegedly causing the breach and the respondent State. The level of this link is not important for present purposes for it has nothing to do with the responsibility model applied by the Court. Attribution, on the other hand, answers a different question: whether the conduct reviewed by the Court is conduct committed by the respondent State. The establishment of attribution then depends upon the link between the conduct reviewed by the court and the respondent State. Attribution pertains to the merits of the judgment and hence jurisdiction logically precedes it.[41] Because, in direct responsibility scenarios, the conduct allegedly causing the breach and the conduct reviewed by the Court are identical, the two questions are conflated. This, however, is not the case in indirect responsibility where the two conducts are different. That is why the disentanglement between the two is of such fundamental importance in cases of provision of competences where indirect responsibility is in play.

(i) Direct Responsibility Before the ECtHR

The starting point of the analysis is the oft-cited *Waite and Kennedy* case.[42] The object of the complaint was the decision of a German court to uphold the immunity of the European Space Agency (ESA). While it was clear that the decision of the court was attributable to Germany, no explicit reference to attribution is made in the ECtHR's analysis. The same goes for the issue of jurisdiction and whether the applicants had rights vis-à-vis Germany. It is suggested here that the Court covertly established Germany's jurisdiction by stating that:

> The Court is of the opinion that where States establish international organisations in order to pursue or strengthen their cooperation in certain fields of activities, and where they attribute to these organisations certain competences and accord them immunities, there may be implications as to the protection of fundamental rights. It would be incompatible with the purpose and object of the Convention, however, if the Contracting States were thereby absolved from their responsibility under the Convention in relation to the field of activity covered by such attribution.[43]

This dictum suggests that while it is the International Organisation that holds certain competences, a Council of Europe member State has jurisdiction with respect to these competences when it transfers these competences to the International Organisation. This statement only confirms that complaints against

[41] *Ilascu v Moldova and Russia*, Application no 48787/99, ECtHR, Judgment of 8 July 2004, [311].

[42] *Waite and Kennedy v Germany*, Application no 26083/94, ECtHR Grand Chamber, Judgment of 18 February 1999, (2000) 30 EHRR 261. Within the judicial system of the Council of Europe, the same approach to responsibility as in *Waite and Kennedy* was taken in *M and Co v Federal Republic of Germany*, Application no 13258/87, European Commission of Human Rights, Decision of 9 February 1990.

[43] ibid [51].

member States that pertain to this field of competence are reviewable by the Court. It says nothing about attribution, nor the international responsibility model applied by the Court. The ECtHR proceeded with its analysis on the merits and found that the conduct of the member State was in conformity with the ECHR. The test it applied in order to determine the existence of breach is not of particular importance for the purposes of present analysis.

What is important for present purposes is to bear in mind that the Court does not perceive the scenario as one of indirect responsibility. Germany's responsibility does not arise for ESA's conduct (Germany does not control ESA) nor for participation in ESA's internationally wrongful act in the sense that a causative link between the International Organisation and the act of the member State is not a prerequisite for the incurring of Germany's international responsibility here. What is crucial for the incurring of member State responsibility is that member State conduct takes place in an area of competence the latter has conferred upon the International Organisation. Since direct responsibility is in play, the above-mentioned quote reaffirms the proposition incorporated in the commentaries to Articles 58 and 59; when joining an International Organisation, member States are directly responsible for own conduct that is incompatible with their international obligations (the *Waite and Kennedy* principle).

The scope of this principle was expanded in the *Matthews* judgment rendered on the same day.[44] The applicant, resident of the dependent territory of Gibraltar, held that the United Kingdom had breached her right to participate in free elections under ECHR, Protocol I, Article 3 because she was disenfranchised from European Parliament elections under European Community (EC, now EU) legislation. The Court upheld the United Kingdom's international responsibility but its analysis was obfuscatory and merits close examination to make it comprehensible.

The entanglement of jurisdiction and attribution perplexed things once again. The UK government argued that the conduct through which the breach occurred is not attributable to the United Kingdom but to the (then) European Community.[45] Only if the United Kingdom had control over the EC act could UK responsibility for the conduct of the International Organisation have unfolded, the government continued.[46] The Court nevertheless rejected the UK argument because it did not perceive the scenario as one of indirect responsibility.[47]

[44] *Matthews v United Kingdom*, Application no 24833/94, ECtHR Grand Chamber, Judgment of 18 February 1999, (2009) 28 EHRR 361.

[45] ibid [26].

[46] ibid. The UK argument is based, albeit with a different wording, on the derivative model of responsibility.

[47] A Stumer, 'Liability of Member States for Acts of International Organizations: Reconsidering the Policy Objections' (2007) 48 *Harvard International Law Journal* 553, 563: 'the responsibility of the Member State is, strictly speaking, not for the act of the international organization, but for the failure to ensure that the transfer of power to the organization was consistent with the State's international obligations'.

Without referring expressly to jurisdiction or attribution, the Court implicitly dealt with these questions in good order in paragraphs 31 to 34 of the judgment. First, it asked whether the United Kingdom could be held responsible under Article 1 (jurisdiction question, paragraph 31) and answered in the affirmative by stating the *Waite and Kennedy* principle (establishment of jurisdiction, paragraph 32). Subsequently, the Court held that the alleged violation flows from international instruments which were freely entered into by the United Kingdom and so the conduct reviewed is not the conduct of the International Organisation but rather the member State conduct of accession to the EC (establishment of conduct attributable to the member State, paragraph 33). Finally, in a synthesis of the above, it expanded the scope of the *Waite and Kennedy* principle: member States remain directly responsible in a field of attributed competence to the International Organisation for own conduct after they have joined the International Organisation, but also for the conduct of transfer of competences itself (the *Matthews* principle, paragraph 34). Once more, the test applied by the Court to judge whether the United Kingdpm has breached its international obligations (the other element of the double basis of an internationally wrongful act) is not important for present purposes as it says nothing about the responsibility model applied by the ECtHR.

The same approach to international responsibility is found in the *Bosphorus* case which has been used by the Court as a point of reference for relevant subsequent case law.[48] In May 1993, an airline company registered in Turkey, Bosphorus Airways, leased a civil aircraft from Yugoslav Airlines. The Irish authorities seized the aircraft during a maintenance stop-over in Ireland. The legal basis for the measure taken by Ireland was an EC Regulation concerning trade between the EC and the Federal Republic of Yugoslavia, which itself was based on UNSC Resolution 820. As a result of this seizure, Bosphorus Airways sued Ireland before the Strasbourg Court.

The ECtHR first had to examine whether it could establish State jurisdiction. Because the aircraft was impounded by Irish authorities on Irish territory, the ECtHR accepted that the company had rights vis-à-vis Ireland and it could assert jurisdiction under Article 1 of the ECHR.[49] Correctly, it held that a member State is:

> responsible under Article 1 of the Convention for all acts and omissions of its organs regardless of whether the act or omission in question was a consequence of domestic law or of the necessity to comply with international legal obligations.[50]

Judge Ress argued in his Concurring Opinion, and I agree, that this was a formulation of the *Matthews* principle as long as international obligations can arise from treaties establishing International Organisations.[51]

[48] *Bosphorus Hava Yollari Turizm v Ireland*, Application no 45036/98, ECtHR Grand Chamber, Judgment of 30 June 2005, (2006) 42 EHRR 1.

[49] ibid [135]–[138].

[50] ibid [153].

[51] ibid Concurring Opinion of Judge Ress, [5].

This dictum nevertheless does not second-guess the attribution question as explained above. But the Court's analysis omits any reference to the question of attribution and conflates these different issues. The finding 'that the impugned interference was not the result of an exercise of discretion by the Irish authorities'[52] should have prevented the Court from attributing the conduct to Ireland. The lack of discretion renders the derivative attribution rule applicable and severs any attribution link between Ireland and the conduct reviewed by the Court (seizure of the aircraft).[53] On this basis, the application should have been declared inadmissible *ratione personae*.

Since the ECtHR ostensibly held that the seizure was attributable to Ireland, it further examined whether Ireland had violated its international obligations. According to the ECtHR, the discretion afforded to member States determines, not the attribution question, but the pattern to be followed in order to assess whether a breach has occurred. Discretionary acts will be reviewed with the usual scrutiny of the Court, while non-discretionary ones through the prism of the 'equivalent protection' presumption.[54] Again, the test applied to determine the breach does not impact the responsibility model in the present instance. The wrongfulness of Ireland's conduct was not dependent upon its link with an EC act and that is why the Court reviews, as in both previous cases, member State conduct and not conduct of the International Organisation. The fact that the Court appealed to the general protection provided by the EC in order to determine the existence of a breach does not imply that the Court is looking for a causative link between the member State act and conduct of the International Organisation, apart from the fact that member State conduct must occur within the fields of competence of the International Organisation.

[52] ibid [148].

[53] On the derivative attribution rule, see Chapter 4.

[54] If the International Organisation provides equivalent protection as the ECHR, the ECtHR will presume that the State did not breach its obligations under the Convention. For an analysis of the presumption, see Verdirame, *The UN and Human Rights* (n 37) 359–71. The reasoning revolved around discretion, inter alia, in the following cases: *Nada v Switzerland*, Application no 10593/08, ECtHR Grand Chamber, Judgment of 12 September 2012, (2013) 56 EHRR 18; *Al-Dulimi and Montana Management Inc v Switzerland*, Application no 5809/08, ECtHR Grand Chamber, Judgment of 21 June 2016, (2016) 55 ILM 1023; *Povse v Austria*, Application no 3890/11, European Commission of Human Rights, Decision of 18 June 2013; *MSS v Belgium and Greece*, Application no 30696/09, ECtHR Grand Chamber, Judgment of 21 January 2011; *Al Jedda v United Kingdom*, Application no 27021/08, ECtHR Grand Chamber, Judgment of 7 July 2011, (2011) 53 EHRR 23; *Cooperative des Agriculteurs de Mayenne and Cooperative Laitiere Maine-Anjou v France*, Application no 16931/04, Europoan Commission of Human Rights, Decision of 10 October 2006. The same reasoning can also be found in *Michaud v France*, Application no 12323/11, ECtHR, Judgment of 6 December 2012. In this case, the Court further noted that the control mechanism provided in an International Organisation (here a preliminary ruling by the ECJ) should be fully brought into play before the presumption of equivalent protection may apply. The *ratio* is similar to the exhaustion of domestic remedies; every opportunity provided in the International Organisation's rules to review the applicant's complaint should be exhausted in order to charge the latter for defective human rights protection, *Michaud* [114]–[115].

The ECtHR may have got the attribution rule wrong, then, however its approach to responsibility in *Bosphorus* is consistent with the one adopted in *Waite and Kennedy* and *Matthews*. The problem of unclear attribution rules is evident in a strain of ECtHR cases and this point is not lost in the second reading of the ARIO.[55] This is the main flaw with the *Behrami and Saramati* case and the other decisions that followed its authority.[56]

Gasparini is also aligned with the direct responsibility approach taken by the Court.[57] The case originated from a labour dispute between NATO and an employee, decided by NATO's administrative tribunal. Specifically, the applicant complained that the International Organisation's administrative tribunal by default (as a result of a structural deficiency) was not offering sufficient ECHR, Article 6 guarantees and the member States (Italy and Belgium being the respondents) were aware of this upon accession to the International Organisation. Therefore, the ECtHR had to determine whether the defendant States violated the ECHR by joining an International Organisation that was not offering human rights guarantees comparable to the ECHR. The Court's reasoning is obfuscatory, a close examination, however, suggests that the Court applied – albeit by stealth – the direct responsibility model.

The member State conduct reviewed in the present instance is the transfer of competences to the International Organisation per se. Nevertheless, this doesn't confer jurisdiction upon the ECtHR as it has to be proven that the applicant had rights vis-à-vis the respondent member State. As discussed above, in order to establish State jurisdiction, the Court must give weight to the link between the respondent member State and the conduct that allegedly caused the breach. The Court held that the conduct causing the structural *lacuna* complained of was in fact the conferral of competences. This suggests two things: first, the conduct that caused the breach is sufficiently linked to Italy and Belgium and hence the complaint falls under the scope of ECHR, Article 1. Second, the conduct that caused the breach is identical to the one reviewed by the Court. This is the reason why the Court, when proceeding with the examination of the case on the merits, omitted (wrongly) any reference to attribution. The Strasbourg Court should have attributed the conduct of conferral of competences to Italy and Belgium and subsequently it should have determined whether this conduct was in breach of the member States obligations under the ECHR. *Gasparini*, then, highlights

[55] ARIO Comment, 88–89, [10]–[11] and authorities cited therein.

[56] *Behrami and Behrami v France/Saramati v France, Germany and Norway*, Application nos 71412/01 and 78166/01, ECtHR Grand Chamber, Decision of 2 May 2007, (2007) 45 EHRR SE10 ('*Behrami and Saramati*'). The judgments that followed *Behrami and Saramati* were *Kasumaj v Greece*, Application no 6974/05, ECtHR, Judgment of 5 July 2007; *Gajić v Germany*, Application no 31616/02, ECtHR, Judgment of 28 August 2007; and *Berić and others v Bosnia*, Application nos 36357/04, 36360/04, 38346/04, 41705/04, 45190/04, 45578/04, 45579/04, 45580/04, 91/05, 97/05, 100/05, 1121/05, 1123/05, 1125/05, 1129/05, 1132/05, 1133/05, 1169/05, 1172/05, 1175/05, 1177/05, 1180/05, 1185/05, 20793/05 and 25496/05, ECtHR, Judgment of 16 October 2007.

[57] *Gasparini v Italy and Belgium*, Application no 10750/03, ECtHR, Judgment of 12 May 2009.

why it is crucial to separate the linkage that pertains to jurisdiction and the one germane to attribution in order to make sense of the relevant case law.

Through the prism of direct responsibility and the distinction between jurisdiction and attribution, *Gasparini* can be distinguished from other similar cases. *Boivin*, for example, concerned a labour dispute between the applicant and the European Organisation for the Safety of Air Navigation which the applicant had taken to the International Labour Organization's Administrative Tribunal.[58] The applicant complained about the conduct of the International Organisation without linking it in any way with member State conduct. Inevitably, then, the Court held that 'the impugned decision thus emanated from an international tribunal outside the *jurisdiction* of the respondent States'[59] (emphasis added). This lack of a link between the impugned decision and the respondent States was the reason *Boivin* was declared inadmissible.[60] After concluding that 'the applicant cannot be said to have been "within the jurisdiction" of the respondent States for the purposes of Article 1 of the Convention', the Court went on to suggest that 'the alleged violations of the Convention cannot therefore be *attributed* to France and Belgium'[61] (emphasis added). This dictum, replicated in a series of subsequent decisions,[62] highlights in the most emphatic way the confusion between the two notions and makes it clear that a distinction between them will add doctrinal clarity in the reasoning and significantly aid the Court in performing its function.

(ii) Indirect Responsibility Before the ECtHR

The same doctrinal issues are entangled in the few cases where the ECtHR has approached member State responsibility from the perspective of indirect responsibility. In *Kokkelvisserij*, the applicant association was engaged in domestic judicial proceedings in the context of which the national court sought a preliminary ECJ ruling.[63] In the procedure before the ECJ, the applicant lacked an opportunity to respond to the Advocate General's opinion and on this basis it complained for a violation of its rights under the ECHR.

First, the Court separated the present case from previous case law on the issue of State jurisdiction. In contrast with *Boivin*, where no member State conduct

[58] *Boivin v 34 Member States of the Council of Europe*, Application no 73250/01, ECtHR, Judgment of 9 September 2008.

[59] ibid 6.

[60] Same reasoning with respect to a completely different set of facts was followed in *Longa v Netherlands*, Application no 33917/12, ECtHR, Judgment of 9 October 2012.

[61] ibid.

[62] *Lopez Cifuentes v Spain*, Application no 18754/06, ECtHR, Judgment of 7 July 2009; *Biret v 15 Member States of the European Union*, Application no 13762/04, ECtHR, Judgment of 9 December 2008; and *Connolly v 15 Member States of the European Union*, Application no 73274/01, ECtHR, Judgment of 9 December 2008.

[63] *Cooperatieve Producentenorganisatie van de Nederlandse Kokkelvisserij UA v Netherlands*, Application no 13645/05, ECtHR, Judgment of 20 January 2009 ('*Kokkelvisserij*').

was linked to the conduct causing the breach, in *Kokkelvisserij*, the respondent State was 'involved' in the intervention by the ECJ because the latter 'had been actively sought by a domestic court in proceedings pending before it'.[64] In this way, the conduct causing the breach (ECJ ruling) was sufficiently linked to the respondent State and hence the applicants had rights vis-à-vis the Netherlands.

The ECtHR's analysis on the merits is slightly more perplexing. The Court held:

> The nexus between a preliminary ruling by the ECJ under Article 234 of the EC Treaty and the domestic proceedings which give rise to it is obvious. It is the domestic court which, finding itself faced with a question of Community law to which it requires an answer in order to give a decision in a case pending before it, seeks the ECJ's assistance in terms of its own choosing; the interpretation which the ECJ then gives of Community law is authoritative and cannot be ignored by the domestic court.[65]

It should be noted that the question to the ECJ for a preliminary ruling is only available to EU Member States. However, the specific State conduct is not an exercise of EU competence from an EU organ. The request for a preliminary ruling is an exercise of competence that lies with the member State of the EU. This is why the Netherlands was acting as a State and not as a member of the EU when its domestic court sought the ECJ's intervention. If one reads between the lines, it looks as if the Court attaches importance to the causative link between the relevant act of the International Organisation (ECJ ruling) and the conduct of the Netherlands (domestic proceedings). I understand this to be an implicit but nevertheless clear formulation of member State responsibility for participation in the internationally wrongful act of an International Organisation.

In order to understand this, one has to bring to the surface some thoughts latent in the Court's reasoning. The ECtHR holds that the main conduct causing the breach is the ECJ ruling. However, the Netherlands will be responsible under the ECtHR, so long as it has intentionally contributed to the commission of a wrongful act of the International Organisation. First, it is evident that the Netherlands intentionally caused the ECJ ruling since they 'actively sought' its rendering. Further, when speaking of a 'nexus' between the International Organisation and the member State conduct, the ECtHR is in fact establishing whether the national courts have contributed to the resulting internationally wrongful act of the International Organisation. The Court does not seek to attribute the ECJ ruling itself to the Netherlands. Therefore, it is the national courts' actions, attributable to the Netherlands, that are reviewed by the ECtHR in the present complaint (conduct reviewed by the Court). *Kokkelvisserij*, then, is an example where the conduct causing the breach and the conduct reviewed by

[64] ibid s B ('The Law') 3, 18.
[65] ibid 20.

the Court do not concur. Through the prism of member State responsibility for participation in the internationally wrongful act of the International Organisation (complicity model), the attribution question was in fact clearly (although implicitly) addressed by the ECtHR.

This responsibility model also explains the focus the analysis placed on the conduct of the International Organisation. It should be reminded that according to the complicity model, the complicit conduct attracts its wrongfulness from the internationally wrongful act of the main actor. Since the wrongfulness of member State conduct can be assessed only if an internationally wrongful act of an International Organisation is established, it is only logical that the Court turned its attention to examining the lawfulness of the International Organisation's conduct. And the tool used by the Court to assess this was the equivalent protection presumption. Probably, this is what the Court had in mind when it stated:

> As a corollary, this presumption [equivalent protection] applies not only to actions taken by a Contracting Party but also to the procedures followed within such an International Organisation and hence to the procedures of the ECJ.

To cite this conclusion as a correlation of the preceding thoughts, which had nothing to do with responsibility for participation in the ECJ's ruling, was a confusing non-sequitur. Commentators have not examined this case through the prism of responsibility for participation in another subject's internationally wrongful act and they lamented the approach taken because it seemed as if the Court was directly reviewing conduct of the International Organisation.[66] Arguably, the reasoning in *Kokkelvisserij* is the result of scattered and unsystematic thoughts because the responsibility model applied by the Court is very unclear. The ECtHR, then, missed the opportunity to clarify its case law in member State responsibility for participation in an internationally wrongful act of an International Organisation.

The same opportunity was missed in the *Lechouritou* decision as this confusing approach was to a certain extent replicated.[67] In this case, the applicants complained that in the context of proceedings against Germany before Greek courts, the CJEU, ruling preliminarily, had violated ECHR, Articles 6, 13 and ECHR, Protocol No 1, Article 1. According to the applicants, the CJEU gave insufficient reasons when declaring the Brussels Convention on Jurisdiction and the Enforcement of Judgments in Civil and Commercial Matters inapplicable. The reasoning of the ECtHR's decision was driven by considerations of judicial economy. The analysis began by saying that it was pertinent to address, first, the question of jurisdiction, but the court would not delve into this matter as the

[66] Ryngaert, 'Oscillating Between Embracing and Avoiding *Bosphorus*' (n 35) 179–81.

[67] *Lechouritou and others v Germany and 26 Member States of the European Union*, Application no 37937/07, ECtHR, Judgment of 3 April 2012.

application fell on different grounds.[68] Thus, it eloquently avoided the matter and jumped into the examination of the complaint on the merits. Skipping also the question of attribution, the ECtHR decided to examine immediately the compatibility of the ECJ ruling with the ECHR, which it found to satisfy the guarantees of Articles 6 and 13. No matter whose conduct the Strasbourg Court was reviewing in the present instance (probably that of the Greek courts), an internationally wrongful act of an International Organisation had not occurred and thus an internationally wrongful act of a member State, which attracts its wrongfulness only when linked with the internationally wrongful act of an International Organisation, cannot arise.

It may be true that the Court's approach in both *Kokkelvisserij* and *Lechouritou* resulted from political expediency. The Court did not try too hard to examine any member State conduct, as in the first place it may have wished to counter the detractors of the EU, and to unambiguously confirm that EU procedures meet human rights standards.[69] This is apparent especially with respect to *Lechouritou*. Be that as it may, political considerations are of little importance when the case law is holistically explained in doctrinal terms. Seen under the lenses of direct and indirect responsibility, the reasonings in the cited case law acquire a new meaning that helps us juxtapose it with the understanding of Article 61 analysed above.

B. Disentangling ECtHR Case Law from Article 61

In the commentaries to ARIO, Article 61, the ILC incorporated certain examples from ECtHR case law as authorities supporting the formulation of the provision. It cited *Waite and Kennedy*, *Bosphorus* and *Gasparini* as examples of 'States being held responsible when they fail to ensure compliance with their obligations under the European Convention of Human Rights in a field where they have attributed competence to an international organization'.[70] The case law cited indeed supports this proposition but this does not necessarily bring these cases under the ambit of Article 61. I argue here that the ILC should have avoided any mention of the ECtHR case law, as the cases cited do not fall within

[68] 'Dans la mesure oul la requête est dirigeie contre les 27 Etats membres de l'Union europeienne, la Cour note que la question se pose de savoir si et dans quelle mesure ces Etats peuvent être tenus responsables de l'arrêt de la Cour de Justice. Elle n'estime cependant pas neicessaire de se prononcer sur cette question car cette partie de la requête doit de toute manielre être rejeteie pour d'autres raisons', ['To the extent that the application is filed against the 27 Member States of the European Union, the Court notes that the question of knowing if and to what extent these States can be held responsible for a judgment of the Court of Justice [of the European Union] arises. Nevertheless, the Court does not consider it necessary to pronounce on this question since this part of the application should in any case be rejected for other reasons'] (author's translation), ibid 5.

[69] Ryngaert, 'Oscillating Between Embracing and Avoiding *Bosphorus*' (n 35) 180.

[70] ARIO Comment, 159–60, [3].

the scope of the provision's application and hence are not pertinent for the drafting of Article 61.

The fundamental difference between Article 61 and the ECtHR jurisprudence cited in the commentaries lies in the responsibility model they address. The three cases mentioned provide evidence that States remain directly responsible by virtue of their own conduct when they join an International Organisation. In this way, the Strasbourg Court attaches minimal or no importance to the causative link between the conduct of the State and the ensuing conduct of the International Organisation causing the breach. The case law cited focuses on the conduct of members as States and especially at the level of the establishment of an International Organisation. The ECtHR ensures that States which create International Organisations cannot do so in such a way as to frustrate or prevent the performance of their own international obligations.[71] In this way, the Court establishes a theory on 'sovereignty transfers' whereby subsisting obligations of member States will act as a limit on what kind of International Organisation they can create.[72]

Article 61, on the other hand, addresses indirect responsibility and is centred on causation. A certain relationship between the acting member State and the conduct of the International Organisation is indispensable for the operation of the provision.[73] The requirement that the member State has to cause a specific conduct of the International Organisation implies that Article 61 does not purport to create a theory of sovereignty transfers. The transfer of competence cannot be the conduct that forms the basis of the internationally wrongful act of the member State in Article 61. First, it can be logically inferred that States are not exercising competence they have already attributed to the International Organisation. Thus, provision of competence per se is in fact conduct taken by States before the particular member State-International Organisation relationship has been established with respect to the competence in play. What is more, the conferral of competence is hardly ever causatively linked to subsequent conduct of the International Organisation. In a *Bosphorus*-like situation, for example, Ireland did not cause the regulation of the EU whereby the aircraft

[71] cf Zemanek's comments in the context of the work of the Institut, noting that States are relatively free to 'write into constituent instruments whatever they want … as long as thereby they do not violate an existing international obligation of their own or design the organization for the purpose of violating international law', Institut de Droit International, (1995) 66-I *Annuaire de l'Institut de Droit International* 328 (Zemanek). See also UNGA, *Summary Record of the 15th Meeting* (n 28) [4] (Switzerland).

[72] I accept Verdirame's definition of a 'sovereignty transfer' as 'the voluntary or involuntary surrender of a previously-held power, right or function characterised as sovereign to another international legal person as part of a legal arrangement designed to last', Verdirame, 'A Normative Theory of Sovereignty Transfers' (n 37) 372 note 2.

[73] Verdirame has identified attribution as a key doctrinal issue that needs clarification in the case law. He argues that the relationship needed in order to connect the act reviewed by the court with the resulting breach remains unclear in the case law. While this criticism is valid, it is targeted towards a different link from the one identified here, Verdirame, *The UN and Human Rights* (n 37) 381.

was impounded. Ditto, in the *Waite and Kennedy* case; Germany did not cause the granting of immunity in the particular instance.

During the drafting process, however, it was suggested that the ILC should place more emphasis on the case law. The European Commission proposed to reinterpret the notion of circumvention under the light of the equivalent protection presumption. The organ of the EU supported an amendment to the direction that 'there was no circumvention if the State transferred powers to an international organization which was not bound by the State's own treaty obligations but whose legal system offered a comparable level of guarantees'.[74] The Special Rapporteur correctly pointed out that this suggestion lies outside the object of the provision.[75] The primary obligation latent in the provision ('to not cause with an intention to avoid compliance an act of an International Organisation') does not specify how the compatibility of member State conduct with the State's international obligations will be determined. This is a matter left entirely to the discretion of every Court and will differ depending on the nature of every obligation. This is why the reference in the commentaries to the equivalent protection standard as pronounced in *Gasparini* is unnecessary and beside the point.

The International Monetary Fund (IMF) on its part relied on the *Bosphorus* judgment to propose that a temporal element should be inserted in Article 61.[76] According to this International Organisation the granting of competence to an International Organisation could only give rise to responsibility by States for an act of the International Organisation if the grant of such competence occurs 'subsequent' to the entry into force of the obligation that is breached. This proposition, however, rests upon the view that it is the granting of competence as such that forms the object of Article 61. The requirement of causing conduct by the member State renders this temporal element redundant. The crucial time for the assessment of the compatibility of the member State's conduct with the State's international obligations is the time the member State commits the causing conduct. In the *Kokkelvisserij* case, for example, it would have made no difference if the Netherlands had attributed the competence for a preliminary ECJ ruling before it adhered to the ECHR. It would still be responsible for its participation in the internationally wrongful act of the International Organisation. It only mattered that the Netherlands intentionally caused the conduct of the International Organisation subsequently to the entry into force of the ECHR.

Given the above, it is not entirely clear how this particular jurisprudence has affected the drafting of Article 61. Since the cases pertain to different

[74] UNGA, 61st Session, Sixth Committee, *Summary Record of the 16th Meeting*, UN doc A/C.6/61/SR.16 (2006) [16].

[75] Gaja Seventh Report (n 27) [78].

[76] ILC, *Responsibility of International Organisations: Comments and Observations Received from International Organizations*, UN doc A/CN.4/582 (2007), reproduced in (2007) 2(1) *YBILC* 17, 28.

responsibility scenarios, any reference to them should have been omitted. Instead, the *Kokkelvisserij* case and the nexus requirement it incorporated should have been considered as a pertinent authority for the introduction of a causation element. What is more, the almost complete lack of relevant case law suggests that the rule advocated by the ILC is still in formation and Article 61 should be considered a progressive development of the law. It is submitted here that the Commission would have assisted this development if it would have drafted Article 61 in corresponding terms with Article 17, as they both address a respectively wide spectrum of scenarios. Thus, a separation between derivative responsibility and responsibility for complicity is necessary in order to make sense of the provision and clearly delineate its scope of application. Arguably, then, the progressive development of the law is captured by the following rule:

> Circumvention of obligations by a State member of an International Organisation
>
> When a State member of an International Organisation has the intention to avoid compliance with its international obligations, it will be responsible:
>
> (a) for conduct of the International Organisation that would have been wrongful if committed by the State, if this conduct results from the restriction of the International Organisation's freedom of action.
>
> (b) for facilitating certain conduct of the International Organisation, if this conduct runs counter to the State's obligations.

IV. CONCLUSION

In this chapter, I attempted an analysis of what has been perhaps the most troubling provision in the ARIO. Article 61 deals with scenarios of circumvention of obligations by member States through the International Organisation. The provision was amended countless times during the drafting process and has been the object of criticism from States, International Organisations and commentators.

Article 61 as adopted is a weird mixture. On the one hand, the ILC has arrived at a wording that is satisfactory because it addresses a wide spectrum of scenarios with a certain doctrinal rigour. The normative elements found within the provision are well-balanced and indispensable for its operation. On the other, the Commission's approach was flawed on a double basis.

First, it was flawed to the extent that it tried to accommodate a wide array of scenarios by drafting a 'package-deal' provision. In order to make sense of the two types of scenarios it covers, I suggested a rule that distinguishes between derivative responsibility and complicity. Therefore, the responsibility models developed in this book are the key to understanding the operation of Article 61.

Second, while Article 61 covers cases of indirect responsibility, ECtHR case law that was used in the commentaries to support the drafting of the provision pertains to direct responsibility. On the basis of the distinction between direct and indirect responsibility, I highlighted the points of convergence between the provision and existing case law and I brought to the surface the thrust of the provision. I hold, then, that the ILC should have avoided in the commentaries any reference to irrelevant ECtHR case law which provoked in its turn some misplaced criticism and a inaccurate understanding of the provision. Instead, an understanding of Article 61 on the basis of the present analysis would have constituted the progressive development of the law in the matter and could potentially transform the provision to a customary rule of international law.

Part III

Interactions Intertwined

7

Responsibility at the Decision-making Level

I. INTRODUCTION

THROUGHOUT THIS BOOK, I have examined certain Articles on the Responsibility of International Organizations (ARIO) provisions on the basis of their accordance with the legal premises of international responsibility. Therefore, the adaptability of the law to real-life scenarios was not the starting-point of the analysis. In this final chapter, I will reverse this principle and I will use decision-making procedures within International Organisations as a case-study to test how my theoretical construction applies to them. The scenarios analysed do not cover only member States' votes but any type of influence a State can exert during these procedures. The starting and end-point of the analysis will be the regulation of the matter within ARIO, Articles 58, 59 and 61 but also within existing case law.

It is fitting to do so with respect to decision-making for three main reasons: first, it is timely to bring Articles 58(2) and 59(2) into the analysis as such procedures were the main reason why these provisions were inserted in the ARIO. The criterion of accordance of State conduct with the rules of the International Organisation they incorporate echoes the threshold I advocated in Chapter 3 for the occurrence of interaction on the basis of membership. It is timely to test its application and examine whether the shielding of member States provided in Articles 58(2) and 59(2) is justified. Second, State conduct during decision-making procedures could occur both inside and outside the particular member State-International Organisation relationship. The type of interaction then shifts in these procedures, and that is why they provide a good illustration of both types of interaction and a figurative way to keep the cleavage as clear as possible. Third, while international responsibility can be established on certain occasions, it will seldom substantiate as jurisdictional bars will inhibit its fruition before a court. Decision-making procedures then are pertinent to keep clear another distinction, that between establishment and implementation of international responsibility.

As I will demonstrate, a thorough understanding of the establishment of international responsibility in the context of decision-making procedures within International Organisations is premised on a *tour d' horizon* of most issues discussed throughout the book. And I think it is only pertinent to conclude the argument, through an applied synthesis of all intermediate findings.

II. CONTROL FROM WITHIN/DERIVATIVE RESPONSIBILITY

A. ARIO, Article 59(2): Rules of the International Organisation as a Threshold

(i) A Two-Layered Responsibility Structure

The International Law Commission (ILC) has expanded the protection afforded towards member States to scenarios that go beyond mere membership. The expansion took place with respect to both 'aid or assistance' and 'direction and control' scenarios. Common paragraph 2 of ARIO, Articles 58 and 59 holds as follows:

> An act by a State member of an international organization done in accordance with the rules of the organization does not as such engage the international responsibility of that State under the terms of this article.

Complicity scenarios under Article 58(2) will be dealt with in the following part, and it should be stressed from the outset that only derivative responsibility is covered by Article 59(2); that is responsibility for conduct of the International Organisation performed under the control of its member States. A corresponding provision does not appear in Article 60 as it is difficult to imagine a coercive act of a member State occurring within the context of an International Organisation in accordance with its rules.[1]

The main consideration of the Commission with the inclusion of Article 59(2) was the regulation of voting patterns within International Organisations and whether under certain circumstances member States' votes in decision-making organs could result in derivative responsibility for conduct of the International Organisation as per Article 59(1).[2] In the post-United Nations era, there have been occasions where the influence exercised by individual member States on International Organisations at the decision-making level was such that

[1] ARIO Comment, 158–59, [3]. The Drafting Committee eloquently stated that: 'It had felt that, as a matter of policy, to suggest that coercion could be undertaken in accordance with the rules of an international organization was unacceptable', ILC, *Provisional Summary Record of the 3097th Meeting*, UN doc A/CN.4/SR.3097 (8 July 2011) 31. The Commission correctly points out that the omission of such a provision does not *ipso facto* render any coercive act necessarily unlawful.

[2] Rao summarised the thrust of the matter during the discussion: 'the real policy reason why the Commission was debating that issue was that wrongful decisions were sometimes pushed through by a group of members of an organization despite fierce opposition from other members. Should the latter really be held responsible for decisions which were subsequently found to be wrongful?', ILC, *Provisional Summary Record of the 2891st Meeting*, UN doc A/CN.4/SR.2891 (2006), reproduced in (2006) 1 *YBILC* 145, 154, [64].

it supposedly undermined the autonomy of the latter. Voting patterns, such as veto votes at the UN Security Council and votes based on quotas at the International Monetary Fund (IMF) Board of Governors, exercise sometimes decisive influence on the outcome of a voting process. A classic example of such influence is how the Soviet Union held sway over the then Warsaw Pact.[3] Will actual direction of an operative kind, at least superficially, in accordance with the rules of the International Organisation, never result in exclusive member State responsibility or even joint responsibility between member States and the International Organisation for the latter's controlled conduct?

The ILC answers this question negatively. The Commission suggests that any member State(s) influence on the conduct of an International Organisation at the decision-making level will not trigger this specific type of responsibility, as long as this occurs in accordance with the internal rules of the International Organisation.[4] Thus, with the inclusion of this provision, the ILC takes a very firm stance in the matter at hand but at the same time it does not invoke any judicial practice to support its assertion.[5] According to Article 59(2), then, the adoption of a decision by the Unified Command of Pact Armed Forces, the organ of the Warsaw Pact in charge of the alliance's military action, to attack the United States, taken in accordance with the rules of the International Organisation, would never trigger the Soviet Union's responsibility for that decision of the International Organisation. In the same vein, had the United Kingdom vetoed UN Security Council Resolution 918 on the prevention of the Rwandan genocide, the permanent member of the Security Council would not have been responsible for the omission of the UN organ. In this latter case, the unlawful inaction of the UN triggers exclusively the international responsibility of the world organisation.

The exculpation of member States for conduct of the International Organisation does not mean that the former are completely immune when voting or otherwise acting within the organisational context. To the contrary, the ILC clarified that member States will still be responsible by virtue of the Articles on State Responsibility (ASR) *qua* States for own conduct regardless of the context in which that act takes place.[6] To return to our previous example,

[3] For more See G Curtis (ed), *Czechoslovakia: A Country Study* (Federal Research Division of the Library of Congress, 1992).

[4] T Grant, 'International Responsibility and the Admission of States to the United Nations' (2009) 30 *Michigan Journal of International Law* 1095, 1146.

[5] Surprisingly, the ILC did not use the ruling of the House of Lords in the International Tin Council (ITC) litigation. The Lords held that the ITC does not function as an 'agent' of its member States when the latter act within the confines of the decision-making processes of the International Organisation. *JH Rayner v Department of Trade and Industry and others and Related Appeals* [1990] 2 AC 515 (per Lord Oliver). This ruling is again of limited value for the purpose of the present analysis because it makes reference to an agency relationship (see Chapter 4 at III B i a, nn 115–19 and accompanying text) and no explanation in legal terms as to why member States are shielded behind the institutional veil was given by the Court.

[6] ARIO Comment, 157, [5].

the United Kingdom would have been responsible on its own accord for vetoing SC Resolution 918, since it is bound by the Genocide Convention. The institutional veil, then, does not shield member States for violations of international obligations incumbent directly upon them, when they occur within the context of an International Organisation.[7] To claim the opposite would suggest that the latter are obligation-free zones for States.

This is clearly demonstrated by the International Court of Justice (ICJ) *Interim Accord* case between the Former Yugoslav Republic of Macedonia (FYROM) and Greece.[8] The two States had signed under UN auspices a bilateral treaty, the 1995 Interim Accord, Article 11(1) of which provides that Greece must not object to the application by or the membership of FYROM in International Organisations of which Greece is a member.[9] The applicant alleged that Greece violated the accord by objecting to FYROM's NATO membership application. Specifically, FYROM expected to receive an invitation to join NATO during the April 2008 NATO Bucharest Summit. The Summit Declaration provided instead that 'an invitation to the former Yugoslav Republic of Macedonia will be extended as soon as a mutually acceptable solution to the name issue has been reached'.[10] The invitation to join the International Organisation can only be extended by unanimous agreement of all NATO members,[11] and the position taken by Greece in the lead-up to the Summit made it clear that Greece opposed the extension of such an invitation.[12] The unanimity required gives Greece the power to direct and control (in the sense of Article 59(1)) with its vote, the decision adopted by NATO.

In its judgment, the Court clearly distinguishes between State responsibility for conduct of the International Organisation (derivative responsibility) and responsibility for own conduct, and this distinction explains why Article 59(2) is not applicable in the case before it. According to the ICJ, FYROM's claim is solely based on the allegation that Greece has violated by its own conduct its obligation under Article 11(1).[13] In this way, 'the consequences it [Greece's conduct] may have on the *actual final decision* of a given organization as to the

[7] As Barros and Ryngaert suggest, member States remain responsible *underneath* the veil, AS Barros and C Ryngaert, 'The Position of Member States in (Autonomous) Institutional Decision-Making: Implications for the Establishment of Responsibility' (2014) 11 *IOLR* 53,70.

[8] *Application of the Interim Accord of 13 September 1995 (Former Yugoslav Republic of Macedonia v Greece)* (Merits) [2011] ICJ Reports 644 ('*Interim Accord*').

[9] 1995 Interim Accord, Art 11(1) provides: 'Upon entry into force of this Interim Accord, the Party of the First Part agrees not to object to the application by or the membership of the Party of the Second Part in international, multilateral and regional organizations and institutions of which the Party of the First Part is a member', Interim Accord between Greece and the Former Yugoslavic Republic of Macedonia, 1891 UNTS 7.

[10] *Bucharest Summit Declaration Issued by the Heads of State and Government Participating in the Meeting of the North Atlantic Council in Bucharest on 3 April 2008*, Press Release (2008)049 [20], available at www.nato.int/docu/pr/2008/p08-049e.html.

[11] North Atlantic Treaty, 1949, 34 UNTS 243, Art 10.

[12] *Interim Accord* (n 8) 668–70, [72]–[83].

[13] ibid 667, [70].

Applicant's membership' are irrelevant for present purposes[14] (emphasis added). Therefore, even when operating within the NATO framework according to the rules of the International Organisation, Greece is not shielded by the institutional veil and remains responsible for own actions.

This two-layered responsibility structure makes clear that States do not give up their international personality when they become members of the International Organisation but instead their international personality continues to exist in parallel with that of the International Organisation.[15] When acting within the context of an International Organisation, State agents perform an international function, as Georges Scelle suggested in his theory of 'role-splitting'.[16] They thus function under a dual but not a double role, in the sense that they are split in 'a Dr Jakyll and Mr Hyde manner, exhibiting a split personality'.[17] While they legally always remain national organs, functionally they operate either as national or as international agents.[18] This approach explains why States, even when dressed up with their institutional garment, are not just bound by the obligations incumbent upon them by the rules of the International Organisation but by the totality of their international obligations as the ILC suggests.[19] Had the Soviet Union voted in favour of attacking the United States in the Unified Command of Pact Armed Forces, it would have been responsible by way of its own vote for a violation of Article 2(4) of the UN Charter, irrespective of the final decision adopted by the organ of the International Organisation.

(ii) Debates in the ILC

In order to put the discussion into perspective though, it is interesting to see how the ILC ended up broadening the protective scope of the institutional veil in scenarios of 'direction and control' within ARIO. Back in 2005, the Special Rapporteur requested comments from States and International Organisations on the general question of member State responsibility in connection with the conduct of the International Organisation.[20] Apart from the problem of responsibility for mere membership examined previously, some few and very

[14] ibid 660, [42].

[15] E Lagrange, *La representation institutionelle dans l'ordre international. Une contribution à la théorie de la personnalité morale des organisations internationals* (Kluwer, 2002) 45.

[16] G Scelle, 'Regies generales du droit de la paix' (1933) 46 *RCADI* 327, 356.

[17] A Cassese, 'Remarks on Scelle's Theory of "Role Splitting" (*dedoublement fonctionnel*) in International Law' (1990) 1 *EJIL* 210, 213.

[18] ibid.

[19] ARIO Comment, 157, [5]. Same logic by the ECtHR in *Waite and Kennedy* when the Court suggested that member States continue to be responsible under the ECHR in the field of activity covered by when they attribute competence to an International Organisation, *Waite and Kennedy v Germany*, Application no 26083/94, ECtHR Grand Chamber, Judgment of 18 February 1999, (2000) 30 EHRR 261, [51].

[20] ILC, *Report of the International Law Commission on the Work of Its 57th Session (2 May–3 June and 11 July–5 August 2005)*, UN doc A/60/10 (2005), reproduced in (2005) 2(2) *YBILC* 1, 13, [26].

differentiated comments were received on the difficult issue of member State responsibility for direction and control, aid or assistance and coercion over conduct of the International Organisation. Common ground in the comments received was that the practical scenario where such considerations may be applicable concerned voting procedures within International Organisations. China was the only State to hold that member States should in principle bear responsibility for an International Organisation's wrongful decision when they vote in favour of it,[21] while a cluster of States held that the opposite principle was the rule but it could be reversed according to the circumstances.[22]

With this background, the Special Rapporteur favoured the second (and majority) approach in his Fourth Report, mainly for two reasons. First, the Special Rapporteur provided a strong policy argument in support of his thesis, by stating that the decision-making process would be severely affected via the establishment of member State responsibility for the casting of a particular vote.[23] It is true that this approach 'would risk a wave of abstentions' within voting mechanisms,[24] and would also 'hamper the reaching of consensus'.[25] Such consequentialist considerations, however, while germane to the present debate, are not directly relevant to the legal analysis attempted here.

Second, a legal argument was evoked in support of this thesis. According to this argument, member State participation in decision-making according to the rules of the International Organisation is covered under the institutional veil and in this way the no-member responsibility rule is rendered applicable in such scenarios.[26] *A contrario*, upholding member State responsibility for acts of the International Organisation on these occasions, would be tantamount to denying the International Organisation's separate legal personality.[27] This line of thinking has a certain appeal, but remains of limited value for present purposes if not analysed in legal terms. As presented by the Special Rapporteur and commentators, the argument is mainly descriptive and does not explain the legal reason why the protective scope of the veil covers the scenarios at hand.[28]

[21] UNGA, 60th Session, Sixth Committee, *Summary Record of the 11th Meeting*, UN doc A/C.6/60/SR.11 (2005) 10, [53] (China).

[22] See comments by Italy, UNGA, 60th Session, Sixth Committee, *Summary Record of the 12th Meeting*, UN doc A/C.6/60/SR.12 (2005) 2, [3]; Belarus, ibid 9, [52]; France, *Summary Record of the 11th Meeting* (n 21) 14, [77]; and Spain, UNGA, 60th Session, Sixth Committee, *Summary Record of the 13th Meeting*, UN doc A/C.6/60/SR.13 (2005) 9–10, [53].

[23] G Gaja, *Fourth Report on Responsibility of International Organizations*, UN doc A/CN.4/564/ (2006) and Add 1 to 2, reproduced in (2006) 2(1) *YBILC* 103 ('Gaja Fourth Report') 124, [93].

[24] J Crawford, *State Responsibility: The General Part* (Cambridge University Press, 2013) 412.

[25] Gaja Fourth Report (n 23) 124, [93].

[26] ILC, *Summary Record of the 2891st Meeting* (n 2) 23.

[27] ibid 7, [67]. See also, C Ryngaert and H Buchanan, 'Member State Responsibility for the Acts of International Organizations' (2011) 7 *Utrecht Law Review* 131, 140; Crawford in milder terms speaks of an 'undermining' and not of a denying altogether of the International Organisation's separate legal personality, *State Responsibility* (n 24) 412.

[28] In Chapter 3 nn 68–69 and accompanying text, I explain why such an approach is not helpful.

The following section argues that an assessment of this argument requires a clear understanding of the relationship between the International Organisation and its member States.

Such an understanding is vital for another reason. The commentaries to Article 59(2) distinguish between conduct that can trigger international responsibility for direction and control and member State participation in International Organisations according to the latter's rules.[29] Nevertheless, participation in decision-making does not cover every aspect of member State participation in the International Organisation, and the commentaries suggest that responsibility can be triggered 'in borderline cases' by other State action within the framework of the International Organisation.[30] *A fortiori*, State action within the organisational framework which is at the same time not in accordance with its rules is possible according to the ILC. The Commission, however, did not back up this distinction with any real-life examples and the sole clarification provided in this direction is that the assessment of whether responsibility is engaged will have to be context-dependent.[31] This renders the distinction hard to fully grasp and several Governments in their comments had called for a clearer distinction to be drawn.[32]

The convoluted line drawn in the commentaries demonstrates that the ILC does not have a clear image of the nature of the relationship between member States and the International Organisation of which they are members. The Commission did not clarify whether States operate *qua* member States only when acting in accordance with the rules of the International Organisation. To put it in clearer terms: is State action within the organisational framework necessary member State action? As stated above, a clarification of the nature of the member State-International Organisation relationship is a necessary premise for an explanation of the institutional veil's protective scope and hence the regulation of the present matter.

When discussing the Fourth Report, members of the Commission agreed with the Special Rapporteur's approach, but saw no reason why a specific mention in this respect should be incorporated in the wording of the (then) Draft Articles. In first reading, then, the Special Rapporteur's point of view is present only in the commentaries to Articles 58 and 59 which (it must be stressed) are exactly the same on the second and final reading of the Articles.[33] When the Draft Articles returned to the Drafting Committee for a second reading, no further clarification was deemed necessary in the commentaries, but the Committee decided

[29] ARIO Comment, 158, [2].

[30] ibid.

[31] The ILC referred to 'the size of the membership' and 'the nature of the involvement' as relevant considerations, ibid 157, [4].

[32] ILC, *Summary Record of the 3097th Meeting* (n 1) 30.

[33] ILC, *Text of the Draft Articles on Responsibility of International Organizations Adopted by the Commission on First Reading*, UN docA/CN.4/L.748/Add.2 (2009), reproduced in 2009 2(2) *YBILC* 19, 71–72.

to include a reference to that respect in the text of the Articles themselves. The principle finally made its way into paragraph 2 of ARIO, Article 59. The provision is rather uncontroversial and does not leave any wiggle-room to argue that derivative responsibility will arise when 'knowledgeable restriction of freedom of action' results from member State conduct taken in accordance with the rules of the International Organisation.

(iii) An Exegesis of the International Organisation's Protective Veil

This section argues that the Article 59(2) rule is justified as there is a clear legal explanation why member States are protected by the International Organisation's institutional veil when they act in accordance with rules of the International Organisation. As explained in Chapter 3, it is the International Organisation's separate personality that operates as a veil and shields member States in the context of the particular member State-International Organisation relationship. The legal exegesis of the protective function of the veil in present scenarios does not rely on general international responsibility rules but rests on the *sui generis* nature of the relationship between member States and the International Organisation of which they are members.[34] The ILC's reluctance to adopt a clear-cut stance on this matter is regrettable.

The starting point of the present enquiry is the fact that International Organisations constitute themselves, like States, legal subjects with separate personality but also legal orders which are separate from general international law.[35] Two distinct features of these legal subjects are of relevance for present purposes. First, they do not possess a general competence, but rather they exercise the specific powers conferred upon them by their members, 'the limits of which are a function of the common interests whose promotion those states entrust to them'.[36] Second, they do not possess the impermeability of States.[37] Albeit not closed, International Organisations are not entirely open structures either, in the sense that States are sometimes shielded when acting within the organisational framework.[38] This is why International Organisations possess a

[34] Grant has suggested that member States do not bear responsibility in present scenarios because of lack of attributability but he fails to provide any explanation as to why this is so, 'International Responsibility and the Admission of States' (n 4) 1147–48.

[35] P Cahier, 'The Internal Legal Order of International Organizations' in RJ Dupuy (ed), *A Handbook on International Organizations* (Martinus Nijhoff, 1998) 377ff; N White, *The Law of International Organizations* (Manchester University Press, 2005) 132.

[36] *Legality of the Use by a State of Nuclear Weapons in Armed Conflict* (Advisory Opinion) [1996] ICJ Reports 66, 78–79. This feature is called the 'principle of speciality', see M Shaw, *International Law* (CUP, 2008) 1306.

[37] C Brölmann, 'A Flat Earth? International Organizations in the System of International Law' (2001) 70 *Nordic Journal of International Law* 319, 322. On the impermeability of States, see ASR, Art 4 and commentaries to this provision.

[38] C Brölmann, *The Institutional Veil in Public International Law: International Organisations and the Law of Treaties* (Hart Publishing, 2007) 30.

transparent quality.[39] This is as far as publicists have managed to go in describing the relationship between member States and the International Organisation from an international law perspective. Nevertheless, such description is by no means a coherent explanation.

Being unable to explain why the institutional personality protects States occasionally, commentators suggested that international law was incapable of providing general rules that regulate the member State-International Organisation relationship. The ILC has recognised this, since it embarked on the drafting of the ARIO.[40] From the early 1990s, when the relevant academic debate was heated due to the demise of the International Tin Council, it was suggested that international law can only revert to the internal law of the International Organisation for the regulation of the member State-International Organisation relationship.[41] The deferral to the constitutional law of the International Organisation favoured by publicists renders the regulation of the said relationship an internal affair.[42] As it will be explained, this does not mean that the relationship is a *non-liquet* for international law but rather that internal rules can have legal ramifications in the international plane.

It is submitted here that the expansion of the veil adopted by the ILC rests on the important distinction put forward in Chapter 3: that between States acting as members, as opposed to members acting as States.[43] First, conduct of States members of an International Organisation can be shielded under the veil only if it occurs as an exercise of competence of the International Organisation according to its rules, that is, within the context of the constitutional framework of the International Organisation. Stumer's example is enlightening in this respect.[44] He argues that if an ad hoc treaty is signed between the International Organisation and some of its members, whereby the latter confer powers on the International Organisation to undertake specific tasks, then the States can incur responsibility for directing and controlling the International Organisation and rightly so. This scenario is not covered by the protective scope of Article 59(2), because States do not operate as members if their conduct

[39] P Weil, 'Cours General de Droit International Public' (1992) 237 *RCADI* 9, 104.

[40] ILC, *Report of the International Law Commission on the Work of Its 55th Session (5 May–6 June and 7 July–8 August 2003)*, UN Doc A/58/10 (2003), reproduced in (2003) 2(2) *YBILC* 1, 23, [10].

[41] R Higgins, Special Rapporteur, 'Report on the Legal Consequences for Member States of the Non-fulfillment by International Organizations of Their Obligations Toward Third Parties' (1995) 66 *Yearbook of the Institute of International Law* 251; CF Amerasinghe, *Principles of the Institutional Law of International Organizations* (CUP, 2005) 259ff; M Hirsch, *The Responsibility of International Organizations Toward Third Parties: Some Basic Principles* (Martinus Nijhoff, 1995) chs 4 and 5; Brölmann, *The Institutional Veil in Public International Law* (n 38) ch 11.3.

[42] ibid (n 37) 331–37.

[43] See Chapter 3 nn 13–16 and accompanying text.

[44] A Stume, 'Liability of Member States for Acts of International Organizations: Reconsidering the Policy Objections' (2007) 48 *Harvard International Law Journal* 553, 561.

pertains to competence that exceeds the confines of the constituent document. In such instances then, International Organisations and member States interact as independent subjects of international law.[45] In decision-making procedures, States act necessarily as members, for every vote cast not in accordance with the constitutional rules of the International Organisation is *ipso facto* not valid. This, however, does not preclude that member States can act both as States and as members in an institutional setting at the same time so long as they exercise different competences.

This proposition nevertheless is prima facie in contradiction with the 'role-splitting' theory on a twofold basis. First, it suggests that member States can perform not only a dual but a double role within the organisational setting, and further that they can abolish their international personality when joining the International Organisation. I suggest that Scelle's theoretical construction does not adequately address the nature of the relationship between member States and the International Organisation. Instead of jettisoning his theory altogether, I propose here that a slightly modified version of it can fully capture the particular relationship under scrutiny.

The double role of States that was rejected under the 'role-splitting' theory must be upheld, because States can wear two different hats at the same time as each one pertains to the exercise of a different competence/function.[46] Other commentators have distinguished between the vote, as an act attributable to the State and the final decision of the International Organisation as an act attributable to the International Organisation, but they do not accept the *dédoublement fonctionelle* of States with respect to the same act.[47] In this way, however, they fail to explain why member States do not bear responsibility for their vote as an influence on the adopted decision of the International Organisation per ARIO, Articles 58(2) and 59(2).

I argue here that the casting of a vote in the organisational framework is the example *par excellence* of States exercising two different functions through the same act. To the extent that voting as such is the expression of the States' own separate will, States exercise own competence, retain their separate legal

[45] As noted by the International Labour Organization: 'a member State may interact with an international organization beyond the scope of its constitutional obligations as a member of the organization; in such cases, the State and the organization relate to each other as two independent subjects of international law', ILC, *Comments and Observations Received from International Organisations*, UN doc A/CN.4/568 (2006) and Add 1, reproduced in (2006) 2(1) *YBILC* 125, 142; in the same vein, see the observations of UNESCO ibid 144–45.

[46] See the Report prepared by the Independent Evaluation Office of the IMF, ch 3 n 15.

[47] Barros and Ryngaert, 'The Position of Member States in (Autonomous) Institutional Decision-Making' (n 7) 71; F Naert, 'Binding International Organisations to Member State Treaties or Responsibility of Member States for Their Own Actions in the Framework of International Organisations' in J Wouters, E Brems, S Smis and P Schmitt (eds), *Accountability for Human Rights Violations by International Organisations* (Intersentia, 2010) 129, 162–66; P Palchetti, 'Sulla Responsabilità di uno Stato per il Voto Espresso in Seno ad Un'Organizzazione Internazionale' (2012) 45 *Rivista di Diritto Internazionale* 352, 354–55.

personality and function as national agents (members as States).[48] To the extent that such a vote is an influence on the expression of the International Organisation's separate will as stipulated in the rules of the International Organisation, States operate within the particular member State-International Organisation relationship; they exercise competence of the International Organisation, their international personality merges with the International Organisation's and they function as member States, hence as international agents (States as members). Thus, States do retain their international legal personality when joining an International Organisation, as Scelle suggested, however they abolish this attribute only insofar as the International Organisation exercises own competence. If it was accepted that member States possess legal personality when directing and controlling the decision-making process of an International Organisation, there would be no reason why they should not bear responsibility for the ensuing act of the International Organisation. According to the analysis of derivative responsibility in Chapter 4, an internationally wrongful act on behalf of member States would have been established and hence member State responsibility should have arisen.

It has been argued that, in voting discretion cases, the doctrine of abuse of rights provides the threshold for the triggering of State responsibility.[49] This is why a special provision on member State responsibility that deals with cases of abuses of rights is needed within ARIO, the argument runs.[50] The ICJ's ruling in the *Admissions* Advisory Opinion[51] and Article 5(b) of the IDI 1995 Lisbon Resolution provide support for such a rule.[52] The inclusion of such a provision, however, is futile mainly for two reasons. First, the 'abuse of rights' doctrine is but an expression of the threshold for member State responsibility advocated here (in accordance with rules of the International Organisation), only tailored to voting discretion scenarios. For example, if a member State of the UN requires as a further condition for its affirmative vote in favour of a state's admission to the UN that another State be admitted simultaneously, such a request constitutes an abuse of the State's voting rights.[53] States cannot validly cast such a vote within the particular procedure. If they do, however, they are not applying the rules of the International Organisation, they are

[48] I Seidl-Hohenveldern, 'Responsibility of Member States of an International Organization for the Acts of that Organization' in I Seidl-Hohenveldern (ed), *Collected Essays on International Investments and on International Organizations* (Kluwer, 1998) 63, 66.

[49] O Murray, 'Piercing the Institutional Veil: The Responsibility of Member States of an International Organization' (2011) 8 *IOLR* 291, 327ff.

[50] ibid 338.

[51] *Conditions of Admission of a State to Membership in the United Nations* (Advisory Opinion) [1948] ICJ Reports 57, 59. For an analysis as to why the ICJ ruling was based on this doctrine, see GDS Taylor, 'Content and Rule Against Abuse of Rights in International Law' (1972) 46 *BYBIL* 323, 343; G Fitzmaurice, 'The Law and Procedure of the International Court of Justice' (1953) 30 *BYBIL* 1, 13.

[52] Higgins, Special Rapporteur, 'Report on the Legal Consequences' (n 41) 445.

[53] *Conditions of Admission* (n 51) 65.

acting outside the constitutional context of the International Organisation – hence not as members – and thus they are not covered under the institutional veil. Second, the purpose of the ILC was to draft provisions that would reflect general responsibility principles and not to put forward tailor-made solutions to specific scenarios.[54]

Overall, it has been argued that the expansion of the protective function of the organisational veil in Article 59(2) is sound from a legal perspective. Instead of drawing convoluted distinctions without any supporting practical examples and referring to 'borderline cases', the ILC should have clearly upheld the threshold of accordance with rules of the International Organisation in the commentaries. Commentators then would not argue that member State responsibility on such occasions would depend upon factual circumstances and especially on the level of member State influence exercised on the International Organisation.[55] If accordance with organisational rules is the criterion for the establishment of member State responsibility, the influence exercised upon the International Organisation is indifferent. Since no judicial practice has authoritatively resolved the matter at hand, it is arguable that States do not have autonomy from the International Organisation when acting in accordance with its rules and hence they remain shielded in respect of organisational acts.[56]

(iv) Double Nature of the Rules of the International Organisation

There are certain inferences to be drawn from this concerning the nature of the rules of the International Organisation in ARIO, Article 59(2). It has been made clear that the rules of the International Organisation have legal ramifications from an international perspective as they affect the international legal status of States. As argued above, States are shielded under the institutional veil for acts of the International Organisation only to the extent that they act in accordance with organisational rules. Under this prism, States become an essential component of the International Organisation and function as member States when they operate in accordance with the rules of the Organisation. This is why the contracting parties to the International Organisation's constituent instrument become member States when they operate in accordance with organisational rules and not by virtue of the conferral of powers.[57] These rules determine when the International Organisation operates autonomously and consequently when States acquire international legal personality while acting within the

[54] ARIO Comment, 159, [2].

[55] Ryngaert and Buchanan, 'Member State Responsibility for the Acts of International Organizations' (n 27) 140; Stumer, 'Liability of Member States for Acts of International Organizations' (n 44) 561; Murray, 'Piercing the Institutional Veil' (n 49) 328ff.

[56] N Blokker, 'International Organizations and their Members: "International Organizations Belong to All their Members and None", Variations on a Theme' (2004) 1 *IOLR* 139, 161.

[57] Against C Ahlborn, 'The Rules of International Organizations and the Law of International Responsibility' (2011) 8 *IOLR* 397, 415.

organisational framework. Then, State conduct not in accordance with the rules of the International Organisation within the organisational framework envisaged by the ARIO is not conduct taken by States as members. That is why the institutional veil does not occasionally protect member States, as submitted by some authors, but always. This attribute of the rules of the International Organisation, however, does not render them international law.

In fact, the Special Rapporteur endorsed the internal law nature of these rules in his Third Report on the ARIO. When commenting on responsibility of an International Organisation for omissions, UNESCO wondered whether the ILC should take into account the fact that organisational conduct 'may simply result from the application of the decision-making process provided under the constitutive act of the international organization concerned'.[58] The General Counsel of the IMF in his turn asked whether an International Organisation would 'be responsible for not taking action, if this non-action is the result of the lawful exercise of their powers by its member States?'[59] The Special Rapporteur held that, as in the case of States, International Organisations are perceived as closed actors and rules of the International Organisation could not exonerate the latter.[60] In this way, the Special Rapporteur merely replicates the second sentence of ASR, Article 3 and thus equates the rules of the International Organisation with internal law.[61]

Nevertheless, this was not the stance adopted by the ILC in the final reading of the ARIO. The Commission refrains on purpose to express a clear-cut view on the issue of the legal nature of the 'rules of the organization' as either internal or international law and this indecision has led to an ambiguous use of this term in various substantive provisions of the ARIO.[62] Provisions on attribution or reparation uphold the internal constitutional nature of rules of the International Organisation, while norms on countermeasures or on the breach of an international obligation consider organisational rules to be part of international law.[63] The second sentence of ASR, Article 3, for example, was not included in the respective ARIO, Article 5 because of the two-dimensional nature of the rules of the International Organisation.[64] Even if the nature of the rules of the International Organisation has not crystallised in the ARIO, it is not contested

[58] ILC, *Comments and Observations 2006* (n 45) 8.

[59] ILC, *Responsibility of International Organizations: Comments and Observations Received from International Organizations*, UN doc A/CN.4/545 (2004), reproduced in (2004) 2(1) *YBILC* 19, 26, [4] (IMF).

[60] G Gaja, *Third Report on Responsibility of International Organizations*, UN doc A/CN.4/553 (2005), reproduced in (2005) 2(1) *YBILC* 7, 10, [10].

[61] ASR, Art 3 reads: 'The characterization of an act of a State as internationally wrongful is governed by international law. Such characterization is not affected by the characterization of the same act as lawful by internal law'.

[62] Ahlborn, 'The Rules of International Organizations' (n 57) 398–99.

[63] ibid 432ff.

[64] ARIO Comment, 80, [2].

that they have a dual dimension and they produce certain effects at the international level.

The shielding of member States by virtue of ARIO, Article 59(2) suggests that, as far as this provision goes, the internal relationship between member States and the International Organisation is not subject to international law. Organisational rules are then perceived to be internal constitutional law and consequently International Organisations are envisaged as closed actors in the particular instance. As 'international law does not permit a State to escape its international responsibilities by a mere process of internal subdivision' why should this principle be different with respect to International Organisations?[65] The difference between the two entities is that constituent parts of States do not possess international legal personality and thus cannot bear international responsibility in the first place. Therefore, the function of internal law is exactly the same in both cases, however, in the case of International Organisations, internal rules shield subjects of international law and that is why they have ramifications that pertain to international law.

The ICJ dealt with the distinction between rules of the organisation that are merely internal and those that have an international law character in its Advisory Opinion on the *Declaration of Independence of Kosovo*.[66] Many intervening governments have questioned whether the Constitutional Framework adopted on behalf of the United Nations Mission in Kosovo (UNMIK) by the Special Representative of the Secretary-General forms part of the applicable international law within the meaning of the General Assembly's question.[67] According to that argument, the Constitutional Framework would not be part of the international law applicable in the present instance and the question of the compatibility of the declaration of independence therewith would thus fall outside the scope of the General Assembly's request. The Court nevertheless upheld the dual nature of the regulations in play. On the one hand, it upheld the international law characterisation of all regulations adopted by the Special Representative by laconically suggesting that these norms ultimately derived their authority and binding force from the United Nations Charter, hence from international law.[68] At the same time, though, the Court admitted the domestic regulatory function of such provisions, thus corroborating their *sui generis* legal status.[69]

[65] ibid 39, [7].

[66] *Accordance with International Law of the Unilateral Declaration of Independence in Respect of Kosovo* (Advisory Opinion) [2010] ICJ Reports 403 ('*Declaration of Independence of Kosovo*').

[67] The question posed by the General Assembly to the ICJ was: 'Is the unilateral declaration of independence by the Provisional Institutions of Self-Government of Kosovo in accordance with international law?', UNGA, Resolution 63/3, UN doc A/RES/63/3 (8 October 2008) ('Request for an Advisory Opinion of the International Court of Justice on whether the unilateral declaration of independence of Kosovo is in accordance with international law').

[68] *Declaration of Independence of Kosovo* (n 66) 439–40, [88].

[69] ibid 440, [89].

A cogent understanding of the nature of organisational rules exceeds the remit of this book. It suffices here to note that such norms provide a valid threshold for the exculpation of member States in scenarios of direction and control covered by Article 59(2). It has been persuasively argued elsewhere that the ILC should have solved the tension between the internal or international law nature of rules of the International Organisation in favour of the former.[70] Be that as it may, the constitutional function of organisational rules, prevalent in Article 59(2), is not incompatible with their nature and generates the necessary autonomy that an International Organisation needs in order to become a subject of international law.

B. Political Influence Beyond the Rules of the International Organisation

(i) Refuting D'Aspremont's 'Overwhelming Control' Threshold

As noted earlier, the ARIO envisaged State conduct not in accordance with rules of the International Organisation within the organisational framework but did not cite any examples to this respect. According to the previous analysis, such conduct will not be covered by the Article 59(2) veil, as member States interact with the International Organisation as independent subjects of international law on these occasions when they perform conduct that exceeds the constitutional confines of the International Organisation. When it comes to decision-making, there exists a form of State participation within the organisational context that is not specifically regulated by rules of the International Organisation. This concerns the political influence exercised by States upon the decision-making process. Since States sometimes control this process through corridor talk, it has to be assessed whether such influence, that lies beyond the reach of organisational rules, is legally relevant for the establishment of State responsibility for acts of the International Organisation.

The argument that political influence over decision-making processes can amount to joint or concurrent responsibility was put forward by d'Aspremont.[71] Specifically, he contended that the control exercised in such instances is problematic if it undermines the autonomy of the International Organisation by abusing the separate legal personality of the International Organisation. The necessary threshold for the establishment of responsibility was according to him 'overwhelming control' over decision-making, which will be present if the influence overrules 'the whole process, thereby stifling any adverse opinion that could be expressed'.[72] The example he used in order to substantiate his

[70] Ahlborn, 'The Rules of International Organizations' (n 57) 435.

[71] J d'Aspremont, 'Abuse of the Legal Personality of International Organizations and the Responsibility of Member States' (2007) 4 *IOLR* 91.

[72] ibid 109.

argument was the case of the dismissal of the Director-General of the Organization for the Prohibition of Chemical Weapons (OPCW) in April 2002, which was deemed illegal by the Administrative Tribunal of the International Labour Organization (ILOAT).[73] The tribunal found that the unlawful decision had been taken '[a]t the insistent request of the United States'.[74] Even though the tribunal was not in a position to conclude that the United States was jointly or concurrently responsible for the wrongful dismissal, d'Aspremont argues that the factual elements in this case constitute evidence of overwhelming control by one State leading to a joint or concurrent responsibility for the International Organisation's wrongful act.

A legal assessment of this argument requires a legal characterisation of political influence from an International Organisation constitutional standpoint, in order to assess whether States act as members on such occasions. As noted earlier, there is no clear legal qualification of such conduct in the rules of any International Organisation, it is therefore open to interpretation whether political pressure is exercised in accordance with organisational rules or not. If one were to adopt *per analogiam* the *Lotus* principle, whereby conduct which is not explicitly prohibited is permitted,[75] one has to conclude that political influence is exercised in accordance with the rules of the International Organisation. However, organisational rules provide not for one but for the *only* way through which decisions can be validly adopted within the context of the International Organisation and this automatically excludes every other type of influence on the decision-making process. Thus, when States exercise political influence they do not act as member States, they interact as independent subjects with the International Organisation and hence their behaviour becomes legally relevant for derivative responsibility purposes if it comes within the scope of Article 59(1).

D'Aspremont disagrees with this proposition and argues that the threshold for the triggering of responsibility differs in two respects from that of 'direction and control' incorporated in Article 59(1). First, according to him the level of control exercised must be akin to coercion and mere domination will not suffice.[76] He fails to provide any specific arguments as to why the intensity of control must be so high, but the overall point is that abuse of legal personality should not be taken lightly and that is why it demands a higher threshold than

[73] ibid.

[74] ILOAT Judgment 2232, 16 July 2003, [15], [16], available at www.ilo.org/dyn/triblex/triblexmain.detail?p_judgment_no=2232.

[75] *Case of the SS Lotus (France v Turkey)* [1927] PCIJ Ser A, No 10 3, 18–21. The Court held that in relation to a specific act, it is not necessary to demonstrate a permissive rule so long as there is no prohibition. Against: Simma in *Declaration of Independence of Kosovo* (n 66) (Separate Opinion of Judge B Simma) [2010] ICJ Reports 478.

[76] Instead of coercion, however, he uses the milder term 'overwhelming control', d'Aspremont, 'Abuse of the Legal Personality of International Organizations' (n 71) 111–12.

mere control.[77] As noted in Chapter 4, however, control of whatever intensity suffices to switch attribution from one legal subject to another. Therefore, the distinction between overwhelming control and control he proposes is not critical for responsibility purposes and he does not suggest any reason why this should be different with respect to the present scenario.

Second, he contends that the requirement of knowledge should be scaled down because States may exert political influence for the realisation of own goals and without being aware that this may lead to the responsibility of the International Organisation.[78] That is why knowledge of their control over the decision-making should suffice for the triggering of responsibility. This criticism, nevertheless, is not germane only to the exercise of political influence in organisational decision-making, but can be warranted in any scenario of direction and control between States or between States and International Organisations. It merely states that a legal subject controls another subject because it suits its own goals and not because it necessarily wants to harm the controlled entity. In the same way, when Germany controlled Italian police in Rome during the Second World War, it may have been unaware that the forcible entry by Italian police forces into the territory of the Holy See in February 1944 would trigger Italy's responsibility.[79] If such criticism is given merit, then all of ASR, Articles 17 and 18, and ARIO, Articles 15, 16, 59(1) and 60 should modify the subjective element they incorporate. As mentioned in Chapter 4, however, the element of knowledge will most probably be presumed in such occasions due to the high level of restriction of freedom exercised and its presence there is justified as an *in extremis* defence mechanism for the controlling entity. Therefore, there is no reason why derivative responsibility for political influence should be regulated by different norms than other derivative responsibility scenarios as d'Aspremont proposes. As an interaction between two independent subjects of international law, political influence is tolerated to the extent that it does not result in 'direction and control' as per Article 59(1), or otherwise in knowledgeable restriction of freedom, as analysed in Chapter 4.

Consequently, political influence upon decision-making falls under the derivative responsibility model and will amount to exclusive State responsibility and not to concurrent or joint responsibility as d'Aspremont suggests. Abuse of legal personality, according to him, 'should not be seen as transforming the act of the organization into an act of the member states'.[80] In this way, attribution of conduct rests with the International Organisation while attribution of

[77] He merely posits in a circular note that '[t]he mere *domination* of one (or a few) state over an international organization or one of its organs is not sufficient either for there to be overwhelming control', ibid 110.

[78] ibid 112.

[79] The argument that the law on occupation is the applicable *lex specialis* in this instance does not affect the application of the ASR, see E Benvenisti, *The International Law on Occupation* (OUP, 2012) 18; ASR Comment, 68, [5].

[80] D'Aspremont, 'Abuse of the Legal Personality of International Organizations' (n 71) 115.

responsibility with the controlling State, he argues. Apart from the fact that attribution of responsibility is not a term of art in the law of international responsibility, it has been explained why restriction of freedom prohibits attribution of conduct to the controlled subject.[81] Thus, for legal purposes, no transformation is taking place as the International Organisation has never acted in a legal sense. In our previous example, then, the illegal dismissal of the Director General of the OPCW was a US act that triggered solely the responsibility of that State.

(ii) Circumvention Through Decision-Making

State responsibility for abuse of the International Organisation's separate legal personality was dealt with by the ILC in ARIO, Article 61. The so-called 'circumvention provision' is mirroring ARIO, Article 17 and deals with scenarios where a State 'avails itself of the separate legal personality of an international organization of which it is a member'.[82] Article 61 reads:

> Circumvention of international obligations of a State member of an international organization
>
> 1. A State member of an international organization incurs international responsibility if, by taking advantage of the fact that the organization has competence in relation to the subject-matter of one of the State's international obligations, it circumvents that obligation by causing the organization to commit an act that, if committed by the State, would have constituted a breach of the obligation.
>
> 2. Paragraph 1 applies whether or not the act in question is internationally wrongful for the international organization.

Prima facie, then, political influence scenarios could fall under its scope and this was recently suggested by a prominent commentator.[83] The analysis of this provision forms the subject-matter of the previous chapter, but it is pertinent to assess here whether circumvention that occurs through decision-making processes of International Organisations is covered by the provision's scope of application.

A chronology of the drafting of the provision makes clear that Article 61 can potentially cover political influence scenarios. Initially, and one has to agree with d'Aspremont in this respect, control at the decision-making level was excluded from the ambit of the then ARIO provision on circumvention.[84] At the time, draft Article 28 referred only to State responsibility for conferral of competence to an International Organisation and this was reflected in the provisional title of the provision.[85] Albeit the Drafting Committee in 2009 removed

[81] See Chapter 4 at III B ii a.
[82] ARIO Comment, 159, [1].
[83] Crawford, *State Responsibility* (n 24) 434.
[84] D'Aspremont, 'Abuse of the Legal Personality of International Organizations' (n 71) 100.
[85] The title of Art 28 was: 'International responsibility in case of provision of competence to an international organization', Gaja Fourth Report (n 23) 11.

the requirement of provision of competence from the title and wording of the provision, the narrow understanding of the abuse of legal personality remained. According to the Chairman of the Committee, the provision of competence is clearly implied in the new wording which stipulates that the International Organisation has competence with respect to the circumvented obligation.[86] In the final reading of the ARIO, Article 28 became Article 61 due to renumbering, its wording made no reference to scenarios of provision of competence, but the commentaries clearly widened the scope of the provision beyond such cases. According to the ILC, circumvention is not limited to provision of competence to the International Organisation and can occur through different types of State conduct.[87] Although such examples were not given by the Commission, circumvention through decision-making cannot be excluded *a priori* from the provision's scope.

As with Article 17, the scope of application of Article 61 consists of both a subjective and an objective element that place it under the umbrella of indirect responsibility. The subjective element incorporated is that of circumvention which, as analysed in Article 17, is higher than knowledge but as a stricter formulation remains within the ambit of this model.[88] The objective element that resurfaces from the wording of the provision is a strong causal link between the ensuing act and State conduct.[89] However, the commentaries offer no explanation as to the exact level of causation required and likewise the debates in the ILC are not enlightening. The ILC replaced 'prompting' with the clearer 'causing' after the first reading of the ARIO. This strengthening of the causation element in Article 61 occurred as it wasn't clear, from the observations received by States and International Organisations, whether the provision required any sort of State influence over the ensuing act of the International Organisation.[90] The ILC holds that the objective standard encompasses restriction of freedom scenarios when it suggests in the commentaries that Article 61 can overlap with Article 59(1) if organisational conduct is caused by the State and is wrongful for the International Organisation.[91]

[86] ILC, 'Responsibility of International Organizations: Statement of the Chairman of the Drafting Committee Mr Marcelo Vázquez-Bermúdez 6 July 2009' available at legal.un.org/ilc/sessions/61/2009_DC_Chairman_RIO_6July2009.pdf 4. The Chairman also explained that it was the Committee's intention to avoid placing too much emphasis on the temporal dimension – the provision of competence preceding the commission of the act – and hence it removed the reference to the provision of competence.

[87] ARIO Comment, 161, [6].

[88] The heated debates at the ILC with regard to the level of the subjective element in Art 61 didn't point to a specific direction. The Special Rapporteur then decided to realign it with the one incorporated in Art 17 in order to avoid confusion and reach consensus, ILC, *Summary Record of the 3097th Meeting* (n 1) 32.

[89] ibid 161, [7].

[90] Austria, for example, held that the provision, as drafted after the first reading, required no causality and was in essence referring to scenarios of State responsibility for acts they did not influence. See ILC, *Responsibility of International Organizations: Comments and Observations Received from Governments*, UN doc A/CN.4/636 (2011) 36 (Austria).

[91] ARIO Comment, 161, [10].

Thus, the abuse of legal personality through political influence described under Article 59(1) will also amount to derivative responsibility under Article 61. The main difference between the scope of application of the two provisions is the level of subjective involvement of the State, which is seemingly higher in Article 61 that incorporates a double subjective standard ('by taking advantage' and 'circumvents'). The additional requirement in Article 61 that the International Organisation must have competence with respect to the obligation in play will always be fulfilled in cases that involve decision-making, because if this was not the case the International Organisation could not validly adopt a decision on the matter in the first place. Nevertheless, Article 61 is clearly distinguished from Article 59(1) as the inclusion of Article 61(2) has an effect akin to that of Article 17(3). Article 59(1) does not cover scenarios of circumvention of obligations whereby the International Organisation is not bound by the norm its conduct violates and Article 61(2) fills this gap.[92] Thus, responsibility for the exercise of political influence at the decision-making level is potentially covered by two ARIO provisions that coexist in an equivalent way to ARIO, Articles 15 and 17; they are partially overlapping and not mutually exclusive.

III. ARIO, ARTICLE 58(2): AID OR ASSISTANCE

A. Members Off the Hook

Regulation of complicity in the ARIO is akin to that of direction and control examined above. ARIO, Article 58(1) is a replica provision of ARIO, Article 14 with the concomitant swap in the position of the actors involved.[93] The first paragraph then covers occasions where States and International Organisations interact as independent subjects of international law. The second paragraph added to Article 58 addresses scenarios whereby States act as members, thus covering their participation in decision-making procedures. The wording of Article 58(2) is identical to that of Article 59(2) examined previously. There is no reason to assume, then, that the threshold for the triggering of responsibility should be different in complicity scenarios; the influence required to trigger responsibility for complicity must exceed that provided by rules of the International Organisation. As explained previously, all votes that can influence decision-making procedures are by definition cast in accordance with organisational rules, thus complicity through voting is excluded outright by the ILC.

Like its counterpart, Article 59(2), the legal basis of this provision is unclear, since no relevant judicial precedents exist. This is evident in the commentaries,

[92] ibid.

[93] ARIO Comment, 156, [1].

where no reference to any source is made and the ILC rule seemingly comes out of thin air. In fact, when commenting on prior drafts of the ARIO, States and International Organisations have expressed opposing views[94] and the same goes for commentators who have resorted to policy arguments in order to address the matter. The ILC's conclusion of the present formulation came about as a weighting of such policy arguments put forward by States and International Organisations.

It is hard to discern the argumentative basis of these *lege ferenda* propositions. Klein suggested that member States' votes in favour of a decision of the International Organisation render them accomplices to the wrongful act,[95] and Ryngaert and Buchanan hold that this should have been the case, while they recognise that under the present formulation of the ARIO, establishment of responsibility does not include votes.[96] Both standpoints seem to echo China's comments and rest on the (according to them) self-evident principle that member States will have to be accountable for the decisions and actions they generally influence. The weak point of this argument is not its obvious circularity but mainly its political nature. The same goes with Crawford's argument in the opposite direction, ie that a broader definition of 'aid or assistance' would provoke a legitimacy crisis within International Organisations and that is why voting should be excluded from the scope of the provision.[97] As highlighted in Chapter 2, however, resort to policy arguments is unnecessary when legal considerations can provide guidance in the regulation of indirect responsibility scenarios.[98]

In complicity scenarios, where member State responsibility results for participation in the internationally wrongful act of an International Organisation and not for the Organisation's conduct, incurrence of member State responsibility for voting seems possible from a legal point of view. The double role performed by States when they vote explains why States do not lose their separate legal personality and bear direct responsibility for the inconsistency of their vote with their international obligations. Article 58(1) incorporates such a primary obligation[99] and it can be argued that States violate this international

[94] See II A ii.

[95] P Klein, *La responsabilite des organizations internationales dans les ordres juridiques internes et en droit des gens* (Bruylant, 1998) 469–70.

[96] They lament the ILC's 'unduly narrow view' on the matter, Ryngaert and Buchanan, 'Member State Responsibility for the Acts of International Organizations' (n 27) 143. Against: Lanovoy who suggests that responsibility for complicity under Art 58 could unfold due to participation in voting procedures. In his analysis, however, he conflates derivative responsibility with responsibility for complicity when he claims that ARIO, Art 58 could be triggered when a State controls the proceedings that lead to the adoption of a decision, V Lanovoy, 'Complicity in an Internationally Wrongful Act' in A Nollkaemper and I Plakokefalos (eds), *Principles of Shared Responsibility in International Law: An Appraisal of the State of the Art* (CUP, 2014) 134, 148–49.

[97] Crawford, *State Responsibility* (n 24) 412.

[98] See Chapter 2 at IV A.

[99] See the analysis of the archetype ASR, Art 16 on which ARIO, Art 58(1) is based in Chapter 4 at III A.

obligation through the act of voting. Nevertheless, this is not the case because the latent obligation directed towards member States within Article 58(1) provides 'to not facilitate with knowing intention the commission of an internationally wrongful act of *an International Organisation* when the same act would have been in breach of the member State's international obligations if committed by the State' (emphasis added). Accordingly, in ARIO, Article 14, the italicised part is replaced by 'a State/another International Organisation' and in ASR, Article 16 by 'another State'; the common denominator of all three being that the main act must be performed by a different subject of international law and not by the accomplice itself. In the scenarios examined here, the ensuing main act is committed by the States themselves by virtue of the personality merging I explained above.[100] So, if State responsibility would arise in the examined scenarios, this would (paradoxically) result in complicity in own conduct. It is safe to argue, then, that no violation of the primary obligation latent within Article 58(1) occurs and thus member States do not incur responsibility for complicity by virtue of their vote.

B. Complicity to the Test: *Chixoy Dam* Case

The implementation of the Chixoy Hydroelectric Dam Project in Guatemala is an illustrative example in this respect. Back in 1975, the newly established military government in Guatemala spent almost US$1 billion in order to construct the Pueblo Viejo-Quixal Hydroelectric Project (or Chixoy Dam Reservoir Project). The project would not have been undertaken but for the involvement of two International Organisations, the World Bank and the Inter-American Development Bank, which funded the construction to a large extent.[101] The two Banks also supervised the project, but the Guatemalan Government was responsible for its implementation on the ground. According to the construction plan, the reservoir of the plant would flood a region historically populated by the Maya Achi tribe.[102] Amidst an internal armed conflict, the government completed

[100] In Chapter 3 at III A, I held that States are inseparable from the International Organisation in such instances.

[101] The Inter-American Development Bank loaned the Guatemalan Government US$175 million and the World Bank US$117. For a detailed account of the loans, see respectively, Inter-American Development Bank, *Project Report, Guatemala, Chixoy River Pueblo Viejo Hydroelectric Project*, Doc PR-676-2-A (2 December 1975), available at www.idbdocs.iadb.org/wsdocs/getdocument.aspx?docnum=862415; and World Bank, *Project Performance Audit Report, Guatemala, Aguacapa Power Project (Loan 1426-GU) and Chixoy Power Project (Loans 1605-GUAND 1605-I-GU)*, Report no 10830 (30 June 1999), available at documents.worldbank.org/curated/en/289341468913902124/pdf/10830-PPAR-REVISED-PUBLIC.pdf.

[102] Report of the Historical Clarification Commission, *Guatemala, Memory of Silence* (United Nations Office for Project Services, 1999) vol VI Annex 1, Illustrative Case No 10, 'Massacre and Elimination of the Community of Río Negro', available at www.aaas.org/sites/default/files/migrate/uploads/mos_en.pdf.

voluntary and forcible relocations of dam-affected communities from the fertile agricultural valleys to the much harsher surrounding highlands. When hundreds of residents refused to relocate, or returned after finding that the conditions of resettlement villages were not what the government had promised, these men, women and children were kidnapped, raped and massacred by paramilitary and military officials between 1980 and 1982.[103] Finally, in January 1983, the sluice gates of the dam were closed and the reservoir began to fill.

The Association for the Integral Development of the Victims of the Violence of the Verapaces, Maya Achí filed on 19 July 2005 on behalf of surviving relatives an application with the Inter-American Commission on Human Rights (IACmHR) against the Guatemalan State for human rights violations that occurred during or resulted from the 1980–1982 massacres.[104] The Commission referred the case to the Inter-American Court of Human Rights (IACtHR)[105] and the latter, in its turn, upheld the responsibility of the Guatemalan State for own acts.[106]

The claimants, however, did not stop there. They correctly distinguished between violations that occurred during the relocation phase and violations that resulted directly from the planning and the construction of the dam. Since only the latter could have been foreseen by the International Organisations involved in the implementation of the project, the claimants filed a parallel second petition before the IACtHR. Represented by three human rights NGOs, they attempted to hold the two International Organisations and their member States responsible as accomplices to the forcible relocation of the Maya Achi that resulted from the construction of the dam.[107] The Secretariat of the IACtHR declared the petition inadmissible on 12 June 2009 ostensibly for lack of jurisdiction,[108] but the petitioners appealed this decision and insisted that member States of the Banks should be held responsible for complicity, since they voted in favour of funding the project.[109] It is worth noting that both International Organisations continued to provide loans for the Chixoy Dam

[103] More than 440 Maya Achi were killed in the village of Rio Negro alone, and the string of extra-judicial killings that claimed up to 5,000 lives between 1980 and 1982 became known as the Rio Negro Massacres. This has been discussed by the Inter-American Commission on Human Rights, *Report on the Situation of Human Rights in the Republic of Guatemala*, Organization of American States doc OEA/Ser. L/V/II.53, doc 21 rev 2 (13 October 1981).

[104] *Rio Negro Massacre v Republic of Guatemala*, Case no 12.649, Report no 86/10, IACmHR Decision of 14 July 2010 (Merits).

[105] IACmHR, Report no 86/10, Case no 12.649 (14 July 2010), available at www.cidh.oas.org/demandas/12.649Eng.pdf.

[106] *Case of the Rio Negro Massacres v Guatemala* (Preliminary Objection, Merits, Reparations and Costs), IACtHR, Judgment of 4 September 2012, available at www.corteidh.or.cr/docs/casos/articulos/seriec_250_ing.pdf.

[107] *Sobrevivientes de la Comunidad de Río Negro y otras comunidades similares en Guatemala (The Chixoy Dam Case)*, IACtHR, Petition no P-894-04 (7 December 2011) (unreported case).

[108] The Secretariat provides no detailed reasoning when rejecting an application at this stage apart from the fact that it does not fulfil admissibility criteria.

[109] Appeal available at 209.240.139.114/wp-content/uploads/2012/01/120119ChixoyPetition.pdf.

Project throughout the construction phase,[110] so officials of the International Organisations and of their member States were or should have been fully aware that local residents' economic, social or cultural rights were violated as a direct result of the project.

Leaving aside any jurisdictional restriction that is posed by the statute of a judicial forum, four different layers of responsibility arise from this set of facts and I will examine them in turn. First, is the issue of responsibility of an International Organisation arising from the funding of the project. The facts of the case clearly bring it under the scope of ARIO, Article 14, as the project would not have been undertaken without the International Organisations' assistance and officials of those International Organisations were aware of the violations when they intentionally financed the construction. The caveat to be borne in mind here is that it is not clear whether the International Organisations themselves are bound by human rights,[111] thus according to the opposability requirement their responsibility may not be triggered in the particular instance.[112]

At a second level, the issue of member State responsibility for the International Organisations' complicit conduct was put forward by the claimants. In their 7 December 2011 appeal, they emphasised the 'disproportionate voting power' on the board of Executive Directors of both the Inter-American Development Bank and the World Bank enjoyed by several States.[113] In essence, the claimants argue that the voting power of certain member States is such that can be equated with direction and control over the actions of the respective International Organisations and that is why these member States should be held responsible under Article 59(1) for controlling the complicit conduct. As reiterated throughout this chapter, however, the responsibility of the member States that comprise the Boards of Executive Directors of both Banks is not grounded on the proportion of their respective voting power. In fact, it is not established at all on account of their participation in decision-making procedures, as member States will not be held responsible even for participation in the wrongful conduct of the International Organisation. By virtue of Article 58(2), member States of the International Organisations which voted in favour of funding the project are

[110] Rights Action, Centre on Housing Rights and Evictions, *Continuing the Struggle for Justice and Accountability in Guatemala: Making Reparations a Reality in the Chixoy Dam Case* (Geneva, 2004), available at www.cohre.org/sites/default/files/guatemala_-_chixoy-report_2004.pdf 36.

[111] On this issue see A McBeth, 'Breaching the Vacuum: A Consideration of the Role of International Human Rights Law in the Operations of the International Financial Institutions' (2006) 10 *International Journal of Human Rights* 390; F Megret and F Hoffman, 'The UN as a Human Rights Violator? Some Reflections on the United Nations Changing Human Rights Responsibilities' (2003) 25 *Human Rights Quarterly* 318.

[112] This discrepancy between organisational and State obligations as a policy argument to drop the opposability requirement was advocated by Cuba (ILC, *Comments and Observations 2011* (n 90) 16 (Cuba)) and the Russian Federation (UNGA, *Summary Record of the 12th Meeting* (n 22) 11, [67]–[69] (Russian Federation). For more on the opposability requirement, see Chapter 4 at III A i b and III B i b.

[113] *Chixoy Dam Case* (n 107) 20 and 39.

not accomplices to the respective organisational acts and thus their responsibility is not triggered.

Irrespective of a State's voting power, State responsibility can arise on account of the inconsistency of the vote itself with the international obligations of the State. As explained above, the ARIO clarify that International Organisations are not obligation-free zones for States and the latter can bear responsibility for own conduct that occurs within the organisational context.[114] Argentina, for example, is a party to the International Covenant on Economic, Social and Cultural Rights (ICESCR) and its first Optional Protocol. When it voted in favour of the Chixoy Dam project in the Inter-American Bank of Development Board of Directors while it knew that local residents would lose their land and shelter, it acted inconsistently with ICESCR, Article 11(1). There is no doubt that the vote is attributable to the said State and hence Argentina committed an internationally wrongful act that triggers its international responsibility.

However, the victims of the violation will not be able to enforce Argentina's international responsibility before the Committee on Economic, Social and Cultural Rights (CESCR), or any human rights body with a jurisdictional clause, because they possess no rights vis-à-vis Argentina. According to Article 2 of the Optional Protocol, 'communications may be submitted by or on behalf of individuals or groups of individuals, under the jurisdiction of a State Party'.[115] In fact, one must clearly distinguish between responsibility and jurisdiction in the present instance.[116] Argentina exercises no 'jurisdiction' over the victims under the spatial or the personal jurisdiction model and that is why the rights of the individuals cannot be asserted against this State.[117] The Chixoy Dam, then, provides a good example where jurisdictional obstacles block the implementation of international responsibility for voting which is otherwise established.[118]

IV. CONCLUSION

In this chapter, I demonstrated that the International Organisation's protective veil extends to situations beyond mere membership. Nevertheless, States

[114] ARIO Comment, 157, [5].

[115] UNGA, Resolution 63/117, UN doc A/RES/63/117 (10 December 2008) (Optional Protocol to the International Covenant on Economic, Social and Cultural Rights).

[116] For a disentanglement of the two see M Milanovic, *Extraterritorial Application of Human Rights Treaties: Law Principles and Policy* (OUP, 2011) 41–53.

[117] For an analysis of the two, see ibid 119ff. For the latest relevant cases not in Milanovic's study, see *Catan and others v Moldova and Russia*, Application nos 43370/04, 8252/05 and 18454/06, ECtHR Grand Chamber, Judgment of 19 October 2012, [115]; *Jaloud v Netherlands*, Application no 47708/08, ECtHR Grand Chamber, Judgment of 24 November 2014, (2015) 60 EHRR 29, [154].

[118] For more on jurisdictional restraints over the establishment of responsibility, see M den Heijer, 'Procedural Aspects of Shared Responsibility in the European Court of Human Rights' (2013) 4 *Journal of International Dispute Settlement* 361.

can be held responsible when they perform conduct within the organisational framework that alters the type of the member State-International Organisation interaction; from interaction on the basis of the particular member State-International Organisation relationship to interaction as independent subjects of international law. The criterion of accordance with the rules of the International Organisation incorporated in ARIO, Articles 58(2) and 59(2), indeed provides a fitting threshold for the establishment of responsibility as it points to the type of interaction in play. The two-layered responsibility structure argued for in the ARIO is informed here by an integrated explanation of the nature of the relationship between International Organisations and their member States but also of the rules of the International Organisation. A salient feature of the analysis attempted here is the functional dualism that underpins State operation within the organisational context. In its turn, this role-splitting affects the establishment of State responsibility.

All the above find expression within decision-making procedures of an International Organisation. Irrespective of the level of influence a member State may exercise upon the decision when it acts as a member (that is, when exercising competence that lies with the International Organisation in accordance with the latter's rules) it is protected by operation of the institutional veil. This is why the distinction between derivative responsibility and complicity is not pertinent in these instances and does not affect the establishment of international responsibility. On the other hand, member States are not protected when they influence the organisational procedure through corridor talk, as the latter lies beyond the regulation of the rules of the International Organisation. And in these instances, indirect responsibility models are potentially applicable, however, the implementation of international responsibility (if established) will very seldom occur due to jurisdictional constraints.

8

Concluding Remarks

International Organisations are a relatively new phenomenon in the international sphere but undoubtedly they are here to stay. The consolidation of this novel form of power, vested in them, 'may conceal the emergence of a new leviathan'.[1] And the creature that we call today 'the international legal order' is comprised of International Organisations but also of States with whom the former interact. Throughout this book, I understood both these actors as subjects of international law, bound by its rules, and bearing legal responsibility for their violation. But this was not the presumption but rather the end-point of my analysis. In essence, the overarching consideration underlying this study has to do with taming the emerging leviathan through legal means. I asked then: is the international legal order capable of restraining those two types of actors that fall under its authority via legal rules that pertain to the establishment of their international responsibility?

I answered affirmatively. My basic argument has been that international responsibility as envisioned by the International Law Commission (ILC) in its two responsibility projects can effectively function as international law's legal accountability mechanism. The breadth of academic criticism targeted towards the Articles on the Responsibility of International Organizations (ARIO) essentially questions this thesis. It is contended that international responsibility cannot capture complex scenarios of non-conformity, such as those involving interaction between member States and the International Organisation of which they are members, because of its inherent limitations. So, my main aim has been the reversal of this perception through an analysis of international responsibility's nature and a concomitant exegesis of its application to the scenarios under scrutiny.

If anything, the notion of international responsibility is not undertheorised. Testament to that is the fact that the Articles on State Responsibility (ASR) are a distillation of 50 years of discussions and of a much longer time of preceding practice. The ILC has provided us through the ASR with a tool with solid legal foundations. However, the ILC in the ARIO, and modern critics, have shied away from those foundations. What has been undertheorised, then, is the connection

[1] G Verdirame, *The UN and Human Rights: Who Guards the Guardians?* (CUP, 2011) 394.

between the ARIO and the ASR. For want of a legal connection, the ILC tried to find the missing link between its two projects in policy argumentation. However, this led to a discussion on an unprincipled basis that inevitably resulted in chaos. The invoking of legal argumentation when dealing with the establishment of international responsibility is therefore my plea.

A pause for reflection is necessary at this point. Why is this return to basics so important? First, because international responsibility is an essential component of the functioning of the international legal order. The attempt to confront the power and authority issues involved in the activities of International Organisations expressed via the ARIO represents overall a commendable effort for the consolidation of international law's normative reach. The application of international responsibility is the only stable process for implementing international law. The way forward should not involve a dismissal of international responsibility as a legal accountability mechanism attached to both States and International Organisations. This would be tantamount to giving up on the international legal order's reach to both subjects. Further, for reasons of judicial practice. The rules regarding the establishment of international responsibility can form a coherent whole and be applied consistently by judicial bodies only when constructed upon legal principles. It is essential for courts to have a guiding light in cases where the law is in a state of formation. The argument that because the ARIO lack a legal basis, their utility is very limited is, as Klabbers infers, 'self-serving'.[2] The outcome of the ILC's work, due to lack of a more authoritative alternative, is already playing an important role in judicial practice (ie the *Nuhanovic* judgments before Dutch courts and the *Behrami* decision of the European Court of Human Rights (ECtHR)).

I do not suffer from the naïve belief that the ILC will re-examine the ARIO on this basis. This is why I do not propose a redrafting of the provisions under scrutiny. The topic has left the ILC and is in the hands of the UN General Assembly. In its 2017 session, the latter commended the ARIO 'to the attention of Governments and international organizations without prejudice to the question of their future adoption or other appropriate action' and deferred the reconsideration of the topic for 2020.[3] At the same time, it invited States and International Organizations 'to submit … written comments on any future action regarding the articles'.[4] This results from the hesitant reactions in the Sixth Committee for the adoption of a convention on the matter, mainly due to the lack of relevant institutional practice that supports the ARIO.[5] This is testament that States feel

[2] J Klabbers, *An Introduction to International Organizations Law* (CUP, 2015) 317.

[3] UNGA, Resolution 72/122, UN doc A/RES/72/122 (10 December 2017) [1] and [3].

[4] ibid [2].

[5] UNGA, 69th Session, Sixth Committee, *Summary Record of the 18th Meeting*, UN doc A/C.6/69/SR.18 (2014) [47]–[80]; M Wood, '"Weighing" the Articles on Responsibility of International Organizations' in M Ragazzi (ed), *Responsibility of International Organizations, Essays in Memory of Sir Ian Brownlie* (Martinus Nijhoff, 2013) 55, 63; on how a weak or strong claim to normativity may affect the 'packaging' or the final form given to the ILC's work, see S Murphy,

a certain unease in treating the ARIO as reflections of the law or its progressive development.

The way forward is neither a turn towards other forms of accountability[6] nor a restructuring of international responsibility on a different basis altogether.[7] It is easy to target the malfunctions or the weak spots of any idea and be dismissive about it. It takes more effort not to give up and attempt to address its weaknesses. Given the multitude of problems international responsibility presents with respect to its implementation (immunities before national courts, lack of a competent international court), a concomitant call for self-control of International Organisations via other forms of institutional accountability is necessary nowadays. Such forms of self-control, however, cannot and do not function as substitutes for legal accountability and they can easily be used as a covert way of getting around the responsibility question.

What is needed, then, is a change of perspective from International Organisations, judicial bodies and lawyers invoking the rules regulating the establishment of international responsibility. I have argued that the ECtHR, for example, can make sense of its jurisprudence that pertains to cases involving interaction between States and International Organisations and put forward this understanding of international responsibility. This does not necessarily require a turn in case law but rather a re-interpretation of relevant cases under existing legal principles. Only if cases keep piling up, if advocacy groups maintain their efforts, and if tinkering with the current approach becomes manifestly insufficient to prevent intolerable results, then a radical change will truly become possible. The rethinking of existing rules will need a concerted effort of academics and practitioners to substantiate. It would be unimaginably damaging for the existence of international law as a legal system, and thus a major blow to its legitimacy, if international responsibility fails to form a coherent set of rules capable of controlling its legal subjects.

'Codification, Progressive Development or Scholarly Analysis: The Art of Packaging the ILC's Work Product' in M Ragazzi (ed), *Responsibility of International Organizations, Essays in Memory of Sir Ian Brownlie* (Martinus Nijhoff, 2013) 29ff.

[6] ILA, *Accountability of International Organizations: Final Report, Berlin Conference* (2004) 154, available at www.ila-hq.org/en/committees/index.cfm/cid/9.

[7] eg the one proposed by D Jacobs and A Nollkaemper, 'Shared Responsibility in International Law: A Conceptual Framework' (2013) 34 *Michigan Journal of International Law* 359.

Appendix

IN THIS APPENDIX, I juxtapose the Articles on the Responsibility of International Organisations (ARIO) provisions I have examined throughout the book (column 2) with the rules which I believe reflect the progressive development of the law in each scenario (column 3). The responsibility scenarios (column 1) are presented in the order they appear in the book. The suggested rules are mainly intended to function as interpretative guidelines for the relevant ARIO provisions.

Column 1 [scenario in play]	**Column 2 [ARIO provision(s)]**	**Column 3 [suggested progressive development of the law]**
Responsibility of a State member of an International Organisation for the Organisation's internationally wrongful acts	*Article 62* 1. A State member of an international organization is responsible for an internationally wrongful act of that organization if: (a) it has accepted responsibility for that act towards the injured party; or (b) it has led the injured party to rely on its responsibility. 2. Any international responsibility of a State under paragraph 1 is presumed to be subsidiary.	*A State member of an International Organisation will be responsible for the internationally wrongful act of this Organisation when it consents to be bound by the legal obligations that arise by virtue of this act.*
Complicity	*Article 14* An international organization which aids or assists a State or another international organization in the commission of an internationally wrongful act by the State or the latter organization is internationally responsible for doing so if: (a) the organization does so with knowledge of the circumstances of the internationally wrongful act; and (b) the act would be internationally wrongful if committed by that organization.	*A State or an International Organisation which facilitates with knowing intention the internationally wrongful act of another State or another International Organisation, is responsible for doing so.*

Column 1 [scenario in play]	Column 2 [ARIO provision(s)]	Column 3 [suggested progressive development of the law]
	Article 58(1) A State which aids or assists an international organization in the commission of an internationally wrongful act by the latter is internationally responsible for doing so if: (a) the State does so with knowledge of the circumstances of the internationally wrongful act; and (b) the act would be internationally wrongful if committed by that State.	
Derivative responsibility	*Article 15* An international organization which directs and controls a State or another international organization in the commission of an internationally wrongful act by the State or the latter organization is internationally responsible for that act if: (a) the former organization does so with knowledge of the circumstances of the internationally wrongful act; and (b) the act would be internationally wrongful if committed by that organization.	1. *A State or an International Organisation which restricts the freedom of action of another State or another International Organisation, is responsible for the conduct committed under conditions of restriction of freedom if:* *(a) it had knowledge of these conditions; and* *(b) the ensuing act would have been wrongful if committed by the former subject.*

Column 1 [scenario in play]	Column 2 [ARIO provision(s)]	Column 3 [suggested progressive development of the law]
	Article 16 An international organization which coerces a State or another international organization to commit an act is internationally responsible for that act if: (a) the act would, but for the coercion, be an internationally wrongful act of the coerced State or international organization; and (b) the coercing international organization does so with knowledge of the circumstances of the act. *Article 59(1)* A State which directs and controls an international organization in the commission of an internationally wrongful act by the latter is internationally responsible for that act if: (a) the State does so with knowledge of the circumstances of the internationally wrongful act; and (b) the act would be internationally wrongful if committed by that State. *Article 60* A State which coerces an international organization to commit an act is internationally responsible for that act if: (a) the act would, but for the coercion, be an internationally wrongful act of the coerced international organization; and (b) the coercing State does so with knowledge of the circumstances of the act.	2. *A State or an International Organisation which restricts the freedom of action of another State or another International Organisation, is responsible for doing so, if:* *(a) it had knowledge that the ensuing act would violate the latter subject's international obligations; and* *(b) the ensuing act would not have been wrongful if committed by the former subject.*

Column 1 [scenario in play]	Column 2 [ARIO provision(s)]	Column 3 [suggested progressive development of the law]
Circumvention of obligations by an International Organisation through its member States	*Article 17* 1. An international organization incurs international responsibility if it circumvents one of its international obligations by adopting a decision binding member States or international organizations to commit an act that would be internationally wrongful if committed by the former organization. 2. An international organization incurs international responsibility if it circumvents one of its international obligations by authorizing member States or international organizations to commit an act that would be internationally wrongful if committed by the former organization and the act in question is committed because of that authorization. 3. Paragraphs 1 and 2 apply whether or not the act in question is internationally wrongful for the member States or international organizations to which the decision or authorization is addressed.	[Article 17 represents the progressive development of the law]

Column 1 [scenario in play]	**Column 2 [ARIO provision(s)]**	**Column 3 [suggested progressive development of the law]**
Circumvention of obligations by a State member of an International Organisation through the International Organisation	*Article 61* 1. A State member of an international organization incurs international responsibility if, by taking advantage of the fact that the organization has competence in relation to the subject-matter of one of the State's international obligations, it circumvents that obligation by causing the organization to commit an act that, if committed by the State, would have constituted a breach of the obligation. 2. Paragraph 1 applies whether or not the act in question is internationally wrongful for the international organization.	*When a State member of an International Organisation has the intention to avoid compliance with its international obligations, it will be responsible:* *(a) for conduct of the International Organisation that would have been wrongful if committed by the State, if this conduct results from the restriction of the International Organisation's freedom of action;* *(b) for facilitating certain conduct of the International Organisation, if this conduct runs counter to the State's obligations.*

Bibliography

(all electronic sources were last accessed the 25th of September 2018)

Books, Book Chapters and Working Papers

Adam, HT, *Les organismes internationaux spécialisés, contribution à la théorie générale des Etablissements publics internationaux* (Librairie Generale de Droit et de Jurisprudence, 1965)

Ago, R, *La responsabilita indiretta nel diritto internazionale* (CEDAM, 1934)

Alvarez, J, *International Organizations as Law-Makers* (OUP, 2005)

Amerasinghe, CF, *Principles of the Institutional Law of International Organizations* (CUP, 2005)

—— 'An Assessment of the ILC's Articles on the Responsibility of International Organizations' in M Ragazzi (ed), *Responsibility of International Organizations, Essays in Memory of Sir Ian Brownlie* (Martinus Nijhoff, 2013) 71

Anzilotti, D, *Corso di diritto internazionale* (CEDAM, 1955) vol I

d'Aspremont J, *Formalism and the Sources of International Law: A Theory of the Ascertainment of Legal Rules* (OUP, 2011)

—— 'A European Law of International Responsibility? The Articles on the Responsibility of International Organizations and the European Union' in V Kosta, N Skoutaris and V Tzevelekos (eds), *The EU Accession to the ECHR* (Hart, 2014) 75

Aust, HA, *Complicity and the Law of State Responsibility* (CUP, 2011)

Barboza, J, *The Environment, Risk and Liability in International Law* (Brill, 2011)

Bederman, DJ, 'Third Party Rights and Obligations in Treaties' in DB Hollis (ed), *The Oxford Guide to Treaties* (OUP, 2012) 328

Benvenisti, E, *The International Law on Occupation* (OUP, 2012)

Blokker, N, 'Preparing Articles on Responsibility of International Organizations: Does the International Law Commission Take International Organizations Seriously? A Mid-Term Review' in J Klabbers and A Wallendahl (eds), *Research Handbook on the Law of International Organizations* (Edward Elgar, 2011) 313

Bobbio, N, 'Nouvelles réflexions sur les normes primaires et secondaires' in N Bobbio (ed), *Études de théorie du droit* (LGDJ, 1988) 198

Bordin, FL, *The Analogy Between States and International Organizations* (CUP, 2018) (forthcoming)

Boyle, A and Chinkin, C, *The Making of International Law* (OUP, 2007)

Brölmann, C, *The Institutional Veil in Public International Law: International Organisations and the Law of Treaties* (Hart Publishing, 2007)

Brownlie I, *System of the Law of Nations: State Responsibility, Part I* (Clarendon Press, 1983)

—— 'State Responsibility: The Problem of Delegation' in K Ginther, G Hafner, W Lang, H Neuhold and L Sucharipa-Behrmann (eds), *Völkerrecht zwischen normativem Anspruch und politischer Realität* (Duncker and Humblot, 1994) 299

—— 'The Responsibility of States for the Acts of International Organizations' in M Ragazzi (ed), *International Responsibility Today, Essays in Memory of Oscar Schachter* (Brill, 2005) 355

Cahier, P, 'La Charte des Nations Unies et les Etats tiers' in A Cassese (ed), *Current Problems of International Law* (1975) 81

—— 'The Internal Legal Order of International Organizations' in RJ Dupuy (ed), *A Handbook on International Organizations* (Martinus Nijhoff, 1998) 377

Cassese, A, *International Law* (OUP, 2005)

Chen, Y, 'Attribution, Causation and Responsibility of International Organizations' in D Sarooshi (ed), *Remedies and Responsibility for the Actions of International Organizations* (Brill, Nijhoff, 2014) 33

Cheng, B, *General Principles of Law as Applied by International Courts and Tribunals* (CUP, 2006)

Chesterman, S, *Who Needs Rules? The Prospects of a Rules-Based International System*, Discussion Paper (Institute for International Law and Justice, NYU Law, 2005)

Combacau, J and Sur, S, *Droit international public* (Monrchrestien, 2004)

Cottereau, G, 'Systèmes juridiques et notion de responsabilité' in *Colloque du Mans, La responsabilité dans le système international* (Pedone, 1991) 21

Crawford, J, *The Creation of States in International Law* (Clarendon Press, 1979)

—— *State Responsibility: The General Part* (Cambridge University Press, 2013)

—— 'The Progressive Development of International Law: History, Theory and Practice' in D Alland, V Chetail, O de Frouville and JE Vinuales (eds), *Unity and Diversity of International Law, Essays in Honour of Professor Pierre-Marie Dupuy* (Martinus Nijhoff, 2014) 1

Crawford, J and Olleson, S, 'The Nature and Forms of International Responsibility' in M Evans (ed), *International Law* (OUP, 2003) 443

Crawford, J and Watkins, J, 'International Responsibility' in S Besson and J Tasioulas (eds), *The Philosophy of International Law* (OUP, 2010) 283

Curtis, G (ed), *Czechoslovakia: A Country Study* (Federal Research Division of the Library of Congress, 1992)

Danilenko, GM, *Law-Making in the International Community* (Martinus Nijhoff, 1993)

Dannenbaum, T, 'Public Power and Preventive Responsibility: Attributing the Wrongs of International Joint Ventures' in A Nollkaemper and D Jacobs (eds), *Distribution of Responsibilities in International Law* (CUP, 2015) 192

Daugirdas, K, 'The International Law Commission Reinvents Itself?' (2014) 108 *AJIL Unbound* 79

David, E, 'Primary and Secondary Rules' in J Crawford, A Pellet and S Olleson (eds), *The Law of International Responsibility* (OUP, 2010) 27

Decaux, E, 'Responsabilité et réparation' in *Colloque du Mans, La responsabilité dans le système international* (Pedone, 1991) 147

Dominicé, C, 'Methodology of International Law' in R Bernhardt (ed), *Encyclopedia of Public International Law* (OUP, 1997) 354

—— 'Attribution of Conduct to Multiple States and the Implication of a State in the Act of Another' in J Crawford, A Pellet and S Olleson (eds), *The Law of International Responsibility* (OUP, 2010) 281

Eagleton, C, *The Responsibility of States in International Law* (New York University Press, 1928)

Eeckhout, P, 'The EU and Its Member States in the WTO: Issues of Responsibility' in L Bartels and F Ortino (eds), *Regional Trade Agreements and the WTO Legal System* 449 (OUP, 2006)

Fitzmaurice, G, 'The Future of Public International Law and of the International Legal System in the Circumstances of Today' in Institute of International Law, *Livre du centenaire 1873–1973: Evolution et perspectives du droit international* (Karger Bâle, 1973) 196

Fox, H, 'The International Court of Justice's Treatment of Acts of the State and in Particular the Attribution of Acts of Individuals to the State' in N Ando, E McWhinney and R Wolfrum (eds), *Liber Amicorum Judge Shigeru Oda* (Kluwer Law International, 2002) 147

Franck, TM, 'The United Nations as Guarantor of International Peace and Security' in C Tomuschat (ed), *The United Nations at Age Fifty: A Legal Perspective* (Kluwer, 1995) 25

Freeman, AV, *The International Responsibility of States for Denial of Justice* (Longmans, 1938)

Gazzini, T, 'The Relationship Between International Legal Personality and Autonomy' in ND White and R Collins (eds), *International Organisations and the Idea of Autonomy* (Cavendish-Routledge, 2010) 199

Guggisberg, S, *The Use of CITES for Commercially-exploited Fish Species: A Solution to Overexploitation and Illegal, Unreported and Unregulated Fishing?* (Springer, 2016)

Hafner, G, 'Is the Topic of Responsibility of International Organizations Ripe for Codification? Some Critical Remarks' in U Fastenrath, R Geiger, DE Khan, A Paulus, S von Schorlemer and C Vedder (eds), *From Bilateralism to Community Interest, Essays in Honour of Judge Bruno Simma* (OUP, 2011) 695

Hart, HLA, *The Concept of Law* (Clarendon Press, 1961)

Heintze, HZ, 'On the Legal Understanding of Autonomy' in M Suksi (ed), *Autonomy: Applications and Implications* (Kluwer Law International, 1998) 7

Hirsch, M, *The Responsibility of International Organizations Toward Third Parties: Some Basic Principles* (Martinus Nijhoff, 1995)

Jackson, M, *Complicity in International Law* (OUP, 2015)

Jimenez de Arechaga, E, *International Responsibility: Manual of Public International Law* (Sorensen, 1968)

Kayser, V, *Launching Space Objects: Issues of Liability and Future Prospects* (Kluwer Academic, 2001)

Kelsen, H, *The Legal Process and International Order* (New Commonwealth Institute Monograph Series, 1935)

Klabbers, J, *An Introduction to International Organizations Law* (CUP, 2015)

Klein, P, *La responsabilite des organizations internationales dans les ordres juridiques internes et en droit des gens* (Bruylant, 1998)

Kolb, R, 'General Principles of Procedural Law' in A Zimmermann, K Oellers-Frahm, C Tomuschat and C Tams (eds), *The Statute of the International Court of Justice: A Commentary* (OUP, 2012), 871

Kosta, V, Skoutaris, N and Tzevelekos, V (eds), *The EU Accession to the ECHR* (Hart, 2014)

Kutz, C, 'Responsibility' in J Coleman and S Shapiro (eds), *The Oxford Handbook of Jurisprudence and Philosophy of Law* (OUP, 2002) 458

Lagrange, E, *La representation institutionelle dans l'ordre international. Une contribution à la théorie de la personnalité morale des organisations internationals* (Kluwer, 2002)

Lanovoy, V, 'Complicity in an Internationally Wrongful Act' in A Nollkaemper and I Plakokefalos (eds), *Principles of Shared Responsibility in International Law: An Appraisal of the State of the Art* (CUP, 2014) 134

—— *Complicity in an Internationally Wrongful Act*, SHARES Research Paper 38 (2014)

Liddell, HG and Scott, R, *An Intermediate Greek-English Lexicon* (Clarendon Press, 1889)

McCorquodale, R, 'International Organizations and International Human Rights Law: One Giant Leap for Humankind' in KH Kaikobad and M Bohlander (eds), *International Law and Power: Perspectives on Legal Order and Justice, Essays in Honour of Colin Warbrick* (Nijhoff, 2009) 141

Merkouris P, *Article 31(3)(c) of the VCLT and the Principle of Systemic Integration: Normative Shadows in Plato's Cave* (Brill, Nijhoff, 2015)

Messineo, F, 'Attribution of Conduct' in A Nollkaemper and I Plakokefalos (eds), *Principles of Shared Responsibility in International Law: An Appraisal of the State of the Art* (CUP, 2014) 60

Milanovic, M, *Extraterritorial Application of Human Rights Treaties: Law Principles and Policy* (OUP, 2011)

Moelle, M, *The International Responsibility of International Organisations: Cooperation in Peacekeeping Operations* (CUP, 2017)

Mosler, H, 'General Principles of Law' in R Bernhardt (ed), *Encyclopedia of Public International Law* (North Holland, 1984) vol 7, 90

Murphy, S, 'Codification, Progressive Development or Scholarly Analysis: The Art of Packaging the ILC's Work Product' in M Ragazzi (ed), *Responsibility of International Organizations, Essays in Memory of Sir Ian Brownlie* (Martinus Nijhoff, 2013) 29

Naert, F, 'Binding International Organisations to Member State Treaties or Responsibility of Member States for Their Own Actions in the Framework of International Organisations' in J Wouters, E Brems, S Smis and P Schmitt (eds), *Accountability for Human Rights Violations by International Organisations* (Intersentia, 2010) 129

Nollkaemper, A, *Responsibility*, Amsterdam Center for International Law Research Paper 2017-03 (2017)

Nolte, G and Aust, H, 'Equivocal Helpers-Complicit States, Mixed Messages and International Law' (2009) 58 *ICLQ* 1

Orakhelashvili, A, 'Division of Reparation Between Responsible Entities' in J Crawford, A Pellet and S Olleson (eds), *The Law of International Responsibility* (OUP, 2010) 647

Pellet, A, 'The Definition of Responsibility in International Law' in J Crawford, A Pellet and S Olleson (eds), *The Law of International Responsibility* (OUP, 2010) 3

—— 'The ILC's Articles on State Responsibility for Internationally Wrongful Acts and Related Texts' in J Crawford, A Pellet and S Olleson (eds), *The Law of International Responsibility* (OUP, 2010) 75

—— 'International Organizations are Definitely Not States: Cursory Remarks on the ILC Articles on the Responsibility of International Organizations' in M Ragazzi (ed), *Responsibility of International Organizations, Essays in Memory of Sir Ian Brownlie* (Martinus Nijhoff, 2013) 41

Pinzauti, G, 'It Takes Two to Tango: States' Conferral of Powers on International Organizations and Its Implications for the Responsibility of the Organization and Its Members' in D Sarooshi (ed), *Remedies and Responsibility for the Actions of International Organizations* (Brill, Nijhoff, 2014) 113

Proulx, VJ, 'An Uneasy Transition? Linkages Between the Law of State Responsibility and the Law Governing the Responsibility of International Organizations' in M Ragazzi (ed), *Responsibility of International Organizations, Essays in Memory of Sir Ian Brownlie* (Martinus Nijhoff, 2013) 109

Raz, J, *The Authority of Law: Essays on Morality and Law* (Clarendon Press, 1979)

Reinhold, S, *Good Faith in International Law*, Bonn Research Chapters on Public International Law no 2/2013 1 (2013)

Reuter, P, *Institutions internationales* (Paris Presses Universitaires, 1955)

Reynolds, FMB, *Bowstead and Reynolds on Agency* (Sweet & Maxwell, 2006)

Rousseau, C, *Principes généraux du droit international public*, vol I, *Sources* (Pedone, 1944)

de Sadeleer, N, 'The Principles of Prevention and Precaution in International Law: Two Heads of the Same Coin?' in M Fitzmaurice, D Ong and P Merkouris (eds), *Research Handbook on International Environmental Law* (Edgar Elgar, 2010) 182

Sands, P and Klein, P, *Bowett's Law of International Institutions* (Sweet and Maxwell, 2001)

Sari, A and Wessel, RA, 'International Responsibility for EU Military Operations: Finding the EU's Place in the Global Accountability Regime' in B Van Vooren, S Blockmans and J Wouters (eds), *The Legal Dimension of Global Governance: What Role for the EU?* (OUP, 2013) 126

Sarooshi, D, *International Organizations and Their Exercise of Sovereign Powers* (OUP, 2007)

Sarvarian A, 'The EU Accession to the ECHR and the Law of International Responsibility' in V Kosta, N Skoutaris and V Tzevelekos (eds), *The EU Accession to the ECHR* (Hart, 2014) 91

Scelle, G, 'Le phénomène juridique du dédoublement fonctionnel' in W Schätzel and JJ Schlochauer (eds), *Rechtsfragen der Internationalen Organisationen* (Festschrift Hans Wehberg, 1956) 324

Schachter, O, *International Law in Theory and Practice* (Martinus Nijhoff, 1991)

Schermers, H and Blokker, N, *International Institutional Law: Unity Within Diversity* (Martinus Nijhoff Publishers, 2011)

Seidl-Hohenveldern, I, *Corporations In and Under International Law* (CUP, 1987)

—— 'Responsibility of Member States of an International Organization for the Acts of that Organization' in I Seidl-Hohenveldern (ed), *Collected Essays on International Investments and on International Organizations* (Kluwer, 1998) 63

Shaw, M, *International Law* (CUP, 2008)

Šturma, P and Bílková, V, 'Targeted Anti-Terrorist Sanctions and Their Implications for International Law Normative and Institutional Coherency' in A Constantinides and N Zaikos (eds), *The Diversity of International Law, Essays in Honour of Professor Kalliopi K Koufa* (MNP, 2009) 217

Talmon, S, 'A Plurality of Responsible Actors: International Responsibility for Acts of the Coalition Provisional Authority in Iraq' in P Shiner and A Williams (eds), *The Iraq War and International Law* (Hart, 2008) 185

—— 'Responsibility of International Organisations: Does the European Community Require Special Treatment?' in M Ragazzi (ed), *Responsibility of International Organizations, Essays in Memory of Sir Ian Brownlie* (Martinus Nijhoff, 2013) 405

Thirlway, H, 'The Sources of International Law' in M Evans (ed), *International Law* (OUP, 2014) 91

Triepel, H, *Völkerrecht und Landesrecht* (Scientia Antiquariat, 1958)

Tzanakopoulos, A, *Disobeying the Security Council. Countermeasures Against Wrongful Sanctions* (OUP, 2011)

Uriarte, JA, 'The Responsibility of International Organizations and International and European Courts and Tribunals: Judicial Review of Security Council Resolutions' in D Sarooshi (ed), *Remedies and Responsibility for the Actions of International Organizations* (Brill, Nijhoff, 2014) 321

de Vattel, E, *The Law of Nations* (Liberty Fund, 2008 [1797])

Verdirame, G, *The UN and Human Rights: Who Guards the Guardians?* (CUP, 2011)

Verdross, A, *Volkerrecht* (Springer, 1964)

Voulgaris, N, 'International Organizations as Autonomous Actors in the Formation of Customary International Law' in S Droubi and J d'Aspremont J (eds), *Perspectives on International Organisations and Formation of Customary International Law* (Manchester University Press, 2018) (forthcoming)

White, N, 'Discerning Separate Will' in W Heere (ed), *From Government to Governance: The Growing Impact of Non-State Actors on the International and European Legal System*, Proceedings of the 2004 Hague Joint ASIL/NVIR Conference (2004) 31

—— *The Law of International Organizations* (Manchester University Press, 2005)

Wood, M, '"Weighing" the Articles on Responsibility of International Organizations' in M Ragazzi (ed), *Responsibility of International Organizations, Essays in Memory of Sir Ian Brownlie* (Martinus Nijhoff, 2013) 55

Wouters, J, Brems, E, Smis, S and Schmitt, P, 'Introductory Remarks' in J Wouters, E Brems, S Smis and P Schmitt (eds), *Accountability for Human Rights Violations by International Organisations* (Intersentia, 2010) 1

Yamada, C, 'Viability of the ILC's Articles Formulated on the Basis of the Articles on State Responsibility' in M Ragazzi (ed), *Responsibility of International Organizations, Essays in Memory of Sir Ian Brownlie* (Martinus Nijhoff, 2013) 89

Yee, S, 'The Responsibility of States Members of an International Organization for its Conduct as a Result of Membership or Their Normal Conduct Associated with Membership' in M Ragazzi (ed), *Responsibility of International Organizations, Essays in Memory of Sir Ian Brownlie* (Martinus Nijhoff, 2013) 435

Articles from Journals and Yearbooks

Addo, M and Grief, N, 'Does Article 3 of the European Convention on Human Rights Enshrine Absolute Rights?' (1998) 9 *EJIL* 510

Ahlborn, C, 'The Rules of International Organizations and the Law of International Responsibility' (2011) 8 *IOLR* 397

—— 'The Use of Analogies in Drafting the Articles on the Responsibility of International Organizations: An Appraisal of the "Copy-Paste Approach"' (2012) 9 *IOLR* 53

Alvarez, J, 'International Organizations: Accountability or Responsibility?', Address at the Canadian Council of International Law, 27 October 2006

—— 'Revisiting the ILC's Draft Rules on International Organization Responsibility' (2011) 105 *American Society of International Law Proceedings* 344

Amerasinghe CF, 'Liability to Third Parties of Member States of International Organizations: Practice, Principle and Juridical Precedent' (1991) 40 *ICLQ* 259

—— 'Comments on the ILC's Draft Articles on the Responsibility of International Organizations' (2012) 9 *IOLR* 29

Amoroso, D, 'Moving Towards Complicity as a Criterion of Attribution of Private Conducts: Imputation to States of Corporate Abuses in the US Case Law' (2011) 24 *Leiden Journal of International Law* 989

Angelini, A, 'A Trouble Shared is a Trouble Halved: How the Structure of Cooperation Matters for the Engagement of Responsibility in the World Bank Partnership Programmes' (2016) 13 *IOLR* 171

d'Argent, P, 'State Organs Placed at the Disposal of the UN, Effective Control, Wrongful Abstention and Dual Attribution of Conduct' (2014) 1 *Questions of International Law* 17

Arsanjani, MH, 'Claims Against International Organizations' (1981) 7 *Yale Journal of World Public Order* 131

d' Aspremont J, 'Abuse of the Legal Personality of International Organizations and the Responsibility of Member States' (2007) 4 *IOLR* 91

—— 'The Articles on the Responsibility of International Organisations: Magnifying the Fissures in the Law of International Responsibility' (2012) 9 *IOLR* 15

—— 'The Idea of "Rules" in the Sources of International Law' (2014) 84 *BYBIL* 103

Barros, AS and Ryngaert, C, 'The Position of Member States in (Autonomous) Institutional Decision-Making, Implications for the Establishment of Responsibility' (2014) 11 *IOLR* 53

Beckett, J, 'Countering Uncertainty and Ending Up/Down Arguments: Prolegomena to a Response to NAIL' (2005) 16 *EJIL* 213

Blokker, N, 'International Organizations and their Members: "International Organizations Belong to All their Members and None", Variations on a Theme' (2004) 1 *IOLR* 139

—— 'Abuse of the Members: Questions Concerning Draft Article 16 of the Draft Articles on Responsibility of International Organisations' (2010) 7 *IOLR* 35

—— 'Member State Responsibility for Wrongdoings of International Organizations. Beacon of Hope or Delusion?' (2015) 12 *IOLR* 319

Bowett, DW, 'Estoppel before International Tribunals and its Relation to Acquiescence' (1957) 33 *BYBIL* 176

Boyle, A, 'State Responsibility and International Liability for Injurious Consequences of Acts Not Prohibited by International Law: A Necessary Distinction?' (1990) 39 *ICLQ* 1

Brölmann, C, 'A Flat Earth? International Organizations in the System of International Law' (2001) 70 *Nordic Journal of International Law* 319

—— 'Member States and International Legal Responsibility: Developments of the Institutional Veil' (2015) 12 *IOLR* 358

de Burca, G, Nollkaemper, A and Canor, I, 'The European Courts and the Security Council: Between Dédoublement Fonctionnel and Balancing of Values: Three Replies to Pasquale De Sena and Maria Chiara Vitucci' (2009) 20 *EJIL* 853

Byers, M, 'Abuse of Rights: An Old Principle, a New Age' (2002) 47 *McGill Law Journal* 389

Cardell, PJ, French, D and White, N, 'Kadi v Council of the European Union' (2009) 58 *ICLQ* 229

Carrillo, N, 'The Links Between the Responsibility of International Organizations and the Quest Towards a More Reasonable and Humane International Legal System' (2010) 7 *IOLR* 441

Cassese, A, 'Remarks on Scelle's Theory of "Role Splitting" (dedoublement fonctionnel) in International Law' (1990) 1 *EJIL* 210

Chandrasekhar, S, 'Cartel in a Can: The Financial Collapse of the International Tin Council' (1989) 10 *Northwestern Journal of International Law and Business* 309

Combacau, J and Alland, D, 'Primary and Secondary Rules in the Law of State Responsibility: Categorizing International Obligations' (1985) 16 *Netherlands Yearbook of International Law* 81

Contartese, C, 'Competence-based Approach, Normative Control and the International Responsibility of the EU and Its Member States: What Does Recent Practice Add to the Debate?' (2018) 15 *IOLR* (forthcoming)

Cottier, T and Müller, JP, 'Estoppel' in *Max Planck Encyclopaedia of Public International Law* (OUP online ed, 2007)

Couzigou, I, 'International Organisations and States Within an Agency Relationship: The Distribution of Responsibility' (2014) 61 *Netherlands International Law Review* 335

Crawford, J, 'The ILC's Articles on Responsibility of States for Internationally Wrongful Acts: A Retrospect' (2002) 96 *AJIL* 874

—— 'State Responsibility' in *Max Planck Encyclopedia of Public International Law* (OUP online ed, 2013)

Criddle, E and Fox-Decent, E, 'A Fiduciary Theory of Jus Cogens' (2009) 34 *Yale Journal of International Law* 331

Dannenbaum, T, 'Translating the Standard of Effective Control into a System of Effective Accountability: How Liability Should be Apportioned for Violations of Human Rights by Member State Troop Contingents Serving as United Nations Peacekeepers' (2010) 51 *Harvard International Law Journal* 113

—— 'Dual Attribution in the Context of Military Operations' (2015) 12 *IOLR* 401

Daugirdas, K, 'The International Law Commission Reinvents Itself?' (2014) 108 *AJIL* 79

—— 'Reputation and the Responsibility of International Organizations' (2014) 25 *EJIL* 991

Dupuy, PM, 'Dioniso Anzilotti and the Law of Responsibility of States' (1992) 3 *EJIL* 139

Eagleton, C, 'International Organization and the Law of Responsibility' (1950) 76 *RCADI* 319

Eeckhout, P, 'Opinion 2/13 on EU Accession to the ECHR and Judicial Dialogue: Autonomy or Autarky' (2015) 38 *Fordham International Law Journal* 955

Evans, M, 'Getting to Grips with Torture' (2002) 51 *ICLQ* 365

Fitzmaurice, G, 'The Law and Procedure of the International Court of Justice' (1953) 30 *BYBIL* 1

Fry, J, 'Coercion, Causation and the Fictional Elements of Indirect State Responsibility' (2007) 40 *Vanderbilt Journal of Transnational Law* 611

Gaja, G, 'Positivism and Dualism in Dionisio Anzilotti' (1992) 3 *EJIL* 123

—— 'General Principles of Law' in *Max Planck Encyclopedia of Public International Law* (OUP online ed, 2013)

—— 'The "Co-respondent Mechanisms" According to the Draft Agreement for the Accession of the EU to the ECHR' in V Kosta, N Skoutaris and V Tzevelekos (eds), *The EU Accession to the ECHR* (Hart, 2014) 341

—— 'Interpreting Articles Adopted by the International Law Commission' (2015) 85 *BYBIL* 10

Gasbarri, L, 'Al-Dulimi and the Competing Concepts of International Organizations' (2016) 1 *European Papers* 1117

Gattini, A, 'Breach of the Obligation to Prevent and Reparation Thereof in the ICJ's Genocide Judgment' (2007) 18 *EJIL* 695

Gazzini, T, 'NATO Coercive Military Activities in the Yugoslav Crisis (1992–1999)' (2001) 12 *EJIL* 369

Geslin, A, 'Réflexions sur la répartition de la responsabilité entre l'organisation internationale et ses etats membres' (2005) 109 *Revue générale de droit international public* 539

Goldie, L, 'Concepts of Strict and Absolute Liability and the Ranking of Liability in Terms of Relative Exposure to Risk' (1985) 16 *Netherlands Yearbook of International Law* 175

Gourgourinis, A, 'General/Particular International Law and Primary/Secondary Rules: Unitary Terminology of a Fragmented System' (2011) 22 *EJIL* 993

Graefrath, B, 'Complicity in the Law of International Responsibility' (1996) 29 *Revue Belge de Droit International* 371

Grant, T, 'International Responsibility and the Admission of States to the United Nations' (2009) 30 *Michigan Journal of International Law* 1095

Guzman, A, 'Against Consent' (2012) 52 *Virginia Journal of International Law* 747

Hartwig, M, 'International Organizations or Institutions, Responsibility and Liability' in *Max Planck Encyclopaedia of Public International Law* (OUP online ed, 2011)

Hassan, T, 'Good Faith in Treaty Formation' (1980) 21 *Vanderbilt Journal of International Law* 443 den Heijer, M, 'Procedural Aspects of Shared Responsibility in the European Court of Human Rights' (2013) 4 *Journal of International Dispute Settlement* 361

Henkin, L, 'International Law: Politics, Values, and Functions' (1989) 216 *RCADI* 9

Hoffmeister, F, 'Litigating Against the European Union and its Member States: Who Responds under the ILC's Draft Articles on International Responsibility of International Organisations?' (2010) 21 *EJIL* 723

Hohfeld, WN, 'Some Fundamental Legal Conceptions as Applied in Judicial Reasoning' (1913) 23 *Yale Law Journal* 16

Horbach, NLJT, 'The Confusion About State Responsibility and International Liability' (1991) 4 *Leiden Journal of International Law* 47

Hund, J, 'Are Social Facts Real?' (1982) 33 *British Journal of Sociology* 270

Jacobs, D and Nollkaemper, A, 'Shared Responsibility in International Law: A Conceptual Framework' (2013) 34 *Michigan Journal of International Law* 359

Johnston, A, 'Frozen in Time? The ECJ Finally Rules on the Kadi Appeal' (2009) 68 *Cambridge Law Journal* 1

Kennedy, D, 'The Sources of International Law' (1987) 2 *American University Journal of International Law and Policy* 1

Klein, NS, 'Multilateral Disputes and the Doctrine of Necessary Parties in the East Timor Case' (1996) 21 *Yale Journal of International Law* 305

Koskenniemi, M, 'Solidarity Measures: State Responsibility as a New International Order?' (2002) 72 *BYBIL* 337

Kuijper, PJ, 'Introduction to the Symposium on Responsibility of International Organisations and of (Member) States: Attributed or Direct Responsibility or Both?' (2010) 7 *IOLR* 9

Lauterpacht, E, 'The Development of the Law of International Organizations by the Decisions of International Tribunals' (1976) 152 *RCADI* 381

Lauterpacht, H, 'Contracts to Break a Contract' (1936) 52 *Law Quarterly Review* 494

—— 'Codification and Development of International Law' (1955) 49 *AJIL* 16

Linderfalk, U, 'State Responsibility and the Primary-Secondary Rules Terminology: The Role of Language for an Understanding of the International Legal System' (2009) 78 *Nordic Journal of International Law* 53

Lock, T, 'Beyond Bosphorus: The European Court of Human Rights' Case Law on the Responsibility of Member States of International Organisations under the European Convention on Human Rights' (2010) 10 *Human Rights Law Review* 529

Lorimer, J, 'Le problème final du droit international' (1877) ix *Revue de Droit International et de Législation Comparée* 161

Lowe, AV, 'Responsibility for the Conduct of Other States' (2002) 101 *Japanese Journal of International Law and Diplomacy* 1

Mallory, I, 'Conduct Unbecoming: The Collapse of the International Tin Agreement' (1990) 5 *American University Journal of International Law and Policy* 835

Mann, FA, 'Reflections on a Commercial Law of Nations' (1957) 33 *BYBIL* 20

Marschik, A, 'Too Much Order? The Impact of Special Secondary Norms on the Unity and Efficacy of the International Legal System' (1998) 9 *EJIL* 212

Martin, JMC, 'The Responsibility of Members Due to Wrongful Acts of International Organizations' (2013) 12 *Chinese Journal of International Law* 679

McBeth, A, 'Breaching the Vacuum: A Consideration of the Role of International Human Rights Law in the Operations of the International Financial Institutions' (2006) 10 *International Journal of Human Rights* 385

McFadden, E, 'The Collapse of Tin: Restructuring a Failed Commodity Agreement' (1986) 80 *AJIL* 811

Megret, F and Hoffman, F, 'The UN as a Human Rights Violator? Some Reflections on the United Nations Changing Human Rights Responsibilities' (2003) 25 *Human Rights Quarterly* 318

Milanovic, M, 'State Responsibility for Genocide: A Follow-Up' (2007) 18 *EJIL* 669

Möldner, M, 'Responsibility of International Organizations, Introducing the ARIO' (2012) 16 *Max Planck Yearbook of United Nations Law* 281

Moynihan, H, 'Aiding and Assisting: The Mental Element Under Article 16 of the International Law Commission's Articles on State Responsibility' (2018) 67 *ICLQ* 455

Murray, O, 'Piercing the Institutional Veil: The Responsibility of Member States of an International Organization' (2011) 8 *IOLR* 291

Narula, S, 'The Right to Food: Holding Global Actors Accountable under International Law' (2006) 44 *Columbia Journal of Transnational Law* 691

Nedeski, N and Nollkaemper, A, 'Responsibility of International Organisations in Connection with Acts of States' (2012) 9 *IOLR* 33

Nolan, M and Sourgens, F, 'Issues of Proof of General Principles of Law in International Arbitration' (2009) 3 *World Arbitration and Mediation Review* 505

Nolte, G, 'From Dionisio Anzilotti to Roberto Ago: The Classical International Law of State Responsibility and the Traditional Primacy of a Bilateral Conception of Inter-State Relations' (2002) 13 *EJIL* 1083

Nissell, A, 'The ILC Articles on State Responsibility: Between Self-Help and Solidarity' (2006) 38 *International Law and Politics* 355

Paasivirta, E, 'Reponsibility of a Member State of an International Organization: Where Will It End? Comments on Article 60 of the ILC Draft on the Responsibility of International Organizations' (2010) 7 *IOLR* 49

—— 'The Responsibility of Member States of International Organizations? A Special Case for the European Union' (2015) 12 *IOLR* 448

Paasivirta, E and Kuijper, PJ, 'Does One Size Fit All? The European Community and the Responsibility of International Organisations' (2005) 36 *Netherlands Yearbook of International Law* 169

Palchetti, P, 'Sulla responsabilità di uno stato per il voto espresso in seno ad un'organizzazione internazionale' (2012) 45 *Rivista di Diritto Internazionale* 352

—— 'Applying the Rules of Attribution in Complex Scenarios: The Case of Partnerships Among International Organizations' (2016) 13 *IOLR* 37

Palombella, L, 'The Rule of Law Beyond the State: Failures, Promises and Theory' (2009) 7 *International Journal of Constitutional Law* 442

Pellet, A, 'Between Codification and Progressive Development of the Law: Some Reflections from the ILC' (2004) 6 *International Law FORUM du Droit International* 15

Pronto, A, 'An Introduction to the Articles on the Responsibility of International Organisations' (2011) 36 *South African Yearbook of International Law* 94

Quigley, J, 'Complicity in International Law: A New Direction in the Law of State Responsibility' (1986) 57 *BYBIL* 77

Reinisch, A, 'Should Judges Second-Guess the UN Security Council' (2009) 35 *IOLR* 257

—— 'Aid or Assistance and Direction and Control Between States and International Organisations in the Commission of Internationally Wrongful Acts' (2010) 7 *IOLR* 63

Ryngaert, C, 'The European Court of Human Rights' Approach to the Responsibility of Member States in Connection with Acts of International Organisations' (2011) 60 *ICLQ* 997

—— 'Oscillating Between Embracing and Avoiding Bosphorus: the European Court of Human Rights on Member State Responsibility for Acts of International Organisations and the Case of the EU' (2014) 39 *European Law Review* 176

Ryngaert, C and Buchanan, H, 'Member State Responsibility for the Acts of International Organizations' (2011) 7 *Utrecht Law Review* 131

Sadurska, R and Chinkin, C, 'The Collapse of the International Tin Council: A Case of State Responsibility?' (1989–1990) 30 *Virginia Journal of International Law* 845

Sands, P, 'The Tin Council Litigation in the English Courts' (1987) 34 *Netherlands International Law Review* 367

Sanxhaktari, V, 'The Implications of the Accession Agreement of the EU to the ECHR' (2014) 5 *Mediterranean Journal of Social Sciences* 135

Sari, A, 'Untangling Extra-Territorial Jurisdiction from International Responsibility in Jaloud v Netherlands: Old Problem, New Solutions?' (2014) 53 *Military Law and the Law of War Review* 287

Sarooshi, D, 'Conferrals by States of Powers on International Organizations: The Case of Agency' (2003) 74 *BYBIL* 308

—— 'The European Courts and the Security Council: Between Dédoublement Fonctionnel and Balancing of Values: A Rejoinder to Gráinne de Burca, André Nollkaemper and Iris Canor' (2009) 20 *EJIL* 889

Scelle, G, 'Regies generales du droit de la paix' (1933) 46 *RCADI* 327

—— 'Quelques réflexions sur l'abolition de la competence de guerre' (1954) *Revue générale de droit international public* 5

Schmalenbach, K, 'International Organizations or Institutions, General Aspects' in *Max Planck Encyclopedia of Public International Law* (OUP online ed, 2014)

Schrodinger, E, 'Die gegenwartige Situation in der Quantenmechanik' (1935) 23 *Naturwissenschaften* 807

Schwarzenberger, G, 'The Fundamental Principles of International Law' (1955) 92 *RCADI* 195

Seidl-Hohenveldern, I, 'Piercing the Corporate Veil of International Organizations: The International Tin Council Case in the English Court of Appeals' (1989) 32 *German Yearbook of International Law* 43

de Sena, P and Vitucci, C, 'The European Courts and the Security Council: Between Dédoublement Fonctionnel and Balancing of Values' (2009) 20 *EJIL* 193

Sereni, AP, 'Agency in International Law' (1940) 34 *AJIL* 638

Simma, B, 'NATO, the UN and the Use of Force: Legal Aspects' (1999) 10 *EJIL* 1

Stumer, A, 'Liability of Member States for Acts of International Organizations: Reconsidering the Policy Objections' (2007) 48 *Harvard International Law Journal* 553

Sucharitkul, S, 'State Responsibility and International Liability under International Law' (1996) 18 *Loyola of Los Angeles International and Comparative Law Review* 821

Taylor, GDS, 'Content and Rule Against Abuse of Rights in International Law' (1972) 46 *BYBIL* 323

Thirlway, H, 'Reflections on Lex Ferenda' (2001) 32 *Netherlands Yearbook of International Law* 3

Tzanakopoulos, A, 'Domestic Courts in International Law: The International Judicial Function of National Courts' (2011) 34 *Loyola of Los Angeles International and Comparative Law Review* 133

Verdirame, G, 'Breaches of the European Convention on Human Rights Resulting from the Conduct of International Organisations' (2008) 2 *European Human Rights Law Review* 209

—— 'A Normative Theory of Sovereignty Transfers' (2013) 49 *Stanford Journal of International Law* 371

de Visscher, C, 'La responsabilité des etats' (1924) 2 *Bibliotheca Visseriana Dissertationum Ius Internationale Illustrantium* 86

Watts, A, 'Codification and Progressive Development of International Law' in R Wolfrum (ed), *Max Planck Encyclopedia of Public International Law* (OUP, 2007)

Weil, P, 'Cours general de droit international public' (1992) 237 *RCADI* 9

Wessel, R and Dekker, I, 'Identities of States in International Organizations' (2015) 12 *IOLR* 293

Widdows, K, 'Security Council Resolutions and Non-Members of the United Nations' (1978) 27 *ICLQ* 459

Wilde, R, 'Enhancing Accountability at the International Level: The Tension Between International Organization and Member State Responsibility and the Underlying Issues at Stake' (2006) 12 *ILSA Journal of International and Comparative Law* 395

Wolfrum, R, 'General International Law (Principles, Rules, and Standards)' in *Max Planck Encyclopedia of Public International Law* (OUP online ed, 2010)

Wood, M, 'International Organizations and Customary International Law' (2015) 48 *Vanderbilt Journal of Transnational Law* 609

Wouters, J and Odermatt, J, 'Are All International Organizations Created Equal? Reflections on the ILC's Draft Articles of Responsibility of International Organizations' (2012) 9 *IOLR* 7

van Zyl Smit, D, 'Punishment and Human Rights in International Criminal Law' (2002) 2 *Human Rights Law Review* 1

Blog Entries

Alvarez, J, 'Misadventures in Subjecthood', *Ejil:Talk!*, 29 September 2010

Milanovic, M, 'European Court Decides Nada v. Switzerland', *Ejil:Talk!*, 14 September 2012

Nollkaemper, A, 'The ECtHR Finds FYROM Responsible in Connection with Torture by the CIA, but on What Basis?', *Ejil:Talk!*, 24 December 2012

Peters, A, 'Targeted Sanctions after Affaire Al Dulimi et Montana Management Inc c Suisse: Is There a Way Out of the Catch-22 for UN Members,' *Ejil:Talk!*, 4 December 2013

Tzanakopoulos, A, 'Sharing Responsibility for UN Targeted Sanctions', *Ejil:Talk!*, 14 February 2013

—— 'Kadi Showdown: Substantive Review of (UN) Sanctions by the ECJ', *Ejil:Talk!*, 19 July 2013

UN Documents

(all electronic documents are accessible through the official documentation system of the United Nations: www.un.org/en/documents/ods/)

Ago, R, *Second Report on State Responsibility*, UN doc A/CN.4/233 (1970), reproduced in (1970) 2(1) *YBILC* 177

—— *Third Report on State Responsibility*, UN doc A/8010/Rev.l (1971) and Add 1–3, reproduced in (1971) 2(1) *YBILC* 199

—— *Seventh Report on State Responsibility*, UN Doc A/CN.4/307 (1978) and Add 1–2 and Corr 1–2, reproduced in (1978) 2(1) *YBILC* 31

—— *Eighth Report on State Responsibility*, UN doc A/CN.4/318 (1979) and Add 1–4, reproduced in (1979) 2(1) *YBILC* 4

—— 'Addendum to the Eighth Report on State Responsibility' (1980) 2(1) *Yearbook of the ILC* 1

Crawford, J, *Second Report on State Responsibility*, UN doc A/CN.4/498 (1999) and Add 1–4, reproduced in (1999) 2(1) *YBILC* 3

Gaja, G, *Third Report on Responsibility of International Organizations*, UN doc A/CN.4/553 (2005), reproduced in (2005) 2(1) *YBILC* 7

—— *Fourth Report on Responsibility of International Organizations*, UN doc A/CN.4/564 (2006) and Add 1–2, reproduced in (2006) 2(1) *YBILC* 103

—— *Seventh Report on Responsibility of International Organizations*, UN doc A/CN.4/610 (2009), reproduced in (2009) 2(1) *YBILC* 73

—— *Eighth Report on Responsibility of International Organizations*, UN doc A/CN.4/640 (2011)

Human Rights Council, *Joint Study on Global Practices in Relation to Secret Detention in the Context of Countering Terrorism*, UN doc A/HRC/13/42 (19 February 2010)

ILC, *Report of the International Law Commission on the Work of Its 23rd session, 26 April–30 July 1971*, UN doc A/8410/REV.1 (1971), reproduced in (1971) 2(1) *YBILC* 275

—— *Report of the International Law Commission on the Work of Its 25th Session (7 May–13 July 1973)*, UN doc A/9010/Rev 1 (1973), reproduced in (1973) 2 *YBILC* 161

—— *Report of the International Law Commission on the Work of Its 27th Session (5 May–25 July 1975)*, UN doc A/10010/Rev l (1975), reproduced in (1975) 2(1) *YBILC* 47

—— *Summary Record of the 1519th Meeting* (18 July 1978), reproduced in (1978) 1 *YBILC* 237

—— *Report of the International Law Commission on the Work of Its 30th Session, 8 May–28 July 1978*, UN doc A/33/10 (1978) reproduced in (1978) 2(2) *YBILC* 74

—— *State Responsibility: Comments of Governments on Part 1 on the Draft Articles on State Responsibility for Internationally Wrongful Acts*, UN doc A/CN.4/342 (1981) and Add 1–4, reproduced in (1981) 2(1) *YBILC* 71

—— *State Responsibility: Comments and Observations Received from Governments*, UN doc A/CN.4/488 (1998) and Add.1–3, reproduced in (1998) 2(1) *YBILC* 81

—— *Summary Record of the 2577th Meeting* (25 May 1999), reproduced in (1999) 1 *YBILC* 67
—— *State Responsibility: Comments and Observations Received from Governments*, UN doc A/CN.4/492 (1999), reproduced in (1999) 2(1) *YBILC* 101
—— *Summary Record of the 2672nd Meeting* (3 May 2001), reproduced in (2001) 1 *YBILC* 34
—— *State Responsibility: Comments and Observations Received from Governments*, UN doc A/CN.4/515 (2001) and Add 1–3, reproduced in (2001) 2(1) *YBILC* 33
—— 'Draft Articles on Responsibility of States for Internationally Wrongful Acts, with Commentaries' (2001) 2(2) *YBILC* 31
—— 'Draft Articles on the Responsibility of States for Internationally Wrongful Acts with Commentaries' (2001) 2(2) *YBILC* 31
—— *Draft Articles on Prevention of Transboundary Harm from Hazardous Activities, with Commentaries*, UN doc A/56/10 (2001), reproduced in (2001) 2(2) *YBILC* 144
—— *Report of the International Law Commission on the Work of Its 55th Session (5 May–6 June and 7 July–8 August 2003)*, UN doc A/58/10 (2003), reproduced in (2003) 2(2) *YBILC* 1
—— *Report of the International Law Commission on the Work of Its 55th Session (2003): Topical Summary of the Discussion Held in the Sixth Committee of the General Assembly During its 58th session, prepared by the Secretariat*, UN doc A/CN.4/537 (2004)
—— *Summary Record of the 2800th Meeting*, UN doc A/CN.4/SR.2800 (18 May 2004), reproduced in (2004) 1 *YBILC* 65
—— *Summary Record of the 2801th Meeting*, UN doc A/CN.4/SR.2801 (19 May 2004), reproduced in (2004) 1 *YBILC* 73
—— *Responsibility of International Organizations: Comments and Observations Received from International Organizations*, UN doc A/CN.4/545 (2004), reproduced in (2004) 2(1) *YBILC* 19
—— *Responsibility of International Organizations: Comments and Observations Received from Governments and International Organizations*, UN doc A/CN/4.556 (2005), reproduced in (2005) 2(1) *YBILC* 27
—— *Report of the International Law Commission on the Work of Its 57th Session (2005): Topical Summary of the Discussion Held in the Sixth Committee of the General Assembly During its 60th Session, prepared by the Secretariat*, UN doc A/CN.4/560 (2005)
—— *Report of the International Law Commission on the Work of Its 57th Session (2 May–3 June and 11 July–5 August 2005)*, UN doc A/60/10 (2005), reproduced in (2005) 2(2) *YBILC* 1
—— *Provisional Summary Record of the 2891st Meeting*, UN doc A/CN.4/SR.2891 (2006), reproduced in (2006) 1 *YBILC* 145
—— *Responsibility of International Organizations: Comments and Observations Received from International Organisations*, UN doc A/CN.4/568 (2006) and Add.1, reproduced in (2006) 2(1) *YBILC* 125
—— *Report of the International Law Commission on the Work of Its 58th Session, 1 May–9 June and 3 July–11 August 2006*, UN doc A/61/10 (2006), reproduced in (2006) 2(2) *YBILC* 1
—— *Draft Principles on the Allocation of Loss in the Case of Transboundary Harm Arising Out of Hazardous Activities, with Commentaries*, UN doc A/61/10 (2006), reproduced in (2006) 2(2) *YBILC* 59
—— *Fragmentation of International Law: Difficulties Arising from the Diversification and Expansion of International Law [Report of the Study Group]*, UN doc A/CN.4/L.682 (13 April 2006)
—— *Provisional Summary of the 2801st Meeting*, UN doc A/CN.4/SR.2801 (19 May 2004)
—— *Responsibility of International Organizations: Comments and Observations Received from International Organizations*, UN doc A/CN.4/582 (2007), reproduced in (2007) 2(1) *YBILC* 17
—— *Provisional Summary Record of the 3015th Meeting*, UN doc A/CN.4/SR.3015 (15 July 2009), reproduced in (2009) 1 *YBILC* 109
—— *Responsibility of International Organizations: Comments and Observations Received from International Organisations*, UN doc A/CN.4/609 (2009), reproduced in (2009) 2(1) *YBILC* 97

—— *Report of the International Law Commission on the Work of Its 61st Session (4 May–5 June and 6 July–7 August 2009)*, UN doc A/64/10 (2009), reproduced in (2009) 2(2) *YBILC* 1
—— *Text of the Draft Articles on Responsibility of International Organizations Adopted by the Commission on First Reading*, UN doc A/CN.4/L.748 (2009) and Add 2, reproduced in 2009 2(2) *YBILC* 19 – *Provisional Summary of the 3081st Meeting*, UN doc A/CN.4/SR.3081 (2011)
—— *Report of the International Law Commission on the Work of Its 63rd Session (26 April–3 June and 4 July–12 August 2011)*, UN doc A/66/10 (2011)
—— *Responsibility of International Organizations: Comments and Observations Received from Governments*, UN doc A/CN.4/636 (2011)
—— *Responsibility of International Organizations: Comments and Observations Received from International Organizations*, UN doc A/CN.4/637 (2011)
—— *Responsibility of International Organizations: Comments and Observations Received from International Organizations*, UN doc A/CN.4/637/Add.1 (2011)
—— 'Draft Articles on Responsibility of International Organisations with Commentaries' (2011) 2(2) *YBILC* 46
—— *Provisional Summary Record of the 3097th Meeting*, UN doc A/CN.4/SR.3097 (8 July 2011)
—— *Report of the International Law Commission on the Work of Its 69th Session (1 May–2 June and 3 July–4 August 2017)*, UN doc A/72/10 (2017)
Quentin-Baxter, R, *Preliminary Report on International Liability for Injurious Consequences Arising Out of Acts Not Prohibited by International Law*, UN doc A/CN.4/334 (1980) and Add 1–2, reproduced in 2(1) *YBILC* 247
—— *Fourth Report on International Liability for Injurious Consequences Arising Out of Acts Not Prohibited by International Law*, UN doc A/CN.4/373 (1983), reproduced in (1983) 2(1) *YBILC* 201
UNGA, 56th Session, *Resolutions and Decisions Adopted by the General Assembly during its Fifty-Sixth Session*, UN doc A/56/49(Vol.I)/Corr.4 (2007)
—— 58th Session, Sixth Committee, *Summary Record of the 14th Meeting*, UN doc A/C.6/58/SR.14 (2003)
—— 60th Session, Sixth Committee, *Summary Record of the 11th Meeting*, UN doc A/C.6/60/SR.11 (2005)
—— 60th Session, Sixth Committee, *Summary Record of the 12th Meeting*, UN doc A/C.6/60/SR.12 (2005)
—— 61st Session, Sixth Committee, *Summary Record of the 13th Meeting*, UN doc A/C.6/60/SR.13 (2006)
—— 61st Session, Sixth Committee, *Summary Record of the 14th Meeting*, UN doc A/C.6/61/SR.14 (2006)
—— 61st Session, Sixth Committee, *Summary Record of the 15th Meeting*, UN doc A/C.6/61/SR.15 (2006)
—— 61st Session, Sixth Committee, *Summary Record of the 16th Meeting*, UN doc A/C.6/61/SR.16 (2006)
—— 66th Session, Sixth Committee, *Summary Record of the 18th Meeting*, UN doc A/C.6/66/SR.18 (2011)
—— 69th Session, Sixth Committee, *Summary Record of the 18th Meeting*, UN doc A/C.6/69/SR.18 (2014)
UN Secretary-General, *A New Approach to Cholera in Haiti*, UN doc A/71/620 (25 November 2016)
Vázquez-Bermúdez, M, 'Responsibility of International Organizations', Statement of the Chairman of the Drafting Committee, 6 July 2009
Wood, M, *Second Report on the Identification of Customary International Law*, UN doc A/CN.4/672 (2014)
—— *Third Report on the Identification of Customary International Law*, UN doc A/CN.4/682 (2015)

International Reports and Other Material

CIA, Office of the Director of National Intelligence, *Summary of the High Value Detainees Program* (2006)

Council of Europe, *Third Negotiation Meeting Between the CDDH Ad Hoc Negotiation Group and the European Commission on the Accession of the European Union to the European Convention on Human Rights: Meeting Report*, Council of Europe doc 47+1(2012)R02 (9 November 2012)

—— *Fifth Negotiation Meeting Between the CDDH Ad Hoc Negotiation Group and the European Commission on the Accession of the European Union to the European Convention on Human Rights, Final Report to the CDDH*, Council of Europe doc 47+1 (2013)008rev2 (10 June 2013)

Higgins, R (Special Rapporteur), 'Report on the Legal Consequences for Member States of the Non-fulfillment by International Organizations of Their Obligations Toward Third Parties' (1995) 66 *Yearbook of the Institute of International Law*

ILA, *Accountability of International Organizations, Final Report* (Berlin Conference, 2004)

IMF, Independent Evaluation Office, *Governance of the IMF: An Evaluation* (2008)

Inter-American Commission on Human Rights, *Report on the Situation of Human Rights in the Republic of Guatemala*, OEA/Ser. L/V/II.53, doc 21 rev 2 (13 October 1981)

North Atlantic Treaty Organization, *Declaration Issued by the Heads of State and Government participating in the Meeting of the North Atlantic Council in Bucharest on 3 April 2008*, Bucharest Summit, Press Release (2008)049, available at www.nato.int/docu/pr/2008/p08-049e.html

Permanent Court of International Justice, Advisory Committee of Jurists, *Procès-verbaux of the Proceedings of the Committee. June 16–July 24th 1920 with Annexes* (Van Langenhuysen, 1920)

Rights Action, Centre on Housing Rights and Evictions, *Continuing the Struggle for Justice and Accountability in Guatemala: Making Reparations a Reality in the Chixoy Dam Case* (Geneva, 2004)

United Nations Office for Project Services, *Guatemala, Memory of Silence, Guatemala, 1999*, vol VI, Annex 1, *Illustrative Case No. 10, Massacre and Elimination of the Community of Río Negro* (Report of the Historical Clarification Commission, 1999)

Index

www.ingramcontent.com/pod-product-compliance
Lightning Source LLC
Chambersburg PA
CBHW071258180926
51613CB00001B/70

Mercury and the Everglades. A Synthesis and Model for Complex Ecosystem Restoration

Curtis D. Pollman • Donald M. Axelrad •
Darren G. Rumbold
Editors

Mercury and the Everglades. A Synthesis and Model for Complex Ecosystem Restoration

Volume III – Temporal Trends of Mercury in the Everglades, Synthesis and Management Implications

Springer

Editors
Curtis D. Pollman
Aqua Lux Lucis, Inc
Gainesville, FL, USA

Donald M. Axelrad
Institute of Public Health
Florida A&M University
Tallahassee, FL, USA

Darren G. Rumbold
Coastal Watershed Institute
Florida Gulf Coast University
Fort Myers, FL, USA

ISBN 978-3-030-55634-1 ISBN 978-3-030-55635-8 (eBook)
https://doi.org/10.1007/978-3-030-55635-8

This Springer imprint is published by the registered company Springer Nature Switzerland AG.
The registered company address is: Gewerbestrasse 11, 6330 Cham, Switzerland

"The Early Ibis Gets the Crayfish" by Brian Garrett

Preface

> If you want to grab the world and run it
> I see that you will not succeed.
> The world is a spiritual vessel, which can't be controlled—Lao Tzu[1]

This book is the culmination of more than a 4-year effort to synthesize essentially 30 years of research into the mercury (Hg) problem in the Everglades. For Hg to enter food webs in aquatic ecosystems such as the Everglades, two things are required: first, of course, is a source of Hg; second is that the Hg in the aquatic ecosystem needs to be either present as or converted to the methylated form. Once Hg is methylated, it can enter the base of aquatic food web and then increasingly bioaccumulate by trophic transfer. This biogeochemical cycling of Hg is complex and involves multiple processes and variables. This cycling with respect to methyl Hg (MeHg) production can also be profoundly influenced by anthropogenic disturbances. For many otherwise pristine aquatic ecosystems, disturbance manifesting in elevated biota Hg concentrations relates primarily to changes in atmospheric inputs of Hg. For the Everglades, however, such disturbance includes not only anthropogenic impacts on atmospheric Hg cycling and deposition, but also direct impacts on the hydrology and water chemistry of the system.

This book is ultimately devoted to understanding the nature and evolution of the Hg problem in the Everglades and the attendant role played by anthropogenic disturbance. Our hope is that synthesizing much of the vast amount of extant research in the Everglades itself can lead to informed approaches and policies by key decision makers toward mitigating the problem. These objectives accordingly are embodied in the sequential exposition of the three volumes comprising this synthesis.

Volume I presented an overview of the Everglades from a physical and ecological perspective and how anthropogenically driven disturbance has changed the system

[1]Lao Tzu (n.d.) Tao Te Ching. Translated by Charles Muller (2005) Barnes and Noble Books, New York, NY.

spatially, hydrologically, and ecologically over the past approximately 140 years. The roots of this disturbance lay in increasing development in south Florida which broadened over time and led to more concerted efforts to both convert natural habitat to agricultural and urban land uses and manage the resultant remnant Everglades hydrologically. The sheer magnitude of these efforts was intimated by Shelton[2], who in 1957 wrote about the "largest low-level pumping station ever constructed" as part of an "enormous flood control and water conservation project" he touted as "one of the greatest examples in America of what man's intelligence and vision can do in converting the erratic forces of nature into solid assets for the vegetable and animal kingdom." While disturbance is an important theme in understanding the mercury problem in the Everglades, the problem would be moot without sources of mercury entering the system. Atmospheric deposition of Hg is the overwhelming pathway for Hg entering the Everglades,[3] and Volume I thus includes chapters on atmospheric cycling of Hg and how key aspects of its cycling serve to exacerbate atmospheric inputs to the Everglades. Volume I also includes chapters on the changing temporal relationship between local and larger scale sources contributing to the Everglades Hg problem and the implications of this current relationship for mitigation through controlling emission sources.

Volume II has two parts, with the first part providing greater context regarding how direct disturbance in the Everglades has or likely has contributed to the Hg problem. The foundation for this assessment lies in understanding how Hg entering the Everglades is transformed and enters the aquatic food web, which in turn links trophic transfer of Hg in terrestrial wildlife to Hg inputs to the marsh. This biogeochemical cycling is critical with respect to how strongly Hg in the Everglades bioaccumulates—the importance of which cannot be overstated. As mentioned earlier, Hg must be present as methyl Hg (MeHg) for it to enter aquatic food webs; since external inputs of Hg to the Everglades are greatly dominated by inorganic Hg rather than MeHg, this Hg in turn must be methylated for it to become problematic. As we saw in Volume II, two water chemistry variables—sulfate and dissolved organic carbon—emerge as playing key roles in the methylation of Hg in the Everglades. In addition, both of these variables—which, along with Hg, George Aiken of the U.S. Geological Survey identified as the "biogeochemical axis of evil" responsible for the global Hg problem—also are profoundly influenced by

---

[2]Shelton WR (1957) Land of the Everglades. Tropical Southern Florida. Department of Agriculture, State of Florida, Tallahassee, FL.

[3]Atkeson TD, Axelrad D, Pollman CD, Keeler G (2003) Integrating atmospheric mercury deposition and aquatic cycling in the Florida Everglades: an approach for conducting a total maximum daily load analysis for an atmospherically derived pollutant. Integrated Summary. Final report submitted to USEPA. Florida Department of Environmental Protection, Tallahassee, FL.

Stober QJ, Thornton K, Jones R, Richards J, Ivey C, Welch R, Madden M, Trexler J, Gaiser E, Scheidt D, Rathbun S (2001) South Florida Ecosystem Assessment: Phase I/II—Everglades stressor interactions: hydropatterns, eutrophication, habitat alteration, and mercury contamination (summary). EPA 904-R-01-002. USEPA Region 4 Science & Ecosystem Support Division, Water Management Division, and Office of Research and Development.

disturbance within the Everglades. The second part of Volume II in turn presents a series of chapters elucidating how Hg bioaccumulates in the Everglades, the magnitude of that bioaccumulation, and the resultant ecological and human health risks.

As the last of three volumes comprising this synthesis, this volume is devoted to the overarching question of how the Hg problem can be mitigated or managed. Similar to the other two volumes, Volume III is organized into two parts. The first part includes the following chapters:

The first two chapters focus on trends observed for two key components of the Everglades Hg problem—trends in atmospheric deposition and trends in aquatic biota and terrestrial wildlife Hg concentrations. The analysis evaluated various datasets for possible long-term and short-term trends. Long-term trends were assessed in Hg accumulation rates in sediment cores (*ca.*1800–2010) and Hg concentrations in the scapular feathers of wading birds, including museum specimens (*ca.* 1910–2010). Analyses of short-term trends include those in wet deposition of atmospheric Hg (*ca.* 1984–2016) and biota, including primarily fish (*ca.* 1980 to 2016). Chapter 3 focuses on the important management question of Hg originating from historical or previous inputs (so-called legacy Hg) and residing in different environmental pools (e.g., Everglades sediments) that can still contribute to Hg biogeochemical cycling and the implications that legacy Hg poses for remediation. Chapter 4 presents an analysis of likely drivers contributing to the temporal dynamics in largemouth bass Hg concentrations using the deterministic Everglades Mercury Cycling Model (E-MCM). Because they use a priori functional, mechanistic relationships in a dynamic modeling framework, models such as E-MCM are considered to be more strongly indicative of cause and effect than empirical models (e.g., linear regression models). While the E-MCM has the ability to be applied across the Everglades as a series of spatially discrete cells, it is quite data intensive. As a result, the model was applied to site 3A-15 within Water Conservation Area 3A because the site was identified during the early days of the South Florida Mercury Science Program (see Preface to Volume I for a discussion of the evolution of the SFMSP) as a Hg "hot-spot" of considerable interest; this interest led to a number of intensive studies led by the U.S. Geological Survey and others[4] that produced

[4]USGS (2018) USGS SOFIA Data Exchange. https://sofia.usgs.gov/projects/index.php?project_url=evergl_merc

Aiken GR, Gilmour CC, Krabbenhoft DP, Orem W (2011) Dissolved organic matter in the Florida Everglades: implications for ecosystem restoration. Crit Rev Environ Sci Technol 41 (S1):217–248.

Krabbenhoft DP (1996) Mercury studies in the Florida Everglades. U.S. Geological Survey Fact Sheet FS-166–196.

sufficient biogeochemical data for parameterizing and calibrating the E-MCM. The part then concludes with a chapter synthesizing key results from the first four chapters.

Several key points emerge from the first part chapters. First is the paradigm that changes in atmospheric deposition of Hg have contributed to changes in biota Hg concentrations and the trends in atmospheric deposition had a local emissions component. Second is that the magnitude of biota Hg concentration changes—both long term and short term—exceeds inferred changes in atmospheric deposition. The implication of this result is that some other variable changing over time is acting in addition to changes in atmospheric deposition to drive biota Hg temporal dynamics. The third key point is that trends in biota Hg vary across the Everglades landscape; this fact is important in assessing the role of changes in water chemistry as causative and the attendant implications of such changes from a mercury mitigation perspective. A fourth key point relates to the impact of legacy Hg on the rate and magnitude of recovery of the Everglades from atmospheric Hg input mitigation. Legacy Hg has two spatial components—large or global scale and local scale. Understanding the very different dynamics these two components expectedly will impose on the Everglades over time has profound implications with respect to Hg mitigation success.

The second part of this volume speaks to the question of trying to mitigate the Everglades problem from a quantitative and philosophical perspective. It contains two chapters that touch upon this question:

Chapter 6: Structural Equation Model for Mercury Cycling in the Everglades
Chapter 7: Mercury Mitigation Management Strategies and Likely Outcomes

The first chapter of this final part uses structural equation modeling (SEM) to identify the biogeochemical variables that most strongly contribute to the methylation of Hg and trophic transfer of MeHg to *Gambusia*[5] within the Everglades marsh. SEM offers several advantages over other modeling approaches for the Everglades Hg problem. First, unlike the E-MCM, the model can be applied across the entirety of the Everglades Protection Area (EvPA) with existing data. Second, similar to mechanistic modeling, SEM relies on *a priori* constructs or pathways. Fitting of the SEM establishes whether the model pathways are statistically significant and supportable; SEM is thus considered to be more informative with respect to cause and

---

Gilmour CC, Riedel GS, Ederington MC, Bell JT, Benoit JM, Gill GA, Stordal MC (1998) Methylmercury concentrations and production rates across a trophic gradient in the northern Everglades. Biogeochemistry 40:327–345.

Hurley JP, Krabbenhoft DP, Cleckner LB, Olson ML, Aiken GR, Rawlik RS (1998) System controls on the aqueous distribution of mercury in the northern Florida Everglades. Biogeochemistry 40:293–310.

[5]*Gambusia* is quite useful as an indicator species because it is both ubiquitous in the Everglades marsh and has a relatively short life span (~1 year). Moreover, *Gambusia* individuals are less widely ranging than larger fish occupying higher trophic level niches. As a result, *Gambusia* Hg concentration dynamics should more closely reflect both smaller spatial and shorter temporal dynamics in Hg biogeochemical cycling.

effect than typical regression models. Moreover, unlike conventional regression modeling, SEM allows for indirect relationships between variables where the effect of a particular variable *A* on a response variable *C* is mediated by the direct interaction of *A* with a third variable *B* that in turn interacts directly with *C*. With respect to Hg biogeochemical cycling, this ability to model indirect effects is important because, for example, the effects of dissolved organic carbon and sulfate on *Gambusia* Hg concentrations are mediated through the effects of both variables on MeHg concentrations.

The SEM in Chap. 6 also lays the predicate for conducting scenario modeling for mitigating the Everglades Hg problem. From a management perspective, it is extremely useful for such modeling to include a quantitative assessment of the uncertainty inherent in the predictions. One such approach that increasingly is gaining broader use is the application of *marginal* analyses. Marginal analyses are used to isolate the effects of single predictive parameter included as part of a multivariate model by holding the other predictive parameters at fixed levels and allowing the predictive parameter of interest to vary across a specified range during the predictive analysis. This allows for the construction of confidence intervals in the predicted values of the response variable (e.g., *Gambusia* Hg concentrations) as a function of the predictive variable of interest (e.g., sulfate). Chapter 7 thus uses marginal analyses coupled with a “reduced form” generalized linear model abstracted from the SEM developed in Chap. 6 to evaluate the effects of reducing sulfate on predicted *Gambusia* Hg concentrations in each of the major hydrologic units within the EvPA. The rationale for recommending and thus focusing on sulfate alone rather than including other variables as the foundation of a strategy for mitigating the Everglades Hg problem is delineated as the chapter begins and reflects broad support for the causative role of sulfate across multiple lines of evidence coupled with the fact that sulfate concentrations are greatly elevated across much of the EvPA.

In the very late 1970s/early 1980s when monitoring of fish tissue Hg concentrations was first initiated, an ongoing and dire Hg problem in the Everglades became immediately manifest. Fish tissue Hg concentrations in the Everglades were among the highest recorded in otherwise pristine systems worldwide (which by their very nature are particularly sensitive to the insults of atmospheric inputs of Hg) coupled with profound impacts to terrestrial wildlife including wading birds and the endangered Florida panther. The story since then, however, provides a glimmer of hope. Since the early 1980s when they were at peak recorded levels, biota Hg concentrations throughout much—albeit not all—of the EvPA declined by upwards to 75%. The variability in spatial and temporal dynamics of biota Hg concentrations in the Everglades further indicates that substantial reductions in biota Hg concentrations can occur rapidly and that variations in biogeochemistry are a major cause of these dynamics. This fact brings us back to the theme of disturbance. Key among the water chemistry variables controlling Hg methylation is sulfate, the occurrence of which within the Everglades is overwhelmingly a product of disturbance. If we have the will, this disturbance can be reversed, and the benefits of reduced Hg concentrations in the Everglades should be reaped quickly.

A few final words are in order. As reflected in the title, we have sought to provide a model for complex ecosystem restoration through this three-volume series. We believe that the state of the science for the Everglades Hg problem is sufficiently robust to offer a clear path forward toward meaningful recovery. Inherent in this title, however, is not just the present state of the science; the title also hints at the future. *Ergo*, this model for complex ecosystem restoration is meaningful only if those charged with the responsibility of managing and safeguarding this singular and irreplaceable natural treasure arise from their passivity and seize the gauntlet of appropriate action.

Gainesville, FL — Curtis D. Pollman
Tallahassee, FL — Donald M. Axelrad
Fort Myers, FL — Darren G. Rumbold

Contents

Contributors

Donald M. Axelrad Florida A&M University, Tallahassee, FL, USA

Donald Beals Reed Harris Environmental Ltd., Oakville, ON, Canada

Mark Cunningham Florida Fish and Wildlife Conservation Commission, Gainesville, FL, USA

Daniel R. Engstrom St. Croix Watershed Research Station, Science Museum of Minnesota, Marine on Saint Croix, MN, USA

Peter C. Frederick University of Florida, Gainesville, FL, USA

Reed C. Harris Reed Harris Environmental Ltd., Oakville, ON, Canada

David Hutchinson Reed Harris Environmental Ltd., Oakville, ON, Canada

Ted Lange Florida Fish and Wildlife Conservation Commission, Eustis, FL, USA

Curtis D. Pollman Aqua Lux Lucis, Inc., Gainesville, FL, USA

Darren G. Rumbold Florida Gulf Coast University, Fort Myers, FL, USA

Chapter 1
Trends in Atmospheric Deposition of Mercury

Curtis D. Pollman and Daniel R. Engstrom

Abstract In Chap. 2 of this volume Lange and Frederick evaluate changes in mercury (Hg) concentrations in Everglades biota to identify the occurrence of temporally coherent trends that ideally can be understood and related to changing process dynamics. To the extent such trends occur in the Everglades, processes that are potentially causative include atmospheric deposition of Hg, changing dynamics in key water quality variables such as sulfate and dissolved organic carbon, and changing hydrology. This overall process of trend identification and elucidation of underlying factors can in turn provide insight on possible strategies for mitigating the problem of excessive biota Hg concentrations in the Everglades. This chapter evaluates whether changes in atmospheric deposition of Hg to the Everglades have occurred in recent years using direct evidence from measured wet deposition and gaseous elemental mercury (GEM). The chapter also considers changes in mercury concentrations recorded in bottom sediments as a proxy for longer-term changes in atmospheric deposition. This latter analysis includes a review of changes observed in aquatic ecosystems from North America and Europe as well as south Florida and the Everglades, and whether recent changes in south Florida reflect large scale processes or reductions in local emissions of Hg.

Keywords Mercury · Wet deposition · Total gaseous mercury · Sediment · Sediment accumulation rates · Lake Annie · R-EMAP

C. D. Pollman (✉)
Aqua Lux Lucis, Inc., Gainesville, FL, USA
e-mail: cpollman@aqualuxlucis.org

D. R. Engstrom
St. Croix Watershed Research Station, Science Museum of Minnesota, Marine on St. Croix, MN, USA
e-mail: dre@umn.edu

C. D. Pollman et al. (eds.), *Mercury and the Everglades. A Synthesis and Model for Complex Ecosystem Restoration*, https://doi.org/10.1007/978-3-030-55635-8_1

1.1 Introduction

Like many otherwise pristine and oligotrophic ecosystems, the Florida Everglades are characterized by high concentrations of mercury (Hg) in fish (Chap. 9, Volume II) and other biota (Chap. 10, Volume II). This problem was first identified in 1989 when a monitoring project by state agencies found Hg in largemouth bass (LMB) from the Florida Everglades to average in excess of 2 mg/kg—well above the Florida Department of Health advisory limits for limited consumption of 0.5 mg/kg. Subsequent to these initial findings, elevated concentrations were found in other Everglades biota, including the endangered Florida panther (Roelke and Glass 1992) and several different species of wading birds (Frederick et al. 1999).

Two types of temporal trend dynamics can be demonstrated for tissue concentrations of Hg in Everglades biota. The first are long-term increases (decadal or greater) of 4 to 6× based on comparing recent concentrations of Hg measured in the scapular feathers of Everglades white ibises (*Eudocimus albus*), great egrets (*Ardea alba*), anhingas (*Anhinga anhinga*) and great blue herons (*Ardea herodias*) to concentrations measured in preserved specimens collected between 1900 and 1980 (Frederick et al. 2004; see also Chap. 2, this volume). The second type of temporal trend involves shorter time scales (less than decadal), and are evidenced primarily through long-term monitoring of fish, including LMB (*Micropterus salmoides*) and mosquitofish (*Gambusia* spp.), and to a lesser extent, wading birds.

As for most aquatic ecosystems, the primary source of Hg to the Florida Everglades is atmospheric deposition. As a result, an obvious hypothesis to test regarding underlying mechanisms for Everglades biota trends is whether long-term and/or short-term variations in the delivery of atmospheric Hg are causative. For example, Atkeson et al. (2005) observed that LMB Hg concentrations declined by ~60% between 1988 and 2000 in the L-35B and L-67A canals, while local emissions between 1991 and 2000 declined by nearly 93%. Atkeson et al. (2005) also found a statistically significant decline in wet deposition fluxes measured between 1993 and 2002,[1] and based on the correspondence between all three trends hypothesized that the decline in local emissions was the primary driver for the biotic response.

Continued monitoring of fish tissue concentrations however indicates that recent, short-term variations in Hg bioaccumulation are complex (Chap. 2, this volume) and reinforces the notion that recent trends may now be dictated more by factors other than local emissions. These factors include variations in atmospheric deposition fluxes of Hg that are occurring because of meteorological patterns (rainfall volume and seasonal distribution). In addition, the Everglades is a highly manipulated system, with perturbations in trophic state (phosphorus concentrations), chloride and sulfate concentrations, and hydrology. All these variables can influence the biogeochemical cycling of Hg. The objective of this chapter is to evaluate both long-term and short-term variations and trends in atmospheric fluxes of Hg to the

[1]Note that the period of record for wet deposition measurements began at the end of a sharp decline in local emissions which peaked in 1991 and had fallen by 65% by the end of 1993.

Everglades which then can be used to help evaluate the drivers dictating Hg bioaccumulation, particularly in terms of helping to inform management strategies and options towards mitigating the Everglades Hg problem. This chapter examines the (indirect) evidence for long-term trends using primarily archival records of Hg accumulation preserved and measured in sediments. The chapter also examines the evidence (both indirect and direct) for short-term trends. As for the long-term trends, the indirect evidence for recent trends is based on dated and measured sediment records of Hg accumulation rates; the direct evidence is based primarily on analyses of Hg wet deposition fluxes and total gaseous elemental Hg (GEM) concentrations in ambient air. The chapter includes data from both the Everglades and study results from other regions including primarily North America to help establish trend robustness and aid in interpretation.

1.2 Trends in Atmospheric Mercury: Concentrations and Fluxes

1.2.1 Gaseous Elemental Mercury

1.2.1.1 North America

Recent temporal trends in GEM concentrations in North America have been analyzed by both Weiss-Penzias et al. (2016) and Zhang et al. (2016). Weiss-Penzias et al. compiled GEM data from 33 sites across the U.S. and Canada they considered representative of background concentrations. Their analysis included data from the National Atmospheric Deposition Program Atmospheric Hg Network (AMNet) and the CAMNet and NatChem networks operated by Environment Canada, as well as a number of individual sites located in western North America. The time period covered by the synthesized data set extended from 1998 through 2013 and included one site from within Florida located in the Florida panhandle. The number of sites with extensive temporal coverage, however, was small and, as a result, Weiss-Penzias et al. conducted their trend analysis across all of their study sites (excluding nine sites for which localized influences were suspected to be important) without distinguishing between site and using monthly median GEM values to construct the time series. Their analysis showed a statistically significant declining trend of 1.5% per year ($p < 0.05$) for the period 1998–2007, with concentrations essentially remaining constant (other than seasonal variability) for the period 2008–2013.

The study conducted by Zhang et al. (2016) was spatially broader than the Weiss-Penzias et al. (2016) study and included not only CAMNet and AMNet sites utilized by Weiss-Penzias et al., but also data from surface sites in Scandinavia and western Europe and the United States, oceanographic cruises in both the north and south Atlantic oceans, free tropospheric measurements from the northern and southern hemispheres, and observations from the Mauna Loa Observatory in Hawaii. Zhang et al. (2016) reported a general decline in GEM concentrations of 1.2 to 2.1% per year since 1990 to the present in northern latitude surface sites. Measurements from the free troposphere above 2 km altitude show no significant decline between 2005 and 2014. Zhang et al. concluded that the difference between surface and free tropospheric GEM trends reflected the influence of declining local emissions on surface sites. This conclusion was further substantiated by changes in simulated Hg0 concentrations between 1990 and 2010 using the Goddard Earth Observing System-Chemistry (GEOS-Chem) model coupled with a global emissions inventory that had been updated to resolve several errors identified in previous inventories by Zhang et al., including the failure to properly account for changes in the speciation of gaseous Hg in emissions related to SO_2 and NO_x emission controls. This updated inventory in turn showed a 20% decreased in total Hg emissions between 1990 and 2010.

1.2.1.2 Florida

Limited data are available to assess the likelihood of any temporal trends in GEM concentrations in Florida. The longest duration monitoring studies include the Florida Atmospheric Mercury Study (FAMS), which included GEM measurements for different time periods at nine stations across Florida between 1992 and 1996, and AMNet monitoring conducted between January 2009 and December 2012 at a site in Pensacola. Two other studies in Florida have included GEM mercury concentrations—the South Florida Atmospheric Mercury Monitoring Study (SoFAMMS) (Dvonch et al. 1999), and monitoring conducted as part of the Florida statewide Hg Total Maximum Daily Load (TMDL) study. SoFAMMS was conducted as an intensive study during August and September 1995 and included five sites located in Dade and Broward counties east of the Everglades Protection Area (EvPA) for which GEM and ambient aerosol measurements were conducted. The statewide Hg TMDL included routine monitoring during 2009 at four locations throughout Florida (Pensacola, Jacksonville, Tampa and Davie). The short duration of the SoFAMMS and statewide Hg TMDL studies minimizes their utility in evaluating temporal trends of any useful length (annual or greater); thus, this analysis focuses on the FAMS and AMNet results.

The FAMS measurements were conducted using gold (Au) coated silica sand traps to collect an integrated sample over 3- to 6-day time intervals (Gill et al. 1995). AMNet sampling for GEM was conducted using gold traps with a 3-h sampling cycle. Similar to Weiss-Penzias et al. (2016), median monthly values from both networks were used for evaluating trends. Because of the large temporal discontinuity between the two data sets, coupled with the relatively short duration of available data for each network (2–3 years), the presence of a likely trend was assessed by comparing the results as two separate time intervals (Fig. 1.1). That analysis shows that the average annual GEM concentration in the Florida panhandle obtained from the monthly medians was slightly higher between 1995 and 1996 (1.33 ng/m^3) compared to 2009–2012 (1.28 mg/m^3), although the difference was not significant.

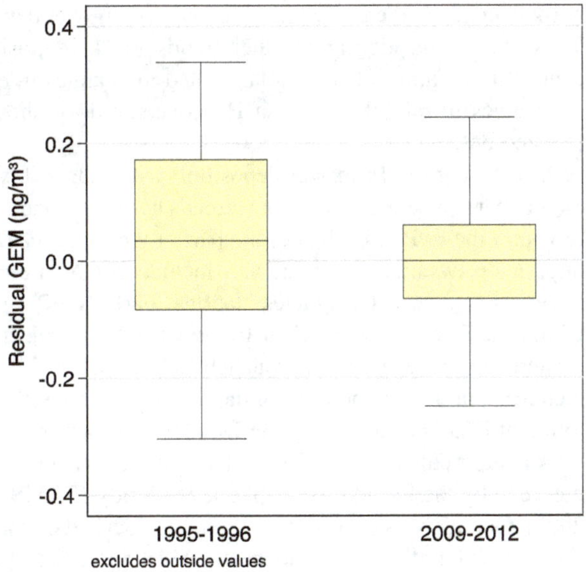

Fig. 1.1 Distribution of monthly median GEM concentrations. The box plot compares the results from two separate monitoring periods [1995–1996 obtained from the FAMS (cf., Gill et al. 1995)] for a site in Caryville in the Florida panhandle, and the AMNet Pensacola site (January 2009 through December 2012)

1.2.2 Wet Deposition

1.2.2.1 The Everglades

Trends in atmospheric Hg deposition ultimately are driven by two components: variations in rainfall dynamics (both volume and seasonal distribution) and changes in the atmospheric signal (*e.g.,* changes in Hg emissions and chemistry supporting the production and occurrence of gaseous oxidized Hg (GOM) in the atmosphere) (see Chap. 3, Volume I). Because aquatic ecosystem response is influenced both by rainfall dynamics (which governs residence time and the ability of the aquatic system to kinetically process Hg inputs) and input concentrations of atmospheric Hg, any evaluation of trends in atmospheric Hg deposition should deconvolute and evaluate the effects of the dynamics of both components. For example, if atmospheric fluxes remain constant over a given time interval despite a reduction in the atmospheric signal of Hg (*i.e.,* by increases in rainfall volume offsetting the reduction in the volume weighted rainfall concentration of Hg), some reduction in aquatic biota Hg concentrations should result nonetheless.

Analyses of trends in atmospheric Hg deposition often focus on changes in the deposition flux (Risch et al. 2012) or annual volume weighted mean concentrations (Prestbo and Gay 2009). Because wet deposition concentrations of Hg are inversely related to precipitation depth (Landis et al. 2002; Prestbo and Gay 2009; Weiss-Penzias et al. 2016), however, and because the variance in precipitation depth greatly exceeds that of Hg concentrations in rainfall, variations in precipitation depth can mask changes in the atmospheric signal driving wet deposition Hg concentrations.[2] Thus, when considering whether trends in Hg deposition reflect a fundamental change in the atmospheric signal related to changes in emission sources, the effect of changes in rainfall depth on Hg concentrations should be first considered and factored out.

Monitoring of Hg in wet deposition with reasonably sufficient long periods of record that can be used to evaluate trends has been conducted at two sites proximal to or within the EvPA. Both sites are part of the Mercury Deposition Network (MDN; http://nadp.sws.uiuc.edu/mdn) and include MDN site FL11 located at the Beard Research Center in Everglades National Park. (ENP) and MDN site FL34 located within the Everglades Nutrient Removal (ENR) project site adjacent to the northwestern perimeter of the Loxahatchee National Wildlife Refuge (LNWR). FL11 includes continuous monitoring data from March 1996 to the present, while monitoring at FL34 began in July 1997 and was discontinued after March 2015.

An important feature of the FL11 site is that monitoring at this location was preceded by the Florida Atmospheric Hg Study (FAMS 1993–1996; Guentzel et al. 2001). Our analysis of wet deposition thus focused on the FL11 site for two reasons. First, by integrating the co-located FAMS and MDN FL11 data, we were able to extend the period of record further back in time during a critical period when emissions of Hg in south Florida were rapidly declining (Fig. 5.1, Chap. 5, Vol. I). Second, preliminary mixed regression modeling (StataCorp 2019) of the effects of seasonal dynamics and rainfall depth on wet deposition concentrations at the two MDN sites strongly indicated no significantly important differences between the two sites.

An essentially continuous record was thus developed from November 1993 through June 2016 of Hg wet deposition fluxes and concentrations at the Beard Research Center within the ENP. In part because the FAMS data consist of integrated monthly wet deposition measurements while the MDN data consist of integrated weekly samples, it was important to demonstrate that the synthesized data were self-consistent with no apparent bias when using the same temporal period of aggregation. Fortunately, monitoring from both studies overlapped for nearly the entirety of 1996, and comparison of monthly results for deposition fluxes demonstrated overall excellent agreement between the two programs (Pollman and Porcella 2003). Subsequent analyses with the two data sets combined however indicated that one observation in the FAMS data set is an outlier and possibly reflects contamination. The Hg concentration for the FAMS observation in question was 71.2 ng/L compared to a volume-weighted mean (VWM) concentration of 12.7 ng/L reported by MDN; the FAMS value was also more than three times higher than any other Hg concentrations recorded for the site as part of the FAMS. As a result, the FAMS results for 1993–1995 (excluding the outlier observation) were concatenated with

[2]For example, the coefficient of variation equals 27.0% in weekly wet deposition Hg concentrations measured at the Beard Research Center between 1996 and 2016 compared to 52.6% for precipitation depth (both variables log-transformed to better approximate normality).

the MDN results for 1996 through mid-2016 to form a nearly continuous period of record for the site that equates to more than 22 calendar years (270 observations out of 272 months).

Trends in atmospheric fluxes of Hg deposited in the Everglades were evaluated via two different methods. First, smoothed time series were constructed using a cross median spline approach to construct cubic spline curves (StataCorp 2019) for Hg deposition, rainfall depth, and VWM Hg concentrations in wet deposition using 12-month running sums (Hg deposition and precipitation depth) and averages (VWM Hg) derived from the integrated FAMS-MDN data set. These results, shown in Fig. 1.2, indicate a somewhat cyclical pattern, with alternating periods of high/low precipitation and antipathetic Hg concentrations. An overall trend of declining Hg deposition might be inferred, but this impression is strongly influenced by conditions at the beginning and end of the monitoring record. Hence, a more rigorous statistical approach is needed to evaluate the long-term pattern.

Second, trends in the change for the observed *vs.* the expected signal in monthly VWM Hg concentrations were constructed using a multivariate analytical approach to develop estimates of the expected signal. The underlying model paradigm considered two important factors that help govern variations in Hg precipitation in rainfall—seasonal dynamics and precipitation dynamics. First, because Hg concentrations in rainfall in the Everglades—as well as elsewhere—have a very strong seasonal component (Guentzel et al. 2001; Mason and Sheu 2000; Keeler et al. 2005; Butler et al. 2008)—seasonal dynamics were incorporated into the model by including the month of sample collection as a categorical variable. Second, the inverse relationship between Hg concentrations and precipitation was included by incorporating log transforms of both variables in the model. The model thus has the following form:

$$Log(Hg_z) = \beta_0 + \beta_1 \cdot Log(P_z) + \beta_{i,z} \cdot Month_i + \varepsilon_z \tag{1.1}$$

where z denotes the individual observation, i denotes the month corresponding to observation z, β are fitted coefficients, and ε_z is the predicted model residual for observation z. Because the model controls for variations in precipitation and month, the assumption is that any temporal trends in ε_z will reflect temporal changes in the source signal ultimately driving rainfall concentrations if Hg.

The model was initially fit using ordinary least square regression (OLS) because of the availability of a variety of diagnostic tools to evaluate model robustness including underlying assumptions of linearity. The OLS modeling was conducted iteratively to identify potential outliers and influential observations based on *hat* leverage and *Cooks D* distance estimates (Hamilton 2013). That analysis led to identifying a total of 6 observations that were excluded from the final model estimation, leaving a total of 264 observations for model estimation.

The final model was fitted using generalized linear modeling (GLM) with a log link function to predict Hg concentrations directly rather than using OLS to predict the log transformed Hg concentration and then back-transforming the predicted

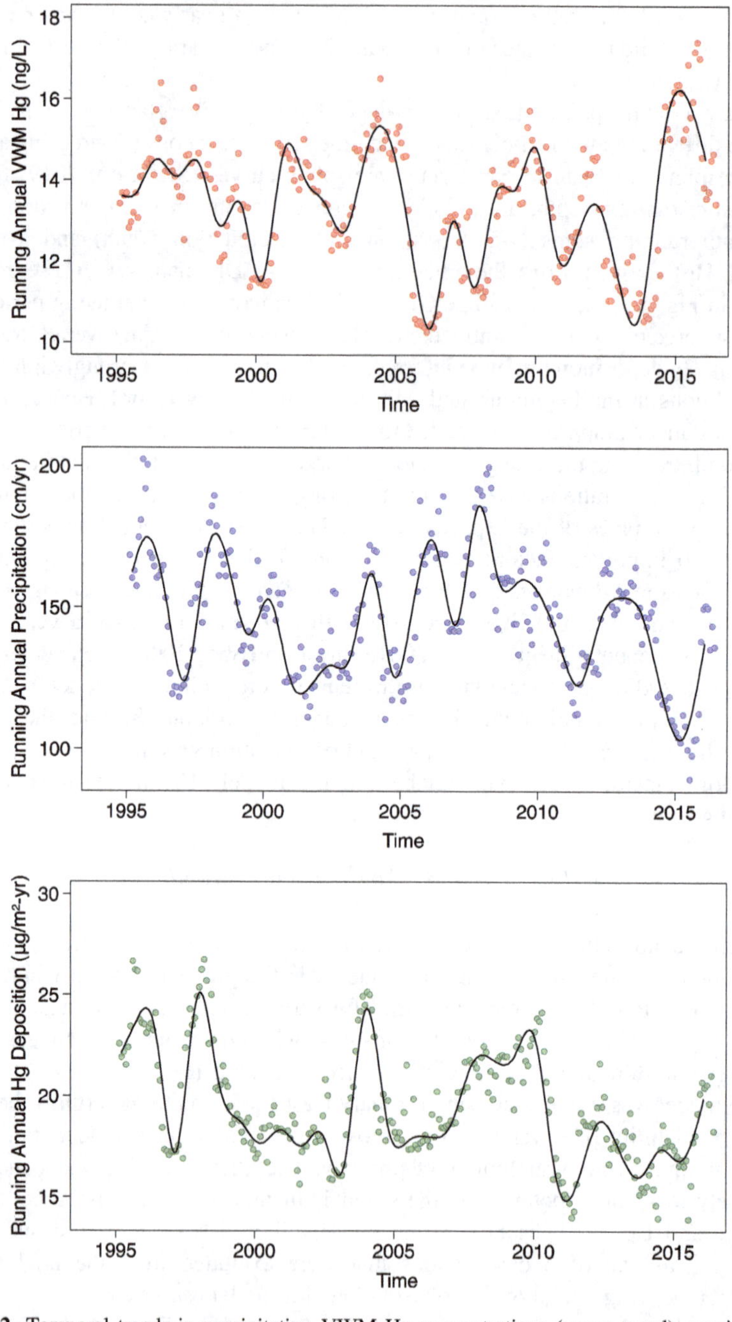

Fig. 1.2 Temporal trends in precipitation VWM Hg concentrations (upper panel), precipitation depth (middle panel), and annual wet deposition Hg flux at Beard Research Center, Everglades National Park. The precipitation depth and deposition flux curves are shown as 12-month running sums of monthly values; the VWM for each observation is calculated from the running sums of both deposition flux and precipitation depth

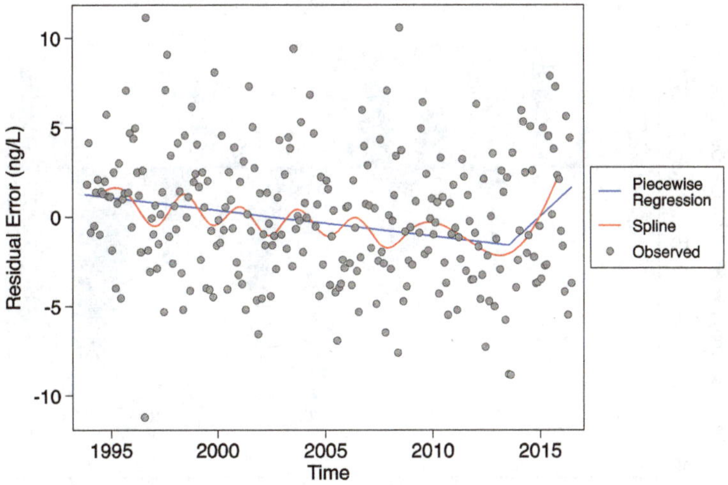

Fig. 1.3 Time series plot of monthly and smoothed GLM model residuals

result to generate the arithmetic concentration. Using GLM to model Hg concentrations directly avoids biases imposed during back-transformation of OLS predictions of log-transformed dependent variables (Duan 1983; Newman 1993). Model estimation using GLM also requires specifying an appropriate expected distribution (*e.g.*, Gaussian or Poisson distribution) for the model errors. Based on results obtained from a modified Park test (Polgreen and Brooks 2012), the final model specified a Poisson distribution for the residual errors.

Variations in the magnitude of the model residuals as a function of time are plotted in Fig. 1.3 for both the individual observations and smoothed values based on a cubic spline (StataCorp 2019). The smoothed residuals show an overall declining trend[3] in the atmospheric deposition signal between late 1993 and *ca.* 2013, with an approximately three-year periodicity of oscillating values superimposed on the trend. Piecewise regression (Mitchell 2012) was conducted to quantify the magnitude of the changes in the signal on both sides of the inflection point (2013.54), which in turn was estimated using non-linear least squares regression. Prior to the inflection point, the linear decline in the Hg signal was −0.146 ng/L-year ($t = 0.001$), while the signal sharply increased after the inflection point (1.106 ng/L-year; $t = 0.026$). Annual variations in the change in the expected deposition flux can be quite large, and potentially can influence ecosystem response for extended time periods. For example, during the interval 1994–1997, excess deposition totaled 7.8 μg/m^2 (9.7% increase), while during the intervals 2005–2007 and 2010–2013,

[3]By definition, model residuals are calculated as the difference between the observed and modeled values. Thus, if a residual value is positive, the model has under-predicted the expected value, and apparent signal influencing the observation is higher than average signal applicable across the data set.

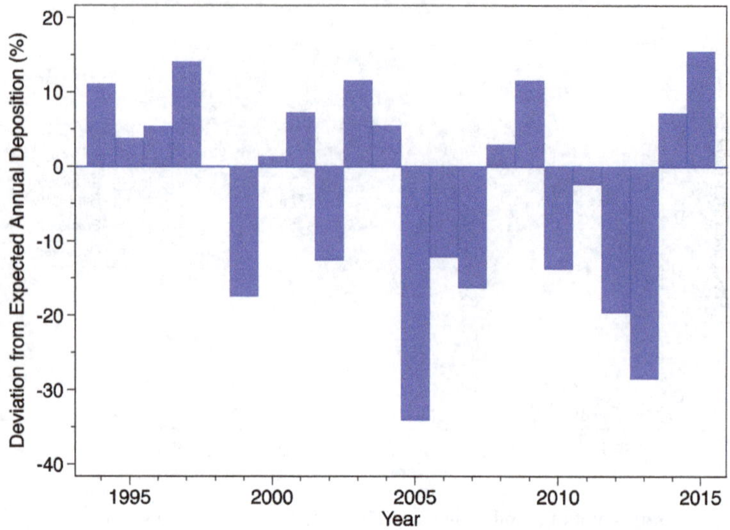

Fig. 1.4 Deviations in the GLM predicted annual wet deposition of Hg from observed values presented as the percent error: (observed – predicted)/observed × 100

the expected deposition flux declined by −11.8 and −10.5 μg/m^2 (17.0 and 13.4%, respectively; Fig. 1.4).

1.3 Trends in Recently Deposited Sediments

1.3.1 North America and Europe

Cores of lake sediments and ombrotrophic (bog) peat have been used to document historical changes in atmospheric Hg deposition at numerous sites throughout North America (Johnson et al. 1986; Johnson 1987; Swain et al. 1992; Rada et al. 1993; Landers et al. 1995, 1998; Lockhart et al. 1995; Lucotte et al. 1995; Engstrom and Swain 1997; Norton et al. 1997; Benoit et al. 1998; Lamborg et al. 2002; Perry et al. 2005; Drevnick et al. 2012a, 2016) and other parts of the globe (Johansson 1985; Renberg 1986; Verta et al. 1989; Jensen and Jensen 1991; Steinnes and Andersson 1991; Meili 1995; Munthe et al. 1995; Bindler et al. 2001a, b; Yang et al. 2010a, b; Drevnick et al. 2012b; Hermanns and Biester 2013; Enrico et al. 2017). Results from these studies converge on a two to fourfold increase in Hg deposition from preindustrial times (*ca.* 1800–1850) to the near-present at locations remote from Hg emission sources. More limited data from sites closer to industrialized areas in North America and Europe (Munthe et al. 1995; Engstrom and Swain 1997; Engstrom et al. 2007) indicate locally higher increases (*ca.* 5 to 10×), while records from the Southern Hemisphere (Biester et al. 2001; Lamborg et al. 2002) and high latitudes in North America (Landers et al. 1995; Lockhart et al. 1995, 1998; Lucotte et al. 1995; Landers et al. 1998; Fitzgerald et al. 2005; Muir et al. 2009; Phillips et al. 2011) show a two to threefold increase.

However, recent studies utilizing longer sediment records suggest substantial increases in Hg emissions (primarily from Hg mining and metallurgy) long before the industrial revolution and by inference imply that present day deposition rates may be elevated more than 10× over true background values (Martinez-Cortizas et al. 1999; Bindler 2003; Givelet et al. 2003; Roos-Barraclough and Shotyk 2003). Nearly all records showing pre-industrial anthropogenic Hg signals are from peat cores, and most of these are European. It should be noted that the reliability of peat cores as recorders of atmospheric Hg deposition is not well established (Biester et al. 2007); these records may be compromised by long-term changes in Hg trapping and retention, diagenetic mobilization, and spatial variability in accumulation within a wetland. Significantly, signals for pre-industrial Hg emissions in North and South America (*e.g.*, post-Columbian gold and silver mining) or northern Europe have not been found in lake sediment records (Bindler et al. 2001a; Lamborg et al. 2002; Engstrom et al. 2014; Fitzgerald et al. 2018), except those highly proximal to the Hg (cinnabar) and silver mining districts in South America (Cooke et al. 2009, 2013; Beal et al. 2013). Furthermore, an expanding compilation of Hg ice-core records also shows global deposition increases largely confined to the industrial period with little evidence of an early mining signal (Beal et al. 2014; Zheng 2015; Kang et al. 2016). These glacial archives include the Upper Fremont ice core—initially presented as evidence for large Hg releases from the North American gold/silver rush of the late nineteenth-century (Schuster et al. 2002)—now recognized as industrial-era emissions under an updated chronology (Chellman et al. 2017).

Most sediment-core studies to date have focused on the magnitude and timing of Hg increases and have paid little attention to whether Hg deposition has declined in recent times in response to reductions in Hg emissions. The earliest investigation that focused on recent deposition trends was that of Engstrom and Swain (1997). They reported significant (25–50%) declines in Hg accumulation in sediment cores from both urban (Minneapolis) and rural (northeastern) Minnesota lakes (four lakes in each region) from peak values in the 1960s and 1970s. The cores were collected *ca.* 1990. Similar declines were not evident in cores from four western Minnesota lakes nor were they found in three cores from southeastern Alaska. The declines were attributed to reductions in Hg use, a decrease in uncontrolled waste incineration, reduced use of coal for home heating, and pollution-control technologies that incidentally capture mercury.

That study was further expanded to include 55 Minnesota lakes, 20 of which were from the Minneapolis-St. Paul metropolitan region, 20 from the forested northeast, and 15 from the agricultural west central part of the state (Engstrom et al. 2007). Results showed that present-day (1991–1996) Hg accumulation rates were substantially higher in the metro and west central regions than in the northeast, largely because of erosional inputs of soil-bound Hg (of atmospheric origin) from disturbed catchments. The study also confirmed the historical reductions in Hg deposition reported by Engstrom and Swain (1997). In the metro region, the decline (correcting for erosional inputs) was about 30% of peak values in the 1970s. A decline of 20–30% was also apparent in restricted areas of northeastern Minnesota (Voyageurs National Park and near the city of Grand Rapids) but not in west central Minnesota or elsewhere in the northeast. The localized nature of the declines implies a reduction in nearby Hg emissions as opposed to regional/continental-scale sources, although improvements in erosion control cannot be ruled out.

In the Great Lakes region, Drevnick et al. (2012a) synthesized data from 104 ^{210}Pb dated sediment cores, in part to examine recent trends in Hg deposition. Cores included inland lakes in the region as well as the Great Lakes. Recent fluxes for the inland lakes, which were selected to include only lakes with relatively undisturbed watersheds, declined about 20% compared to peak flux rates which generally occurred in the late 1980s. Similarly, recent Hg accumulation rates for offshore areas of Lake Superior, which Drevnick et al. conclude reflect primarily atmospheric deposition, also show a nearly 20% decline. Current wet deposition fluxes are generally uniform across the region and, as a result, Drevnick et al. suggest (1) that local and regional sources of Hg emissions have been important sources of Hg deposition compared to global sources, and (2) regional and local controls have been effective at reducing influxes of Hg to lakes in Great Lakes area. This effectiveness occurred regardless of watershed size; likewise, the ratio of watershed area to lake surface area had no effect on either relative changes in recent Hg accumulation or the year in which peak Hg accumulation fluxes occurred. These aspects of the sedimentary record, coupled with the fact that recent measured wet deposition fluxes show no decline, lead Drevnick et al. (2012a) to conclude that the recent trends in Hg sediment accumulation are likely responding to declines in Hg atmospheric deposition that occurred decades earlier.

Sediment-core evidence for recent declines in Hg deposition also have been reported for the northeastern US. The most recent of these studies by Fitzgerald et al. (2018) of a varved and precisely dated sediment record from coastal Rhode Island showed a 60% decline in Hg accumulation since the early 1970s when the Hg flux was roughly 15× preindustrial values. This historical reconstruction of local industrial emissions was substantiated by parallel trends in polycyclic aromatic hydrocarbons (PAHs), lead (Pb) and its isotopes.

Earlier work by Kamman and Engstrom (2002) documented similar declines in Hg accumulation over the last one to two decades in cores from seven of ten study lakes in New Hampshire and Vermont. In contrast to the results for the Great Lakes which showed no watershed effect (Drevnick et al. 2012a), the declines were greatest in lakes with proportionally small watersheds, indicating sustained export of historically deposited Hg from watershed soils is buffering the response in lakes with proportionally larger watersheds. Very similar results have been reported by Lorey (2001) for eight lakes in the Adirondack region of upstate New York. These lakes were originally cored in 1982 as part of EPRI's Paleolimnological Investigation of Recent Lake Acidification (PIRLA) study to document historical trends in lake pH, and subsequent analysis of sedimentary Hg by Lorey and Driscoll (1999) revealed a 3.5-fold increase in Hg accumulation since preindustrial times. New cores collected in 1998 showed recent declines in Hg accumulation of 14–71% (average = 33%)

from peak values between 1973 and 1990 at seven of the eight sites; Hg concentrations declined at all eight sites. As in the study of Kamman and Engstrom (2002), watershed inputs of Hg have become a greater portion of the Hg load to the lakes as direct atmospheric deposition has declined. These latter two studies demonstrated how the response of sedimentary records to reduced atmospheric deposition can be muted by continued export of "legacy Hg" from a large upland soil-Hg reservoir. Most significant for this analysis is the regional nature of the observed Hg declines which implies a response to large-scale reductions in industrial Hg emissions from the northeastern US.

Similar conclusions have been drawn from lake sediment records in Sweden, where recent declines in Hg concentrations are temporally consistent with observed reductions in atmospheric Hg deposition (since the 1980s) (Munthe et al. 1995; Bindler et al. 2001a). Bindler et al. (2001a) analyzed cores from nine lakes in Sweden to determine whether recent sediment concentrations have declined in response to declining fluxes of atmospheric Hg. Cores were collected from six forest lakes distributed along a depositional transect traversing southern and northern Sweden, and three mountain lakes in northern Sweden. Increases in Hg concentration in the sedimentary record occurred concurrent with the appearance of spheroidal carbonaceous fly ash particles (SCP) derived from fossil-fuel combustion. Hg and SCP correlate strongly in the cores ($r = 0.67$ to 0.91). No dating was reported, and only concentrations of Hg rather than fluxes were reported. Eight of the nine lakes sampled showed maximum Hg concentrations below the surficial sediment interval, with Hg concentrations declining towards the sediment-water interface. These results are contrasted with the earlier survey of Johansson (1985), who measured maximum Hg concentrations in the surface 0 to 1 cm interval in a series of cores collected in 1979. Spatial gradients in enrichment factors of Hg in sediments are consistent with gradients observed in atmospheric deposition measured at a limited number of stations across Scandinavia. Hg concentrations in sediments from lakes in southwestern Sweden appear to be more affected by essentially more localized sources, while cores from lakes in central and northern Sweden likely reflect broader, hemispheric scales of Hg pollution. Cores collected in west Greenland by Bindler et al. (2001b) also provide some evidence of recent declines in Hg depositional fluxes.

1.3.2 The Everglades and South Florida

1.3.2.1 Sediment Core Studies

Several investigators have reconstructed mercury deposition in south Florida from sediment cores (Delfino et al. 1993; Rood et al. 1995), but these studies used wetland-soils rather than lake sediments as the historic archive and were conducted too early to detect recent declines in Hg deposition. Results of this core work showed an average fivefold increase in Hg flux from the turn of the last century (pre-1900) to

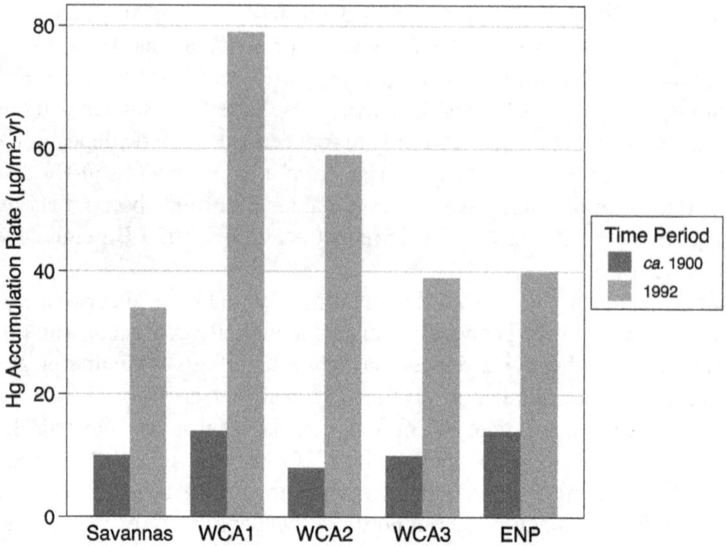

Fig. 1.5 Average historical (*ca.* 1900) and recent (1992) Hg accumulation rates in major regions of the Everglades (Water Conservation areas and Everglades National Park) and the Savannas marsh northeast of the Everglades. Data from Rood et al. (1995)

present-day (*ca.* 1985–1992), which suggests the effect of local emission impacts, but unconformities in the peat and large variability among cores limited a more detailed spatial or temporal analysis (Fig. 1.5). Basin-wide averages of the modern enrichment ratio ranged from 4.0 for Water Conservation Area 3 (WCA) to 8.7 for WCA-2. The enrichment ratio for two cores collected from the Savannas Marsh, which is a linear coastal wetland located in Lucie and St. Martin counties and is approximately 50 km north of West Palm Beach, averaged 3.4 and was closer to ratios observed at more background sites in North America.

Kang et al. (2000; see also Kang 1999) collected cores from Florida Bay and the coastal margin of the southwest Everglades, including Coot Bay, Oyster Bay, and Shark River Slough. Dating was conducted using ^{210}Pb, and verified using ^{137}Cs as a marker for peak atmospheric fallout during the early 1960s. Cores were collected in 1994 and early 1998, and thus are not as useful as more recent cores for elucidating trends that may have emerged during the 1990s. Kang et al. (2000) used downcore concentrations of total organic carbon (TOC) and aluminum (Al) to calculate non-excess (non-anthropogenic) inputs of Hg. These fluxes were used to calculate excess Hg (anthropogenic) from total fluxes. The core from Coot Bay showed an excess flux of approximately 17 μg/m^2-year, which peaked around 1930 and remained constant until the time of the study. The core from NW Oyster Bay had an excess flux that peaked at much higher levels (approaching 60 μg/m^2-year) around 1960, and then declined to about 21 μg/m^2-year by *ca.* 1990.

Robbins et al. (2000) collected sediments in May 1994 and February 1995 from depositional zones at three sites in the central portion of Florida Bay and dated the

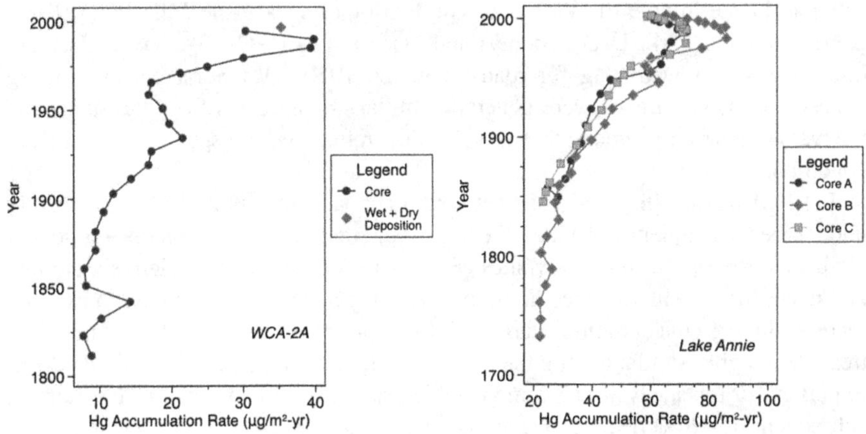

Fig. 1.6 Hg accumulation rates in sediment cores from site F3 in WCA-2A (left-hand panel) and Lake Annie (right-hand panel) located approximately 40 km northwest of the western edge of Lake Okeechobee. The WCA-2A results are for a single core analyzed by Abelak et al. (unpublished data obtained from T. Atkeson, personal communication). The Lake Annie results comprise three cores analyzed by Engstrom et al. (2003)

cores using $^{210}Pb/^{226}Ra$. Using a model to calculate lags between the delivery of atmospheric particles and subsequent mixing and permanent deposition in the sediments produced a series of profiles that agreed very well with ^{137}Cs, Pu, Pb and coral Pb distributions. Robbins et al. calculate that the characteristic integration time for ^{137}Cs, Pu, and stable lead is 16 years. This will have the effect of both muting and spreading peaks within the sedimentary record derived from Florida Bay, and should have some bearing on the interpretation of the Kang et al. cores collected from the same region.

Abelak et al. (unpublished data provided through T. Atkeson) also collected a sediment core from site F3 in WCA-2A. Site F3 is a moderately eutrophied site along a nutrient gradient located downstream from the S-10C structure supplying water to WCA-2A (F3 itself is located 5.58 km downstream from the structure). Phosphorus concentrations averaged 29 μg P/L between 1998 and 2000 (unpublished data from SFWMD, outliers removed) compared to essentially background concentrations averaging 8 μg P/L at site U3 (10.8 km downstream from S-10C). Hg net accumulation as a function of time is shown in Fig. 1.6. These preliminary results indicate that the net flux of Hg peaked during 1985–1990 at approximately 40 $\mu g/m^2$-year, and then declined by about 25% to approximately 30 $\mu g/m^2$-year by mid 1994. No error statistics are available to evaluate the uncertainty in these estimates.

The most relevant information regarding recent trends in Hg deposition for south Florida comes from the study of Engstrom et al. (2003). Multiple sediment cores from four lakes and ponds in south Florida were collected in 2002 and 2003 to reconstruct recent trends in atmospheric Hg deposition. The study sites include Lake Annie, a small (37 ha) seepage lake located on the Archbold Biological Station, Highlands County (Sacks et al. 1998), and Gator Lake, a small (0.2 ha) karst sinkhole in the middle of WCA-3A. The two other sites, Nine Mile Pond (Everglades National Park, Dade County) and Gary Ponds (WCA-3A, Dade Co.), are borrow pits that were dug for road-fill in the 1950s. Temporal changes in Hg concentrations and fluxes were generally similar among cores from the same site, but varied markedly among basins, possibly reflecting site-specific depositional conditions.

Lake Annie, with near-constant sediment accumulation and a relatively undisturbed catchment, provides the most coherent and robust reconstruction of Hg deposition of the four study sites (Fig. 1.6). The profiles are relatively smooth and unconfused, with changes in atmospheric Hg deposition are recorded as a 3× increase in Hg concentration (and flux) from preindustrial to modern times. The trends are highly similar among the three cores in both timing and magnitude. Most important for this analysis is a demonstrable peak in Hg flux during the 1980s and a subsequent 13–20% decline beginning in the mid-1990s. This decline was well defined in each core by 5–6 stratigraphic analyses over a sediment depth of 5–6 cm. The results from Lake Annie appear to confirm the decline in Hg accumulation (*ca.* 1990) evident in the F3 core in WCA-2A reported by Abelak et al., (unpublished data). The decline suggested by the Abelak et al. core is limited to the uppermost core interval and so is less secure than the longer stratigraphic trends (declines) in the Annie cores.

The Lake Annie results suggest that Hg deposition peaked in central Florida at the time of maximum Hg emissions from local sources in south Florida. The reduction in Hg accumulation recorded in Lake Annie, however, is substantially lower than the greater than 90% decline in Hg emissions reported for Broward, Dade, and Palm Beach counties over the same time period. The more modest decline in the sediment cores suggests that Lake Annie receives much of its Hg from continental or global sources. This is evidenced by the relatively low modern enrichment ratio of 3×, which is similar to enrichment ratios that have been observed in other lakes considered to be representative of global background impacts. By comparison, the modern enrichment ratios for sites in the Everglades are higher and ranged from an average of 4.0 for WCA-3 to 8.7 for WCA-2 (Rood et al. 1995).

Although the Lake Annie and the Abelak et al. core show similar temporal patterns, the comparison of the two sets of results shows a striking discrepancy in the magnitude of the fluxes. Atkeson et al. (2005) estimated that the total (wet plus dry) deposition flux of atmospheric Hg approximated 35.3 $\mu g/m^3$ during 1996, which differs from the most recent sediment accumulation rates recorded at site F3 (*i.e.*, mid-1994) by about 16%. In contrast, fluxes recorded in the Lake Annie sediments are about 2.5–3 times higher than the F3 fluxes. The much larger fluxes in the Lake Annie cores are likely the result of sediment focusing—the preferential deposition of fine-grained sediments (and Hg) into deeper parts of the lake basin where the cores were collected. A focusing correction based on the ratio of ^{210}Pb flux in the sediment cores (0.74 ± 0.04 pCi cm^{-2} $year^{-1}$) to that measured in atmospheric deposition (0.24 ± 0.04 pCi cm^{-2} $year^{-1}$; Lamborg et al. 2013) brings the Annie fluxes more closely in line with those at F3.

The other three sites studied by Engstrom et al. (2003), although closer to local emission sources, are less ideal sedimentary recorders than Lake Annie. All exhibit highly variable sedimentation rates that reflect changes in the local catchment and confound the interpretation of recent trends in Hg deposition. Post-1995 declines in Hg concentration, evident in the cores from Gator Lake, are obscured in flux calculations by increasing litterfall from the development of fringing woody vegetation. The two man-made basins—Nine Mile Pond and Gary Ponds—show no evidence of declining Hg flux or concentration in recent sediments. Transient changes in sediment accumulation associated with basin maturation, however, are evident at both sites and complicate the Hg record.

Present-day Hg accumulation in the sediments at all four sites is 3–10 times higher than contemporary wet deposition of Hg in south Florida. Hg fluxes are highest in those basins with the largest perimeter to area ratios (Gator Lake and the Gary Ponds). Dry deposition on catchment vegetation or stomatal uptake of GEM and subsequent delivery in throughfall and litterfall is the likely source of this large Hg flux. These catchment inputs may make it difficult to detect modest changes in atmospheric loading.

1.3.2.2 R-EMAP Surficial Sediment Surveys

The Regional Environmental Monitoring and Assessment Program (R-EMAP) conducted by the USEPA in the Everglades includes data on soil and sediment Hg concentrations that potentially can be used to help establish whether Hg concentrations in surficial soils within the EvPA have changed over recent time. The R-EMAP Everglades effort included collecting water, sediment, and biota samples throughout the marsh to both establish its status with respect to ecosystem health and provide a basis for determining the effectiveness of efforts designed to restore the Everglades (Scheidt and Kalla 2007). Everglades marsh sampling began in 1995 and included both the wet and dry seasons (each season comprising a cycle). A total of nine sampling cycles were conducted (five wet and four dry), with the most recent conducted in 2014 (wet period only). The REMAP program utilized a randomized tessellation stratified (RTS) design (Stevens 1997) for selecting sites which was designed for the purpose of inferring the distribution of critical water quality and other ecosystem health-related parameters throughout the Everglades. R-EMAP data for all nine cycles were obtained directly from Peter Kalla with the USEPA (personal communication, March 20, 2008 and January 30, 2017) and can be downloaded from the Internet (USEPA 2019).

Variations in Hg concentrations in submerged soil and sediment are strongly influenced by organic carbon concentrations (Kang et al. 2000; Kamman et al. 2005; Nater and Grigal 1992), as illustrated for a suite of 129 lakes sampled across Florida by the Florida Department of Environmental Protection (FDEP 2013) (Fig. 1.7). As a result, soil and sediment Hg concentrations can vary greatly within a region—even if the atmospheric deposition signal is uniform—based on factors that influence the physical depositional environment and overall particle dynamics.

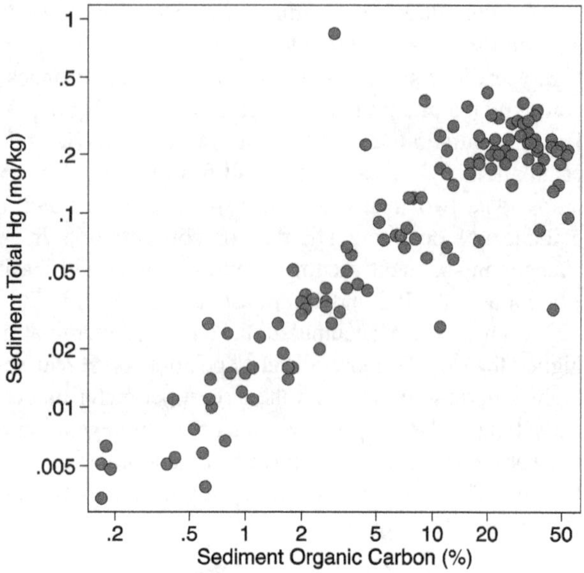

Fig. 1.7 Relationship between concentrations of total Hg and organic carbon in Florida lake sediments. $N = 129$. Data from FDEP (2013)

Although sediment organic carbon measurements were not conducted for each of nine the R-EMAP wet-dry cycles, R-EMAP did include two variables that reflect the depositional environment (erosional or depositional) and overall soil composition—soil bulk density and ash-free dry weight. Thus, the effects of bulk density and ash-free dry weight on variations in soil Hg were estimated through linear regression (all variables log-transformed; $N = 973$). Wet/dry season dynamics also were included as a dummy variable, resulting in model with following form:

$$Hg_{soil} = \beta_0 + \beta_1 \cdot BD + \beta_2 \cdot AFDW + \beta_3 \cdot Season \tag{1.2}$$

Residuals from the model ($r^2 = 0.727$; $p < 0.0001$) were then evaluated across time to evaluate any temporal trends. Initial analyses indicated that the distribution of the residuals was relatively homogeneous prior to and including 2005; as a result, the final evaluation separated the residuals into two temporal groups: 1995 through 2005; and 2014 (Fig. 1.8).

ANOVA results indicate that the soil Hg residuals were significantly higher (*i.e.,* soil Hg signal was higher) ($p = 0.001$) during the 2014 sampling. Interpreting these results in the context of recent changes in the Hg depositional signal, however, is problematic. The R-EMAP soil samples were collected by using a coring tube to sample the top 10 cm of the soil profile. Triplicate samples from each site were combined and homogenized before extracting subsamples for chemical analysis (P. Kalla, personal communication, August 23, 2017). As a result, the R-EMAP soil samples represent a Hg signal integrated over an extended period of time. Based on a separate survey of Hg concentrations measured in surficial soils throughout the Everglades, Cohen et al. (2009) estimated that the inventory of soil Hg expressed on

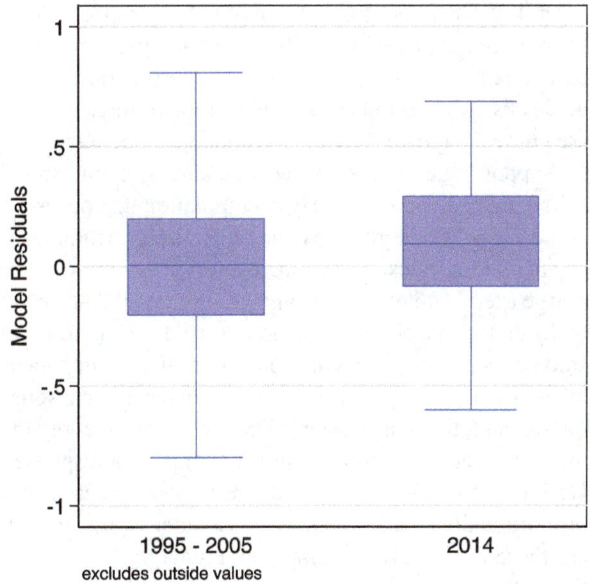

Fig. 1.8 Comparison of the distribution of soil Hg model residuals (see Eq. (2)) for surficial Everglades soils for the time intervals 1995–2005 and 2014. Data from the USEPA R-EMAP program and confined to the EvPA. $N = 973$

an areal basis and extending to a depth of 10 cm equated to approximate 100 times contemporary wet deposition fluxes. This means that, as new sediment is deposited, an equivalent amount of historical sediment (based on thickness) likely deposited somewhere between ~1900 and ~1950 is concomitantly buried below the 10 cm sampling horizon. Because the Hg flux within this historical time frame is likely well below the current Hg flux, the newly deposited material should in essence result in a higher inventory of Hg between 0 and 10 cm, even if the most recent Hg signal represents a continued *decline* in the deposition flux compared to the peak deposition flux occurring *ca.* 1990–1994. Restated, if the change in the soil Hg residuals was negative and statistically significant, that change would strongly support a large, recent decline in Hg deposition. That the signal was positive and significant does not negate the possibility that a recent decline in the Hg signal has nonetheless occurred.

1.4 Conclusions

Long-term records of changes in sediment Hg accumulation rates for a multitude of sites located principally through North America and Europe clearly indicate that current background atmospheric deposition fluxes of Hg are ~2 to 4× greater than fluxes that occurred during preindustrial times. Similar increases in fluxes have been recorded in Lake Annie in south central Florida (3×). Modern enrichment ratios in the Everglades are higher, based on both a comparison of Hg accumulation rates for pre-1900 sediments compared to sediments for the time interval 1985–1992 for samples collected throughout the Everglades (average enrichment ratios ranging from 4.0 to 8.7 for WCA-3 and WCA-2, respectively; Rood et al. 1995) and data from a core collected in WCA-2 and analyzed by Abelak et al. (unpublished data; enrichment ratio ~ 4). The higher modern enrichment ratios observed in the Everglades likely reflect near-field depositional impacts from local emission sources that are currently greatly reduced or no longer operational.

Supporting evidence for recent changes in atmospheric mercury deposition rates following peak periods of Hg accumulation that occurred during primarily the 1980s and early 1990s is given by the rather well documented declines in recent mercury accumulation rates in sediments observed in Minnesota, the Great Lakes, the northeastern United States, and Scandinavia. The nature of the declines (*i.e.*, due to local factors or larger scale sources) is variable depending upon the systems studied. For example, localized changes in mercury accumulation rates in Minnesota lake sediments suggest principally changes in local sources. In both the Great Lakes region and the northeastern US, however, the regional nature of the observed mercury accumulation rates in lakes implies a response to large-scale reductions in Hg emissions. Declines in the northeastern lakes tend to be greatest in lakes with proportionally small watersheds—in other words, the lakes that are most responsive are those that receive a comparatively larger fraction of their mercury load directly from atmospheric deposition. The dampened response in lakes with relatively larger watersheds is likely due to sustained export of Hg from watershed soils originally derived from atmospheric deposition over long periods of time.

Within Florida, two separate sources of information indicate that atmospheric fluxes of mercury have declined during the 1990s through the present. The first line of evidence is based on statistical modeling of wet deposition fluxes in Everglades National Park from late 1993 through 2016. Piecewise regression of the residuals obtained from that modeling indicates two distinct periods of change in the mercury signal owing to factors other than seasonal dynamics and rainfall. The first period, which extends from late 1993 to mid-2013, was characterized by a significant decline in the VWM mercury signal approximating 2.3 ng/L by the end of the interval; this decline equates to 18% of the observed VWM concentration of 12.7 ng/L for the entire interval. The second period, which extends from mid-2013 through 2016, was characterized by a comparatively sharp increase in the Hg signal; this increase also approximated 3 ng/L. As a result, the current Hg signal in wet deposition differs little from the wet deposition signal at the beginning of the period of record, although significant variations occurred within the overall time period.

The second piece of evidence indicative of recent changes in atmospheric deposition fluxes of Hg in south Florida is provided by sediment cores collected by Engstrom et al. (2003) from Lake Annie. Results from those cores show an unambiguous and monotonic decline in sediment mercury accumulation rates of 13–20% beginning in the mid-1990s through 2002 when the cores were collected. Because of the location of Lake Annie relative to the south Florida urban fringe, it likely has not been appreciably impacted by the large reductions of emissions in that area of greater than 90%, and the measured decline is more likely representative of change in the global background. As mentioned previously, this is evidenced by the relatively low modern enrichment ratio of 3×, which is similar to enrichment ratios that have been observed in other lakes considered to be representative of global background impacts. By comparison, the modern enrichment ratios for sites in the Everglades are higher and ranged from an average of 4.0 for WCA-3 to 8.7 for WCA-2 (Rood et al. 1995).

From a management perspective, how these changes in deposition correspond to the temporal dynamics of biota Hg concentrations in the Everglades is of course a critical question. For example, concentrations of Hg in LMB collected from Site 3A-15 located within WCA3A—and which was then considered to be a "hot-spot" for elevated Hg concentrations—declined nearly monotonically from 1.24 to 0.78 mg/kg between 1996 and the mid- to late 1990s. The declines in LMB concentration during this period are matched by similar declines observed in other areas of the Everglades (Chap. 2, this volume) and generally correspond to trends in the Hg atmospheric signal we have elucidated here. In the absence of other data, this would suggest that the LMB trends were caused by the changes in atmospheric Hg deposition. At the same time, however, large declines in sulfate concentrations also were observed at 3A-15. Because of the causative role of sulfate as a driver of Hg methylation in the Everglades (see Chaps. 1, 3, and 6 in Volume II), the roles of both changing sulfate and atmospheric deposition on Hg dynamics thus must be considered and deconvoluted. This is done by Harris et al. (Chap. 4, this volume) for Site 3A-15 using a mechanistic, dynamic Hg cycling model calibrated to the site. Chap. 5 (this volume) further synthesizes the information on trends in biota developed in Chap. 2 in conjunction with the role of legacy Hg (Chap. 3 this volume) and atmospheric deposition to help address the overarching question of cause and effect.

References

Atkeson TD, Pollman CD, Axelrad DR (2005) Chapter 26. Recent trends in mercury emissions, deposition, and biota in the Florida everglades: a monitoring and modeling analysis. In: Pirrone N, Mahaffey KR (eds) Dynamics of mercury pollution on regional and global scales: atmospheric processes and human exposures around the world. Springer, New York, pp 637–655

Beal SA, Jackson BP, Kelly MA, Stroup JS, Landis JD (2013) Effects of historical and modern mining on mercury deposition in southeastern Peru. Environ Sci Technol. https://doi.org/10.1021/es402317x

Beal SA, Kelly MA, Stroup JS, Jackson BP, Lowell TV, Tapia PM (2014) Natural and anthropogenic variations in atmospheric mercury deposition during the Holocene near Quelccaya Ice Cap, Peru. Glob Biogeochem Cycles 2014. https://doi.org/10.1002/2013GB004780

Benoit JM, Fitzgerald WF, Damman AWH (1998) The biogeochemistry of an ombrotrophic bog: evaluation of use as an archive of atmospheric mercury deposition. Environ Res 78:118–133

Biester H, Kilian R, Franzen C, Woda C, Mangini A, Schöler HF (2001) Elevated mercury accumulation in a peat bog of the Magellanic Moorlands, Chile (53°S) - an anthropogenic signal from the Southern Hemisphere. Earth Planet Sci Lett 201:609–620

Biester H, Bindler R, Martinez-Cortizas A, Engstrom DR (2007) Modeling the past atmospheric deposition of mercury using natural archives. Environ Sci Technol 2007(41):4851–4860

Bindler R (2003) Estimating the natural background atmospheric deposition rate of mercury utilizing ombrotrophic bogs in southern Sweden. Environ Sci Technol 37:40–46

Bindler R, Olofsson C, Renberg I, Frech W (2001a) Temporal trends in mercury accumulation in lake sediments in Sweden. Water Air Soil Pollut Focus 1:343–355

Bindler R, Renberg I, Appleby PG, Anderson NJ, Rose NL (2001b) Mercury accumulation rates and spatial patterns in lake sediments from West Greenland: a coast to ice margin transect. Environ Sci Technol 35:1736–1741

Butler TJ, Cohen MD, Vermeylen FM, Likens GE, Schmeltz D, Artz RS (2008) Regional precipitation mercury trends in the eastern USA, 1998–2005: declines in the Northeast and Midwest, no trend in the Southeast. Atmos Environ 42:1582–1592

Chellman N, McConnell JR, Arienzo M, Pederson GT, Aarons SM, Csank A (2017) Reassessment of the Upper Fremont Glacier ice-core chronologies by synchronizing of ice-core-water isotopes to a nearby tree-ring chronology. Environ Sci Technol 51(8):4230–4238

Cohen MJ, Lamsal S, Osborne TZ, Bonzongo JCJ, Newman S, Reddy KR (2009) Soil total mercury concentrations across the Greater Everglades. Soil Sci Soc Am J 73:675–685

Cooke CA, Balcom PH, Biester H, Wolfe AP (2009) Over three millennia of mercury pollution in the Peruvian Andes. Proc Natl Acad Sci 106(22):8830–8834

Cooke CA, Hintelmann H, Ague JJ, Burger R, Biester H, Sachs JP, Engstrom DR (2013) Use and legacy of mercury in the Andes. Environ Sci Technol 47:4181–4188

Delfino JJ, Crisman TL, Gottgens JF, Rood BE, Earle CDA (1993) Spatial and temporal distribution of mercury in Everglades and Okefenokee wetland sediments. Department of Environmental Engineering Sciences, University of Florida, Gainesville

Drevnick PE, Engstrom DR, Driscoll CT, Swain EB, Balogh SJ, Kamman NC, Long DT, Mui DGC, Parsons MJ, Rolfhus KR, Rossmann R (2012a) Spatial and temporal patterns of mercury accumulation in lacustrine sediments across the Laurentian Great Lakes region. Environ Pollut 161:252–260

Drevnick PE, Yang H, Lamborg CH, Rose NL (2012b) Net atmospheric mercury deposition to Svalbard: estimates from lacustrine sediments. Atmos Environ 59:509–513

Drevnick PE, Cooke CA, Barraza D, Blais JM, Coale KH, Cumming BF, Curtis CJ, Das B, Donahue WF, Eagles-Smith CA, Engstrom DR, Fitzgerald WF, Furl CV, Gray JE, Hall RI, Jackson TA, Laird KR, Lockhart WL, Macdonald RW, Mast MA, Mathieum C, Muir DCG, Outridge PM, Reinemann SA, Rothenberg SE, Ruiz-Fernández AC, Louis VLS, Sanders RD, Sanei H, Skierszkane EK, Van Metre PC, Veverica TJ, Wiklund JA, Wolfe BB (2016) Spatiotemporal patterns of mercury accumulation in lake sediments of western North America. Sci Tot Environ 568:1157–1170

Duan N (1983) Smearing estimate: a nonparametric retransformation method. J Am Stat Assoc 78 (383):605–610

Dvonch JT, Graney JR, Keeler GI, Stevens RK (1999) Use of elemental tracers to source apportion mercury in South Florida precipitation. Environ Sci Technol 33:4522–4527

Engstrom DR, Swain EB (1997) Recent declines in atmospheric mercury deposition in the upper Midwest. Environ Sci Technol 312:960–967

Engstrom DR, Pollman CD, Fitzgerald WF, Balcom PH (2003) Evaluation of recent trends in atmospheric mercury deposition in South Florida from lake sediment records. Final Research Report Florida Department of Environmental Protection, Tallahassee, FL

Engstrom DR, Swain EB, Balogh SJ (2007) History of mercury inputs to Minnesota lakes: influences of watershed disturbance and localized atmospheric deposition. Limnol Oceanogr 52:2467–2483

Engstrom DR, Fitzgerald WF, Cooke CA, Lamborg CH, Drevnick PE, Swain EB, Balogh SJ, Balcom PH (2014) Atmospheric Hg emissions from preindustrial gold and silver extraction in the Americas: a reevaluation from lake-sediment archives. Environ Sci Technol 48:6533–6543

Enrico M, Le Roux G, Heimbürger L-E, Van Beek P, Souhaut M, Chmeleff J, Sonke J (2017) Holocene atmospheric mercury levels reconstructed from peat bog mercury stable isotopes. Environ Sci Technol. https://doi.org/10.1021/acs.est.6b05804

Fitzgerald WF, Engstrom DR, Lamborg CH, Tseng C-M, Balcom PH (2005) Modern and historic atmospheric mercury fluxes in northern Alaska: global sources and Arctic depletion. Environ Sci Technol 39:557–568

Fitzgerald WF, Engstrom DR, Hammerschmidt CR, Lamborg CH, Balcom PH, Lima-Braun AL, Bothner MH, Reddy CM (2018) Global and local sources of mercury deposition in coastal New England reconstructed from a multiproxy, high resolution, estuarine sediment record. Environ Sci Technol 52:7614–7620

Florida Department of Environmental Protection (FDEP) (2013). http://www.dep.state.fl.us/water/tmdl/docs/tmdls/mercury/Mercury-TMDL.pdf

Frederick PC, Spalding MG, Sepulveda MS, Williams GE Jr, Nico L, Robbins R (1999) Exposure of Great Egret nestlings to mercury through diet in the Everglades of Florida. Environ Toxicol Chem 18:1940–1947

Frederick PC, Hylton BA, Heath JA, Spalding MG (2004) A historical record of mercury contamination in southern Florida as inferred from avian feather tissue. Environ Toxicol Chem 23:1474–1478

Gill GA, Guentzel JL, Landing WM, Pollman CD (1995) Total gaseous mercury measurements in Florida: the FAMS project (1992–1994). Water Air Soil Pollut 80:235–244

Givelet N, Roos-Barraclough F, Shotyk W (2003) Predominant anthropogenic sources and rates of atmospheric mercury accumulation in southern Ontario recorded by peat cores from three bogs: comparison with natural "background" values (past 8000 years). J Environ Monit 5:935–949

Guentzel JL, Landing WM, Gill GA, Pollman CD (2001) Processes influencing rainfall deposition of mercury in Florida: the FAMS Project (1992–1996). Environ Sci Technol 35:863–873

Hamilton LC (2013) Statistics with Stata: updated for Version 12, 8th edn. Brooks/Cole, Boston, 473 pp

Hermanns Y-M, Biester H (2013) Anthropogenic mercury signals in lake sediments from southernmost Patagonia, Chile. Sci Tot Environ 445–446:126–135

Jensen A, Jensen A (1991) Historical deposition rates of mercury in Scandinavia estimated by dating and measurement of mercury in cores of peat bogs. Water Air Soil Pollut 56:769–777

Johansson K (1985) Mercury in sediment in Swedish forest lakes. Verhandlungen der Internationalen Vereinigung für theoretische und angewandte Limnologie 22:2359–2363

Johnson MG (1987) Trace element loadings to sediments of fourteen Ontario lakes and correlations with concentrations in fish. Can J Fish Aquat Sci 44:3–13

Johnson MG, Culp LR, George SE (1986) Temporal and spatial trends in metal loadings to sediments of the Turkey Lakes, Ontario. Can J Fish Aquat Sci 43:754–762

Kamman NC, Engstrom DR (2002) Historical and present fluxes of mercury to Vermont and New Hampshire lakes inferred from 210Pb dated sediment cores. Atmos Environ 36:1599–1609

Kamman NC, Chalmers A, Clair TA, Major A, Moore RB, Norton SA, Shanley JB (2005) Factors influencing mercury in freshwater surface sediments of northeastern North America. Ecotoxicology 14:101–111

Kang W-J (1999) Inputs of sediment and mercury to the lower Everglades and Florida Bay: a temporal and spatial perspective. M.S. thesis, Division of Marine & Environmental Systems, Florida Institute of Technology, Melbourne, FL

Kang W-J, Trefry JH, Nielsen TA, Wanless HR (2000) Direct atmospheric inputs versus runoff fluxes of mercury to the lower Everglades and Florida Bay. Environ Sci Technol 34:4058–4063

Kang S, Huang J, Wang F, Zhang Q, Zhang Y, Li C, Wang L, Chen P, Sharma C, Li Q, Sillanpää M, Hou J, Xu B, Guo J (2016) Atmospheric mercury depositional chronology reconstructed from lake sediment and ice cores in the Himalayas and Tibetan Plateau. Environ Sci Technol 50:2859–2869

Keeler GJ, Gratz LE, Al-Wali K (2005) Long-term atmospheric mercury wet deposition at Underhill, VT. Ecotoxicology 14:71–83

Lamborg CH, Fitzgerald WF, Damman AWH, Benoit JM, Balcom PH, Engstrom DR (2002) Modern and historic atmospheric mercury fluxes in both hemispheres: global and regional mercury cycling implications. Glob Biogeochem Cycles 16:1104. https://doi.org/10.1029/2001GB1847

Lamborg CH, Engstrom DR, Fitzgerald WF, Balcom PH (2013) Apportioning global and non-global components of mercury deposition through ^{210}Pb indexing. Sci Tot Environ 448:132–140

Landers DH, Ford J, Gubala C, Monetti M, Lasorsa BK, Martinson J (1995) Mercury in vegetation and lake-sediments from the U.S. Arctic. Water Air Soil Pollut 80:591–601

Landers DH, Gubala C, Verta M, Lucotte M, Johansson K, Vlasova T, Lockhart WL (1998) Using lake sediment mercury flux ratios to evaluate the regional and continental dimensions of mercury deposition in arctic and boreal ecosystems. Atmos Environ 32:919–928

Landis MS, Vette AF, Keeler GJ (2002) Atmospheric mercury in the Lake Michigan Basin: influence of the Chicago/Gary urban area. Environ Sci Technol 36:4508–4517

Lockhart WL, Wilkinson P, Billeck BN, Hunt RV, Wagemann R, Brunskill GJ (1995) Current and historical inputs of mercury to high-latitude lakes in Canada and to Hudson Bay. Water Air Soil Pollut 80:603–610

Lockhart WL, Wilkinson P, Billeck BN, Dannel RA, Hunt RV, Brunskill GJ, Delaronde J, St. Louis V (1998) Fluxes of mercury to lake sediments in central and northern Canada inferred from dated sediment cores. Biogeochemistry 40:163–173

Lorey PM (2001) The determination of ultra trace levels of mercury in environmental samples in the Northeastern U.S.: inferring the past, present, and future of atmospheric mercury deposition. Ph. D. Syracuse University, Syracuse, NY

Lorey P, Driscoll CT (1999) Historical trends of mercury deposition in Adirondack lakes. Environ Sci Technol. https://doi.org/10.1021/es9800277

Lucotte M, Mucci A, Hillaire-Marcel C, Pichet P, Grondin A (1995) Anthropogenic mercury enrichment in remote lakes of northern Québec (Canada). Water Air Soil Pollut 80:467–476

Martinez-Cortizas A, Pontevedra-Pombal X, Garcia-Rodeja E, Novoa-Munoz JC, Shotyk W (1999) Mercury in a Spanish Peat Bog: archive of climate change and atmospheric metal deposition. Science 284:939942

Mason RP, Sheu GR (2000) Annual and seasonal trends in mercury deposition in Maryland. Atmos Environ 34:1691–1701

Meili M (1995) Preindustrial atmospheric deposition of mercury - uncertain rates from lake sediment and peat cores. Water Air Soil Pollut 80:637–640

Mitchell MN (2012) Interpreting and visualizing regression models using Stata. Stata Press, Plano, TX, 558 pp

Muir DCG, Wang X, Yang F, Nguyen N, Jackson TA, Evans MS, Douglas M, Kock G, Lamoureux S, Pienitz R (2009) Spatial trends and historical deposition of mercury in eastern and northern Canada inferred from lake sediment cores. Environ Sci Technol 43(13):4802–4809

Munthe J, Hultberg H, Lee Y-H, Parkman H, Iverfeldt Å, Renberg I (1995) Trends of mercury and methylmercury in deposition, run-off water and sediments in relation to experimental manipulations and acidification. Water Air Soil Pollut 85(2):743–748

Nater EA, Grigal DF (1992) Regional trends in mercury distribution across the Great Lakes states, north central USA. Nature 358:139–140

Newman MC (1993) Regression analysis of log-transformed data: statistical bias and its correction. Environ Toxicol Chem 12:1129–1133

Norton SA, Evans GC, Kahl JS (1997) Comparison of Hg and Pb fluxes to hummocks and Hollows of ombrotrophic Big Heath Bog and to nearby Sargent Mt. Pond, Maine, USA. Water Air Soil Pollut 100:271–286

Perry E, Norton SA, Kamman NC, Lorey PM, Driscoll CT (2005) Deconstruction of historic mercury accumulation in lake sediments, northeastern United States. Ecotoxicology 14:85–99

Phillips VJA, St. Louis V, Cooke CA, Vinebrooke RD, Hobbs WO (2011) Increased mercury loading to western Canadian alpine lakes over the past 150 years. Environ Sci Technol 45:2042–2047

Polgreen LA, Brooks JM (2012) Estimating incremental costs with skew: a cautionary note. Appl Health Econ Policy 10(5):319–329

Pollman CD, Porcella DB (2003) Assessment of trends in mercury-related data sets. J Phys IV France 107:1083–1090

Prestbo EM, Gay DA (2009) Wet deposition of mercury in the US and Canada, 1996–2005: results and analysis of the NADP mercury deposition network (MDN). Atmos Environ 43:4223–4233

Rada RG, Powell DE, Wiener JG (1993) Whole-lake burdens and spatial distribution of mercury in surficial sediments in Wisconsin seepage lakes. Can J Fish Aquat Sci 50:865–873

Renberg I (1986) Concentration and annual accumulation of heavy metals in lake sediments: their significance in studies of the history of heavy metal pollution. Hydrobiologia 143:379–385

Risch MR, Gay DA, Fowler KK, Keeler GJ, Backus SM, Blanchard P, Barres JA, Dvonch TJ (2012) Spatial patterns and temporal trends in mercury concentrations, precipitation depths, and mercury wet deposition in the North American Great Lakes region, 2002–2008. Environ Pollut 161:261–271

Robbins JA, Holmes C, Halley R, Bothner M, Shinn E, Graney J, Keeler G, tenBrink M, Oralandini KA, Rudnick D (2000) Time averaged fluxes of lead and fallout radionuclides to sediments in Florida Bay. J Geophys Res 105(C12):28,805–28.821

Roelke M, Glass CM (1992) Florida panther biomedical evaluation. Florida Game and Fresh Water Fish Commission, Tallahasee, FL

Rood BE, Gottgens JF, Delfino JJ, Earle CD, Crisman TL (1995) Mercury accumulation trends in Florida Everglades and Savannas Marsh flooded soils. Water Air Soil Pollut 80:981–990

Roos-Barraclough F, Shotyk W (2003) Millennial-scale records of atmospheric mercury deposition obtained from ombrotrophic and minerotrophic peatlands in the Swiss Jura Mountains. Environ Sci Technol 37:235–244

Sacks LA, Swancar A, Lee TM (1998) Estimating groundwater exchange with lakes using water-budget and chemical mass-balance approaches for ten lakes in ridge areas of Polk and Highlands counties, Florida. U.S. Geological Survey Water-Resources Investigations Report 98-4133

Scheidt DJ, Kalla PI (2007) Evergladees ecosystem assessment: water management and quality, eutrophication, mercury contamination, soils and habitat: monitoring for adaptive management: a R-EMAP status report. USEPA Region 4, Athens, GA. EPA 904-R-07-001. 98 pp. http://www.epa.gov/region4/sesd/reports/epa904r07001/epa904r07001.pdf

Schuster PF, Krabbenhoft DP, Naftz DL, Cecil LD, Olson ML, Dewild JF, Susong DD, Green JR, Abbott ML (2002) Atmospheric mercury deposition during the last 270 years: a glacial ice core record of natural and anthropogenic sources. Environ Sci Technol 36:2303–2310

StataCorp (2019) Stata statistical software: Release 16. StataCorp LLC, College Station, TX

Steinnes E, Andersson EM (1991) Atmospheric deposition of mercury in Norway: temporal and spatial trends. Water Air Soil Pollut 56:391–404

Stevens DL Jr (1997) Variable density grid-based sampling designs for continuous spatial populations. Environmetrics 8:167–195

Swain EB, Engstrom DR, Brigham ME, Henning TA, Brezonik PL (1992) Increasing rates of atmospheric mercury deposition in midcontinental North America. Science 257:784–787

USEPA (2019). https://www.epa.gov/everglades/everglades-ecosystem-assessment-water-management-and-quality-eutrophication-mercury

Verta M, Tolonen K, Simola H (1989) History of heavy metal pollution in Finland as recorded by lake sediments. Sci Total Environ 87/88:1–18

Weiss-Penzias P, Gay DA, Brigham ME, Parsons MT, Gustin MS, ter Schure A (2016) Trends in mercury wet deposition and mercury air concentrations across the U.S. and Canada. Sci Total Environ 568:546–556

Yang H, Battarbee RW, Turner SD, Rose NL, Derwent RG, Wu G, Yang R (2010a) Historical reconstruction of mercury pollution across the Tibetan Plateau using lake sediments. Environ Sci Technol 44(8):2918–2924

Yang H, Engstrom DR, Rose NL (2010b) Recent changes in atmospheric mercury deposition recorded in the sediments of remote equatorial lakes in the Rwenzori Mountains, Uganda. Environ Sci Technol 44:6570–6575

Zhang Y, Jacob DJ, Horowitz HM, Chen L, Amos HM, Krabbenhoft DP, Slemr F, Louis VLS, Sunderland EM (2016) Observed decrease in atmospheric mercury explained by global decline in anthropogenic emissions. Proc Natl Acad Sci 113(3):526–531

Zheng J (2015) Archives of total mercury reconstructed with ice and snow from Greenland and the Canadian High Arctic. Sci Total Environ 509–510:133–144

Chapter 2
Temporal Changes in Mercury Concentrations in Everglades Biota

Ted Lange, Darren G. Rumbold, Peter C. Frederick, Mark Cunningham, and Curtis D. Pollman

Abstract Mercury in Everglades food webs poses human health and ecological risks most notably to anglers, hunters and fish-eating wildlife. These risks vary spatial and temporally across the Everglades landscape. The purpose of this chapter is to present an evaluation of temporal trends in mercury bioaccumulation within specific links in Everglades food webs. Emphasis is given to assessing temporal trends in biotically important species (see Chap. 8, Vol. II for food web descriptions of mosquitofish, largemouth bass, wading birds, and the Florida panther); however, multiple additional species along a gradient of trophic levels and habitats are considered in the context of the recognized high degree of spatial variability in bioaccumulation across the Everglades.

Keywords Freshwater fish · Alligator · Wading birds · Florida panther · Raccoon · Marine fish · Temporal trend · Spatial variability

T. Lange (✉)
Florida Fish and Wildlife Conservation Commission, Eustis, FL, USA
e-mail: ted.lange@mywfc.com

D. G. Rumbold
Florida Gulf Coast University, Fort Myers, FL, USA
e-mail: drumbold@fgcu.edu

P. C. Frederick
University of Florida, Gainseville, FL, USA
e-mail: pfred@ufl.edu

M. Cunningham
Florida Fish and Wildlife Conservation Commission, Gainesville, FL, USA
e-mail: mark.cunningham@myfwc.com

C. D. Pollman
Aqua Lux Lucis Inc., Gainseville, FL, USA
e-mail: cpollman@aqualuxlucis.org

C. D. Pollman et al. (eds.), *Mercury and the Everglades. A Synthesis and Model for Complex Ecosystem Restoration*, https://doi.org/10.1007/978-3-030-55635-8_2

2.1 Introduction

Monitoring temporal trends in concentrations of mercury (Hg) in biota is critical in assessing responses to changes in loadings of Hg to the Everglades from atmospheric or other sources (Wiener et al. 2007). Such data are often utilized, or even a result of, monitoring to assess risks to wildlife and humans who consume fish, as well as to assess health risks to top-predator fish themselves (see Chaps. 10 and 11 of Vol. II). This chapter focuses on four important Everglades animal groups for which details of their food habits, dietary Hg concentrations, and Hg exposures are well established and reported in Chap. 8 Vol. II. Moreover, temporal analyses of Hg concentrations in several additional species from freshwater, marine, and terrestrial habitats are presented.

In selecting biological indicators of temporal change in Hg levels, applicability to risk assessment as well as a broad geographical distribution in the area of interest are of paramount importance. The indicator species selected, eastern mosquitofish (*Gambusia holbrooki*), Florida largemouth bass (*Micropterus salmoides floridanus*), several species of long-legged wading birds, and the Florida panther (*Puma concolor coryi*) are well established, generally widely distributed, and have well understood life-history characteristics. All have natural histories in some way tied to the unique cycle of flooding and drying across the Everglades landscape including our focus on the impounded Water Conservation Areas (WCA) and Everglades National Park (ENP). Mosquitofish are perhaps the most widely distributed fish in the Everglades, occurring wherever surface water is present while serving as a critically important prey item for piscivorous fish and wildlife. Florida largemouth bass are a piscivorous predator near the top of the aquatic food web. Bass are a premier sport fish in Florida, grow to trophy size in the Everglades, and represent a vector for human exposure. Wading birds, including white ibises (*Eudocimus albus*), great egrets (*Ardea alba*), and great blue herons (*Ardea herodias*), are some of the most iconic species representing the biological values that led to the creation of ENP. Wading birds, like bass, are top level aquatic predators that forage over large areas of the Everglades in search of a wide range of fish and invertebrate prey. Diets are highly dependent upon bird species, location, prey animal size and prey species availability which in turn vary in response to seasonal flooding and drying cycles. The well-studied Florida panther (*Felis concolor coryi*) is a regional apex predator that is more important in lands surrounding the Everglades, such as Big Cypress Swamp, where they prey primarily on deer and feral swine; however, decreases in their primary prey base coupled with longer hydroperiods may be causing them to select prey more closely associated with the aquatic food web. These species, along with the American alligator (*Alligator mississippiensis*), raccoon (*Procyon lotor*), and several estuarine dependent fish species provide a broad range of trophic interactions across varying ecological niches within the Everglades from which to assess temporal trends in Hg bioaccumulation.

2.2 Freshwater Everglades

2.2.1 Mosquitofish

Eastern mosquitofish Hg data is included in the South Florida Ecosystem Assessment Project's Regional Environmental Monitoring and Assessment Program (R-EMAP) conducted by the USEPA Region 4 in the Everglades. Life-history and Hg dynamics of mosquitofish are described in detail in Chap. 8, Vol. II. The R-EMAP project sought to establish baseline marsh conditions for Hg concentrations in water, sediment and biota to assess the effects of greater Everglades restoration efforts (Scheidt and Kalla 2007). Everglades marshes do not support a diverse assemblage of organisms (Lodge 1994) but mosquitofish are abundant and widely distributed across the Everglades ecosystem (Loftus and Kushlan 1987). Mosquitofish have a lifespan of only a few months (Haake and Dean 1983) but because of an omnivorous diet they bioaccumulate high concentrations of methylmercury (MeHg) (Chap. 8, Vol. II). Local environmental factors and seasonal hydrology lead to highly variable gradients in Hg across the Everglades landscape (Cleckner et al. 1998; Loftus 2000, Chap. 8, Vol. II).

R-EMAP survey results revealed higher total Hg (THg) concentrations in marsh collected mosquitofish, with 62% exceeding the 0.1 mg/kg predator protection criterion (Eisler 1987), compared to only 17% from canals (Stober et al. 2001). Marsh habitat "hotspots" in south-central WCA3 and Shark River Slough (SRS) in ENP led Stober et al. (2001) to the rational conclusion that marsh habitats were the primary source of Hg contamination.

Spatial gradients in mosquitofish THg concentrations in the R-EMAP study area were assessed during baseline studies in 1995–1996, and again during 1999, 2005 and finally in 2014 providing a multi-decadal temporal assessment of bioaccumulation across the EvPA (Kalla and Scheidt 2017). Mercury burdens in mosquitofish declined sharply in the Everglades over this period as the THg estimates for wet-season marsh areas shifted towards significantly lower concentrations (Fig. 2.1; Kalla and Scheidt 2017). In 2014, the percentage of marsh with mosquitofish exceeding the predator protection criteria of 0.077 mg/kg (USEPA 1997) reached a sample period low of 13% compared to in-excess of 70% in 1995 (Fig. 2.1). Clearly, THg concentrations in mosquitofish were much reduced compared to 1995, and much of the decline occurred after 2005 (Fig. 2.1).

2.2.2 Largemouth Bass

The Florida largemouth bass (hereafter bass or LMB) is the native black bass species in the Everglades ecosystem. Because of their popularity as a sport fish, ability to integrate Hg over wide temporal and spatial scales, and role as an apex predator, bass are a useful bioindicator of Hg bioaccumulation (Wiener et al. 2007). Long-term data

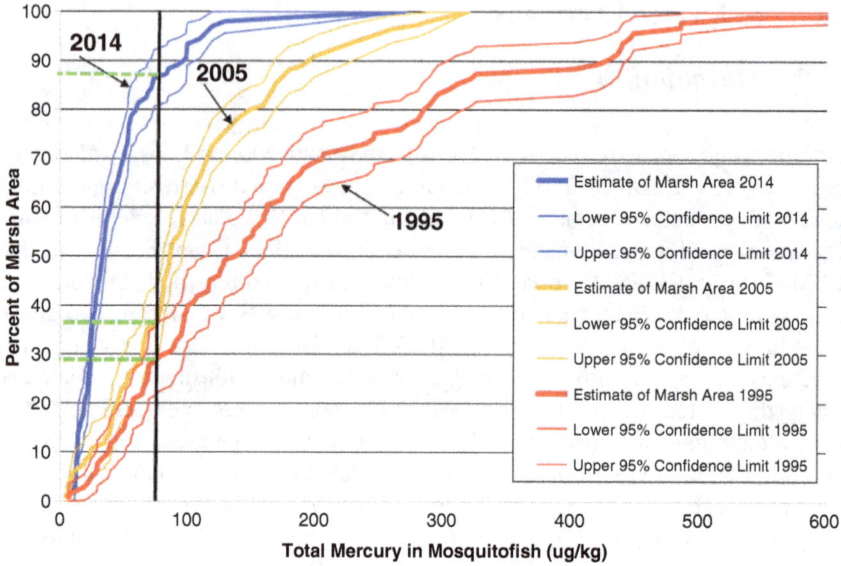

Fig. 2.1 Cumulative distribution function (CDF) curves of THg in mosquitofish in the wet season, showing changes over the course of R-EMAP (adapted from Kalla and Scheidt 2017). The solid black vertical line in the figure is the 77 μg/kg (0.077 mg/kg) predator protection criterion (USEPA 1997). The dashed green horizontal lines are the corresponding y-intercepts, showing the proportion of the system below the criterion. In 2014, the intercept was at 87% and only 13% of the marsh was above 77 μg/kg in mosquitofish. The apparent differences among the curves are statistically significant ($p < 0.05$, Wald F, FWC pers. comm.). Analysis of variance indicated that the lower concentrations observed in 2014 compared to 2005 cannot be explained by fish length or weight (Kalla and Scheidt 2017)

on LMB THg concentrations are available from the South Florida Water Management District (SFWMD) (1998–2018) and Florida Fish and Wildlife Conservation Commission (FWC) (1988–2018); both data sets are described in Chap. 9, Vol. II.

Using all bass data collected by FWC and SFWMD between 1988 and 2018 provided 4975 bass collected from 61 sampling areas in WCAs 1, 2, and 3 and 872 from 2 sampling sites in SRS in ENP (Table 2.1). Both monitoring programs targeted bass ranging from 200 to 500 mm in length, but SRS bass were, on average, slightly larger (Table 2.1). The range of sizes collected were similar and represent bass that can be readily and legally harvested for consumption. Therefore, these collections can be employed to describe broad temporal trends in potential human exposure to Hg via consumption of fish. Bass median THg from the WCA sites ranged from 0.30 to 1.80 mg/kg and declined steadily from the late 1980s to the early 2000s (Fig. 2.2, top). Since 2000 the median THg in bass from the WCAs has varied minimally and ranged between 0.30 and 0.56 mg/kg. Correspondingly, high values in individual fish (outliers in excess of the 90th percentile) have decreased since 2000 yet remain high relative to the human health criterion (0.3 mg/kg). During the same time period, the median THg in bass from SRS in ENP varied between 0.77

Table 2.1 Total mercury concentrations (mg/kg) in bass muscle tissue from the Water Conservation Areas (WCA) and Shark River Slough (SRS) in Everglades National Park

	WCAs	SRS
Sites	61	2
Sample size	4975	872
Mean total length in mm (range)	290 (98–596)	333 (169–538)
Median THg (range)	0.45 (0.30–1.80)	1.19 (0.77–1.88)
Mean THg (s.d.)	0.59 (0.48)	1.31 (0.67)
Individual bass THg range	0.01–4.36	0.19–4.80

Sites include both canal and marsh sites in Fig. 2.3 and additional locations sampled between 1988 and 2018 through biomonitoring programs of South Florida Water Management District and Florida Fish and Wildlife Conservation Commission

and 1.88 mg/kg (Fig. 2.2, bottom). In SRS, THg in bass varied among years; however, there is scant evidence of any specific trends in bioaccumulation with Hg levels in nearly all bass well in excess of human health criteria.

Assessing trends in a large-bodied, highly mobile predator (i.e. bass), can be problematic, requiring accounting for variations in fish size distributions and MeHg bioavailability across the landscape. Bass THg increases with fish size and age (Lange et al. 1994), requiring normalization among collections with varying size distributions to assess temporal and spatial trends (Wiener et al. 2007). Bass integrate Hg in their diet over time and space as they move in response to hydroperiods (Chap. 8, Vol. II); however, strong site fidelity has been demonstrated during tracking studies with bass remaining in marsh slough habitat in spite of receding water levels (Fury et al. 2001). Based on habitat differences in food webs and Hg bioaccumulation (Chap. 8, Vol. II) as well as a north to south increasing trend in Hg concentrations in fish and wildlife (Chap. 9, Vol. II), sampling program biases, including site selection inconsistencies among years, must be accounted for. Because of these potential biases, trends in WCA bass were evaluated at specific sites within both canal and marsh habitats using bass THg concentration normalized to age.

Exploratory analyses indicated that bass THg are linearly related to age once both variables have been log-transformed. Normalization was conducted by using a generalized linear model (GLM) that regressed bass THg tissue concentrations against the log-transformed age using a log link function (StataCorp 2017), rather than using ordinary least squares (OLS) with the dependent variable log-transformed. The latter approach can lead to biased estimates of the model coefficients, particularly if the residuals are heteroskedastic (Santos Silva and Tenreyro 2006). The error distribution was assumed to follow a Poisson distribution, and model estimation was conducted using the Huber White sandwich estimator of variance, which is more robust to some forms of model misspecification (*cf.* Gould 2011). The GLM model also included interaction terms for site and sampling year necessary for evaluating changes in the normalized concentrations (calculated for both age-1 and age-3) over both time and site.

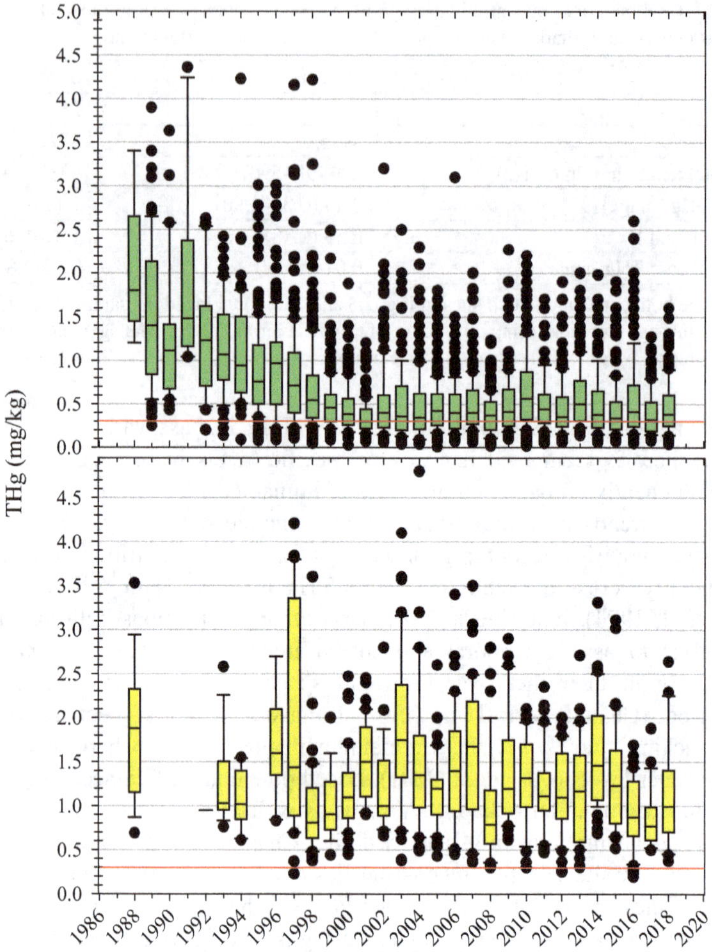

Fig. 2.2 Annual summaries of largemouth bass (bass) THg from the Everglades Protection Area including Water Conservation Areas (WCA) 1, 2, and 3 (top) and Shark River Slough (SRS) in Everglades National Park (bottom) between 1989 and 2018 (see Table 2.1). Boxes represent the median, 25th and 75th percentiles, whiskers the tenth and 90th percentiles and points are outliers. The red lines are USEPA (2001) MeHg criterion for protection of human health (0.3 mg/kg). Adapted and updated from Axelrad et al. (2011)

Temporal trends for select canal (L7, L35B, and L67A) and interior marsh sites (LOXF1, WCA2U3, and CA315) within WCA1, WCA2, and WCA3 respectively, and SRS sites (L67F1 and ENPNP) within the ENP (Fig. 2.3) were constructed using kernel-weighted local polynomial smoothing (StataCorp 2017). The sites were selected based on having a long-term period of record for monitoring that extended at least as far back as 1998 or earlier coupled with largely continuous monitoring since towards the present. The smoothing was conducted separately for each of the two hydrologic types and the ENP group of sites by aggregating the standardized

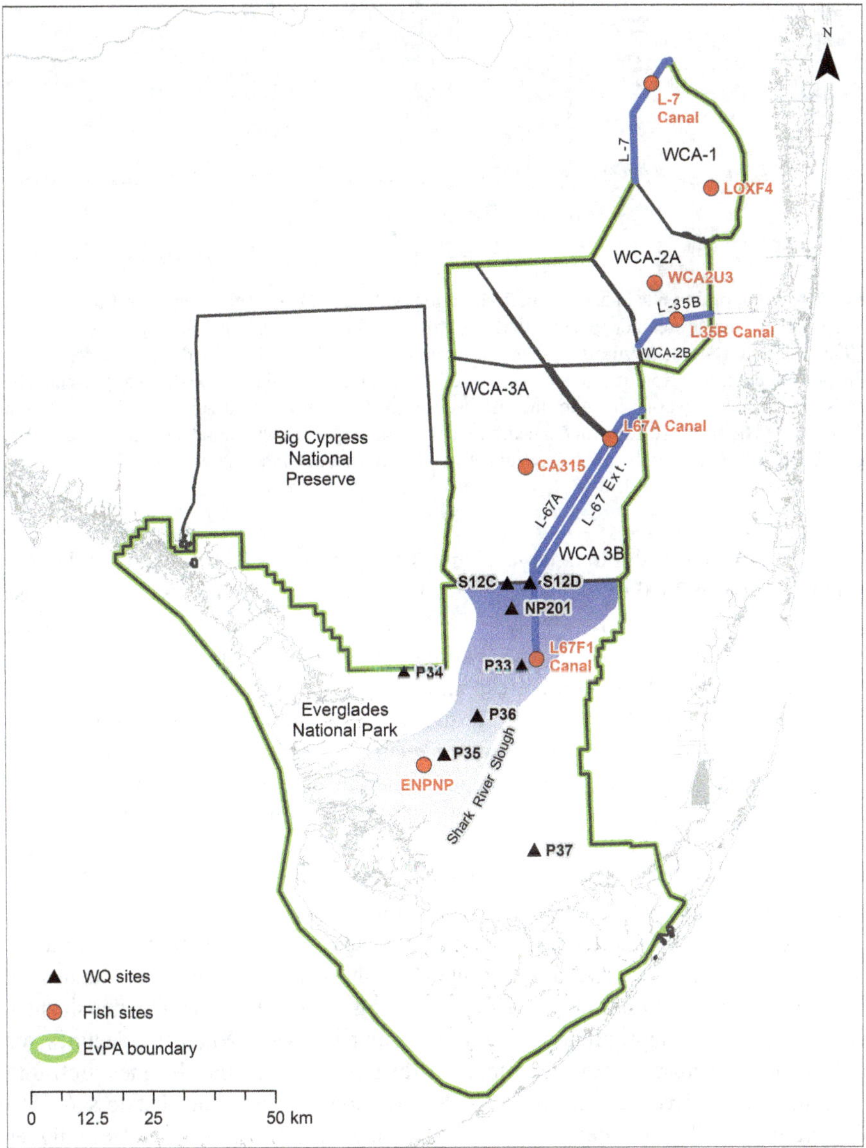

Fig. 2.3 Map of Everglades Protection Area (EvPA) with fish and water quality (WQ) sample sites

estimates for age-3 fish across sites within each grouping type. Prior to data aggregation, the standardized age-3 data for each site were normalized to express the fish tissue THg at each point in time as a fractional change relative to the overall mean for the time interval of 2000 to 2017 (the most current date in the data set for the sites analyzed). The 2000–2017-time interval was selected as the normalization

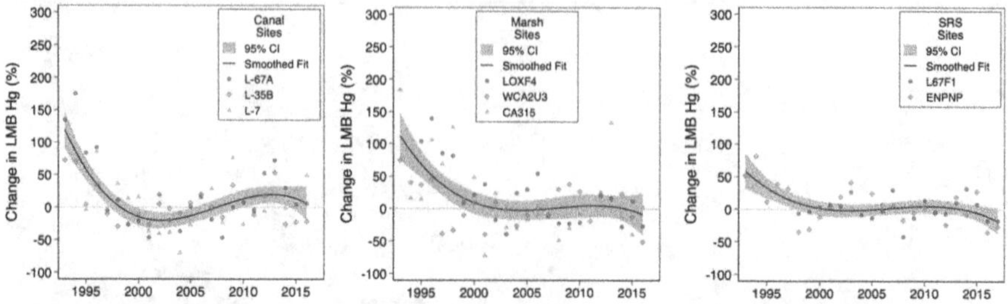

Fig. 2.4 Temporal trends in age-normalized largemouth bass THg at select canal (left-hand panel; 1989–2016); marsh (center panel; 1993–2016) and Shark River Slough (right-hand panel; 1993–2017) long-term monitoring sites (see sites in Fig. 2.3). Each individual value represents the percent deviation from mean age-normalized concentration for the period 2000 to present. The canal and marsh locations include one site each in Water Conservation Areas (WCA) 1, 2, and 3. Smoothed trends were constructed using kernel-weighted local polynomial smoothing (see text); gray bands associated with each curve represent 95% confidence intervals

base for two reasons. First, large changes in fish tissue THg over time largely occurred prior to 2000 (*c.f.*, Fig. 2.2). Second, normalizing to fish tissue THg across a large interval characterized by a fair amount of variability yet showing no overt overall trend provides a more robust estimate for the base normalization concentration rather an individual point corresponding to a given year.

The smoothed trends are shown for the canal, marsh and SRS site groupings in Fig. 2.4. All three site groupings showed relatively similar trends—namely higher THg in bass in the early 1990s trending downwards towards relatively stable concentrations beginning *ca.* 2000. The relative magnitude of the declines during the 1990s appears to differ consistently across the three groups, with the largest relative decline observed for the canal sites, followed by the marsh sites. The SRS sites showed the least amount of relative decline.

The difference between the canal and marsh sites however is simply an artifact of the shorter period of record embodied in the marsh sites. For example, the canal sites showed declines approximating 70% beginning in 1989, while the marsh sites showed a decline approximating 50% beginning in 1993. When the declines for both canal and marsh sites are compared relative to 1993, the declines are quite similar. The relative decline in the SRS sites however is somewhat less (~35% decline from 1993) and may reflect differing biogeochemistry that results in higher THg in LMB in SRS compared to sites north of the ENP. These differences are explored in Chap. 5 (this volume).

2.2.3 Wading Birds

Long-legged wading birds have offered perhaps the longest record of Hg exposure in the food web of any Everglades biotic sampling medium. This is because it is

Table 2.2 Total mercury concentrations (mg/kg) in feather samples of piscivorous birds from the Everglades comparing the same species from pre-1980s and post-1999

	Anhinga	Great egret	White ibis	Great blue heron
Pre-1980s				
Mean	1.86	2.77	1.04	3.34
SD	2.72	3.64	0.77	3.34
Median	0.78	1.50	0.86	2.35
n	21	7	33	12
Post-1990				
Mean	10.03	19.84	7.47	21.03
SD	9.11	12.45	4.58	15.98
Median	6.50	18.00	7.10	19.00
n	7	37	98	49
Z[a]	3.475	3.834	7.508	4.264
P	0.00007	0.00001	0.00001	0.00001

SD standard deviation
From Frederick et al. (2004)

possible to use museum specimens as historical indicators of Hg burdens. Growing feathers readily take up Hg from the blood stream and then form a stable, covalent bond with feather tissue (Thompson and Furness 1989). Museum skins can therefore be used as an excellent long-term record of Hg availability (Burger 1993; Monteiro and Furness 1995). Frederick et al. (2004) sampled scapular feathers from preserved skins of Everglades white ibises great egrets, anhingas (*Anhinga anhinga*) and great blue herons between 1900 and 2000 and found dramatic increases (4–6X) in feather THg between pre- and post-1980 samples (Table 2.2) in all species. All four species demonstrated the same temporal pattern, with THg being stable and low until the late 1980s, followed by a large increase thereafter (Fig. 2.5). This pattern was quite different from the global pattern of monotonic increase in THg since the industrial revolution (Frederick et al. 2004) and has been important evidence implicating local sources as a main cause of contamination in the Everglades (Frederick et al. 2005). High THg in wading bird feathers was also one of the first illustrations that the Everglades had high Hg availability.

More recent shifts in both temporal and spatial patterns of contamination have been demonstrated by annual, sampling of great egret chick feathers in the central Everglades since 1994. Scapular feathers were collected from chicks sampled when they left the nest but were not yet able to fly (28–35 days of age). Since chicks are confined to the colony until this point, chick feathers are representative of Hg exposure from food gathered from the surrounding area by attending adults (Frederick et al. 1999; Spalding et al. 2000). Considerable variation is seen in annual colony-specific means (Fig. 2.6), and geographic variation is usually much larger than variation among individual nests within a colony (Frederick et al. 1999; Zabala et al. 2019).

Prior to 1998, standard-age great egret chick feathers averaged 15.3 mg/kg fresh weight (fw), while 1998–2013 feathers averaged 7.1 mg/kg fw THg, an approximate

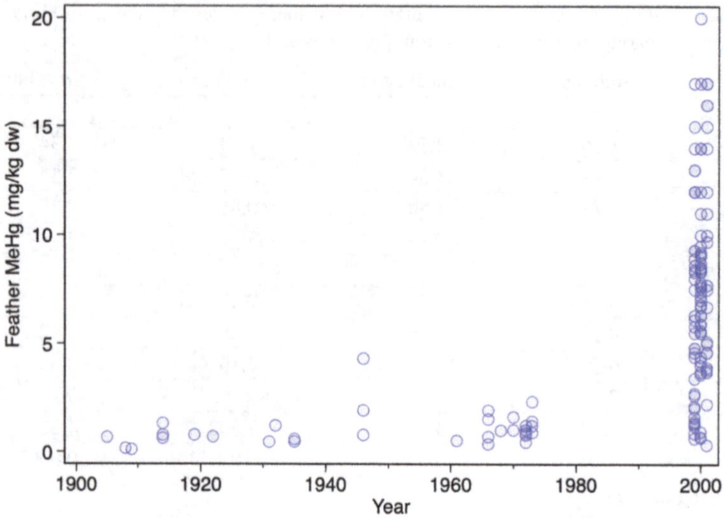

Fig. 2.5 Methylmercury concentrations in feathers of white ibises collected in south Florida, 1900–2000. Adapted from Frederick et al. (2004)

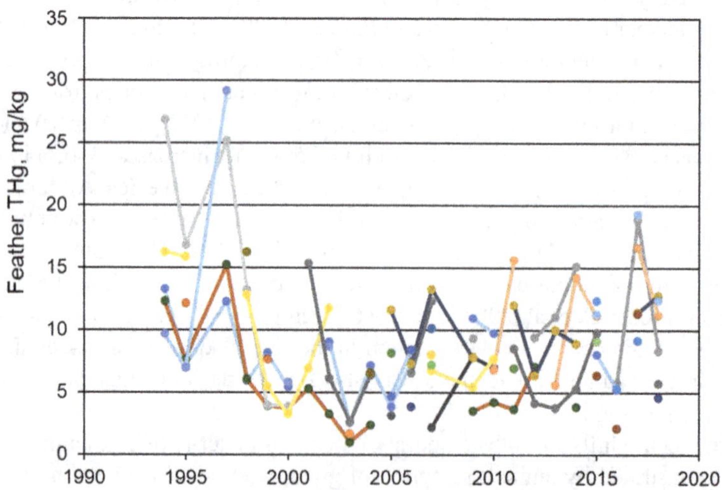

Fig. 2.6 Feather THg from great egret nestlings collected annually from Everglades breeding colonies. Different colored lines represent trendlines in different colonies. Not all colonies were active in all years of the study

halving of the exposure, at least in WCA 3 (Fig. 2.7). This temporal shift matches up fairly well with general trends in bass THg during the same period and locations, which is described above. While this is not surprising since great egrets are largely piscivorous, it is worth noting that the two independent sampling programs both detected the same temporal trend over a large area of the Everglades.

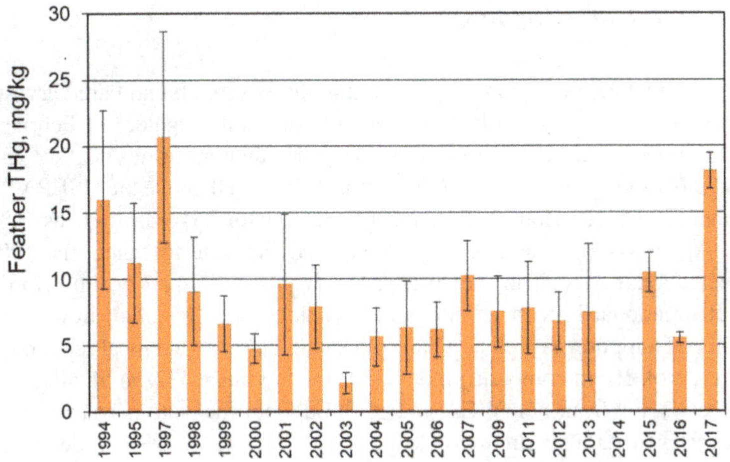

Fig. 2.7 Averages of colony-wide great egret chick feather THg (1994–2017) from wading bird breeding colonies in freshwater areas of the Everglades. Each year represents an average of values from 3 to 6 colonies, each colony is represented by 8–30 samples from individual nests. Error bars are 1 standard deviation, no data were collected in 2014

The years 2015 and 2017 showed an apparent marked increase in regional Hg exposure for great egrets. It is not clear whether these 2 years represent a true regional shift towards greater Hg exposure, or are an artifact of changing regional sampling, since not all colonies are active or accessible in all years. Both 2015 and 2017 had relatively high reproductive parameters, an indication that food was abundant and available. High food intake is one path by which mercury exposure may increase for nestlings. In contrast, the 2016 nesting season was an El Nino year, in which surface water did not recede, food was poorly available, and nestings showed all the hallmarks of food stress. That year showed one of the lowest average THg on record.

The available record of Hg exposure in Everglades wading birds suggests that this taxa group can reflect variation in Hg availability at large geographic scales, a valuable tool in such a large wetland complex. Besides being of value as an indicator of contamination, these data can also function as a measure of population health for wading birds. Mercury exposure is increasingly well defined as a parameter known to affect avian health, endocrinology and reproduction (Wolfe et al. 1998; Scheuhammer et al. 2007; Evers et al. 2008). The field of Hg effects research in birds has progressed considerably in recent years (Fuchsman et al. 2017; Ackerman et al. 2016; Whitney and Cristol 2017) to the point of defining effects levels, and even to linking exposure to population level responses, in some cases specifically to the avian species breeding in the Everglades (Frederick and Jayasena 2011). This ability to translate regional exposure to biological effects levels therefore has direct relevance for Everglades restoration and can serve as a model for understanding net effects of Hg on wetland wildlife in other systems.

2.2.4 American Alligator

American alligators are important predators in the Everglades and are harvested for consumption by humans. Early FWC surveys of adult alligators in February and June 1989 revealed mean THg in tail muscle of alligators from WCAs 2 and 3 of 2.12 and 2.60 mg/kg, respectively (Hord et al. 1990), well above the USEPA 0.3 mg/kg human health criterion. Individual alligators with THg as high as 3.88 and 3.58 mg/kg in WCAs 2 and 3, respectively, led the state to cancel the 1989 and 1990 recreational harvest in the Everglades to protect human health (Hord et al. 1990). Recreational harvest of alligators has since been restored; however, advisories on consumption as well as a ban on the sale of harvested meat remain in place (Chap. 11, Vol. II). In comparison, during 1989, the mean THg in 58 alligator meat samples collected from non-WCA waters throughout the state in managed harvest areas was 0.39 with a maximum of 1.40 mg/kg (Hord et al. 1990) underscoring the fact other waters in Florida, like the Everglades, have a high degree of sensitivity to Hg bioaccumulation. Results of several biomonitoring programs suggest that the greater Everglades (WCAs and freshwater reaches of ENP) are most susceptible to bioaccumulation of Hg in alligators. Ogden et al. (1974) reported that THg in alligator eggs greatly exceeded levels found in their estuarine counterpart, the American Crocodile (*Crocodylus acutus*); however, this could have been a function of differences in species life histories rather than habitat related. Between 2008 and 2010, average THg in alligator muscle tissue in Stormwater Treatment Areas (STAs) 1 W, 5, and 3/4 were 0.084, 0.113, and 0.277 mg/kg with a maximum concentration of 0.77 mg/kg (Axelrad et al. 2011), all much lower than concentrations observed in WCA alligators (for discussion of why STAs are low in Hg, see Chap. 3, Vol. II).

Surveys by FWC during the 1990 and 1996 statewide alligator harvest showed decreases in THg in adult alligators in WCA 3 as compared to the 1989 levels with concentrations declining to 1.90 mg/kg south of Alligator Alley and 1.62 north of the Alley (Fig. 2.8). FWC data from 2011 suggests a modest decline from 2.12 to 1.28 mg/kg in WCA 2 and an area-wide decline from 2.60 to 2.18 mg/kg in WCA 3 over two decades. Similarly, Rumbold et al. (2002) surveyed THg in sub-adult alligators from northern WCA-3 in 1999 and reported a statistically significant decline in THg in tail muscle compared to similar sized alligators surveyed in 1994 by Yanochko et al. (1997). Rumbold et al. (2002) noted higher concentrations of THg in both liver and muscle tissue in alligators collected from ENP. Despite subtle declines in THg in both adult and sub-adult alligators in the WCAs, they continue to serve as a sentinel for Hg bioaccumulation in an apex predator that represents an exposure route to both humans and wildlife.

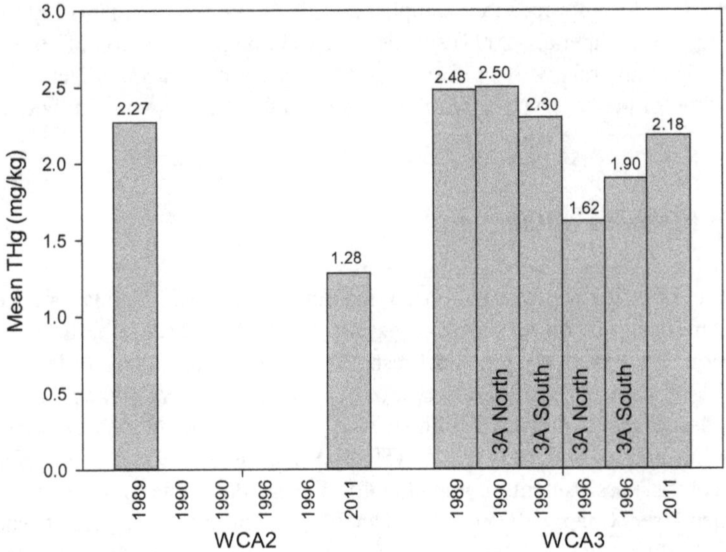

Fig. 2.8 Mean THg in American alligator tail muscle tissue from sampling events on Water Conservation Areas (WCA) 2 (left) and 3 (right) during 1989–2011 (Hord et al. 1990 and FWC, unpublished data)

2.2.5 *Raccoons*

Porcella et al. (2004) contrasted THg in south Florida raccoon hair from museum specimens collected prior to 1960 with animals trapped in 2000. Comparisons were also made with archived samples collected by Roelke et al. (1991) in 1990. Raccoons were chosen to assess historic patterns of Hg exposure because of the abundance and distribution of raccoons in present-day environments of concern and in museum collections. Likewise, concern over raccoons as a vector of Hg contamination to the endangered Florida panther (Chap. 8, Vol. II) was a motivating factor in selecting raccoons. Museum (n = 54) and current (n = 118) hair samples as well as other tissue samples were also analyzed for MeHg.

Of several tissues analyzed, Porcella et al. (2004) found the highest THg levels in liver and hair; however, liver was almost entirely (93%) inorganic Hg while hair was almost all MeHg (99%). The high inorganic Hg content of liver tissue suggests that it acts as a site of sequestration and demthylation/detoxification while hair serves as an efficient mechanism for eliminating MeHg (Clarkson 1994). Not surprisingly, they found high spatial variability (20×) with the highest levels in raccoons from SRS. Temporal differences in MeHg depended on location with some areas having higher MeHg in museum specimens (Long Pine Key and SRS north of US41) while other areas, particularly SRS south of US41 had higher concentrations in modern specimens (mean was 11.2 mg/kg in 1947–1948 as compared to a mean of 26.7 mg/kg in 2000; Porcella et al. 2004). Yet, these levels were low compared to those reported by

Roelke et al. (1991) for raccoons sampled in ENP (south of US 41) in 1990 (mean of 72 mg/kg). Porcella et al. (2004) surmised that although deposition of Hg to South Florida is spatially relatively uniform, seasonal variations in raccoon diet were likely responsible for the observed differences in temporal patterns among individual sites.

2.2.6 Florida Panther

In 1978 the Florida panther, the only remaining *P. concolor* population in eastern North America, was on the brink of extinction. To help determine threats to this population, the Florida Game and Fresh Water Fish Commission (GFC, now the Florida Fish and Wildlife Conservation Commission [FWC]) began collecting various tissues from panthers examined at necropsy or capture. Tissues were subsequently subsampled and analyzed for THg by Roelke et al. (1991) for one of the first ecological risk assessments completed for Everglades biota (for review of risk assessment, see Chap. 10, Vol. II). The FWC continues to collect tissues and routinely collects hair for Hg determination. Roelke et al. (1991) reported THg ranging as high as 130 mg/kg in hair from a panther sampled in 1989 but found levels highly variably among individuals and in panthers from different regions. Levels of Hg in hair differed significantly by location with highest levels occurring in panthers from SRS (Geometric mean of hair-Hg in 8 panthers was 55.5 mg/kg) and lowest levels in panthers captured north of Alligator Alley (GM for 43 panthers was 1.8 mg/kg). This spatial variability in Hg biomagnification and resulting levels in top predators is consistent with the patterns described above for fishes, birds, and other biota and is consistent with what is known about variability in methylation biogeochemistry leading to hotspots (for review, see Chap. 1, Vol. II). Additionally, panthers occupy different habitats, which affect their diet and Hg exposure (for review, see Chap. 8, Vol. II). Spatial variation in biomagnification at the start of the monitoring program obviously influences the way temporal trends should be assessed. In data summaries, Roelke et al. (1991) categorized capture location by different regions (7–11 areas) to maximize sample size for a given tissue, but in several analyses grouped them into five regions (north of Alligator Alley, Fakahatchee Strand State Reserve, Raccoon Point, SRS and Long Pine Key). Since late 1980s sampling effort has varied over the years and the focus shifted to different areas. For example, few panthers have been sampled recently from SRS in ENP. There are various reasons for this spatial bias in recent sampling of panthers, including poor habitat in WCA-3A (due to high water levels), the ephemeral nature of the Everglades panther population, logistical constraints, and increased focus on the larger western population. Nonetheless, this sampling bias must be considered in assessing long-term trends in THg. To increase sample size for temporal trend analysis, capture location has been consolidated to just four regions (Fig. 2.9). Hair-THg data (those having necessary metadata) from 1986 through to 2015 are summarized in Fig. 2.9; the highest hair-THg reported by Roelke et al. (1991) can be found assigned to the SE region. Interestingly, the highest THg value (i.e., 100 mg/

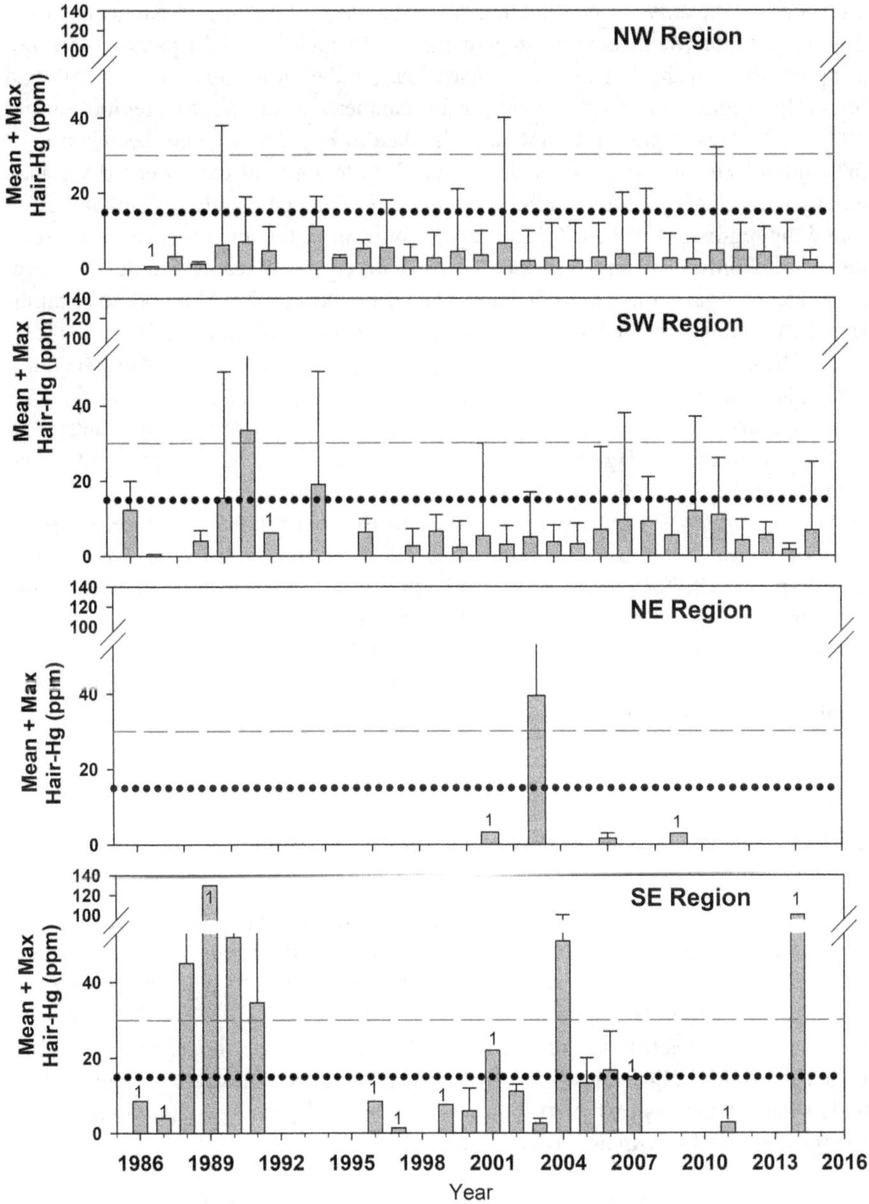

Fig. 2.9 Annual average hair-THg (and maximum concentration shown by whisker in ppm) in Florida panthers sampled from different regions of south Florida from 1986 to 2015 (regions defined north-south by Interstate 75 and east-west by eastern BCNP boundary). Often only one ($n = 1$ labeled on graph) or no panthers caught in a given year. Also shown are toxicity reference values for terrestrial mammals based on results of different literature reviews or models (Eccles et al. 2017; Basu 2012)

kg) observed recently (from 2008 to 2015) was in a panther hit by a car near Francis Taylor Wildlife Management Area in this same region. While panthers are not sampled often in the NE region, at least one panther from this area in 2003 had hair-THg within the range observed in panthers from the SE region during 1987–1991. It is important to note that the data in Fig. 2.9 have not been censored or standardized for age or sex and this may lead to some of the observed variance among individuals. While a preliminary analysis of the data collected up until 2007 found the regression of hair-THg on age significant in one region (Brandon 2011), the R^2 was only 0.06 and the slope was negative, which seems counter intuitive. More recent regressions based on larger data sets (through 2015) found no relationship between age and hair-THg in panthers from the NW region ($F = 3.11, 292$; $p = 0.08$) or SW region ($F = 1.71, 189$; $p = 0.2$). This lack of age affect (i.e., not seeing an increase in THg with increasing panther age as is observed in fish, for example) may be a result, in part, to the tremendous capacity for panthers to fortuitously sequester Hg in their hair. Repeated sampling of hair from individual panthers reveals dramatic changes in hair-THg over time.

When individual hair-THg data were regressed over date of capture, temporal trends were non-significant: SE region $F = 1.6, 1, 36$; $p = 0.2$; SW region $F = 1.8, 1, 189$; $p = 0.18$; NW region $F = 3.2, 1, 292$; $p = 0.07$. It is clear that individual panthers in some areas of south Florida are still highly exposed to Hg. Given declines in the deer population in some areas (Garrison et al. 2011) and possible shifts in prey selection (Caudill et al. 2019), exposure to Hg will likely continue to be significant threat to panthers in the Everglades population.

2.3 Everglades Estuaries and Coastal Waters

The freshwater Everglades and downstream estuarine waters of the Florida Bay and other south Florida coastal ecosystems are closely linked through regional hydrology. Flow of fresh water to south Florida estuaries serve to deliver nutrients for primary production and to reduce salinity (McIvor et al. 1994), but flows of freshwater have been much reduced in certain cases in the managed Everglades. Because of this, Hg trends in these ecotonal and coastal areas are critical to understand in the context of restoration of historic hydrologic conditions to the Everglades and downstream coastal waters.

2.3.1 Temporal Trends in Hg Levels in Marine Species from South Florida

As mentioned in Chap. 10 (Vol. II) of this book, Florida's Hg problem extends beyond the freshwater Everglades through the estuaries and out into the coastal waters. In fact, the first fish consumption advisory issued by the Florida Department of Health and Rehabilitative Services (now known as the Florida Department of Health or FDOH) in 1991was not for a freshwater fish but instead recommended limited consumption of sharks due to high Hg. Sharks (all species in Florida waters) remain on the FDOH's fish consumption advisory list in 2019 along with 58 other marine fish species, many of which are recreationally or commercially important (FDOH 2019).

Marine biota have been surveyed along Florida's coasts for THg in their tissues by various entities to assess risk to human consumers, to investigate sources and influential factors affecting biomagnification of MeHg and, to a lesser extent, to assess temporal trends. Temporal trend analysis must be done with care, however, because levels will vary due to various aspects of the sampled population (i.e., species, size, age, exposure duration) and because Hg biomagnification is so spatially highly variable. Consequently, comparisons should be done on animals of the same age (or size as a proxy) or through statistical analysis that can partition the variability in Hg due to difference in age and will be limited by the availability of long-term data sets for a given species within a specific region. For example, Adams et al. (2003) in a survey of fish THg in Everglades coastal waters, Florida Bay and the Keys noted lower median THg in red drum (*Sciaenops ocellatus*) from estuarine regions to the north (mean 0.17–0.30 mg/kg) than in the Keys/Florida Bay region (mean 0.52 mg/kg). Additionally, they reported the occurrence of "hot spots" for mercury bioaccumulation within Florida Bay where localized samples of spotted seatrout (*Cynoscion nebulosus*) contained higher THg than the surrounding sample region.

2.3.2 *Trends in Hg Levels in Florida Bay Biota*

Total mercury concentrations have been surveyed intermittently in several species of marine fishes in Florida Bay by federal and state agencies since 1998. Crevalle jack (*Caranx hippos*) and gray snappers (*Lutjanus griseus*) were two species often surveyed. Figure 2.10 presents results from four surveys of jacks from 1998 to 2008. As evident from the graph, sampled populations differed in size; however, certain data sets did not exhibit a statistically significant relationship between size and THg and, consequently, ANCOVA was not available to assess the data statistically. Visual inspection of the data, however, reveals very little evidence of a temporal trend in THg of jacks of similar size since 1998. Figure 2.11 shows similar issues were encountered in attempting to compare THg in gray snapper collected from 1993 through 2008. Nonetheless, similar to the jacks, there was no obvious long-term trend in THg in snapper (Fig. 2.11).

The absence of a temporal trend, with THg levels remaining elevated, in fishes of northeastern Florida Bay was recently supported by a survey of fish-eating osprey (*Pandion haliaetus*) in Florida Bay. Total mercury in feathers collected during 2014

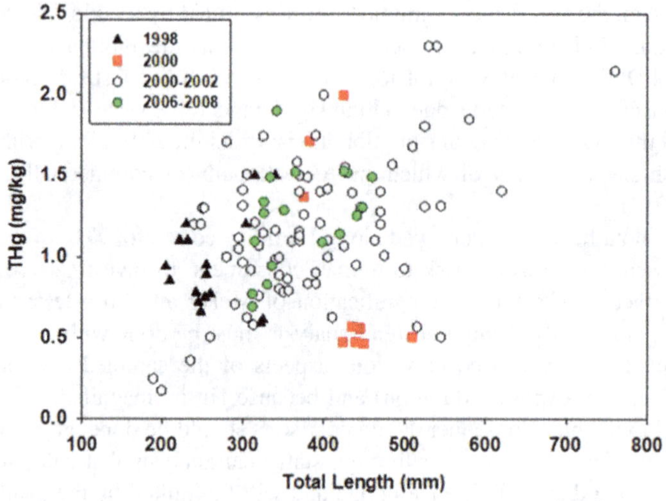

Fig. 2.10 Total mercury in crevalle jack (*Caranx hippos*), a marine fish, caught in northeastern Florida Bay from 1998 to 2008 (1998: Strom and Graves 2001; 2000: Evans and Crumley 2005; 2000–2002; Evans and Rumbold unpublished; 2006–2008; Adams et al. 2018)

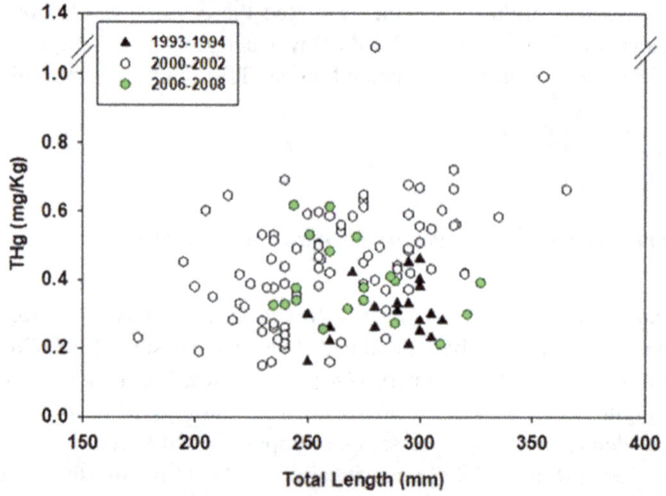

Fig. 2.11 Total mercury in gray snapper (*Lutjanus griseus*), a marine fish, caught in northeastern Florida Bay from 1998 to 2008 (1993–1994: Strom and Graves 2001; 2000–2002 Evans and Rumbold unpublished; 2006–2008; Adams et al. 2018)

did not differ from THg in feathers collected in 2000–2001 by Lounsbury-Billie et al. (2008, as cited by Rumbold et al. 2017).

Additionally, recent reports of exceptionally high THg in sharks (Matulik et al. 2017) and bottlenose dolphin (*Tursiops truncates*, Damseaux et al. 2017) in the bay are further evidence that Florida Bay remains a Hg hotspot.

2.3.3 Trends in Mercury in Fishes in Southwest Florida Estuaries

Short term trends in THg in fishes from two southwest Florida estuaries were mixed—with one showing an increase and the other a decrease over a period of about 6 years demonstrating the dynamic nature of Hg levels in Florida. Gray snappers collected in a survey at the mouth of the Caloosahatchee River Estuary in 2011–2015 had 48% higher THg than gray snappers caught by Adams et al. (2018) from 2006 to 2008 (Rumbold et al. 2018). This difference was statistically significant ($F = 23.5, 1, 122; p < 0.001$) even though they were smaller in size ($F = 10.2, 1, 122; p < 0.01$; significant interaction prevented use of ANCOVA). Although crevalle jacks caught during these same two surveys did not differ significantly in THg ($F = 2.01, 1, 82; p = 0.16$), the jacks caught in 2006–2008 were 45% larger ($F = 7.6, 1, 82; p < 0.01$) and would have been expected to have higher THg simply due to their larger size (and presumably greater age). Adams et al. (2018) also report that THg in these species in the offshore gulf regions did not differ between the 2007–2008 and 2014–2015 sampling periods.

In contrast, THg decreased in both gray snappers and crevalle jacks collected at the mouth of Shark River Estuary in 2011–2015 as compared to 2006–2008. Total mercury decreased by 70% in snappers in 2011–2015 as compared to similar sized fishes collected in 2006–2008 ($F = 32.4, 1, 129; p < 0.001$; size did not differ: $F = 0.1, 1, 129; p = 0.75$). Likewise, THg was 26% lower in jacks caught in 2011–2015 as compared to 2006–2008 (ANOVA $F = 99.8, 1, 90; p < 0.001$). However, common snook (*Centropomus undecimalis*) caught near the headwaters of Shark River Estuary (North Prong), while highly variable through the years (1993–2015; parsed in three-year periods; $F = 3.8$, $df = 6, 68$, $p = 0.002$), did not exhibit a monotonic temporal trend in least square mean (LSM) for THg (1996–1998, 2007–2009 and 2013–215 were periods with elevated THg >1 mg/kg for snook with a TL of 645 mm).

As mentioned above, the first advisory in Florida recommending limited consumption of fishes due to elevated Hg was issued on May 13, 1991, after shark fillets sold in retail markets was found to contain high levels of Hg (Florida Department of Health and Rehabilitative Services). A follow-up survey completed in 1992 confirmed high Hg levels in wild-caught sharks, with higher levels generally occurring in sharks from the southern part of the state (Hueter et al. 1995). FWC has continued monitoring Hg in Florida sharks (Adams et al. 2003). More recently, Rumbold et al. (2014) sampled adult sharks from southwest Florida coastal waters from 2010 to 2013 and found much higher levels in blacktip sharks (*Carcharhinus limbatus*, mean = 2.65 mg/kg) as compared to blacktips sampled in this area by Hueter et al. (1995) and Adams et al. (2003). Average THg were also higher in 2010–2013 for blacknose sharks (*C. acronotus*), bull sharks (*C. leucas*), sharpnose (*Rhizoprionodon terraenovae*) and tiger sharks (*Galeocerdo cuvier*) (for review, see Rumbold et al. 2014). Matulik et al. (2017) also found higher THg in sharks from Florida Bay as compared sharks caught years earlier by Adams et al. (2003). Furthermore, a research study (Reistad 2018) that sampled sharks in Charlotte Harbor in 2015 reported THg in juvenile blacktips (0.836 mg/kg) that was higher than the average level in slightly older blacktips (0.79 mg/kg, pool of juveniles and young adults) sampled from the area from 1989–2001 by Adams et al. (2003).

2.4 Conclusions

To summarize, sampling of mosquitofish across the Everglades periodically by USEPA R-EMAP showed a trend of declining Hg residues with markedly lower levels in 2005 and then again in 2014 as compared to 1995–1996. Based on more densely packed data from monitoring THg in bass on an annual basis it appears there was a breakpoint in the general decreasing trend in 2000, after which, levels stabilized for several years but began to increase in 2005 only to show a hint of a downturn more recently. Bass from certain areas, particularly from Shark River Slough in ENP did not show the same trend in THg. Mercury levels decreased in great egret feathers from the mid-1990s and were near their lowest levels in 2000 but have subsequently increased, albeit somewhat variably, with 2017 levels the second highest observed (only feathers in 1997 had higher levels). Mercury levels in tail muscle of alligators also showed similar trends—decreasing from mid-1990s to 1999 and then began to increase. Raccoons collected in 2000 exhibited much lower THg than animals collected in 1990 but have not been sampled more recently. While changes in spatial sampling have hampered trend analysis in panthers, very high levels continue to be observed occasionally. While most data sets of Hg residues in Florida's marine biota are not as long as those from monitoring freshwater system, sharks are the exception and while data gaps do not allow us to assess breakpoints, current levels appear to be higher now than in 1992. There was no evidence of any trend, decreasing or increasing, in THg levels in Florida Bay biota where some of the highest levels in the state, and possibly the world, are still being observed.

Thus, it is clear that biota in most areas of the freshwater Everglades have shown marked and statistically significant declines in THg since the mid-1990s; however, levels continue to be spatially highly variable. Yet, not all areas showed the same decline in THg and, more troublesome, recently THg in biota in some areas are trending higher. Current THg in Florida biota remain higher than many other areas of North America (e.g., Rumbold et al. 2014, 2017, 2018; Chap. 9, Vol. II) and continue to represent a risk to wildlife (Chap. 10, Vol. II) and humans (Chap. 11, Vol. II) who eat locally caught fish. The question is then what are the factors responsible for the decreasing Hg trends in biota in some areas but not in others, and can we exploit those factors as a possible means of mitigating the Hg problem in south Florida (for potential answers see, Chaps. 4, 5 and 7, this volume).

References

Ackerman JT, Eagles-Smith CA, Herzog MP, Hartman CA, Peterson SH, Evers DC, Jackson AK, Elliott JE, Vander Pol SS, Bryan CE (2016) Avian mercury exposure and toxicological risk across western North America: a synthesis. Sci Total Environ 568:749–769

Adams DH, McMichael RH, Henderson GE (2003) Mercury levels in marine and estuarine fishes of Florida 1989–2001. In: FFWC (ed) Florida Marine Research Institute, p 57

Adams DH, Tremain DM, Evans DW (2018) Large-scale assessment of mercury in sentinel estuarine fishes of the Florida Everglades and adjacent coastal ecosystems. Bull Mar Sci. https://doi.org/10.5343/bms.2017.1160

Axelrad DM, Lange T, Gabriel M (2011) Chapter 3B: Mercury and sulfur monitoring, research and environmental assessment for the Florida Everglades. In: South Florida Environmental Report, South Florida Water Management District, West Palm Beach, FL. https://www.sfwmd.gov/science-data/scientific-publications-sfer. Accessed 19 July 2012

Basu N (2012) Piscivorous mammalian wildlife as sentinels of methylmercury exposure and neurotoxicity in humans. In: Ceccatelli S, Aschner M (eds) Methylmercury and neurotoxicity, current topics in neurotoxicity, vol 2. Springer, Boston, MA, pp 357–370

Brandon AL (2011) Spatial and temporal trends in mercury concentrations in the blood and hair of Florida panthers (*Puma concolor coryi*). Unpublished MS Thesis. Florida Gulf Coast University. Ft. Myers, FL

Burger J (1993) Metals in avian feathers: bioindicators of environmental pollution. Rev Environ Toxicol 5:203–311

Caudill G, Onorato DP, Cunningham MW, Caudill D, Leone EH, Smith LM, Jansen D (2019) Temporal trends in Florida panther food habits. Hum Wildl Interact 13(1):87–97

Clarkson TW (1994) The toxicology of mercury and its compounds. In: Watras CJ, Huckabee JW (eds) Mercury pollution: integration and synthesis. CRC Press, Boca Raton, FL, pp 631–641

Cleckner LB, Garrison PJ, Hurley JP, Olson ML, Krabbenhoft DP (1998) Trophic transfer of methyl mercury in the northern Florida Everglades. Biogeochemistry 40(2/3):347–361

Damseaux F, Kiszka JJ, Heithaus MR et al (2017) Spatial variation in the accumulation of POPs and mercury in bottlenose dolphins of the lower Florida keys and the coastal Everglades (South Florida). Environ Pollut 220:577–587

Eccles KM, Thomas PJ, Chan HM (2017) Predictive meta-regressions relating mercury tissue concentrations of freshwater piscivorous mammals. Environ Toxicol Chem 36(9):2377–2384. https://doi.org/10.1002/etc.3775

Eisler R (1987) Mercury hazards to fish, wildlife, and invertebrates: a synoptic review. U.S. Fish and Wildlife Service Biological Report 85(1.10), 90 pp

Evans DW, Crumley PH (2005) Mercury in Florida bay fish: spatial distribution of elevated concentrations and possible linkages to Everglades restoration. Bull Mar Sci 77(3):321–346

Evers DC, Savoy LJ, Desorbo CR, Yates DE, Hanson W, Taylor KM, Siegel LS, Cooley JH, Bank MS, Major A, Munney K, Mower BF, Vogel HS, Schoch N, Pokras M, Goodale MW, Fair J (2008) Adverse effects from environmental mercury loads on breeding common loons. Ecotoxicology 17:69–81

Florida Department of Health (FDOH) (2019) Your guide to eating fish caught in Florida. http://www.floridahealth.gov/. Accessed 25 November 2019

Frederick PC, Jayasena N (2011) Altered pairing behaviour and reproductive success in white ibises exposed to environmentally relevant concentrations of methylmercury. Proc Biol Sci R Soc 278:1851–1857

Frederick PC, Spalding MG, Sepulveda MS, Williams GE Jr, Nico L, Robbins R (1999) Exposure of great egret nestlings to mercury through diet in the Everglades of Florida. Environ Toxicol Chem 18:1940–1947

Frederick PC, Hylton BA, Heath JA, Spalding MG (2004) A historical record of mercury contamination in southern Florida as inferred from avian feather tissue. Environ Toxicol Chem 23:1474–1478

Frederick PC, Axelrad D, Atkeson T, Pollman C (2005) Contaminants research and policy: the Everglades mercury story. Natl Wetlands Newsl 27:3

Fuchsman PC, Brown LE, Henning MH, Bock MJ, Magar VS (2017) Toxicity reference values for methylmercury effects on avian reproduction: critical review and analysis. Environ Toxicol Chem 36:294–319

Fury JR, Roettiger T, Morello F (2001) Everglades Region Fisheries Investigations Project Completion Report. Florida and Wildlife Conservation Commission. Project F-56, Everglades Fisheries Investigations 1998-2001, 23pp

Garrison E, Leone EH, Smith K, Bartareau T, Bozzo J, Sobczak R, Jackson D (2011) Analysis of Hydrological Impacts on White-Tailed Deer in the Stairsteps Unit, Big Cypress National Preserve, 21pp

Gould WW (2011) Use poisson rather than regress; tell a friend. The Stata Blog: Not Elsewhere Classified. http://blog.stata.com/2011/08/22/use-poisson-rather-than-regress-tell-a-friend/

Haake PW, Dean JM (1983) Age and growth of four Everglades fishes using otolith techniques. Technical report SFRC-83/03, Everglades National Park, Homestead, FL

Hord LJ, Jennings M, Brunell, A (1990) Mercury contamination of Florida alligators. In: Proceedings of the 10th Working Meeting of the Crocodile Specialist Group of the Species Survival Commission of the World Conservation Union convened at Gainesville, FL, 23–27 April 1990

Hueter RE, Fong WG, Henderson G, French M, Manire CA (1995) Methylmercury concentration in shark muscle by species, size and distribution of sharks in Florida coatal waters. Water Air Soil Pollut 80:893–899

Kalla PI, Scheidt DJ (2017) Everglades ecosystem assessment – Phase IV, 2014: data reduction and initial synthesis. United States Environmental Protection Agency, Science and Ecosystem Support Division, Athens, GA. SESD Project 14–0380, 58pp

Lange TR, Royals HE, Connor LL (1994) Mercury accumulation in largemouth bass (*Micropterus salmoides*) in a Florida Lake. Arch Environ Contamin Toxicol 27:466–471

Lodge TE (1994) The Everglades handbook: understanding the ecosystem. St. Lucie Press, Delray Beach, FL

Loftus WF (2000) Accumulation and fate of mercury in an ever-glades aquatic food web. PhD dissertation, Florida International University

Loftus WF, Kushlan JA (1987) Freshwater fishes of southern Florida. Bull Florida State Mus Biol Sci 31(4):147–344

Matulik AG, Kerstetter DW, Hammerschlag N, Divoll T, Hammerschmidt CR, Evers DC (2017) Bioaccumulation and biomagnification of mercury and methylmercury in four sympatric coastal sharks in a protected subtropical lagoon. Mar Pollut Bull 116(1–2):357–364

McIvor C, Ley J, Bjork R (1994) Changes in freshwater inflow from the Evergaldes to Florida Bay including effects on biota and biotic processes: a review. In: Davis SM, Ogden JC (eds) Everglades: the ecosystem and its restoration. St. Luci Press, Delray Beach, pp117–148

Monteiro LR, Furness RW (1995) Seabirds as monitors of mercury in the marine environment. Water Air Soil Pollut 80:851–870

Ogden JC, Robertson WB Jr, Davis GE, Schmidt TW (1974) Pesticide, polychlorinated biphenols and heavy metals in Upper Food Chain Levels, Everglades National Park and Vicinity. National Park Service, Everglades National Park, Homestead, FL

Porcella DB, Zilliouz EJ, Grieb TM, Newman JR, West GB (2004) Retrospective study of mercury in Raccoons (*Procyon lotor*) in South Florida. Ecotoxicology 13:207–221

Reistad NA (2018) Mercury Exposure Pathways and Risks for Neonatal and Juvenile Blacktip Sharks (*Carcharhinus limbatus*) of Charlotte Harbor. Unpublished Master Thesis. Florida Gulf Coast University, pp 44

Roelke M, Schultz D, Facemire C, Sundlof S, Royals H (1991) Mercury contamination in Florida panthers. Prepared by the Technical Subcommittee of the Florida Panther Interagency Committee, 26pp

Rumbold DG, Fink LE, Laine KA, Niemczyk SL, Chandrasekhar T, Wankel SD, Kendall C (2002) Levels of mercury in alligators (*Alligator mississippiensis*) collected along a transect through the Florida Everglades. Sci Total Environ 297:239–252

Rumbold D, Wasno R, Hammerschlag N, Volety A (2014) Mercury accumulation in sharks from the coastal waters of Southwest Florida. Arch Environ Contam Toxicol 67:402–412

Rumbold DG, Miller KE, Dellinger TA, Haas N (2017) Mercury concentrations in feathers of adult and nestling osprey (*Pandion haliaetus*) from coastal and freshwater environments of Florida. Arch Environ Contam Toxicol 72:31–38

Rumbold DG, Lange TR, Richard D, DelPizzo G, Hass N (2018) Mercury biomagnification through food webs along a salinity gradient down-estuary from a biological hotspot. Estuar Coast Shelf Sci 200:116–125

Santos Silva JMC, Tenreyro S (2006) The log of gravity. Rev Econ Stat 88(4):641–658

Scheidt DJ, Kalla PI (2007) Everglades ecosystem assessment: water management and quality, eutrophication, mercury contamination, soils and habitat: monitoring for adaptive management: a R-EMAP status report. USEPA Region 4, Athens, GA. EPA 904-R-07-001, 98pp

Scheuhammer AM, Meyer MW, Sandheinrich MB, Murray MW (2007) Effects of environmental methylmercury on the health of wild birds, mammals, and fish. Ambio 36:12–18

Spalding MG, Frederick PC, McGill HC, Bouton SN, McDowell LR (2000) Methylmercury accumulation in tissues and its effects on growth and appetite in captive Great Egrets. J Wildl Dis 36:411–422

StataCorp (2017) Stata statistical software: release 15. StataCorp LLC, College Station, TX

Stober QJ, Thornton K,Jones R, Richards J, Ivey C, Welch R, Madden M, Trexler J, Gaiser E, Scheidt D, Rathbun S (2001) South Florida ecosystem assessment: phase I/II (technical report) – Everglades stressor interactions: Hydropatterns, eutrophication, habitat alteration, and mercury contamination. EPA 904-R-01-003

Strom DG, Graves GA (2001) A comparison of mercury in estuarine fish between Florida Bay and the Indian River Lagoon, Florida, USA. Estuaries 24:597–609

Thompson DR, Furness RW (1989) Comparison of the levels of total and organic mercury in seabird feathers. Mar Pollut Bull 20:577–579

USEPA (1997) Mercury study report to Congress. Volume VI: an ecological assessment for anthropogenic mercury emissions in the United States. USEPA Office of Air Quality Planning & Standards and Office of Research and Development. EPA-452/R-97-008

USEPA (2001) Water quality criterion for the protection of human health: methylmercury. Washington, DC, EPA/823/R-01-001

Whitney MC, Cristol DA (2017) Impacts of sublethal mercury exposure on birds: a detailed review. Rev Environ Contam Toxicol 244:113–163

Wiener JG, Bodaly RA, Brown SS, Lucotte M, Newman MC, Porcella DB et al (2007) Monitoring and evaluating trends in methylmercury accumulation in aquatic biota. In: Harris R, Krabbenhoft DB, Mason R, Murray MW, Reash R, Saltman T (eds) Ecosystem responses to mercury contamination: indicators of change: Society of Environmental Toxicology and Chemistry (SETAC) North America Workshop on Mercury Monitoring and Assessment. CRC Press, New York, pp 47–87

Wolfe MF, Schwarzbach S, Sulaiman RA (1998) Effects of mercury on wildlife: a comprehensive review. Environ Toxicol Chem 17:146–160

Yanochko GM, Jago CH, Brisbin IL Jr (1997) Tissue mercury concentrations in alligators (*Alligator mississippiensis*) from the Florida Everglades and the Savannah River site, South Carolina. Arch Environ Contam Toxicol 32:323–328

Zabala JA, Meade M, Frederick PC (2019) Variation in nestling feather mercury concentrations at individual, brood, and breeding colony levels: implications for sampling mercury in birds. Sci Total Environ 671:617–621

Chapter 3
Legacy Mercury

Curtis D. Pollman and Daniel R. Engstrom

Abstract Legacy mercury (Hg) refers to Hg in the environment that originated with antecedent or historical releases and has the potential to continue to impact the environment over time after the source—*e.g.,* atmospheric emissions or industrial releases—has been reduced or eliminated. Depending upon its magnitude and where in the environment it is stored, legacy Hg can affect the cycling of Hg with a turnover time of centuries at the global scale to a few years or decades at watershed or more localized levels. This chapter examines how legacy Hg can impact Hg cycling and recovery in the Everglades. This analysis includes examining the current global cycling of Hg and how disequilibrium related to legacy Hg is expected to continue to influence rates of atmospheric deposition well beyond current and anticipated efforts to reduce anthropogenic emissions. The chapter also considers the question of legacy Hg stored in Everglades soils and sediments and the likelihood that such legacy Hg will militate against restoration efforts over shorter time scales (years).

Keywords Methylmercury · Gaseous elemental mercury · Global cycle · Emissions reduction scenario · Sediments · Recovery · Box model · Deep ocean turnover · R-EMAP

3.1 Introduction

From a conceptual perspective, mitigating or reducing the mercury (Hg) burden in Everglades biota and its associated, cascading impacts can be approached by several different strategies. Perhaps the most obvious—but not necessarily the most

C. D. Pollman (✉)
Aqua Lux Lucis, Inc., Gainesville, FL, USA
e-mail: cpollman@aqualuxlucis.org

D. R. Engstrom
St. Croix Watershed Research Station, Science Museum of Minnesota, Marine on St. Croix, MN, USA
e-mail: dre@umn.edu

C. D. Pollman et al. (eds.), *Mercury and the Everglades. A Synthesis and Model for Complex Ecosystem Restoration*, https://doi.org/10.1007/978-3-030-55635-8_3

achievable—approach is to reduce the amount of inorganic Hg available to drive methylation. The idea of controlling Hg as a possible mitigation strategy has four supporting components: (1) direct atmospheric inputs are the primary source of Hg to the Everglades (see Sect. 3.3.1); (2) current atmospheric deposition fluxes to the Everglades are likely 3 times or more higher than fluxes that occurred in preindustrial times (Chap. 1, this volume); (3) the relationship between Hg concentrations and Hg methylation is likely linear (Chap. 1, Volume II); and (4) decreases in concentrations of Hg in aquatic biota and related wildlife corresponding (or in response) to declining inputs of atmospheric Hg are well-documented in both North America and Scandinavia (*e.g.*, Johansson et al. 2001; Monson et al. 2011; Blukacz-Richards et al. 2017).

A second approach to mitigating the Hg burden in Everglades biota considers ongoing anthropogenic perturbations to the Everglades that have affected the biogeochemical cycling of Hg and its bioaccumulation in the Everglades independent of changing atmospheric inputs of Hg. Perhaps the most striking and important example of such a perturbation has been widespread increases in surface water sulfate concentrations resulting primarily from the use of fertilizer amendments to manipulate soil pH in the Everglades Agricultural Area (EAA) and, to a lesser extent, hydrologic changes to the EAA landscape that have resulted in the upward migration of sulfate-enriched connate seawater in some of the major canals draining the EAA (see Chaps. 2 and 3, Volume II for a discussion of sources and the causal link between sulfate and Hg methylation, respectively). This chapter considers the first strategy, and more specifically, the possible effects of historical, anthropogenically enriched earth-surface reservoirs (*legacy* Hg) as a modifying factor on the effect of changing atmospheric emissions on the deposition flux dynamics and on ecosystem response to those changes in deposition.

How quickly the Hg burden in Everglades biota will respond to a change in a driving variable is largely a function of how rapidly the pool or reservoir of the driving variable turns over—*i.e.*, its residence time—in the environment. Assuming well-mixed dynamics within the pool and a stepped change in inputs, the magnitude of the driving variable pool will approximate equilibrium with its new inputs within three residence times. Thus, if the pool of legacy Hg governing methylation and Hg bioaccumulation is 10 years, the temporal response of the ecosystem to a stepped decrease in Hg inputs expectedly will follow an exponential decay curve that will approximate the new steady state within 30 years.

From a landscape or spatial perspective, legacy Hg in the environment can influence changes in the aquatic Hg signal driving methylation through both large scale and local scale processes. Large scale process pathways consider the global atmospheric cycling of Hg and the oxidation of gaseous elemental Hg (GEM) to Hg (II), which is readily scavenged from the atmosphere and deposited to the landscape via wet and dry deposition. The two primary pools of legacy Hg that influence atmospheric deposition of Hg through continued releases or re-emissions into the atmosphere and subsequent deposition include terrestrial soils and the oceans. Localized scale processes consider the storage or burden of deposited Hg in upland soils and sediments within the water body of interest that, at least in concept, can continually serve as a substrate to drive methylation until deep burial removes Hg from either the zone of active transport from upland soils to the aquatic ecosystem, or from the zone of methylation in surficial sediments that also are actively exchanging with the water column.

3.2 Legacy Hg Effects on Atmospheric Deposition of Hg

The global cycling of atmospheric Hg involves coupling of the atmosphere and its processing of elemental Hg and Hg(II) (gaseous and particulate) to terrestrial (Mason 2009; Zhang et al. 2016) and oceanic pools of Hg (Mason and Sheu 2002; Strode et al. 2007), as well as releases of geologically-derived Hg (*e.g.,* volcanic emissions and geothermal releases; Schroeder and Munthe 1998; Mason 2009). An early example of a conceptual model that embodied these concepts and considered the effects of legacy re-emissions on atmospheric cycling of Hg was presented by Schroeder and Munthe (1998). Improved understanding and parameterization of these processes have led to the development of numerical global Hg cycling models that have been used to estimate fluxes between the atmospheric, oceanic and terrestrial pools and how changing emission scenarios will likely affect atmospheric deposition fluxes of Hg. Two key examples of such models are the Global/Regional Atmospheric Heavy Metals (GRAHM) model (Dastoor et al. 2015) and the Goddard Earth Observing System (GEOS-Chem) model (Selin et al. 2008).

Amos et al. (2013) have developed a global biogeochemical Hg box model based on GEOS-Chem as implemented by Streets et al. (2011). The Amos et al. model couples the time-dependent dynamics of Hg turnover and exchange among oceanic, terrestrial and atmospheric reservoirs and comprises 7 boxes, including three different pools of Hg associated with surficial soils and vegetation, three oceanic pools (surface, subsurface, and deep ocean), and the atmosphere (Fig. 3.1). The model also includes geogenic emissions (*i.e.,* volcanic emissions, crustal weathering and degassing) as an external input because the deep mineral reservoir supporting these emissions has a very long residence time (~ 1×10^9 years).

The relatively simple structure of the Amos et al. box model makes it well suited for evaluating different emission scenarios and how legacy Hg stored in different reservoirs will quantitatively affect atmospheric deposition fluxes over time. For example, Amos et al. simulated the changes in atmospheric deposition fluxes if 2008 emission fluxes from anthropogenic sources were held constant, completely eliminated, reduced by 50%, or increased according to emissions projected forward to 2050 developed by Streets et al. (2009). The Streets et al. (2009) emission scenarios were the first projections of future Hg emissions published in the open literature and were based in part on a series of energy and fuel use forecasts developed by Streets et al. (2004) and which were predicated on growth scenarios developed by the Intergovernmental Panel on Climate Change (IPCC).

A more recent set of global Hg emission scenarios projected forward to 2050 has been developed by Rafaj et al. (2013). In this case future emissions were based on

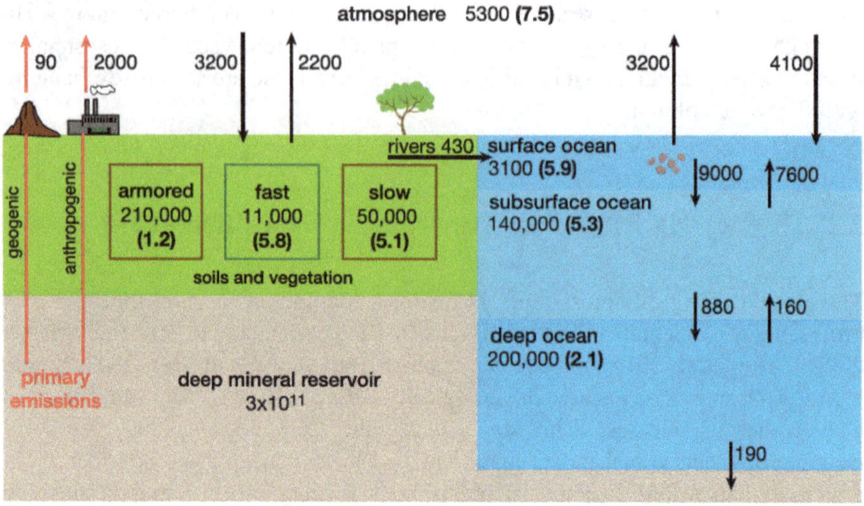

Fig. 3.1 Box model developed by Amos et al. (2013) to depict global cycling of Hg. Fluxes (Mg/year) and reservoir storages (Mg) represent estimated conditions in 2008. Values in () represent estimated enrichment ratios (current to natural) in each reservoir. See Amos et al. (2013) for a more detailed schematic depicting fluxes from the three individual terrestrial reservoirs. Reprinted with permission

projections of energy consumption that reflected either a continuation of current governmental energy and climate policies, or implementation of climate policies to limit the increase in average global temperatures by 2050 to about 2 °C. Superimposed on these two broad scenarios were various degrees of Hg emission reduction strategies that considered individual country initiatives to control air pollution, full adoption of the best available technologies to control emissions of Hg by 2030 and beyond, and elimination of Hg emissions associated with artisanal small-scale gold mining activities.

We have used the Rafaj et al. (2013) projected emissions as input to the Amos et al. (2013) box model to illustrate some key aspects of the effects of legacy Hg in the terrestrial and oceanic pools on likely changes in global depositional fluxes of atmospheric Hg. The original parameterization of the Amos et al. (2013) model subsequently has been revised both by Amos et al. (2014) and Song et al. (2015) (Table 3.1). Primary variable changes implemented by Amos et al. (2014) included increasing gross GEM fluxes to and from the ocean surface and reducing GEM losses from terrestrial compartments by an order of magnitude. Using the Amos et al. (2014) inputs as a starting point, Song et al. (2015) further re-parameterized the model using inverse modeling to optimize the model inputs and coefficients. Parameter changes implemented by Song et al. (2015) include mass exchange between the surface and subsurface ocean water and shifts in GEM fluxes to and from terrestrial reservoirs towards values that more closely approximate the original gaseous exchange fluxes used by Amos et al. (2013).

Table 3.1 Hg reservoir magnitudes (Mg) and mass fluxes (Mg/year) between reservoirs used in the Amos et al. (2013) 7-box Hg global biogeochemical cycling model and as re-parameterized by Amos et al. (2014) and Song et al. (2015)

Reservoir/flux component	Amos et al. (2013)	Amos et al. (2013)	Song et al. (2015)
Atmosphere	5000	5000	4400
Hg(II) deposition to ocean	3900	3600	4000
Hg(0) deposition to ocean	40	1700	1500
Hg(II) deposition to land	1500	1500	1620
Hg(0) deposition to land	1500	1500	1320
Surface ocean	2900	2900	4100
Hg(0) evasion	3000	4700	4800
Particle settling to subsurface ocean	3300	3300	340
Water transfer to subsurface ocean	5100	5100	7300
Subsurface ocean	130,000	130,000	123,000
Particle settling to deep ocean	480	480	460
Water transfer to surface ocean	7100	7100	7000
Water transfer to deep ocean	340	340	320
Deep ocean	220,000	220,000	220,000
Burial to deep sediments	210	210	210
Water transfer to subsurface ocean	180	180	180
Fast terrestrial pool	9600	9600	9600
Evasion due to respiration of organic carbon	460	45	360
Photochemical re-emission of deposited Hg	850	85	680
Biomass burning	290	290	200
Transfer to slow pool	330	330	330
Transfer to armored pool	10	10	10
River runoff to surface ocean	365	710	710
Slow soil pool	35,000	35,000	35,000
Evasion due to respiration of organic carbon	250	25	200
Biomass burning	8	8	6
Transfer to fast pool	210	210	210
River runoff to surface ocean	10	20	20
Armored soil pool	190,000	190,000	190,000
Evasion due to respiration of organic carbon	25	3	20
Biomass burning	4	4	3
Transfer to fast pool	15	15	15
River runoff to surface ocean	5	10	10
Deep mineral reservoir	3E+11	3E+11	3E+11
Geogenic emission	90	90	90

We have used the model parameterization developed by Song et al. (2015) for our analysis. The model was initialized with storages for the various Hg reservoirs specified by Song et al. (2015) with the assumption that those storages are applicable to 2008. Anthropogenic emissions were initialized at 2270 Mg/year based on Horowitz et al. (2017). Emission trajectories forward in time were based on percentage increases between 2005 and 2050 obtained from Rafaj et al. (2013) and were constructed using linear interpolation to apply the relative changes in the trajectories from 2008 forward. Four emission trajectories were developed based on Rafaj et al. (2013) projections:

- Baseline scenario—This scenario is based on full implementation by 2030 of legislative controls on Hg emissions currently in place for each of the 162 countries included in the Rafaj et al. analysis. It also assumes no further strengthening of those reductions between 2030 and 2050.
- Climate mitigation scenario—This scenario imposes further emission reductions on the baseline scenario by including the effects of the implementation of climate policies to limit the increase in average global temperatures by 2050 to about 2 °C. It also includes the effects of imposing other control measures considered by Rafaj et al. (2013) to be the maximum feasibly possible but excludes any controls on emissions related to artisanal small-scale gold mining.
- Maximum reduction scenario—This scenario includes the cessation of Hg emissions related to artisanal small-scale gold mining coupled with the climate mitigation scenario.
- Zero emissions scenario—This scenario superimposes a complete reduction in all direct anthropogenic emissions. The initial trajectory follows the maximum reduction scenario emissions until 2020, followed by a linear decrease to zero emissions achieved in 2030. The effects of completely eliminating all direct anthropogenic emissions was also considered by Amos et al. (2013) and illustrates the temporal lag imposed by legacy Hg on returning to natural, steady state atmospheric deposition fluxes.

The emission trajectories were extended to 2100 by assuming that the estimated anthropogenic emissions predicted for 2050 remained constant thereafter (Fig. 3.2). Simulated changes in global Hg deposition normalized to 2008 for each of the four scenarios are shown in Fig. 3.3.

The simulations illustrate several key points about the global Hg cycle. First, and as discussed by Amos et al. (2013), global Hg dynamics are in disequilibrium; restated, the storages of Hg in the different terrestrial and oceanic reservoirs are not in equilibrium with current emission levels. This is perhaps best shown by the climate mitigation scenario, which assumes that global emissions decrease by 14% by 2030, return to approximately 2008 emission levels by 2050, and then remain constant.[1] Under this scenario, atmospheric deposition fluxes are stable through

[1]The upwards shift in the climate mitigation emissions scenario projected between 2030 and 2050 is due to projected increases in artisanal small-scale gold mining not removed under this scenario.

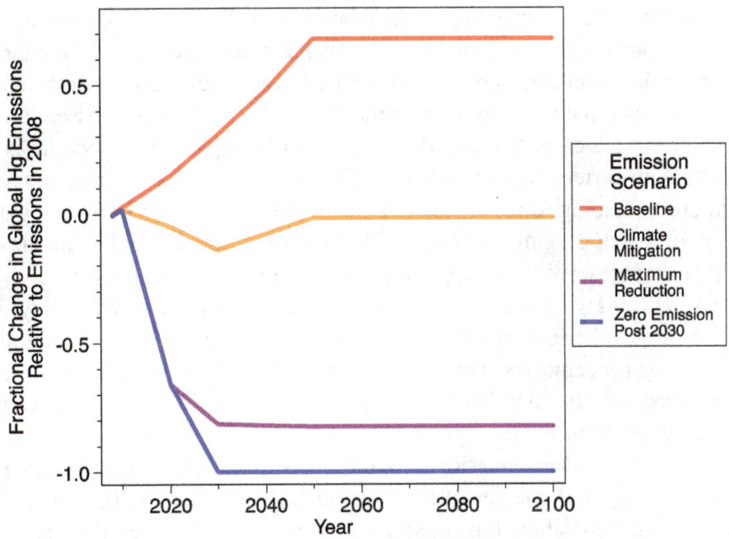

Fig. 3.2 Global Hg emission trajectory scenarios used as input to the Amos et al. (2013) box model. The initial year in the scenarios is 2008, which corresponds to the year for which Amos et al. detailed storages in each of the model compartments. Values shown are fractional change in emissions relative to emissions in 2008 obtained from Rafaj et al. (2013), with 2008 emissions corresponding to the value used by Amos et al. (2000 Mg/year)

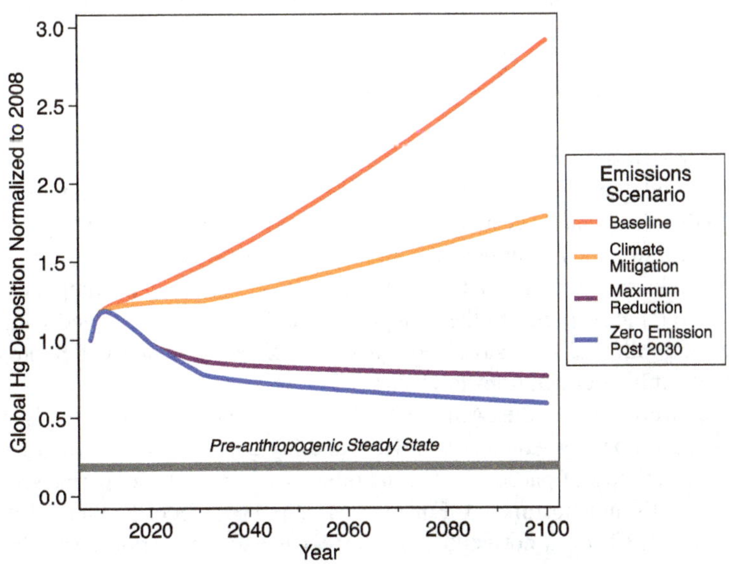

Fig. 3.3 Simulated changes in global atmospheric deposition fluxes of Hg relative to modeled deposition in 2008. Each curve show the effects of different Hg emission scenarios, with the zero emission curve illustrating the effects of legacy Hg imposed on deposition dynamics after 2030 (when anthropogenic emissions are assumed to be wholly eliminated)

2030 but do not decline in response to the relatively small decreases in emissions prior to 2030. Deposition fluxes then begin to increase monotonically throughout the remainder of the simulation despite constant emissions after 2050. Both the initial stable response and the increase in deposition following the return to essentially 2008 emissions levels indicates that the global system of coupled Hg reservoirs is not at steady-state with current deposition fluxes. This of course is not surprising given that, based on current storages and fluxes out, residence times in the terrestrial slow and armored pools are approximately 70 and 3900 years respectively and in the subsurface and deep oceanic reservoirs are approximately 16 and 560 years respectively.

Second, legacy Hg stored in terrestrial and oceanic reservoirs will delay the full response of atmospheric deposition fluxes to sustained changes in direct anthropogenic emissions for centuries. This is illustrated by Fig. 3.3 which shows for the zero emissions scenario the simulated changes in atmospheric deposition relative to steady state deposition fluxes expected to have occurred prior to the release of any anthropogenically related emissions. While deposition fluxes decay fairly rapidly between 2010 and 2030, the rate of decay is much less rapid after 2030. By 2100, the predicted global deposition flux is still approximately 2.8 times the natural flux. 500 years into the simulation, atmospheric deposition is still 1.7 times natural levels.

The effect of legacy Hg and disequilibrium is such that current anthropogenic emissions (based on Horowitz et al. 2017) need to be immediately reduced by approximately 50% or more to ensure that global atmospheric deposition remains below current levels through 2050 (Fig. 3.4). Long-term simulations (20,000 years), however, indicate that anthropogenic emissions need to be reduced to less than 18% of current levels for steady state atmospheric deposition fluxes to approximate current levels (Fig. 3.5). This long-term dynamic reflects the slow buffering of perturbations in atmospheric emissions imposed by the long residence time terrestrial and oceanic reservoirs.

The long-term simulation shown in Fig. 3.5 also illustrates an important aspect of the global model discussed by Amos et al. (2013). The atmospheric box turns over quite rapidly (less than 1 year) but is also coupled to far more slowly responding boxes. As a result, the response of the atmospheric box to changes in anthropogenic emissions released directly to the atmosphere has two overall components—an initial, quite rapid response to the change in emissions that is achieved within less than 3 years, followed by a sustained, far slower response which will approximate steady state only after centuries have passed.

One concern about the Amos et al. (2013) model that extends to the re-parameterizations by Amos et al. (2014) and Song et al. (2015) is the likelihood that net burial fluxes of particulate Hg in both coastal and pelagic marine sediments are substantially underestimated. For example, the box model as implemented by Amos et al. (2013) does not explicitly consider net sedimentation losses from the surface ocean although pelagic net sedimentation fluxes approximating 210 Mg/year are included. In contrast, Zaferani et al. (2018) estimate global net Hg accumulation rates ranging from 850 to 1166 Mg/year based on measured accumulation rates in diatom ooze sediments.

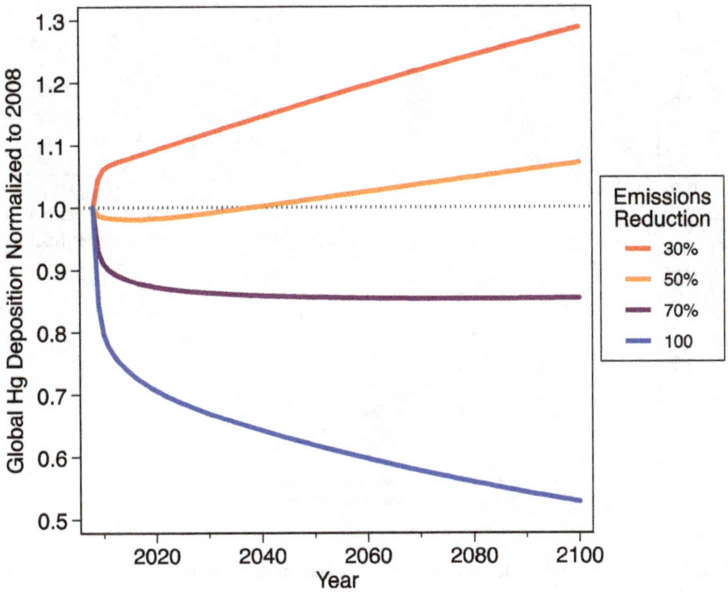

Fig. 3.4 Simulated changes in global atmospheric deposition fluxes of Hg relative to modeled deposition in 2008 to stepped reductions in anthropogenic emissions (30, 50, 70, and 100%). Fluxes are normalized to the total Hg deposition flux predicted to occur at the beginning of the simulation (2008)

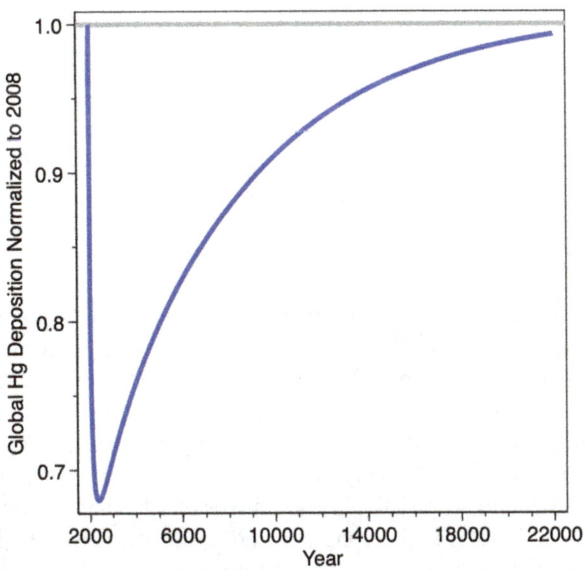

Fig. 3.5 Long-term (20,000 years) simulation of the effects on global atmospheric Hg deposition of a stepped 82.5% reduction in all direct anthropogenic Hg emissions to the atmospheric beginning in 2008

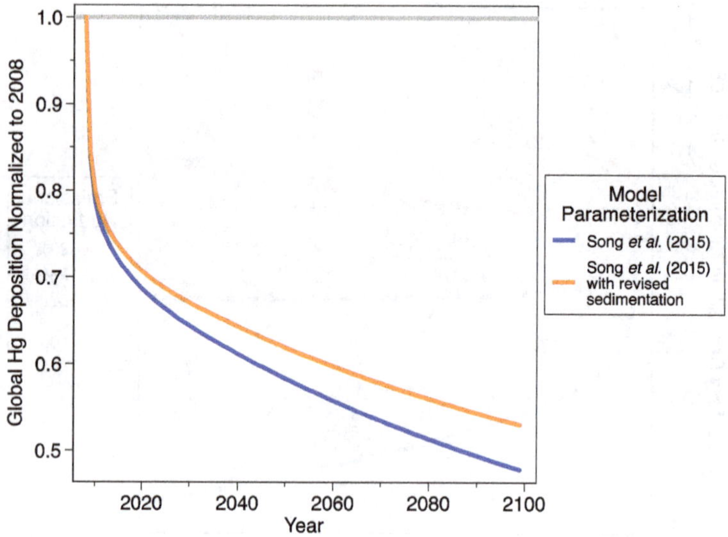

Fig. 3.6 Effects of including increased Hg sedimentation in coastal and pelagic sediments according to Outridge et al. (2018)

Table 3.2 Effect of different published parameterizations of the 7-box global Hg cycling model on total Hg residence times in each of the three oceanic compartments included in the model

	Total Hg residence time (year)		
Model parameterization	Surface	Subsurface	Deep
Amos et al. (2013)	0.254	16.4	564
Amos et al. (2014)	0.221	16.4	564
Song et al. (2015)	0.233	16.7	564
Song et al. (2015) with Outridge et al. (2018) net sedimentation	0.229	16.7	282

Also included is the effect of adding Hg net sedimentation losses to the surface ocean layer and increasing the deep ocean layer net sedimentation losses used by Outridge et al. (2018) and applied to the Song et al. (2015) parameterization

This apparent underestimation of marine sedimentation losses can result in substantially slower response times by the deep ocean layer than might otherwise be predicted assuming faster burial rates and thus a more protracted and greater effect of legacy Hg on the recovery of atmospheric deposition fluxes in response to emissions reductions. This is illustrated by comparing the total Hg residence time for the deep ocean layer for different model parameterizations, including one that incorporates coastal and deep sedimentation fluxes of 200 and 600 Mg/year utilized by Outridge et al. (2018) into the Song et al. (2015) model (Fig. 3.6; Table 3.2).

Because net sedimentation is a relatively minor flux of Hg out of the surface ocean layer, including it explicitly in the box model has very little effect on the surface ocean layer Hg residence time. On the other hand, increasing net sedimentation losses in the deep ocean layer (without any further modifications to the model) cuts the Hg residence time by a factor of two (from 564 to 282 years). While the practical consequences of this shift in the Hg residence time of the deep ocean may be relatively minor over the near-term (several decades) with respect to legacy fluxes and response to perturbations in atmospheric inputs, the sensitivity of the residence time estimate to this single variable highlights the need for improved understanding of marine Hg cycling. Indeed, as noted by Outridge et al. (2018), until this understanding is improved, "prediction of the timeline and effects of global emission reductions will remain uncertain."

3.3 Watershed and In situ Scale Legacy Effects on Hg Biogeochemical Cycling

Legacy Hg that can influence aquatic cycling at a watershed scale broadly includes two different types of pools: (1) Hg stored within upland catchment soils; and (2) Hg stored in sediments within the aquatic ecosystem itself. In this section we briefly examine how legacy Hg within both of these pools can influence aquatic ecosystem recovery in response to declining Hg atmospheric inputs. The section then concludes with an analysis of the legacy Hg question specific to the Everglades.

3.3.1 Legacy Hg Stored in Upland Soils and Catchments

Hg methylation and other key processes of the biogeochemical cycling of Hg in aquatic ecosystems, including the Everglades, is linearly constrained or limited by the bioavailability of Hg(II) (Orihel et al. 2006, 2007; Gilmour et al. 2004). Previously deposited Hg stored in upland soils and catchments is thus relevant only if the legacy Hg is or can be exported in a bioavailable form, or if the Hg exported has been already methylated, principally as the Hg flows through riparian wetlands. Isotopic addition studies conducted at a watershed scale as part of the METAALICUS Project (Mercury Experiment to Assess Atmospheric Loading in Canada and the United States; Harris et al. 2007) have shown that newly deposited Hg behaves differently than aged, strongly bound Hg resident in soil and vegetation (Hintelmann et al. 2002).

The response dynamics of aquatic ecosystems to changing inputs of atmospheric Hg can be complicated, and ultimately depend on the geochemical and hydrologic characteristics of the individual ecosystem (Munthe et al. 2007; Brigham et al. 2014). Larger watersheds with comparatively smaller volumes of surface water appear to be less responsive (Lorey and Driscoll 1999; Kamman and Engstrom 2002; Mills et al. 2009), in all likelihood because of the larger amounts of Hg stored in watershed soils (Grigal 2002). Consistent with the results from METAALICUS indicating that the export of deposited Hg from upland soils proceeds slowly (Harris et al. 2007), simulation studies indicate that temporal lags in response to changing atmospheric fluxes of Hg are longest for systems with larger watersheds, while seepage lakes (which receive the majority of their hydrologic income from precipitation falling directly on the lake surface) respond more rapidly (Knightes et al. 2009). The lag in response is driven by the effective travel time of infiltrating precipitation moving through the soil column and laterally to the receptor water body; it also can reflect release of legacy Hg when atmospheric inputs are reduced. As a result, current concentrations of Hg in some aquatic ecosystems may reflect changes in atmospheric inputs of Hg that occurred decades earlier (Drevnick et al. 2012) and have yet to come to equilibrium with current atmospheric inputs (Mills et al. 2009).

3.3.2 Legacy Hg Stored in Aquatic Ecosystem Sediments

The importance of sediments in aquatic ecosystems serving as an internal source of contaminant resupply long after external inputs of the contaminant have been reduced or eliminated is well established for a number of contaminants, including perhaps most notably phosphorus (*e.g.*, Imboden and Lerman 1978; Nurnberg 1991; Mehner et al. 2008). Not surprisingly, there is some evidence that Hg deposited in surficial lake sediments can modulate or retard the response of aquatic ecosystems to changes in atmospheric inputs (Orihel et al. 2008). How important this legacy Hg is in modifying the dynamic response of aquatic ecosystems to changing inputs in turn has been argued to be related to how recently the Hg was deposited ("new" *vs.* "aged" Hg)—at least in part.

Compared to "aged" Hg, new "Hg" is highly reactive, resulting in more rapid biogeochemical processing in aquatic ecosystems (Poulain et al. 2006). For example, new Hg is preferentially adsorbed by suspended particulates in the water column, resulting in more rapid delivery to the sediment-water interface and enhanced rates of methylation (Chadwick et al. 2013). Aging of new Hg appears to be related to redox processes involving Fe and Mn near the oxic-anoxic boundary near the sediment-water interface (Chadwick et al. 2013).

Mesocosm studies using isotopic additions of Hg indicate that methylation of Hg stored in lake sediments continues over time, and theoretically can influence or retard aquatic ecosystem recovery dynamics (Orihel et al. 2008). Nonetheless—and consistent with the "new" Hg paradigm—the recovery of aquatic ecosystems in response to changing external inputs of Hg may not be substantively influenced by legacy Hg stored in surficial sediments. For example, Hodson et al. (2014) found that Hg concentrations in amphipods and fish in a lake previously contaminated with Hg originating from industrial activity were not related to surficial sediment concentrations of total Hg and methylmercury (MeHg); they further concluded that mitigation strategies should focus more on limiting external loadings rather than remediating the sediments.

The "new" vs. "aged" Hg paradigm, however, is not firmly supported by the literature. There are clear examples of legacy Hg derived from localized anthropogenic activities that can continue to adversely impact aquatic ecosystems decades after the localized releases were terminated (Foxgrover et al. 2019; Brent and Berberich 2014). A particularly striking example is the lower Penobscot River and upper estuary located in Maine (USA). Between 1967 and 2000, this site received between 6 to 12 tonnes of Hg directly discharged from a local chlor-alkali plant when the plant was operational (Kopec et al. 2019). Most of this Hg was released before the early 1970s when the plant's chlor-alkali cells were operational (Rudd et al. 2018). Nearly five decades later, elevated Hg concentrations continue to persist in the sediments. This persistence is driven by a "mobile pool" of legacy Hg that remains trapped in the upper estuary and continues to release Hg that in turn is deposited to surface sediments. Hg methylation in these surficial sediments occurs largely in the uppermost 3–5 cm in response to ongoing deposition of fresh, labile organic matter. As a result, high concentrations of Hg are observed in biota, including invertebrates, fish, and marsh birds with sediment-based food webs (Rudd et al. 2018; Kopec et al. 2019). Rudd et al. (2018) concluded that methylation of legacy Hg was the problem driving elevated biota Hg concentrations in the estuary and that the issue of "new" *vs.* "old" Hg more appropriately reflected whether the location of the Hg was favorable for methylation (see also Foxgrover et al. 2019). Similarly, localized contamination from releases of inorganic Hg into the South River (Virginia, USA) act as a continuing source of Hg to downstream portions of the river, resulting in more distributed methylation and increasing biota Hg concentrations downstream rather than serving as localized hotspots of methylation (Brent and Berberich 2014).

Modeling studies indicate that the vertical thickness of the surficial sediment lens comprising exchangeable, reactive or labile Hg that actively supports in situ methylation can exert a profound effect on aquatic ecosystem recovery following Hg load reductions (USEPA 2006; Knightes et al. 2009). For example, the dynamic Mercury Cycling Model (MCM) was used to compare the response time required to approach steady state (defined by the predicted concentration at *time* = 150 years) for two different exchange depth scenarios (USEPA 2006) in Devils Lake, WI. The first scenario considered the active exchange depth extended to 3 cm, which was the exchange depth typically used in MCM simulations prior to the Devils Lake study. The second scenario considered the exchange depth extending to only 3 mm, and was motivated by the then emerging evidence from METAALICUS that aquatic ecosystems react very rapidly to new inputs of Hg. The results from the MCM simulations indicate that, at least for Devils Lake, the time required to reach 95% of the predicted steady state response is quite sensitive to the magnitude of legacy Hg represented by the two different exchange depths (9.8 vs. 52 years; Fig. 3.7).

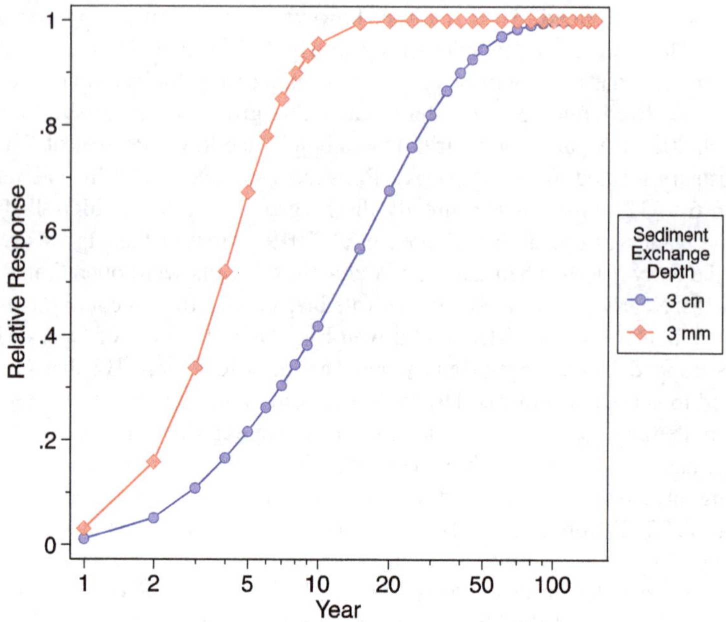

Fig. 3.7 Relative response in age 5 walleye MeHg concentrations predicted in Devil's Lake to a 50% reduction in atmospheric deposition inputs. Simulations were conducted using the dynamic MCM model (USEPA 2006). Plot compares two scenarios: the red curve shows the response assuming a 3 mm sediment exchange depth; the blue curve shows the response assuming a 3 cm sediment exchange depth. Time to reach 95% of the full response (defined here by the response at 150 years) is 9.8 and 51.9 years, respectively

3.3.3 Legacy Hg Stored in Everglades Soils and Sediment

3.3.3.1 Role of Everglades Sediments

Atmospheric sources of wet and dry deposition have long been considered the primary sources of mercury to the Everglades (Stober et al. 2001). More recently, Julian (in review) has estimated that wet deposition fluxes alone exceed surface water inputs throughout the Everglades Protection Area (EvPA) by ratios ranging from 47.5:1 to 49:1 for the period May 2015 through April 2016. Given that these input ratios only consider wet deposition and ignore dry deposition processes including stomatal uptake of GEM, the importance of direct deposition inputs is likely even higher. As a result, legacy Hg from a watershed scale perspective likely assumes any real significance with respect to that stored in the soils and sediments within the EvPA only, with continuing contributions from other upland sources expected to be comparatively minor.

Some insight into the possible role of sediment buffering of Hg methylation dynamics in the Everglades is afforded by model hindcasting using the Everglades version of the MCM (E-MCM; Harris et al. 2020; see also Chap. 4, this volume) at site 3A-15 within Water Conservation Area 3A. The hindcasting simulations were conducted to discriminate between different hypotheses regarding the drivers for temporal changes in largemouth bass concentrations of Hg observed at 3A-15, including changes in atmospheric deposition. The simulations indicate that changes in atmospheric deposition inferred from sediment core analyses may account for recent changes in largemouth bass Hg concentrations, but only if the size of the pool of Hg(II) that is readily bioavailable in surficial sediments for methylation is relatively small and turns over quickly. Simulations conducted with active sediment layers 3–5 cm thick resulted in response dynamics for MeHg that were simply too slow to match observations. Using a thinner sediment layer of 3 mm resulted in faster responses for Hg concentrations in sediments and improved concordance between observed and predicted biota concentrations over time. With recent sediment accumulation rates in the Everglades approximating 2.33 mm/year for relatively undisturbed sites (mean value, with standard deviation equal to 0.24 mm/year; Craft and Richardson 1993), such a thin active layer would reach equilibrium with a change in external Hg inputs in approximately 4 years. If we assume that the uncertainty in the estimated depth of the active sediment layer is log normally distributed and equates to a standard deviation of 100%, the aggregated uncertainty in the equilibrium response time ranges from approximately 0.9–12 years (upper and lower 10% quantiles).

A final question about legacy Hg stored in Everglades sediments considers the effects of sulfidization of dissolved organic matter (DOM) as a consequence of anthropogenic inputs of sulfate into the EvPA, originating largely from the EAA, and its impact on methylation of sediment Hg. Based on his review of experimental evidence from in situ Everglades mesocosms indicating DOM stimulates Hg methylation from sediment Hg, Graham (Chap. 4, Volume II) hypothesized that sulfidized DOM, which is more aromatic and more reactive, "could continue to mobilize legacy Hg" and that this possibility "has implications for ecosystem management and is worthy of further study."

3.3.3.2 Magnitude of Hg Stored in Everglades Sediments

To date, two studies have been conducted quantifying Hg concentrations in soils and sediments across the entirety of the EvPA. The first is the R-EMAP program (see also Sect. 1.3.2.2 in Chap. 1, this volume), which began in 1995 and has included nine sampling cycles over wet and dry periods in the marsh (five wet and four dry) to date, including the most recent sampling conducted during the wet season in 2014. R-EMAP has sampled 983 sites within the EvPA with valid analytical results for sediment total Hg samples. The second study was conducted by Cohen et al. (2009), who sampled 424 sites across the EvPA between May 2003 and January 2004. Both studies analyzed surficial soil/sediment samples integrated over 0–10 cm depth (if the bottom substrate allowed sampler penetration to that depth); both studies also used randomized stratification schemes to select sites for sampling. Median sediment total Hg concentrations between the R-EMAP and the Cohen et al. studies

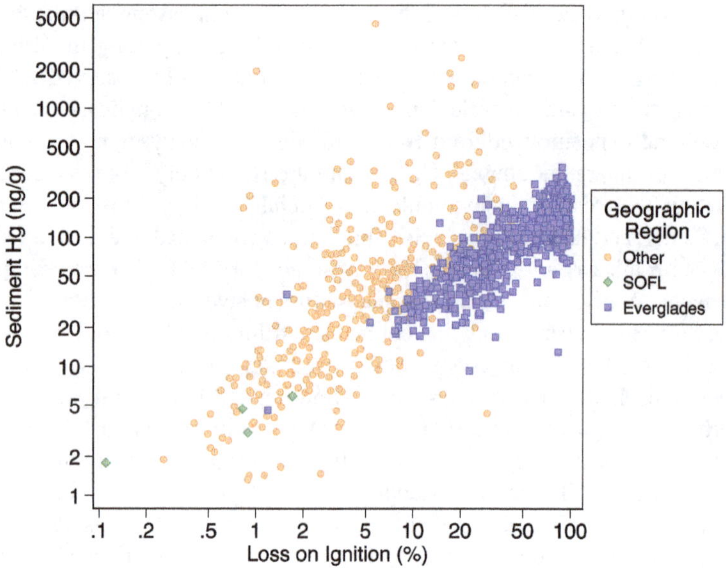

Fig. 3.8 Relationship between sediment concentrations of total Hg and loss on ignition. Everglades data from R-EMAP (1995–2014; $N = 979$). Other data and SOFL (south Florida) data from Bauch et al. (2009; 1998–2005; $N = 620$)

agree rather closely (130 *vs.* 126 ng/g respectively), although a comparison of mean values (127 *vs.* 189 ng/g) and maximum values (350 *vs.* 917 ng/g) indicates that the Cohen et al. included more sites greatly enriched with sediment Hg.

The spatial occurrence of Hg in surficial sediments in the Everglades is largely driven by the association of Hg with particulate organic matter and its accretion in bottom sediments. Correlations between sediment Hg and soil organic content (as represented by ash-free dry weight or loss on ignition (LOI)) were nearly identical ($r^2 = 0.70$ and 0.66, for R-EMAP EvPA sites and "unimpacted" sites sampled by Cohen et al. (2009), respectively). Whether higher rates of atmospheric deposition of Hg in south Florida also contribute to elevated sediment Hg in the Everglades can be examined by comparing the relationship between sediment Hg and organic matter content in Everglades with that of other regions in the United States. As part of the USGS National Water Quality Assessment (NAWQA) Program, Bauch et al. (2009) compiled sediment chemistry including total Hg and LOI from 46 different regions within the US, including four sites in south Florida, between 1998 and 2005. Figure 3.8 shows the relationship between sediment Hg and LOI for both the NAWQA sites and the R-EMAP sites. The plot clearly indicates that the sediment Hg normalized to LOI for the Everglades is lower compared to most other sites in the US.

Intercepts obtained from mixed linear regression (StataCorp 2017) also show that the values for the R-EMAP and NAWQA south Florida sites (SOFL) are nearly identical. Additional modeling of a subset of the NAWQA sites that have published estimates of regional wet deposition of Hg (16 regions, $N = 332$; see Krabbenhoft et al. 1999, for the wet deposition estimates) was conducted using Hg wet deposition and latitude in addition to LOI as independent variables. That modeling shows that latitude is a strong, positive determinant of sediment Hg, although sediment organic content is still the dominant variable (standardized β coefficients $= 0.27$ and 0.55, respectively). The relationship of sediment Hg with wet deposition was significant ($p = 0.002$), but *negative* and not robust based on an analysis of the residuals. Together, the modeling indicates that surficial sediment Hg concentrations at a given location in the Everglades are governed primarily by the accumulation of sediment organic matter and, secondarily, latitudinal effects; any effects of local atmospheric deposition fluxes of Hg are minor compared to these other two variables. These results are similar to that of Obrist et al. (2011), who found that soil Hg concentrations across the continental U.S. were not strongly related to Hg deposition but rather increased with soil carbon, latitude, precipitation quantity and clay content.

3.4 Conclusions

Legacy Hg that can influence the dynamic response and recovery of aquatic ecosystems comprises a series of earth-surface pools that differ profoundly in terms of spatial scale, turnover, and magnitude. Large-scale pools (oceanic and terrestrial) influence atmospheric cycling of Hg and, because atmospheric inputs of Hg to the Everglades have only relatively small contributions from local and state-wide sources (<10%; see Chap. 6, Volume I), the effect of these large-scale reservoirs on the Everglades will be quantitatively similar to their impacts on the global cycling of atmospheric Hg. Simulation studies suggest that global deposition fluxes of Hg are not in equilibrium with current emissions, and the effect of this disequilibrium is such that current anthropogenic emissions need to be immediately reduced by at least 50% to ensure that global atmospheric deposition fluxes of Hg remain below current levels through 2050. Based on currently projected emission trajectories, however, it is more likely that emissions will increase during that time frame.

Hg stored in upland catchment soils and sediments within the aquatic ecosystem also constitute legacy Hg reservoirs that can potentially influence ecosystem response to mitigation measures. However, because Hg inputs to the Everglades are dominated to a very large extent by atmospheric deposition directly to the EvPA, with very small contributions from upland runoff (<5%), legacy Hg associated with upland soils should not be particularly problematic or limiting on how rapidly the Everglades recovers in response to changes in atmospheric inputs. The quantitative effects of sediments are less well constrained or understood. The effect of legacy Hg stored in Everglades sediments is governed by the size and turnover of labile, reactive Hg—so-called "new" Hg. Moreover, the temporal variability of MeHg and biota Hg concentrations observed in a number of locations within the Everglades can be large over very short time frames. Modeling studies conducted with the E-MCM to evaluate cause and effect relationships that can account for these dynamics in turn indicate that the legacy pool likely comprises an active surficial sediment layer that is only a few millimeters thick (Chap. 4, this volume); this translates to a likely response time to achieve near steady state (within 95%) of less than 12 years.

It is important to understand that the legacy Hg question is ultimately one of response timing and, *ceteris paribus*, that the long-term response of aquatic ecosystems including the Everglades will be governed by the external inputs. While legacy Hg stored in Everglades sediments is probably not a limiting concern with respect to the short-term recovery of the Everglades to changing Hg inputs, the effects of legacy Hg stored in oceanic and terrestrial pools that are in disequilibrium and slowly turning over likely will limit the effectiveness of current strategies based on reducing global emissions. Atmospheric deposition fluxes—both globally and in the Everglades—thus will likely continue to increase, at least through 2050. These results suggest that mitigation strategies for resolving the Hg problem in the Everglades that rely on reducing atmospheric inputs alone will not be effective—indeed such strategies will likely see the problem exacerbated over the next several decades. Alternative strategies that take advantage of key aspects of Hg biochemical cycling in the Everglades would seem more prudent and warranted.

References

Amos HM, Jacob DJ, Streets DG, Sunderland EM (2013) Legacy impacts of all-time anthropogenic emissions on the global mercury cycle. Global Biogeochem Cycles 27:1–12. https://doi.org/10.1002/gbc.20040

Amos HM, Jacob DJ, Kocman D, Horowitz HM, Zhang Y, Dutkiewicz S, Horvat M, Corbitt ES, Krabbenhoft DP, Sunderland EM (2014) Global biogeochemical implications of mercury discharges from rivers and sediment burial. Environ Sci Technol 48:9514–9522. https://doi.org/10.1021/es502134t

Bauch NJ, Chasar LC, Scudder BC, Moran PW, Hitt KJ, Brigham ME, Lutz MA, Wentz DA (2009) Data on mercury in water, bed sediment, and fish from streams across the United States, 1998–2005: U.S. Geological Survey Data Series 307, 33 p

Blukacz-Richards EA, Visha A, Graham ML, McGoldrick DL, de Solla SR, Moore DJ, Arhonditis GB (2017) Mercury levels in herring gulls and fish: 42 years of spatio-temporal trends in the Great Lakes. Chemosphere 172:476–487

Brent RN, Berberich DA (2014) Use of artificial stream mesocosms to investigate mercury uptake in the South River, Virginia, USA. Arch Environ Contam Toxicol 66:201–212

Brigham ME, Sandheinrich MB, Gay DA, Maki RP, Krabbenhoft DP, Wiener JG (2014) Lacustrine responses to decreasing wet mercury deposition rates – results from a case study in northern Minnesota. Environ Sci Technol 48:6115–6123. https://doi.org/10.1021/es500301a

Chadwick SP, Babiarz CL, Hurley JP, Armstrong DE (2013) Importance of hypolimnetic cycling in aging of "new" mercury in a northern temperate lake. Sci Total Environ 448:176–188. https://doi.org/10.1016/j.scitotenv.2012.10.069

Cohen MJ, Lamsal S, Osborne TZ, Bonzongo JCJ, Newman S, Reddy KR (2009) Soil total mercury concentrations across the Everglades. Soil Sci Soc Am J 73(2):675–685. https://doi.org/10.2136/sssaj2008.0126

Craft CB, Richardson CJ (1993) Peat accretion and N, P, and organic C accumulation in nutrient-enriched and unenriched Everglades peatlands. Ecol Appl 3(3):446–458

Dastoor A, Ryzhkov A, Durnford D, Lehnherr I, Steffen A, Morrison H (2015) Atmospheric mercury in the Canadian Arctic. Part II: insight from modeling. Sci Total Environ 509–501:16–27

Drevnick PE, Engstrom DR, Driscoll CT, Swain EB, Balogh SJ, Kamman NC, Long DT, Mui DGC, Parsons MJ, Rolfhus KR, Rossmann R (2012) Spatial and temporal patterns of mercury accumulation in lacustrine sediments across the Laurentian Great Lakes region. Environ Poll 161:252–260

Foxgrover AC, Marvin-DiPasquale M, Jaffe BE, Fregoso TA (2019) Slough evolution and legacy mercury remobilization induced by wetland restoration in South San Francisco Bay. Estuar Coast Shelf Sci 220:1–19

Gilmour CC, Krabbenhoft DP, Orem WO (2004) Mesocosm studies to quantify how methylmercury responds to changes in mercury, sulfur, and nutrient loading. 2004 Everglades Consolidated Report Appendix 3B-3, 15 pp

Grigal DF (2002) Inputs and outputs of mercury from terrestrial watersheds: a review. Environ Rev 39:1–39

Harris RC, Rudd JMW, Amyot M, Babiarz CL, Beaty KG, Blanchfield PJ, Bodaly RA, Branfireun BA, Gilmour CC, Graydon JA, Heyes A, Hintelmann H, Hurley JP, Kelly CA, Krabbenhoft DP, Lindberg SE, Mason RP, Paterson MJ, Podemski CL, Robinson A, Sandilands KA, Southworth GR, Louis VLS, Tatem MT (2007) Whole-ecosystem study shows rapid fish-mercury response to changes in mercury deposition. PNAS 104(42):16586–16591

Hintelmann H, Harris R, Heyes A, Hurley JP, Kelly CA, Krabbenhoft DP, Lindberg S, Rudd JWM, Scott KJ, Louis VLS (2002) Reactivity and mobility of new and old mercury deposition in a Boreal forest ecosystem during the first year of the METAALICUS study. Environ Sci Technol 36(23):5034–5040

Hodson PV, Norris K, Berquist M, Campbell LM, Ridal JJ (2014) Mercury concentrations in amphipods and fish of the Saint Lawrence River (Canada) are unrelated to concentrations of legacy mercury in sediments. Sci Total Environ 494-495:218–228

Horowitz HM, Jacob DJ, Zhang Y, Dibble TS, Slemr F, Amos HM, Schmidt JA, Corbitt ES, Marais EA, Sunderland EM (2017) A new mechanism for atmospheric mercury redox chemistry: implications for the global mercury budget. Atmos Chem Phys 17:6353–6371. https://doi.org/10.5194/acp-17-6353-2017

Imboden DM, Lerman A (1978) Chapter 11. Chemical models of lakes. In: Lerman A (ed) Lakes: chemistry, geology, and physics. Springer, New York, pp 241–356

Johansson K, Bergbäck B, Tyler G (2001) Impact of atmospheric long range transport of lead, mercury and cadmium on the Swedish forest environment. Water Air Soil Poll Focus 1:279–297

Julian P (in review) Atmospheric mercury deposition trends. In: Julian P, Gu B, Weaver K (eds) Chapter 3B: Mercury and sulfur environmental assessment for the Everglades. 2017 South Florida environmental report – volume I. South Florida Water Management District, West Palm Beach, FL, pp 3B-30–3B-34

Kamman NC, Engstrom DR (2002) Historical and present fluxes of mercury to Vermont and New Hampshire lakes inferred from 210Pb dated sediment cores. Atmos Environ 36:1599–1609

Knightes CD, Sunderland EM, Barber MC, Johnston JM, Ambrose RB Jr (2009) Application of ecosystem scale fate and bioaccumulation models to predict fish mercury response times to changes in atmospheric deposition. Environ Toxicol Chem 28(4):881–893

Kopec AD, Kidd KA, Fisher NS, Bowen M, Francis C, Payne K, Bodaly RA (2019) Spatial and temporal trends of mercury in the aquatic food web of the lower Penobscot River, Maine, USA, affected by a chlor-alkali plant. Sci Tot Environ 649:770–791

Krabbenhoft DP, Wiener JG, Brumbaugh WG, Olson ML, DeWild JF, Sabin TJ (1999) A national pilot study of mercury contamination of aquatic ecosystems along multiple gradients. In: U.S. Geological Survey Toxic Substances Hydrology Program – Proceedings of the Technical Meeting, Charleston, South Carolina, March 8–12, 1999 – Volume 2 of Contamination of Hydrologic Systems and Related Ecosystems: U.S. Geological Survey Water-Resources Investigations Report 99-4018B, pp 147–160

Lorey P, Driscoll CT (1999) Historical trends of mercury deposition in Adirondack lakes. Environ Sci Technol 33:718–722

Mason R (2009) Mercury emissions from natural processes and their importance in the global mercury cycle. In: Pirrone N, Mason R (eds) Mercury fate and transport in the global atmosphere. Springer, New York, pp 173–191

Mason RP, Sheu GR (2002) Role of the ocean in the global mercury cycle. Global Biogeochem Cycle 16(4):1093. https://doi.org/10.1029/2001GB001440

Mehner T, Diekmann M, Gonsiorczyk T, Kasprzak P, Koschel R, Krienitz L, Rumpf M, Schulz M, Wauer G (2008) Rapid recovery from eutrophication of a stratified lake by disruption of internal nutrient load. Ecosystems 11(7):1142–1156

Mills RB, Paterson AM, Blais JM, Lean DRS, Smol JP, Mierle G (2009) Factors influencing the achievement of steady state in mercury contamination among lakes and catchments of south-Central Ontario. Can J Fish Aquat Sci 66:187–200

Monson BA, Staples DF, Bhavsar SP, Holsen TM, Schrank CS, Moses SK, McGoldrick DJ, Backus SM, Williams KA (2011) Spatiotemporal trends of mercury in walleye and largemouth bassfrom the Laurentian Great Lakes Region. Ecotoxicology 20:1555–1567

Munthe J, Bodaly RA, Branfireun BA, Driscoll CT, Gilmour CC, Harris R, Horvat M, Lucotte M, Malm O (2007) Recovery of mercury-contaminated fisheries. Ambio 36(1):33–44

Nurnberg GK (1991) Phosphorus from internal sources in the Laurentian Great Lakes, and the concept of threshold external load. J Great Lakes Res 17(1):132–140

Obrist D, Johnson DW, Lindberg SE, Luo Y, Hararuk O, Bracho R, Battles JJ, Dail DB, Edmonds RL, Monson RK, Ollinger SV, Pallardy SG, Pregitzer KS, Todd DE (2011) Mercury distribution across 14 U.S. forests. Part I: spatial patterns of concentrations in biomass, litter, and soils. Environ Sci Technol 45:3974–3981

Orihel DM, Paterson MJ, Gilmour CC, Bodaly RA, Blanchfield PJ, Hintelmann H, Harris RC, Rudd JWM (2006) Effect of loading rate on the fate of mercury in littoral mesocosms. Environ Sci Technol 40:5992–6000

Orihel DM, Paterson MJ, Blanchfield PJ, Bodaly RA, Hintelmann H (2007) Relationship between inorganic mercury loading and methylmercury accumulation by aquatic biota. Environ Sci Technol 41:4952–4958

Orihel DM, Paterson MJ, Blanchfield PJ, Bodaly RA, Gilmour CC, Hintelmann H (2008) Temporal changes in the distribution, methylation, and bioaccumulation of newly deposited mercury in an aquatic ecosystem. Environ Pollut 154:77–88

Outridge PM, Mason RP, Wang F, Guerrero S, Hëimburge-Boavida LE (2018) Updated global and oceanic mercury budgets for the United Nations Global Mercury Assessment 2018. Environ Sci Technol 52:11466–11477

Poulain AJ, Orihel DM, Amyot M, Paterson MJ, Hintelmann H, Southworth GR (2006) Relationship between the loading rate of inorganic mercury to aquatic ecosystems and dissolved gaseous mercury production and evasion. Chemosphere 65:2199–2207

Rafaj P, Bertok I, Cofala J, Schöpp W (2013) Scenarios of global mercury emissions from anthropogenic sources. Atmos Environ 79:472–479. https://doi.org/10.1016/j.atmosenv.2013.06.042

Rudd JMW, Bodaly RA, Fisher NS, Kelly CA, Kopec D, Whipple C (2018) Fifty years after its discharge, methylation of legacy mercury trapped in the Penobscot estuary sustains high mercury in biota. Sci Tot Environ 642:1340–1352

Schroeder W, Munthe J (1998) Atmospheric mercury – an overview. Atmos Environ 32 (5):809–822

Selin NE, Jacob DJ, Yantosca RM, Strode S, Jaeglé L, Sunderland EM (2008) Global 3-D land-ocean-atmosphere model for mercury: present-day versus preindustrial cycles and anthropogenic enrichment factors for deposition. Global Biogeochem Cycle 22:GB2011. https://doi.org/10.1029/2007GB003040

Song S, Selin NE, Soerensen AL, Angot H, Artz R, Brooks S, Brunke E-G, Conley G, Dommergue A, Ebinghaus R, Holsen TM, Jaffe DA, Kang S, Kelley P, Luke WT,

Magand O, Marumoto K, Pfaffhuber KA, Ren X, Sheu G-R, Slemr F, Warneke T, Weigelt A, Weiss-Penzias P, Wip DC, Zhang Q (2015) Top-down constraints on atmospheric mercury emissions and implications for global biogeochemical cycling. Atmos Chem Phys 15:7103–7125. https://doi.org/10.5194/acp-15-7103-2015

StataCorp (2017) Stata statistical software: release 15. StataCorp LP, College Station, TX

Stober QJ, Thornton K, Jones R, Richards J, Ivey C, Welch R, Madden M, Trexler J, Gaiser E, Scheidt D, Rathbun S (2001) South Florida Ecosystem Assessment: Phase I/II – Everglades stressor interactions: hydropatterns, eutrophication, habitat alteration, and mercury contamination (summary). EPA 904-R-01-002. USEPA Region 4 Science & Ecosystem Support Division, Water Management Division, and Office of Research and Development

Streets DG, Bond TC, Lee T, Jang C (2004) On the future of carbonaceous aerosols. J Geophys Res 109:D24212. https://doi.org/10.1029/2004JD004902

Streets DG, Zhang Q, Wu Y (2009) Projections of global mercury emissions in 2050. Environ Sci Technol 43(8):2983–2988. https://doi.org/10.1021/es802474j

Streets DG, Devane MK, Lu Z, Bond TC, Sunderland EM, Jacobs DJ (2011) All-time releases of mercury to the atmosphere from human activities. Environ Sci Technol 45(24):10485–10491

Strode SA, Jaegle L, Selin NE, Jacob DJ, Park RJ, Yantosca RM, Mason RP, Slemr F (2007) Air-sea exchange in the global mercury cycle. Global Biogeochem Cycles 21:GB1017. https://doi.org/10.1029/2006GB002766

USEPA (2006) Mercury inputs and cycling in Devils Lake, Wisconsin: a pilot study for conducting a maximum total maximum daily load analysis for an atmospherically-derived pollutant. Watershed Branch, Office of Wetlands, Oceans and Watersheds, U.S. Environmental Protection Agency, Washington, DC

Zaferani S, Pérez-Rodríguez M, Biester H (2018) Diatom ooze – a large marine mercury sink. Science 361:797–800. https://doi.org/10.1126/science.aat2735

Zhang H, Holmes CD, Wu S (2016) Impacts of changes in climate, land use and land cover on atmospheric mercury. Atmos Environ 141:230–244

Chapter 4
Simulating Mercury Cycling in the Florida Everglades: A Case Study

Reed C. Harris, David Hutchinson, Curtis D. Pollman, and Don Beals

Abstract A mechanistic model of mercury cycling was applied to an Everglades marsh to help assess the role of sulfate on methylmercury concentrations in surface waters. The Everglades Mercury Cycling Model (E-MCM) was applied to site 3A-15, located in the interior of Water Conservation Area 3A. This site experienced declines in fish mercury and water column sulfate concentrations during the late 1990s and early 2000s. The model analysis focused on 1995–2003, but simulations began earlier to accommodate the potential for pre-1995 conditions to affect mercury concentrations afterwards. Simulations assuming sulfate affected methylation matched the observed decline in methylmercury in surface waters better than simulations with no sulfate effect. The analysis also suggested other factors may have contributed to the decline of surface water methylmercury concentrations at 3A-15, including potential legacy effects of mercury loads to the marsh prior to 1995, and changes to other water quality conditions. Greater confidence is assigned to the predicted effect of declining sulfate than changes in atmospheric mercury deposition, because deposition rates prior to 1996 were constructed using indirect means, and the duration of legacy effects is uncertain.

Keywords Model · E-MCM · Methylation · Sulfate · Methylmercury · Simulation · Atmospheric deposition

4.1 Introduction

Elevated fish mercury (Hg) concentrations have been observed in the Florida Everglades since 1989 when a monitoring project by state agencies found Hg concentrations above 2 μg/g in largemouth bass (LMB) (Axelrad et al. 2007). This

R. C. Harris (✉) · D. Hutchinson · D. Beals
Reed Harris Environmental Ltd., Oakville, ON, Canada

C. D. Pollman
Aqua Lux Lucis, Inc., Gainesville, FL, USA

C. D. Pollman et al. (eds.), *Mercury and the Everglades. A Synthesis and Model for Complex Ecosystem Restoration*, https://doi.org/10.1007/978-3-030-55635-8_4

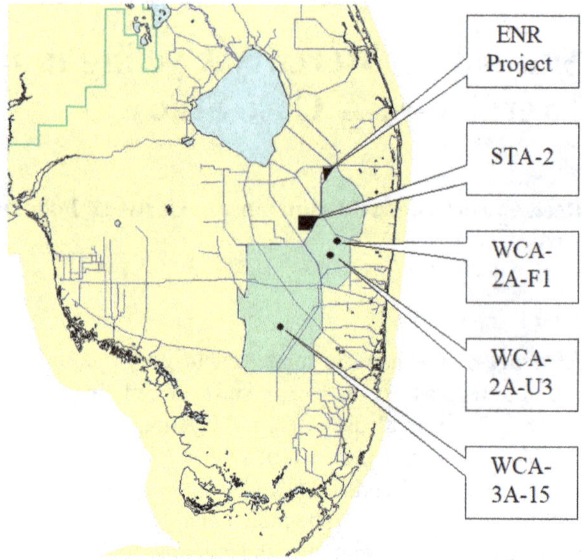

Fig. 4.1 Everglades sites modeled with E-MCM

level was well above the 1989 Florida Department of Health fish consumption guidance recommending that the public limit their consumption of fish with a concentration above 0.5 μg/g to one meal per month for women of childbearing age and children, and one meal per week for men. Hg concentrations in largemouth bass declined substantially throughout much of the Everglades in the early 1990s until *ca.* 2003, including canal and interior marsh sites (Axelrad et al. 2007; Chaps. 2 and 5 this volume). A wide range of factors has been considered to explain these trends, including changes in atmospheric Hg deposition, hydrology, particle dynamics, water chemistry and food web structure [see Chaps. 3, 4 and 6 (Vol. II), Chaps. 5 and 6 (this Volume)]. To assist in the analysis, a mechanistic model of Hg cycling and bioaccumulation known as the Everglades Mercury Cycling Model (E-MCM, Harris et al. 2003; Tetra Tech 1999b) was applied to several sites in the Everglades (Fig. 4.1), spanning a range of environmental conditions.

In the analysis described here, E-MCM was applied to site 3A-15 located in the interior of Water Conservation Area (WCA) 3A. This site was chosen because it was studied intensively by the US Geological Survey and others (*e.g.* USGS 2018; Aiken et al. 2011; Krabbenhoft 1996; Gilmour et al. 1998; Hurley et al. 1998), and declines were observed in fish Hg and sulfate concentrations in surface waters during the late 1990s and early 2000s (Fig. 4.2). Hg concentrations in 3 year old largemouth bass declined 50% or more from the mid-1990s to 2005 (Chap. 2, this volume; Axelrad et al. 2007). Sulfate concentrations declined from ~3 to 6 mg/L in 1994–1995 to less than 0.1 mg/L by 2003 (Pollman et al. 2006; Krabbenhoft et al. 2008). Together, these two features of site 3A-15 provided an opportunity to test causality hypotheses regarding changes in biota Hg concentrations. An important objective of the application of E-MCM to site 3A-15 was to test the hypothesis that observed declines in fish Hg concentrations at site 3A-15 were influenced by declining sulfate

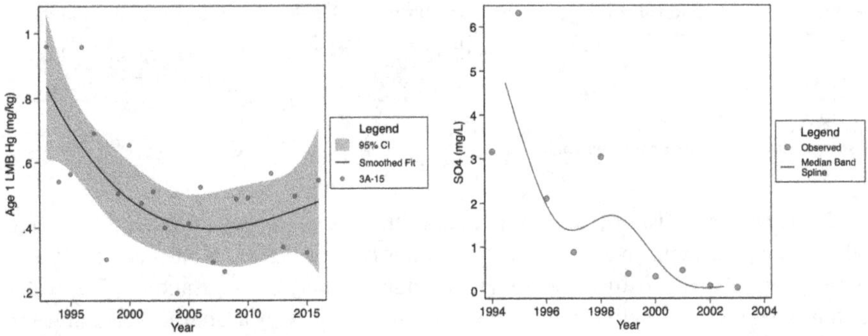

Fig. 4.2 Time series plots of (1) tissue concentrations of Hg in largemouth bass, normalized to age 1 year (left-hand panel) and (2) sulfate concentrations (right-hand panel) at site 3A-15. Fish tissue concentrations courtesy of Ted Lange, Florida Fish and Wildlife Conservation Commission (FFWCC). Sulfate concentrations are annual mean concentrations obtained from South Florida Water Management District's DBHYDRO online database (SFWMD 2019)

concentrations. Sulfur interactions with methylmercury (MeHg) production and concentrations have been examined for many years, *e.g* Gilmour et al. 1998 (see also Chaps. 1 and 3, Vol. II).

4.2 Approach and Methods

4.2.1 Modeling Approach

The overall study approach involved developing four model calibrations at site 3A-15 and assessing which calibration produced the better fit to observed MeHg concentrations in surface waters from 1995 to 2003. The calibrations used different assumptions regarding the effect of sulfate on methylation, and different estimates of atmospheric Hg deposition from 1930 to 1995, which allowed the cycling of legacy Hg to be included in the analysis.

The model simulated inorganic Hg and MeHg concentrations and fluxes in water, sediments and biota. The overall calibration of Hg cycling was, for the most part, carried out in the following sequence:

- Inorganic Hg(II) and Hg(0) in water and sediments
- MeHg in water and sediments
- MeHg in the food web.

This calibration order was used because MeHg in the food web depends on MeHg in water and sediments, which in turn depend on inorganic Hg in water and sediments. Checks were also carried out whether later steps in the calibration, *e.g.* calibrating MeHg, affected earlier components, *e.g.* inorganic Hg. Iteration was used to manually obtain reasonable results for each of the three major calibration components.

Table 4.1 Assumptions regarding sulfate and atmospheric Hg deposition in 4 model calibrations

	Contributions to 3A-15 atmospheric deposition in 1996	
Sulfate effect	70% local: 30% global	30% local: 70% global
Sulfate affects methylation	✓	✓
Sulfate does not affect methylation	✓	✓

This chapter focuses on the component of the overall model calibration related to MeHg concentrations in surface waters, primarily the roles of sulfate and changes to atmospheric Hg deposition on MeHg production and concentrations. The water column MeHg calibration was carried out manually with a goal of matching the observed decline from 1995 to 2003. While the analysis focused on 1995–2003, simulations began in 1930 to accommodate the potential for pre-1995 conditions to affect MeHg concentrations and trends afterwards.

Sulfate-reducing bacteria are well known to produce MeHg in some situations, but other microbes can also methylate inorganic Hg(II) (Chap. 3, Vol. II) and the influence of sulfate reduction on overall MeHg production in the Everglades has been debated (Chaps. 3 and 6, Vol. II). Inorganic Hg loading can also affect MeHg concentrations (Munthe et al. 2007; Harris et al. 2007). As discussed later in the chapter (see also Chap. 1, this volume), there is indirect evidence that atmospheric Hg deposition was higher prior to 1994 than monitored afterwards. Depending on the timescale that previously deposited Hg can affect current conditions, systematic changes in Hg deposition prior to 1995 (the beginning of the calibration period) could potentially affect the temporal pattern for Hg concentrations and MeHg production at site 3A-15 in 1995 and afterwards. For these reasons, four alternative calibrations were developed with different assumptions regarding the effect of sulfate on Hg methylation and different estimates of atmospheric Hg deposition, and compared to observations (Table 4.1).

4.2.1.1 Effect of Cell Size

Because the 3A-15 research site did not have clear physical boundaries, a representative 1 km × 1 km marsh area was simulated. Conditions were assumed to be horizontally uniform anywhere within the modeled area. The size of the cell selected for modeling has the potential to influence the relative importance of external inputs versus in situ production in a single cell model analysis. From the perspective of the overall Everglades, direct atmospheric Hg deposition is the primary source of inorganic Hg (Stober et al. 2001). If a representative sub-area of the Everglades is examined, *e.g.* a 1 km^2 area, water would travel through this area faster than through the Everglades as a whole, but atmospheric Hg loading rates remain the same on an areal basis. Inflows would become more important sources of inorganic Hg and MeHg in budgets for the smaller area. Ideally this issue is accommodated by having a model that includes many connected cells which cumulatively reflect the overall dominance of atmospheric deposition while also reflecting spatial differences and

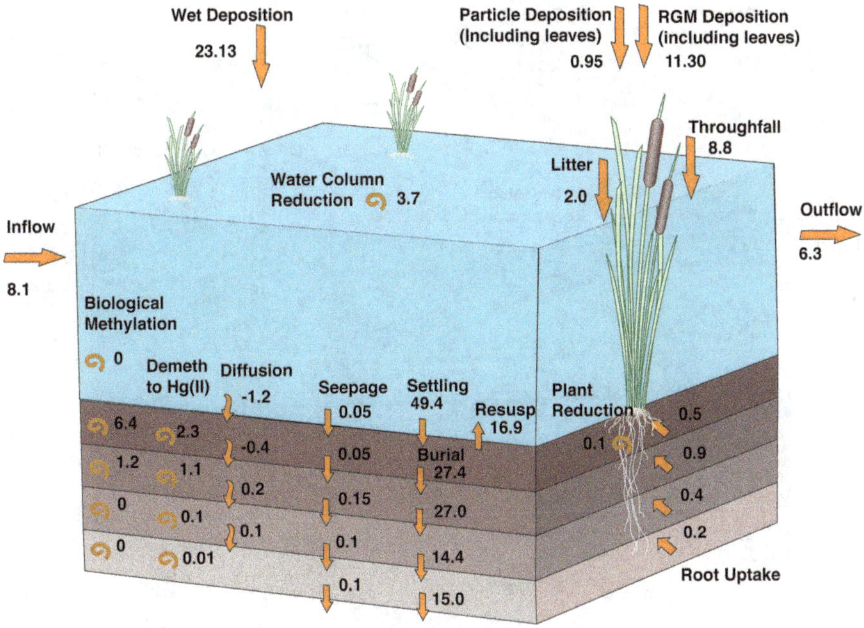

Fig. 4.3 Simulated inorganic Hg(II) fluxes (μg/m^2/year) for 3A-15, based on estimates for site conditions and Hg loads *ca.* 2000 and assuming these conditions were stable over a period of years to decades (from Harris et al. 2000)

processes that are important within each cell. For site 3A-15, a preliminary single-cell steady state analysis with E-MCM (Harris et al. 2000) assumed that site conditions and Hg loads *ca.* 2000 were stable over a period of years to decades. The analysis estimated that atmospheric deposition was the largest source of inorganic Hg in a 1 km^2 cell (Fig. 4.3), while in situ production was the largest source of MeHg (Fig. 4.4). The model analysis presented in this chapter differed from the steady state analysis by considering the fact that conditions changed over time. The implications of the assumed cell size are further discussed in the results section of the chapter.

4.2.1.2 Thickness of Surface Sediment Layer

The surface layer of sediments was assumed to be the primary site of in situ methylation and was assigned a thickness of 3 mm. Using a thinner sediment layer resulted in faster responses for Hg concentrations in sediments following changes in external loading (*e.g.*, it takes less time to replace the contents of a 3 mm well-mixed layer than a 3 cm layer). Implications for the assumed thickness of the surface sediment layer are further examined in the Discussion section of this chapter (see also Chap. 3, this volume).

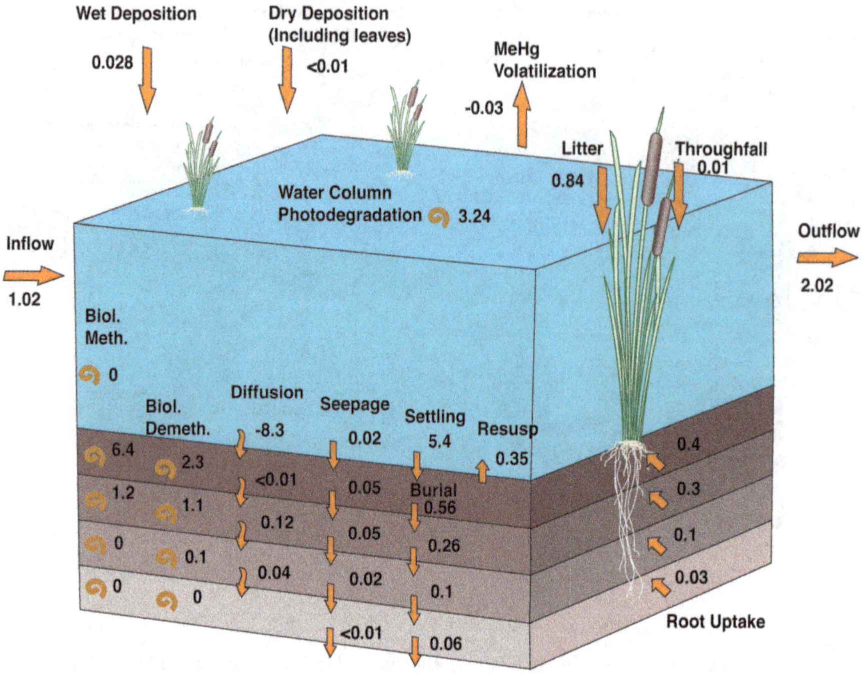

Fig. 4.4 Simulated MeHg fluxes (μg/m^2/year) for 3A-15, based on estimates for site conditions and Hg loads *ca.* 2000 and assuming these conditions were stable over a period of years to decades (from Harris et al. 2000)

4.2.2 Model Description

The Everglades Mercury Cycling Model (E-MCM) simulates mercury cycling and bioaccumulation in marsh areas of the Florida Everglades (Fig. 4.5). It emerged from an earlier version of the model developed for lakes (Hudson et al. 1994; Tetra Tech 1999a), with processes and compartments added to reflect additional features affecting Hg cycling and bioaccumulation in Everglades marshes. These included shallow waters, a warm subtropical climate, high sun exposure, neutral to alkaline pH, high concentrations of dissolved organic carbon, the presence of periphyton, sawgrass, cattails and water lilies, and a wide range of nutrient levels and primary production (Atkeson et al. 2003).

E-MCM is a Windows™-based mechanistic simulation model. As described by Atkeson et al. (2003), a mass balance approach is used to predict time-dependent concentrations for three forms of Hg: inorganic Hg(II), MeHg and elemental Hg. Model compartments include the water column (dissolved and particle phases), three macrophyte species (cattails, sawgrass, water lilies), four sediment layers and a food web. Major processes are shown in Fig. 4.5, including surface inflows and outflows, vertical groundwater flow, Hg partitioning between solids and dissolved complexes, particulate settling, resuspension and burial, macrophyte related fluxes

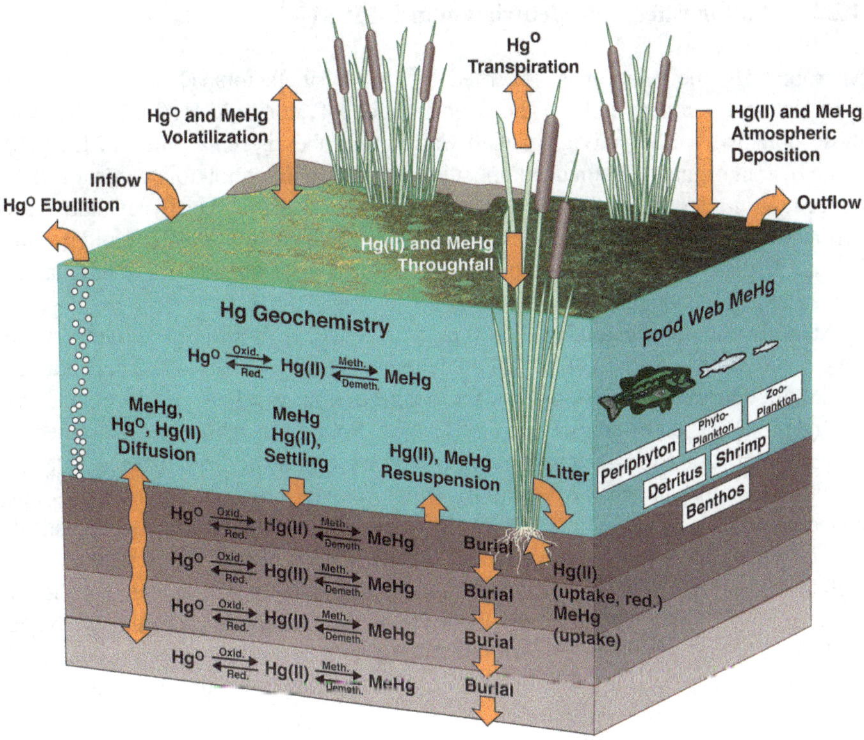

Fig. 4.5 Biogeochemical cycling of Hg in E-MCM

(throughfall, litter, root uptake, transpiration), atmospheric deposition, air/water gaseous exchange, in situ transformations (methylation, demethylation, MeHg photodegradation, Hg(II) photoreduction), Hg(II) and MeHg kinetics in plankton, and MeHg fluxes in fish populations (uptake via food and water, excretion, egestion, mortality, fishing).

Hg concentrations in the atmosphere are input as boundary conditions and used to calculate gaseous exchange at the air/water interface, wet deposition, and dry deposition of particles and reactive gaseous Hg. A simplified food web includes detritus, periphyton, phytoplankton, zooplankton, benthos, shrimp, mosquitofish, bluegill/warmouth sunfish (grouped together), and largemouth bass. Fish Hg concentrations tend to increase with age and are followed in each year class (up to 20 cohorts) for each species. Bioenergetics equations developed for individual fish at the University of Wisconsin (Hanson et al. 1997) were modified to consider temperature dependent growth and coupled to MeHg fluxes (Harris and Bodaly 1998). Fluxes for individual fish were then extended to simulate MeHg fluxes for year classes and entire populations.

4.2.2.1 Sulfur Effects on Methylation in E-MCM

Microbial Hg methylation is governed by two basic factors: (1) the activity of methylating microbes, and (2) the concentration of inorganic Hg(II) available to those organisms. The activity of methylating microbes is represented in E-MCM using overall organic carbon decomposition rates, with an option to include a sulfate concentration dependency. The concentration of inorganic Hg(II) available for methylation is predicted in E-MCM using thermodynamic speciation. For this study, all dissolved Hg(II) complexes were assumed available for methylation, including Hg(II) bound to dissolved organic carbon (DOC).

Methylation of inorganic Hg(II) was assumed to occur in surface sediments at site 3A-15, and optionally had either (a) no dependency or (b) a first order dependency on sulfate concentration in pore waters, where doubling sulfate would double the methylation rate, other factors remaining equal. Pore water sulfate was assumed to vary in proportion to surface water concentrations. It is recognized that methylation would more mechanistically depend on sulfate reduction rates, rather than sulfate concentrations. At sites such as site 3A-15 where organic carbon supply is plentiful, sulfate reduction is more likely limited by the supply of electron acceptors, *e.g.* sulfate, rather than organic carbon. In this situation, more sulfate can potentially result in more sulfate reduction and methylation. For the purposes of this study, an analysis relating methylation to sulfate concentration was considered capable of providing insights into the role of increased sulfate loading and concentrations on MeHg production and concentrations.

Lastly, as discussed in Chap. 1 of Vol. II, higher rates of sulfate reduction can lead to increasing pore water sulfide concentrations which in turn can limit Hg methylation by reducing the availability of inorganic Hg(II) (Orem et al. 2011; Benoit et al. 1999). This leads to an expected optimal combination of sulfur-related conditions for methylation (in cases where sulfate reduction plays a role) with sulfate reduction active but not elevated to the point of producing a large inhibitory sulfide effect (Chaps. 3 and 6, Vol. II). Orem et al. (2011) indicated that sulfide is inhibitory to methylation at concentrations >1 mg/L. Pore water sulfide concentrations in surface sediments at site 3A-15 from 1995 to 2004 were less than 0.4 mg/L, and typically less than 0.1 mg/L (USGS 2018). For this model analysis it was assumed that sulfide did not inhibit methylation at site 3A-15. We therefore carried out simulations testing the hypothesis that methylation varied linearly with sulfate concentration, other factors being equal. Because methylation rates cannot be measured directly under ambient conditions, concentrations of filtered MeHg in water were used as the primary metric for model calibration.

4.2.3 Water Conservation Area 3A-15 Site Description

Water Conservation Area 3A is located in the Everglades ~50 km west of Fort Lauderdale and has an area of approximately 2000 km^2 (Abtew et al. 2005). Ambient water chemistry data from 1978 to 2003 (Cl, SO_4, DOC, pH, and total phosphorus) and rainfall data (Figs. 4.6, 4.7, 4.8, and 4.9) were obtained from the South Florida Water Management District's DBHYDRO on-line data base (SFWMD 2019). The period of record and completeness of the data sets varied for

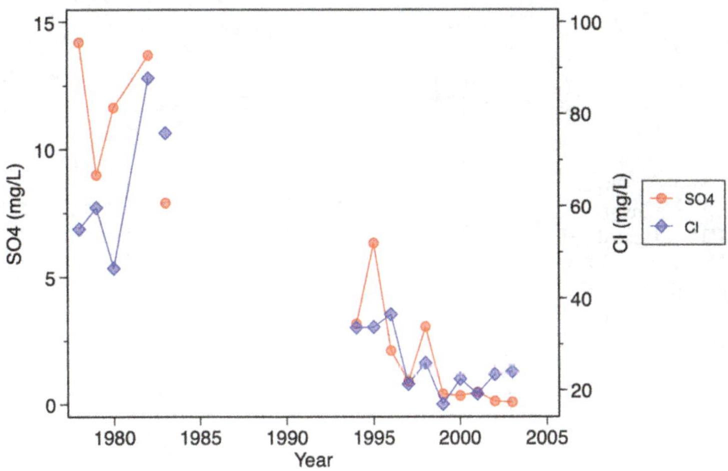

Fig. 4.6 Long-term trends (1978–2003) in annual mean concentrations of chloride and sulfate concentrations at site 3A-15. Data courtesy of SFWMD

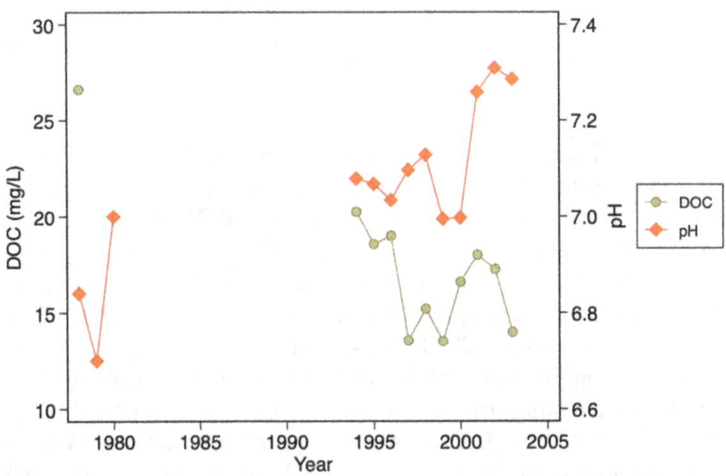

Fig. 4.7 Long-term trends (1978–2003) in annual mean concentrations of DOC concentrations and pH at site 3A-15. Data courtesy of SFWMD

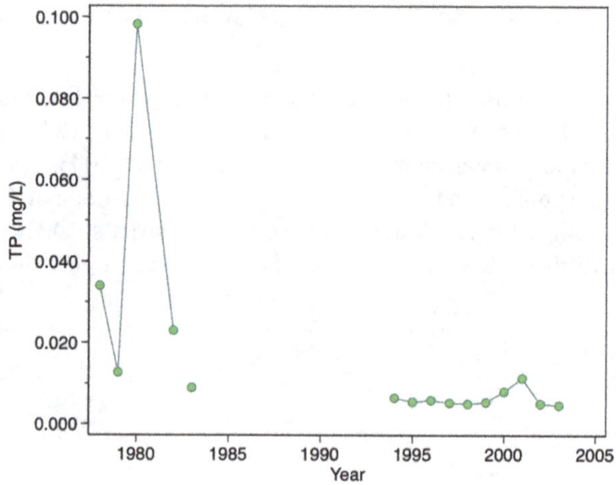

Fig. 4.8 Long-term trends (1978–2003) in annual mean concentrations of total phosphorus at site 3A-15. Data courtesy of SFWMD

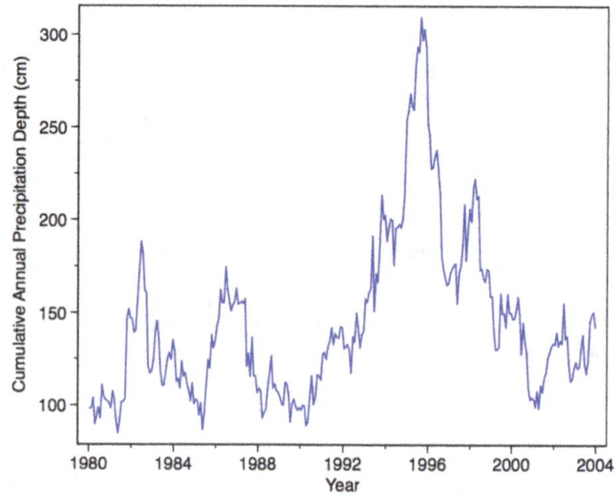

Fig. 4.9 Annual rainfall at site 3A-4/3A-S located near Site 3A-15 for 1980–2003. Values are rolling annual sums calculated monthly. Data courtesy of SFWMD

each parameter. Missing observations between reporting intervals were estimated using linear interpolation between nearest neighboring observations in time.

Between 1980 and 2000, and particularly after 1995, sulfate concentrations dropped dramatically at site 3A-15 (Fig. 4.6), apparently due to changes in hydrologic routing of water enriched in sulfate and chloride derived from the Everglades Agricultural Area (and as evidenced by concomitant declining trends in chloride). During the late 1990s and early 2000s, the site was low in primary productivity (total phosphorus less than 10 μg/L), with significant dissolved organic carbon levels (13–19 mg/L) and circumneutral pH (Fig. 4.7). Largemouth bass are the top trophic level fish species at the site. Because it was considered a "hot-spot" with elevated fish Hg concentrations, site 3A-15 was also the location of intense research in the mid to late 1990s. Moreover, and similar to other Everglades long-term monitoring sites maintained by the FFWCC since the early 1990s, this site also experienced a large decline in fish tissue Hg concentrations (~ 50%; see Fig. 4.2 and Chap. 5, this volume) that stabilized by *ca.* 2005.

4.2.3.1 Atmospheric Hg Deposition

Several datasets were used to construct time series model inputs for atmospheric Hg deposition. These datasets included direct measurements of wet deposition, inferred total deposition fluxes derived from sediment cores, estimated contributions of dry deposition, and changes in local Hg emission fluxes. Because the periods of record varied for different types of data, the approaches used to estimate Hg deposition also varied for different time periods.

Direct measurements of wet deposition fluxes were used to construct the Hg deposition trajectory for the time period between 1996 and 2003 using data collected at the Beard Research Center in Everglades National Park (ENP). The primary data source was the Mercury Deposition Network (NADP 2017), which began monitoring in the ENP in spring 1996, supplemented with data from the co-located Beard Research Center site included as part of the Florida Atmospheric Monitoring Study (Guentzel et al. 2001) to yield a complete monitoring record for 1996.

Prior to 1996, local and regional/global contributions to wet Hg deposition were estimated separately and combined to produce a total estimate of wet deposition. Total deposition fluxes attributable to global sources for the period 1930–1996 were inferred from sediment accumulation rates of Hg measured by Engstrom et al. (2003) (see Fig. 1.6 in Chap. 1, this volume) in cores collected from Lake Annie, a comparatively pristine seepage lake located about 150 km NW of the Palm Beach County urban fringe. This estimation assumes that changes in atmospheric Hg deposition recorded in the Lake Annie sediments predominantly reflect changes in the global signal. The average modern enrichment ratio (ER) of *ca.* 3.0 in Lake Annie sediments is consistent with ER values converging between 2 and 4 at locations remote from Hg emission sources (Chap. 1, this volume). Changes in local inputs between 1980 and 1996 were derived from the south Florida emissions inventory compiled by RMB Associates (2002) (Fig. 4.10; see also Chap. 5, Vol. I). Local inputs preceding 1980 were based on a mercury material usage or flows analysis developed for south Florida by Husar and Husar (2002). Actual usages developed by Husar and Husar for 1980 were scaled to the 1980 emissions calculated by RMB Associates; this scaling factor then was used to infer local contributions from 1930 through 1979.

Two deposition trajectories were constructed. The first assumed that the contribution from local sources was 70% in 1996 and the remaining 30% was from global sources, while the second trajectory assumed that the percentage inputs were reversed. Trajectories for total deposition were constructed for 1930 to 1996 using the relative change trajectories for local and global inputs, and assuming that wet deposition at site 3A-15 in 1996 was equivalent to the measured wet deposition flux measured at the Beard Research Station (15.2 $\mu g/m^2$). The global trajectory derived from the Lake Annie cores was then scaled by a uniform factor based on the ratio

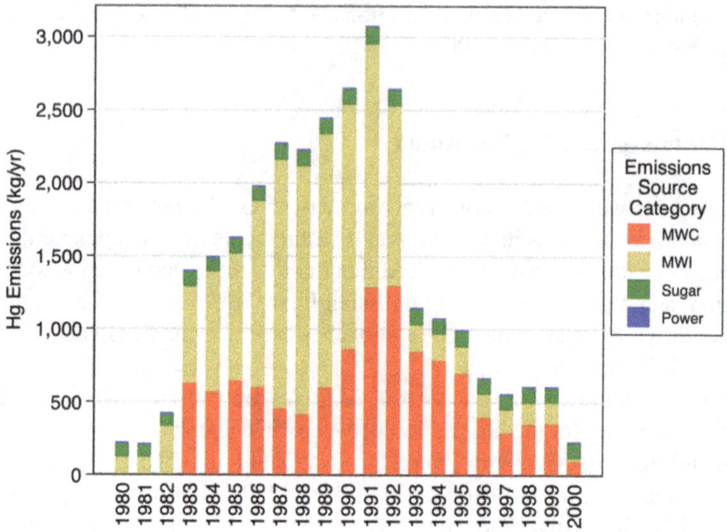

Fig. 4.10 Total Hg emissions estimated for south Florida (Dade, Broward and Palm Beach counties) for 1980–2000. Emissions based on plant operating data and emission factors. Source categories include municipal waste combustion (MWC), power generation, medical waste incineration (MWI) and sugar processing. From RMB Associates (2002); see Chap. 5, Vol. I

between the FAMS/MDN wet deposition flux for 1996 and the Hg sediment accumulation rate obtained for the same time period. The total deposition trajectory then was constructed using the global:local relative change trajectories to add in the appropriate amount of local deposition to the global background deposition.

Lastly, E-MCM model input deposition trajectories were adjusted to account for dry deposition. Dry deposition inputs were based on assuming that dry:wet deposition ratios remained constant over time and are equivalent to 0.53, which is the ratio Atkeson et al. (2003) calculated based on dry deposition modeling conducted by Keeler et al. (2000) for south Florida for 1995–1996 and concomitant measured wet deposition fluxes. This ratio likely varies to some extent over time, as follows. First, the predicted dry deposition flux used to develop the dry:wet deposition ratio was largely associated with gaseous oxidized Hg (GOM). Second, GOM concentrations in the atmosphere have a short residence time, and would more likely contribute to local rather than global deposition. Third, the contributions of local and global inputs to Hg deposition were estimated to change with time. This combination of conditions could therefore lead to changes over time in the dry:wet Hg deposition ratio.

The resulting synthesized total deposition trajectories for Hg are shown in Fig. 4.11. Note that both trajectories are identical from 1996 through 2003 because both are based on observed wet deposition fluxes measured at Beard Research Station for that period and use the same approach to estimate dry deposition.

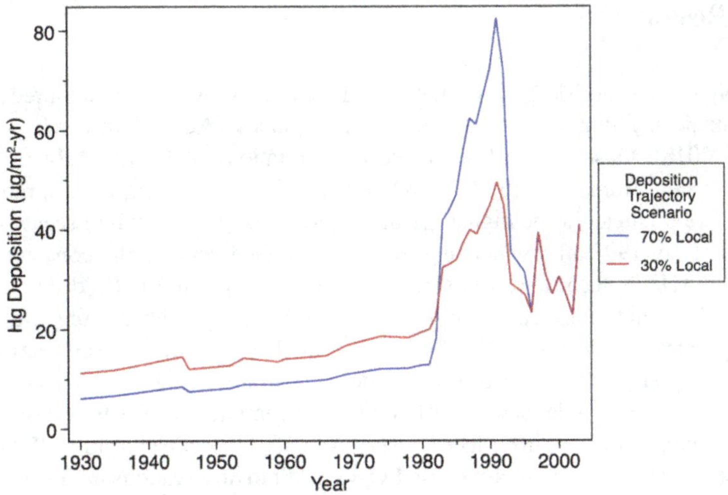

Fig. 4.11 Inferred atmospheric Hg deposition (wet + dry) trajectories. Blue curve shows trajectory when local emissions are assumed equivalent to 70% of the total deposition signal in 1996. Red curve shows same except that the relative local:global signal contributions in 1996 are reversed (*i.e.* 30% local)

4.2.3.2 Hg Loads from Inflows

Observed declines in MeHg and inorganic Hg(II) concentrations at site 3A-15 in the late 1990s and early 2000s also likely occurred in inflows to the modeled area. Limited measurements of Hg(II) and MeHg concentrations were available from site 3A-33 approximately 30 km upstream of 3A-15. Average concentrations for 7 samples collected from December 1996 to November 1999 were 2.14 ng/L for Hg (II) and 0.27 ng/L for MeHg. It was assumed that the relative rate of decline of inflowing Hg concentrations would be similar to the rate of decline predicted by E-MCM in 3A-15 surface waters. Time trajectories for inflow MeHg and inorganic Hg(II) concentrations were adjusted iteratively to follow the relative rate of change predicted in 3A-15 surface waters, while maintaining the observed average inflow concentrations for the period from 1997 to 1999. This approach was considered valid if inflow was not the dominant predicted source of MeHg or Hg(II) at site 3A-15. If this condition was satisfied, then the temporal pattern predicted in surface waters at site 3A-15 would not be dictated by the temporal pattern assigned to inflows. If inflows were the dominant source of MeHg or Hg(II) to the model domain, the temporal pattern predicted in surface waters would be dominated by the temporal pattern of inflows, which would lead to a circular (invalid) approach.

4.3 Results

Total Hg (THg) and MeHg concentrations in surface waters were measured during the Aquatic Cycling of Mercury in the Everglades (ACME) research program (USGS 2018). Observed and simulated concentrations of filtered THg in 3A-15 surface waters from 1995 to 2003 are shown in Fig. 4.12. THg concentrations in water were predicted to be higher for the 70:30 (local:global source) scenario until approximately 1997 after which all scenarios predicted very similar concentrations. Predicted THg concentrations in surface sediments (top 3 mm) also differed in the early 1990s and converged by roughly 2000, see predicted pore water Hg (II) concentrations in Fig. 4.13. Pore water Hg(II) concentrations are relevant for predicted MeHg trends, because the model was configured assuming that surface sediment methylation depended partly on the concentration of Hg(II) in pore water.

MeHg concentrations in surface waters at site 3A-15 declined from 1995 to 2003, see observations and a non-parametric LOWESS fit to observations in Fig. 4.14. The four calibrations of E-MCM to surface water MeHg concentrations at 3A-15 all reflected the observed decline from 1995 to 2003, but to varying degrees. The best fit to observations was the calibration with a sulfate effect on methylation and the 70:30 trajectory for Hg deposition (Fig. 4.14 and Table 4.2) . This calibration also closely matched an exponential fit to the field data (not shown) although there is no reason to assume *a priori* that MeHg concentrations should have declined in an exponential manner. Calibrations with a sulfate effect on methylation had higher MeHg concentrations in water and a greater rate of decline than simulations with no sulfate effect, better fitting observations. The 70:30 (local:global source) calibrations resulted in higher peak concentrations of inorganic Hg(II) and MeHg in surface waters and declined faster in the early to mid-1990s than their counterpart 30:70 (local:global source) calibrations, again better fitting observations.

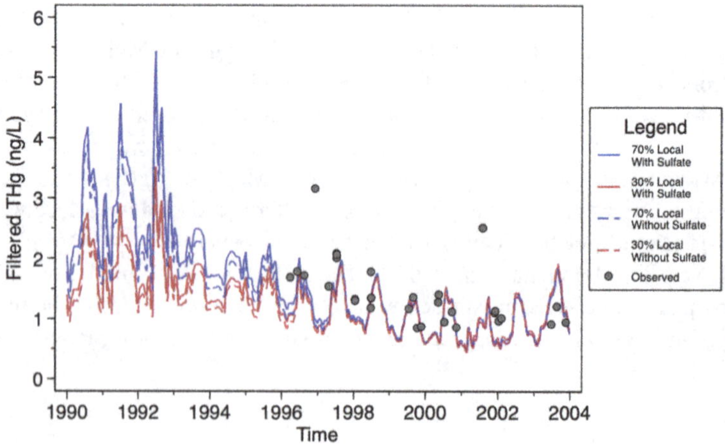

Fig. 4.12 Simulated and observed concentrations of filtered THg in 3A-15 surface waters from 1990–2003. Observations from USGS (2018)

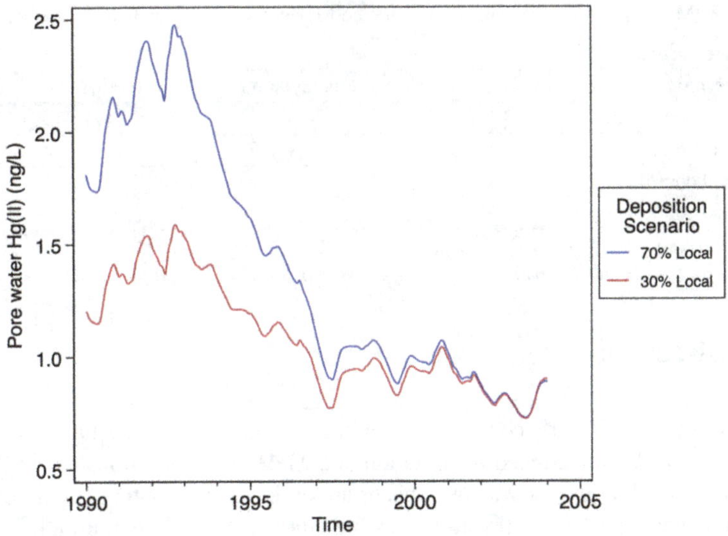

Fig. 4.13 Predicted Hg(II) concentrations in surface sediment pore waters (top 3 mm) for 2 Hg deposition scenarios. No field data available for top 3 mm specifically, which may have different concentrations than samples integrated over different depths

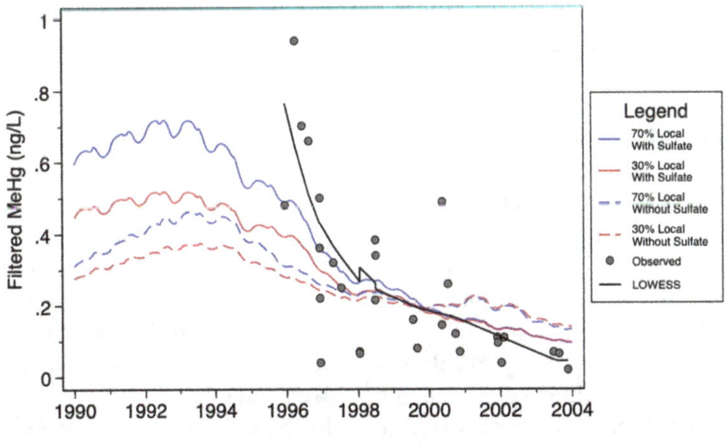

Fig. 4.14 Observed and E-MCM calibrated concentrations of filtered MeHg in 3A-15 surface waters for 1995–2003. Observations from USGS (2018)

The trajectory for atmospheric Hg deposition prior to 1994 (70:30 vs 30:70 local: global source) had little effect on predicted MeHg concentrations in water after 1997. A sulfate effect on methylation did however influence predicted MeHg concentrations in surface waters throughout the simulations (Fig. 4.14).

Table 4.2 Model performance statistics for filtered MeHg concentrations in surface waters

Calibration scenario			
Hg deposition	Sulfate effect on methylation	RMSE	Bias
70% local contribution	Yes	0.147	0.006
70% local contribution	No	0.172	0.035
30% local contribution	Yes	0.205	0.042
30% local contribution	No	0.216	0.047

Lower values of RMSE and bias are better
RMSE = root mean square error

4.4 Discussion

These model results are consistent with the hypothesis that declines in sulfate loading in the 1990s reduced methylation and MeHg concentrations at site 3A-15. The model calibration for MeHg concentrations in surface waters better reflected observed declines when methylation was linked to sulfate concentration (Fig. 4.14, Table 4.2).

The model results also suggest other factors may have played a role in the decline of surface water MeHg concentrations at 3A-15, potentially including Hg loading rates to the marsh prior to 1995 and changes to other water quality conditions. The calibration with the combined effects of a sulfate dependency on methylation and the estimated 70:30 (local:global source) trajectory for atmospheric deposition provided the best fit to observations of the 4 calibrations (Fig. 4.14). More confidence is assigned to the predicted contribution of declining sulfate than changes in Hg deposition. This is because the decline in sulfate concentrations at 3A-15 from 1996 to 2003 was measured directly. The contribution of atmospheric Hg deposition to declines in simulated MeHg concentrations in surface waters from 1995 to 2003 was related to legacy effects from higher Hg deposition rates in the early 1990s, inferred from indirect evidence. Furthermore, the influence of Hg deposition prior to the simulation period was related to model assumptions affecting the duration of legacy effects. For example, how long would it take Hg(II) concentrations in sediments, and importantly Hg(II) concentrations available for methylation to respond to a change in Hg deposition (discussed further below)?

DOC and chloride concentrations also declined from 1995 to 2003 at site 3A-15, while pH rose slightly (Figs. 4.6 and 4.7). DOC is well documented to have a strong influence on Hg cycling in aquatic systems, with competing influences that could increase or decrease MeHg concentrations, depending on the setting and environmental compartment of interest. In this analysis, simulations assumed DOC-bound Hg(II) in pore water was included in the pool available for methylation. Higher DOC concentrations led to more methylation, all else being equal. A sensitivity simulation indicated that declining water column DOC levels in simulations tended towards lower predicted surface water MeHg in the filtered phase. It is less clear whether declining DOC would also have contributed to declining fish Hg concentrations. E-MCM was calibrated with MeHg bound to DOC assumed to be unavailable for uptake by plankton, consistent with reports of higher bioaccumulation factors (BAFs) for MeHg in plankton and fish at lower DOC concentrations (*e.g.* Watras et al. 1998). Predicted declines in filtered MeHg would be at least partially offset in the food web due to higher BAFs. Declining chloride was not predicted to have a meaningful effect on MeHg in surface waters, although it may have had more influence on the availability of dissolved MeHg for uptake by the food web.

The effect of cell size on model results was also examined. The largest predicted source of MeHg at 3A-15 in the early 1990s was in situ production in sediments. In later years of the simulation, MeHg production declined dramatically due to the decline of sulfate concentrations. Predicted MeHg concentration in surface waters depended more on assumed declines in inflowing MeHg concentration, and less on processes occurring within the model domain. Furthermore, there is uncertainty whether the model assumption that methylation had a first order dependency on sulfate concentration would be valid at extremely low sulfate concentrations prevalent in later years of the simulation. If sulfate concentrations approached zero, would methylation rates to do the same? A number of methylating bacteria have been identified in addition to sulfate reducers (*e.g.* Gilmour et al. 2018; Fleming et al. 2006; Kerin et al. 2006), including bacteria with the ability to methylate in the absence of sulfate within WCA-3A (Bae et al. 2014; see also Chap. 3, Vol. II). For these reasons, the model results for the early years of the simulation, when the rate of decline of MeHg in water was greatest, are viewed as having greater reliability.

A further consideration is the time required for various steps to occur between changes in sulfate or inorganic Hg loading and MeHg concentrations in surface waters. In model simulations, methylation responded immediately to assigned declines in surface water sulfate concentration, as it was assumed that pore water sulfate concentrations and sulfate reduction responded immediately to changes in surface water sulfate. Hg(II) in contrast exists primarily in the solid phase in surface sediments. The pool of Hg(II) available for methylation, even if in dissolved form, has some connection with solid phase Hg(II) through partitioning. This connectivity has the potential to slow the pore water Hg(II) response to changes in Hg(II) loading. In the simulations presented here, Hg(II) in sediments was fully and instantly exchangeable between solids and pore water. In a mixed sediment layer a few cm thick, it would have taken decades for Hg(II) concentrations to respond to changes in loading. To allow the model to predict a rate of decline of MeHg concentrations in water consistent with observations, the surface sediment layer in the model was assigned a thickness of 3 mm. This allowed Hg(II) concentrations in pore water to respond more quickly than if a thicker sediment layer had been used. As a result, legacy effects of changes to Hg deposition lasted a few years, in terms of the time for sediment Hg(II) concentrations to respond in the model (Fig. 4.13). The true duration of legacy effects could be shorter or longer. An alternative mechanism to allow the pool of Hg(II) available for methylation to respond faster would be to have slow desorption of Hg(II) from solids. This would reduce the buffering effect of solid phase Hg(II) on the response of dissolved Hg(II) in pore water. In this scheme, a well-mixed surface sediment layer on the order of a few cm thick could experience rapid changes in pore water Hg(II) but much slower (decadal) changes in solid phase

Hg. Hg methylation, to the extent it depends on dissolved Hg(II), could be decoupled from the response time for Hg on sediment solids. A third possibility is that some component of in situ methylation at site 3A-15 occurs in the water column, where Hg (II) concentrations and methylation would respond more quickly to changes in loading.

4.5 Conclusions

A mechanistic model analysis was carried out to examine the role of declining sulfate on MeHg concentrations in surface waters at site 3A-15 observed from 1995 to 2003. The analysis supports the hypothesis that declines in sulfate contributed to declining MeHg production and concentrations at the site. The analysis also estimated that atmospheric Hg deposition could have declined in the early 1990s and contributed to declining MeHg production and concentrations at 3A-15. This prediction is assigned less confidence than the sulfate effect because declines in sulfate were measured directly while atmospheric Hg deposition rates and trends prior to 1994 had to be constructed using indirect means, and the duration of legacy effects is not accurately quantified.

Time has passed since this work was originally carried out, and advances have since been made in the understanding of the mercury cycle. The treatment of mercury cycling in the E-MCM model was sufficient to provide the insights reported here, but additional research on the following topics would help in understanding and in modeling the magnitude and timing of the response of MeHg concentrations in the Everglades following changes in sulfate loading and atmospheric Hg deposition: (1) the pool of Hg(II) available for methylation, (2) the kinetics of Hg (II) adsorption and desorption between solids and the dissolved phase, and associated effects on Hg(II) availability for methylation, (3) the active depth of sediments relevant to MeHg supply to overlying waters, and (4) the extent to which overall methylation in the Everglades depends on sulfate reduction, or on non-sulfate reducing microbes, especially at very low sulfate levels. Some work was done previously to soft-link results from a model of geochemical sulfur cycling with a model of mercury cycling and bioaccumulation (Gilmour et al. 2007). Additional progress to develop model frameworks that simulate the environmental drivers of mercury cycling as well as the mercury cycle itself, would lead to an improved predictive capability.

References

Abtew W, Huebner RS, Ciuca V (2005) 2005 South Florida Environmental Report. Chapter 5: Hydrology of the South Florida Environment. South Florida Water Management District, West Palm Beach, FL

Aiken GR, Gilmour CC, Krabbenhoft DP, Orem W (2011) Dissolved organic matter in the Florida Everglades: implications for ecosystem restoration. Crit Rev Environ Sci Technol 41 (S1):217–248

Atkeson TD, Axelrad DM, Pollman CD, Keeler GJ (2003) Integrating atmospheric mercury deposition with aquatic cycling in the Florida Everglades: an approach for conducting a total maximum daily load analysis for an atmospherically derived pollutant. Integrated Summary, Final Report. Prepared by the Florida Department of Environmental Protection, University of Michigan Air Quality Laboratory, and Tetra Tech Inc., 247 pp

Axelrad DM, Atkeson TD, Lange T, Pollman CD, Gilmour CC, Orem WH, Mendelssohn IA, Frederick PC, Krabbenhoft DP, Aiken GR, Scheidt DJ, Kalla PI (2007) Mercury monitoring, research and environmental assessment in South Florida. Chapter 3B in 2005 South Florida Environmental Report

Bae H, Dierberg FE, Ogram A (2014) Syntrophs dominate sequences associated with the mercury-methylating gene hgcA in the Water Conservation Areas of the Florida Everglades. Appl Environ Microbiol 80:6517–6526

Benoit JM, Gilmour CC, Mason RP, Heyes A (1999) Sulfide controls on mercury speciation and bioavailability to methylating bacteria in sediment pore waters. Environ Sci Technol 33:951–957

Engstrom DR, Pollman CD, Fitzgerald WF, Balcom PH (2003) Evaluation of recent trends in atmospheric mercury deposition in south Florida from lake sediment records. Final Report. Florida Department of Environmental Protection, Tallahassee, FL

Fleming EJ, Mack EE, Green PG, Nelson DC (2006) Mercury methylation from unexpected sources: molybdate-inhibited freshwater sediments and an iron-reducing bacterium. Appl Environ Microbiol 72(1):457–464

Gilmour CC, Riedel GS, Ederington MC, Bell JT, Benoit JM, Gill GA, Stordal MC (1998) Methylmercury concentrations and production rates across a trophic gradient in the northern Everglades. Biogeochemistry 40:327–345

Gilmour C, Roden E, Harris R (2007) Approaches to modeling sulfate reduction and methylmercury production in the Everglades. Tasks 5 and 6. MAP for RECOVER Section 3.6.4.4. Final Report

Gilmour CC, Bullock AL, McBurney A, Podar M, Elias DA (2018) Robust mercury methylation across diverse methanogenic archaea. mBio 9:e02403-17

Guentzel JL, Landing WM, Gill GA, Pollman CD (2001) Processes influencing rainfall deposition of mercury in Florida: The FAMS Project (1992-1996). Environ Sci Technol 35:863–873

Hanson PC, Johnson TB, Schindler DE, Kitchell JF (1997) Fish Bioenergetics 3.0. Wisconsin Sea Grant Institute

Harris RC, Bodaly RA (1998) Temperature, growth and dietary effects on fish mercury dynamics in two Ontario lakes. Biogeochemistry 40(2/3):175–187

Harris R, Pollman C, Hutchinson D, Beals D (2000) Florida Pilot Mercury Total Maximum Daily Load (TMDL) Study: application of the Everglades Mercury Cycling Model (E-MCM) to Site WCA 3A-15. Prepared for the United States Environmental Protection Agency and Florida Department of Environmental Protection

Harris R, Pollman C, Beals D, Hutchinson D (2003) Modeling mercury cycling and bioaccumulation in Everglades Marshes with the Everglades Mercury Cycling Model (E-MCM). Final Report. Prepared for the Florida Department of Environmental Protection and the South Florida Water Management District

Harris RC, Rudd JWM, Amyot M, Babiarz C, Beaty KG, Blanchfield PJ, Bodaly RA, Branfireun BA, Gilmour CC, Graydon JA, Heyes A, Hintelmann H, Hurley JP, Kelly CA, Krabbenhoft DP, Lindberg SE, Mason RP, Paterson MJ, Podemski CL, Robinson A, Sandilands KA, Southworth GR, St. Louis VL, Tate MT (2007) Whole-ecosystem study shows rapid fish-mercury response to changes in mercury deposition. Proc Natl Acad Sci USA 104(42):16586–16591

Hudson RJM, Gherini SA, Watras CJ, Porcella DB (1994) Modeling the biogeochemical cycle of mercury in lakes: the Mercury Cycling Model (MCM) and its application to the MTL study lakes. In: Watras CJ, Huckabee JW (eds) Mercury pollution - integration and synthesis. CRC Press, Boca Raton, FL

Hurley JP, Krabbenhoft DP, Cleckner LB, Olson ML, Aiken GR, Rawlik RS Jr (1998) System controls on the aqueous distribution of mercury in the northern Florida Everglades. Biogeochemistry 40:293–310

Husar JD, Husar RB (2002) Trends of anthropogenic mercury mass flows and emissions in Florida. Final Report, Lantern Corporation, Clayton, MO

Keeler GJ, Marsik FJ, Al-Wali KI, Dvonch JT (2000). Project final technical report - Modeled deposition of speciated mercury to the SFWMD Water Conservation Area 3A: 22 June 1995 to 21 June 1996. Project description and results. The University of Michigan Air Quality Laboratory. Ann Arbor, MI

Kerin EJ, Gilmour CC, Roden E, Suzuki MT, Coates JD, Mason RP (2006) Mercury methylation by dissimilatory iron-reducing bacteria. Appl Environ Microbiol 2006:7919–7921

Krabbenhoft DP (1996) Mercury studies in the Florida Everglades. U.S. Geological Survey Fact Sheet FS-166-96

Krabbenhoft DP, Orem W, Aiken G, Gilmour C, Scheidt D, Kalla P, Rumbold D, Lange T (2008) A review of mercury monitoring and research activities in the Everglades, 1995–2008. Presented at the Greater Everglades Ecosystem Restoration (GEER) Conference

Munthe J, Bodaly RA, Branfireun B, Driscoll CT, Gilmour CC, Harris R, Horvat M, Lucotte M, Malm O (2007) Recovery of mercury-contaminated fisheries. Ambio 36(1):33–44

National Atmospheric Deposition Program (NADP) (2017) Mercury Deposition Network (MDN). NADP Program Office. Illinois State Water Survey, University of Illinois, Champaign, IL. Available at http://nadp.sws.uiuc.edu/mdn

Orem W, Gilmour C, Axelrad D, Krabbenhoft D, Scheidt D, Kalla P, McCormick P, Gabriel M, Aiken G (2011) Sulfur in the South Florida ecosystem: distribution, sources, biogeochemistry, impacts, and management for restoration. Crit Rev Environ Sci Technol 41(S1):249–288

Pollman CD, Harris RC, Porcella DB, Hutchinson D (2006) Have changes in atmospheric deposition caused concomitant changes in largemouth bass concentrations in the Florida Everglades – a model Hindcast Analysis. Final report submitted to Florida Electric Power Coordinating Group, Tampa, FL. Submitted by Tetra Tech, Inc., Lafayette, CA

RMB Consulting & Research, Inc (2002) Atmospheric mercury emissions from major point sources – Broward, Dade, and Palm Beach Counties, 1980-000. Final Report, RMB Consulting & Research, Inc., Raleigh, NC

South Florida Water Management District (SFWMD) (2019) Online database. http://my.sfwmd.gov/dbhydroplsql/show_dbkey_info.main_menu. Accessed 2 July 2019

Stober QJ, Thornton K, Jones R, Richards J, Ivey C, Welch R, Madden M, Trexler J, Gaiser E, Scheidt D, Rathbun S (2001) South Florida Ecosystem Assessment: Phase I/II – Everglades Stressor Interactions: Hydropatterns, Eutrophication, Habitat Alteration, and Mercury Contamination (Summary). EPA 904-R-01-002. USEPA Region 4 Science & Ecosystem Support Division, Water Management Division, and Office of Research and Development

Tetra Tech Inc (1999a) Dynamic mercury cycling model for Windows 95/NT. A model for mercury cycling in lakes – D-MCM Version 1.0 – User's Guide and Technical Reference. Prepared for EPRI

Tetra Tech Inc (1999b) Everglades mercury cycling model for Windows 95/NT. A Model for Mercury Cycling in Everglades Marsh Areas – Draft User's Guide and Technical Reference. Version 1.0 Beta. Prepared for the United States Environmental Protection Agency

USGS (2018) USGS SOFIA Data Exchange. https://sofia.usgs.gov/projects/index.php?project_url=evergl_merc

Watras CJ, Back RC, Halvorsen S, Hudson RJM, Morrison KA, Wente SP (1998) Bioaccumulation of mercury in pelagic freshwater food webs. STOTEN 219:183–208

Chapter 5
Temporal Changes in the Mercury Signal in the Everglades: A Synthesis

Curtis D. Pollman

Abstract Analyzing temporal trends for a response variable can help elucidate causality. Analyzing temporal trends can also help elucidate time scales of response and factors influencing those time scales. This part of the book (for which this is the culminating chapter) comprises a series of papers devoted to trends in the *alpha* and the *omega* of the Everglades mercury (Hg) biogeochemical cycle—atmospheric inputs of Hg and the accumulation of Hg in biota. This part of the book also includes a chapter on legacy Hg previously released into the environment and its likely impacts on mitigating the Everglades Hg problem depending upon whether the legacy Hg is stored globally or locally within the Everglades. Lastly this part of the book includes a chapter in which a mechanistic or deterministic model is used to analyze possible factors contributing to a short-term decline in largemouth bass concentrations of Hg observed at a marsh site within the Everglades. The present chapter integrates key findings from each of these chapters in an effort to both help define causality and how legacy Hg can influence or impede the rate at which the Everglades can recover in response to mitigation efforts.

Keywords Everglades restoration · Wading bird mercury · Largemouth bass mercury · *Gambusia* mercury · Sulfate · Long-term trends · Short-term trends · Legacy mercury

5.1 Introduction

When considering the likelihood of success of different management strategies to resolve or mitigate the Everglades mercury (Hg) problem, there are two key questions that decision makers need to contend with. First of course is the issue of causality; second is the issue of the time scale of recovery. Considerable effort has

C. D. Pollman (✉)
Aqua Lux Lucis, Inc., Gainesville, FL, USA
e-mail: cpollman@aqualuxlucis.org

C. D. Pollman et al. (eds.), *Mercury and the Everglades. A Synthesis and Model for Complex Ecosystem Restoration*, https://doi.org/10.1007/978-3-030-55635-8_5

been devoted in this compendium to the issue of causality from both mechanistic (Chaps. 1, 3, 4, 5 and 6 in Vol. II) and empirical (Chap. 6, Vol. II and Chap. 6, this volume) perspectives. In the latter case, this effort includes using statistical models to evaluate whether a hypothesized relationship between a causal variable (including sulfate in particular) and a Hg-related response variable (*e.g.*, surface water methyl Hg (MeHg) or fish tissue Hg concentrations) across time and space are both significant and consistent with our underlying mechanistic understanding of the structural nature of that relationship.

The analysis of temporal trends can further elucidate causality. This part of Vol. III presents three chapters devoted to Hg trends, including: Chap. 1 (atmospheric deposition trends); Chap. 2 (fish, wading bird and other biota trends); and Chap. 4 (a mechanistic modeling analysis of MeHg trends at site 3A15 in WCA-3A using the Everglades Mercury Cycling Model [E-MCM]). A fourth chapter in this part (Chap. 3) looks at the question of legacy Hg—*i.e.,* excess (anthropogenic) Hg historically released into the environment—and whether this legacy Hg (which is stored in various reservoirs ranging in scale from highly localized to global) can militate against Hg mitigation efforts in the Everglades. This chapter integrates key findings from each of these chapters in an effort to bring some insight to the question of causality with respect to Hg biota dynamics in the Everglades. The chapter begins with an evaluation of long-term trends (decadal extending back to nearly before the advent of major cultural disturbances initiated in the Everglades in the late 1800s) and then considers the relationship between short-term dynamics of both largemouth bass (LMB) and *Gambusia* spp. (mosquitofish) Hg concentrations and potential driving variables, including atmospheric deposition of Hg and sulfate concentrations. The chapter then concludes with some comments on the question of how quickly the Everglades could recover from current levels of Hg exposure.

5.2 Long-Term Trends

5.2.1 Biota

Perhaps the most robust dataset available for evaluating the magnitude of changes in Hg exposure and bioaccumulation within the Everglades between pre-cultural and current conditions is embodied in the retrospective study by Frederick et al. (2004) of Hg concentrations in four different species of wading birds measured in the scapular feathers of archived museum specimens. The Frederick et al. (2004) study is useful not only because it compared feather Hg concentrations in archived specimens from multiple points in time between 1912 and 2000, but because—as noted in Chap. 2 (this volume)—the "available record of Hg exposure in Everglades wading birds suggests that these taxa can reflect variation in Hg availability at large geographic scales." As discussed by Frederick et al. (2004; see also Chap. 2, this volume), the trajectory of feather Hg concentrations across all four species studied was consistent over time, with low and relatively stable concentrations observed

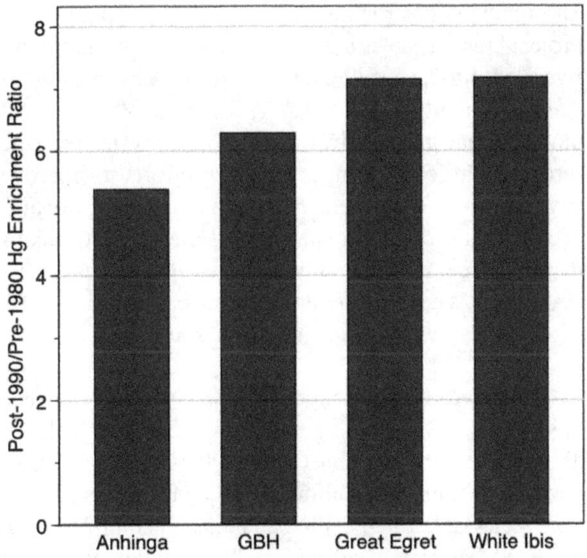

Fig. 5.1 Enrichment ratios (ER) calculated as the ratio of mean scapular feather Hg concentrations for post-1990 and pre-1980 specimens for the four species of Everglades wading birds included in the Frederick et al. (2004) retrospective study. *GBH* Great Blue Heron

between the earliest points in the period of record until *ca.* 1980 (<2.8 mg/kg for anhingas, white ibises, and great egrets; <3.3 mg/kg for great blue herons). Concentrations in specimens collected after 1990 increased sharply, with enrichment ratios (ER) comparing mean pre- and post-1980 concentrations ranging from 5.4 (anhingas) to 7.2 (white ibises) (Fig. 5.1). When compared to historically low levels, these large post-1980 increases were suggestive to Frederick et al. (2004) of "partial evidence for a threshold of reproductive impairment."

5.2.2 *Disturbance and Changes in Water Chemistry*

Major disturbances to the Everglades that have impacted the biogeochemical cycling of Hg include disturbances originating within (*e.g.*, hydrologic and land use patterns/practices) and external to the ecosystem (*e.g.*, atmospheric cycling of Hg and resultant changes in atmospheric deposition fluxes of Hg). As discussed by Rumbold in Chap. 2 of Vol. I, the hydrology of the Everglades has been fundamentally altered through a series of activities designed to drain land both for agricultural purposes and to facilitate or enable urban development. The first major efforts to drain the Everglades began in 1881 and, by 1917, the Miami, North New River, Hillsborough and West Palm Beach canals from Lake Okeechobee through the Everglades to the Atlantic Ocean were completed. As evidenced by drought conditions between 1931 and 1945, these hydrologic changes to the Everglades led to overdrainage. These changes also were inadequate for controlling flooding resulting from extreme rainfall events. As a result, these hydrologic problems led to the initiation of the Central and Southern Florida Project for Flood Control and other Purposes (CSF Project).

Through the construction of perimeter levees and flood control structures, the CSF Project created the structural features that define the major hydrologic units of the Everglades today, including the Water Conservation Areas (WCAs) and the Everglades Agricultural Area (EAA) (Chap. 2, Vol. I). By 1963 most of the hydrologic modifications imposed by the CSF Project were completed. Between 1965 and 1973, further hydrologic changes included efforts to improve conveyance and meet the environmental water demands of Everglades National Park (ENP). Lastly, in 1979 backpumping of excess water from the EAA to Lake Okeechobee—which was a major source of nutrient loading (and likely sulfate loading) to the lake—was terminated as a land/water table management process. This resulted in the redirection of all excess water from the EAA southward to the Everglades Protection Area (EvPA).

These hydrologic changes to the Everglades have been accompanied by changes in water quality, including major ions (Chap. 2, Vol. I), nutrients (Chap. 5, Vol. II), dissolved organic carbon (DOC; Chap. 4, Vol.II) and sulfate (Chap. 2, Vol. II). Perhaps the most compelling evidence for these overall changes is given by annual time series data for specific conductance compiled by Flora and Rosendahl (1982) collected between 1959 and 1979 at Station P33 located in Shark River Slough (SRS) nearly 16 km south of the S-12D structure and augmented with monthly data collected by the South Florida Water Management District (SFWMD) from the same location between October 1985 and March 2019 (DBHYDRO 2019b). Results from the concatenated data sets (using annual mean values for the SFWMD data to be consistent with annual values presented by Flora and Rosendahl) show a steep monotonic increase in specific conductance between 1959 and 1979 from ~240 to 630 μS/cm followed by variable levels oscillating around a mean value of 550 μS/cm between 1985 and the present (Fig. 5.2). These changes translate to an increase in overall ionic strength of 230%. A comparison of Ca and Na/K concentrations measured in 1939 and cited by Love (1955) with values measured by Flora and Rosendahl (1982) suggests that substantive changes in major ion chemistry likely had not occurred within the northern ENP until at least the late 1950s. Indeed, Miller et al. (2004) concluded that increases in chloride that accompanied the increases in specific conductance were the result of increased hydrologic inputs of high conductivity water from the north by the L-67 canals which were constructed in 1962 and further extended 15.3 km south of Tamiami Trail to within 4.8 km of site P33 in 1966–1967.

The changes in major ion chemistry reflected in Fig. 5.2 likely included large increases in sulfate concentrations. This is shown in Fig. 5.3, which shows box plots of both chloride and sulfate concentrations measured in 1985–1986 with the values for Shark River Canal at the Tamiami Bridge Canal in 1939 reported by Love (1955). Those results suggest Cl and SO4 increases by 1985–1986 approximating 350% and 250% respectively. More detailed (~monthly) time series data for sulfate concentrations at P33 presented by Miller et al. (2004) show highly variable but generally increasing sulfate concentrations between 1960 through 1985 (maximum values around 10 mg/L) followed by a stepped increase in minimum values from <2 mg/L to between 3 and 5 mg/L mg/L and an increase in maximum values to

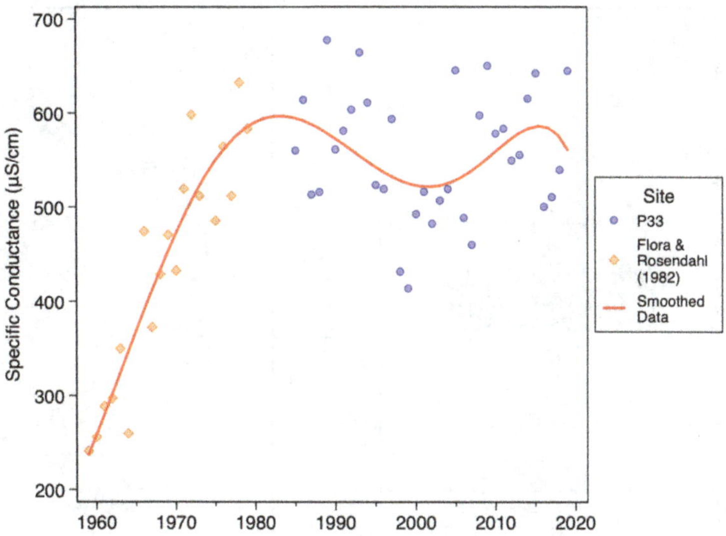

Fig. 5.2 Temporal trends in specific conductance at site P33 located in SRS approximately 16 km south from the S-12D structure discharging into the ENP. Annual average data abstracted from Flora and Rosendahl (1982) for 1959–1979 and DBHYDRO for 1985–2019. Smoothing conducted using local polynomial smoothing (Epanechnikov kernel function; kernel $n = 6$; StataCorp, 2019)

between 10 and 25 mg/L beginning in 1986. Miller et al. (2004) attributed the increases in sulfate to increased flow under Tamiami Trail.

As mentioned earlier, another major disturbance to the Everglades *vis-à-vis* Hg cycling relates to changes in atmospheric deposition of Hg over time as the result of anthropogenic activity. As discussed in both Chap. 6 (Vol. I) and Chap. 1 (this volume), the temporal trends in atmospheric deposition of Hg suggest a pattern of localized enhanced deposition superimposed on a longer-term pattern dominated by large scale atmospheric cycling. This is evidenced by comparing sediment core data for Hg accumulation rates for cores collected in Lake Annie (located north of Lake Okeechobee approximately 203 km from the northern edge of WCA-2A and thus less likely to reflect any significant impacts from local emission sources originating from the south Florida urban fringe within Miami-Dade, Broward and Palm Beach counties) and WCA-2A (Fig. 5.4) which lies directly west of and much closer to the south Florida urban fringe. To facilitate a comparison between the two sets of sediment core data, the accumulation fluxes for each individual core as a function of time have all been normalized to *ca.* 1910 by dividing each point in the core time series by the flux observed proximal to or during 1910. The normalized sediment accumulation rates show good concordance between Lake Annie and WCA-2A until *ca.* 1980, when the signal for WCA-2A increases more rapidly. This divergence corresponds to a large increase in local emissions due primarily to medical waste incineration and municipal waste combustion that began around 1981 in the south Florida urban fringe (RMB 2002; see Chap. 5, Vol. I). The implication of these

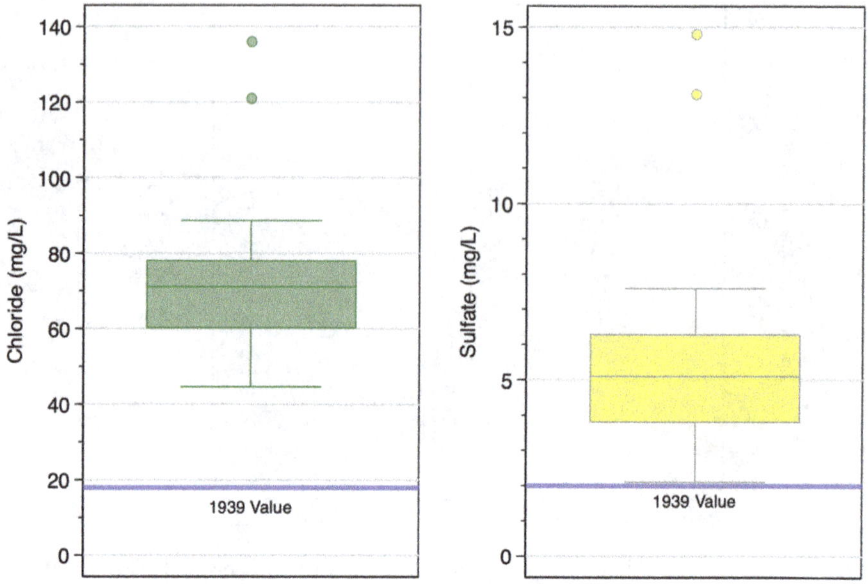

Fig. 5.3 Box plots of monthly concentrations of chloride (left-hand panel) and sulfate (right-hand panel) measured at site P33 during 1985–1986 ($N = 15$) by the SFWMD (DBHYDRO, 2019b). Superimposed on each box plot are the historical values reported by Love (1955) for a single sample collected in 1939 from "Shark River Canal at Tamiami Trail Bridge" (blue horizontal line). Each filled box delimits the interquartile range (25 to 75%) of the distribution. Whiskers are calculated based on the interquartile range x 1.5 and modified based on whether the values of the largest or smallest observation lie within or outside the whiskers (StataCorp. 2019)

results is that the Everglades experienced a period of substantially enhanced fluxes of atmospheric deposition of Hg relative to global background that originated from the south Florida urban fringe. The likelihood of this localized source impact on Hg enrichment is further substantiated by sediment cores collected by Rood et al. (1995) throughout the Everglades. Results from these cores—which were collected prior to the large declines in atmospheric deposition indicated by the Lake Annie and the WCA-2A cores shown in Fig. 5.4—show modern enrichment ratios (ER) ranging from 4.0 for WCA-3 to 8.7 for WCA-2 (average values for each major hydrologic unit). In contrast, the ER for two cores collected from the Savannas Marsh (a linear coastal wetland located in Lucie and St. Martin counties approximately 50 km north of West Palm Beach), averaged 3.4 and was closer to ER values observed at more background sites in North America (Chap. 1, this volume).

Disturbance in the form of atmospheric deposition also includes changes in atmospheric loadings of sulfate in Florida which have likely increased by perhaps 350% (*ca.* 1990) relative to pre-cultural (*ca.* 1880) deposition fluxes because of large increases in anthropogenic emissions of atmospheric SO_2 (Husar 1986 and personal communication).

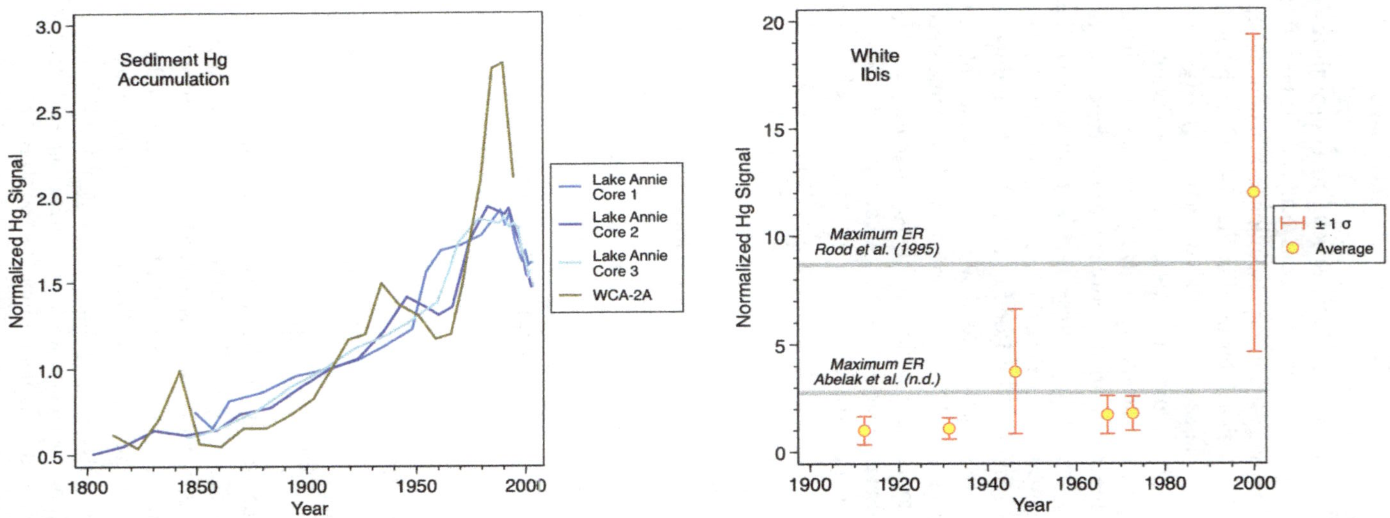

Fig. 5.4 Comparison of normalized Hg accumulation rates in Everglades sediment cores with normalized Hg concentrations measured in the scapular feathers of white ibis specimens. The normalized signal for each core is calculated as the enrichment ratio (ER) of the annual Hg accumulation rate at a given point in time relative to the accumulation rate measured in the core interval most closely approximating *ca.* 1910. White ibis ER results are normalized to *ca.* 1912 to provide a direct comparison with the sediment core results. Left-hand panel—results from sediment cores collected from Lake Annie (3 replicates) and WCA-2A as a function of time. Right-hand panel—white ibis ER values between 1912 and 2000 with maximum ER values from the WCA-2A core and the Rood et al. (1995) cores superimposed. Maximum ER for the Rood et al. (1995) data corresponds to the maximum average ER observed for the different major hydrologic units within the Everglades. White ibis ER results are from concentrations published by Frederick et al. (2004). Lake Annie core data from Engstrom et al. (2003); WCA-2A core data from Abelak et al. (unpublished data provided through T. Atkeson)

5.2.3 *Long-Term Trends Synthesis*

Because of the availability of substantially more specimens both with respect to points in time and total number of individual specimens analyzed, the Frederick et al. (2004) white ibis data can provide a higher resolution evaluation of temporal changes than shown in Fig. 5.1. This is illustrated in Fig. 5.4, which integrates the white ibis Hg data with changes in sediment-inferred atmospheric Hg fluxes over time. Similar to the sediment Hg accumulation rates, the concentrations of Hg in white ibis feathers are incorporated into the figure as ER values (normalized to *ca.* 1912), thus enabling a more direct comparison between the disturbance trajectory for Hg inputs to the Everglades and white ibis response. The comparison illustrates several key points. First, the mean white ibis ER of 12.0 $\pm$ 7.4 in 2000 exceeds the maximum average ER of 8.7 reported by Rood et al. (1995) for sediment cores within WCA-2. It should be noted that the Rood et al. ER values are likely biased somewhat high relative to using *ca.* 1910 as the normalizing base value since Rood et al. (1995) used *ca.* 1900 to define historic conditions. Examining the Hg accumulation trajectories for the Lake Annie and WCA-2A cores over this time interval suggests this bias is on the order of 10% or more; accounting for this bias would in turn indicate that the maximum ER for the Rood et al. (1995) data for WCA-2 is $\leq$7.9. Coupled with (uncorrected) average ER values for the other major hydrologic units ranging from 4.0 to 7.9, this result strengthens the likelihood that the white ibis ER values exceed expected ER values based solely on increases in atmospheric deposition that occurred in the Everglades (including localized emissions impacts). More specifically, the elevated white ibis ER in 2000 in excess of values that can be directly attributed to atmospheric deposition indicate the effect of a concomitant disturbance that served to magnify the effects of increased atmospheric inputs of Hg. This concomitant disturbance may reflect increased sulfate loadings that likely peaked (particularly in the ENP) around 1980–1990 (Fig. 5.2).

5.3 Short-Term Dynamics

5.3.1 *Largemouth Bass*

The monitoring of Hg concentrations in the tissues of largemouth bass (LMB) conducted by Lange and colleagues (Chap. 2, this volume) provides an essentially continuous annual record for this metric for several marsh stations between the early 1990s and the present. Figure 5.5 includes temporal trends for two of these sites—LOXF4 located essentially in the center of WCA1 (the Loxahatchee National Wildlife Refuge) and 3A15 located deep in the interior of WCA3. Very early in the evolution of the South Florida Mercury Science Program (see Preface to Vol. I), site 3A15 was initially considered an aquatic biota Hg "hot-spot" because of very high fish tissue Hg concentrations (*e.g.*, average annual LMB Hg concentrations

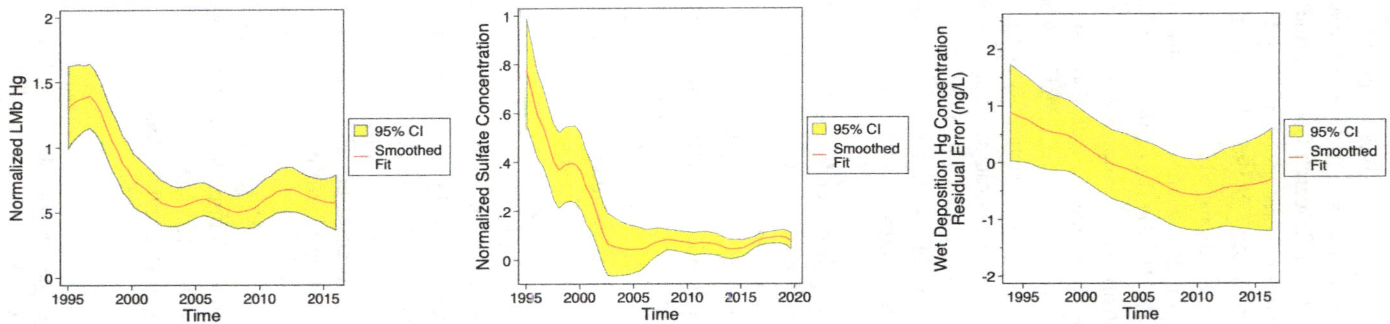

Fig. 5.5 Temporal changes in LMB Hg concentrations (left-hand panel), surface water sulfate concentrations (middle panel) and the Hg signal in wet deposition not accounted for by seasonal dynamics and rainfall variations over time (right-hand panel; see also Sect. 1.2.2.1 and Fig. 1.3 in Chap. 1, this volume). The plots for LMB Hg and sulfate concentrations were constructed using annual average data for sites 3A15 and LOXF4. The plot for the Hg signal in wet deposition was constructed using monthly data. Smoothing for all three variables was conducted using kernel-weighted local polynomial regression and includes 95% confidence intervals (CI) for each smoothed curve (StataCorp, 2019)

equal to 1.10 ± 0.30 mg/kg between 1993 and 1998) and became a focal point of considerable cause and effect analysis when LMB concentrations declined by ~50% by 2001 (Chap. 4, this volume). Also included in Fig. 5.5 are trends for Hg wet deposition fluxes measured at the Beard Research Center in the ENP (Chap. 1, this volume) and surface water sulfate concentrations obtained from the SFWMD DBHYDRO online data base (DBHYDRO 2019c). The trends for both the LMB Hg and surface water sulfate concentrations were normalized to 1995 values by dividing each individual observation by the mean concentration observed during 1995 for the respective two sites. The Hg wet deposition trend in Fig. 5.5 shows the change in the Hg signal in wet deposition over time after accounting for the effects of variations in rainfall depth and seasonal dynamics (see also Sect. 1.2.2.1 and Fig. 1.3 in Chap. 1, this volume). The trends for all three variables were smoothed using kernel-weighted local polynomial regression (StataCorp 2019). Because the LMB Hg and sulfate concentration plots were constructed using average annual data, the bandwidth for the smoothing was set to the minimum value of 1 to minimize oversmoothing. For the plot of the Hg signal in wet deposition, which was constructed using monthly data, the bandwidth was set to 3 to help filter out the noise in the monthly variations.

A quick comparison of the smoothed trends for both LMB Hg and sulfate concentrations shows that both variables dropped sharply between 1995 and 2002/2003, followed by stabilized concentrations throughout the remainder of the period of record. The magnitude of the LMB Hg decline during this interval was between 40% and 52%.[1] The relative decline in sulfate concentrations was even more striking and averaged in excess of 90%. This general concordance of trends across years and magnitude suggests a causative role for sulfate. The Hg signal in wet deposition showed a more sustained decline that continued nearly a decade longer until mid-2013; the signal subsequently was followed by an apparent increase. The decline in the volume weighted mean (VWM) Hg signal between late 1993 approximated 2.3 ng/L by the end of the interval. This decline equates to 18% of the observed VWM concentration of 12.7 ng/L for the entire interval and appears to be far too modest to account for the large biota Hg changes. Declines in Hg deposition in Everglades beginning in the mid- to late-1980s however appear to be far more substantial (Fig. 5.4) than estimated from the more limited record of available direct wet deposition measurements used to construct Fig. 5.5, and model hindcasting conducted with the dynamic E-MCM discussed in Chap. 4 (this volume) suggests that changes in atmospheric deposition of Hg related to declines in local Hg emissions from the south Florida urban fringe coupled with declines in surface water sulfate concentrations are both likely important contributors to the pronounced decline in LMB Hg concentrations at 3A15. The fact that these patterns are consistent when extended to LOXF4 further strengthens this conclusion.

[1]The decline is even higher depending when the overall decline is based on maximal values observed during the 1990–1999 decade. For example, the decline in average annual concentrations at 3A15 was 63% based on using 1993 and 2003 as reference points.

5.3.2 Gambusia

Monitoring of *Gambusia* Hg concentrations conducted in the EvPA by the USEPA as part of its Regional Environmental Monitoring and Assessment Program (R-EMAP; Scheidt and Kalla 2007; Kalla and Scheidt 2017) provides a rich albeit somewhat discontinuous data set for evaluating short term temporal dynamics across the EvPA—both within specific hydrologic units as well as across the system as a whole. Whole system inferences are possible because the R-EMAP project used a randomized sampling scheme specifically designed to provide such inferences. Synoptic sampling was conducted during relatively narrow time intervals at the end of both wet and dry seasons in 1995, 1996, 1999 and 2005, and at the end of the wet season only in 2014.

Analysis of variance (ANOVA) of *Gambusia* Hg concentrations indicates that significant differences occurred between different R-EMAP sampling years and that these differences were more pronounced than overall differences related to hydroperiod. This analysis was conducted on log-transformed concentrations to better approximate normality and used the subset of R-EMAP values screened by Pollman (2014) to remove outlier observations ($N = 579$). Outliers were identified through linear regression and *post hoc* analyses (*e.g.,* Cook's *D* and leverage tests, and analyses of the distribution of model residuals; see Hamilton 2013) to identify influential observations that inappropriately biased model estimation and significance. The analysis was also restricted to the four R-EMAP cycle years that included both wet and dry hydroperiod sampling (1995, 1996, 1999, and 2005). *F* values for year effects were highly significant ($F = 44.12$; $p < 0.0001$); effects related to hydroperiod alone and the interaction between hydroperiod and year were insignificant ($F = 0.07$; $p = 0.7896$) and substantially less important ($F = 9.48$; $p < 0.0001$) compared to the effects of R-EMAP cycle year alone, respectively. The general trend of declining concentrations between 1995 and 2005 is shown for both seasonal cycles in Fig. 5.6. The figure also illustrates that seasonal differences across years were not consistent with respect negative or positive effects.

When the analysis of the effects of R-EMAP cycle year is extended to include the complete range of wet hydroperiod sampling (*i.e.,* 1995–2014), the range of differences is magnified and striking. This is illustrated by Figs. 5.7 and 5.8, which show the distribution of *Gambusia* Hg concentrations during the wet season for each R-EMAP cycle year for the EvPA excluding WCA-2A (designated EvPA*) and WCA-2A, respectively. The results for WCA-2A are presented separately because water chemistry (including sulfate) in WCA-2A is more profoundly impacted by discharges from the EAA than other regions within the EvPA. For example, sulfate concentrations during the wet season for the EvPA* between 1995 and 2005 averaged 5.5 ± 10.0 mg/L compared to 38.2 ± 30.0 mg/L for WCA-2A.

Within the EvPA*, the overall distribution of *Gambusia* Hg concentrations consistently declined between 1995 through 2005, with a further, more pronounced decline observed in 2014 (median concentrations in 1995, 1996, 1999, 2005 and 2014 of 153, 166, 128, 88 and 35 ng/g, respectively). The relative magnitude of the

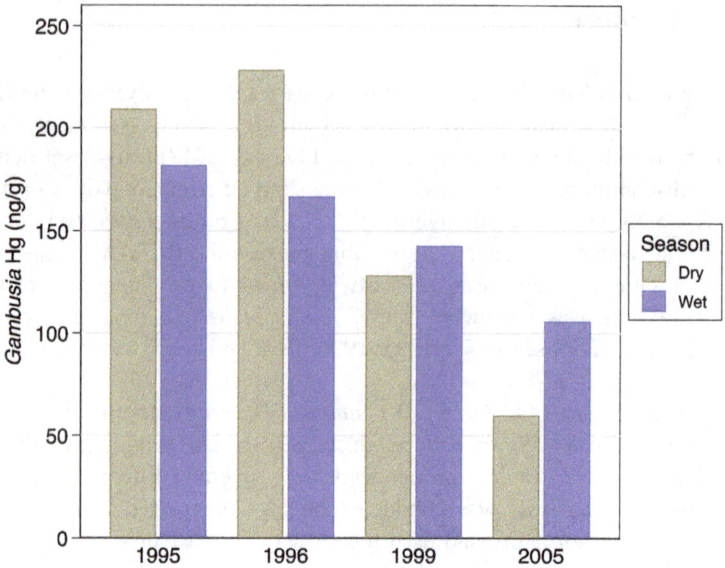

Fig. 5.6 Bar chart of mean values of *Gambusia* Hg concentrations in the EvPA as a function of year and season, 1995–2005. Data from USEPA R-EMAP sampling conducted in the Everglades (Scheidt and Kalla, 2007) as modified by Pollman (2014) to remove outliers. $N = 579$

declines in *Gambusia* Hg between 1995 and 2005 are similar to the declines observed in LMB Hg in marsh sites other than SRS) with long-term monitoring (Fig. 5.5; see also Figs. 2.2 and 2.3 in Chap.2, this volume). It is important to emphasize, however, that these overall declines do not equate to system-wide declines in the EvPA*. Not surprisingly, given that spatial variations in *Gambusia* Hg concentrations occur (Scheidt and Kalla 2007; Kalla and Scheidt 2017), spatial variations in temporal response have been identified (Pollman 2012). Such spatial heterogeneity in temporal response is discussed in Sect. 5.3.3.

According to Kalla and Scheidt (2017), the sharp decline in 2014 cannot be ascribed to changes in body weight or length of *Gambusia*. As a result, the decline likely reflects some biogeochemical factor (or factors) that has altered MeHg production and/or trophic transfer. This likelihood is reinforced by similar, statistically significant declines in MeHg concentrations (Kalla and Scheidt 2017).

Key variables that have been shown to influence Hg methylation in the Everglades include dissolved organic carbon (DOC; alternatively dissolved organic matter or DOM) and sulfate (Chaps. 1, 3, 4 and 6, Vol. II). The likelihood that either of these two variables are important contributors to the temporal trends in *Gambusia* Hg can be qualitatively assessed by evaluating whether the overall trends in the annual distributions of DOC and sulfate agree with the annual trends in *Gambusia* Hg concentrations. This is shown for the distributions during the wet season in Figs. 5.7 and 5.8 for both the EvPA* and WCA2 respectively for sulfate, while Fig. 5.9 shows the comparison with DOC for both regions. Figures 5.7 and 5.8

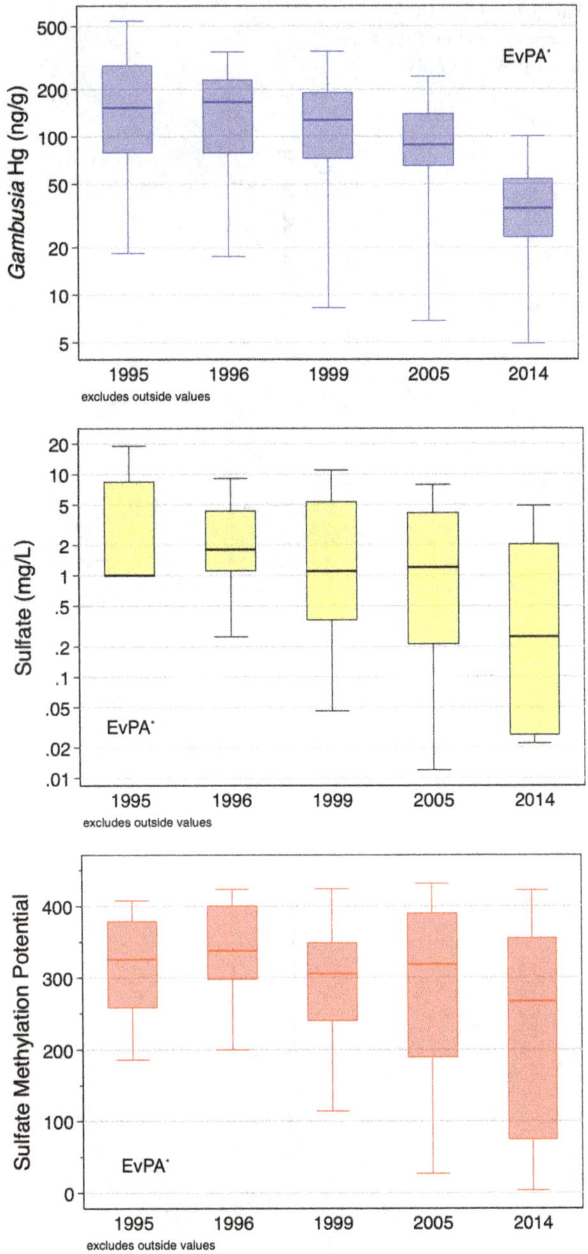

Fig. 5.7 Box plots of *Gambusia* Hg (top panel), surface water sulfate concentrations (middle panel) and sulfate methylation potential (bottom panel) during the wet season in the EvPA exclusive of WCA2 (*i.e.*, EvPA*) as a function of sampling year. USEPA R-EMAP data from Scheidt and Kalla (2007) and Kalla and Scheidt (2017). Values outside the whiskers have been excluded (see Fig. 5.3 for explanation)

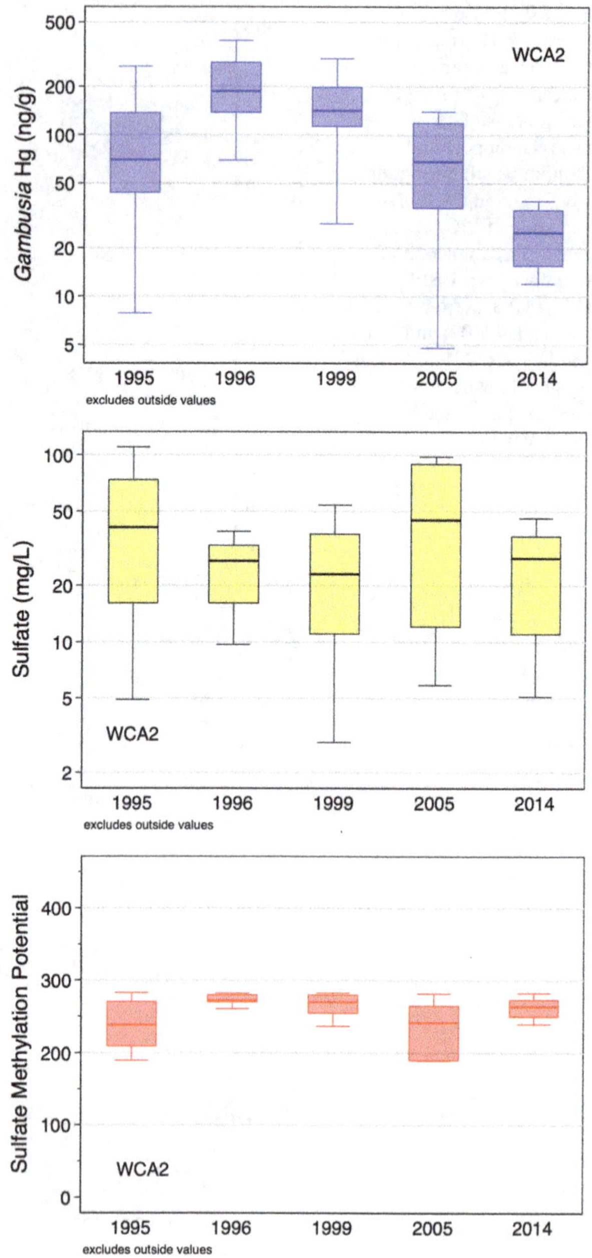

Fig. 5.8 Same as Fig. 5.7, except that the plot includes data for WCA2 only

also include box plots of the computed "sulfate methylation potential" based on non-linear transformations of sulfate concentrations to reflect its unimodal effect on

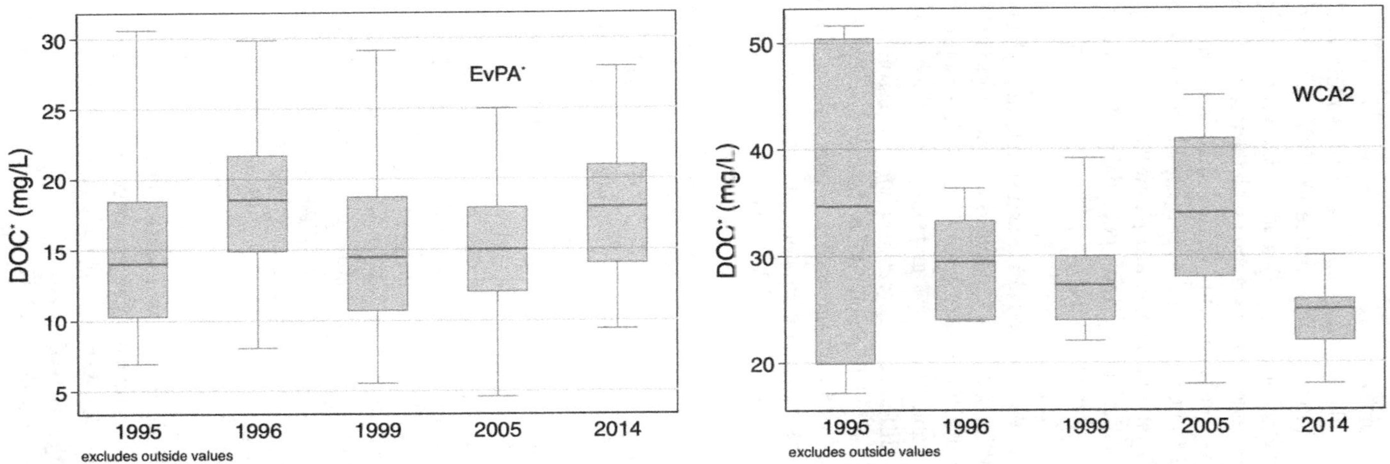

Fig. 5.9 Box plots of DOC* (DOC or TOC depending upon R-EMAP cycle year; see Chap. 6, this volume) for the EvPA* (left-hand panel) and WCA2 (right-hand panel) during the wet season as a function of sampling year. USEPA R-EMAP data from Scheidt and Kalla (2007) and Kalla and Scheidt (2017)

Hg methylation and its subsequent bioaccumulation in *Gambusia* (Pollman 2014; see also Chap. 6, this volume).

For the EvPA*, overall declining trends in both sulfate and its transformed analogue, sulfate methylation potential, match up well with the overall pattern of declining *Gambusia* Hg concentrations. Trends in DOC for the EvPA*, however, are not consistent and do not appear to correspond with the trends in *Gambusia* Hg. This qualitative assessment is consistent with the quantitative structural equation model (SEM) results developed in Chap. 6 (this volume), which considers different interaction (including mediated and competing) pathways between different variables and demonstrated that sulfate methylation potential was the most important independent water chemistry variable influencing Hg methylation and *Gambusia* Hg bioaccumulation in the EvPA.

For WCA2, consistent declines in sulfate and sulfate methylation potential were not observed between 1995 and 2014 and thus do not appear to be a major causative factor. Indeed, compared to the rest of the EvPA, sulfate methylation potential in WCA2 was far more stable (Figs. 5.7 and 5.8, respectively) with a very slight increase in 2014 (1.1% difference between median wet season values for 2005 and 2014). This increase in methylation potential is the calculated product of reductions in ambient sulfate concentrations from earlier, higher values that were greatly and further in excess of the estimated sulfate concentration likely to result in maximal methylation rates (2.8 mg/L for WCA-2A; Table 2, Chap. 7, this volume).

DOC in WCA2, however, underwent a major and significant decline in 2014 (Fig. 5.9). As illustrated by spatial gradients across the EvPA, DOC exported from the EAA is a major source for DOC in WCA2 (*cf.* Scheidt and Kalla 2007). This DOC not only is important as a general driver of Hg methylation (Chap. 6, Vol. II) but, because the DOC derived from the EAA is both more highly sulfidized and more aromatic, its effects on methylation are, *ceteris paribus*, enhanced as well (Chap. 4, Vol. II). As a result, the large decline in the overall distribution of DOC in WCA2 in 2014 likely is a contributing factor to the concomitant *Gambusia* Hg decline.

The large decline in sulfate that occurred in the EvPA* in 2014 is almost certainly a direct consequence of decreased loadings of sulfate exported from the EAA. This is illustrated by Fig. 5.10 which shows changes in annual fluxes of sulfate discharged through S-8 control structure on the Miami Canal as the canal enters WCA-3A immediately south of the EAA. The fluxes are shown as a 12-month cumulative running sum from 1994 through 2017. Compared to the time intervals of other R-EMAP wet season sampling events, the sampling conducted in later 2014 immediately followed a period of exceptionally low sulfate discharges. This period of low discharge was driven by an extended drought that began in April 2014 and continued through mid-2015 (Fig. 1.2b in Chap. 1, this volume). Despite the prolonged drought, the stage levels during the wet season in 2014 were not unusually low, nor were the stage dynamics unusually accentuated (Fig. 5.11). It thus seems rather unlikely that stage dynamics were an appreciable direct contributor to the large declines in *Gambusia* Hg observed in 2014.

Figure 5.12 shows the distribution of TP concentrations during the wet season for each of the five R-EMAP sampling years. This plot is included because of the

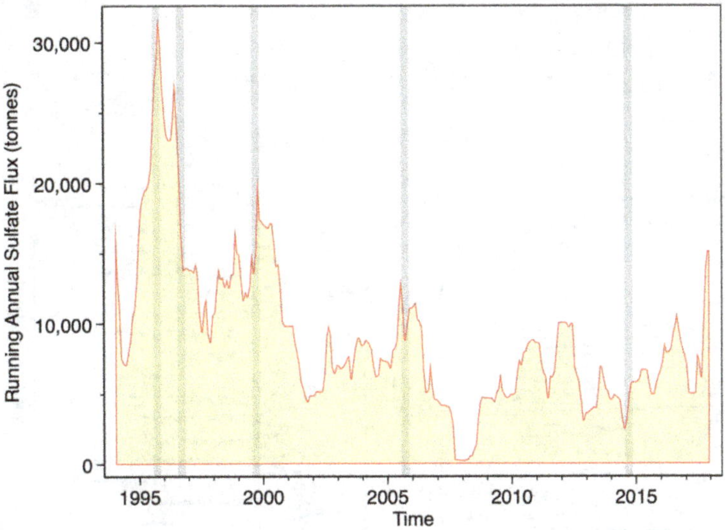

Fig. 5.10 Running annual fluxes of sulfate discharged through the S8 structure on the Miami Canal leaving the EAA and entering WCA-3A. Data from DBHYDRO (2019a). Gray vertical bars show the sampling times when wet season sampling was conducted by the USEPA for R-EMAP

historical and contentious interest in phosphorus dynamics on Hg cycling in the Everglades that was particularly pronounced from the mid-1990s through the mid-2000s (Chap. 6, Vol. II). Wet season concentrations in TP dropped appreciably between 1995 and 1996 (median concentrations of 12 and 5 μg/L, respectively) within the EvPA* but then increased somewhat during 1999 and remained stable through 2005 and 2014 (median concentration in 2014 = 6 μg/L). TP concentrations in WCA2 showed essentially no consistent pattern (median concentrations in 1995 and 2014 were 11 and 9 μg/L, respectively). The shift in distributions in TP over time essentially show no correspondence with the shifts in *Gambusia* Hg concentrations including, in particular, the large fish tissue Hg declines observed in 2014. This is consistent with analyses of the bivariate relationship between *Gambusia* Hg concentrations and surface water TP concentrations shown in Chap. 6 (Vol. II) and more comprehensive SEM modeling developed elsewhere in this volume (Chap. 6) which show no substantial relationship—direct or mediated—between the two variables.

5.3.3 *Spatial Heterogeneity in Temporal Trends*

Although there are general patterns of concordant short-term temporal trends across much of the Everglades landscape (*e.g.*, trends in major canals and marsh sites in the LNWR, WCA2, and WCA3 for LMB Hg concentrations; Fig. 2.3 in Chap. 2, this volume), there is a component of spatial heterogeneity that also is important. For example, although there is evidence of monotonic declines in age-3 normalized

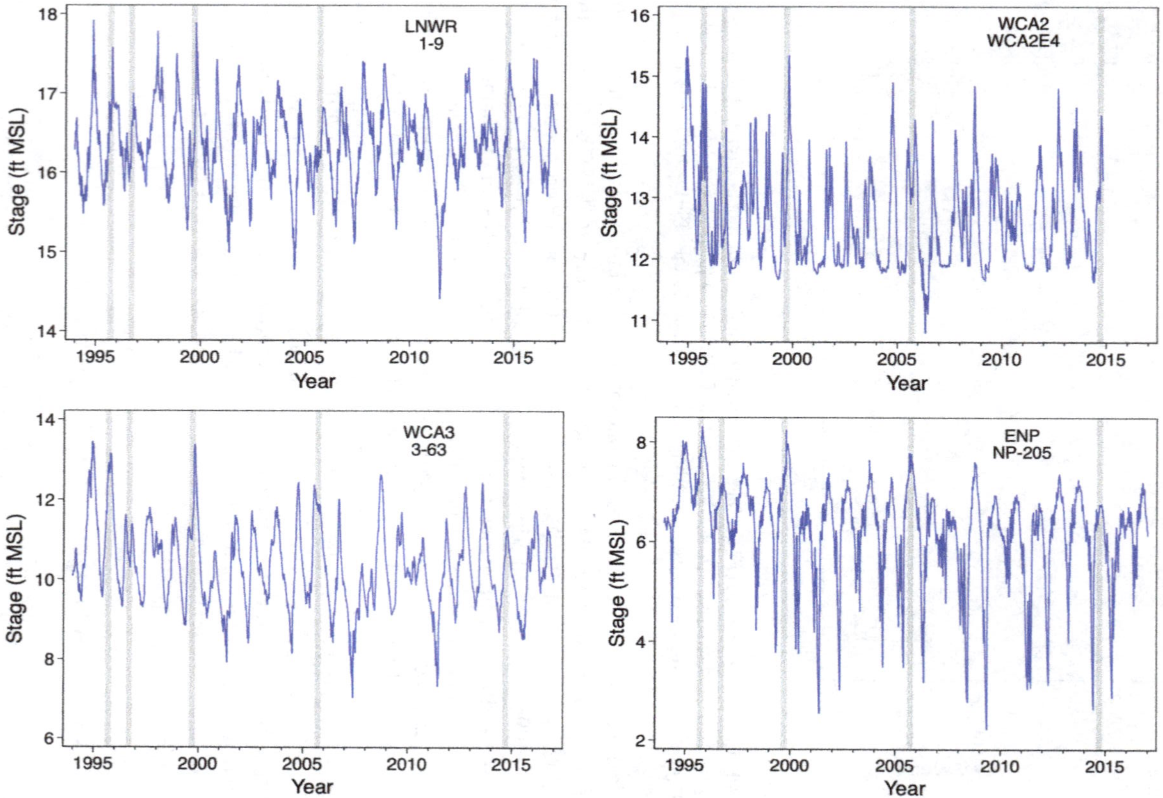

Fig. 5.11 Stage dynamics between 1994 and 2017 at interior marsh stations in the LNWR (upper left-hand panel), WCA2 (upper right-hand panel), WCA3 (lower left-hand panel), and ENP (lower right-hand panel). Gray vertical bars show when R-EMAP wet season sampling was conducted. Values for daily stage measurements obtained from DBHYDRO (2019c)

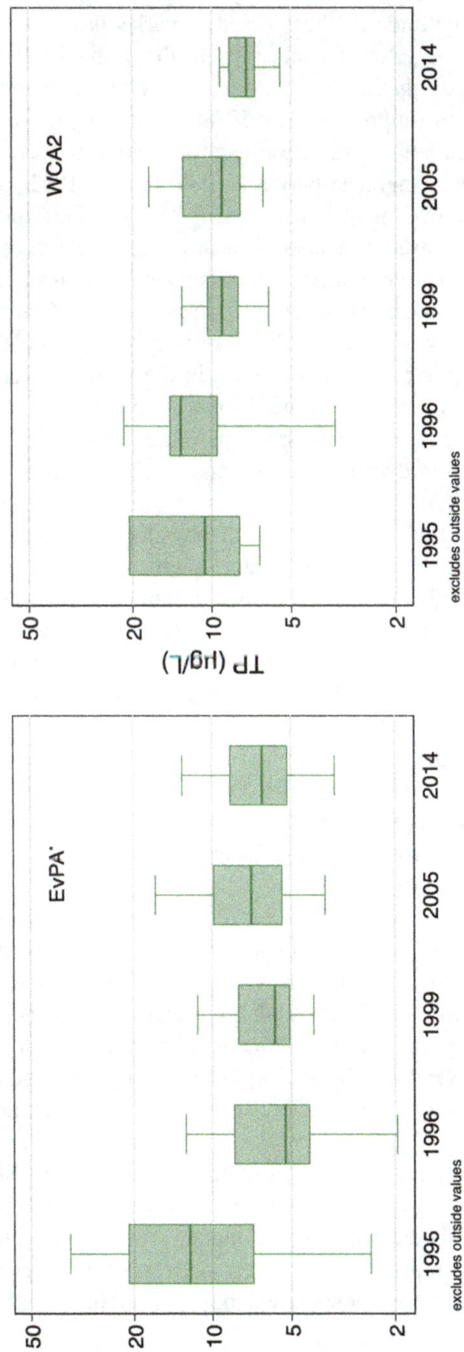

Fig. 5.12 Same as Fig. 5.9, except the variable plotted is the concentration of TP

LMB Hg concentrations during the entirety of the 1990s throughout much of the EvPA, the relative magnitude of those declines varies based on whether the sites were located within the ENP. Canal sites north of the ENP showed declines approximating 70% during the 1990s. Marsh sites north of the ENP showed a smaller relative decline (approximately 50%) relative to the above canal sites, although this difference is the product of a shorter period of record that missed the declines captured in the canal data between 1989 through 1992. In contrast, marsh sites within SRS in the ENP is somewhat less (~35% decline from 1993).

The R-EMAP *Gambusia* data also indicate spatial heterogeneity in temporal responses. Based on direct comparison of changes in *Gambusia* Hg concentrations of proximal R-EMAP sampling locations sampled in 1995 and 2005, Pollman (2012) noted spatial clustering of sites with respect to magnitude and direction of change. This clustering is particularly evident in the more southern portions of the ENP where several locations showed net *increases* in *Gambusia* Hg between 1995 and 2005 *vis-à-vis* the more northern portions of the ENP which are located more closely to surface water discharges from the S-12 structures and showed net decreases (Fig. 5.13).

These spatially variable responses in the freshwater portions of the EvPA almost certainly reflect spatial differences in water chemistry. This is supported by the ability of the SEM developed in Chap. 6 (this volume; see Fig. 6.6) to successfully capture a significant fraction of the variability in *Gambusia* Hg concentrations both spatially across the EvPA and over time. Moreover, the generalized linear model (GLM) developed by Pollman (2012) as a predecessor to the SEM was able to capture general locations of "hotspots" defined by their response between 1995 and 2005 reasonably well although concentration shifts in some spatial clusters were showed poorer agreement. This lack of precision at a more refined spatial level is not surprising and underscores the fact that the utility of empirical models developed using cross-sectional data for predicting changes lies more in predicting generalized rather than individual site responses.

The two estuarine systems within the EvPA for which relatively long-term fish data sets are available to evaluate short-term trends had mixed results. The SRS estuary showed a 70% decrease in gray snapper Hg concentrations for the period 2011–2015 compared to 2006–2008, while gray snappers collected from the Caloosahatchee River estuary showed a 48% increase between the same time intervals. Based on intermittent sampling beginning in 1998, clear temporal trends in either direction within Florida Bay, which also is part of the EvPA, are not evident. These differences likely are due to the more fully marine nature of Florida Bay and thus more stable water chemistry (including sulfate) compared to the SRS and Caloosahatchee River estuaries which are defined by freshwater inputs derived from their respective watersheds mixed with marine inputs. Collectively, these results again point to processes affecting biogeochemistry on a more local level than a broader scale factor such as shifts in atmospheric deposition of Hg as causative factors.

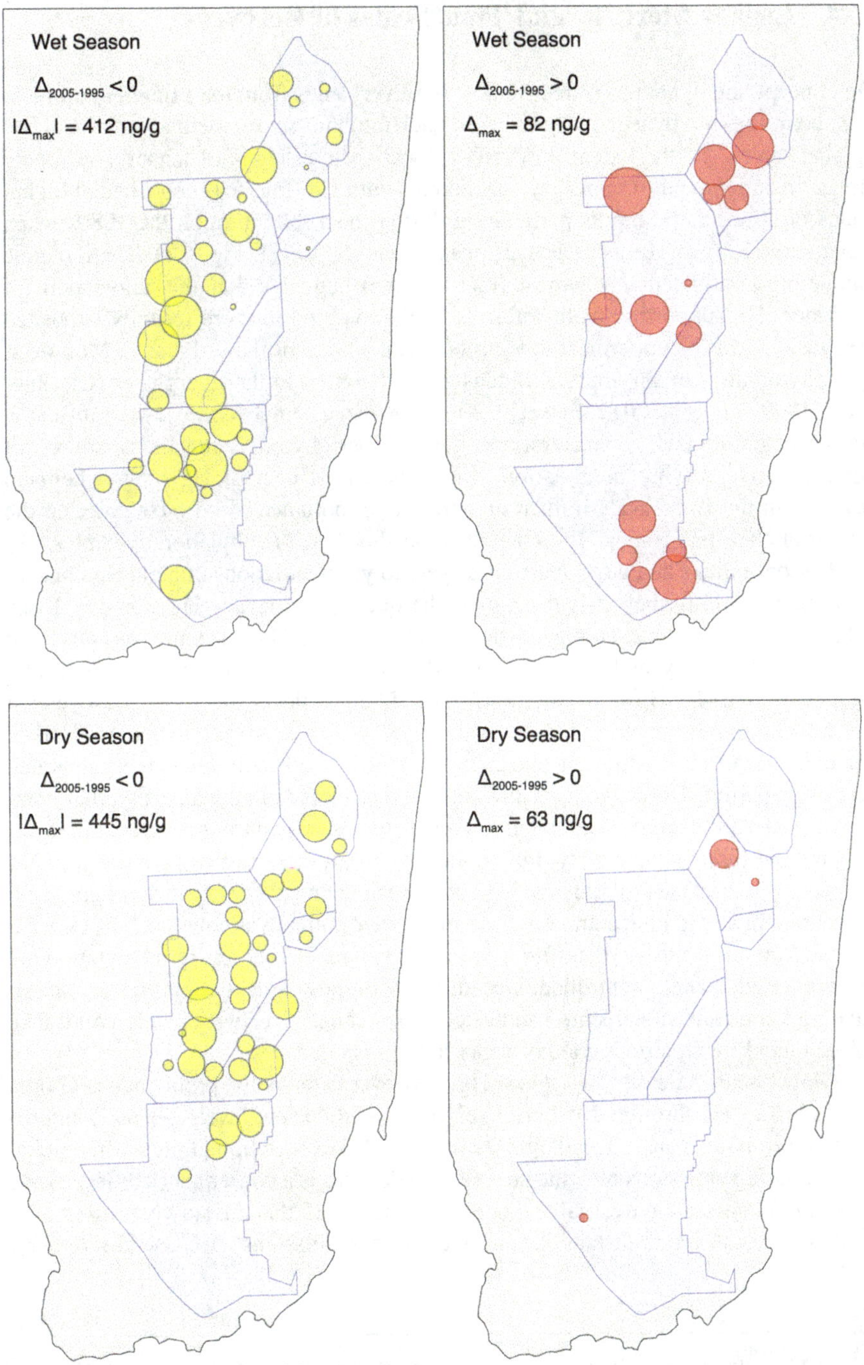

Fig. 5.13 Spatial distribution of observed changes in *Gambusia* Hg concentrations between 1995 and 2005 for closely located (across time) R-EMAP sites. Upper two panels—changes for wet season samples; lower two panels—changes for dry season samples. Changes in concentration (Δ) calculated as $\Delta = C_{2005} - C_{1995}$ where C equals the *Gambusia* Hg concentration (ng/g). Right

5.4 Legacy Mercury and Time Scales of Recovery

In concept, the dynamics of recovery of the Everglades from the extant Hg problem can be influenced by legacy Hg released back into the environment at both local and global scales. To the extent they occur, local scale releases of legacy Hg largely relate to enrichment of upper layer sediments with Hg (Fig. 5.4) deposited at higher rates of atmospheric inputs particularly during the 1960s through the 1980s when local emissions of Hg were at their peak (Chap. 5, Vol. I, Fig. 5.1). The dynamic modeling conducted in Chap. 4 (this volume) suggests that the active pool of sediment Hg supporting methylation is likely confined to more recently deposited Hg residing in the uppermost few cm or surface layer of the sediments. Moreover, periphyton also are an important locus of methylation in the Everglades (Cleckner et al. 1999; Yin et al. 2012; Bae et al. 2019; see also Chap. 3, Vol. II); since diffusion of water column Hg concentrations into the periphyton is the likely source of inorganic Hg driving methylation, this important aspect of Hg biogeochemical cycling in the Everglades further supports the importance of new Hg entering the system rather than legacy Hg as a control on short-term methylation dynamics.

Discontinuities and large short-term (year to year) variations in biota Hg concentrations provide further insight *vis-à-vis* the question of legacy Hg stored in Everglades sediments. For example, the decline in *Gambusia* Hg concentrations observed in 2014 after a 9-year hiatus in R-EMAP sampling is not matched by a similar response in LMB Hg concentrations. This likely reflects the short life cycle of *Gambusia* (approximately 1 year; Mukherjee et al. 2014) while the LMB data include samples from different age cohorts and thus a substantially longer integrated exposure period. These two facts also suggest that short-term dynamics (perhaps less than 1 year) can exert profound impacts on Hg exposure and trophic transfer in lower trophic tier biota. Collectively, the implication of all these results is that legacy Hg stored in Everglades sediments will not preclude recovery of the system from excessive biota Hg concentrations assuming other critical variables such as external inputs from atmospheric deposition or excess sulfate effects on Hg methylation are otherwise adequately controlled. Depending upon how quickly appropriate mitigative measures are implemented and effectively realized, recovery likely could take place quickly with a time scale of years rather than decades.

Global scale releases of legacy Hg, however, are likely problematic. Global emissions of Hg through 2050 are likely to exceed current levels—even if anthropogenic emissions are reduced by a factor of 2. This expectation of increasing global emissions Hg emissions over the next several decades is a consequence of legacy Hg stored in large-scale terrestrial and oceanic pools of Hg that are slowly turning over and, as a result, are in disequilibrium with current emissions. Because atmospheric

---

Fig. 5.13 (continued) panels show the absolute values for negative (yellow filled circles) and positive (red filled circles) Δ, respectively. Circle size is proportional to the magnitude of the change in *Gambusia* concentration. Redrawn from Pollman (2012)

inputs of Hg to the Everglades have only relatively small contributions from local and state-wide sources (<10%; see Chap. 6, Vol. I), the effect of these large-scale reservoirs on the Everglades expectedly will be quantitatively similar to their impacts on the global cycling of atmospheric Hg.

5.5 Summary and Conclusions

Dynamic modeling using the mechanistic E-MCM suggests that regulation-driven, sharp reductions in local emissions of Hg helped drive the monotonic declines in fish Hg observed between 1989 and 2000. That modeling also suggests that reductions in water column sulfate concentrations helped drive that response. Likewise, large relative increases in the concentration of Hg in the feathers of wading birds recorded between *ca.* 1912 and 2000 that greatly exceed the relative changes in atmospheric inputs of Hg inferred from surficial sediment concentrations of Hg indicate that other factors substantially contributed to or helped accentuate the effects of atmospheric Hg on Everglades biota Hg. The variable that appears to most significantly contribute to this accentuation also is sulfate. This role is supported by evaluating concomitant trends in water chemistry and *Gambusia* Hg concentrations; it is also supported by structural equation modeling (Chap. 6, this volume) that quantitatively identifies the importance of sulfate driving both methylation and ultimately *Gambusia* Hg concentrations.

Legacy Hg stored in surficial Everglades marsh sediments is not expected to substantially impede efforts to mitigate the Everglades Hg problem. Moreover, the magnitude of short-term variations in biota Hg concentrations indicates that, assuming atmospheric inputs of Hg do not increase substantially, mitigation efforts that are able to effect a significant change in a causative biogeochemical variable such as sulfate will achieve meaningful reductions in biota Hg over similarly short time scales (*e.g.*, 1–2 years).

Legacy Hg stored in global pools, including the deep oceans in particular, tells a different story for recovery. The likelihood that atmospheric Hg deposition will increase largely because of the disequilibrium and slow turnover of legacy Hg in global ocean pool indicates that managers charged with the protection of Everglades will need to focus on other components of the Hg cycle in the system—including sulfate in particular—that are not only highly important to methylation and/or trophic transfer but also are sufficiently perturbed such that mitigation of the perturbation is sufficiently reasonable to lead to meaningful ecosystem recovery.

References

Bae H-S, Dierberg FE, Ogram A (2019) Periphyton and flocculent materials are important ecological compartments supporting abundant and diverse mercury methylator assemblages in the

Florida Everglades. Appl Environ Microbiol 85:e00156–e00119. https://doi.org/10.1128/AEM.00156-19

Cleckner LB, Gilmour CC, Hurley JP, Krabbenhoft DP (1999) Mercury methylation in periphyton of the Florida Everglades. Limnol Oceanogr 44:1815–1825

DBHYDRO (2019a). https://my.sfwmd.gov/dbhydroplsql/show_dbkey_info.show_station_info?v_station=S8_P. Accessed 9 April 2019

DBHYDRO (2019b). http://my.sfwmd.gov/dbhydroplsql/show_dbkey_info.main_menu. Accessed 14 April 2019

DBHYDRO (2019c). http://my.sfwmd.gov/dbhydroplsql/show_dbkey_info.main_menu. Accessed 2 July 2019

Engstrom, DR, Pollman CD, Fitzgerald WF, Balcom PH (2003) Evaluation of recent trends in atmospheric mercury deposition in south Florida from lake sediment records. Final Report. Florida Department of Environmental Protection, Tallahassee, FL

Flora MD, Rosendahl PC (1982) Historical changes in the conductivity and ionic characteristics of the Shark River Slough, Everglades National Park, Florida, U.S.A. Hydrobiologia 97:249–254

Frederick PC, Hylton BA, Heath JA, Spalding MG (2004) A historical record of mercury contamination in southern Florida as inferred from avian feather tissue. Environ Toxicol Chem 23:1474–1478

Hamilton LC (2013) Statistics with STATA: updated for version 12, 8th edn. Brooks/Cole, Boston

Husar RB (1986) Emissions of sulfur dioxide and nitrogen oxides and trends for eastern North America. In: Acid deposition long-term trends. National Research Council, National Academy Press, Washington, DC

Kalla PI, Scheidt DJ (2017) Everglades ecosystem assessment – Phase IV, 2014: data reduction and initial synthesis. U.S. EPA, Science and Ecosystem Support Division, Athens, GA. SESD 14-0380, 58 pp

Love SK (1955) Quality of ground and surface waters - with special reference to the geology and ground water of the interior Miami area. In: Parker, GG, Ferguson GE, Love SK (eds) Water Resources of Southeastern Florida. Geological Survey Water-Supply Paper 1255, United States Government Printing Office, Washington, DC, pp 727–826

Miller RD, McPherson BF, Sobczak R, Clark C (2004) Water quality in Big Cypress National Preserve and Everglades National Park—trends and spatial characteristics of selected constituents. Water Resources Investigations Report 03-4249. U.S. Department of the Interior, U.S. Geological Survey, Reston, VA

Mukherjee S, Heithaus MR, Trexler JC, Ray-Mukherjee J, Vaudo J (2014) Perceived risk of predation affects reproductive life-history traits in *Gambusia holbrooki*, but not in *Heterandria formosa*. PLoS One 9(2):e88832. https://doi.org/10.1371/journal.pone.0088832

Pollman CD (2012) Modeling sulfate and *Gambusia* mercury relationships in the Everglades – final report. Florida Department of Environmental Protection, Tallahassee

Pollman CD (2014) Mercury cycling and trophic state in aquatic ecosystems: implications from structural equation modeling. Sci Tot Environ 499:62–73

RMB Consulting & Research, Inc. (RMB) (2002) Atmospheric mercury emissions from major point sources – Broward, Dade, and Palm Beach Counties, 1980-2000. Final Report. RMB Consulting & Research, Inc., Raleigh, NC

Rood BE, Gottgens JF, Delfino JJ, Earle CD, Crisman TL (1995) Mercury accumulation trends in Florida Everglades and Savannas Marsh flooded soils. Water Air Soil Pollut 80:981–990

Scheidt DJ, Kalla PI (2007) Everglades ecosystem assessment: water management and quality, eutrophication, mercury contamination, soils and habitat: monitoring for adaptive management: a R-EMAP status report. USEPA Region 4, Athens, GA. EPA 904-R-07-001. 98 pp. http://www.epa.gov/region4/sesd/reports/epa904r07001/epa904r07001.pdf

StataCorp (2019) Stata Statistical Software: Release 16. StataCorp LLC, College Station, TX

Yin L, Yongguan Y, Liu G, Tachiev G, Roelant D, Jiang G et al (2012) Estimation of the major source and sink of methylmercury in the Florida Everglades. Environ Sci Technol 46:5885–5893

Chapter 6
Structural Equation Model for Mercury Cycling in the Everglades

Curtis D. Pollman

Abstract This chapter uses structural equation (SE) modeling as a tool to empirically evaluate the key water quality variables—and thus processes—that govern the methylation of mercury and its transfer into *Gambusia* spp. (mosquitofish) across the Everglades landscape. The modeling builds upon previous SE modeling conducted by Pollman (Sci Tot Environ 499:62–73, 2014) by expanding the original data set used in model construction to include the most recent Regional Environmental Model and Assessment Program (R-EMAP) sampling results from 2014. These more recent data were used to both *post hoc* validate and subsequently revise the original model. Key aspects of this modeling form the underpinnings of a reduced-form management model developed and applied in Chap. 7 (this volume).

Keywords Methylmercury · Sulfate · Dissolved organic matter · Sulfide · *Gambusia*

6.1 Introduction

In Chap. 1 of Volume II Orem et al. present a conceptual model of the primary processes governing the cycling and trophic transfer of mercury (Hg) through the food web in aquatic ecosystems, including the Everglades. The biogeochemical constructs embodied in the conceptual model also comprise the foundational underpinnings of the only extant mechanistic model applied to the Everglades—*viz.* the Everglades Mercury Cycling model (E-MCM). While considerable effort was expended to extend and calibrate the E-MCM to the Everglades, from a practical perspective its application to simulating Hg dynamics in the Everglades never extended beyond the historically important "hotspot" located in WCA-3A-15 centrally located in WCA-3A (see Chap. 4, this volume) and several sites along the phosphorus gradient in WCA-2A (see Chap. 6, Volume II). As a result, the E-MCM

C. D. Pollman (✉)
Aqua Lux Lucis, Inc., Gainesville, FL, USA
e-mail: cpollman@aqualuxlucis.org

C. D. Pollman et al. (eds.), *Mercury and the Everglades. A Synthesis and Model for Complex Ecosystem Restoration*, https://doi.org/10.1007/978-3-030-55635-8_6

is useful as a mechanistic tool for hypothesis testing over limited spatial domains within the Everglades, including evaluating how fish tissue Hg concentrations will respond to changes in atmospheric inputs (Atkeson et al. 2005) and other variables such as phosphorus, dissolved organic carbon (DOC), and sulfate (Chap. 4, this volume). Although the E-MCM has been applied as a spatially segmented, hydrologically interconnected model across WCA-2A (Pollman et al. 2002), its calibration to only a small number of sites currently precludes its utility to make predictions across the entirety of the Everglades Protection Area (EvPA).

An alternative approach towards resolving the spatial heterogeneity problem is offered by the structural equation model (SEM) developed by Pollman (2014) to predict the bioaccumulation of Hg in mosquitofish (*Gambusia* spp.) within the Everglades. There are two fundamental advantages inherent in the development of the SEM. First, the model was constructed using data collected from the USEPA's Regional Environmental Monitoring and Assessment Program (R-EMAP) program implemented for the Everglades. The R-EMAP effort in the Everglades included collecting water quality, sediment, and biota samples throughout the marsh to establish its status with respect to ecosystem health and provide a basis for determining the effectiveness of efforts designed to restore the Everglades (Scheidt and Kalla 2007). R-EMAP Everglades data used to construct the SEM developed by Pollman (2014) included samples collected from 579 marsh sites between 1995 and 2005 across eight sampling cycles (four wet and four dry seasons).

The second advantage lies in the nature of structural equation (SE) modeling itself. While there is a rich history of using multivariate statistical models—and multiple linear regression models in particular—to analyze the relationship between fish tissue Hg concentrations and independent variables such as pH, DOC, and methylmercury (MeHg) concentrations, such models often are problematic as quantitative management tools. This is because the model relationships ultimately involve indirect or mediated pathways as well as direct pathways (Fig. 1.1 in Chap. 1, Volume II). SE modeling allows for complete and simultaneous modeling of all the relationships inherent in a system of linear regression equations, while ordinary least squares regression (OLS) is restricted to a single regression equation (Ullman 2007). As a result, OLS generally is not well-suited to model mediated relationships involving multiple dependent variables such as those embodied in the aquatic cycling of Hg.

Subsequent to when the Pollman (2014) SE modeling was originally developed and published, the R-EMAP program released data from an additional round of sampling conducted during the wet season of 2014 (Kalla and Scheidt 2017). The availability of these new data provides an opportunity to *post hoc* further validate the model and evaluate whether further modifications are appropriate and necessary. The objective of this chapter thus is to conduct both analyses, with the idea that the updated model can serve as a framework for assessing how management strategies such as reducing sulfate inputs to the EvPA will likely change MeHg concentrations in *Gambusia*.

6.2 Data Synthesis

The original SEM developed by Pollman (2014) included four variables considered as independent or *exogenous*: surface water DOC, surface water sulfate transformed (transformed to represent the unimodal relationship between sulfate and Hg methylation potential), surficial soil organic matter content (represented by soil ash-free dry weight) and pore water sulfide concentrations. The model also included surface water MeHg, periphyton MeHg, soil MeHg, and soil total Hg concentrations as dependent or *endogenous* variables. Model variables that were included for collection and analysis during the most recent R-EMAP cycle (Cycle 11) were consistent with previous cycles with two exceptions—pore water sulfide and periphyton MeHg. During Cycle 11, R-EMAP sampled bottom water located immediately above the sediment-water interface as a surrogate for estimating pore water sulfide concentrations—the latter of which were measured during Cycles 4 through 7 in surficial sediment interstitial waters sampled using a syringe equipped with a 0.45 μM filter. Cycle 11 sampling, which was conducted during the end of the wet season (September) 2014, included samples from 119 sites within the EvPA.

As part of transitioning to sampling bottom water sulfide concentrations, the R-EMAP program collected both bottom and pore water simultaneously from 10 sites in 2015 and 2016 (triplicate samples from 9 sites, and duplicates from an additional site for a total N equal to 29). The objective of the sampling was to validate the use of bottom water sampling as an inferential method for pore water sulfide. Preliminary plots of pore water sulfide (PW) values as a function of bottom water sulfide (BW) concentrations and highlighting the year the sample was collected indicated that the model for defining the relationship between BW and PW needs to include *year* as an effect. Our goal however is to estimate the part of the model that defines the general relationship between BW and PW that is *fixed*—in other words, independent of the *year* effect which ostensibly is *random*. As a result, mixed level regression (Hox 2010; StataCorp 2019) was conducted to isolate the fixed effect of BW on PW. Lastly, because inspection of preliminary model residuals indicated that log-transformation of both variables was preferred, the modeling was conducted with both variables log-transformed. Figure 6.1, which shows the relationship between observed and predicted values, illustrates that the modeled relationship is quite good (apparent $r^2 = 0.944$; $p < 0.0001$).

The fixed relationship between BW and PW was then used to initially infer PW values for Cycle 11. A comparison of the inferred PW values as a function of surface water sulfate concentrations with observed values from earlier cycles indicated a slight offset in the Cycle 11 results. This offset is consistent with the mixed model structure including random effects associated with time. Additional modeling of PW concentrations as a quadratic function of surface water sulfate concentrations (both variables log-transformed) and coupled with a dummy variable defining whether the sample was collected during Cycle 11 was used to estimate the random effect offset for Cycle 11. A comparison of the final estimated PW values for Cycle

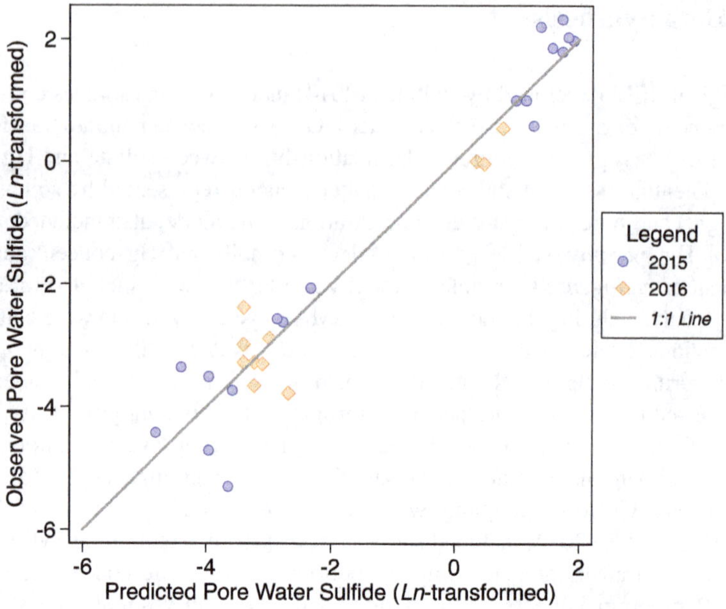

Fig. 6.1 Comparison of observed pore water sulfide concentrations with predicted values obtained from the mixed level regression model using bottom water sulfide concentrations as the independent variable. Predicted values include both fixed effects related to bottom water sulfide concentrations alone and random effects associated with the year the samples were collected. Solid line shows the expected 1:1 agreement line

11 incorporating this offset and observed PW values for previous cycles as a function of surface water sulfate concentrations is shown in Fig. 6.2.

Periphyton MeHg concentrations were included in the original model as the mean of the measured concentrations observed at a given site across the three major types comprising the periphyton community (floating, epiphytic, and benthic) sampled when present. Cycle 11 sampling included all three periphyton assemblage components as two variables—one explicitly for benthic periphyton, and the other as a composite of floating and epiphytic periphyton. In order to make the Cycle 11 data as equivalent as possible to the data from the other cycles, MeHg concentrations for periphyton collected during Cycle 11 were calculated as a weighted mean as follows:

$$PP_{Hg} = \frac{2 \cdot FEPP_{Hg} + BPP_{Hg}}{3}$$

where PP_{Hg} is the mean MeHg concentration for the entire periphyton community, $FEPP_{\mathrm{Hg}}$ is the MeHg concentration for the composite variable representing floating and epiphytic periphyton, and BPP_{Hg} is the MeHg concentration for benthic periphyton present at the site. If a given site included measurements for only one of the two variables, that value was used directly as the measure of MeHg concentrations in the periphyton community at the site.

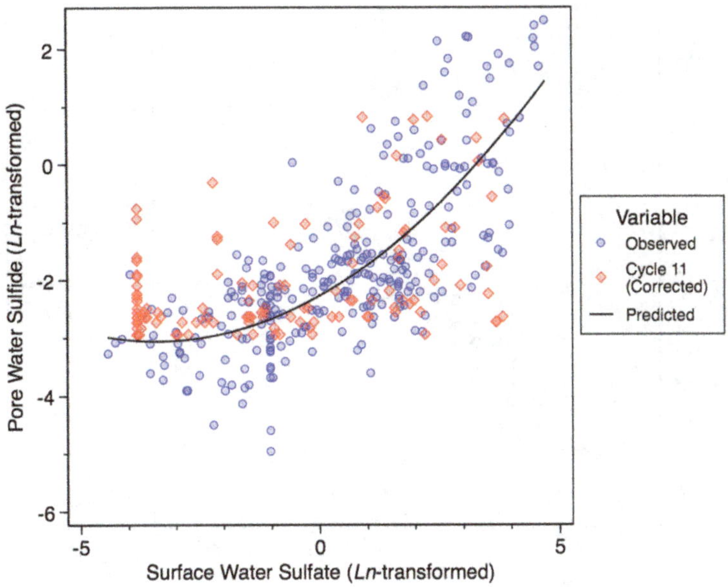

Fig. 6.2 Comparison of inferred (Cycle 11) and observed pore water sulfide concentrations as a function of surface water sulfate concentrations. Inferred values obtained from mixed regression model defining fixed effects between bottom water sulfide concentrations as the dependent variable and pore water sulfide concentrations. Inferred values are corrected to account for random effects related to time of sampling

A final consideration in synthesizing the R-EMAP data across the different cycles relates to organic carbon concentrations. Organic carbon in the water column was measured during R-EMAP as total organic carbon (TOC) during Cycles 0–5, and as DOC during Cycles 6–7. As a result, Pollman (2014) concatenated these two variables into a single variable. Julian (2014) suggests that combining the R-EMAP results for TOC and DOC into a single variable complicates the use of the synthesized variable because TOC comprises particulate organic carbon as well as the dissolved fraction. Whether this concern has any practical significance can be directly tested using Cycle 11 data, which includes contemporaneous measurements for both DOC and TOC at 117 stations. An analysis of whether any appreciable bias is imposed by utilizing DOC values in the synthesized variable was conducted using a paired *t test*. Those results indicate that the mean difference between the Cycle 11 TOC and DOC measurements was −0.03 mg/L (TOC minus DOC; 2.6%) and statistically indistinguishable from 0 ($p = 0.760$). Figure 6.3 plots a direct comparison of the two variables and further illustrates that, as far as the R-EMAP data are concerned, TOC and DOC are essentially equivalent measurements within the EvPA.

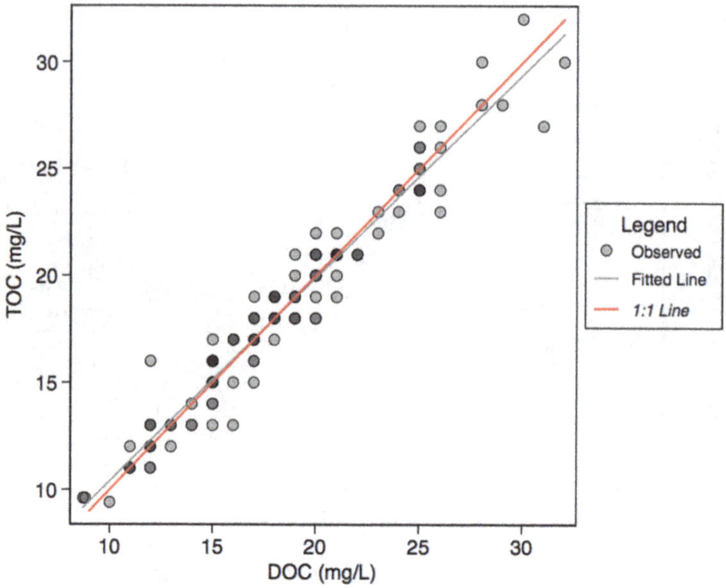

Fig. 6.3 Bivariate comparison of surface water TOC and DOC concentrations measured as part of R-EMAP during Cycle 11. Comparison includes fitted regression line ($r^2 = 0.946$; $p < 0.0001$) and expected 1:1 line obtained if TOC and DOC measurements are providing essentially equivalent results. Darker circles show multiple overlying observations ($N = 117$)

6.3 Model Structure and Estimation

6.3.1 Initial Modifications to Pollman (2014) Model

In the original SEM developed by Pollman (2014), it was noted that Hg concentrations predicted for *Gambusia* collected within the ENP were biased low (observed values greater than predicted). In addition, separate mixed or multi-level modeling of the relationship between *Gambusia* Hg and the variables directly linked to *Gambusia* Hg by the SEM suggests this spatial bias is better represented as an additive intercept that changes with region rather than by changes in the fundamental relationships (by modifying the slopes) for the variables retained in the model. As a result, the original SEM was modified to include a categorical variable that divides the spatial domain of the model into two entities—the ENP, and the remainder of the EvPA.

The model incorporates two variable effects that appear to be spatially distinct to the ENP (Fig. 6.4). The first effect is associated with somewhat elevated soil Hg concentrations relative to soil organic matter content. As discussed in Chap. 3 of this volume, soil Hg concentrations throughout the Everglades—as well as in other aquatic ecosystems—are closely related to soil organic matter content, which in turn reflects the physical depositional environment and its effect on size sorting of settling and accreting particles. When considering that ash-free dry weight of

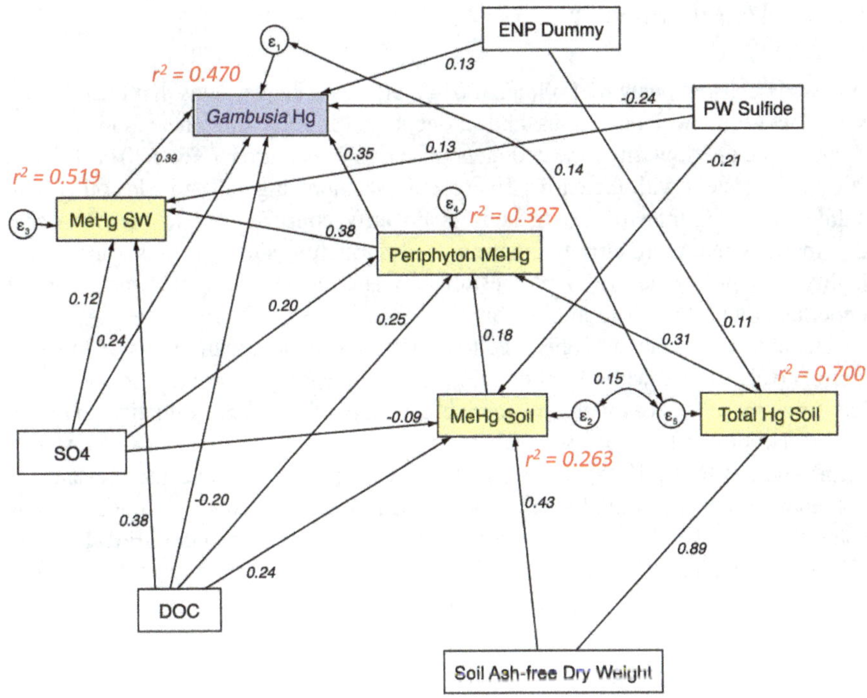

Fig. 6.4 Path diagram delineating the functional inter-variable relationships for the Everglades SEM of *Gambusia* Hg concentrations fitted to R-EMAP Cycles 0–7 data. Filled boxes denote dependent (endogenous) variables. Path coefficients, which are expressed as standardized values, are all significant (bootstrapped standard errors) at $p < 0.001$ except for the pore water sulfide to surface water and soil MeHg paths ($p = 0.049$ and 0.002, respectively), soil MeHg to periphyton MeHg path ($p = 0.001$), the ENP dummy variable relationship with *Gambusia* Hg ($p = 0.001$), and the sulfate methylation potential relationship with soil MeHg concentrations ($p = 0.008$). $N = 579$

surficial soils in the ENP averages 38.9%, this elevation in the soil Hg signal is nearly 8%.

The second effect is associated with elevated *Gambusia* Hg in the ENP relative to other regions within the EvPA once the differential effects of sulfate, DOC, soil organic matter content, and pore water sulfide have been considered. It is not clear at this juncture why this elevation occurs—for example, it could relate to food web characteristics unique to the ENP—but the effect is fairly substantial. For example, the model predicts *Gambusia* Hg concentrations averaging 145 ng/g in the ENP if the categorical effect of location within the ENP is included in the prediction; excluding the ascribed categorical effect results in an average predicted concentration of 112 ng/g (~23% lower).

The structure of the SEM is shown in Fig. 6.4. The model was fit to the same suite of 579 R-EMAP sites used by Pollman (2014) in his calibration of the original model. The model was fitted using Stata 16 (StataCorp 2019), and model fit was evaluated using a number of fit statistics generated by Stata.

6.3.2 *Model Linearity*

As discussed previously by Pollman (2014), SE modeling assumes that the relationships between the endogenous and exogenous variables are linear and that the multivariate distribution of the endogenous variables is normal (Kline 2011; Ullman 2007). Consistent with the earlier Everglades SE modeling, all variables other than sulfate were log-transformed to address linearity concerns and to yield variable distributions that more closely approximated normality, although multivariate normality was not achieved. Model estimation approaches that subsequently were undertaken with this issue in mind are discussed in Sect. 6.3.3.

The ability to evaluate adherence to underlying model assumptions of linearity are relatively limited with SE modeling. Multiple linear regression (MLR), however, has a rich set of tools available to conduct a variety of *post hoc* evaluative analyses. Given the similarities between path analysis (of which the Everglades SEM is a form) and MLR (Li 1975), Pollman (2014) verified linearity and the presence of potential outliers by initially conducting MLR on *Gambusia* Hg concentrations using the same variables used to directly model *Gambusia* Hg in the SEM. Pollman (2014) then validated assumptions of linearity by constructing augmented component plus residuals (ACPR) plots (Hamilton 2013).

6.3.2.1 Sulfate Transformation

As discussed in detail in Chaps. 1, 3 and 6 in Volume II, the relationship between sulfate and Hg methylation is complex, and is generally considered to reflect a balance between two different processes. These processes include the stimulation of sulfate-reducing bacteria (SRB) activity involved in Hg methylation by increasing sulfate concentrations when sulfate availability is otherwise limiting, thus producing higher concentrations of MeHg. It also includes the concomitant and competing effect of increasing sulfide production as a sink limiting the availability of dissolved inorganic Hg necessary for methylation. Together, these competing, antagonistic effects result in a unimodal relationship between sulfate and Hg methylation, with maximum methylation occurring at an optimum level of sulfate. At sulfate levels above this optimum, sulfide increasingly inhibits methylation; at sulfate levels below this maximum, the constraining effects of sulfate availability on SRB activity dominates (Gilmour and Henry 1991).

Previous work by Pollman (2012) demonstrated that the relationship between *Gambusia* Hg and sulfate concentrations based on the R-EMAP data was nonlinear, and that the outer response envelope could be described by a unimodally shaped curve. Because the chemical character of DOC changes across the Everglades landscape (Hoch et al. 2001)—which in turn should change how DOC complexes with inorganic Hg (the necessary precursor for Hg methylation; see Chap. 4, Volume II)—Pollman (2012) used cubic spline smoothing to define individual curves of sulfate-related methylation potential for the four major hydrologic units within the

EvPA. The resulting curves developed by Pollman (2012) subsequently were used to transform sulfate so that the linearity of the relationship between biota Hg and surface water MeHg concentrations and transformed sulfate was greatly improved compared to the original relationships with sulfate.

6.3.3 Model Estimation

All statistical analyses, including SE modeling, were conducted using Stata 16 (StataCorp 2019). Estimation was conducted using maximum likelihood with missing values (MLMV). The full suite of model variables was not available for all the observations used for model estimation, and the MLMV method allows for observations with missing values to be included (other estimation methods invoke listwise deletion) by assuming the missing values are randomly distributed throughout the data set and that the joint or multivariate distribution of the variables is normal. Plots of sites with and without missing variable values suggest that both types of sites are fairly evenly distributed throughout the model spatial domain.

As mentioned previously, log-transformations of the SEM variables resulted in improved but not fully compliant distributions with respect to normality. Deviations from multivariate normality can be problematic because incorrect estimates of the precision of the various model coefficients can result when the method of model estimation assumes multivariate normality. Multivariate non-normality can also influence the overall significance of the model fit (Kline 2011).

One estimation approach that makes no assumptions about data normality is the *arbitrary* or *asymptotic distribution free* (*adf*) method (Browne 1984; Kline 2011; Acock 2013). This method requires that all the observations used in the model include values for all the model variables. In addition, as discussed by Kline (2011), the *adf* method generally requires a large number of observations for the results to be reasonably accurate; this can result in excess of 200 to 500 observations needed for even relatively simple models. Together, both of these constraints preclude the *adf* method as an attractive estimation method for our model.

Other approaches towards model estimation include: (1) correcting the model test statistics using a normal corrected normal theory method such as the Satorra-Bentler statistic (Tomarken and Waller 2005; Kline 2011; StataCorp 2019) and (2) bootstrapping (Kline 2011; Tomarken and Waller 2005; McIntosh 2007; Acock 2013). The Satorra-Bentler technique corrects the χ^2 statistic used to define overall goodness of model fit (see Sect. 6.3.4) by adjusting the estimate based on the kurtosis of the data (Kline 2011). Bootstrapping, which uses repeated sampling with replacement of the individual observations to produce estimates of the standard errors and resulting significance of the model coefficients, makes no assumptions regarding multivariate normality. As a result, bootstrapping produces more robust estimates of coefficient confidence. The Satorra-Bentler technique is not available in Stata when the MLMV method is used for model estimation; as a result, bootstrapping was used to estimate coefficient signficance. Bootstrapping was conducted using 1000 replications and model path relationships which did not emerge from the boostrapping with significance levels intact ($p < 0.05$) were eliminated from the model.

6.3.4 Assessment of Goodness of Fit

The goal of SE modeling is to reproduce the observed covariance matrix for the variables in the model. As a result, assessing the goodness of model fit characteristically involves evaluating the discrepancy between the fitted and the observed covariance matrices. The χ^2 test is the approach most used to evaluate the overall fit of SEMs (Grace 2008) and, following Pollman (2014), was used here as the initial criterion for assessing the adequacy of the fitted model. Alternative fit indices to supplement the χ^2 test include both absolute and incremental or approximate fit indices. Absolute fit indices are generally indicators of the proportions of the observed covariance matrix explained by the model, while incremental fit indices measure the relative improvement in model fit when the model in question is compared to a so-called baseline model (typically a model in which all the observed variables are uncorrelated) (Hu and Bentler 1999; Kline 2011). Stata calculates alternative fit indices of both types, including the root mean squared error of approximation (RMSEA), the comparative fit index (CFI) and the Tucker-Lewis index (TLI), and these metrics were also considered as part of the model evaluation process. The target value often cited for the RMSEA is 0.05, while values greater than 0.95 are recommended for both the CFI and TLI (Hu and Bentler 1999; Acock 2013). A χ^2 p value <0.05 was used as the threshold for rejecting the null hypothesis and thus rejecting the model (*e.g.*, Hu and Bentler 1999; Hayduk and Glaser 2000; Bizzi et al. 2013).

6.4 Model Results

6.4.1 Model Fitted with R-EMAP Cycles 0–7 Data

6.4.1.1 Model Goodness of Fit

Model goodness of fit statistics for the SEM depicted in Fig. 6.4 are summarized in Table 6.1. Given the degrees of freedom in the model (13), the model χ^2 (13.475) was acceptably low ($p = 0.412$). In addition, the various approximate fit indices all indicate that the overall fit of the SEM is acceptable as well. More specifically, the probability that the RMSEA is less than the critical value of 0.05 (*cf.*, Kline 2011) is 0.985; likewise, both the CFI and TLI exceed the recommended target minimum value of 0.95 (Hu and Bentler 1999; Acock 2013). All path coefficients were significant at $p < 0.001$ except for the pore water sulfide to surface water and

Table 6.1 Goodness of fit statistics for the Everglades SEMs

Metric	Cycles 0–7	Cycles 0–11
$\chi 2$—Degrees of freedom	13	15
$\chi 2$	13.475	14.819
$p > \chi 2$	0.412	0.465
RMSEA*	0.008	< 0.001
90% CI**, lower bound	<0.001	< 0.001
90% CI, upper bound	0.042	0.035
p RMSEA ≤ 0.05	0.985	0.998
Comparative Fit Index	1.000	1.000
Tucker-Lewis Index	0.999	1.000
Residuals coefficient of determination	0.882	0.906
Gambusia Hg (ln-transformed) coefficient of determination	0.470	0.520
N	579	698

*RMSEA** root mean squared error of approximation; *CI*** confidence interval

soil MeHg paths ($p = 0.049$ and 0.002, respectively), the soil MeHg to periphyton path ($p = 0.001$), the ENP dummy variable relationship with *Gambusia* Hg ($p = 0.001$), and the sulfate methylation potential relationship with soil MeHg concentrations ($p = 0.008$). Coefficients of determination (r^2) for the endogenous variables ranged from 0.263 for soil MeHg to 0.700 for soil total Hg, with the value for *Gambusia* Hg equal to 0.470.

6.4.1.2 Validation of Cycles 0–7 Model

Model validation was conducted in two phases. The first step involved conducting a "leave one out cross validation" (LOOCV) or jackknife analysis where the SEM was refit by withholding a single observation from model estimation, and then using the refit model to predict the log-transformed value for *Gambusia* Hg of the withheld observation. This process was repeated for each of the Cycles 0–7 observations ($N = 579$) used by Pollman (2014) in his original model development.

LOOCV conducted with the full suite of 579 sites used for initial calibration indicates that the SEM is robust within the Cycle 0 through 7 calibration period. A comparison of the out-of-sample predictions with the predicted values for *Gambusia* Hg (log-transformed) from the model fitted with the full data set shows excellent agreement with no obvious outlying or influential observations. Likewise, a comparison of the root mean square error (RMSE) for the fully fitted model with the out-of-sample predictions for *Gambusia* Hg concentrations shows only minor degradation in model performance (RMSE = 0.372 and 0.383 for the fully calibrated and out-of-sample predictions, respectively).

The second validation step involved using the most recent R-EMAP data (Cycle 11; $N = 119$) to conduct out-of-sample predictions. The Cycle 11 data were collected during a period of both reduced surface water discharge from the EAA and lower water depths compared to previous sampling cycles (Kalla and Scheidt 2017). Two of the key model response variables—*Gambusia* Hg and surface water MeHg concentrations—were substantially lower during Cycle 11 (Fig. 6.5), and using the Cycle 11 data to conduct out-of-sample predictions is thus particularly useful in terms of helping to: (1) validate the basic structure of the SEM and its robustness; (2) define modifications to the model to improve its performance; and (3) identify key gaps in understanding.

Figure 6.6 compares the observed concentrations for *Gambusia* Hg, surface water MeHg and periphyton MeHg as a function of predicted values. In brief, the model performs reasonably well predicting periphyton MeHg during Cycle 11. While the model does predict declines in both *Gambusia* Hg and surface water MeHg, the magnitudes of these declines are under-predicted. This result suggests that another factor (or factors) not included in the model contributed further to the decline in both response variables. This result also suggests that an improvement to the model would be to include a dichotomous categorical variable that acknowledges this effect and thus allows for better partitioning of forcing variable effects on these two key endogenous variables.

6.4.2 Revised SEM for Cycles 0–11

6.4.2.1 Model Revisions

The SEM for the Cycles 0–7 model was thus modified to include a categorical variable that separated the data into two groups: Cycles 0–7 and Cycle 11. The model was recalibrated, and model coefficients were checked for robustness as described previously. This resulted in eliminating the pathway between pore water sulfide and surface water MeHg. With the exception of the pathways associated with the categorical variable for Cycle 11, the revised model otherwise remained intact. As expected, the categorical variable for Cycle 11 effect on surface water MeHg and *Gambusia* Hg was negative.[1] In addition, the model included positive effects on soil methyl and total Hg concentrations during Cycle 11 (Fig. 6.7), perhaps due to increased oxidation of surficial soil organic matter associated with the lower water stages that prevailed through much of the EvPA prior to when Cycle 11 sampling was conducted (see Chap. 5, this volume).

It should be noted that the model continues to represent pore water sulfide as an exogenous variable. From a biogeochemical perspective, it is clear that the presence and magnitude of sulfate in the water column is a necessary driver of pore water sulfide and thus it would be more appropriate and satisfying to incorporate that functional relationship into the model (*cf.* Pollman et al. 2017). The difficulty with

[1]The categorical variable was set equal to 1 for samples collected during Cycles 0–7, and equal to 0 for samples collected during Cycle 11. Thus, for example, the positive standard coefficient shown between the categorical variable and surface water MeHg concentrations shown in Fig. 6.6 depicts a *negative* effect superimposed during Cycle 11.

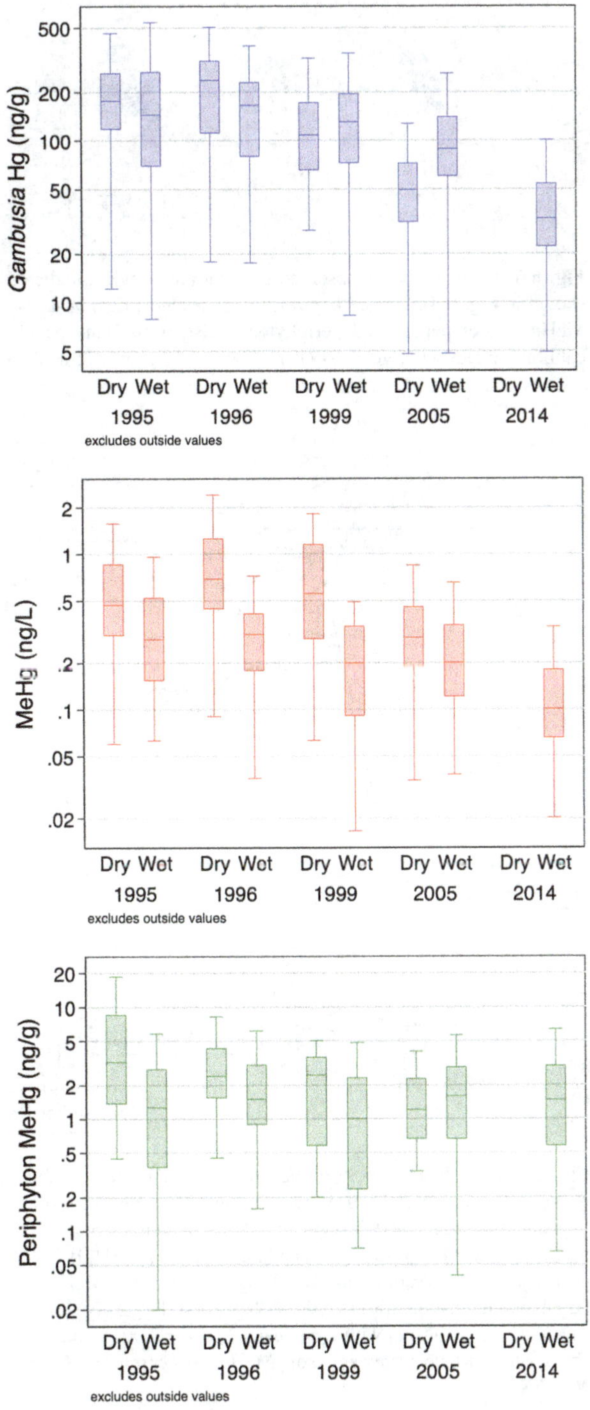

Fig. 6.5 Box plots showing the change in the distribution of *Gambusia* Hg (upper panel), surface water MeHg (middle panel) and periphyton MeHg (lower panel) concentrations over time based on the R-EMAP data

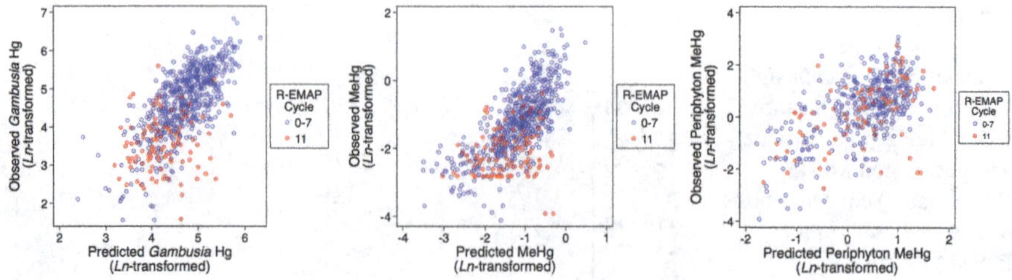

Fig. 6.6 Comparison of observed concentrations with predicted values obtained from the SEM shown in Fig. 6.4 for three key response variables: *Gambusia* Hg (left-hand panel); surface water MeHg (center panel); and periphyton MeHg (right-hand panel). Figure includes results for the calibration data set (Cycles 0–7) and Cycle 11 out-of-sample data set

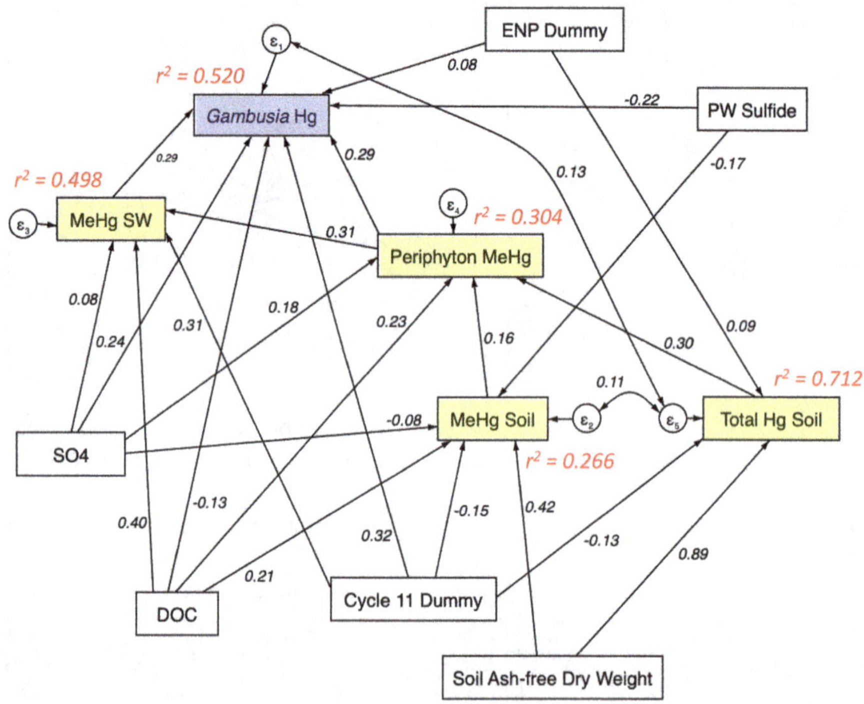

Fig. 6.7 Path diagram delineating the functional inter-variable relationships for the Everglades SEM of *Gambusia* Hg concentrations fitted to R-EMAP Cycles 0–11 data. Filled boxes denote dependent (endogenous) variables. Path coefficients, which are expressed as standardized values, are all significant (bootstrapped standard errors) at $p < 0.001$ except for the pore water sulfide to soil MeHg path ($p = 0.002$), the soil MeHg to periphyton MeHg path ($p = 0.001$), the ENP dummy variable relationships with *Gambusia* Hg and soil total Hg ($p = 0.012$ and 0.001, respectively), the TOC/DOC relationship with *Gambusia* Hg ($p = 0.001$), and sulfate methylation potential relationships with surface water and soil MeHg concentrations ($p = 0.005$ and 0.011, respectively). $N = 698$

incorporating pore water sulfide as an endogenous variable dependent in part on surface water sulfate concentrations is that the Cycle 11 pore water sulfide concentrations used as input to the model already are inferred values based in part on surface water sulfate concentrations. This would lead to spurious correlation and an overstatement of the significance of the pathway and, of course, compromise the overall integrity of the model fit statistics.

6.4.2.2 Model Results

Model fit statistics for the Cycle 0–11 model are presented in Table 6.1. Although the model χ^2 for the Cycle 0–11 model is slightly higher than the value obtained for the Cycle 0–7 model (14.819 *vs.* 13.475), the significance of the Cycle 0–11 model is improved ($p = 0.465$ *vs.* 0.412, respectively) because of the more parsimonious structure of the Cycle 0–11 model. Likewise, the remaining fit statistics for the Cycle 0–11 model are also equivalent or improved as well.

LOOCV was also conducted on the Cycle 0–11 model to evaluate the robustness of the predictions for *Gambusia* Hg (log-transformed). Those results show little difference in the RMSE for the fully calibrated and cross-validated predictions, with RMSE values of 0.646 *vs.* 0.655, respectively.

The path model diagrams for both the Cycle 0–7 and 0–11 models include the standardized coefficient quantifying the directed relationship between the two variables comprising a given path. Standardized coefficients give the corresponding response for a dependent variable—with the response normalized to the standard deviation of the dependent variable—when a given independent variable has been increased by a single standard deviation. As a result, standardized coefficients are useful for comparing the relative importance or strength of association of different independent variables, while the unstandardized coefficients reflect the actual form of the relationship (Acock 2013).

A convenient approach towards illustrating the direct and indirect effects of different variables in a SEM that influence a given dependent variable is to construct a string diagram[2] using the standardized coefficients. In constructing the string diagram for the purposes of this chapter, the total effect of a driving variable on a response variable is the sum of the direct effect (which is given by the standardized coefficient, β for the direct path) and the indirect effect (which is the product of the β for the indirect path and the β for the contributing direct path). Figure 6.8 presents a string diagram that has been constructed for the Cycle 0–11 model and illustrates the relative effects of the external forcing variables and the intermediary variables that modify those forcing effects on *Gambusia* Hg concentrations.

[2] An early example in the limnological literature of the use of string diagrams is provided by Charles and Christie (1991). In this case, string diagrams were used to compare the individual contributions of major ion depletion and enrichment to the overall process of stream and lake acidification.

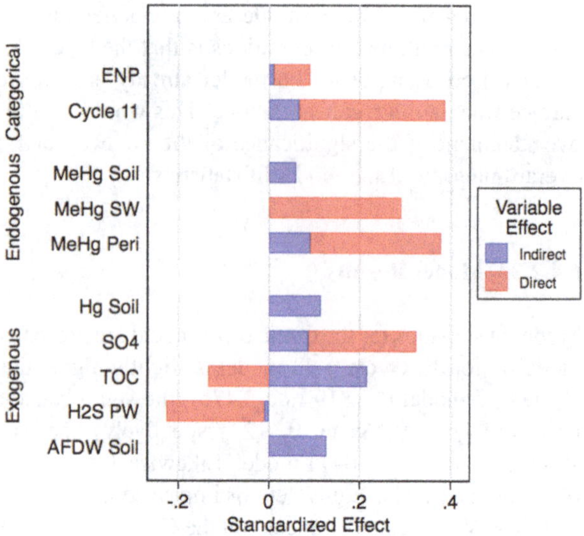

Fig. 6.8 String diagram showing the magnitude and direction of the standardized effect of the endogenous and exogenous variables influencing *Gambusia* Hg concentrations in Cycles 0–11 SEM (Fig. 6.7)

The results illustrate several important points. First, the model indicates that the magnitude of MeHg production exerts the largest influence on the bioaccumulation of MeHg in *Gambusia.* Variations in periphyton MeHg concentrations are the most important, followed closely by the effect of variations in MeHg concentrations in the water column. This, of course, is not surprising, and is consistent with our conceptual understanding of the biogeochemical cycling of Hg and the trophic transfer of MeHg in the Everglades food web (Chaps. 1 and 8 in Volume II; Chap. 4 in this volume). For example, Cleckner et al. (1999) demonstrated that periphyton can be an important locus for *in situ* methylation in the Everglades, while Yin et al. (2012) in turn demonstrated that the periphyton can be a significant contributor to water column concentrations of MeHg. The direct, positive effect of surface water MeHg concentrations on *Gambusia* Hg may reflect to some extent gill uptake of dissolved MeHg, although bioenergetics modeling suggests that this pathway is comparatively small (Harris et al. 2001). The more likely mechanism underlying this pathway is that the pathway is mediated, and that the mediating variable (or variables) has not been included in the model. Because the *Gambusia* diet comprises largely zooplankton, small insects and insect larvae, mediating variables likely would include phytoplankton in the water column as well as zooplankton and the insect components of their diet.

A second key result illustrated by the string diagram is that sulfur (*i.e.,* surface water sulfate and pore water sulfide) and TOC dynamics are far more important as external forcing variables than the other two exogenous variables (soil AFDW and soil total Hg) included in the model. As seen in Pollman's (2014) original model and the Cycle 0–7 model, the effects of sulfur and TOC are complex, and both exert competing negative and positive influences on *Gambusia* Hg concentrations depending upon the pathway.

Consistent with the conceptual model articulated for the Everglades (Chap. 1, Volume II), the effect of unimodally transformed sulfate on both surface water and periphyton MeHg concentrations is positive ($\beta = 0.08$ and 0.18, respectively). The conceptual model posits that net MeHg production in the Everglades reflects a balance between the stimulatory effects of increasing sulfate concentrations on microbially-mediated sulfate reduction and inhibition of Hg methylation as sulfide produced by sulfate reduction accumulates (Gilmour and Henry 1991). Conceptually this translates to a unimodal relationship that has indeed been both validated previously through testing of model specification and robustness by Pollman (2014) and further confirmed by this model.

Other key aspects of the effects of sulfur dynamics on Hg biogeochemical cycling suggested by the model include:

1. A direct, positive effect of sulfate methylation potential on *Gambusia* Hg concentrations. This relationship is similar to the nonlinear relationship observed by Gabriel et al. (2014) between sulfate and Hg concentrations in several different trophic levels of fish (including *Gambusia*) in the Everglades. As discussed by Pollman (2014), the mechanism underlying this pathway is not clear, and likely reflects an additional, mediated pathway with a variable not included in the model.
2. Increasing pore water sulfide concentrations negatively affect soil MeHg concentrations. This inhibition has been widely noted in a number of aquatic ecosystems, including the Everglades (Orem et al. 2011), and is likely due to decreases in concentrations of neutral Hg(II)-sulfide complexes as sulfide concentrations increase (Benoit et al. 1999; Liu et al. 2009).
3. Increasing pore water sulfide also appears to inhibit the bioaccumulation of *Gambusia* Hg. This is consistent with the notion articulated above that an additional mediated pathway for MeHg production and bioaccumulation is missing from the model.

The direct effect of TOC on *Gambusia* Hg concentrations is negative ($\beta = -0.13$), and probably reflects limitations imposed on the bioavailability of MeHg imposed by higher concentrations of TOC (*e.g.,* Watras et al. 1995, 1998; Gorski et al. 2008).

The effects of TOC on *Gambusia* Hg through mediated pathways included in the model are all related to MeHg production (*i.e.,* MeHg in surface water, soil, and periphyton) and are all positive. These mediated effects are consistent with DOC serving as a substrate driving the activity of sulfate-reducing bacteria, or through the effects of DOC maintaining the bioavailability of neutrally charged Hg(II)-sulfide complexes in the presence of sulfide (Graham et al. 2012) necessary to drive methylation.

While the indirect and direct pathways for the effect of TOC on *Gambusia* Hg are highly significant ($p \leq 0.001$), the competing, antagonistic effects obscure the importance of TOC when considering its total effect in isolation of the individual pathways ($p = 0.037$). Likewise, a simple bivariate plot of *Gambusia* Hg concentrations as a function of TOC (both log-transformed) suggests that any relationship

Fig. 6.9 Bivariate plot of *Gambusia* Hg concentrations as a function of surface water TOC/DOC concentrations

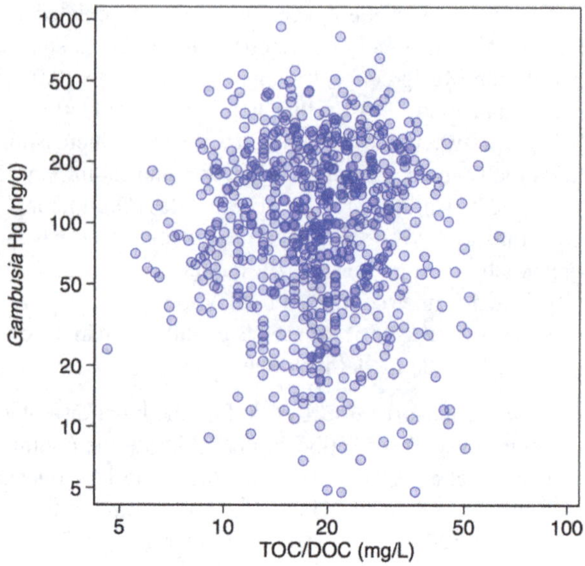

between these two variables is non-existent (Fig. 6.9). These two facts together illustrate the virtue and importance of SE modeling for elucidating complex structural relationships such as those inherent in the biogeochemical cycling of Hg. Moreover, these facts also demonstrate that using traditional ordinary least squares (OLS) regression to simulate biota Hg concentrations has an inherent problem with proper model specification because of the inability of OLS regression to consider mediated relationships.

The final key result from extending the model to include the Cycle 11 R-EMAP data is that the model still requires further development to gain a more complete understanding of the multitude of factors that govern the magnitude and temporal dynamics of Hg bioaccumulation in aquatic biota in the Everglades. The importance of the dummy variable defining Cycle 11 samples ($\beta = 0.32$ and 0.39 for direct and total effects, respectively) indicates that the model is lacking one or more variables necessary to fully account for large declines in *Gambusia* Hg concentration that occurred during Cycle 11 (Fig. 6.5). The model suggests that declines in sulfate methylation potential can account for a substantial portion of the decline, but that other factors need to be considered as well. These factors may be related (at least in part) to more extreme hydrologic conditions (low water coverage and depths) that occurred during Cycle 11 that were most pronounced in WCA3 and the ENP. This is examined in detail in Chap. 5 (this volume) which, based on analyses conducted with both the dynamic E-MCM and the Cycle 0–11 SEM, discusses the drivers of temporal changes in fish tissue Hg concentrations observed in the Everglades.

6.5 Discussion and Conclusions

R-EMAP sampling of the EvPA during the 2014 wet season afforded an opportunity to further validate the SEM that Pollman (2014) originally developed to help elucidate the underlying biogeochemical factors leading to Hg bioaccumulation in *Gambusia* within the Everglades marsh. The original model, which was based on R-EMAP data collected between 1995 and 2005, indicated that the dominant influence on fish tissue Hg is related to variations in the MeHg signal. The dominant external forcing variable, however, was related to methylation potential defined by unimodal transformations of surface water sulfate concentrations and, to a somewhat lesser effect, the effects of pore water sulfide. The original model also demonstrated that the effect of DOC on *Gambusia* Hg concentrations was exerted through multiple and antagonistic pathways, including facilitated transport of total Hg and MeHg, enhanced rates of methylation, and limitations imposed on bioavailability.

The unimodal transformations of sulfate were conducted uniquely for each major hydrologic unit to empirically account for geographic differences in sulfate-dependent methylation potential (Pollman 2012). The original SEM nonetheless still retained some spatial predictive bias with the model showing a stronger tendency to under-predict concentrations along a north-south gradient in the EvPA. As a result, the SEM was revised to include a dichotomous categorical variable to help quantify these effects and eliminate the bias. The dichotomous variable suggests two factors that are significantly different ($p < 0.001$) in the ENP compared to other major hydrologic units within the EvPA: (1) the total Hg signal in surficial ENP soils is elevated by nearly 10% compared to other EvPA regions when normalized to soil organic matter content; and (2) *ceteris paribus*, concentrations of Hg in *Gambusia* relative to other regions within the EvPA also are elevated. Why both of these differences occur is unclear and should be topics of further research.

Out-of-sample predictions using the 2014 wet season R-EMAP data demonstrated that the model performs reasonably well for predicting periphyton MeHg concentrations, but generally under-predicted the magnitudes of the very substantial declines observed for both surface water MeHg and *Gambusia* Hg concentration during that period. As a result, a second dichotomous categorical variable was incorporated into the model that specified whether an observation was collected during the 2014 wet season, and the model was refit to the full suite of R-EMAP sampling cycles to help quantify this effect. This resulted in improved model performance with respect to overall model fit statistics, including the coefficient of determination for *Gambusia* Hg (0.520 *vs.* 0.470).

Of the four exogenous variables included in the revised SEM (soil total Hg, sulfate methylation potential, surface water TOC and pore water sulfide), the sulfur-related variables were dominant. Increasing sulfate methylation potential resulted in higher *Gambusia* Hg concentrations through both indirect (periphyton MeHg and surface water MeHg) and direct pathways. The direct pathway connection likely reflects an additional, mediated pathway with a variable not included in the model. Increasing sulfide concentrations resulted in reductions in *Gambusia* Hg concentrations through primarily a direct pathway. Similar to and consistent with the direct pathway for sulfate methylation potential effects, the direct pathway for sulfide affecting *Gambusia* Hg concentrations also suggests a mediated pathway with a response variable not included in the model.

The dichotomous variable used to isolate effects related to the 2014 wet season indicates that these effects are substantial. The inclusion of the dichotomous variable also quantitatively underscores that some process as yet identified played a major role with respect to the large declines observed throughout the EvPA during the 2014 wet season. Given that the 2014 wet season R-EMAP sampling campaign was conducted during a period of substantially reduced water levels in the ENP and WCA3, hydrology may be contributing factor but, because water levels were not reduced in the LNWR or WCA2 (Kalla and Scheidt 2017), changes in water levels do not seem to account for the ubiquitous nature of the decline. With the exception of WCA2, sulfate methylation potentials were also substantially lower throughout the EvPA. Hydrology and declining sulfate inputs to the EvPA thus can account for much but not all of the profound declines in *Gambusia* Hg observed in 2014. This is explored more fully in Chap. 5 (this volume).

Lastly, the revised (Cycles 0–11) SEM includes pore water sulfide as an exogenous variable. Because surface water sulfate concentrations ultimately govern the magnitude to which pore water sulfide concentrations can develop, using the SEM as a management tool to evaluate the likely impacts of sulfate-mitigation strategies ideally would include pore water sulfide as an endogenous variable. In concept, the model would thus include the direct interactions of sulfate with both pore water sulfide and its direct effects on methylation. The fact that pore water sulfide concentrations for Cycle 11 were inferred from surface water sulfate however precludes its use in the revised model as an endogenous variable. The intent of this modeling, however, was in part to isolate the effects of otherwise unquantified or missing variables not included in the original SEM that might help explain the large declines in *Gambusia* Hg and surface water MeHg observed in 2014. Restricting the data used for model estimation to only those observations preceding 2014 thus would have compromised its ability to evaluate possible causes for these large declines.

References

Acock AC (2013) Discovering structural equation modeling using Stata, Revised edn. Stata Press, College Station, TX. 306 pp

Atkeson TD, Pollman CD, Axelrad DM (2005) Trends in mercury emissions, deposition, and biota in the Florida Everglades: a monitoring and modeling analysis. In: Pirrone N, Mahaffey K (eds) Dynamics of mercury pollution on regional and global scales atmospheric processes and human exposures around the world. Springer, New York

Benoit JM, Gilmour CC, Mason RP, Heyes A (1999) Sulfide controls on mercury speciation and bioavailability to methylating bacteria in sediment pore waters. Environ Sci Technol 33:951–957

Bizzi S, Surridge BWJ, Lerner DN (2013) Structural equation modeling: a novel statistical framework for exploring the spatial distribution of benthic macroinvertebrate in riverine ecosystems. River Res Appl 29:743–759
Browne MW (1984) Asymptotically distribution-free methods for the analysis of covariance structures. Br J Math Stat Psychol 37(1):62–83
Charles DF, Christie S (eds) (1991) Acidic deposition and aquatic ecosystems: regional case studies. Springer-Verlag, New York
Cleckner LB, Gilmour CC, Hurley JP, Krabbenhoft DP (1999) Mercury methylation in periphyton of the Florida Everglades. Limnol Oceanogr 44:1815–1825
Gabriel MC, Howard N, Osborne TZ (2014) Fish mercury and surface water sulfate relationships in the Everglades protection area. Environ Manag 53:583–593
Gilmour C, Henry E (1991) Mercury methylation in aquatic systems affected by acid deposition. Environ Pollut 71:131–169
Gorski PR, Armstrong DE, Hurley JP, Krabbenhoft DP (2008) Influence of natural dissolved organic carbon on the bioavailability of mercury to a freshwater alga. Environ Pollut 154:116–123
Grace JB (2008) Structural equation modeling for observational studies. J Wildl Manag 72:14–22
Graham AM, Aiken Graham AM, Aiken GR, Gilmour CC (2012) Dissolved organic matter enhances microbial mercury methylation under sulfidic conditions. Environ Sci Technol 465:2715–2723. https://doi.org/10.1021/es203658f
Hamilton LC (2013) Statistics with Stata: updated for version 12, 8th edn. Brooks/Cole, Boston, 473 pp
Harris R, Pollman CD, Hutchinson D, Beals D (2001) Florida Pilot Mercury Total Maximum Daily Load (TMDL) Study: application of the Everglades Mercury Cycling Model (E-MCM) to Site WCA 3A-15. Report to the Florida Department of Environmental Protection, Tallahassee, FL. Submitted by Tetra Tech, Inc., Lafayette, CA
Hayduk LA, Glaser DN (2000) Jiving the four-step, waltzing around factor analysis, and other serious fun. Struct Equ Model 7:1–35
Hoch AR, Reddy MM, Aiken GR (2001) Calcite crystal growth inhibition by humic substances with emphasis on hydrophobic acids from the Florida Everglades. Geochim Cosmochim Acta 64(1):61–72
Hox JJ (2010) Multilevel analysis: techniques and applications, 2nd edn. Routledge, New York
Hu L, Bentler PM (1999) Cutoff criteria for fit indexes in covariance structure analysis: conventional criteria versus new alternatives. Struct Equ Model 6:1–55
Julian P (2014) Reply to "Mercury bioaccumulation and bioaccumulation factors for Everglades mosquitofish as related to sulfate: a re-analysis of Julian II (2013)". Bull Environ Contam Toxicol. https://doi.org/10.1007/s00128-014-1389-0
Kalla PI, Scheidt DJ (2017) Everglades ecosystem assessment – Phase IV, 2014: data reduction and initial synthesis. U.S. EPA, Science and Ecosystem Support Division, Athens, GA. SESD 14-0380. 58 pp. https://www.epa.gov/sites/production/files/2017-07/epa_everglades_emap_2014_data.xlsx
Kline RB (2011) Principles and practice of structural equation modeling, 3rd edn. The Guilford Press, New York
Li CC (1975) Path analysis – a primer. Boxwood Press, Pacific Grove, CA, 346 pp
Liu J, Valsaraj KT, Delaune RD (2009) Inhibition of mercury methylation by iron sulfides in an anoxic sediment. Environ Eng Sci 26(4):833–840. https://doi.org/10.1089/ees.2008.0243
McIntosh CN (2007) Rethinking fit assessment in structural equation modelling: a commentary and elaboration on Barrett (2007). Personal Individ Differ 42:859–867
Orem W, Gilmour C, Axelrad D, Krabbenhoft D, Scheidt D, Kalla P, McCormick P, Gabriel M, Aiken G (2011) Sulfur in the South Florida ecosystem: distribution, sources, biogeochemistry, impacts, and management for restoration. Crit Rev Environ Sci Technol 41:249–288
Pollman CD (2012) Modeling sulfate and Gambusia mercury relationships in the Everglades – final report. Florida Department of Environmental Protection, Tallahassee

Pollman CD (2014) Mercury cycling and trophic state in aquatic ecosystems: implications from structural equation modeling. Sci Tot Environ 499:62–73

Pollman CD, Harris RC, Beals D, Hutchinson D (2002) Modeling spatial and temporal dynamics of mercury in the Everglades: proof-of-concept. Final report submitted to U.S. Environmental Protection Agency, Ecosystems Research Division, National Exposure Research Laboratory, Athens, Georgia. Tetra Tech, Inc., Lafayette, CA. Submitted by Tetra Tech, Inc., Lafayette, CA

Pollman CD, Swain EB, Bale D, Myrbo A, Monson P, Shore M (2017) The evolution of sulfide in shallow aquatic ecosystem sediments – an analysis of the roles of sulfate, organic carbon, iron and feedback constraints using structural equation modeling. J Geophys Res Biogeosci 122. https://doi.org/10.1002/2017JG003785

Scheidt DJ, Kalla PI (2007) Everglades ecosystem assessment: water management and quality, eutrophication, mercury contamination, soils and habitat: monitoring for adaptive management: a R-EMAP status report. USEPA Region 4, Athens, GA. EPA 904-R-07-001. 98 pp. http://www.epa.gov/region4/sesd/reports/epa904r07001/epa904r07001.pdf

StataCorp (2019) Stata statistical software: release 16. StataCorp LP, College Station, TX

Tomarken AJ, Waller NG (2005) Structural equation modeling: strengths, limitations, and misconceptions. Annu Rev Clin Psychol 1:31–65

Ullman JB (2007) Structural equation modeling, Chapter 14. In: Tabachnick BG, Fidell LS (eds) Using multivariate statistics, 5th edn. Allyn & Bacon, Boston, MA, pp 676–780

Watras CJ, Morrison KA, Host JS, Bloom NS (1995) Concentration of mercury species in relationship to other site-specific factors in the surface waters of northern Wisconsin lakes. Limnol Oceanogr 40:553–565

Watras CJ, Back RC, Halvorsen S et al (1998) Bioaccumulation of mercury in pelagic freshwater food webs. Sci Total Environ 219:183–208

Yin L, Yongguan Y, Liu G, Tachiev G, Roelant D, Jiang G, Cai Y (2012) Estimation of the major source and sink of methylmercury in the Florida Everglades. Environ Sci Technol 46:5885–5893

Chapter 7
Mercury Mitigation Management Strategies and Likely Outcomes

Curtis D. Pollman, Donald M. Axelrad, and Darren G. Rumbold

Abstract This chapter examines the suite of major perturbations impacting the Everglades that have direct or indirect connections to mercury (Hg) cycling and trophic transfer leading to unacceptably high biota Hg concentrations and considers the likely efficacy of controlling a given perturbation as a management strategy for mitigating the Hg problem. From a conceptual perspective, reducing sulfate contamination in the Everglades emerges as the only viable mitigation strategy. Based on a reduced form model derived from the structural equation model presented in Chap. 6 (this volume), this chapter presents the likely response and uncertainty of *Gambusia* Hg concentrations to reductions in surface water sulfate concentrations.

Keywords Mercury mitigation · Sulfate · *Gambusia* mercury · Atmospheric deposition · Trophic state · Hydrologic disturbance · Biodilution · Generalized linear modeling · Marginal analysis

7.1 Introduction

The mercury (Hg) problem in the Everglades is the net result of an inherently vulnerable aquatic ecosystem exposed to multiple environmental insults. The foundation of this vulnerability is the ultra-oligotrophic nature of the Everglades. In aquatic ecosystems in general, trophic state influences the transfer of Hg and its

C. D. Pollman (✉)
Aqua Lux Lucis, Inc., Gainesville, FL, USA
e-mail: cpollman@aqualuxlucis.org

D. M. Axelrad
College of Pharmacy, Institute of Public Health, Florida A&M University, Tallahassee, FL, USA
e-mail: donald.axelrad@famu.edu

D. G. Rumbold
Florida Gulf Coast University, Ft. Myers, FL, USA
e-mail: drumbold@fgcu.edu

C. D. Pollman et al. (eds.), *Mercury and the Everglades. A Synthesis and Model for Complex Ecosystem Restoration*, https://doi.org/10.1007/978-3-030-55635-8_7

bioaccumulation through the food web via two fundamental processes. The first process relates to the methylation of Hg, the entry of methylmercury (MeHg) into the base of the food web, and the degree to which it initially bioaccumulates. The second process relates to the trophic transfer of Hg through the food web and its resultant bioaccumulation or biomagnification once it has entered the base. By their very nature—less productivity leading to lower biodilution at the base of the food web and extended, complex food webs leading to higher levels of trophic transfer—ultra-oligotrophic aquatic ecosystems such as the remnant Everglades are particularly sensitive to atmospheric inputs of Hg compared to more eutrophic systems. In addition, there are other perturbations to the Everglades that have influenced biogeochemical cycling of Hg and its methylation. These include increased inputs of anthropogenic phosphorus and sulfate, of which the latter demonstrably influences MeHg production. In addition, the hydrology of the Everglades has been radically transformed from a system that historically was characterized by sheet flow responding naturally to antecedent rainfall, to a highly controlled system that has altered the natural hydroperiod of wetting and drying for much of the Everglades, and which likely has resulted in periodic, pulsed increases in Hg methylation. The following gives a brief review of these perturbations as they relate to Hg cycling and whether management strategies that target these perturbations are likely to be effective with respect to mitigating the Everglades Hg problem. Based on these assessments, controlling surface water sulfate concentrations emerges as the only potentially viable option with any reasonable benefits over the near term. The chapter then examines the predicted effects and policy implications of reducing sulfate concentrations on fish tissue Hg concentrations.

7.2 Biota Mercury Control Strategies

7.2.1 Atmospheric Mercury Deposition

Atmospheric deposition fluxes of Hg to the Everglades are substantially higher than most other regions in United States (Chap. 4, Vol. I), despite the fact that contributions to those fluxes from local sources are quite small (<7% and likely closer to 3% or less; see Chap. 5, Vol. I). The higher deposition fluxes of atmospheric Hg in the Everglades are driven by two factors. The first factor relates to the prevalence of tall, convective storms in south Florida that, because of their height, can ventilate both the upper as well as lower troposphere and scavenge the higher concentrations of gaseous oxidized Hg present in the free troposphere; the second factor is generally higher annual fluxes of precipitation relative to the rest of the conterminous US other than the northern coastal region of the Gulf of Mexico.

Because local emissions comprise such a small fraction of the total atmospheric deposition flux, further limiting or even wholly eliminating these emissions will have only a minor mitigative effect on the Everglades Hg problem. Thus, any strategy that contemplates reducing depositional fluxes of atmospheric Hg must include reductions in global emissions. This of course is beyond the reach of managers and decision makers charged with protecting the Everglades. Moreover, legacy Hg stored in oceanic and terrestrial pools that are in disequilibrium and slowly turning over likely will limit effectiveness of current strategies based on limiting global emissions (Chap. 3, this volume). Atmospheric deposition fluxes—both globally and in the Everglades—thus will likely continue to increase, at least through 2050. These results suggest that mitigation strategies for resolving the Hg problem in the Everglades that rely on reducing atmospheric inputs alone will not be effective—indeed such strategies will likely see the problem exacerbated over the next several decades. Other strategies that take advantage of key aspects of Hg biochemical cycling in the Everglades would seem more prudent and warranted.

7.2.2 Trophic State Manipulation: Phosphorus Inputs

On the basis of early analyses linking increasing fish tissue Hg concentrations to declining TP concentrations across a gradient from the S-10 structures leading to the interior of WCA-2A, it has been argued that nutrient enrichment is protective against elevated biota Hg concentrations and that reducing nutrient inputs entering the Everglades from surface water sources such as the Everglades Agricultural Area (EAA) will be counter-productive with respect to the Hg problem (Green and Perko 2001). The foundation of this argument is the notion that increasing trophic state leads to increased particle production and simplification of food webs, and thus less biomagnification of Hg at the base of the food web (biodilution) and less biomagnification through trophic transfer (food web simplification). An example of the inverse relationship between *Gambusia* Hg concentrations and ambient surface water TP concentrations observed along the phosphorus gradient in WCA-2A is shown in Fig. 7.1.

There are multiple problems with ascribing a significant cause and effect to this inverse relationship. First, as illustrated by Fig. 7.1, the inverse relationship does not hold over time. This is apparent from examining the data from 1999 and 2000. Second, the bivariate analysis ignores the effects of other variables which, when accounted for in a more expanded statistical framework, result in the apparent phosphorus effect vanishing. This is illustrated in the structural equation (SE) modeling conducted by Pollman (2014) who found no statistically significant effect of surface water total phosphorus concentrations on any aspect of Hg cycling included in his model, much less an effect of *Gambusia* Hg concentrations. Third, when the analysis of the bivariate relationship between surface water TP and *Gambusia* Hg concentrations is expanded spatially across the Everglades Protection Area (EvPA) and across time, the inverse relationship seen in limited data across the WCA-2A nutrient gradient again vanishes. This is illustrated in Fig. 7.2 which shows the distribution of *Gambusia* Hg concentrations as a function of categorical levels of TP concentrations for different major hydrologic units within the EvPA based on USEPA R-EMAP data, Cycles 0–11 (1995–2014). Lastly, while evidence

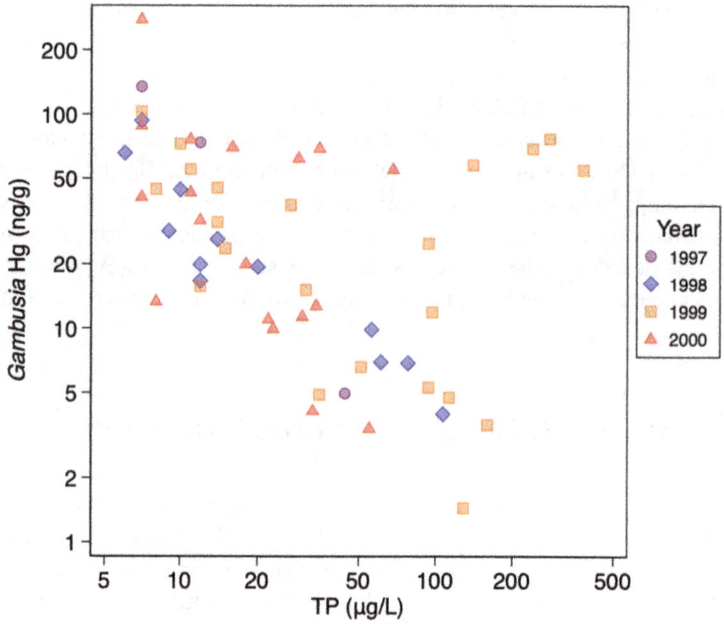

Fig. 7.1 Bivariate plot of *Gambusia* Hg concentrations as a function of TP concentrations across the TP gradient in WCA-2A, 1997 through 2000. TP concentrations represent data averaged across the 2 months preceding the date of fish collection coupled with data collected the same month of fish collection. Data courtesy of SFWMD (L. Fink, personal communication)

supporting food web simplification in lakes in response to incipient eutrophication is evident, such evidence for the Everglades in lacking (Chap. 7, Vol. II).

In addition to the fact that there is no significant supporting evidence for the efficacy of increased TP as a mitigative strategy for the Everglades Hg problem, there are a number of problems posed by nutrient enrichment that decision makers charged with protecting the Everglades must consider. These problems encompass a variety of ecological and geochemical effects, including (Chaps. 5 and 6, Vol. II):

- Shifts in the vegetative community structure, including large scale excursions of cattail (*Typha* spp.) into habitat historically dominated by sawgrass and changes in the species composition of periphyton. The latter includes declines in the cyano-bacteria (commonly known as blue-green algae) that dominate calcareous periphyton that function as a key component of the primary producer community. These shifts in vegetation community structure also have cascading effects on habitat quality that affect other components of the ecosystem, including wading birds.
- Shifts in the quality of organic matter and increased vegetation decomposition rates where cattail has invaded.
- Shifts in phosphorus recycling dynamics, including reduced phosphorus accretion in soils and sediments (and thus higher phosphorus concentrations) in areas

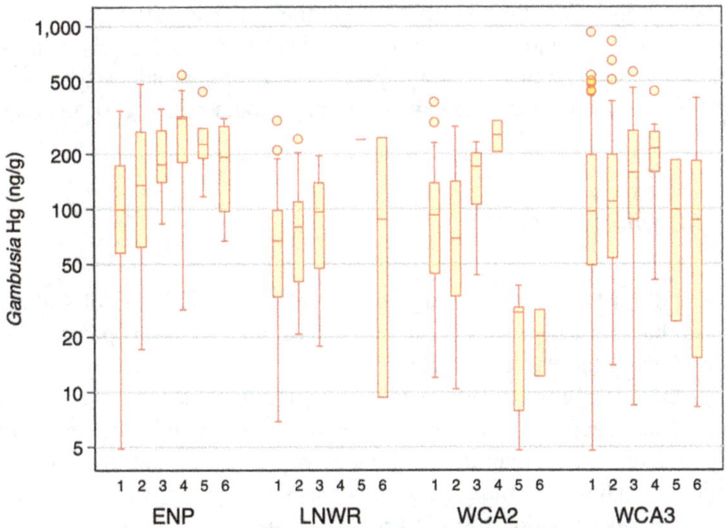

Fig. 7.2 Box plot of the bivariate relationship observed between *Gambusia* Hg concentrations and surface water TP concentrations. Data from the USEPA R-EMAP, Cycles 0–11, and include the suite of 698 sites used in the SE modeling presented in Chap. 6, this volume. Box plot shows the distribution of *Gambusia* Hg concentration within increasing categories of TP concentrations for different major hydrologic units in the EvPA. TP categories are defined as follows: Category 1: TP $\leq$ 10 μg/L; Category 2: 10 $<$ TP $\leq$ 20 μg/L; Category 3. 20 $<$ TP $\leq$ 30 μg/L; Category 4: 30 $<$ TP $\leq$ 40 μg/L; Category 5: 40 $<$ TP $\leq$ 50 μg/L; Category 6: TP $>$ 50 μg/L

where the calcareous periphyton mats are lost or fail to develop in response to elevated phosphorus inputs.

- Reductions in dissolved oxygen concentrations due to increased rates of organic matter decomposition. These reductions can have profound impacts on all components of the aquatic community. For example, the microbial community will by necessity shift towards using terminal electron acceptors other than oxygen to metabolize organic matter once oxygen levels have become depleted. This alters the geochemical dynamics of the surficial sediment environment and has important implications for Hg methylation—both stimulatory and reducing depending upon how much sulfide is produced through dissimilatory reduction of sulfate as a terminal electron acceptor. In addition, reductions in dissolved oxygen concentration can exert direct, deleterious effects on aquatic biota including fish based on their respective tolerances of low dissolved oxygen concentrations.
- While high concentrations of sulfide that can develop under nutrient-enriched conditions can inhibit Hg methylation, it also has associated toxic effects on aquatic biota, including sawgrass, invertebrates and fish.

All of these trophic state-related effects strongly argue against using nutrient enrichment as a Hg mitigative strategy for the Everglades. Thus, while biodilution and food web simplification related to eutrophication have resulted in lower biota Hg concentrations in lakes, the evidence supporting such a mitigative effect in the Everglades is lacking and the cost to the Everglades in terms of changing habitat, ecosystem structure and function is too great. As a result, trophic state manipulation using nutrient enrichment as a mitigative strategy should be categorically dismissed.

7.2.3 Sulfate Inputs

There are several key and necessary aspects related to the issue of sulfate in the Everglades that make the idea of reducing sulfate concentrations potentially attractive for mitigating the Everglades Hg problem.

First is the causal role of sulfate in driving Hg methylation. This role is well-documented and supported by a broad range of studies conducted on a variety of aquatic ecosystems, including the Everglades (see Chap. 3, Vol. II). These include observational studies over time that link changes in Hg methylation to changes in sulfate inputs; manipulation (dose-response) studies (laboratory scale and *in situ* mesocosms), geochemical modeling including E-MCM hindcast modeling of Hg trends in the interior of WCA3 (Chap. 4, this volume), and cross-sectional studies that, from a statistical perspective, robustly link surface water sulfate concentrations to both MeHg and fish Hg concentrations in the Everglades (Chap. 6, Vol. II).

Second is the fact that sulfate concentrations are greatly elevated throughout much of the Everglades. While we have no direct information on actual concentrations of sulfate that would be representative of pre-cultural conditions in the Everglades, we can infer an upper limit on what those concentrations likely were based on current sulfate concentrations in areas of the remnant Everglades that are least impacted by surface water discharges that carry elevated sulfate. Using the synoptic survey from the USEPA's R-EMAP program conducted during 9 sampling cycles (5 separate years) between 1995 and 2014, 95% of the sites sampled[1] had surface water sulfate concentrations in excess of an assumed background concentration 0.022 mg/L. For half of these sites, sulfate is enriched by a factor of at least 68, and for 25% of the sites, the enrichment factor is 300.

The third aspect of sulfate dynamics in the Everglades that supports reducing sulfate concentrations as a means to mitigate the Hg problem relates to sources and whether those sources can be controlled. Excess sulfate in the Everglades ultimately reflects inputs from three potential sources: (1) sulfur derived from soil amendments applied to agricultural lands located primarily in the EAA and to a lesser extent sources discharging into Lake Okeechobee, including sources within the Kissimmee River watershed; (2) connate seawater related to the construction of several of the canals draining the EAA; and (3) atmospheric deposition which includes excess sulfate derived from emissions of SO_2 released into the atmosphere from the

[1]This analysis is based on data for 696 R-EMAP sites within the Everglades Protection Area that were used to construct the structural equation model presented in Chap. 6, this volume.

combustion of fossil fuel. The predominant source of excess sulfate to the EvPA is surface water discharges originating from or passing through the EAA which contain sulfur originating largely from land application, including soil oxidation releases of legacy applications of sulfur. Connate seawater fluxes may be appreciable as well, although their significance remains uncertain (Pollman 2012). Lastly, although the atmospheric deposition fluxes of sulfate are enhanced relative to pre-cultural levels, the contributions from this pathway to the Everglades as a whole are minor (<5%; see Chap. 2, Vol. II).

7.2.4 Other Control Strategies

Hydrologic Management As mentioned previously, the hydrology of the Everglades has shifted from sheetflow to a highly managed system with attendant disruptions to the historical variations in hydroperiod cycling from inundation to exposure and drying. This likely has resulted in periodic, pulsed increases in Hg methylation in excess of naturally occurring rates prevalent during the course of a more normal hydrologic regime. Although managing quantity, timing and distribution of source waters to reduce methylation does not seem feasible on system-wide basis, it should, however, be considered for localized hotspots (*cf.* Rumbold and Fink 2006).

Other Strategies Other strategies such as adding nitrate as an alternative terminal electron acceptor, and binding Hg to prevent it from being released, methylated, or entering the food web through the application of activated carbon, iron amendments, or coagulation with metal-based salts have been used elsewhere in cases of where the sources of Hg are highly localized (*e.g.*, chlor-alkali plants, Hg use in gold mining). Because Hg inputs to the Everglades are almost entirely due to direct depositional fluxes from the atmosphere, the sheer spatial scale of treating elevated Hg concentrations precludes the practicality of these strategies. Moreover, there is also a significant risk of unintended consequences from these actions.

Of the various strategies that we have articulated as possibly mitigating the Everglades Hg problem, reducing sulfate concentrations clearly holds the most promise. This is because of the fundamental role of sulfate as a driver for Hg methylation coupled with the fact that excess sulfate in the Everglades is both widespread and predominantly related to cultural disturbances (land use and hydrologic) within the watershed and thus inherently controllable. Lastly—and equally important—targeting sulfate loadings to the freshwater Everglades poses the lowest risk of unintended consequences compared to other approaches that focus on trophic state manipulation, hydrologic manipulation, or in situ treatment. Sulfate load reductions also would mitigate the sulfide toxicity problem. As a result, the rest of this chapter quantitatively explores the implications of reducing surface water sulfate on *Gambusia* Hg concentrations using a statistical model specifically designed and applied to isolate the effects of sulfate.

7.3 Controlling Sulfate as a Mitigation Strategy

7.3.1 Sulfate Management Model for the Everglades: Overview

Ideally, using a statistical model to predict the effects of a management strategy such as controlling sulfate concentrations in the Everglades to mitigate Hg bioaccumulation in biota includes several features.

1. The model structure should be based on mechanistically observed or hypothesized constructs.
2. The model should be demonstrably robust and structurally consistent with the underlying assumptions inherent in fitting the model. For example, if the model is estimated using ordinary least squares (OLS) regression, the relationships between the dependent variable and each of the model independent variables should be linear, the independent variables should be uncorrelated with one another, and the model residuals should be independent, with constant variance and normally distributed.
3. When used to predict the effects of the independent variable of interest on the response variable, the effects of other variables should be appropriately isolated, and the inherent uncertainty in the model predictions quantified. This type of analysis, otherwise known as a *marginal effect analysis*, is particularly useful for evaluating mitigation strategies for the Everglades because the analysis recognizes that a given strategy for controlling the variable of interest will have a different effect depending upon the antecedent conditions dictated by the other variables in the model.

The structural equation model (SEM) presented in Chap. 6, this volume, is particularly useful in helping to elucidate the complexities of the relationship between sulfur and MeHg cycling in the Everglades, including quantifying the relative importance of each modeled pathway and the indirect and direct effects. From a management perspective, however, a limitation of using SE modeling to conduct marginal analyses on the effect of varying sulfate concentrations is that the sulfate effect is unimodal (*cf.* Chaps. 3 and 6, Vol. II). This unimodal relationship requires an appropriate transformation of sulfate to satisfy the inherent linearity constraints imposed on the relationships between MeHg and *Gambusia* Hg concentrations as response variables and transformed sulfate (Pollman and Axelrad 2014; Pollman 2014). While marginal analyses can be conducted directly on the transformed sulfate variable (for example, to answer the question how *Gambusia* Hg concentrations are expected to change given a 50% reduction in transformed sulfate concentrations), relating a given value of the transformed sulfate variable to a back-transformed concentration of sulfate is problematic because the back-transformation will yield two possible sulfate values. This is because the unimodal transformation by definition yields a methylation potential maximum at some sulfate concentration, $SO4_{critical}$. As a result, for any given methylation potential below the

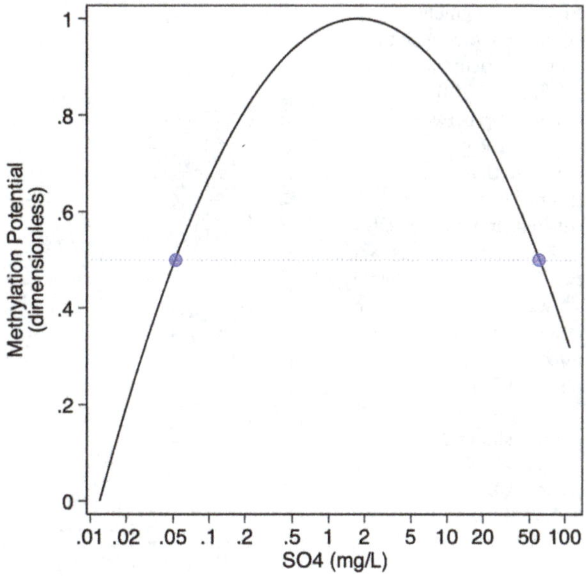

Fig. 7.3 Conceptual plot illustrating the unimodal relationship between surface water sulfate concentrations and the potential for Hg methylation (and, by extension, aquatic biota Hg concentrations). In this model, the maximum potential for Hg methylation occurs at sulfate concentrations ($SO4_{critical}$) equal to 2 mg/L

maximum, the same potential is defined by two concentrations (each concentration lying to either side of $SO4_{critical}$; see Fig. 7.3). As we shall see later on (Sect. 7.2.2), this has important consequences with respect to the question of reducing sulfate concentrations as a MeHg mitigation strategy in the Everglades.

One solution to the marginal analysis problem is to include sulfate in a model of *Gambusia* Hg as an interaction term. Model estimation using continuous interaction terms is, however, quite limited with the current generation of SEM estimation methods, and extremely difficult to implement for the Everglades SEM. On the other hand, interactions terms can be easily implemented as part of a generalized linear model (GLM) and facilitate meaningful analyses of marginal effects in which the analyses are conducted directly as a function of the variable itself prior to the linearizing transformation.

As a result, we accordingly have constructed a relatively simple *reduced form* model to serve as a management tool for evaluating the marginal effects and uncertainty of differing reduction strategies for controlling sulfate concentrations alone and the expected effect on *Gambusia* Hg concentrations. This management model was constructed using the same data from R-EMAP used to construct the SEM. The model includes categorical effect variables for the major hydrologic subunits in the EvPA to account for overall regional effects influencing *Gambusia* Hg concentrations in addition to sulfate-related effects. Recognizing that there are likely variable effects related to time that were not included in the SEM, sampling year was also included as a categorical variable. The model thus has the following form:

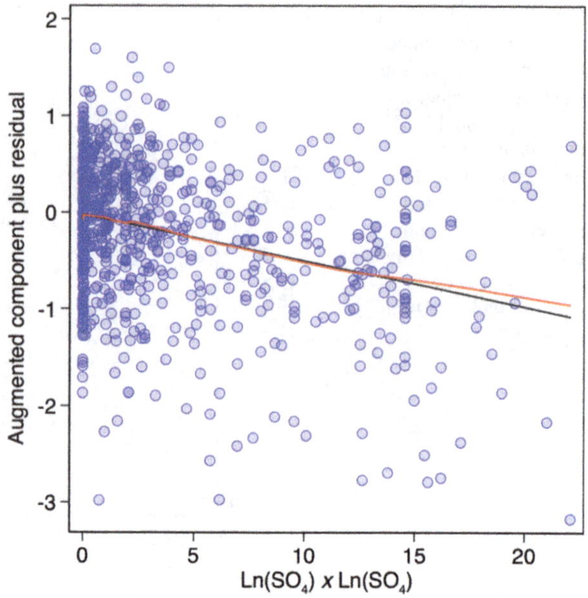

Fig. 7.4 Augmented component plus residuals plot constructed to evaluate the linearity of the relationship between *Gambusia* Hg concentrations (ln-transformed) and squared (ln-transformed) sulfate concentrations. See Eq. 7.1. Solid black line shows the expected linear relationship based on the fitted model coefficients obtained from the OLS estimation of Eq. 7.1; solid red line shows the smoothed LOWESS curve fitted to the ACPR data

$$Ln(Hg_{Gambusia}) = \beta_0 + \beta_1 \cdot Ln(SO_4) \cdot Ln(SO_4) + \beta_{2,R} \cdot Ln(SO_4) \cdot Region + \beta_{3,R} \cdot Region + \beta_{4,Y} \cdot Year \quad (7.1)$$

where $Hg_{Gambusia}$ is the *Gambusia* tissue Hg concentration, *Region* is the categorical variable for hydrologic subunit, *Year* is the categorical variable for sampling year, and β is the fitted coefficient for each model term. Both *Gambusia* Hg and sulfate concentrations are log transformed to satisfy linearity constraints. The interaction of sulfate fits a unimodal (quadratic) sulfate relationship that, because of the interaction of sulfate with region (coupled with the individual sulfate term), is also defined by a unique value for sulfate that imposes a maximal response within each region.

This linear form of the reduced model was initially fitted using OLS regression in order to test the validity of the key assumption regarding linearity between the interaction term for sulfate and *Gambusia* Hg. Overall goodness of fit (adjusted r^2) of the model was 0.407; the significance of the estimated coefficient for the sulfate interaction term was $p < 0.001$. Linearity was tested by constructing an augmented component plus residual (ACPR) plot (StataCorp 2017). ACPR analyses are an extension of component plus residual (CPR) plots that in turn are constructed by plotting the sum of the model residuals plus the expected contribution from the component variable of interest as a function of the component variable. ACPR plots are constructed by "augmenting" the CPR with a quadratic term that improves the ability to detect underlying non-linearities (Mallows 1986). The ACPR plot for the sulfate-*Gambusia* Hg model (Fig. 7.4) includes a linear line that shows the expected relationship of the augmented component plus residual with the quadratic term for

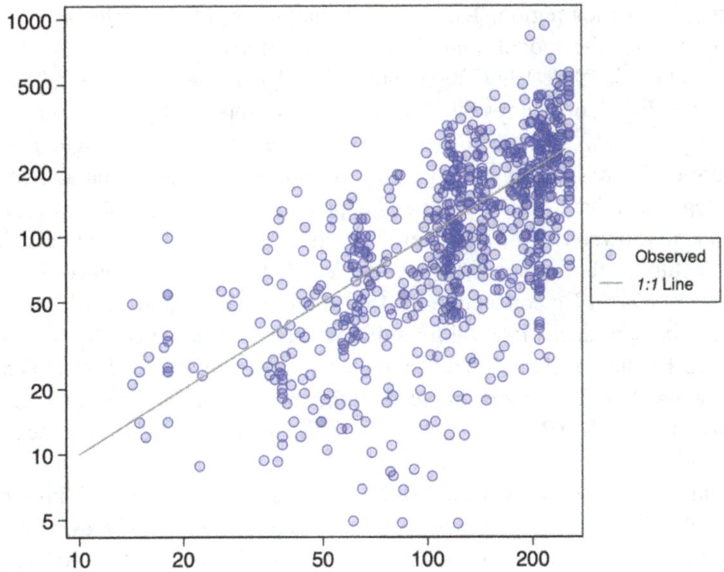

Fig. 7.5 Comparison of observed *Gambusia* Hg concentrations with predicted values obtained from the GLM using a log link function. Solid gray line shows the expected fit assuming perfect agreement between observed and predicted values

sulfate obtained from the fitted model; superimposed on the plot is a non-parametric locally-weighted smoothed scatterplot (LOWESS) curve fitted to the data as well. If the relationship is fully linear, then the expected linear response curve and the LOWESS curves should be identical. With the exception of very minor tailing that is an artifact of the LOWESS curve responding to the very small number of values at the end of distribution of the squared sulfate values, the curves match up extremely well, and the linearity of the sulfate transformation is well-supported.

Final model estimation was conducted using generalized linear modeling (GLM) by regressing *Gambusia* Hg fish tissue concentrations against the independent variables in Eq. (7.1) using a log link function (StataCorp 2017), rather than using ordinary least squares (OLS) with the dependent variable log-transformed. GLM with a log link function to model *Gambusia* Hg was utilized because using OLS to model log-transformed *Gambusia* Hg would require back-transformation. This latter approach can lead to biased predictions (Newman 1993; Manning 1998; Manning and Mullahy 1999; Santos Silva and Tenreyro 2006). The error distribution for the model was assumed to follow a Poisson distribution, and model estimation was conducted using the Huber-White sandwich estimator of variance, and which is more robust to some forms of model misspecification (*cf.* Gould 2011). A comparison of observed *Gambusia* Hg concentrations with predicted values obtained from the GLM is shown in Fig. 7.5.

Marginal analyses were conducted to show the predicted effect and associated uncertainty of changes in sulfate concentrations on the average concentration of Hg in *Gambusia* for each region. The marginal analyses were conducted separately for each region with the model year fixed at each of the 5 years of R-EMAP data availability (1995, 1996, 1999, 2005, and 2014). The results from the 2005 analysis are shown in Fig. 7.6. The results illustrate several important points. First, with the exclusion of WCA2, the 95% prediction confidence interval for *Gambusia* Hg concentrations is reasonably narrow, thus providing confidence that sulfate reduction strategies can have a significant and appreciable effect if sulfate concentrations are sufficiently lowered. This is further illustrated in Table 7.1 which summarizes the average width of the upper and lower limits of the 95% confidence interval for predicted *Gambusia* Hg concentrations for sulfate concentrations restricted to 2 mg/L or less. The confidence interval for sulfate concentrations below 10 mg/L is large for WCA2 because it has a limited number of observations in this concentration range (see also Fig. 7.6). For example, the minimum sulfate concentration in WCA2 throughout the R-EMAP program was 2.9 mg/L, and the 5% quantile concentration was 5.3 mg/L.

Second, the values for $SO4_{critical}$ differ depending upon region within the Everglades (Table 7.2). The largest $SO4_{critical}$ value is for the ENP and may be related to the fact that the organic matter content (as estimated by the ash-free dry weight) of the surficial soils in the ENP is substantially lower compared to other parts of the Everglades (Fig. 7.7). Indeed, separate regression modeling of pore water sulfide concentrations indicates that pore water sulfide concentrations increase as a joint function of increasing sediment organic matter content and surface water sulfate concentrations (Fig. 7.8). Sulfate of course is necessary for sulfate reduction to occur, while increasing sediment organic matter supports higher rates of microbial metabolic activity, including that of sulfate reducers. For the ENP, the amount of sulfate necessarily present in the water column to result in an equivalent amount of pore water sulfide concentrations observed in other parts of the Everglades is thus substantially higher. The estimated $SO4_{critical}$ for WCA2 is also higher compared to the LNWR and WCA3 but is likely biased high because of the lack of observations below 2.9 mg/L for the region.

7.3.2 *Application of the Sulfate Management Model for the Everglades*

The sulfate management model was used to predict the expected average change in *Gambusia* Hg concentrations throughout the EvPA in response to different surface water sulfate concentration reduction scenarios. Each reduction scenario assumed a fixed relative reduction in the amount of sulfate present at a given location in the EvPA relative to a defined background concentration (see next section):

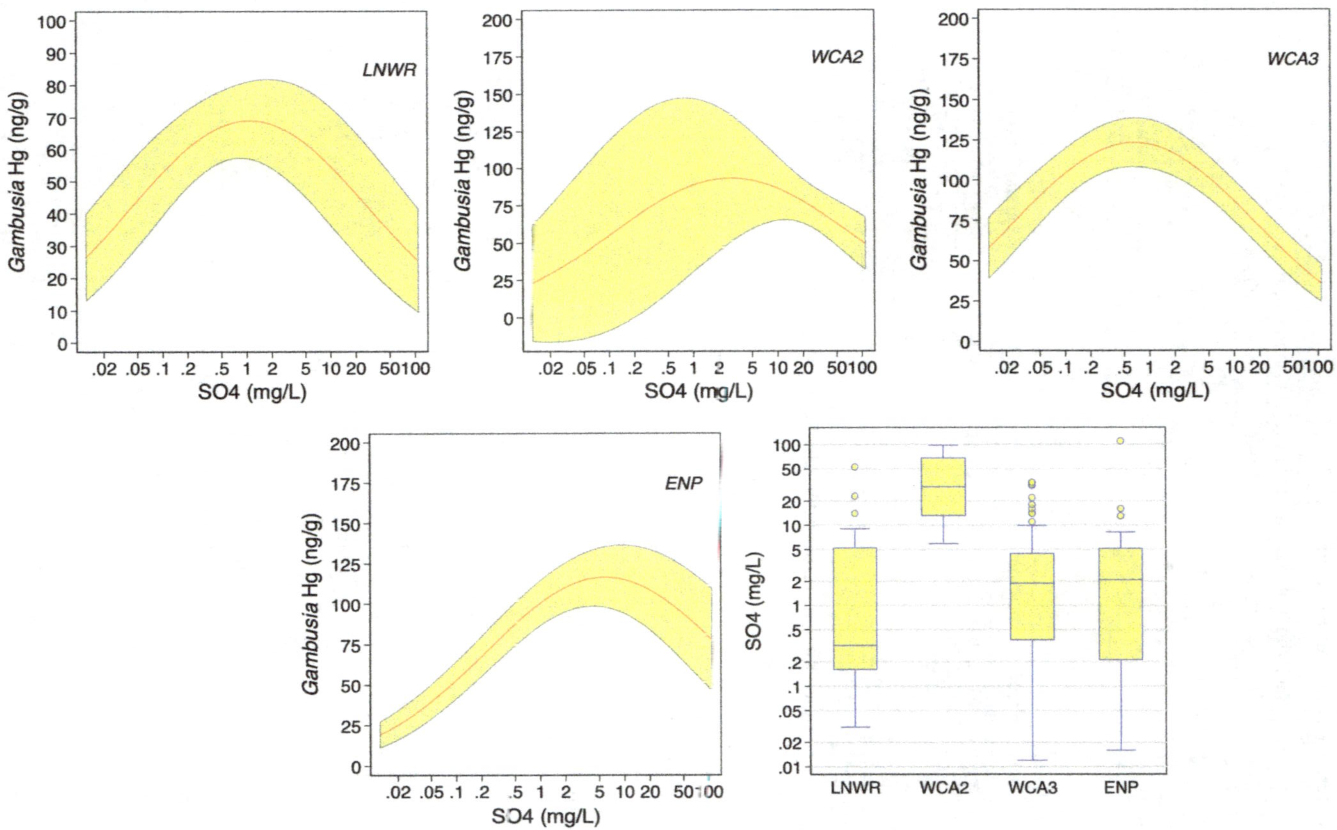

Fig. 7.6 Marginal analysis of the predicted effects of sulfate on average *Gambusia* Hg concentrations for different major hydrologic subunits in the Everglades. Confidence intervals (95%) about the mean predicted concentration are shown as yellow bands. Predictions are fixed for 2005 average conditions. The figure also includes a box plot of surface water sulfate concentrations observed in each hydrologic subunit during 2005

Table 7.1 Average uncertainty (half-width of the 95% confidence interval) in predicted *Gambusia* Hg concentrations (ng/g) obtained from GLM *Gambusia* Hg-sulfate model marginal analyses for predictions restricted to sulfate concentrations ≤2 mg/L

	Average half-width of *Gambusia* Hg (ng/g) Confidence Interval (95%)				
Region	1995	1996	1999	2005	2014
LNWR	27	25	21	13	8
WCA2	123	114	91	58	31
WCA3	39	33	27	16	11
ENP	23	22	17	12	8

Table 7.2 Estimated $SO4_{critical}$ concentrations predicted to result in maximum *Gambusia* Hg concentrations as a function of location (major hydrologic subunit or region) in the Everglades

Everglades region	Minimum observed sulfate (mg/L)	$SO4_{critical}$ (mg/L)	95% CI (mg/L)
LNWR	0.022	1.10	0.35–3.79
WCA2	2.9	2.84	0.29–35.1
WCA3	0.012	0.67	0.39–1.05
ENP	0.016	5.91	2.8–18.3

$SO4_{critical}$ obtained from fitting the model defined by Eq. (7.1) to the R-EMAP data

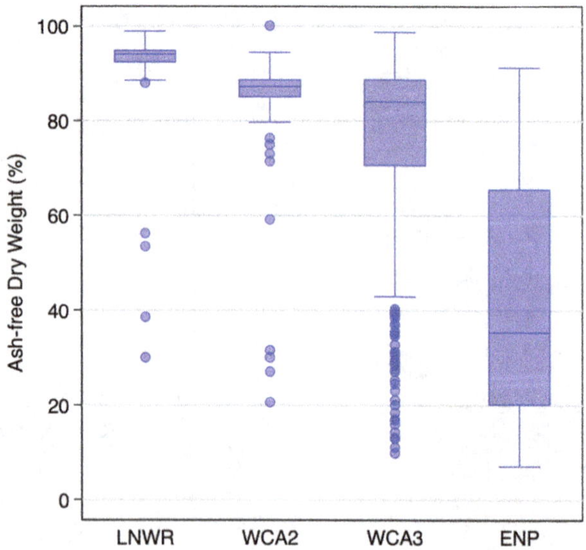

Fig. 7.7 Box plot of the distribution soil organic matter content as measured by ash-free dry weight for different major hydrologic subunits in the Everglades. Data from USEPA R-EMAP program, 1995–2014 ($N = 695$)

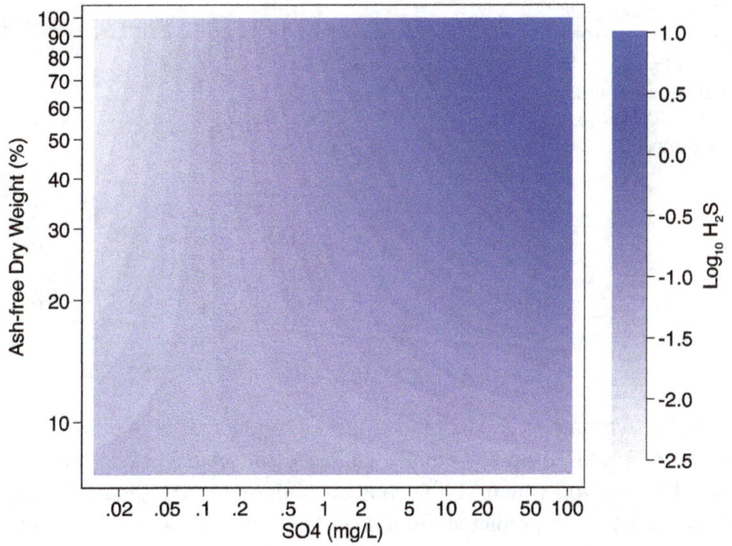

Fig. 7.8 Modeled pore water H_2S concentrations (log_{10}-transformed) as a joint function of surface water sulfate concentrations and sediment organic matter content expressed as ash-free dry weight. Data from R-EMAP Cycles 0–7

$$SO4_{i,excess} = SO4_i - SO4_{bkgrnd} \tag{7.2}$$

$$SO4_{i,reduced} = \frac{SO4_{i,excess}}{f_{reduction}} + SO4_{bkgrnd} \tag{7.3}$$

where $SO4_i$ is the concentration of sulfate at a given location, *i*, $SO4_{bkgrnd}$ is the assumed background concentration that would occur in the absence of any anthropogenic loadings that are related to land use practices, including the use of sulfur soil amendments in the EAA (Chap. 2, Vol. II), $f_{reduction}$ is the assumed reduction in loading factor, $SO4_{i,excess}$ is the excess sulfate relative to $SO4_{bkgrnd}$ and $SO4_{i,reduced}$ is the resultant reduced concentration of sulfate at location *i*. The R-EMAP data can be used to help define $SO4_{bkgrnd}$. An analysis of the overall distribution of sulfate concentrations included in the R-EMAP data used to construct the management model ($N = 696$) indicates that the 90th percentile concentration in the EvPA is 0.11 mg/L (*i.e.*, 10% of the sites have concentrations $\leq$0.11 mg/L). Using data from all of the R-EMAP cycles to define a 10% lower quantile however imposes a positive bias in the results because of high analytical method detection limits (MDL) for sulfate during Cycles 0 through 3 (Table 7.3). If we thus confine the analysis to cycles in which the MDL is below 0.1 mg/L (namely, Cycles 4 through 11), the 5% and 10% quantile values are 0.022 and 0.036 mg/L.

The management scenario modeling was conducted using 0.036 mg/L as $SO4_{bkgrnd}$. If ambient sulfate concentrations were below $SO4_{bkgrnd}$, no change in

Table 7.3 Minimum and lower quantile (5 and 10%) sulfate concentrations in the R-EMAP data subset used to construct the SEM/sulfate management models

Cycle	N	Minimum	5% quantile	10% quantile
0	79	1	1	1
1	94	1	1	1
2	56	0.25	0.25	0.25
3	73	0.25	0.9	1
4	23	0.06	0.1	0.1
5	91	0.046	0.13	0.3
6	56	0.029	0.039	0.075
7	107	0.012	0.031	0.054
11	117	0.022	0.022	0.022
4-11	394	0.012	0.022	0.036

ambient sulfate was imposed. The modeling was conducted for 696 sites—including each of the 684 sites used to initially calibrate the management model plus an additional 12 sites for which sulfate but not *Gambusia* Hg data were available. The difference between predicted *Gambusia* Hg concentrations with no change in sulfate concentration compared to the predicted *Gambusia* Hg concentrations based on the assumed reduction in ambient sulfate concentrations was then calculated.

The model was applied using each model calibration year (1995, 1996, 1999, 2005 and 2014) as a fixed effect to evaluate the predicted response to sulfate reductions across a range of environmental conditions. Since ambient sulfate concentrations vary across time as well, the ambient sulfate concentration measured at each site sampled during a given year was used to define a comparative "no-management effect" baseline.

Two sulfate management scenarios were initially modeled. The first imposed a 50% reduction in excess sulfate concentrations ($f_{reduction} = 2$); the second imposed a 90% reduction in excess sulfate concentrations ($f_{reduction} = 10$). The "average" predicted change was based on the difference between the predicted baseline *Gambusia* Hg concentration and the predicted concentration after the sulfate reduction had been imposed:

$$\Delta Hg_{Gambusia,i} = Hg_{Gambusia,scenario,i} - Hg_{Gambusia,baseline,i} \tag{7.4}$$

where $Hg_{Gambusia,baseline,i}$ is the predicted *Gambusia* Hg concentration corresponding to baseline conditions at site *i*, $Hg_{Gambusia,scenario,i}$ is the predicted *Gambusia* Hg concentration based on the reduced sulfate concentration at site *i* that results from the reduction scenario, $SO4_{reduced,i}$, and $\Delta Hg_{Gambusia,i}$ is the difference between the two predicted values. The difference is an *average* predicted change because the model is predicting a mean response for each site.

Average predicted changes in *Gambusia* Hg are shown as a function of location in Fig. 7.9 ($f_{reduction} = 2$) and Fig. 7.10 ($f_{reduction} = 10$). Predicted changes in *Gambusia* Hg concentrations for the 50% reduction scenario ranged from a maximal decrease of 20 ng/g to a maximal increase of 35 ng/g. More sites were predicted to show an increase rather than a decrease in *Gambusia* Hg concentrations (361 *vs.*

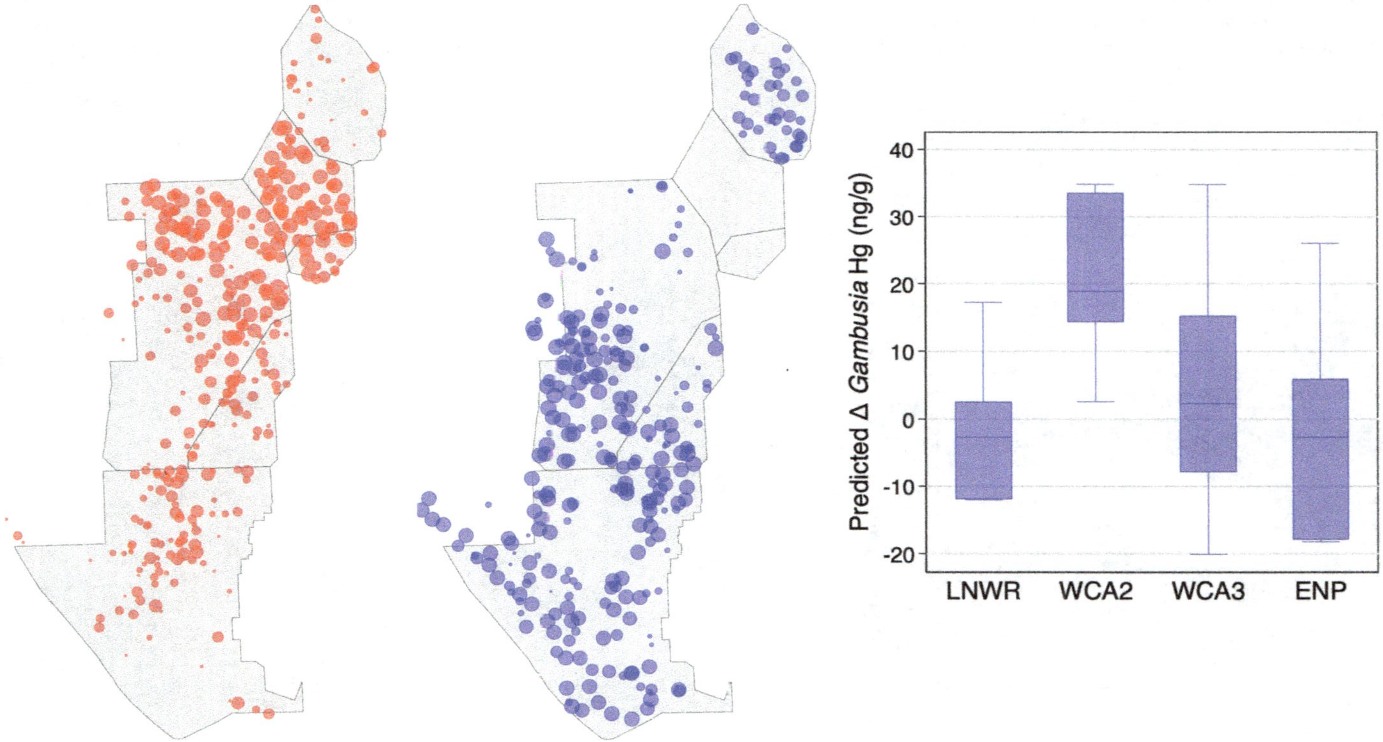

Fig. 7.9 Spatial distribution of predicted changes in *Gambusia* Hg concentrations throughout the EvPA based on $f_{reduction} = 2$ (50% reduction in excess sulfate concentrations). Background sulfate assumed to equal to 0.036 mg/L. Area of each circle is proportional the magnitude of predicted change. Left-hand panel—predicted increases in *Gambusia* Hg concentrations (maximum increase = 35 ng/g; *N* sites = 361); right-hand panel—predicted decreases in *Gambusia* Hg concentrations (maximum decrease = 20 ng/g; *N* sites = 335). Box plot shows the distribution of predicted changes in *Gambusia* Hg concentrations for each major hydrologic subunit

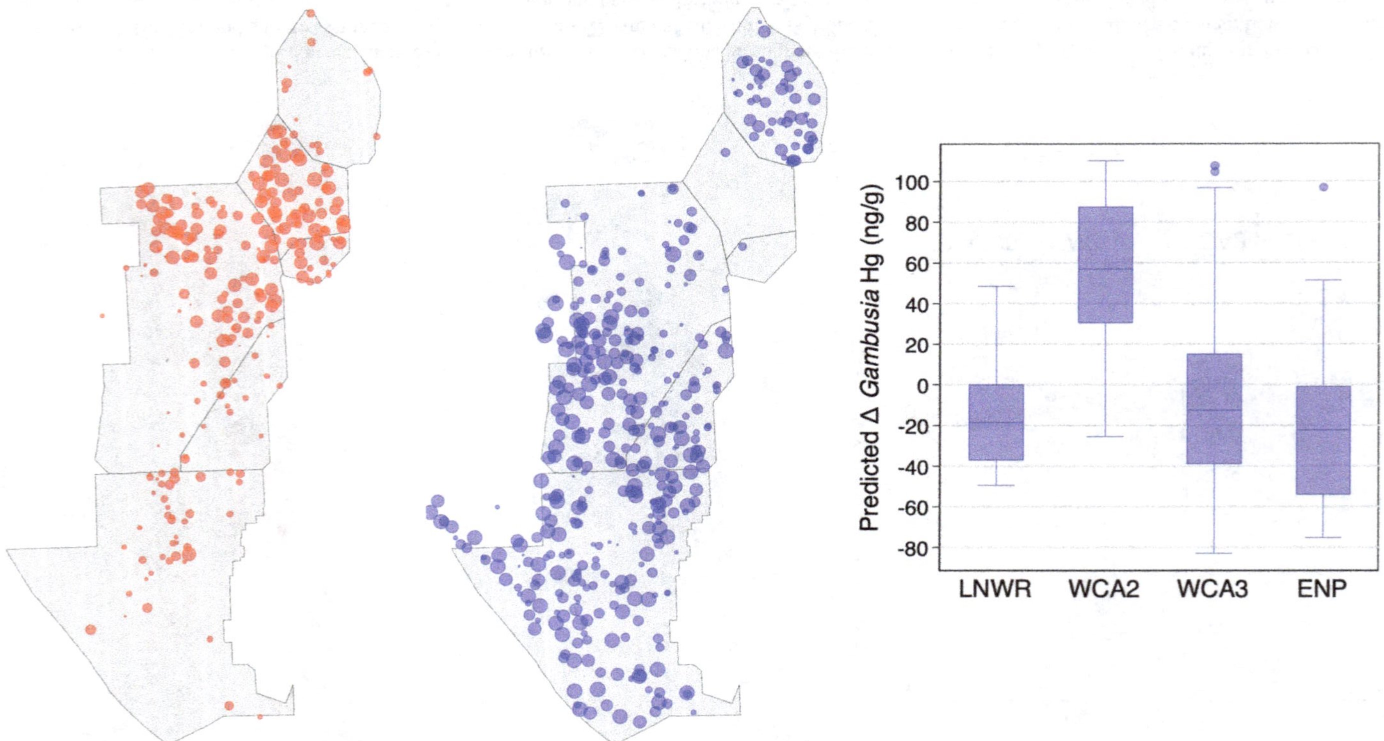

Fig. 7.10 Spatial distribution of predicted changes in *Gambusia* Hg concentrations throughout the EvPA based on $f_{reduction} = 10$ (90% reduction in excess sulfate concentrations). Background sulfate assumed to equal to 0.036 mg/L. Area of each circle is proportional to the magnitude of predicted change. Left-hand panel—predicted increases in *Gambusia* Hg concentrations (maximum increase = 110 ng/g; *N* sites = 241); right-hand panel—predicted decreases in *Gambusia* Hg concentrations (maximum decrease = 83 ng/g; *N* sites = 455). Box plot shows the distribution of predicted changes in *Gambusia* Hg concentrations for each major hydrologic subunit

335 sites, respectively), with an overall average *increase* in concentrations of 2.6 ng/g despite the reduction in ambient sulfate concentrations. This is a consequence of the unimodal nature of the sulfate-Hg methylation relationship coupled with very high ambient sulfate concentrations occurring throughout much of the EvPA well in excess of the modeled sulfate methylation maxima. For example, all of the 70 sites in WCA2 had ambient sulfate concentrations in excess of the estimated sulfate maximum of 2.72 mg/L. Decreasing the excess sulfate concentration by 50% still resulted in 66 sites with sulfate concentrations in excess of the sulfate maximum. This had the effect of pushing the sulfate concentrations of the 66 sites closer to the sulfate maximum, and thus resulted in higher predicted *Gambusia* Hg concentrations.

The 90% excess sulfate reduction scenario resulted in more widespread and larger reductions in *Gambusia* Hg concentrations. Nearly two-thirds of the sites had predicted reductions. Sites with predicted increases were concentrated again in WCA2 and the northern to east central parts of WCA3. The maximum predicted decrease in *Gambusia* Hg concentrations was 83 ng/g, and the maximum predicted increase was 110 ng/g. Concentration changes across all the sites equated to an average reduction of 7.8 ng/g, compared to average overall increase of 2.6 ng/g for the 50% reduction scenario. The largest reductions are predicted for the ENP (median reduction equals 22 ng/g) followed by the LNWR and WCA3 (median reductions of 19 and 13 ng/g, respectively).

When considering the possible efficacy of different sulfate management scenarios as a mitigative strategy for the problem of high biota Hg concentrations in the Everglades, the modeling results illustrate several key points. First, the unimodal relationship between surface water sulfate concentrations and Hg methylation means that the effect of lowering sulfate can have an undesired, antagonistic effect depending upon location within the EvPA. For sites where ambient sulfate concentrations are below the sulfate maximum $SO4_{critical}$, reductions in excess sulfate should—all other factors being constant—result in concomitant reductions in *Gambusia* Hg. Conversely, for sites where ambient sulfate concentrations are above $SO4_{critical}$, reductions in excess sulfate will not achieve the desired effect of *Gambusia* Hg reductions unless the resultant sulfate concentration is sufficiently well below $SO4_{critical}$. Consider as an example a management scenario in which excess sulfate concentrations are reduced by 50%. This scenario results in a large fraction of the R-EMAP sites still remaining above $SO4_{critical}$ (Fig. 7.11). Moreover, the post-reduction sulfate concentrations for all of these sites lie closer to $SO4_{critical}$, which results in predicted increases in *Gambusia* Hg concentrations. Because sulfate concentrations throughout most of the Everglades during R-EMAP have been at least an order of magnitude above expected background concentrations, even a 90% reduction scenario still results in over 25% of the R-EMAP sites across time lying within or above the range of expected $SO4_{critical}$ concentrations.

A second issue that has management implications is the true value of the $SO4_{bkgrnd}$ concentration and its use in setting target reductions in sulfate loading. Using $SO4_{bkgrnd}$ equal to 0.022 rather 0.036 mg/L results in larger average predicted declines in *Gambusia* Hg for a given $f_{reduction}$. As an example, the average decline for the 90% excess sulfate reduction scenario changes from 7.8 to 10.5 ng/g.

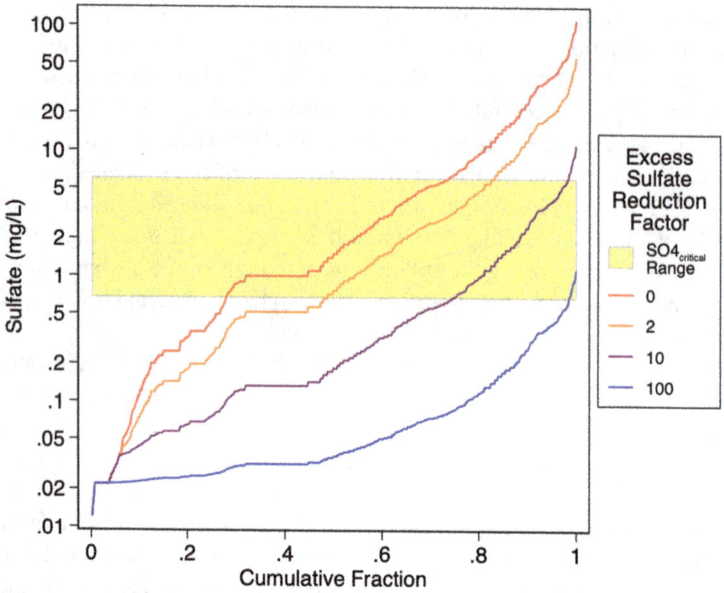

Fig. 7.11 Cumulative distribution of sulfate concentrations measured during R-EMAP across the EvPA with different reduction scenarios imposed on excess sulfate concentrations. For $f_{reduction}$ factors of 2 and 10, $SO4_{bkgrnd}$ was assumed to equal 0.036 mg/L. For $f_{reduction}$ factors equal to 100, $SO4_{bkgrnd}$ was assumed to equal 0.022 mg/L

In all likelihood, an assumption of $SO4_{bkgrnd}$ equal to 0.022 mg/L is still biased high. This bias becomes apparent based on two considerations. First, sulfate concentrations in the interior of the LNWR can lie below ≤0.022 mg/L, despite the fact that sulfate concentrations in the interior are influenced by surface water drainage from the EAA into the marsh (Chen et al. 2012; Wang et al. 2012) as well as atmospheric deposition. Second, atmospheric loadings of sulfate in Florida have likely increased by perhaps 350% (*ca.* 1990) relative to pre-cultural (*ca.* 1880) deposition fluxes because of large increases in anthropogenic emissions of SO_2 (Husar 1986 and personal communication).

A final simulation was thus conducted in which excess sulfate concentrations were reduced by 99% relative to $SO4_{bkgrnd}$ equal to 0.022 mg/L. This reduction results in the distribution of sulfate concentrations almost entirely (>98%) lying below the lowest $SO4_{critical}$ concentration (0.67 mg/L) (Fig. 7.11). As a result, the number of sites with predicted reductions in *Gambusia* Hg increases to 578 (83%), including improved overall reductions (both spatially and distribution of magnitude) in WCA2 (Fig. 7.12). Overall, the predicted magnitude in changes in *Gambusia* Hg improved to an average reduction of 47 ng/g. Moreover, when the predicted concentrations for *Gambusia* Hg (rather than the change in concentration) are plotted as distributions (box plots) across model year and region for both the 90% and 99% excess sulfate reduction scenarios, the differences are striking (Fig. 7.13). For example, the median *Gambusia* Hg concentration for the EvPA excluding WCA2 is predicted to decline from 49 ng/g in the absence of any sulfate reductions to 41 and

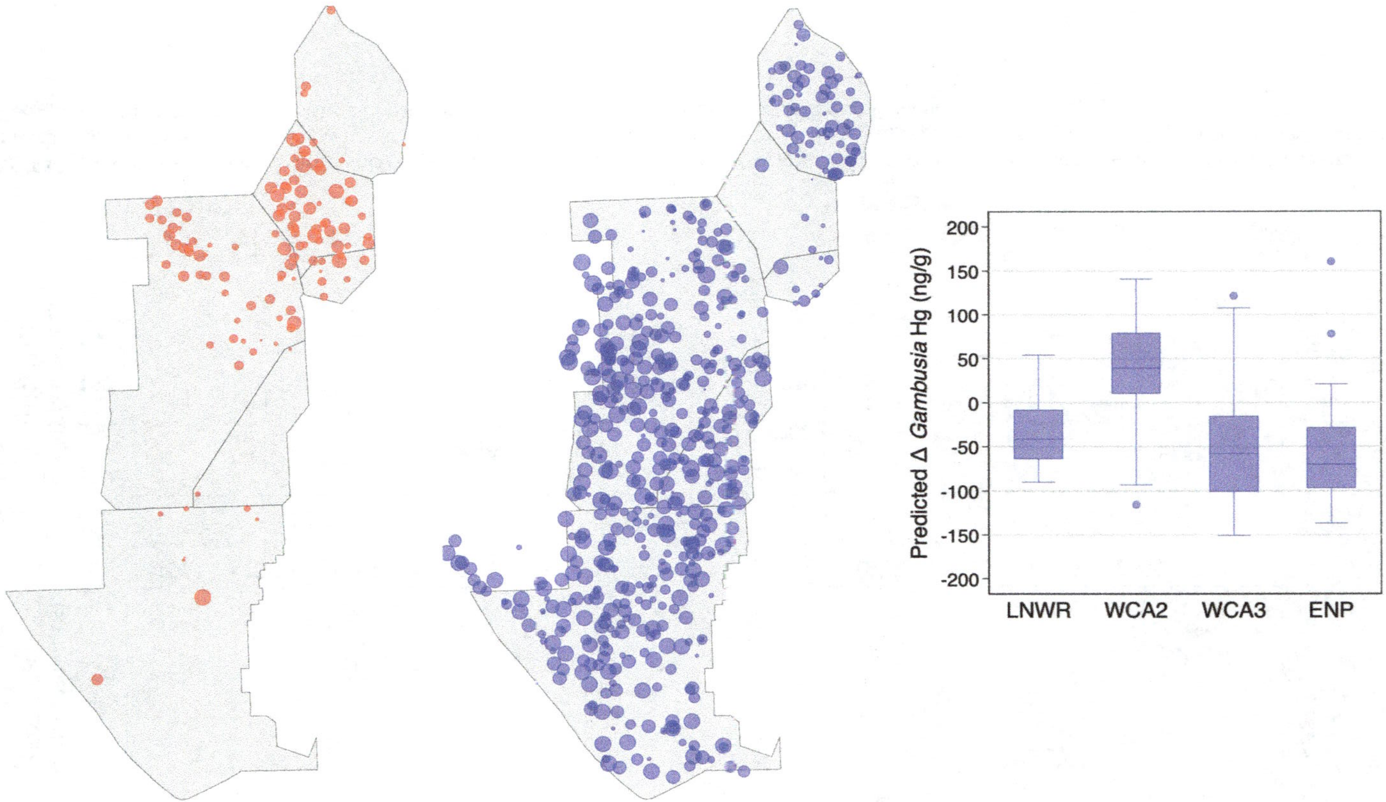

Fig. 7.12 Spatial distribution of predicted changes in *Gambusia* Hg concentrations throughout the EvPA based on $f_{reduction} = 100$ (99% reduction in excess sulfate concentrations). Background sulfate assumed to equal to 0.022 mg/L. Area of each circle is proportional to the magnitude of predicted change. Left-hand panel—predicted increases in *Gambusia* Hg concentrations (maximum increase = 161 ng/g; *N* sites = 118); right-hand panel—predicted decreases in *Gambusia* Hg concentrations (maximum decrease = 151 ng/g; *N* sites = 578). Box plot shows the distribution of predicted changes in *Gambusia* Hg concentrations for each major hydrologic subunit

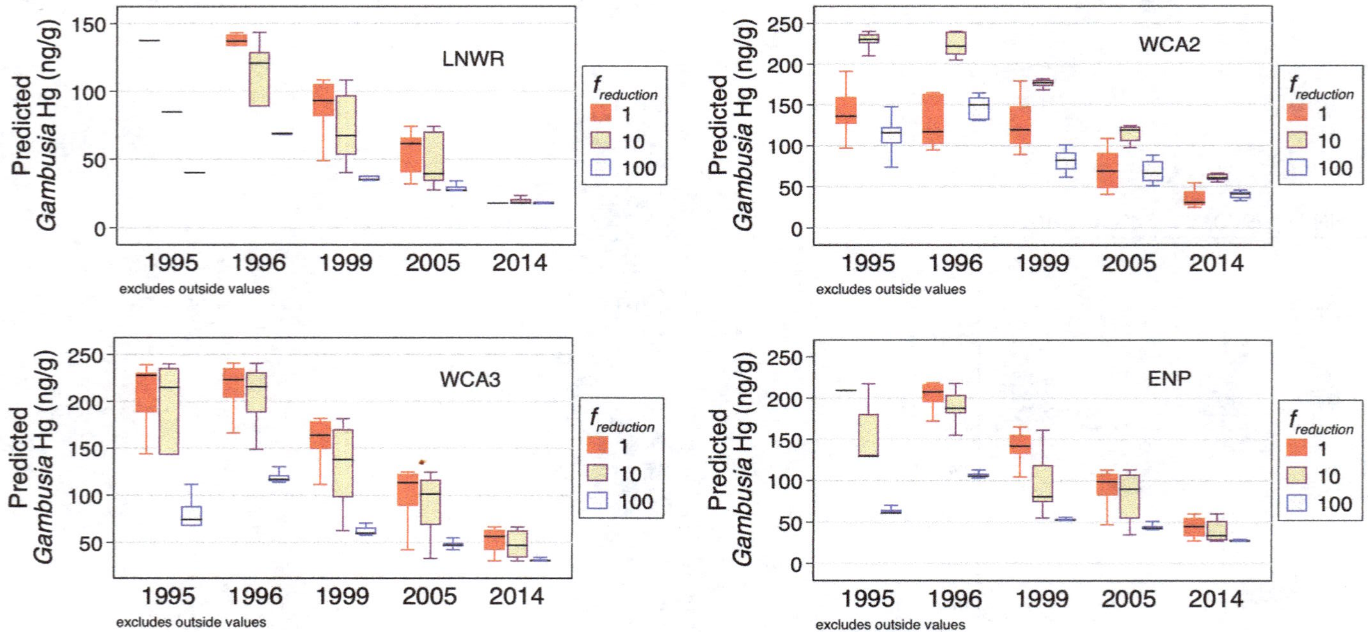

Fig. 7.13 Box plots showing the distribution of predicted *Gambusia* Hg concentrations by simulation year for each major hydrologic subunit. Three simulated regimens are shown: (1) no reduction in excess sulfate ($f_{reduction} = 1$); (2) a 90% reduction ($f_{reduction} = 10$) in excess sulfate; and (3) a 99% reduction ($f_{reduction} = 100$) in excess sulfate. Black horizontal bars shown median predictions for each data grouping

31 ng/g for the 90% and 99% excess sulfate reduction scenarios, respectively. These results underscore the necessity of large reductions (>90%) in excess sulfate to achieve broad, consistent reductions in aquatic biota Hg concentrations in the Everglades.

7.4 Conclusions

The problem of elevated Hg concentrations in Everglades biota has two anthropogenically related components—high fluxes of atmospheric Hg serving as a necessary pre-requisite for Hg methylation to occur; and greatly elevated sulfate concentrations relative to expected background concentrations that are nearly ubiquitous throughout the EvPA, and which stimulate the activity of sulfate-reducing bacteria largely responsible for the methylation of Hg in the Everglades. Atmospheric fluxes of Hg may have been elevated as much as five times by the early 1990s compared to pre-industrial fluxes, and more likely have declined to a factor of ~3× in response to local emission reductions. These flux reductions appear to explain at least in part the reductions in largemouth bass Hg concentrations approximating 60% in long-term monitoring sites between 1989 and 2003 (Chaps. 2, 4 and 5, this volume). Although the atmospheric signal is still substantially elevated, a strategy that relies upon reductions of atmospheric Hg emissions to further mitigate the Everglades Hg problem has two hurdles that essentially nullify its utility. First, Hg emissions originating within Florida contribute only a minor fraction (3 to 7%; Chap. 5, Vol. I) to atmospheric deposition fluxes of Hg in the Everglades. As a result, the effect of complete reductions in Florida emissions on Hg cycling in the Everglades would be nearly inconsequential. Second, legacy Hg stored in oceanic and terrestrial pools that are slowly turning over likely will limit the effectiveness of current strategies based on limiting global emissions. Atmospheric deposition fluxes—both globally and in the Everglades—thus will likely continue to increase, at least through 2050.

Simulations with the sulfate management model indicate that imposing reductions in excess sulfate loadings to the EvPA can yield meaningful benefits as a mitigative strategy for the Everglades Hg problem, but only if the commitment by policy makers to reduce loadings is substantial (>90%). Lower reductions—at least with respect to the Hg problem—will likely lead to mixed results with little overall improvements in the EvPA. This is particularly true in WCA2 and the northeastern WCA3 where sulfate concentrations are so greatly elevated relative to background concentrations. While the sulfate management model can be used as a tool to help evaluate the effect of assumed reductions in surface water sulfate concentrations, it does not address the logistical problem of how sulfate can best be managed as a mitigative strategy. Elevated sulfate concentrations throughout the EvPA are largely related to land use practices in the EAA and the Kissimmee River basin, including the use of sulfur as a soil amendment to adjust soil pH and improve the availability of soil phosphorus for plant uptake; it also is present in other agricultural chemicals including sulfur-based fungicides. Secondary sources include likely fluxes of connate seawater related to the construction of several of the canals draining the EAA as well as atmospheric deposition fluxes of anthropogenically-derived sulfate.

Given both the perceived need for sulfur soil amendments and the importance of EAA-associated fluxes to the EvPA, Orem (Chap. 2 of Vol. II) thus has proposed several possible strategies for reducing sulfate fluxes from the EAA. These strategies include the implementation of best management practices (BMPs) to reduce the agricultural usage and runoff of elemental sulfur and sulfate. A second strategy proposed by Orem is to redesign stormwater treatment areas (STAs) currently in use to capture and mitigate phosphorus-enriched releases from the EAA through plant uptake (including uptake by emergent, submerged and floating macrophytes) to remove sulfate as well. This would have the additional benefit of reducing ongoing releases of legacy sulfur stored in EAA soils originating from historical practices that otherwise would not be affected by BMPs designed to reduce current usage of elemental sulfur and sulfate. Sulfate removal by STAs could proceed via two routes—direct plant uptake to satisfy nutritional needs and losses of sulfate through sulfate reduction—but would require changing the hydraulic dynamics to increase residence time and perhaps the addition of iron to sequester sulfides forming in the sediments. The third strategy proposed by Orem is the use of permeable reactive barriers (PRBs) implemented *in situ* to passively remove sulfate. As noted by Orem, the use of PRBs to remove sulfate is a relatively new concept and would require pilot testing before implementation.

These strategies all are predicated on the assumption that the primary source of anthropogenic, excess sulfate exported to the EvPA is the EAA. Although this assumption is supported by several different and independent lines of evidence detailed in Chap. 2 (Vol. II), as Orem notes "a mass balance that includes detailed information on sulfur sources to the canals and Everglades marshes will be crucial for any attempts to mitigate this serious contamination problem." Such a mass balance requires "[a] more detailed accounting of all sulfur used in the EAA, a more thorough investigation of the actual contributions of groundwater and where groundwater comes to the surface, and a better understanding of release of sulfur from soil oxidation." Unfortunately, while it has been understood for more than a decade that sulfate loading reductions could potentially serve as a mitigative strategy for the Everglades MeHg problem,[2] neither the State of Florida nor the Federal

[2]Reductions in sulfate loadings sufficient to lead to mitigating the MeHg problem also may have the concomitant benefit of reducing sulfide toxicity to both Everglades aquatic flora and fauna (see Chap. 2, Vol. II). This benefit is predicated on the following. First, pore water sulfide concentrations generally follow surface water concentrations of sulfate (Orem et al. 2011) and are elevated in areas heavily impacted by excess sulfate inputs. In these areas, pore water sulfide concentrations can exceed background concentrations of <1 μg/L by over two to as high as four orders of magnitude. Second, these elevated levels of pore water sulfide can greatly exceed aquatic toxicity thresholds (Chap. 2, Vol. II). Third, although the quantitative relationship between pore water sulfide concentrations and ambient concentrations of surface water sulfate has not been developed for the Everglades, the production of sulfide in marsh sediments expectedly should be a direct function of sulfate (cf., Pollman et al. 2017). Given the low concentrations of pore water sulfide throughout areas of the Everglades much less impacted by sulfate inputs, it thus is highly likely that appropriate reductions of sulfate inputs should lead to substantially less toxic exposure to sulfide.

government have yet to seriously engage in the first step towards assessing the feasibility of this option, *viz.* developing accurate sulfur budgets for the Everglades.

As we conclude this final chapter, we would like to leave the reader with a few thoughts. This three-volume series is the culmination of a four-year effort to synthesize 30 years of research on the Everglades Hg problem. This chapter marks the conclusion of that synthesis effort, which by design has been about what the extant science has to tell us about the causes and evolution of the Hg problem, where the problem is likely heading in the decades to come, and how decision makers can mitigate the problem. Indeed, this hope has been deeply entrenched in the book title and its reference to "... a model for complex ecosystem restoration." Unfortunately, this effort is only one side of the coin for solving the Everglades Hg problem. The second side of the coin is *right* action by those entrusted with preserving the integrity and sanctity of this incredibly valuable and iconic global treasure. It is clear from the available research on Hg biogeochemical cycling and biota Hg concentrations that the Everglades has the ability to respond quickly and effectively to perturbations. Moreover, this science is both mature and robust. As a result, this should give us hope that the Hg problem can indeed be effectively managed and reduced; however, such hope will be justified only if we as a society—including in particular key decision makers—have the will and perseverance to undertake and tread upon the course of right action.

References

Chen C, Meselhe E, Waldon M (2012) Assessment of mineral concentration impacts from pumped stormwater on an Everglades wetland, Florida, USA – using a spatially-explicit model. J Hydrol 452-453:25–39. https://doi.org/10.1016/j.jhydrol.2012.05.016

Gould WW (2011) Use poisson rather than regress: tell a friend. The Stata Blog: Not Elsewhere Classified. http://blog.stata.com/2011/08/22/use-poisson-rather-than-regress-tell-a-friend

Green WH, Perko GV (2001) Good science or myopia: will the 1991 Everglades settlement lead to an optimal restoration or will phosphorus reductions be taken too far? St. Thomas Law Rev 13:697–727

Husar RB (1986) Emissions of sulfur dioxide and nitrogen oxides and trends for eastern North America. In: Acid deposition long-term trends. National Research Council, National Academy Press, Washington, DC

Mallows CL (1986) Augmented partial residuals. Technometrics 28:313–319

Manning WG (1998) The logged dependent variable, heteroscedasticity, and the retransformation problem. J Health Econ 17:283–295

Manning WG, Mullahy J (1999) Estimating Log models: to transform or not to transform? Technical Working Paper 246. National Bureau of Economic Research, Cambridge, MA

Newman MC (1993) Regression analysis of log-transformed data: statistical bias and its correction. Environ Toxicol Chem 12:1129–1133

Orem W, Gilmour C, Axelrad D, Krabbenhoft D, Scheidt D, Kalla P, McCormick P, Gabriel M, Aiken G (2011) Sulfur in the South Florida ecosystem: distribution, sources, biogeochemistry, impacts, and management for restoration. Rev Environ Sci Technol 41(S1):249–288

Pollman CD (2012) Modeling sulfate and Gambusia mercury relationships in the Everglades – final report. Florida Department of Environmental Protection, Tallahassee

Pollman CD (2014) Mercury cycling and trophic state in aquatic ecosystems: implications from structural equation modeling. Sci Tot Environ 499:62–73

Pollman CD, Axelrad DM (2014) Mercury bioaccumulation and bioaccumulation factors for Everglades Mosquitofish as related to sulfate: a reanalysis of Julian II (2013). Bull Environ Contam Toxicol. https://doi.org/10.1007/s00128-014-1384

Pollman CD, Swain EB, Bale D, Myrbo A, Monson P, Shore M (2017) The evolution of sulfide in shallow aquatic ecosystem sediments – an analysis of the roles of sulfate, organic carbon, iron and feedback constraints using structural equation modeling. J Geophys Res Biogeosci. https://doi.org/10.1002/2017JG003785

Rumbold DG, Fink LE (2006) Extreme spatial variability and unprecedented methylmercury concentrations within a constructed wetland. Environ Monitor Assess 112(1–3):115–123

Santos Silva JMC, Tenreyro S (2006) The log of gravity. Rev Econ Stat 88(4):641–658

StataCorp (2017) Stata statistical software: release 15. StataCorp LLC, College Station, TX

Wang H, Meselhe EA, Waldon MG, Harwell MC, Chen C (2012) Compartment-based hydrodynamics and water quality modeling of a Northern Everglades Wetland, Florida, USA. Ecol Model 247:273–285. https://doi.org/10.1016/j.ecolmodel.2012.09.007

CPSIA information can be obtained
at www.ICGtesting.com
Printed in the USA
BVHW060944091220
595241BV00020B/27

9 783030 556341